BASICS OF NIGERIAN LABOUR RELATIONS DYNAMICS

BASICS OF NIGERIAN LABOUR RELATIONS DYNAMICS

Dafe Otobo

malthouse

Malthouse Press Limited

Lagos, Benin, Ibadan, Jos, Port-Harcourt, Zaria

First Published 2025
ISBN (paperback): 978-978-61135-2-4
ISBN (e-book): 978-978-61135-3-1

Published and manufactured in Nigeria by
Malthouse Press Limited
7 Adele Road, Off Warehouse Road,
Apapa, Lagos Mainland, Nigeria
E-mail: malthouselagos@gmail.com
Website: malthouselagos.com
Facebook:@malthouselagos
Twitter:@malthouselagos
Instagram:@malthouselagos
Tel: 0802 600 3203

ACNOWLEDGEMENTS

The materials assembled in this volume bring very pleasant memories surrounding each and every one, colleagues, friends and acquaintances in the trades unions, employers' associations, NECA, the MDAs, major companies in the oil and gas industry, manufacturing, banking and finance, professional bodies, academia, international development agencies (e.g. DFID), some agencies of the United Nations Organisation (ILO, ARLAC, UNDP especially), and others who invited my random thoughts on some vexed or topical issue, and still others who involved me in workshops, conferences and committees over the last five decades. I owe them immense gratitude.

PREFACE

The main attempt here is to provide a ready and comprehensive source at one glance of the essential twists and turns since the 1890s of attempts by critical socio-political and economic actors in what has become Nigeria to secure, promote and protect respective interests, especially in determining pattern and quantum of remuneration at work. These events and activities cover early colonial period, post–World Wars colonial labour relations, the First Republic, the military regimes, post-military dictatorships period till recently.

The reader will notice, with some unease or shock or amazement, how employment and labour relations issues, strategies and tactics deployed by state authorities through their relevant and law enforcement agencies, private employers and organised labour in respect thereof have not substantially changed directions despite series of "protests", ensuing "reforms", "development plans", "national independence", military dictatorships, retreat of military regimes, and enthronement of a said democratic system of governance over the last century.

In all of these, the critical linkages between internal and external socioeconomic conditions can hardly be overstated, internal benefactors attempting to dominate the local socio-political landscape and rationalise such continuously in the "national" interest.

Please sit back, see how, what, and when internal political authorities, employers, and workers and their organisations entangled and disentangled themselves continuously with external interests chipping in till the early 1990s. The companion volume to this work, *Contemporary Nigerian Trade Unions and Trade Unionism*, to be released later in the year offers essential gist of workers and their organisations from 1990s to date. Happy reading!

THE AUTHOR

Educated at the University of Ibadan (BSc Soc), The London School of Economics & Political Science (MSc Econs), and the University of Oxford, (DPhil Econs), Professor Dafe Otobo began his teaching career at the University of Ibadan, and moved on to the University of Lagos, Employment Relations & HRM Department from where he recently retired. He is also the President of the Nigerian Industrial & Employment Relations Association (NIERA), and former Member, Executive Committee of the International Labour and Employment Relations Association, Geneva, Switzerland, and member of African Books Collective, Oxford Council of Management.

He has done extensive consulting and training since 1980 in both the public and private sectors, and with various international development agencies (EU, DFID, German Friedrich Ebert Foundation) and UNO agencies (ILO, UNDP, African Regional Labour Administration Centre ARLAC, Zimbabwe).

Some public sector engagements include the 1981 Presidential Commission on Federal Polytechnics, Advanced Teachers, Training and Technical Colleges (Adamolekun Commission), Presidential Committee on Consolidation of Emoluments in the Public Sector (Chief Shonekan Committee) 2005-2006; the Presidential Commission on Consolidation of Emoluments in the Public Sector 2005-2006; Presidential Panel on Wages, Salaries and Emolument Relativity in the Public Sector (Professor Edozien Panel) 2005; Member of the team of experts to review and produce a draft Labour/Employment Policy for ECOWAS Commission (2008); Member of the Vision-20-20 Employment Thematic Group Subcommittee (2009); Consultant on Industrial Relations to the National Committee of Experts on Parameters for Wage Determination in the Federal Public Service established by Mr President (2009); and to the 2024 Tripartite Committee on National Minimum Wage; Member of ECOWAS Experts of Public Service Delivery; Consultant to the NUC and UNDP on Mainstreaming Human Development Studies in Curricula of Nigerian Universities (2010-2012); Consultant to the Federal Ministry of Labour and its agencies/parastatals; Consultant engaged by the Federal Environmental Protection Agency (FEPA), later Federal Ministry of Environment, as a Socio-Economist, on environmental impact assessment of various development projects especially in the Oil and Gas and manufacturing industries. Various training programmes for NNPC Group for over thirty years, including presentations at successive Chief Officers' Courses, the Department of Petroleum Resources (DPR), NAPIMS, NEPA, and Ministry of Power, and the Trade Unions, especially NUPENG, National Union of Civil Engineering, Construction, Furniture and Wood Workers (NUCECFWW), PENGASSAN, Textile Workers Union, SESCAN, and NLC.

ABBREVIATIONS AND ACRONYMS

AATUF	All-African Trade Union Federation
AAUCTU	All-African Union of Christian Trade Unions
ACSTWU	African Civil Servants Technical Workers' Union
AFL	American Federation of Labour
AFL-CIO	American Federation of Labour and Congress of Industrial Organisations
AG	Action Group
ANTUF	All Nigeria Trade Union Federation
ASUU	Academic Staff Union of Universities
ATUC	African Trades Union Confederation
AUCCTU	All-Union Central Council of Trade Unions
CBN	Central Bank of Nigeria
CDO	Collateralized Debt Obligations
CFAO	Compagnie Francaise de l'Afrique Occidentale
CFTC	Confederation Francaise des Travailleurs Chretiens
CGT	Confederation Generale du Travail
CGT-FO	Confederation du Travail-Ford Ouvriere
CIO	Congress of Industrial Organisations
COLA	Cost of Living Allowances
CONMESS	Consolidated Medical Salary Structure
COR states	Cross-River, Ogoja and Rivers
CSTWU	Civil Service Technical Workers Union
CWC	Central Working Committee
DFRRI	Directorate of Food, Rural Roads and Infrastructure
DGB	Deutsch Gewerkschaftsbund
DNA	Det norske Arbeiderparti (Norwegian Labour Party)
ECOWAS	Economic Community of West African States
FES	Friedrich-Ebert Stiftung
FESSAN	Federation of Senior Staff Association of Nigeria
FTUN	Federated Trades Unions of Nigeria
GATT	General Agreements on Tariff and Trade

IAP	Industrial Arbitration Panel
ICFTU	International Confederation of Free Trade Unions
IFATU	International Confederation of Arab Trade Unions
IFCTU	International Federation of Christian Trade Unions
ILO	International Labour Organisation
IMF	International Monetary Fund
ING	Interim National Government
ITS	International Trades Secretariats
ITUC	International Trade Union Congress
IULC	Independent United Labour Congress
JAC	Joint Action Committee
JCC	Joint Consultative Committees
JIC	Joint Industrial Councils
LO	Landsorganisasjon
LP	Labour Party
LUF	Labour Unity Front
MAMSER	Directorate of Mass Mobilisation
MAN	Manufacturers' Association of Nigeria
MBS	Mortgage-based Securities
NACCIMA	Nigerian Association of Chambers of Commerce, Industry, Mines and Agriculture
NAPEP	National Poverty Eradication Programme
NASU	Non-Academic Staff Union
NCNC	National Council for Nigeria and the Camerouns
NCTUN	National Council of Trade Unions in Nigeria
NDE	National Directorate of Employment
NEC	National Executive Council
NECA	Nigeria Employers Consultative Association
NEPA	National Electric Power Authority
NFL	Northern Federation of Labour
NGO	Non-Governmental Organisation
NIC	National Industrial Court
NITEL	Nigeria Telecommunications
NLAC	National Labour Advisory Committee
NLC	Nigeria Labour Congress
NNDP	Nigerian National Democratic Party
NNFL	Nigerian National Federation of Labour
NNPC	Nigeria National Petroleum Corporation
NPC	Northern People's Congress
NPF	National Provident Fund

NRC	National Republican Convention
NSITF	National Social Insurance and Trust Fund
NSIWC	National Salaries, Income & Wages Commission
NTUC	Nigerian Trade Union Congress
NUBIFIE	National Union of Bank, Insurance and Financial Institutions Employees
NUPENG	National Union of Petroleum and Gas Workers
NUT	Nigerian Union of Teachers
NWC	Nigerian Workers' Council
NYM	Nigerian Youth Movement
OATUU	Organization of African Trade Union Unity
OECD	Organization for Economic Co-operation and Development
OPEC	Organisation of Petroleum Exporting Countries
ORIT	Inter-American Regional Organisation of Workers (ICFTU)
PENGASSAN	Petroleum and Natural Gas Senior Staff Association
PWD	Public Works Department
PZ	Paterson Zochonis
RILU	Red International of Labour Unions
RMAFC	Revenue Mobilisation Allocation and Fiscal Commission
RNC	Royal Niger Company
SAP	Structural Adjustment Programme
SCTU	Supreme Council of Trade Unions
SCOA	Societe Commerciale de L'Ouest Africain
SDP	Social Democratic Party
SESCAN	Senior Staff Consultative Association of Nigerian
SFEM	Second Tier Foreign Exchange Market
SWAFP	Socialist Workers and Farmers' Party
TUC	Trade Union Congress
TUCN	Trades Union Congress of Nigeria
UAC	United Africa Company
UCCLO	United Committee of Central Labour Organizations
ULCN	United Labour Congress of Nigeria
UMBC	United Middle Belt Congress
UNAMAG	Amalgamated Union of UAC African Workers
UNO	United Nations Organisation
USS	University System Scale
UTC	Union Trading Company
WCL	World Confederation of Labour
WFTU	World Federation of Trade Unions
WTO	World Trade Organisation

CONTENTS

INTRODUCTION

Chapter 1

MODELS OF UNIONISM AND INSTITUTIONAL MANIFESTATIONS: *ORIGINS AND CHARACTERISTICS*

The impulses released by the 1870 Franco-Prussian war accentuated a quest for colonial possessions which was formalised at the Berlin West African Conference of 1884-5. That Conference recognised disparate 'spheres of influence' based on numerous, but mostly fictitious, 'treaties' which were signed by European traders and companies with some African rulers and impostors on behalf of the metropolitan countries concerned. The now well-known 'Scramble for Africa' that followed led to what the British euphemistically described as 'pacification', a misnomer for the systematic subjugation of indigenous political authorities and economic undercutting of established and powerful local traders by European interests.[1]

Pertaining to the area that later became Nigeria, the main weapon utilized by the British was the Royal Niger Company (RNC). The Company was formed in 1879 as the United African Company (UAC) but changed its name to the National African Company when it changed hands in 1881. In 1883 there were only four firms in the Niger area, two of which were French; these were all absorbed by the National African Company in 1884 which, we are persuaded, 'greatly strengthened British diplomatic action' at the Berlin Conference.[2] As spheres of influence could only be respected by rivals upon effective occupation, the military conquest of these areas was only a matter of time.

Due to a variety of reasons that need not detain us and especially the fact of the dominance of capitalist economic ideology of *laissez faire* which sought non-, or-minimum government interference in economic matters, Britain refrained from immediate colonization and followed the path blazed by the East India Company. A Royal Charter was granted the National African Company which thereafter became the Royal Niger Company in 1886, an arrangement which Geary has likened to 'a slum landlord who

---

1. See Dike, K. O., *Trade and Politics in the Niger Delta*, OUP, 1956; Crowder, M *The Story of Nigeria*, Faber, London, 1966 edn.
2. Geary, W. N. M., *Nigeria Under British Rule*, Frank Cass, London, 1965 New Impr, p. 178.

employs an agent to collect rent, whom he remunerates by commission.'[3] By 1887 such local capitalist traders as Jaja of Opobo and Oko Jumbo who constituted rival economic forces had been banished and deported by British officials, leaving the way clear for European, but mostly British, traders. But the Royal Niger Company proceeded to establish a virtual monopoly by sheer physical and military might: it bombarded neighbouring territories with gunboats and subjected their rulers to its political authority. These areas were then declared the 'Protectorate of Southern Nigeria' in 1890.

Accompanying this military exercise was the economic blockade mounted against those areas that traded with other firms and itinerant European traders: soon enough most trade was passing through the Company's own 'customs and trading' stations strategically located along the Niger Basin. Nana of the Itsekiri, one of the most powerful men in the western delta of the Niger and who resisted encroachments of the Company and of the new 'protectorate' was deported to the Gold Coast in 1894. By cleverly exploiting rivalry and feuding among the Yoruba groups of people, British Governors in Lagos (Lagos had been 'ceded' to Britain in 1862) managed to bring the area under British influence - but not until the 'problem' of Oyo was 'finally settled by a punitive expedition despatched by the Royal Niger Company' late in 1893.[4]

With the formation of the West African Frontier Force by Britain in 1887 under the command of a colonel Lugard (an employee of the Company), the self-imposed task of grabbing as much territory as possible was made manifestly easier for the Company. It had captured Ilorin and Bida while a detachment of the West African Frontier Force took and burnt down Benin in the same years.[5] Thereafter, British troops routinely sacked the Hausa-/Fulani emirates, areas which were then declared the 'Protectorate of Northern Nigeria' in 1906. Both Southern and Northern Protectorates were amalgamated in 1914 by Lugard in the name of Nigeria.

The rather sudden appearance of a rudimentary colonial administrative framework and the withdrawal of the Royal Charter from the Company because of its monopoly of trade and local bitterness engendered by its general conduct encouraged many more non-mining firms to move into Nigeria. The cut-throat competition that ensued reduced their number, through amalgamation and liquidation, from 197 to 46 by 1936, of which only fourteen had an unbroken existence.[6] A good example of businessmen

---

[3] Ibid., p. 198.

[4] Crowder, M., *The Story of Nigeria, op. cit.*, p. 109.

[5] For more details see Ryder, A., Benin and the Europeans, Longman, London, 1965 Mars, J., 'Extra-Territorial Enterprises' in Perham, M. (ed), Mining, Commerce, & Finance in Nigeria, Faber & Faber, London, 1948, pp. 51-2.

[6] Mars, J. , 'Extra-Territorial enterprises' in Perham, M. (ed), Mining, Commerce, & Finance in Nigeria, Faber & Faber, London, 1948, pp. 51-2

who exploited difficulties of other firms was a W.H. Lever, a Liverpool soap magnate, who acquired the Niger Company in 1919, and upon failing to take over the African & Eastern Trading Corporation (which itself was the product of a merger of the African Association, Miller Bros. and F & A Swanzy in 1919), persuaded it into a merger to form a most powerful United African Company (UAC) in 1929.[7] By 1930 therefore an oligopoly dominated by the UAC had been created.

The First World War, the Bolshevik Revolution of 1917-8, the creation of the International Labour Office (later the International Labour Organization) in 1919 as part of the League of Nations, and the economic depression of the 1930s led to extensive revision of the capitalist economic doctrine of *(laissez-faire in* Europe and North America. For the colonial powers, the, economic depression drove home two main lessons: a) it had the unintended consequence of creating a pool of labour that sought wage employment and constituted both a social and political problem in colonial urban areas; b) that for their own economies to avoid (rather predictable) slumps, it was necessary to generate consumption-oriented economies in the colonies to absorb manufactured products.[8]

As manifested in British policy, it meant discouraging the setting up of manufacturing industries in the colonies, encouraging peasant farmers to expand their production of export crops and who, at any rate, provided the 'leading sector' in generating demand for imports, and compelling generally recalcitrant colonial employers to treat labour 'decently' in order to avoid a disruption of mining and other commercial activities essential to the metropolitan economy - hence the Colonial Development and Welfare Acts. A residual factor was, of course, the shattering of confidence in the invisible mechanism of the 'market' in allocating scarce resources and the human sufferings which accompanied the slump necessarily brought a more interventionist reaction from most metropolitan governments, if only to avoid political repercussions at home. In all, British strategic and global considerations, peculiar problems confronting the colonial administration (discussed elsewhere) and the needs and activities of British and other European firms were all to impinge on the course and development of the Nigerian labour movement.

But more relevantly to this process were the ideological consequences of the Second World War, especially as what emerged as 'Western Europe' was not keen on the dismantling of the capitalist structures and mode of production already established, albeit shakily, on a greater surface area of the modern world. The end of the war not only signalled the end of Nazism but also heralded the demise of colonialism and the propagation of highly

---

[7] Ibid., pp. 51-2; Hopkins, A. G., *An Economic History of West Africa,* Longman London, 1973; p. 199.
[8] This was held back in Nigeria by low producer prices and colonial fiscal stringency.

infectious ideals of 'freedom', 'democracy' and recognition of the 'right of a people to self-determination.'

The traditional big-power quest for 'spheres of influence' became compounded by heightening ideological differences. Logically, and predictably, the immediate post-war period saw a marked shift of focus towards the leadership and internal administration of trade unions and political parties in colonial territories. Decolonization, once grudgingly recognized as an inevitable process had to be accomplished, as interestingly described, 'within the framework of Western Alliance.'[9] The open ideological rift in Europe of 1949 made more and more imperative the control of or influence over the outcome of political opposition in the colonies. Whatever influence colonial administrations and employers had over protest movements, especially the trade unions, were now to be supplemented by efforts of more specialized bodies and agencies.

CLASSIFICATION OF EXTERNAL INSTITUTIONAL MANIFESTATIONS

It is clearly outside the scope of this chapter to discuss in any great detail the philosophies of both ideological blocs, but it may be worth mentioning frequently projected crucial difference, namely, the degree of coercion o amount of consensus evidenced in both 'societies' with specific reference to decision-making and choice of alternatives in both political and socio economic spheres. From all indications, the Eastern bloc's policy of economic modernization under conditions of extremely centralized planning and control seem to have involved a minimum of consensus. This has led the West to describe itself as 'free', 'democratic' and 'pluralistic', implying the existence of greater degree of consensus and freedom in its kind of society.

This is necessarily an over-simplification and clearly contains elements of distortion. Main differences could be sought by contrasting roles played by political parties, governments, trade unions, and the institution of the ownership of the means of production, apart from other institutional arrangements. Surely, the issue of consensus versus coercion can be quit deceptive: the industrial revolution in Europe or Britain was no less coercive, in many aspects, both internally and externally (slave trade and colonialism) The 'freedoms' that prevailed in post-war Western Europe and North America were hardly available to a majority of the people in the crucial centuries during; which profound economic changes were wrought.

For our immediate purposes external influences may be broken into five main categories: colonial administration, international labour organizations diplomatic missions, foreign national union centres and Pan-African labour

[9] Lynd, G. E. (pseudonym), The *Politics of African Trade Unionism*, Praeger, New Yorl 1968, p. 146.

organizations. As the colonial administration category scarcely needs further clarification, brief comments on the others would be appropriate.

International Labour Organizations

International labour organizations refer to such bodies as the WFTU, the ICFTU and the International Federation of Christian Trade Unions - IFCTU (renamed World Confederation of Labour). The International Federation of Trade Unions, for the most part, was an association of European trade unions It agreed in 1945 to unite with the 'Red' International of Labour Unions (RILU to form the World Federation of Trade Unions (WFTU). This was at the suggestion of the British Trades Union Congress.[10] The British TUC eve went so far as to convene a special colonial trade union conference a few days before the preliminary World Trade Union Conference opened in London in February 1945 in order to bring as many colonial trade unions as possible into the new body.[11] The intensification of ideological differences led to the break-up of the WFTU in 1949, with the British, American and the non-communist European trade unions forming the ICFTU. The rump WFTU was reconstituted under the influence of the Soviet Union.[12] Although the International Federation of Christian Trade Unions (IFCTU) was formed in 1908 and organized unions on a denominational Christian basis, it was 'reorganized' in 1946 in light of ideological developments and joined in the fight for affiliates.[13] The other two bodies in this category are the International Confederation of Arab Trade Unions (ICFTU)[14] and the International Trades Secretariat (ITS). The latter are organizations of unions in specific trades and industries that cut across countries and continents, the three biggest being the International Transport Workers Federation, the Miners International Federation, and the International Metal Workers Federation.[15]

Foreign National Union Centres

A few examples are given here to exemplify the range of interests involved rather than an exhaustive list. Prominent in this group have been the British TUC, Confederation Francaise des Travailleurs Chretiens (CFTC) Confederation Generale du Travail (CGT), Confederation du Travail-Ford

[10] Roberts, B. C., *Labour in the Tropical Territories* , op cit., p. 157.

[11] Padmore, G., *Pan-Africanism or Communism?* Dennis Dobson, New York, 1956, p. 15

[12] For a more detailed coverage of the dissensions within the WFTU and the founding of the ICFTU, see Foster, W. E., *The World Trade Union Movement,* International Publishers, 1956; Lorwin, L., The International Labour Movement, Harper, New York 1953. For the ICFTU see Windmuller, J. P., 'ICFTU, Ten Years After', *ILRA* VOL I4, 1960.

[13] It had to later modify its policies so as to attract 'non-Christian' trade unions.

[14] For further details see Belling, W. A., *Pan-Arabism and Labour,* Harvard University press, 1960.

[15] See Lorwin L. L., 'The International Trades Secretariat', *Annals of the American Academy of Political and Social Science, vol.* 310, March 1957. Also, Steinbach, Regional Organisations of International Labour', *Annals of the American Academy* 'Regional Or *of Political and Social Science, vol.* 310, March 1957.

Ouvriere (CGT-FO), American Federation of Labour-Congress of Industrial Organizations (AFL-CIO), the Soviet All-Union Central Council of Trade Unions (AUCCTU), All-China Confederation of Trade Unions, West German Deutsch Gewerkschaftsbund (DGB), East German Federation of Labour, Israeli Histadrut, the Ghana Trades Union Congress, and Canadian Federation of Labour. They have all actively tried to influence central trade unionism in Nigeria.[16]

Diplomatic missions

The means by which most governments achieve their foreign policy goal: are varied. Customarily, most of them have 'labour attaches' under diplomatic cover in their embassies; their duties though not spelt out are generall1 expected to include the monitoring of developments in the host country's labour scene. In the› view of national interests and ideological sympathies, it mal be naive to assume that labour attaches merely observe, especially in area where the foreign government has extensive economic interests. Suffice it to say at this point that some trade union leaders in Nigeria developed unusually close relations with members of some diplomatic missions.

Pan-African Labour Organizations

The relevant pan-African labour organizations are the All-African Trade Union Federation (AATUF), the African Trades Union Confederation (ATUC) and the All-African Union of Christian Trade Unions (AAUCTU). The AATUF was formed in May 1961 in Casablanca after a series of preparatory meeting: that went under the title: 'Conference of African Peoples'.[17] In the main it arose in response to the activities of both the ICFTU and WFTU in Africa even if influenced and coloured by the patent political ambitions of Dr. Kwame Nkrumah and Sekou Toure, the circumstances of which are discusses elsewhere.[18] Conversely, both the ICFTU and ICFTU created the ATUC and AAUCTU to undercut the AATUF. All three organizations expended considerable amount of financial and other resources in quest of affiliate in Africa.

Conspicuously missing from the list are the League of Nations, the United Nations Organization (UNO) and its agencies and the International Labour Office (later Organization). The first two influenced developments in

---

[16] For a general review of their activities see Meynaud, J. & Salah-B4 y, A., *Trade Unionism in Africa*, Methuen, London, 1974. A not very satisfactory book is Lynd G.E., *The Politics of African Unionism*, Praeger, New York, 1964. For a rather slanted view see Lichtblau, G. E., 'Communist Labor Offensive in Former Colonial Territories', *I.L.R..R.., vol.* 15, April 1962. For the history of the international organisations themselves, see Lorwin, L. L. The *International Labor Movement*, Harper, New York, 1953; Windmuller, J. P., 'ICFTU: Ten Years After', *LLR.R., vol.* 14, 1960;and Lichtblau, G. E., 'The WFTU', *Social Research, vol.* 25 (1), 1958.

[17] The first conference of African peoples was held in Accra in December 1958 where the idea of a Pan-African trade union organisation was first mooted.

[18] See pages 73-75.

the colonies with their concept of 'trusteeship', acceptance of the principle of self-determination and the setting up of committees on racism, decolonization W apartheid. The ILO, formed in 1919 as part of the League of Nations made a substantial impact on colonial unionism for it was far easier to establish the violation of any of its convention than, say, the violations of political frights. The 1940s and 1950s saw colonial administrations and employer› struggling somewhat uncomfortably to comply with the ILO's provision; covering such items as forced labour and freedom to organize and to collective bargaining.[19] Although it is possible to identify the ILO's 'model' of industrial relations with a general 'western model', it cannot be said to have participated in the ideological business of 'capturing' trade unions in target areas. It, therefore, must be emphasized that this study is mainly preoccupied with the impact of the Cold War (or all that went under the name) on central trade unionism in Nigeria. To this extent, these organizations and their agencies ire ignored.

OBJECTIVES OF FOREIGN INFLUENCE

In discussing the objectives of foreign influences, analysis is mostly restricted to the area of industrial relations relevant to the subject of this study. The objective fact to be noted is that never in recorded history (or more aptly since the Industrial Revolution and emergence of trade unions) except since World War II have such systematic and purposeful strategies been pursued to guide the growth of labour organizations in other countries. The means used in pursuing these strategies have been varied and not easily all overt in nature. Professor Windmuller has noted that:

> The exercise of influence over labour organizations in underdeveloped countries has become a large-scale international operation. It is a full-time occupation for hundred of people, it is highly competitive, and it even contains elements of melodrama a indicated by the use of secret training schools, undercover agents, and forge documents.[20]

Windmuller further identified three main objectives of the external factors the propagation of a model, the infusion of a suitable, ideological orientation and the creation of technically proficient organizations.[21]

---

[19] For the influence of the ILO conventions on Nigerian Labour Legislation see *International Labour Review,* vol. 82, July 1960 and vol. 83, April 1961, on its impact on Asian Countries. For the history of the ILO itself see Johnson, G. A., *The ILO,* Europa Publications, London, 1970.

[20] Windmuller, J., 'External Influences on Labour Organisations in Underdeveloped Countries,' *ILRR, vol.* 16, July 1963, p. 572.

[21] Ibid, p. 569.

The preceding section of this Chapter gives but a brief sketch of the organizations that make up the foreign influences. For the purposes of this study the IFCTU (or WCL), the ITS and the ICFTU are rolled into one group vis-a-vis the WFTU. This kind of simplification makes it possible that subtle but meaningful differences existing between these organizations may be over-looked. From the Cold War angle, however, such differences may be disregarded since all three organizations have the aim of containing what is generally announced to be 'communism'. As it turns out, an undefined 'communist-style trade unionism' is nothing more than militant unionism that tends to threaten profits by increasing labour costs, advocating the ending of foreign control of resources and production processes (meaning multi-national and foreign companies) and, in few instances, abolition of private ownership of means of production.

Even a casual study of the ICFTU, IFCTU and ITSs shows that existing relationships are not restricted to ideological empathy alone. The activities of the ICFTU are reinforced in scope and depth through interlocking relationships with the various ITSs. There exists a system of mutual representation in the Executive Boards of both organizations, buttressed by a consultative council composed of officials drawn from the organizations, apart from the sizable financial contributions made by the ITS to the Regional fund of the ICFTU for 'organizing' in Africa and Asia.[22] Lorwin, in fact, argues that the ITS have 'proved themselves staunch supporters of democratic principles and have played an important part in the struggle against communist infiltration.'[23] Indeed, the ITSs are not only 'ideologically linked with the ICFTU', they also 'accept the ICFTU as the overall policy-making organization.' [24]

On the other hand, relations between the IFCTU (or WCL) and the ICFTU have not always been friendly. The leaders of the ICFTU have sneeringly described the former as a 'midget international' and have upbraided it fox its alleged 'neutralism', especially when some religious 'principles' could be compromised. The leaders of the IFCTU have in reply expressed 'pride in poverty' and have made insinuations about the 'mysterious flow of gold' into the coffers of the ICFTU, a hint at the large financial contributions made by American trade unions. But in practice-¨the IFCTU tends to back the actions of the ICFTU in the UNO and in other

---

[22] Lorwin, R. L., The International Labour Movement, Harper, New York 1953

[23] Ibid., p. 8. This is obviously a misrepresentation of the nature of international rivalry. In Nigeria, as is elsewhere, the issue has been more of rivalry *within* the capitalist camp than anything else. The competition between Britain, United States of America, Japan, France and W. Germany for resources and investment outlets has become more acute. Potential communist support for groups that seek to eliminate 'foreign control' becomes the bogey, conveniently explained in terms of 'Cold War' and 'spread of communism'.

[24] Windmuller, J. P., 'ICFTU: Ten Years After', op cit., p. 271.

international organizations.[25] March 1974, it was agreed that a joint ICFTU/WCL working committee or executive level be created, the objectives of which would be to study meant of developing further co-operation between both organizations and to seek ways and means for unification. This proposal was subsequently ratified b) the ICFTU Executive Board in May 1974 and by the WCL Confederal Committee in October 1974.[26]

More importantly, the AFL-CIO has consistently disagreed with other members of the ICFTU over a range of issues. The 'fight' against communism colonial issues (such as the rate of decolonization, the Algerian war of independence, the so-called Mau Mau uprising in Kenya, among others) and aid programmes' have all provided areas where opinions and strategies tender to differ. Professor Roberts flatly stated:

> The AFL-CIO have made it abundantly clear that they believe that the European union have not waged war vigorously enough on Communism and colonialism...and they have shown at times reluctance to increase their contributions to the ICFTU fund until assured of changes in is policy.[27]

Apart from affecting financial contributions, this orientation has had some other concrete manifestations. Windmuller has associated the 'revised estimate' of Mr Oldenbroek's (then incumbent General Secretary of the ICFTU) qualification to retain his job by American unions to the 'disappointingly slow progress of the ICFTU's strength and influence as the standard bearer of global trade unionism in the struggle against the forces of communism.'[28] It may be unnecessary to add that Oldenbroek subsequently lost his job.

It is also instructive that even Oldenbroek's successor ran into similar difficulty. At the March 1955 Executive Board meeting an open breach between the AFL-CIO and Omer Becu, the new General Secretary, became apparent. George Meany, President of the AFL-CIO, attacked the ICFTU, describing it as 'a complete and absolute bureaucracy, inept in the way it functions' and complained that money donated by his organization of the (ICFTU) was lying unused in banks. The main issue, however, was that the (ICFTU) appeared not sufficiently committed to the 'war against communism.'[29] Meg Roberts has succinctly summed up the situation:

---

[25] Lorwin, L. L., *The International Labour Movement, op. cit.,* p. 330.
[26] ICFTU Eleventh World Congress, Report on Activities 1972-1974, Brussels, pp. 26-27.
[27] Roberts, B. C., *Labour in the Tropical Territories of the Commonwealth*, Bell, London, 1964, p. 160.
[28] Windmuller, ICFTU, *op. cit., p.* 258.
[29] Davies, I., *African Trade Unions, op.* cit., p. 207.

> The British TUC accuses the Americans of using ICFTU funds for the purposes of Cold War; of offering assistance not necessarily where it will be most useful to union purposes, but where it will be most effective against communist influence. A subsidiary accusation is that American anti-colonialism which takes the form of discouraging union-to-union assistance is a cover for the attempt to replace the ICFTU. This feeling is so strong that the British TUC has this year refused to contribute to the ICFTU Solidarity Fund.[30]

The common membership of the ICFTU has not performed the miracle of eliminating national rivalries. A direct consequence of this is that' the AFL-CIO, the West German DGB, the Israeli Histadrut, the Belgian General Federation of Labour (FGTB), the British TUC and others also operate independently outside the framework of the ICFTU. This is not to say that such display of disunity and 'ideological deviation' is restricted to the CFTU. Although the Soviet Union plays a guiding role which the Americas unions never had in the ICFTU (though they aspired to it) the East Germans Czechoslovaks, Polish, and Bulgarians also make contacts and give aid outside the WFTU. The separate activities of the Chinese are taken for granted. In view of this, it could be argued that governmental and international trade union diplomacy has veered increasingly from polarized power and ideological East-West axis to regional and bilateral relations. But the seeming clad between self-interest and ideological commitment, underlined by tactical considerations, though substantial in certain areas of interest, takes place within recognized and understood framework. Thus, for example, the American, and other Western allies may disagree over the rate of decolonization but the problem of decolonization *per se* has to be settled within the political systems of the colonial, powers and the Western alliance.

Special attention will be paid to the American AFL-CIO not only because of its wide-ranging activities outside the framework of the ICFTU (like the Soviet AUCCTU) but it is one of those organizations that has found it difficult to conceive of its external relations in non-Cold War terms. A more important reason, however, is the dominant position it has achieved in the realm of central trade unionism in Nigeria, and the fact that since the AFL-CIO withdrew from the ICFTU on February 28, 1959, it has tended to function independently almost an 'international labour organization' in its own right.

On December 31, 1955, eight days after his election as President of the AFL-CIO, George Meany declared in a foreign policy address that there could be no 'neutrals' in the struggle between communism and

[30] Roberts, M., 'African Trade Unions in Transition' *World Today, vol.* 17, 1961, p. 450.

democracy.[31] Even at a much earlier period, before both the AFL and the CIO merged, the AFL maintained a 'Free Trade Union Committee' which undertook 'independent activities'. Notwithstanding gentle hints and open prodding by turns from the ICFTU and from European trade unions, and of course from the CIO, the AFL maintained this committee and its 'independent activities' abroad with undiminished aggressiveness. These 'independent activities' began shortly before the creation of the all embracing WFTU (in 1945) and during the WFTU period, the AFL considered itself as 'practically the only anti-communist force' in international trade union affairs.[32]

It is relevant to note the AFL-CIO's basic orientation in both policy arc actions. Article II, section 7 of its constitution talks about 'giving constructive aid in promoting the cause of peace and freedom in the world and to aid assist and co-operate with free and democratic labour movements throughout the world'. Such grand declarations may have been coloured by the euphoria, which ensued at the end of the Second World War, but a cursory review of its activities in the Third World, especially Nigeria, shows that three decade have not revealed any change in its outlook. The AFL-CIO still appears to hinge its policies to the set of ideas which the AFL and CIO explicitly agree on as a common basis for a foreign policy:

a) that Free labour movements can exist and prosper only in a democratic soil Totalitarian forces of the Right and Left threaten the very existence of the democracies, but the deadliest threat stems from the expansive and ruthless power of international communism led by the Soviet Union. The democratic nations must meet the danger collectively and with firm resolve...;
b) that the economically underdeveloped countries of the world must be give sufficient economic, technical and financial assistance to enable them to construe viable economic systems. Continued poverty, inequality and hopelessness will alienate people friendly to our cause and increase communist strength…; and
c) colonialism as a way of governing underdeveloped areas has become obsolete an is in any event immoral. The aspirations of colonial peoples for self-government and political independence cannot be denied except at the certain risk of enhancing the appeal of communism . . .[33]

The world has come a long way since 1955. Virtually all colonial territories gained political independence without becoming communist, while America domination and flexing of its military muscle in reaction to

---

[31] Windmuller, J. P., 'Foreign Affairs and the AFL-CIO', *ILRR*, April 1956, p. 419.

[32] Windmuller, J. P., Foreign Affairs, *op. cit.*, p. 424.

[33] Windmuller, 'Foreign Affairs and the AFL-CIO', p. 425. For a review of AFL-CIO constitution see *ILRR, vol.* 9, Oct. 1955.

its own pet 'domino-theory' of spread of communism has been substantially counter-productive: has created many more communist regimes than any time since the Soviet Union swept through Eastern Europe. Contrary to what Windmuller has tried to argue,[34] this fixation -about 'communist intentions' would, for the American trade unions, logically make international trade union diplomacy complementary to and integrated with government's foreign policy. Ioan Davies takes this point further by pointing out that if Europeans can be seen trying desperately to insist on trade union 'principles' (for whatever reason of their own), Americans are disposed to preventing 'communist subversion and take-over.' And to do this, the whole apparatus of the state, management and the unions must be harnessed (as happens) in a common effort.[35] Ioan Davies forgot to add that in this 'struggle', the so-called 'totalitarian forces of the Right' become allies and 'very existence of democracy' and 'totalitarian forces of the Right' become synonymous with 'American interests' (or British or German interests, as the case may be) and any groups, apart from militant unionists, remotely representing a 'threat' to such interests become either 'communists' or 'totalitarian forces of the Left'. This perspective thus denies the real possibility of socialist or national movements dedicated to termination of at least, 'foreign domination'. In this regard, it is little wonder that prominent American labour leaders such as George Meany and Walter Reuther are alleged to have very strong links with the American Central Intelligence Agency (CIA).[36]

THE TWO VIEWS OF TRADE UNIONISM

The two divergent interpretations of trade unionism, for the purpose of this study, will be referred to as 'Communist' and 'Western' - the former coinciding with views of Soviet Union and other socialist countries on the one hand, and 'Western' referring to non-communist European countries in North American sub-continent. Both views can be regarded as effectively represented at international level by the WFTU and ICFTU, respectively. This neat division into two camps may be qualified: firstly, views on trade unionism are not identical in all countries located in any one camp. Trade unionism in Yugoslavia is not quite the same as that in Soviet Union, just as trade unionism in the United States of America is a far cry from that in Britain.

---

[34] Windmuller, J. P., 'External influences', p. 567-568.

[35] Davies, I., *African Trade Unions*, p. 208-209.

[36] Agee, P., *Inside the Company: CIA Diary*, Penguin, Harmondsworth, 1974, p. 75 just to mention only one source. The American United Auto Workers (AUW) only withdrew from the AFL-CIO after Reuther's death.

Secondly, contradictory views on trade unionism exist within individual countries themselves. To illustrate the point, some sections of society in Britain can be found clamouring for 'responsible' trade unionism while other raise the spectre of worker-controlled factories.[37] Perhaps in a more striking vein, some sections of the French labour movement - trade unions under the control of the CGT, which is affiliated to the WFTU - officially regard their brand of unionism as not only economic exercise but as a revolutionary political struggle as well. Like the Communist Party, they are armed with a blue-print for a complete economic and political restructuring of their society.

Thirdly, legal definition of a trade union or what constitutes one is not the same in all countries, with possible exception of communist countries.[38] Lastly, whereas some countries in both camps have 'industrial' and 'craft unions', both Britain and the United States of America have the separate problem of 'multi-unionism' and 'business' unionism.[39] Despite these qualifications, it is still possible to discern a common outlook exclusive to any one of the camps in terms of what they regard as 'proper' trade unionism or the ideas propagated in connection thereof.

The Communist View

The Communist view of trade unionism given here is largely derived from the International Labour Office report on the trade union movement in Soviet Union, and other incidental works as well as from official pronouncements. As the International Labour Office (ILO) report noted, after the 1921 period – with the introduction of the Russian New Economic Plan – actual practice departed from theory both in the organization of the trade unions and in their departed from theory both in the organization other trade unions and in their economic and social activities.[40] It also becomes apparent that the Communist theory of trade unionism presents two distinct aspects which differ according to whether action is contemplated under a capitalist or proletarian regime. This is significant to the extent that different strategies and tactics are adopted by trade unions under differing circumstances.

---

[37] See the Conservative Party's *Fair Deal at Work*, 1968 for 'responsible' trade unionism orientation. For both views, Flanders, A., *Management and Unions*, *op. cit.*, p. 40.

[38] The total working population are usually organized into industrial unions – there are no employers' organizations. The 1968 Royal Commission's Report has defined a trade union as "any combination, whether temporary or permanent, the principal objects of which are under its constitutional statutory objects, namely the regulation of regulation of relations between workmen and masters, or between workmen and workmen, or between masters and masters, or the imposing of restrictive conditions on the conduct of any trade or business, and also the provisions of benefits to members." This definition thus includes employer organizations.

[39] For a discussion of 'union types' see Turner, H.A., 'The Morphology of Trade Unionism' in McCarthy, W.E.J., (ed) *Unions*, Penguin, 1972.

[40] International Labour Office, Geneva, 1927, Preface.

Under Capitalist Regime

Apart from organizing the masses with a view to improving material situation and conditions of labour in general, it is the duty of the revolutionary trade unions to unite, discipline and educate the masses with a view to 'the abolition of capitalism' and to progress towards the 'creation of a socialist regime.'[41] As for trade union structure, it is expected that the question of outstanding importance is to convert the craft unions into industrial unions. "One undertaking, one union" must be the motto of the revolutionary trade unions. By this system all classes of workers in an undertaking or factory will form a compact group in face of the employers.[42] On the question of trade union 'neutrality' or political involvement, the theory states in unambiguous terms that:

> the revolutionary socialists have always been hostile to the idea of trade union neutrality and the independence of the revolutionary proletariat, knowing full well that under the names of neutrality and independence towards revolutionary socialism was concealed the bourgeois and reformist idea of separating political action from economic struggle of the proletariat. For this reason the idea of the independence of the trade union movement must be energetically and resolutely rejected.[43]

Communist objections to the 'neutrality' of the trade unions lie in who may be termed the 'incorporation thesis'. Trade unions, being manifestation of class antagonisms in an industrial setting, are logically required to occupy themselves 'fighting' capital owners and the bourgeois state for power instead of' accepting a permanent delimitation of 'spheres of influence' - thereby stifling out any revolutionary political activities. The 'inevitability' of co-operation between antagonistic forces in industry was since pointed out by Trotsky:

> There is one common feature in the development, or more correctly, the degeneration of modern trade union organisations in the entire world: it is their drawing closely to and growing together with the state power. The process is equally characteristic of the neutral, the Social-Democratic, the Communist and "anarchist" trade unions. This fact alone shows that the tendency towards "growing together" is

[41] Ibid., p. 20.

[42] ILO Report, *op. cit.*, p. 50

[43] Resolutions and Statutes adopted by the First International Congress of Revolutionary Trade Unions cited in ILO report, *op. cit.*

> intrinsic not in this or that doctrine as such but it derives from social conditions common for all unions.[44]

The 'growing together' phenomenon is acceptable in a proletarian-controlled polity (since the proletariat theoretically have power and means of production) whereas a similar occurrence under a capitalist regime would not only present a 'contradiction' but also constitutes 'exploitation' only made possible by combined prevalence of 'false consciousness' on the part of workers and the omnipotence of capital and bourgeois state. From this standpoint, a symbiotic relationship between trade unions, bourgeois state and management at best represent a strategy, a peaceful interlude in an otherwise thorny road to socialism. Or, the trade unions could become 'lieutenants of capital in to intensified exploitation of the workers.[45] In sum, 'the ideas of direct action, pressure brought to bear on capital and the State by the masses, and to overthrow of capitalism by social revolution, do great honour to the revolutionary trade unions and constitute the practical side of their general principles.'[46]

Under a Proletarian Regime

As soon as a successful revolution is achieved the trade unions are expected streamline their activities so as to consolidate the 'gains of the revolution'. Meaning that:

> After the political revolution the trade unions must take up a central position in politics and in a certain sense they must even become the main political organisation. They become the founder of the new society. . . The trade unions must educate the masses and lead them to share in the government of the country. That is why nationalisation of the trade unions is inevitable.[47]

> Trade union neutrality becomes impossible, for in theory;

> The strongest and most powerful organisation is to be found in the State organisation of the working classes or, in other words, the Society power. Therefore the trade unions and cooperative organisations must transform themselves into economic sections and organs of the State power…[48]

Even the use of Strikes as a revolutionary weapon changes too:

---

[44] Trotsky, Trade Unions in the Epoch of Imperialist Decay, 1948; also quoted in Hyman, R. *Marxism and the Sociology of Trade Unionism, op. cit.*, p. 19.

[45] 'The Trade Unions in Britain (1933) in *Leon Trotsky on the Trade Unions*, 1969, p. 54.

[46] ILO Report, 1929, *op. cit.*, p. 26.

[47] Ibid., p. 51.

[48] Bucharin and Preobrazhensky, *The A.B.C. of Communism*, p. 280.

> Having carried out a successful revolution, and dispossessed the middle classes, and converted the factories and undertakings into public property, is it possible that the workers con template making demands, supported by strikes and disorder in industry, on their own government? Such action would be contradictory to all common sense. Therefore it is perfectly logical that the strike must henceforth be rejected as a weapon by the Russian trade unions.[49]

The ILO mission to the USSR in 1960 partially verified the fact that strikes were not officially prohibited but was reminded that in any case 'workers did not have to resort to strike action and there was nobody for them to strike against, since the means of production belonged to them.'[50]

Trade unionism is thus not restricted to 'job consciousness' for 'in the plan of struggle of the working class the economic movement and political activity are inseparably intertwined.'[51] But the unions have other functions, as Lenin revealed in his critique of Trotsky:

> But the trade unions...are educational organisations, organisations that enlist, that train; they are schools, schools of administration, schools of management, schools of communism. The place the trade unions occupy in the system of the dictatorship of the proletariat is...between the Party and the State power.[52]

Summarizing, Lozovsky noted that:

> The moment is supposed only to follow the ideological policy given by the Communist Party. It differs from British trade unionism in that it has never at any period been a purely economic, purely corporate movement. Again, it differs from the reformist theory in that it has never aimed at a gradual evolution fro m capitalism to socialism. And it differs from anarcho-syndicalism in that it is not opposed to the State in abstract metaphysical meaning of the word. The only State to which Russian trade unionism is opposed is the composition of the State which interests it...Thus it is that we can agree with the anarcho-syndicalists concerning class aims, the evolutionary tactics to be adopted, and the direct action of one class against another. At the same time, however, we see eye to eye with the Germanic trade unions as far as centralisation is concerned, when this is understood as a

---

[49] Lozovsky, *The Russian Trade Unions and the N.. E. P.*, Paris, 1922, Report, *op. cit.*

[50] ILO Report, *Trade Union Situations in the USSR.*, Geneva, 1960, pp, 65-66.

[51] Lozovsky, A., 'The Role of the Trade Unions in the General Class Struggle of the Proletariat' in McCarthy, W. E. J. (ed), *Unions, op* cit., p. 52. For a general coverage Deutsch, I., *Soviet Trade*, Brown, E. C. ,*Soviet Trade Unions and Labour Relations*, Harvard University Press, Cambridge, Mass., 1966.

[52] Lenin quoted in Sorensen, J.B., *Life and Death of Soviet Trade Unionism*, Atherton Press, New York, 1969, p. 85.

> maximum concentration of our force. We have much less in common with Anglo-Saxon trade union principles, and perhaps only with the tenacity with which those unions lead an economic struggle.[53]

Since we are, in this analysis, only concerned to present contrasting views on trade unionism, a further critique of this view may be unnecessary. One could point out with Professor Harold Laski, however that 'the abstraction is based upon the assumption that the government is aiming at the welfare of the common people, and that its interpretation of that welfare is indisputable.'[54]

The Western View of Trade Unionism

The Western view of trade unionism is effectively summarized by G.D.H. Cole:

> This second idea of trade unionism is that it exists in order to protect and advance the interest of a defined group of workers who possess some special skill or other mark of distinction from the general mass of labour, so that they can hope by a close combination of those who possess this special qualification to secure better terms of employment and a higher status than would be possible if each man acted alone. The aim of those who hold this view is to create for themselves a limited monopoly of labour, in order to improve its price, just as capitalists endeavour by combination to exact a monopoly profit. There is in this type of Trade Unionism no set intention to change the economic system, but only a will to make it work better from the standpoint of the particular group. Nor is there any solid desire to build up a solid combination of the whole working class for it is clearly impossible for all of them to exact special privileges.[55]

Thus unlike communist countries (and Sweden) where the total working population is organized into trade unions, only segments of the working population are organized in Western countries. In Britain, the working populations not only partially organized, there has been intense lobbying in recent years in support of legislation that would legalize the right of the individual to refrain from joining any union if he so desired.[56]

Writing with specific reference to the United States of America, Bruce Millen has noted that:

---

[53] Lozovsky, The Universal Trade Union Movement before and after the War, p. 24-25, quoted in 1927, ILO Report, op *cit.*

[54] Laski, A., *Trade Unions in the New Society*, Allen and Unwin, London, 1950, p. 11.

[55] Cole, G. D. H., *British Trade Unionism Today*, Victor Gollancz, London, 1938, pp. 535-536.

[56] The 1971 Industrial Relations Act, for example.

> The term "free and independent trade unionism" which thereafter became the policy beacon for both government and organized labour assistance to labour movements abroad has never been precisely defined, except as expressed in the Benton Amendment. But in general it seems to imply a model of unionism that a) is primarily, if not exclusively concerned with economic function of collective bargaining to win benefits for workers, b) is not linked with or/and controlled by a government or political party, c) has no communist connections.[57]

The slogan 'free and independent trade unionism' features prominently in the literature of all he affiliates of the ICFTU, which describes itself as the embodiment of the 'international free trade union movement' – a status now equally shared by the AFL-CIO. But Millen's subsequent remarks seem interesting:

> The only labour movement in the world whose operations accord with all three specifications (as outlined above) is that of the U.S.A…But in the context of the Cold War this is in itself a political stance…The "free and independent" slogan as used by American union representatives and government officials alike, seems essentially a statement of faith and hope – faith in the democratic process as the U.S.A. knows it, and hope for the future of the new countries.[58]

Describing the British scene, Professor Banks identifies the general principles and ideology of trade unionism at the present time as:

> a) regarding collective bargaining and the protection the interests of union members against employers as its main function; b) remaining independent of all employers for purposes of negotiations; c) being prepared to use all forms of industrial actions, including strikes, to achieve its aims; d) describing itself to be a trade union; e) registering itself as a trade union; f) affiliating to the TUC; and g) affiliating to the Labour Party.[59]

It is doubtful whether Bank's last condition holds true in view of the fact that the reins of power do change hands quite regularly between the Labour and Conservative parties, and the fact that the latter has of recent set out to woo trade unions into its fold. Unions' participation in the body politic is expected, for 'they may decide by a majority to support a political party... It

[57] Millen, B. H., the Political Role of Labour in Developing Countries, The Brooking Institution, Washington, 1963, p. 5

[58] Ibid., p. 5

[59] Banks, J. A., *Trade Unionism*, Collier and Macmillan, London, 1974, pp. 5-6

reflects no more than a recognition that they must engage in political as well as industrial action to further their own objectives, and taking sides is the best strategy because it produces best results.'[60] Unions' 'involvement' in politics is thus seen only in terms of counteracting the harmful aspects of the activities of other interest groups, such as employers' associations or government that could encroach on the rights of workers – say, by lobbying for a legislation that could hamper union development or reduce social welfare benefits.

The 'role' of the State is generally seen as that of a neutral arbiter but since the adoption of Keynesian 'basket of tools' economic strategies, notably monetary (fiscal and incomes) and full employment policies, such a view has become less convincing: governments now have their own 'interests' and usually tend to influence industrial relations in a particular direction. As Harold Laski put it':

> The area in which the government of a capitalist country can be neutral, it is said, still more the area in which it can be favourable to the workers, is necessarily small. Both the law and the administration of a capitalist society are directed essentially to the support of the employers; it is therefore natural for the unions to insist upon their right to as fully independent a judgement as they can make, because, normally the scales are weighted against the interest of the workers.[61]

The hub of this model of industrial relations or trade unionism is collective bargaining.[62] Apart from general policy guidelines - in this era of economic planning - terms and conditions of work should be settled within the enterprises, between management and workers' representatives. Committees and various other bodies are created to look into wages and other disputes that may arise. These efforts are usually supplemented by government's own arbitration boards and the like. But in the United States of America there is a strong preference for private organizations that specialize in arbitration, and the courts show a strong presence during bargaining occasions as collective agreements are often legally binding.

In Britain, however, the courts play a minimal role in settling disputes because of the 'voluntary' tradition.[63] Voluntarism is generally held to mean

---

[60] Flanders, A., *Management and Unions*, op cit., p. 39

[61] Laski, H., *Trade Unions in the New Society*, op cit., p. 10

[62] For a useful treatment of this concept see Flanders, A., (ed) *Collective Bargaining*, Harmondsworth, penguin, 1969. See also Fox A., *Man Mismanagement*, Hutchinson, London, 1974, pp. 122-144 for an interesting overview; Chamberlain and Kuhn, *Collective Bargaining*, McGraw-Hill, New York, 1965 for an American perspective. For disputes procedures see March, A.I. & McCarty, W. E. J., disputes procedures in British Industry, Research Paper No. 2, part 2, Royal Commission on Trade Unions and Employers' Associations, 1966.

[63] See Flanders, A., 'The Tradition of Voluntarism,' BJIR. vol. 12 (3), 1974.

the preference of employers and workers for collective bargaining to State regulation as a means of determining wages and other conditions of employment. Collective agreements are far from being final and detailed legalistically drafted documents that cover specified periods of time. An agreement is regarded essentially as a stage in the continuing process of negotiation with the present points or conditions representing workable compromises or minima to be maintained, but open to revision as other factors crop up. In some cases, 'agreements' are often informal trade practices and customs or local bargains struck by shop stewards. In summary, collective bargaining in Britain is a dynamic, on-going process that leaves room for differences among workgroups in terms of occupational status and bargaining power, while incorporating the synthesis of the attitudes and orientations of a people which are firmly rooted in their tradition. Thus all that is needed are, as trade unions are supposed to see the situation, minimum laws or statutes to ensure the freedom of the parties to bargain collectively in pursuit of their interest. In the Western view, therefore, trade unions are not expected to be revolutionary in their outlook, should be solely concerned with 'bread and butter' issues and strikes should be undertaken in a 'responsible' fashion. A Royal Commission lists the following as trade union objectives: collective bargaining and political lobbying, improved terms of employment, improved physical environment at work, greater employment opportunities and national prosperity, security of income and improved social services and a voice in government.[64] The whole tenor of this brand of unionism has been captured by Banks in his description:

> Trade unionists, then, play their part in the historical process by organising successfully for economic reforms which reduce the number of capitalists facing them, but they need not intend to achieve this, nor need they be aware that it is a consequence of their action. Strikes which result in a shorter working week or in an increase in wages which the employer finds difficult to pass on to consumer, may not be designed to cause him to search for new ways of maintaining his share of surplus labour by forcing less efficient or less ruthless competitors out of business, in so far as this occurs, polarisation without pauperisation is intensified. Political agitation which leads to an extension of the Factory Acts, or to measures to prevent destitution or unemployment, may equally be carried on without the further understanding that an accompanying result is the amassing of the control of more and more capital in fewer and fewer hands. Such

---

[64] Royal Commission on Trade Unions and Employers' Associations, 1966, pp. 32-39. For union objectives in America see Barbash, J., *The Practice of Unionism*, Harper & Bro, 1956

trade union activities, economic and political, are *not* revolutionary in the class-conscious sense of that term, unless they are informed by the clear understanding that anew social system, structurally different from capitalism, is the inevitable outcome.[65]

One must note, however, that the activities of some trade unions do not conform to this popular view of trade unionism, a development commented on by Paul Ferris, Professor Vic Allen and Richard Hyman, among others.[66]

In concluding this section, attention is again drawn to the fact that one of the main aims is to review critically the attempts to introduce the divergent interpretations of trade unionism into the Nigerian labour movement. It is usually difficult to identify the link between the activities of the international labour organizations and their conception of 'proper' unionism, which can only be inferred from their official pronouncements and areas and organisations which receive their 'aid' and other forms of assistance. It is reasonable to assume that recipients of all forms of aid and assistance from any one of the external donors either conform closely to the expectations of the donor, in terms of organisational structure and general outlook, or are expected or hoped to do so. There *are* deliberate attempts at indoctrinating trade unions leaders even though not of an extensive nature:

those who do receive fairly systematic ideological training are mainly students in the labour colleges. The donors expect, however, that the influence of this training will extend far beyond these students, for it is assumed that, after finishing their studies at the colleges, they will transmit what they have learned in their own countries through formal instructional programmes which they themselves create or through their actions as leaders.[67]

Aid may be given to 'hostile' organizations with the hope that such organizations may modify their policies over a period of time. The fact that 'subversion' and 'infiltration' feature rather frequently in the language of in labour organizations in describing the activities of rival bodies would seem to indicate the donor's expectations and intentions and yardstick by which its own activities many be based. Competitive 'assistance' from external

---

[65] Banks, J. A., *Marxist Sociology in Action,* Faber and Faber, London, 1970, g. 52. Emphasis mine.

[66] Ferris, P., *The New Militants: Crisis in the Trade Unions,* Penguin, Harmondsworth, V.L. Allen, *Militant Trade Unionism,* Merlin, London, 1966; Hyman, R .*The Workers' Union,* Clarendon Press, 1971; *Industrial Relations: A Marxist Introduction, op cit.*:- and Lane, T. & Roberts, K., *Strike at Pilkingtons,* Fontana, London, 1971. On strikes see Knowles, K.G.J.C., *Strikes: a Study in Industrial Conflict,* Blackwell, Oxford 1952; Kornhauser, A., Dubin, R., and Ross, A. M. (eds), *Industrial Conflict,* McGraw-Hill, New York, 1954; Hyman, R., *Strikes,* Fontana, London, 1972.

[67] Jacobson, H. K., 'Ventures in Polity Shaping: External Assistance to Labour Movements in Developing Countries' in Cox, R. (ed), *International Organisation: World Politics,* Macmillan, London, 1969, p. 202

sources has come in various forms: as direct financial grants, payment of wages and salaries of union staff, of office equipment, as payment for the secondment of trade union 'experts' or 'organizers' , or in the form of finances for visits and scholarships.[68]

The 'aid relationship' itself remains crucial for the achievement of donor's goals:

> ...donors are prepared to voice their opinions on the recipient's situation and development projects...This sort of donor role falls somewhere between giving and exerting pressure. Advice is normally offered with the expectation of action taken in accordance with the advice given...Pressure is normally backed by form of sanction to ensure that certain actions follow. This sort of contact by aid-giver puts the recipient in a position where he is questioned, challenged and harassed.[69]

To what extent this relationship constitutes 'intervention' is extensively commented upon by Krassowski:

> Intervention is based on the simple idea that the donor...there are two main varieties. Country's superior range of skills, great technical capacity, and longer development experience enable it to exercise a beneficial supervisory role both in the use of aid and in the formulation of development policies. This may be called the "influence and control" approach. It rests on the notion of "performance criteria"; specific advice is given, and aid is made, explicitly or implicitly,, conditional upon a satisfactory reaction to the advice. The second variety may be called "involvement" and takes as its starting point the fact that aid contacts act as a stimulus to the receiving country. The involvement approach seeks to maximize these points of contact in an all-embracing aid relationship. The approach sees the donor as bringing a certain view and a set of values, and confronting the recipient with them. The resulting clash of views and attitudes helps to stimulate the recipient's thinking and action.[70]

These two 'approaches' are relevant in the context of the activities of the colonial administration, labour and trade union officers, foreign national union centres, and those of the international labour organizations in Nigeria.

---

[68] Zack, A., *Labour Training in Developing Countries*, Praeger, New York, 1964, p. 26

[69] Krassowski, A., *The Aid Relationship*, Overseas Development Institute, London, 1968, p. 13

[70] Krasssowski, A., *AID*, *op cit.*, p. 17. For a theoretical approach see Morgenthau, H. J., 'A Political Theory of Foreign Aid', *American Political Science Review*, vol. 56, 1962, p. 301-309.

The 'Labour Colleges' themselves in which special training is given to labour leaders are widely scattered around the globe. The ICFTU main training centres have been: a) Labour Relations Institute of the University of Puerto Rico (set up in 1951 in co-operation with ORIT - the Inter-American regional organisation of the ICFTU; b) ICFTU Asian Trade Union College, Calcutta, India (established in 1949); c) Labour Education Centre, University of the Philippines (established in 1952 by the United States Foreign Operations Administration); d) ICFTU African Labour College, Kampala, Uganda (established in 1958 but closed by government of President Obote in mid-1960s); e) Histadrut's Afro-Asian Labour Institute, Tel Aviv, Israel (jointly organized by the American AFL-CIO and the British TUC); and the ICFTU Inter-American Residential Institute for Labour Studies, Mexico City, (established in 1962 for the training of teachers, labour journalists an sponsored by ORIT). The Ruskin College, Oxford and the Department of Industrial Relations at the London School of Economics also provided similar facilities under the aegis of the British TUC. The AFL-CIO also utilized Harvard University in its programmes, while the WFTU depended on the Patrice Lumumba Friendship University in Moscow and other training centres in Leipzig, Prague and Bulgaria. Whether these 'colleges' and other 'aid programmes' achieved a 'transfer' of certain 'values', 'attitudes' and 'organizational structures' is another matter - perhaps to those "trained".

But it should be noted, however, that there exists no clear separation between external 'influences' view of, and assumptions about 'institutional transfers and views propagated in most academic analyses of Nigerian trade union scene Indeed, the latter often provide the theoretical arguments with which external factor habitually 'explains' its outlook and activities. Apart from extensive documentation on the legal/institutional framework of the Nigerian trade union scene, most writers and academic analyses have stayed satisfied with identifying and listing 'ills' and 'weaknesses', departure points from a assumed prototype. Constant reference thus will be made to major studies (and to a few tangential literature) on Nigerian industrial relations, and critically assessed as if they are part and parcel of external 'influences'.[71]

---

[71] Major literature include Yesufu, T. M. *An Introduction to Industrial Relations in Nigeria,* OUP fqr NISER, 1962; Warren, W. M., 'Urban Real Wages and the Nigerian Trade Union Movement', *E.D.C.C. , vols. 15* (1) 1966 and 17 (4) 1969; Berg, E. J. & Butler, J. 'Trade Unions' in Coleman, J. S. & Rosberg, C. G. *(eds) Political Parties and National Integration in Tropical Africa,* Univ. of California Press, Bekerley & Los Angeles, 1964; Kilby, P., *Industrialisation in an Open Economy: Nigeria 1945-1966,* Cambridge University Press, 1969; Anababa, W., *The Trade Union Movement in Nigeria,* Ethiope, Benin City, 1969; Cohen, R., *Labour and Politics in Nigeria,* Heinemann, London, 1974; Peace, A., 'Industrial Protest in Nigeria' in Kadt, de E. & Williams, G. P. (eds) *Sociology and Development,* Tavistock, London, 1974; and articles by Peace and Lubeck in Sandbrook, R & Cohen, R. (eds) *The Development of An African Working Class,* Longman, London, 1975.

TRADE UNIONISM

Chapter 2

TRADE UNIONS DURING EARLY COLONISATION

HISTORICAL BACKGROUND

The creation of a wage-earning labour force in Nigeria is directly traceable to historical relations between Africa and Europe, especially the trade that flourished from the 1700s. This trade introduced money wages which coexisted with the use of cowrie shells as a medium of exchange even into the twentieth century and created a pool of ex-slaves, dispossessed persons who clustered around powerful local traders and functioned variously as porters, guards, clerks, errand boys and armed thugs as occasion demanded 9. Remuneration was mostly in kind; imported food items, clothing, spirits and other odd trading items such as mirrors.

The situation of the 'employees' of European traders and firms was difficult to determine. Individual traders were a rough lot. From 1830 to 1900 firms, mostly British, French, German and Swedish, operated independently in Nigeria and were often the only link between the territory and metropolitan governments and commercial interests (Geary, 1965, 197; Crowder, 1968, 127).[1]

Pre-European craft unions or guilds could not form the basis for union organisation because they had been destroyed by the extensive disorganisation of various Nigerian societies caused by centuries of slave trading and by the flooding of these areas with cheap European metal hardware and other products. The free hand granted to commercial firms in line with the prevailing economic ideology of *laissez-faire* has resulted in the survival of few records of early Nigerian workers' organisations save that workers were housed in 'company yards' and fully protected by 'company troops' from indignant outbursts from the indigenous population and rival firms (Dike, 1956; Crowder, 1968).[2]

---

[1] Geary, W.N.M. *Nigeria Under Colonial Rule*, Frank Cass, London, 1965; Crowder, M., *West Africa Under Colonial Rule*, Hutchinson, 1968

[2] Dike, K.O., *Trade and Politics in the Niger Delta 1830-85*, Oxford, 1956, Crowder, M., *West Africa Under Colonial Rule, op. cit.*

European rivalries before and after the 1884-1885 Berlin West African Conference which led to the well-known scramble for African territories dramatically changed the whole picture. Between 1860 and 1910 (Lagos was seized by the British in 1862) most of Africa and Nigeria were militarily occupied following so-called 'pacification' exercises as a result of which all indigenous political authorities lost their sovereignties. The establishment of a rudimentary colonial administration greatly accelerated the creation of an African wage labour force because of its infrastructural activities, mostly in the building of houses, construction of roads, bridges, ports, railways, and other works of public importance.

In summary, there is little evidence of the effective establishment of workers' organisations before 1870. Incipient organisations appeared by the 1890s (Hopkins 1966; Hughes & Cohen, 1978);[3] effective organisations emerged only from the First World War period (Roberts, 1964, 17-8).[4] The Southern Nigeria Civil Service Union appeared in 1912, changing its name to Civil Service Union in 1914 when both the Southern and Northern Nigeria administrations were amalgamated under Colonel Lugard in 1914. There followed in 1931 the Nigerian Union of Teachers and the Railway Workers Union.

The nature of the state itself bore directly on its relations with the nascent trade unions at this early stage. Four factors require emphasis. First, the somewhat shaky colonial administration was essentially a military regime, deriving immediate support from the 'West African Frontier Force' which was for a time under the direct command of Colonel Lugard. It was thus authoritarian and dictatorial by definition. Second, the period also coincided with the military conquest of Nigeria which formally ended with the sacking of the Hausa-Fulani emirates and the declaration in 1906 that they constituted the 'Protectorate of Northern Nigeria' and with the amalgamation of the Southern and Northern Protectorates in 1914 (Crowder, 1966). The arbitrariness of governmental decisions under war conditions requires no elaboration. Pressure was continually applied by the state to secure the conformity of organised interest groups. Third, and flowing from the above reasons, is that in a new political order largely based on force, and thus lacking political legitimacy, organised interest groups, particularly trade unions, logically bore the brunt of government hostility, their activities being regarded as destabilising of the colonial regime whose prime interest lay in the rapid exploitation of resources and its supply of raw

---

[3] Hopkins, A.G. The Lagos Strike of 1897: an Exploration in Nigerian Labour History,' *Past & Present*, vol. 35, 1966; Hughes, A. and Cohen, R. 'An Emerging Nigerian Working Class: The Lagos Experience, 1897-1939,' in Gutkind, P., Cohen, R. and Copans, J, (eds) *African Labour History* (Beverly Hills and London, 1979);

[4] Roberts, B.C., *Labour in the Tropical Territories of the Commonwealth*, Bell, 1964

materials to European industries. Fourth and last, the colonial administration at this point made no pretence that it was governing in the interest of the citizen. Welfare schemes and social legislation were of little interest to it. Thus workers and their organisations (as well as the complementary activities of nationalist politicians) had to fight for the establishment of a basic floor of industrial rights and access to social amenities.

The colonial administration's labour policy was simple and straightforward; employment was regarded as casual and impermanent, a reflection of the seasonal nature of construction and other infrastructural activities. Labour was forcibly recruited directly by the military or indirectly through traditional rulers and was not appropriately compensated. The widespread 'disappearance' of these workers and protests over their status compelled the colonial administration to pay wages, but very low wages indeed. Limited funds and demands by foreign firms for a better and adequate infrastructure and for social amenities ruled out for colonial administration a reversal of such a low-wage policy. Between June 1900 and January 1902 approximately 6,500 labourers left Lagos to work on the Sekondi railway and gold mines of the Gold Coast where the rate of pay was higher (Hopkins, 1966, 149). By 1909 labour shortage in Lagos was sufficiently acute enough for the authorities to give serious consideration to the possibility of importing Indian labour into West Africa (ibid.).

Two main arguments were used in justification of a low wage policy: a) that peasants transformed into workers were farmers by occupation, could feed themselves and thus need not rely on their wages; and b) that there existed a backward sloping supply curve for native workers. African workers, it was claimed, had specific and limited wants and would only work enough to obtain sufficient money to satisfy these wants; they would then disappear. If wages were kept low, their services would, therefore, be available for a much longer time. Governor McCallum of Lagos Colony claimed, indeed, that their wages were too high. His reduction of the wages of workers in the Public Works Department provoked a bitter strike in 1897 (Hopkins, *op cit.,* 136).

Various developments tended to undermine the low wage policy between 1900 and the outbreak of the First World War. The bureaucracy of the Lagos Colony had been expanded to cover the rest of the country and civil servants formed a trade union to protect their interests. The administration's own policy of paying European civil servants more than their African counterparts served as one protest-inducing element, the latter arguing for 'equal pay for equal work'. Secondly, these were hard and inflation-ridden times. Shortages and scarcity of funds at the beginning of the First World War pushed the administration into adopting an incomes and prices policy, a policy so ineffectual that it did no more than elicit protests from workers. The administration's discriminatory grant of 'war bonus' to European civil servants only added fuel to such protests. The importance of civil servants in the colonial system, the fear of undermining the war effort in which the colonies played the crucial part of supplying raw materials, along with more effective industrial protests, made wage reviews inevitable and encouraged the administration to devise a more systematic approach to grievances in the fledging public sector.

Such realism on the part of state functionaries, brought about by the logic of war and confrontation with an external enemy, was encouraged by the Colonial Office in London with its enactment of a series of Colonial Development Welfare Acts, the first appearing in 1929. The enactment of the 1929 Colonial Development Act by the Labour Government signalled a slight modification of the *laissez faire* philosophy but it was primarily 'to promote commerce with, and to relieve economic depression in the United Kingdom and to stimulate agricultural and industrial activity in the colonial territories' (cited in Ekundare, 1973, 21).[5] It also meant that the colonial administration could draw on the funds provided under the Act to offset the costs of constructing roads and railway lines helpful in the transportation of agricultural and mineral products. Labour legislation and administration in Nigeria up to 1938 provided only negative protection against open abuse of employment conditions, compensation for injury, the employment of women at night and of the employment of children under sixteen. It did little for the betterment of living conditions at all (Bowers, 1948, 8).[6]

The Colonial Development and Welfare Act of 1940 (as amended in 1945), elaborated on a dispatch of the Secretary of State for the Colonies to all colonial governors which requested that economic surpluses derived from colonies be passed on to the colonial workers in the form of improved social services. It required that any colony desiring to benefit from UK funds should enact laws to facilitate the establishment and functioning of trade unions and ensure that wage levels were reasonable. In Nigeria a Trade Union Ordinance had been enacted in 1938, followed by the establishment of a labour inspectorate in October 1939 and a Trade Disputes (Arbitration and Inquiry) Ordinance in 1941. The Colonial Administration benefited to the extent of £23 million for financing its Ten-Year Development Plan in 1945, a sum it attracted by expanding its organisation for labour inspection (Akpala,1971, 23).[7]

---

[5] Ekundare, R.O., *An Economic History of Nigeria, 1860-1960*, Methuen, London, 1973

[6] Bowers P. 'The Mining Industry', in PERHAM, M. (ed.), *Mining, Commerce and Finance in Nigeria*, Faber & Faber, 1948.

[7] Akpala, A. 'Industrial Relations Policies in Nigeria', *Genieve Afrique*, vol. 10(1), 1971

The position of the private sector in this period was akin to that of an outsider. It followed the prevailing capitalist ideology of laissez-faire which in the main argued non-governmental involvement or interference in economic affairs. As Lugard (now Lord Lugard) himself officially admitted, employers did what they liked, jointly and arbitrarily fixing the prices of imported commodities and those at which peasant farmers could sell their cash crops, a situation which produced wages generally lower than those in government establishments (Report on Amalgamation 1920, 31-35). Matters were hardly helped by the underdeveloped state of trade unionism in the private sector, the first trade union, the Kano Mercantile Clerks Union, emerging only in 1941 - almost three decades after the first emergence of a union in the public sector.

On the whole the relationship between state and trade unions was characterised by intense hostility, by the intermittent and violent use of strikes and by the free use of police and troops on striking workers. Trade unions were denied legal recognition and the unilateral imposition of terms and conditions of work by employers was the norm in spite of fierce worker resistance. Furthermore, official labour policy was itself constrained by metropolitan politics and global strategic and economic considerations. This tended to introduce an element of unpredictability into state-union relations as London responded to situations created by European rivalry and British industrial upheavals.

LABOUR-MANAGEMENT RELATIONS

Within each 'enterprise', labour-management relations tended to reflect the conditions and ideology of the times. The four main industries, concerned were, in present day parlance, construction, mining, agriculture and commerce. The state dominated the first while private firms controlled the other three. The firms or companies were themselves small both in terms of capital and labour employed, except for the United Africa Company and John Holt which had country-wide branches and featured prominently in all industries. Between 1890 and 1938 fewer than 5o companies survived competition and the economic depression of the 1930s.

Colonial management was, as revealed by Franz Fanon (1967)[8] and others, suffused with paternalism and racial bigotry; early European colonists were rarely-genteel or progressive in their attitudes to labour. Most subscribed to what Alan Fox (1973)[9] has described as 'unitary' ideology - seeing all employees as members of one 'family', or 'team' sharing a common destiny and regarding dissent or protest as 'irrational', if not

---

[8] Fanon, F. *The Wretched of the Earth*, Penguin, 1973.

[9] 'Industrial Relations: A Social Critique of Pluralist Ideology' in J. Child (ed.), *Man and Organisation*, George Allen 8; Unwin, London, 1973

traitorous. Strong personal attachment to some employers was not unusual in the case of favoured staff, but a considerable number of people working for private firms were employed on a temporary basis only (Egboh, 1968, 67).[10] Otherwise, most labour was forcibly recruited.

Little effort was directed at motivating or developing employees, especially in the private sector. Of the Royal Niger Company (1896-1900), Geary noted "it was a hard master to its employees...and...there does not linger about its rule the mellow memories attaching to 'John Company' in India" (1965,197). Nor did it 'take any steps towards educating or civilizing the natives or raising their standard of life;...it did not set up and subsidize schools; but it maintained such peace and order on the Niger that missionaries could work' (ibid.).

However primitive much of the labour force may have been, the casual and insecure nature of its employment could hardly have been justified. European officials and employers seemed to delight in painting pictures of primitiveness, savagery and a lack of interest in work as a justification for the work of thousands of men without explicitly stated terms and conditions of employment. Employees and forcibly recruited labour appeared far more in need of some kind of formally stated terms of work and negotiating or disputes procedures than either the employers or the administrators themselves.

By 1930, almost the only group of workers that had anything close to 'terms of employment' were some of those engaged by the colonial administration, either as clerks in the civil service or as skilled and semi-skilled workers attached to the railways, ports and other public utilities. Trade unionism was treated as subversion, particularly in private establishments, nor was 'joint consultation' or 'collective bargaining' tolerated by management. Even in the colonial administration, despite the official recognition extended to the Civil Service Union, Union of Teachers and the Marine Workers' Organization, union activities were generally regarded as a 'threat to law and order' or a potential source of 'disruption'. As a corollary, industrial agitation automatically became a matter for the troops and other law enforcement agencies: voluntary conciliation and arbitration were simply out of the question. Workers in the private sector had to depend on the whims and caprices of employers to earn a regular wage, to obtain a rise or to get promotion.

UNIONS AND MEMBERS

Union tactics were understandably influenced by the members' own perceptions of the situation and by the objective facts of the situation. The

[10] The Early Years of Trade Unionism in Nigeria', *African Quarterly*, Vol.8(i), 1968; 'Trade Union Education in Nigeria, 1940-1964', *African Studies Review*, Vol. XIV( ), 1968.

leadership of the Civil Service Union was originally dominated by 'senior' African bureaucrats who, as earlier noted, remained satisfied with writing the occasional memorandum on the amelioration of existing terms of service and with petitioning against the award of 'war bonus' to expatriate civil servants alone. It took nineteen years for artisans, technicians and other occupational groups to achieve an open break with this kind of leadership and form the Railway Workers' Union and the Nigerian Union of Teachers in 1931. These groups of workers felt that the Civil Service Union was not adequately protecting their interests. Even before the formation of the Railway Workers' Union, a mechanics' union formed by the artisan railroad employees of the Nigerian Railway went on strike in I92I against a threatened reduction in wages and won a concession thereby (Coleman,1958, 212).[11]

What did workers expect from their unions and what did the unions actually achieve at that time? The few unions which existed took organizational root only in the 1930 and 1940s. It was individual workers and strategically located occupational groups which bore the brunt of state and employer hostility. The core of the working class that emerged by 1940 was relatively divorced from the white collar leadership of the Civil Service Union. Indeed, as Yesufu (1962)[12] has pointed out, the Civil Service Union was not only formed by senior African members of the public service but restricted its membership to 'officials down to and including those of the rank of first class', although it claimed to protect the interests of civil servants generally (1962,34). In practice the union as then constituted was an exclusive body comprising the 'few Africans in top posts' and its conservative posturing, including its no-strike policy, reflected its membership's perceptions of their place in the colonial order. The same could be said of the membership of the Nigerian Union of Teachers, with its exclusive definition of occupational interests. The distinction between 'white' and 'blue' collar workers thus took on a deeply invidious connotation in the colonial order with its emphasis on literacy in European languages and crass mimicry of European mores and modes of dressing, a cross-cultural balancing act that early Nigerian and African bureaucrats and professionals took very seriously indeed.

There were indeed difficulties for workers in recognising and defining their own interests for representational purposes. The colonial order represented a new society, the white man's creation, which differed in many significant respects from traditional practice. The stratification of society which emerged was in response to criteria previously unfamiliar; paid

[11] Coleman, J.S., *Nigeria: Background to Nationalism*, Univ. of California Press, Berkeley & Los Angeles, 1958

[12] Yesufu, T.M., *An Introduction to Industrial Relations in Nigeria*, OUP for NISER, 1962

employment itself was a novelty. In such an agonising and psychologically disorienting situation, made worse by military conquest and forced labour, perceptions of individual rights were less clear than they may nowadays be. Egboh has perceptively observed of early Nigerian workers, especially in the private sector, that 'many employees...never thought they were part of this new social order and might have felt that in it they had no rights of their own which could be defended' (1968,66).[13] On the reverse of the coin, in the presence of troops and of a company's own constabulary, the rights of private ownership could hardly have been more pointedly asserted.

In defence of their interests workers instinctively devised tactics to avoid the worst of the situation and to secure redress where possible. Those forcibly recruited as individuals and in groups deserted in large numbers to escape long hours, low wages, and economic insecurity made worse by the introduction of taxes by the colonial administration in the late 1920s which were payable in cash. The latter imposition sparked off riots in many Nigerian cities. Spontaneous strikes broke out. Gradually during the First World War such actions became better organised and effective.

Two factors which pushed workers into greater activity were the soaring cost of living resulting from the war of 1914-1918 and the devastating effects of the economic depression which began in late 192os. Strikes and protests centred on wage increases and job security. Where unions existed, tactics were also influenced by organizational politics and general discrimination in favour of expatriate staff. The Civil Service Union persistently protested against the reluctance of the authorities to advance the careers of its members and the disparity in pay which existed between qualified Nigerian and expatriate staff performing similar jobs. These formed 'orbits of coercive comparison', a situation seized upon by vocal nationalist politicians to the embarrassment of a succession of colonial governors, whose reactions in turn served to impose limits on trade union actions and demands.

In concluding this section, we may note that workers and their organizations at this time were striving to assert their presence against employer resistance which was equally fierce, and entrenched rather along the lines earlier suggested by Lester (1958).[14] It was a volatile political situation; 'firms' were often no more than armed gangs or groups. It was only in 1930 that an oligopoly dominated by the UAC was formed from a merger of three powerful companies.' Furthermore, the failure of emergent trade unions adequately to take care of workers' needs arising from colonial urban society led ultimately to the emergence of ethnic and tribal associations which began to play an increasingly important role in the lives of many urban workers. Finally, the colonial administration was also in

---

[13] *Op. cit.*

[14] LESTER, R.A., *As Unions Mature*, Princeton University Press, 1958

process of imposing its rule and machinery on a countrywide basis. It therefore paid little attention to the rights of indigenous political authorities or workers' organizations. All protests groups were ruthlessly dealt with and any concessions gained by such groups owed little to officially progressive attitudes; when a compromise was reached the self-interest and countervailing power of organized and unorganized workers were a more potent force than reason, tolerance and understanding.

Chapter 3

TRADE UNIONISM IN POST-DEPRESSION PERIOD, 1939-1960

The worldwide economic depression came and went and the Second World War was fought and won without substantial changes in Nigeria's colonial status. Nevertheless a great deal happened between 1939 and 1960 to put Nigerian industrial relations on a surer footing and to lay the foundation for subsequent developments. We now explore these developments insofar as they impinged on the role of trade unions. As before, union-government relations are first examined, followed by those at labour-management level and by the union-member situation.

UNION-GOVERNMENT RELATIONS

During this period pressure from the Colonial Office, war-induced social and economic conditions, the dynamic and momentum of so-called independence movements, ideological squabbles in Europe and more effective workers' protests, all served to affect union-government relations.

The Passfield Memorandum of 1930 had marked a watershed of colonial unionism. In his capacity as Secretary of State for the Colonies, Lord Passfield (formerly Mr. Sydney Webb), expressed in his despatch to all colonial governors the view that unions were to be expected as a natural and legitimate development. He suggested trade union legislation along the lines of the United Kingdom Trade Union Act of 1871. Practically all colonial administrations delayed or resisted the passing of such an Act and conceded only under great pressure from the Colonial Office (Yesufu, 1962, 29).[1]

The reaction in Nigeria to the Passfield Memorandum was characteristic of colonial employers everywhere:

> `The views of the Nigerian government, as well as those of the European employers who were consulted, were that the wage-earning population was still too small, that the tribal system of mutual assistance provided all the necessary protection which local workers then needed, and that the country was far from ready for

[1] Yesufu, T.M., *An Introduction to Industrial Relations in Nigeria*, OUP/Niser, 1962

> the type of legislation which the 'civilised world' had evolved only after a considerable period of years, (Yesufu, 1962, 29-30).[2]

Pressure from workers and the tempting offer of funds for the colony's development programme (set aside by the Colonial Development and Welfare Acts) enabled the colonial administration to see its way towards a trade union ordinance which came into force on April 7, 1939. Although the Ordinance provided for the usual 'immunities' in the British tradition, some of its clauses reduced the legal standing of unions to precarious proportions. The Registrar had general powers to call for special returns and to institute criminal or civil proceedings in connection therewith. It even stipulated that no illiterate person might be appointed to the office of President, Secretary or Treasurer (Yesufu, *op. cit.,* 29-32 for details), and unions were to be compulsorily registered. Compulsory registration was a conspicuous departure from trade union practice in Britain. Nevertheless, the ordinance was an important piece of legislation which achieved the reclassification and upgrading of unions from the 'level of guerrilla struggle to more institutionalised, if administratively suspect, organisations' (loan Davies, 1966, 31).[3]

Despite stringent wartime conditions and the semi-legal status of unions, the 1939-45 World War proved to be a boon to their development. The explanation for this is two-fold: firstly, the Trade Union Ordinance, with all its imperfections, had given them some legal status and provided encouragement for workers to join where conditions were favourable; secondly, the war brought untold hardship both to workers and the general public in the form of acute shortages of basic commodities and a fall in real wages *(Annual Report,* 1942, 5-6; 1943, 11; 1944, 4). The price of the few food items available rose sharply and workers joined unions in great numbers, particularly when rationing began in Lagos (Oyemakinde, 1973 for details).[4]

This period was characterised by intermittent work stoppages which were often effective even though they were usually short and frequently led to the arrest and banishment of union leaders. The colonial administration initially introduced a palliative by granting cost-of-living allowances (COLA) to many workers. As the war dragged on, however, and as living conditions worsened and budgets became tighter, such allowances progressively failed to keep up with inflation and demands for more awards resulted. The administration then asked the unions to defer claims until the war ended. By this time, however, an augmented and increasingly militant membership had

[2] Ibid.

[3] *African Trade Unions*, Penguin, Harmondsworth, 1966.

[4] Oyemakinde, W., The Pullen Marketing Scheme: A Trial in Food Price Control in Nigeria, *Journal of Historical Society of Nigeria*, vol. 6, 1973

come to interpret the administration's inadequate response to mean lack of interest in the welfare of workers. This unacceptable state of affairs culminated in the 1945 general strike which involved over 42,000 workers *(Annual Report,* 1945). The rising cost of living aside, it is possible that workers, realising the extent of their contribution to the war effort and thus their strategic importance, exploited the situation not only by extracting cost-of-living awards but also by securing recognition for their unions.

The Second World War brought in its wake some agonising changes in attitudes. The victory of democracy and freedom over dictatorship made the retention of colonies more morally indefensible than ever. Developing *pari passu* was the heightened socio-political consciousness of African or indigenous populations. The war not only de-mystified the 'invincibility' of the coloniser (the German occupation of Belgium and parts of France and De Gaulle's flight to Africa were common knowledge); those Africans who had fought side by side with European troops had experienced different values at work. The non-representativeness of the coloniser's values and his failure to portray the humane democratic aspects of Western societies became more pronounced, a distinction emphasized by Western propaganda in the colonies which focused on the fight against oppression and abhorrence of the treatment meted out to the Jews. Such an emphasis served to highlight more than ever racial inequalities. Predictably, the relative deprivation experienced by the ex-servicemen made them the earliest vocal 'nationalists' in the immediate post-war situation. Many of them became union members.

A potent and singular factor in the situation of relevance to our area of interest was the post-war ideological polarisation in Europe. This development raised the spectre of 'communist infiltration' and the consequent creation of that hardly inconceivable, being (from the Western point of view) the 'African Communist'. Quantification of the catalytic role of the feared or actual presence of communists in post-war socio-political developments in the colonies is hardly possible. But the resultant rivalry between the two ideological blocs and the unceasing denunciation of 'colonialism' and 'imperialism' both by the communist and Americans camps undeniably pushed even the most paternalistic colonial administration into accepting a growing number of modest political and industrial reforms. Nor was the significance of the formal independence of India and of the Chinese revolution of 1948 lost on anyone.

Two immediate consequences were the intervention of the state in industrial matters and increased external pressure on both colonial administration and trade unions. The notion of the neutrality of the state in industrial relations as embodied in the pluralist doctrine required extensive revision to be of any analytical value in so extreme a situation. The post-war period therefore saw a more positive and calculated approach to the socio-political problems of the colonies by both metropolitan and colonial administrations. This supersession of the deliberate content of colonial policies was linked with the desire to control or influence the outcome of emerging political movements. The 1930 Passfield Memorandum could rightly be regarded as marking the beginning of the 'deliberate phase' which had now ended.

The British government, through the colonial administration, sought strenuously to divorce trade unionism from what it saw as 'politics' (Roberts, 1964, 89).[5] The British Trades Union Congress (BTUC) was particularly active as an instrument of government policy. Its role has been described in these terms:

> `the trade union movement has played a unique role in British colonial policy which contrasts strongly with French, Belgian and Dutch experience. For over twenty-five years the TUC and individual unions have not only been consulted on labour relations policy; they have in effect (through the system of Labour Officers and participation of the Colonial Advisory Board) been part of the Colonial Administration...' (Davies, 1958, 32).[6]

Between the Colonial Office and British TUC there had 'slowly evolved a theory of the role of trade unions which stresses the importance of effective democracy within trade union movements and seeks to maintain the independence of trade unionists from government control' (ibid.,34 1946) In 46 this anxiety was also shared by the Tudor Davies Commission, set up to review wages as a result of the 1945 General Strike, which concluded that 'it is no use...asking the question: Is the time ripe for trade unions in Nigeria? The point is that trade unions are in existence in Nigeria *de facto* and *de jure* and the real issue is not whether they are to be destroyed, but how they are to be directed into right paths.' (Report,1946, para. 88).

In pursuance of this objective and when the declaration of war had made the more effective utilisation of labour imperative, a Department of Labour was set up in 1942 in Lagos on the recommendation of Major Orde Brown. By 1954 it had mushroomed into a complete ministry, boasting a complete set of ranks from minister and commissioner of labour to assistant trade union officer.

In practical terms the colonial administration was forced to treat workers and their organisations in a much more serious fashion. It could ill-afford in war-time widespread disruption of production, particularly in the tin

---

[5] Roberts, B.C., *Labour in the Tropical Territories of the Commonwealth*, Bell, 1964

[6] *Op. cit.*

mining industry which had assumed greater and greater importance as the Japanese threatened (and later overran) tin mines for that metal which had hitherto met the bulk of British demand

Attention was directed both to the leadership and the internal workings of trade unions. The Trade Unions Congress of Nigeria (TUC) that came into being in 1943 was accorded immediate recognition by the administration, and a system of monthly meetings between its Working Committee and the Department of Labour was formally instituted. The cordial state of relations and the effectiveness of the TUC were duly acknowledged by the administration when it announced that the 'TUC has rendered considerable assistance to the Department of Labour in the settlement of disputes and the general application of labour standards' *(Annual Report,* 1943,18). Aside from this, the TUC's influence on labour legislation is instanced by the postponement, at its request, of a proposed law that would have increased the powers of the Registrar of Trade Unions (Uvieghara, 1976,32).[7]

At the TUC's 1943 inaugural conference, two resolutions called on the colonial administration to nationalise the mining industry and demanded workers' representation on the Legislative Council, a body comprising of hand-picked men from among police, European firms and traditional rulers which 'advised' the Governor. At the 1944 conference, described as 'remarkable for its representative character, the high quality of its debates and the wide range of subjects discussed' (Ananaba, 1969, 4).[8] Considerable attention was also devoted to socioeconomic issues affecting workers. Some of the resolutions adopted concerned the resettlement and rehabilitation of ex-servicemen, scholarships for training Nigerians for responsible positions in the public service and industry, social security schemes, labour participation in schemes for achieving good industrial relations, the revision of wages of two shillings and sixpence per diem, slum clearance, the provision of adequate dwelling houses for workers, effective rent control and the amendment of the Workmen's Compensation Ordinance to provide improved rates of compensation for industrial and occupational accidents and to cover cases of industrial and occupational diseases which were outside the scope of the existing ordinance (Ananaba, *op.cit.*,42).

As may be expected, aspirations ran ahead of concrete achievements. Nevertheless, given the times and by comparison with the formulations of nationalist politicians, many of the demands of trade union leaders were epoch making indeed. Unfortunately the multifarious pressures brought to bear on the leadership led to factionalism within the trade union ranks, the first open breach coinciding with the rift in the international labour

[7] *Trade Union Law in Nigeria*, Ethiope, 1976

[8] Ananaba, W. *The Trade. Union Movement in Nigeria*, Ethiope Publishing Company, Benin, 1969

movement in 1947 in line with the ideological preferences of European governments. Apart from such short-lived central bodies as the Nigerian Labour Congress (1949-1951) and the All Nigerian Trade Union Federation (1953-1956), two mutually hostile and competing central labour organisations, backed internationally by opposing ideological blocs emerged, the Committee of Trade Unions (1947), renamed the Nigerian National Federation of Labour in 1949, and the Committee of ICFTU Affiliated Unions in 1956 (renamed National Council of Trade Unions of Nigeria in 1957). Leaders of these organisations were consulted by the colonial administration, and were picked to represent Nigerian workers in such internal tripartite bodies as wages boards, and for conferences abroad (e.g. ILO annual conferences). Such union leaders were also likely recipients of scholarships provided by the administration, the ICFTU, and various western labour organisations. It has since been established that these organisations largely survived on financial and other aid from however, viewed with some misgiving by the colonial administration, employers and British officials, not only because of the organisation's continued interest in the political future of Nigeria but also because of its talk of 'imparting political knowledge to workers', of 'socialist government' and its encouragement 'of a World Parliament of the working class'. Its newspaper, *Labour Champion* not only had 'Toward the creation of the Socialist Republic' as its motto; it also, according to official sources, 'showed strong political interest, notably in communism, and carried on for some weeks without any advertisements' *(Annual Report,* 1950-1, para. 36).

The NLC, formed on May 25 1950 and representing all unions, established political links with the NCNC and was affiliated internationally to the communist-controlled World Federation of Trade Unions." The metropolitan goal of 'divorcing union leaders from politicians' was totally disregarded when some members of the NLC leadership stood and won seats at the 195o Lagos municipal elections. The All Nigeria Trade Union Federation (ANTUF), which succeeded the NLC as an all-embracing central body, remained formally neutral in respect of international affiliations and instead forged links with the Accra-based pan-African All African Trade Union Federation, an organisation that sought to neutralise both the ICFTU and the WFTU in the affairs of African unions. This neutral stance was in itself sufficient reason for pro-ICFTU labour leaders to break away in 1956.

The division of top union leaders into warring camps did nothing to restrain the activities of workers themselves. The hardships imposed by the second world war in the form of rising prices, food shortages and compulsory recruitment led to a series of workers' protests that culminated in the 1945 General Strike. Between 1940 and 1960 there were 528 officially recorded strikes, the great majority occurring in the burgeoning public sector between 1950-196o. Such strikes were more widespread in the latter period, largely in reaction to rapid `Nigerianisation' of the state machine with attendant problems of regrading and because of the competitive wage fixing efforts of rival regional political parties (Ezera, 1960; Yesufu, 1962).[9]

By 1941 the colonial administration had attempted to contain the situation by a Trades Dispute (Arbitration and Inquiry) Ordinance, a measure rendered largely ineffectual by the draconian provisions contained in the Emergency Powers (Defence) Act, 1939. The 1941 Act, however, initiated the first elaborate price control ever attempted and by 1943 the Nigerian General Defence (Control of Prices)

Regulation had established special markets in Lagos and Apapa (referred to as 'Pullen Markets'). These Pullen Markets, as it was officially admitted, 'were not intended to feed the whole of Lagos but to provide enough food to act as a stabiliser by forcing other traders to lower their prices in order to compete with the government retailers' *(Annual Report,* 1943, 7). But wages were frozen despite spiralling prices whilst institutional avenues for negotiation were almost nil.

In this regard the 1946 Tudor Davies Commission recommended that a special *ad hoc* body to be named the 'Negotiating Committee' should be established consisting of representatives of various government departments and trade unions and that provision should be made for machinery for the settlement of disputes by arbitration. It concluded that the 'cause of trouble in Nigeria has been, not recognition of the principles of trade unionism, but a decision as to what type of trade union should be registered and recognised'. Matters of wages and conditions of employment should entirely be the responsibility of a reconstituted Labour Department, and all stages, from conciliation to final enforcement, should be in its hands' *(Report,* 1946, pp.26-27).

Although Provincial Wage Committees had been established since 1941, they had hardly ever been used. The colonial administration showed a strong preference for wages commissions as a mode of determining terms of employment in the public sector. Subsequent political development, rapid `Nigerianisation of the Civil Service and other arms of the state, and more effective unionism hurried the pace at which a loose institutional framework was being erected. In 1946 the Harragin Commission reviewed the salaries of established government staff whilst the Miller Committee looked into the wage rates of daily-paid labourers

Following the Harragin recommendations the Cowan Enquiry of 1948 investigated and reported on methods of negotiation between government and employees in state-owned industrial establishments. It introduced

---

[9] Ezera, K, *Constitutional Developments in Nigeria*, CUP, 1960; Yesufu, An Introduction to *Industrial Relations in Nigeria, op. cit.*

'Whitley Councils': a Junior Whitley Council (A) for clerical and other office employees, and a Junior Whitley Council (B) for industrial or manual workers. Yesufu argues that the 'Whitley Councils became, so to speak, the machinery for collective bargaining whereas the departmental committees became consultative committees (1962, 52).[10] This was an exaggeration. Official testimony recognised their limited impact, noting that the Whitley Councils 'ran into severe difficulties because of dissatisfaction on the management side' *(Annual Report,* 1949-50, W. Ananaba, 1969,72).

By 1953 therefore, after a decade of intense worker protests and activity by labour and trade union officers, the finishing touches were being put to institutional mechanisms for processing grievances. By 1960, 212 standing committees for joint consultation and 'collective bargaining', covering an aggregate of 207,582 employees, had been established (Yesufu, *op. cit.*, 53). Although these committees covered about thirty per cent of the wage-earning population, Sonubi has observed that there was little evidence that they were being `actively used' (1971,182).[11] In fact the colonial administration wound up the decade by appointing two wages commissions, the Mbanefo Commission (1959) for Federal, Northern and Eastern governments, and the Morgan Commission (1960) for the Western Region government.

In summary the decades 1939-1960 witnessed the willingness of the colonial administration to deal directly with unions in the public sector and was a period in which official attention was paid to union administration and leadership. Indeed, the colonial administration's pre-occupation with the divorce of trade unionism from politics became obsessive. In 1945 it was warned that 'the Chief Commissioners (Police) have given it as their opinion that there can be no comfortable line of demarcation between labour affairs and politics....and that in consequence, labour policy becomes mainly the concern of the Provincial Administration itself...' (Department of Labour *Quarterly Review,* 1945). In practice this meant that henceforth the activities of the trade unions, the work of the Labour Department, and indeed the whole field of industrial relations were to be subjected, above all else, to political considerations (Yesufu, 1962,138).

Little official interest was shown in 'collective bargaining' in the private sector, and in the public sector only in the obviously weak forms of Whitley Councils and consultative committees. Administrative fiat and wages commissions were more favoured approaches. Military administration and wartime experience gave birth to extensive use of troops and police on workers, the worst incident by far being the killing of 21 striking miners and

---

[10] *Op. cit.*

[11] Trade Disputes in Nigeria 1966-1971, *Nigerian Journal of Economic and Social Studies*, vol. 15, No. 2, July 1973

the wounding of 51 others at Enugu in 1949. In general, union-government relations were in a constant state of flux, reflecting the internal dynamics of a colonial economy as influenced by external political, economical and ideological considerations.

Labour-Management Relations

In this section the private sector is examined to complement the attention paid to the public sector in the preceding section. As already noted private employers were mostly opposed to the original 1938 Trade Union Ordinance. Their prejudices could hardly have been expected to disappear overnight. The colonial administration under Lord Lugard remained aloof from the private sector in most economic matters, except when troops were needed to recruit compulsory labour or to suppress worker protests. This attitude persisted long after Lugard's departure. The private sector stayed 'private' for the colonial administration until the 1945 general strike when, under the protective umbrella of the Tudor Davies Commission, the first national union in the private sector emerged in the form of ;he Amalgamated Union of UAC African Workers (UNAMAG). Paternalism still reigned supreme and trade union and labour officers had great difficulty in persuading employers to adopt negotiating machinery and pay regular wages.

The private sector was small, including a handful of plantations in the agricultural sector, textile, general retail trade, transportation (mostly land and sea), mining (tin and columbite) and an export trade in agricultural produce. All these activities were dominated by a handful of firms. The plantations owned by the UAC and John Holt Ltd. operated under less than satisfactory conditions, a situation the colonial administration did not seem to mind at all, particularly arbitrary dismissals and rapid personnel turnover which it considered to be ideal for 'the constant coming and going of labourers [is] a system which has its advantages in which the labour force can be increased or decreased without provoking labour difficulties' *(Annual Report,* 1942, 3). Subsequent developments were to dispel such illusions.

Unions did not emerge in the agricultural sector until the late 195os because of the migrant nature of this type of labour and 'a tendency in mining and plantations to regard the labour force as comparable with a military force, to be housed in barracks and kept under semi-military discipline' (Hodgkin, 1956,119).[12] By 1953 conditions were so intolerable to workers that strikes broke out in all plantations *(Annual Report,* 1953/4, 21) despite the fact that this period also produced boom conditions for primary produce from which some firms, marketing boards and individuals that owned large cocoa, cotton and groundnut farms made fortunes. All

[12] Hodgkin, T., *Nationalism in Colonial Africa* (London, 1956)

plantations were subsequently taken over by the government and wages and other terms of employment regulated as in equivalent jobs in other departments.

The commercial sector remained largely unorganised and conditions of employment for the most part notoriously bad. Until a few years ago both retail and wholesale trades were dominated by the UAC, John Holt Ltd., Paterson & Zochonis, Chellarams and a small group of Indian and Syrian traders. Between 1946 and 1960 the commercial sector saw some of the most intense struggles by workers for recognition of their organisations despite the fact that both the UAC and John Holt Ltd. (which also operated all ports in Nigeria except Lagos) had the highest paid workers in the private sector.

The UAC set the pace for other firms by establishing negotiations with the Amalgamated Union of UAC African Workers (UNAMAG) in 1946. However, a series of disagreements between the union and management, punctuated by numerous stoppages throughout 1948 and 1949, eventually exploded into a nation-wide strike by all branches of the union. The strike was broken with some difficulty 'by management by means of intimidation and the fear of intimidation by workers' *(Annual Report,* 1950/1, 29-30). After the strike the UAC management refused to have further dealings with union officials and according to official testimony UNAMAG 'was emasculated as a result of the actions of its officials and in the strike' *(*ibid., 30). Thereafter, we are informed, the company introduced 'joint consultation' in the absence of 'a properly organised union' (ibid.,30*).* 'In theory', Peter Kilby observed, these 'joint consultative committees explained management's policies to the workers and discussed matters of productivity' (1969, 292).[13]

The UAC did without unions till 1955 when it cautiously extended recognition to a single 'house' union in Lagos. A national union embracing all UAC workers was formed only in 1957 after Mr. F. Kanu `requested and was granted permission by the company' (Kilby, *op.cit.,* 292). The emergent Associated Companies African Workers Union `negotiated' eight national agreements with the UAC between 1959 and 1962, at which point the company unilaterally decentralised its bargaining in favour of 55 individual company agreements in line with its new organisational structure. So much for 'collective bargaining' in the private sector!

It is essential to recognise that the UAC was perhaps at the most liberal end of the spectrum in dealing with workers and their incipient organisations. The Nigerian Tobacco Company (NTC), for example, recognised its union in 1945 and though it met union officials every two years, signed its first collective agreements only in 1953 and in respect to lay-

[13] Kilby, P., *Industrialisation in an Open Economy: Nigeria 1945-66* (Cambridge, 1969).

off procedures! (Kilby, *op. cit*, 299) It finally agreed to a joint industrial council in 1957, also signing a comprehensive agreement covering wages and other conditions that was to be re-negotiated every two years. Thus an interval of twelve years elapsed between formal recognition and the negotiation of a collective agreement of real substance.

Some firms were willing to recognise unions within their establishments but refused to discuss terms of employment or any other conditions until they had approval from their headquarters in Paris, London or wherever their 'home base' might be. In 1942 Metal Containers (W.A.) Ltd. refused to pay cost-of-living allowance (COLA) the absence of instructions from London. When its angry workers went on strike, they were arrested by the police and charged under the Nigeria General Defence Regulation of 1941 *(Annual Report,* 1942, 11). In the case of French companies Roberts & de Bellecombe point out that 'it was impossible for even a detail to be modified without the securing of telegraphic authorisation from France' (1967, 43).[14]

The norm, of course, was strong opposition by employers to unionisation and when it proved impossible to stem the tide, `associations' and 'house unions' were imposed on workers of the more docile sort. Employees found it necessary to resort to extreme measures to match their employers' extreme unwillingness to extend recognition: it took a visit to Britain by the president of the Nigerian Union of Seamen and discussions there with shipping companies having interests in West Africa for the union to gain recognition in 1954 (*Annual Report*, 1954-5, 16).

The mining industry, dominated by tin and coal, saw especially acrimonious labour-management relations. The coal mines near Enugu were fully under the control of the colonial administration but managed day-to-day by a Colliery Board. Relationships between miners and colliery management had long been strained. According to Ananaba (1976) this was 'partly because of the management's opposition to the existence of a militant trade union' (1967, 98). The same writer gives a detailed account of a situation which seems to have evolved from a refusal to recognise unions, arbitrary dismissals, physical assault on some workers by members of colliery management, refusal by the latter to negotiate, and strikes over systems of payment.

Until 1950 the Enugu Colliery was apparently administered as an integral part of the Nigerian Railway, a situation which seemed likely to ensure the autonomous existence of a miners' union. In practice the position was different. A Colliery Workers' Union, formed in 1940, eventually sought effective recognition in the place of a Colliery Surface Improvement Union. The latter had the backing of management and organised only timekeepers,

[14] Roberts, B.C. & Greyfie de Bellecomb, *Collective Bargaining in African Countries*, International Institute for Labour Studies, Macmillan, London, 1967

who constituted the lowest rung of management. In addition to conciliators appointed by the Department of Labour, 'disputes procedures' and 'negotiating machinery' seem to have included everything from attempts by management to involve village heads, local councillors to the use of police and troops (Ananaba, *op. cit.*, 10ff). In spite of the establishment of a Whitley Council in the coal mining industry early in 1949, 21 striking miners were shot dead with 51 others wounded in November of the same year. The Fitzgerald Commission which looked into the circumstances surrounding such an appalling act dealt at length with labour-management relations in the mines, noting weak and inefficient union leadership, lack of basic conciliation facilities and the highhandedness of colliery management.

Between 1945 and 1960, the story was largely one of various strategies adopted by colliery management to discredit union officials and their organisations and of fragmentation action by workers into successive unions, particularly the Nigerian Coal Miners Union, which made spirited attempts to make their presence felt. The methods and tactics adopted by both sides were often unsavoury, reflecting little of the discussion and consultation ideally regarded as the essence of labour-management relations.

The tin-mining situation has been admirably described and discussed by Bill Freund (1981). Many companies were active at the mines under the protective umbrella of both the colonial administration and the UAC, the latter as successor to the Niger Company, a condition of the termination of its Royal Charter in 1890 (granted in 1886) being an entitlement to a percentage of the proceeds of the industry, though the company was concerned neither with prospecting nor the payment of miners' wages."

At the tin mines, union structure was mostly determined by that of the mining companies, workers in each company forming their own separate union. Freund notes that the first labour inspector in the Plateau in 1941, C.H. Croasdale, 'tried to convince mine managers that unions were a natural development whose recognition would avoid disorder and industrial action' (1981,179). The Governor, Sir Arthur Richards, thought that 'reasonably sane unions' should be 'encouraged', but many British officials based on the Plateau resisted the establishment of the Labour Board 'as a form of dangerous outside interference' (*ibid.,180*). In 1944 most workers 'were still frightened of joining the unions', with the Resident in Jos continuing to feel that 'he or some other provincial officer was far more suited to represent labourers than any trades union members' (*ibid.*, 81).

A particularly striking feature of the early orientation of trade union leadership in the mining area, Freund further observed, was 'the centrality of struggle for better wages' (ibid., 79), implying limited objectives on the part of workers. Against a background of forced and semi-forced labour, with elders, clan heads, Emirs, labour contractors and prison officials as the main recruiting agents, it was exceedingly difficult to get employers to pay wages at all. As has generally been recognised, wages were offered as a result of mass desertions (and attendant shortage of labour for most of the time), and such wages were low indeed. Freund himself cites several instances of employers and subcontractors going back on previously agreed rates of pay, whilst others juggled the task system in such a way that miners received less than the Local Council of the Nigerian Chamber of Mines had offered (*op. cit.,* p. 38).[15] As for physical conditions of employment which most employers were loath to ameliorate, 'conditions in the camps were deplorable. Overcrowding was severe and men huddled in the huts to keep themselves warm...Contagious disease, notably cerebrospinal meningitis and small pox, were rife.' (ibid.)

By default the colonial administration's comparatively higher wage scales became regarded as 'fair wages' and public sector wage awards made by various tribunals provoked strikes in the mines as miners sought equivalent increases (ibid., 182). The achievement of parity with government workers became almost a negotiating principle until the 1960s when pay of the middle and upper levels overtook prevailing rates. Management-union relations were at best acrimonious as employers sought to reduce overall costs and survive competition, while miners and their organisations demanded shorter hours, better health facilities, an end to the use of forced labour and arbitrary dismissals, and improved holidays and other fringe benefits. Labour and other colonial officers were recognised as instruments for containing 'subversive' political groups and workers, constrained to persuade a motley group of private employers to pay wages and maintain a semblance of disputes and conflict- regulating machinery. Political developments, accentuated ethnic animosities and the coercive and divisive activities of colonial law enforcement agencies were all contributory factors to the fragmentation of the trade union movement which characterised the mining situation in the 1950s (Freund, *op. cit.,*184). Given the shaky hold over the Plateau of the ruling party in Northern Region, its government consistently intervened in wage settlements. Because of state intervention from 1960, 'real wages for labour in the tin mines increased substantially when compared with their abysmal level of the 1940s' (ibid., 189) .

The conduct of some union officials at this time left much to be desired. Some took personal objection to particular members of management and sought to express their animosity by threatening strikes. Many union officials, in the commercial sector in particular, tended to become 'secretary' to a number of unions at the same time in order to earn a sizeable income and gain a sufficient power base, thus generating possible conflicts of interest and casting doubts on their commitment to the labour movement.

---

[15] Freund, B., *Labour and Capital in Nigerian Tin Mines*, Longman, 1981, 174ff

Additionally, union officials were claimed by official sources on many occasions to have presented 'a long list of points in dispute and letters couched in discourteous and unhelpful terms...instead of reasoned arguments' (*Annual* Report, 1955/6, 20). Such complaints paid little attention to the absence for a long period of grievance procedures and negotiating machinery, a state of affairs that could only serve to encourage confrontational strategies and the presentation of a 'long list of points in dispute' whenever a possible audience presented itself. The point was aptly put by the late Alhaji Adebola of the now defunct United Labour Congress of Nigeria (ULCN). 'The colonialists did not want to give recognition to trade unions and as a result trade union leaders developed a hostile complex in their dealings with management..' (*West African Pilot,* 1964 Sept. 2, 5 & 8). This applied with equal force to the private sector where, it should be emphasized, such a *modus operandi* directly related to the strong arm tactics and hostility of employers to unionisation and union officials.

Unions and Members

The acquisition of individual identity in the colonial context was inevitably far more difficult and complex than it is today. Paid employment was still limited in scope and a new experience for the bulk of workers; so were the attendant socio-psychological adjustments to the seemingly unlimited subjection of self to an individual employer, to a faceless group of employers, to arbitrary industrial discipline, to unaccustomed authority relations in the workplace and to subsistence solely based on meagre wages. The 'guinea pigs' of the proletarianisation process, systematically alienated from their peasant roots, found themselves caught in a vortex of conflicting emotions and values.

The political situation in the 1940s was characterised both by volatility and potential for development. The National Council for Nigeria and the Cameroons (later, National Convention of Nigerian Citizens) emerged in 1943 as the first serious political party and a number of quasi-pressure groups and other voluntary associations followed in its wake. A vision of the possibility of self-rule sparked off competitive theorising on the strategies to be adopted to achieve it and how best Nigerian policy could be organised. The net effect was that actors on the social scene played many roles, some of them conflicting. There was every reason to believe that ethnic or so-called tribal associations were far more influential than nascent political parties; indeed, the former often made up the basis for the latter (see Ezera, K., 1960; Dudley, B., 1973).[16]

Workers and their organisations could hardly remain insulated from

[16] Ezera, K., *Constitutional Developments..., op. cit.*; Dudley, B.J., *Instability and Political Order- Politics and Crisis in Nigeria*, Ibadan, 1973.

these cross-pressures. The TUC itself foundered on the issue of affiliation to the NCNC. Trade unionists, as the property of emerging political elites, were not expected to betray *any* form of nationalism! Furthermore, colonial society was largely urban-based, and urban areas were understandably cultural and ethnic melting pots. T.M. Yesufu (1962) notes how the activities of ethnic associations tended to supplement those of trade unions, although there is considerable evidence to show how the two types of organisations developed in parallel one with the other.

> `The workers own tribal organisation, or 'improvement' union in the town provides benefits in desperate cases, financially assists those who want to get married, pays the burial expenses of a deceased parent, makes a present on the occasion of a new babe, honours the worker elevated to a chieftaincy and repatriates the destitute. Some tribal organisations award scholarships to the young educated worker or to the children of others. It is this that explains the seeming paradox that whereas the worker will not regularly subscribe to the funds of a trade union (apparently because he is too poor) he does pay regular subscription to the fund of his tribal `union'; and the contributions here are usually higher than those required by the trade union ...Thus the trade union is caught in a vicious circle; it is deprived of funds because the services which it ought to render are provided by non-industrial organisations supported by the workers and it cannot provide rival services because it has not funds' (cited in Sklar, R., 1963, footnote).[17]

This passage reveals, among other things, some of Yesufu's preconceived notions about what trade unions 'ought' to do, a model emphasizing economic benefits to members in line with the generalised Western model of the late nineteenth century.

Independent observers and official reports have both tended to indict union officials of maladministration, authoritarianism, misuse of union funds, and nepotism.' [9] Except for some interesting exchanges between Bill Warren and Eliot Berg, on the one hand, and Peter Kilby and John Weeks on the other, very little attention has been paid to relationships between union officials and their members and to the positive contribution made by the unions to the betterment of the workers' condition.[18] That unions survived

---

[17] Sklar, R., Nigerian Political Parties, Princeton University Press, 1963

[18] Warren, W.M. 'Urban Real Wages and the Nigerian Trade Union Movement, 1939-1960', *Economic Development and Cultural Change*, vol. 15(1), October 1966.: 2) 'Urban Real Wages and the Nigerian Trade Union Movement, 1939-1960: A Rejoinder', *Economic Development and Cultural Change*, vol. 17(4), 1969; Berg, E.J. 'Urban Real Wage and the Nigerian Trade Union Movement 1939-1960: A Comment', *Economic Development and Cultural Change, (EDCC)*, vol. 17(4), 1969; Kilby, P. 'Industrial Relations and Wage Determination: Failure of the Anglo-Saxon Model', *Journal of Developing Areas*

at all against the overwhelming odds earlier mentioned would suggest, at worst, that workers shared a basic belief and interest in them as useful devices to advance their interests. Given the scenario in the tin mines as outlined by Bill Freund (1981), for example, no improvement in the physical treatment of workers and in their conditions of employment would have been possible without worker protests, union activities and the catalytic activities of labour officers of the Department of Labour.

Given differentials in pay, skill and tasks, the pervasive hostility of employers and their labour-control strategies and the suspicions of the Department of Labour, colonial administrators and law enforcement agencies, unions could seldom claim the support of all the workers in the establishments they organised. For its part the colonial administration seemed to believe that all workers at this period thought of unions as 'a stick to beat their employers with in the extortion of higher wages' *(Annual Report*, 1943, 19). In the context of employer dependence on forced and convict labour for several decades and of their consequent reluctance to pay reasonable wages, it would be surprising if such a view did not contain more than a grain of truth. The fact, however, that the Colonial Office and colonial administration devoted so many human and material resources to influencing the activities of the trade unions would in itself point to the fact that the workers' use of their unions went beyond simple demands for wage increases.

The Nigerian workers' commitment to their unions has been subject to critical remarks from several observers who have tended to base their judgements on an index of membership financial support. Warmington (1960), Yesufu (1962), Kayode (1973) and Cohen (1974) have observed that union members gained minimal material benefits, Yesufu and Cohen noting in addition that workers' support for unions tended to increase during and immediately following a period of intense wages agitation (Yesufu, 1962, 67; Cohen, 1974,128). Such a focus on material rewards from union membership has served to divert attention from other socio-psychological factors of equal importance to members. The size of a union's funds is not necessarily an indication of its effectiveness in the vigorous pursuit of workers' demands. With the experience of British and American unions behind him, Warmington (1960) in his study of the Cameroons Developed Corporation Workers' Union (said to be one of the best and largest unions

---

(JDA)., vol. 1(14), July 1967.; 'A Reply to John F. Weeks' Comment', JDA, vol. 3(1), October 1968.; 'Further Comment on the Kilby/Weeks Debate: Final Observations', JDA, vol. 5(2), January 1971; Weeks, J. 'A Comment on P. Kilby: Industrial Relations and Wage Determination', *Journal of Developing Areas*, vol. 3(1), 1968.; 'Further Comment on the Kilby/Weeks Debate: An Empirical Rejoinder', *Journal of Developing Areas*, vol. 5(2), Jan. 1971.

in Nigeria at the time), was somewhat surprised to find that a union could survive without adequate subscriptions and that 'accounting methods were unsatisfactory and the financial position of the union for appreciable periods at a time appeared to be strained, and much worse than might have been expected from the amount of support being given to the union by its members' (1960, 33; also quoted in Yesufu, *op. cit.*, 66).

Eliot Berg (1959), pushing this line of inquiry somewhat further, recognised just how misleading it was to view workers' commitment to their unions and to assess union effectiveness solely in terms of financial contributions and resources. If this were the case, colonial (and some post-colonial) unions could hardly have sustained strikes either. But this was clearly not the case. Berg recorded a typical strike situation in this way:

> `Considerable discipline is exhibited during stoppages. It is ordinarily not prudent for an African to present himself for work during these protest demonstrations. Racial alignments become crystal clear: Europeans are almost always at work and Africans are not. On both sides, it is something of an act of treachery to desert one's camp. Often the protest tends to become generalised, starting as a demonstration against a decision of the employers or the Administration proper...Thus during these protest demonstrations the African urban community tends to close its ranks. Ethnic particularism and union ideological differences tend to be submerged in the common African struggle against the European employers and administration, (in Galenson, W., 1959, 226).[19]

Despite this, the impact of strikes and protests was often limited. Unions were not capable of forcing employers to shut down, however widespread a work stoppage might be, because of the presence of European workers in key positions. Employers could easily break strikes in a labour market characterised by oversupply and in a relatively undifferentiated and non-industrialised economy. In addition, the breaking of strikes under the 'emergency powers' of the Administration, which preceded 'negotiations', frequently resulted in the death and banishment of trade union leaders and the destruction of unions. All this was achieved by the deregistration of unions by the Department of Labour, by the free use of troops and police by the colonial administration, by widespread victimisation of union members and by the refusal of employers to meet union officials. Strikes were therefore usually more effective in the public sector where 'essential services' remained paralysed and the administration had little choice but to negotiate with its own employees on whom the colonial order substantially depended.

[19] Galenson, W. *Labor in Developing Countries*, Univ. of California Press, Berkeley & Los Angeles, 1963

The effectiveness of work stoppages in the small private sector had therefore little to do with the size of strike funds or the regular payment of union dues: it depended on the availability of alternative sources of livelihood which determined the ability to stay away from the job. The hard core of workers who now depended solely on their wages for survival were in the event the more skilled who had relatively secure employment and possessed a not inconsiderable bargaining leverage; the mass of unskilled and daily-paid labour, given the spasmodic and seasonal nature of their employment, drifted from place to place, hardly stayed long enough in any one job to be active and to pay regular dues to their union. This paradox of 'organisationally and financially weak' unions constantly wresting concessions from private and public employers has led several observers to talk of the 'political' methods of Nigerian unions, despite the obvious disregard of politicians and political parties for organised labour since early 1950s.[2]' Be that as it may, the limited impact of scanty financial resources on union tactics could not persist in the face of a rapid proletarianisation process and of the dramatic impoverishment of rural areas and the consequent near elimination of alternatives to wage employment. Increased foreign investment, the growth of the private sector, the bloated nature of the state apparatus, the pattern of public expenditure and more effective unionisation all set the stage for the post-Independence (or post-colonial) phase to which we now turn.

Chapter 4

THE TRADES UNIONS IN THE PERIOD 1960-1985

GOVERNMENT-UNIONS RELATIONS

The government's reaction to workers was largely determined by the nature of the post-colonial state, itself a subject of great controversy.[1] The dominant view sees the post-colonial state as a continuation of the previous colonial structure. The decolonisation process is said to have mainly involved the filtering up to positions of power of a congeries of pro-Western indigenous groups, an amalgam of 'modern' and traditional' elites. These elites, by virtue of formal Western education and economic interests, are said to have perpetuated foreign and private domination of the economy. The state and its functionaries were thus committed, by the logic of the situation, to resisting any — forces that could threaten current economic and political arrangements, particularly any activities geared to the reduction of profits and the security of investments. The argument then proceeds that these elites, have been propped up politically and economically by multinational companies and metropolitan governments and, being essentially parasitic on their respective populations, have been an unlikely spearhead for any drive for meaningful economic development and independence.[2]

On the ground, there were in 1960 three main political parties – the National Congress of Nigerian Citizens (NCNC), the Northern People's Congress (NPC), the Action Group (AG) and these drew their main support from the Eastern Region Northern Region, and Western Region and respectively. They strenuously sought to incorporate all other dissenting groups within these political regions, an attempt that was accompanied by widespread physical violence, arson and general insecurity by 1963.[3] In order to weaken the Action Group, the Midwest Region was hived off from the Western Region in 1963. There followed a hotly disputed and abortive national census, and a badly managed and rigged Western Region election

[1] ALAVI, H, 'The State in Postcolonial Societies', *New Left Review*, Vol. 74, 1972.
[2] Ibid.
[3] COHEN, R., *Labour and Politics in Nigeria*, Heinemann, 1974.

that resulted in a state of emergency being declared in the area by the federal government. Direct rule from Lagos followed. Finally the stalemated 1965 federal elections gave birth to a 'government of national unity' which was toppled a few months later on 15 January 1966 in a military coup.

Within seven months the military had broken into open factions with a counter-coup, a situation that rapidly deteriorated into a bloody Civil War by July 1967. A starved and disillusioned rebel army surrendered three years later on 15 January 1970, bringing to a close one of the most heart-rending phases of Nigerian social history.

It has generally been acknowledged that politicians of the so-called First Republic had little time for anything but the spoils of office. A goodly number of labour leaders had in fact been politically compromised as staunch party members, members of parliament and senators under the aegis of particular political parties. Lower level union leaders and organisers effectively kept together a resentful and aggrieved organised labour force in spite of the factionalisation at the central level represented by the existence of two (and later four) central labour organisations.

The Trades Union Congress of Nigeria (TUCN) and the Nigerian Trades Union Congress (NTUC), the rival central labour bodies, had in 1961 presented memoranda to the Federal Government asking for a review of wages and salaries and the regrouping of house unions into twenty-five industrial and general unions. The government showed little interest in these and other issues raised by workers and their representatives, being solely preoccupied with the emasculation of political opposition. Its proposed 'Preventive Detention Act' was roundly opposed and defeated and as thuggery and political violence mounted, leading members of the Federal opposition, including Chief Awolowo, were arrested, tried and jailed for 'treason'.

As in colonial times, little use was made of internal machinery for processing grievances in the public sector. Characteristically tribunals were established only after major or persistent workers' protests. The Morgan Commission was set up in the wake of the 1964 general strike; the Adebo Commission in 1970-2; the Udoji Commission in 1974; the Onosode Commission for federal parastatals in 1981; the Cookey Commission for universities in 1982; and the Adamolekun Commission for federal polytechnics, advanced and technical teachers colleges in 1982.

Where industrial conflict was concerned, the strategies adopted by successive governments differed only slightly in the extent to which strong arm tactics were adopted by police and troops. In his minority report on the 1964 general strike, T. M. Yesufu noted the 'mounting dissatisfaction with the role of the police during strikes' (1964, p. 31). During the civil war the military government promulgated Decrees 21 (of 1968) and 53 (of 1969) which banned strikes and related activities, and institutionalised a police intervention while making provision for limited conciliation. Arbitration and conciliation services were later fully provided for in the 1976 Trade Disputes Decree which created a standing Industrial Arbitration Tribunal (now Panel) and a National Industrial Court. The decree substituted compulsory arbitration for the previously voluntary type, making it unlawful for workers to remain on strike while mediation, conciliation and arbitration processes were in progress. It thus sought by this roundabout but unsubtle way to make strikes illegal.

Given the relative instability of the political order arid of the state, the amount of attention paid to the structure and government of workers' organisations bordered on the excessive. The Balewa administration (1960-65) attempted, somewhat weakly, to play off leading labour leaders against one another, a ploy that was neutralised by the formation of the Joint Action Committee of all labour leaders in 1963. Whilst the short-lived military administration of Major-General Aguiyi-Ironsi sought the greater unity of the labour movement, the General was himself quite emphatic in his denunciation of strikes and lockouts which he thought disturbed the prevailing 'peaceful and orderly atmosphere' (*West Africa*, 12 Feb. 1966, 19).

The Gowon, Murtala and Obasanjo regimes were more decisive in the area of labour control strategies. Galloping inflation and the extensive dislocation of peasant life and organised labour occasioned by the civil war gave cause for protests; yet a wage freeze was imposed by 1968. Overt workers' protests at the end of war, followed by Adebo awards, found the government in an even greater quandary. Increases in pay served to enlarge its wage bill. Small as these were in the context of soaring prices, they led to demands for further increases. The whole situation was exacerbated by the failure of the Price Control Board and the Nigerian Supply Company to keep down prices and increase the supply of milk, sugar, salt and other commodities in short supply. A vicious cycle was thus created: the raging inflation made workers push for further increases in the public sector, awards for which workers in the private sector (particularly those at the bottom of the scale) then went on strike, compelling employers to implement and thus further increase the anguish of the government.

A hard-pressed government produced various labour constraining measures. It acquired the power to compel employers to recognise trade unions, made check-off compulsory, and half-heartedly attempted to control foreign domination of the economy by means of indigenisation decrees (Nigerian Enterprises Promotion Decrees) which sought to transfer controlling shared in various enterprises into Nigerian hands whilst forbidding and limiting foreign participation in other sectors of the economy.

As implemented, the indigenisation decrees enabled the government to acquire shares in many enterprises, thereby blurring the distinction between the private and public sectors. As its economic tentacles spread across the economy so did its concern over workers and their activities. The government undertook a 're-organisation' of less than a thousand 'house unions' into forty-two national and industrial unions in 1976, just as it appointed the Adebiyi Tribunal to probe the finances and activities of prominent labour leaders and of rival central labour organisations. As a result eleven prominent labour leaders were banned from unionism for life.[4] The Trade Disputes Decree No. 7 of 1976 spelt out 'official limited intervention' in labour matters. Judging by the way the government intervened in the appointment of full-time 'secretaries' to the new unions and by its refusal to recognise the Nigerian Labour Congress founded by workers' representatives in December 1975, its barely concealed intention was to ensure a more predictable central labour leadership.

As government found it increasingly difficult to implement its incomes policy so did it adopt a stronger anti-union posture. As various sectors of the economy became affected by industrial disputes so did the government promulgate decrees to regulate them. In anticipation of industrial action by bank workers it produced a Trade Dispute (Essential Services) Decree on 21 May 1976 which not only empowered it to dissolve trade unions that contravened its provisions but also specified an 'essential services' category so widely defined as to include virtually the whole of the public sector and financial institutions (insurance and banks) in the private sector. The National Union of Nigerian Bank Employees was proscribed on 27 May 1976 after a strike. Strikers at the Peugeot Car assembly plant in Kaduna were jailed and their union dissolved (*West Africa*, 6 March 1978, 478). Section II(i) of the Trade Union Act prohibited workers in insurance, banking, telecommunications, the armed forces and police from belonging to trade unions. Also extremely severe and repressive was the Petroleum Production and Distribution (Anti-sabotage) Act No.15 of 1977 which classified strikes by tanker drivers and petroleum workers as 'criminal' and made strikers liable to imprisonment without trial.

The Trade Unions (Amendment) Act No.22 of 1978 and the Labour (Amendment) Act No.21 of 1978 which extended recognition to the NLC as the only central labour organisation, created an automatic and compulsory check-off system for paying union dues and sanctioned the creation of industrial unions, came under a determined attack from the business community. The attack lost much of its steam as the military, along with

[4] Abiodun, M.O. *Restructuring of Trade Unions in Nigeria, 1976-1978*, p. 11

aspiring politicians, became preoccupied with the mechanics of handing over the reins of government to an elected civilian administration. Notwithstanding, the Nigerian Civil Service Union on May 1979 simultaneously declared a trade dispute with the Federal Government and gave it twenty-one days within which to restore the car loans that had been suspended by General Murtala's administration. The government, in order to buy time, referred the matter to the Industrial Arbitration Panel (IAP) and went on with its business of announcing the budget, a budget that was roundly denounced by the leader of the civil service union though initially supported by the NLC leadership. In the end, the NLC took the wind out of the sails of the Civil Service Union by issuing a 21-day ultimatum to the military administration within which to restore car loans, review rent and transport allowances and fix a national minimum wage. Talks between both sides ensued, and the compromise reached included a 60 naira national monthly minimum wage and continuing review of rent subsidy, car loans and transport allowances.

The lull was short lived as organised labour, through the NLC, demanded from the recently elected President Shehu Shagari some form of commitment to the general welfare of labour. More concerned about establishing his own political authority and that of his political party, the National Party of Nigeria (NPN), the President refused to be drawn into any dialogue. This seeming complacency was broken by 10 January 1980 when the NLC gave another ultimatum demanding that the government should reach a settlement on outstanding issues by 31 March or face a general strike.

The President responded by declaring by administrative fiat a new 100 naira monthly minimum wage in order to stave off a national stoppage. This was followed by talks between representatives of government and the NLC in which agreement was reached on rent subsidies and a transport allowance, with the national minimum wage and car loan issues referred to a tripartite committee comprising the NLC, government and employers' representatives and the National Economic Council (a body comprising all 19 state governors, former heads of state and chief justices and some prominent traditional rulers, chaired by the vice-president) respectively.

Exploiting the goodwill among workers created by revised fringe benefits and a national minimum monthly wage, the government counterattacked on 15 April 1980 with an incomes policy which classified workers simply as 'junior' and 'senior', the former category covering those earning up to ₦3,000 per annum. A single price increase a year was allowed provided that it was not more than 5% and that the Incomes Board had been notified thirty (30) days in advance. For increases above this norm, as well as a review of current fringe benefits and the creation of new types, the permission of the Minister for Employment, Labour & Productivity was required. And arrears from any pay negotiations could not be back-dated beyond the beginning of the financial year, wage increases themselves being restricted to an upper ceiling of 15 per cent.

In practice the government was not in a position, in terms of manpower and political will, to implement such an incomes policy.

Secondly, the largely trading subsidiaries of multi-national companies were too entrenched in the system to yield to effective monitoring, quite apart from the fact that many legislators sat on their boards and had extensive business interests. In the end rapidly rising prices, exceeding 300 per cent within two months in the case of some commodities, blew the policy to pieces.

The upshot was incessant criticism by labour leaders of what remained of the government's incomes policy and particularly of the perceived fall in the general standard of living which was seen as a consequence of official policies. The debate over an appropriate national minimum wage was renewed with increased vigour, the NLC suggesting the sum of ₦300 per month. This time legislators, through the Labour Committees of both the House of Representatives and of the Senate, showed some interest in the matter, seeking on the one hand to upstage the President and on the other to ensure a lower figure. With the Industrial Arbitration Panel (IAP) still dragging its feet over the car loan issue, the NLC held its biennial conference in Kano in late February 1981. Sunmonu retained the presidency of the organization and a resolution in favour of a general strike by May 1981 was unanimously adopted, should outstanding issues not be adequately tackled by the government. The general strike commenced on 11 May, lasted only two days, involved almost a million workers and was effective. The points in dispute included the 300 naira monthly minimum wage, total restoration of the car loan and basic allowances and a minimum pension not less than the minimum monthly wage. Negotiations that enabled the NLC to call off the strike drew in representatives of the government, the National Assembly and employers, agreements being reached on transport allowances while other issues were referred to both the National Assembly and the Industrial Court. The National Assembly subsequently fixed a new national minimum wage of ₦125 naira a month.

The situation immediately after the general strike witnessed attempts by powerful sections of both the Senate and House of Representatives and the business community to achieve a repeal of the Trade Unions Act No.31 of 1973, the Trade Unions (Amendment) Act No.22 of 1978 and the Labour (Amendment) Act No. 2 I of 1978. The object of repeal was to reduce union funds by making payment of union dues optional, to threaten the current structure and life of the forty-two national unions by withdrawing recognition and to facilitate the creation of another central labour organization in order to weaken the NLC and the labour movement in general. The repeal of the Acts was prevented by effective lobbying on the part of the NLC and the ability of a good many legislators to appreciate the possible consequences of such a decision against a background of an increasingly disenchanting and corrupt political process, shortages of various food items and truly galloping inflation. President Shagari's administration was overthrown by the military on 31 December 1983.

The succeeding military administration of Major General Buhari was noticeably sterner in its approach to labour issues. An ongoing massive retirement exercise in the public sector threw at least 50,000 into the labour market during 1984 alone, with the prospect of more sackings and redundancies to come. This policy went hand in hand with the government unilaterally cutting back on and, in some cases, suspending, existing fringe benefits. This took ominous forms in the States where military governors, in seeking to outdo each other in dynamism, put forward quite outrageous proposals. The governor of Imo State, Brigadier Ike Nwachukwu, for example, sought a complete downward revision of basic pay rates of public servants by proposing to link monthly wages to the amount of the subventions paid into the state's treasury each month. Since oil revenues were on the decline and subventions to each of the nineteen states correspondingly diminishing, the 'Imo Formula', as it was dubbed, sought therefore to reduce take home pay by 40 per cent, the resultant loss of pay to be restored only when 'the economy picked up.' The policy was reluctantly abandoned by the governor in the face of protests and general condemnation.

Lt. Colonel David Mark of Niger State met with some success in the drive to erode 'terms of employment'. As in Bendel State, civil servants were two months behind in payment of salaries, while fringe benefits had been suspended since January 1985 on account of 'poor state finances'. Tired of sending petitions on this matter the local chapter of the Nigerian Labour Congress (NLC) called workers out on strike on 26 July 1985, a strike which failed as armed policemen stood guard over all government offices and parastatals, while the governor threatened to sack all those who did not turn up for work. The permanent secretary in the state's Ministry of Information, Mallam Aliu Umar, attributed the collapse of the strike to the 'unrealistic demands of labour leaders', generously noting that 'it would have been "pardonable" if the labour leaders had been demanding the payment of all entitlements due to retrenched workers rather than calling for the restoration of suspended fringe benefits' (*The Guardian*, July 27 1985, p.16). Apart from those in the private sector, only an insignificant proportion (less than one-half of one per cent) of retrenched workers in the public sector received their entitlements upon termination. The NLC has recently indicated interest in this issue and had resolved to toughen its stance over it and over continuing retrenchment.

Although the Industrial Arbitration Panel still continued to tackle some cases, mostly from the private sector, the Buhari military administration was ruthless in dealing with public sector strikes. The 1984 strike by Nigeria Airways pilots was smashed by the authorities, forty-nine pilots, including officers of their union, being dismissed for participating in the stoppage. The military administration went a step further in the case of striking doctors in March 1985. All doctors working in state hospitals were dismissed and required to re-apply for their jobs, these 'new' jobs involving a loss in seniority and previous experience, and to sign an undertaking not to go on strike. Some doctors lost their jobs while the Nigerian Medical Association (NMA) was itself proscribed and its officials placed under indefinite detention.

The intervention of the NLC, led to a 'compromise' which involved asking doctors to re-apply for jobs, but the administration still refused to heed pleas for the release of the detained NMA officers, notably Professor Beko Ransome-Kuti.

LABOUR-MANAGEMENT RELATIONS

Labour-management relations have been conditioned largely by the following factors:

a) the import substitution strategy for industrialisation as implemented by various Nigerian governments;
b) attempts at Nigerianisation of the economy;
c) poorly implemented incomes policies over the years;
d) hostile anti-labour legislation.

The import-substitution strategy has been based partly on the assumption that colonial trade significantly influenced the taste of 'consumers' and also that there already exists a market for particular commodities. Given these assumptions the policy has emerged that the importation of such items shall continue until demand (or size of market) has grown enough to warrant local manufacture. Local factories are then to be protected by a high wall of tariffs until their products become competitive enough. The possible advantages of this strategy as advocated by its proponents are numerous but are of little interest to us. Of relevance are the structure of the economy attendant upon its implementation in Nigeria, government industrial policies in this regard and how these have affected labour-management relations.

In effect, the economy has become dominated by the subsidiaries of multinational companies which originally sold in Nigeria finished products imported from parent companies in Europe, Japan and North America. In line with new official policy, these companies were encouraged to establish assembly plants and to undertake some processing of primary products. The important factor from the Nigerian point of view is that these plants operated in most instances on the basis of securing over ninety per cent of inputs, in most instances from abroad, and that the state of labour-management relations in the so-called manufacturing sector, in spite of existing collective agreements and other understandings, hinged on the ease or otherwise with which companies could secure import licences. Between 1960 and 1983, with the exception of the Civil War years of 1967 to 1970, no great problems were encountered in this regard. There were a number of reasons for this - the relatively strong position of these companies within the economy, the corrupt practices of relevant bureaucrats, the indiscriminate issue of import licences by politicians as political patronage and pay-off, the availability of large amounts of foreign exchange derived from crude oil sales in the latter part of the period.

The same considerations applied with equal force to most of the retail and wholesale sector which depended solely on imported items, leaving only the huge public sector, banking, and petroleum industries (exploration, production and marketing) less affected by the 'politics of import licences.'

From about 1983 such understandings, collective agreements, and 'custom and practice' were generally being abandoned by employers in the face of a dearth of import licences resulting from rapid depletion of the country's foreign reserves by President Shagari's administration. This also coincided with a slump in oil prices and declining oil revenue. Wages were frozen, arrears of up to six months were owed to workers, particularly in the public sector, and thousands of workers lost their jobs through dramatic 'rationalisations' and 're-organisations'. When the externally derived economic depression set in, even such 'big' companies as the United African Company (UAC), Paterson & Zochonis (PZ), Lever Brothers and Guinness Nigeria Ltd., all noted for their more enlightened approach to personnel issues, disgorged more than a third of their total workforce into the ranks of the unemployed, the more extreme example being the Swiss-dominated trading company R. T. Briscoe Nigeria Ltd., which reduced its workforce from 5,000 to fewer than 500 between 1982 and 1984. Even where some of the stronger unions wrested 'concessions' from particular managements, this had more to do with timing and the spread of such massive redundancies than to principle or scale.

As for the demand for the 'Africanisation' or 'Nigerianisation' of the economy this stretches back to the early years of colonial nationalism to its legal origins and the Nigerian Enterprises Promotion Decrees of which the first was enacted in 1972. This series of decrees sought to transfer ownership and control of equity shares into Nigerian hands by compelling foreign investors to relinquish between sixty and one hundred per cent of their shares, depending on the type of business. Because only a few Nigerians could afford these shares, the state acquired controlling interests in banks, insurance companies, and petroleum-producing companies, while exercising exclusive jurisdiction over the mining of minerals, iron and steel production, telecommunications, postal services and the generation and supply of electricity.

An obvious consequence was a change in management structure, Nigerians replacing, and in some cases outnumbering, expatriates. A second development, perhaps of more important consequence for labour-management relations, was the subjection of employment policies to political considerations as reflected in the official policy of 'federal character' - a euphemism for ethnic balancing of personnel. A third consideration was the subjection of the policies and objectives of such companies to the dictates of successive governments, governments themselves plagued by ethnic rivalries, corruption and quarrels over the spoils of office. Fourth and last, the existence of the state as a major shareholder meant a substantial merging of both private and public sectors, making industrial and labour policies increasingly the prey of political expediency.

Although the nature of the above factors makes it utterly impossible to isolate their respective autonomous impacts, pointers can easily be discerned. Managements have been plagued by insecurity due to sudden changes in personnel, promotions and appointments not strictly based on experience, competence and recommended procedures, and disciplinary actions effectively neutralised by political pressure or lobbying. Dissatisfaction with such unpredictable internal motivational and disciplinary systems seems to have had two immediate consequences: first a noticeable increase in extra-organisational activities for pecuniary reward (called 'private practice'), almost as an insurance against distorted or frustrated career expectations; and the growth of ethnic chauvinism as one of the primordial sentiments to be exploited in order 'to get ahead'.

Secondly, the 'Nigerianisation' of managements and ensuing personal and ethnic rivalries has led to insufficient attention being paid to the grievances and expectations of non-managerial grades usually designated 'junior staff' or 'junior workers'. Factions of management have taken sides with striking or disputing workers and their unions against other factions siding with the managing director, personnel manager or director and the board of directors. In a few instances workers and their unions have been drawn into strictly intra-management conflicts, with the affected management personnel and unions writing petitions against 'management', citing alleged 'corrupt' or 'unpatriotic' action and decisions. In most 'parastatals' and in private companies where the state owns a significant amount of equity shares, petition-writing has been raised to an art form, becoming the main source of information upon which a goodly number of policies are based.

Thirdly, where 'terms of employment', 'grievance settlement' and 'collective bargaining' are concerned, particular managements seem to have exploited the ambiguity of the position of the state (or government) as the ultimate arbiter of their fate. On the one hand, they have argued their inability to offer a lasting solution to any set of problems or proposals, feigning impotence before political authority even when something could have been done. On the other hand, in some of the administratively less autonomous parastatals, practically every little detail has been presented for approval by the relevant ministry, bureaucrats in turn referring all decisions to political heads. Public sector negotiations in Nigeria have become characterised by frustrating delays due to lack of mandate on the part of 'management' or representatives of government and the tendency on the part of the core ministries (finance, establishment, employment, labour and productivity office and the cabinet office or office of the president) to subject agreements, to further review and negotiations. This is the more dramatically so when a general wage review is based on the recommendations of an officially constituted wage tribunal, or negotiated agreements result from general strikes.[5]

What is left of the 'pure' private sector in Nigeria has not remained unaffected by these pressures even if their consequences have been less destabilising. Since individuals and companies are legally free to appoint whomsoever they wish, the employment of relatives and kinsmen has hardly been an issue at all: in practice, subsidiaries of multinational companies employ expatriates drawn from their home bases and can be said to have blazed the trail in this regard, showing a strong preference for personnel from wherever the company is located both in Nigeria and home base (e.g. a majority of expatriates employed by Guinness (Nigeria) Ltd are inevitably Irish and probably drawn from Dublin). What can reasonably be said is that Nigerian majority share-holders in the private sector have a freer hand in getting rid of the personnel for any reason and, since their driving force remains the profit motive, some attempts have been made to ensure a measure of competence, effectiveness, and relevance of personnel irrespective of ethnic or racial background.

The same scope for development has also been evident in negotiations on existing terms of employment, representatives of management enjoying the confidence of boards and fully mandated to strike agreements with workers'

---

[5] Sonubi, O.Machinery for Salaries and Wages Administration in Nigeria,' *Quarterly Journal of Administration*, Ife, Vol.6, 1971

representatives. Such mandates have also been deployed with some single-mindedness, especially in establishments where even the initial stirring of unionism have been snuffed out with the permanent intention of the unilateral dictation of the terms and conditions of employment. As Sonubi (1973) has correctly observed, about 50 per cent of disputes have centred on terms of employment and anti-unionism.[6] And where unionism has taken root, it is not uncommon, as the Morgan Commission of 1964 noted, for employers or managements '...to resort to all sorts of practices to make it difficult for their employees to participate actively in the affairs of trade unions, employing all sorts of dubious means, 'for example, fostering the formation of splinter groups and also of paying loyalty bonuses' (Report, 1964, 4, para 13). The former tactic has become immeasurably more difficult to use since the 1976-77 reorganisation exercise and instead efforts have been directed at splitting the branch unions at the individual plant level, diverting the national union's attention and energies to domestic squabbles, as it were. Like the former 'house unions', branch unions are far more susceptible to pressure than national unions because the overwhelming majority of branch union officers are employees and are personally exposed to an array of coercive measures at the disposal of management.

The subject of poorly implemented incomes policies over the years is a well-covered topic and only a few remarks will be made here on the backwash created for labour-management relations. The major planks of particular incomes policies have oscillated between wage freezes and pay norms of 5% and 15 per cent and the use of wage tribunals to establish basic thresholds of entitlements among the different categories of employees as previously discussed. These measures have had a mixed impact on labour-management relations and can be regarded as positive or negative depending on the point of view. In spite of this, it would be correct to maintain that pressures for and against incomes policies have ultimately, after discussions and strike activity, led to the protection of weak and unorganised groups of workers in the form of minimum pay rates and pension arrangements.

On the other hand, the apparent ineffectiveness of the Price Control Board in checking arbitrary and very frequent price increases by retailers, in preventing shortages of various widely consumed food items as a result of hoarding, in improving a poor distribution system and in preventing shortfalls in supply that the ineffectual Nigeria National Supply Company has woefully failed to make up, - all these have served to exacerbate labour-management relations as workers have constantly demanded reviews of basic rates and fringe benefits in the face of rapidly deteriorating living standards.

---

[6] Sonubi, O.,'Trade Disputes in Nigeria, 1966-1971', *The Nigerian Journal of Social and Economic Studies* (NJESS), Vol.!5(2), 1973.

The wages tribunals have thus served the dual purposes of establishing minimum rates (which most employers have opposed as increasing labour costs) and of distorting differentials which affected workers have opposed and frequently struck against. The latter has been a somewhat unintended consequence for those in lower pay brackets since government has consistently maintained that its intention has always been to narrow the gap between the top and bottom pay scales. Despite this the failure of a good many employers to implement tribunal wage awards, seems to have fuelled the demand for a legally binding national minimum wage. The enactment of such a minimum wage, though useful in itself, has hardly solved the problem of low wages and of daily paid workers. The legislation itself has provided a loophole, since it applies only to employers of fifty workers or more. Considering that over 70 per cent of employers in the country employ fewer than fifty workers, little comfort can be drawn from the minimum wage legislation as currently constituted. Perhaps its only saving grace is that most of the organized labour force is distributed among a handful of companies in both the public and private sector of the economy. In this respect the periods 1967-1970 and 1980-1984 have probably been the worst years of the worst two decades. It is thus not surprising that these two decades have seen the greatest number of strikes, of wage tribunals, of incomes policies and of anti-labour provisions in legislation.

Some anti-labour legislation has undoubtedly been passed in the 'national interest'. This has been the period in which the political and economic elites have had great difficulty in working out 'the rules of the game', failure to do so having led to civil war in one instance and to four military coups. What constitutes 'the national interest' remains as elusive as ever, and anti-labour legislation may usefully be viewed as a by-product of ongoing crisis within the Nigerian body politic.

As nearly all labour legislations impose a measure of constraint on workers and their organisations, a few examples may serve to illustrate the situation. The provision for the compulsory registration of unions is the first. A trade union which has not been registered or which has ceased to be registered may not lawfully perform any act in furtherance of its purposes. This clause, contained in the original 1938 Trades Union Ordinance and reinforced in all subsequent legislation governing the formation and administration of trade unions, has been used by successive governments to prevent or slow down the rate of unionisation, to neutralise those sections of organized labour considered too radical or troublesome and to influence the composition of union leadership, particularly at the centre. Innumerable strikes, protest demonstrations, marches and litigation have resulted from the use of the registration (and de-registration) process to control the labour movement. On the discouragement of union growth, Professor Uvieghara

(1976)[7] has discussed the abortive attempt of government in 1970 to prevent unionisation of customs preventive staff when the acting Registrar of Trade Unions not only refused to register the union but also declined to offer reasons for his decision. Upon successful litigation by union officials, the government countered on 29 April 1970 by passing Decree No.27, the Trade Unions (Amendment) Decree which, among other provisions, prohibited persons in certain establishments from forming or joining trade unions and in the Customs Preventive Service or in any other service of the Federal or State Governments authorised to bear arms (Uvieghara, 1976,96). Section 2 of the Act specifically dissolved that union. Likewise the National Union of Bank Employees (NUMBE) was proscribed on 27 May 1976 after a strike. Strikers at the Peugeot car assembly plant in Kaduna were jailed and their union dissolved (*West Africa*, 6 March 1978, 476).

The government refused to register the NLC formed on 17 December 1975 as a central labour organisation. It was not enamoured of the emergent leadership, and also banned the four central bodies (ULCN, NTUC, LUF and NWC) that had merged to constitute that all-embracing body. The government, consequent upon the submission of the Adebiyi Report already discussed, decreed the Trade Unions (Disqualification of Certain Persons) Act No. i5 of 1977 which singled out eleven trade unionists, including veteran Michael Imoudu, and prohibited them from trade union activity for life.

It will be recalled that by 1972 the first of the indigenisation decrees had been passed and post-Adebo Awards strikes lingered on while pre-Udoji strikes were raging. To check mounting protests and to protect its increasing investments in the private sector, the Trade Union Act No.31 of 1973 was enacted by the government, its section II (i) adding workers in insurance, banking, and telecommunications to the growing list of sectors banned from forming trade unions.

In response to the increasing number of strikes, the Trade Disputes Decree No. 7 of 1976 admitted of the 'official limited intervention' in labour matters, made arbitration compulsory and indirectly sought to declare strikes illegal by insisting in its section 13 that none of the parties to an industrial dispute could engage in any form of industrial action while mediation, conciliation and arbitration were in progress! To make the point quite clear in the petroleum industry from which the government derived most of its revenue, the Petroleum Production and Distribution (Anti-sabotage) Decree No. 15 of 1977 classified strikes by tanker drivers and

---

[7] UVIEGHARA, E.E., *Trade Union Law in Nigeria*, Ethiope, Benin City, 1976

petroleum workers as 'criminal' and subjected them to the penalty of imprisonment without trial.

The epoch-making 're-organisation' of the less than one thousand trade (house) unions into forty-two national unions between 1976 and 1978 by the military administration was a far from subtle attempt to influence the labour movement's leadership and aspirations. Firstly, the deliberate naming of each union in the enabling decree has made it extremely difficult to form new unions, even in previously unorganized sectors. Secondly, the government was fought to a standstill in its attempt to infuse pro-government unionists into the executives of the new unions throughout 1976 and 1977 (Otobo, 1981, 68).[8] Thirdly, alarmed at trade union potential, the government deliberately and legally created two sets of unions with exclusive memberships: the famous forty-two national unions could only organize 'junior workers' while the nineteen others were designated 'senior stair associations. Fourthly, reinforcing this false dichotomy, the decree stipulated that only the forty-two unions organizing so-called junior workers could be members of the NLC. In 1984 two unions, including the Academic Staff Union of Universities (ASUU), defied this provision by becoming members of the NLC.

Finally, the Registrar of Trade Unions has brought some of his extensive powers to bear on various sections of the organized labour movement. The most celebrated weapon in his arsenal has been the right to insist on regular yearly returns by unions, a legal provision especially misapplied in the case of the NLC in the years 1981, 1982, and 1983 when the NLC's yearly accounts as submitted were rejected by the Registrar of Trade Unions on the grounds that he had not appointed the auditors. The NLC simply ignored him, prompting him to threaten to de-register the organization. Litigation instigated by some unions on this issue is still pending in the courts. Be that as it may, it should be realised that not all labour legislation has necessarily been, detrimental to the interests of labour. The tactics of employers and other developments in society have from time to time pushed workers and their unions into pressing for various items of protective legislation, a good example being the compulsory check-off system for union dues.

Workers, having demanded this since the 1940s finally got it in 1973. Some of these positive aspects are mentioned below but a serious treatment of labour laws in Nigeria may be found in Emiola (1980) and Uvieghara (1976).[9]

---

[8] OTOBO, D., The Nigerian General Strike of 1981', *Review of African Political Economy*, NO.22, 198

[9] EMIOLA, A., *Nigerian Labour Law*, University of Ibadan Press, 1980; UVIEGHARA, E.E., *Trade Union Law in Nigeria*, Ethiope, *op. cit.*

In summary labour-management relations have been a mixture of anger, bitterness, conflict and uneasiness, at least on the part of workers and unions. The private sector between the years 1960 and 1969 was small and, of all the evidence available, permeated by employers' paternalism (Yesufu, 1962; Roberts, 1964, Kilby, 1969; Ananaba, 1969; Cohen, 1974),[10] the 1964 General Strike notwithstanding. The situation was worse in the small Nigerian-owned and operated concerns which had sprung up in their thousands either as agents (wholesale and retailing) or contractors and sub-contractors to these subsidiaries of multinational companies, or as 'consultants' and contractors to various arms of the state, and usually both. Here the job was far less secure, unionism actively discouraged, arbitrariness and authoritarianism easy substitutes for mutually established procedures of any sort. Workers who were owed (and denied) wages were the norm, with employers in the construction industry and stevedoring as worst offenders. Most of these concerns began to collapse as import licences became scarcer and government payment for completed projects and jobs trickled in and then stopped altogether.

Employers had it even easier during the Civil War years of 1967 to 1970 when state coercive powers were maximally applied on organised labour in the form of a ban on strikes and related activities, the detention of some workers and labour leaders without trial, a wage freeze despite soaring prices, the free use of troops and police on striking workers and the destruction of some unions. The dissatisfaction generated by the Adebo and Udoji awards elicited corresponding repressive legislation from government, which increasingly showed interest in union leadership, finances and administration. Private employers themselves were to decry the erosion of collective bargaining processed by official wage increases and seemed uncomfortable about the existence of a national minimum wage, while the economic recession provided a golden opportunity for massive retrenchments and redundancies.

UNION-MEMBERSHIP RELATIONS

Union-membership relations underwent many changes in this period. The typical state of affairs between 1938 and 1964, as characterised by observers of the scene, was the domination of small and numerous unions by a handful of professional union 'secretaries' or organisers on the one hand, and 'house unions' (restricting membership to a branch or section of a

---

[10] YESUFU, T.M., *An Introduction to Industrial Relations in Nigeria*, OUP for the Nigerian Institute of Social and Economic Research, London, 1962; ROBERTS, B.C, *Labour in the Tropical Territories of the Commonwealth*, Bell, London, 1964; KILBY, P., *Industrialization in an Open Economy: Nigeria 1945-1966*, CUP, 1969; ANANABA, W., *The Trade Union Movement in Nigeria*, Ethiope, Benin City, 1969; COHEN, R., *Labour and Politics in Nigeria*, Heinemann, 1974

company) kept firmly in check by managements. Professional secretaries 'organised' more than one union at a time in order to earn a sizable income. In neither type of union was any strict distinction made between personal and union funds, elections, where held, were often rigged or led to disagreements and consequent factionalisations. Union finances were paltry due to smallness, non-payment or irregular payment of union dues and the diversion of such funds to personal use. There was widespread apathy among union members who were said to be mostly illiterate and led by barely literate union officials with ethnic associations as rival foci of loyalty (Roper, 1958; Warmington, 1960; Yesufu, 1962; Davies, 1966; Smock, 1969; Ananaba, 1969; Kilby, 1969; Cohen, 1974).[11]

Most generalized impressions contain gross inaccuracies. The preceding image of Nigerian trade unions, their leadership and membership, is one such. As Adrian Peace (1979) has correctly pointed out, house unions were not peculiar to the early 1960s; indeed, it was not until the second half of the decade that they began to make their presence felt, particularly after the politicians had forfeited most of their legitimacy and after the 1964 General Strike (1979, p.109ff). The tremendous growth of the economy and especially of the private sector between 1970 and 1976 was accompanied by a corresponding rise in the number of unions, unions different in character from earlier ones. In the first place, the work force was made up mostly of younger men and women and of the relatively better educated. Secondly, younger and more aggressive union leaders had replaced older ones. Thirdly, an increasingly complex economy and more effective unions seem to have convinced several managements of the inevitability of higher levels of co-operation and consultation with workers' representatives. Lastly, the successive political crises briefly mentioned previously, and major economic developments, compelled governments to adopt a more critical posture toward employers and workers, showing more than a passing interest in such issues as union recognition, check-off and union finances, arbitration, and the reorganisation of house unions. Ensuing legislation has substantially changed the complexion of Nigerian industrial relations.

---

[11] ROPER, R.I. *Labour Problems in West Africa,* Penguin, 1958; Warmington, W.A., *A West African Trade Union, OUP, London, 1960;* YESUFU, T.M., *An Introduction to Industrial Relations in Nigeria, op. cit.;* DAVIES, I., *African Trade Unions,* Penguin, Harmondsworth, 1966; SMOCK, D.R., Conflict and Control in an African Trade Union: A Study of the Nigerian Coal Miners' Union, Hoover Institution, Stanford, 1969; ANANABA, W., *The Trade Union Movement in Nigeria,* Ethiope, Benin City, 1969; KILBY, P., *Industrialization in an Open Economy: Nigeria 1944-1966,* Cambridge University Press, 1969; COHEN, R., *Labour and Politics in Nigeria,* Heinemann, 1974;

How did the house unions really fare in the early nineteen sixties? For this we turn again to Adrian Peace (1979) whose study is the most recent on the subject and embraced the Ikeja Industrial Estate which contains almost half of the organised labour force in Lagos. In their earlier years, Peace argues, most functions were carried out by elected union presidents and one or two of their closest associates. Such leaders made few attempts to involve the labour force at large in decision-making and many workers who were union members in the mid-1960s affirm that they had little idea of day to day developments unless the leaders were arguing among themselves. Consequently, although their unions gained formal recognition, workers' demands were modest. Growing disenchantment among rank and file then led to changes in leadership. Workers now elected to representative office were men who were much the same as the workers themselves. They were less likely to use their offices as stepping stones to mobility within the workplace and in the wider community outside as was prevalent in the 1940s and 1950s. As part and parcel of a more democratic style, union presidents began to convene general meetings several times a year, and at times of dispute even two or three in quick succession, in order that ordinary workers could voice their opinions and where most issues could be put to a formal vote. Workers nowadays frequently argue that as major issues are extensively discussed on the shop floor, frequent attendance at union meetings is somewhat unnecessary and that the close relationship between leaders and followers which the house system allows has been crucial in allowing workers to advance their shared interests (*op. cit.,* 109-123).

How these were shared objectives achieved? Early demands concerned such issues as safety, canteen facilities and the opportunity for workers to have some choice as to when they might take holidays (ibid., 113). The new crop of union leaders improved on this approach: 'the new men managed to make some progress on the issue of general wage levels and did so either by threatening strike action, or in some cases, by bringing production to a halt. They pressed for general wage increases across the board'. And 'house union leaders were now consulted by employers on major changes pending within factories,....rather than waiting to be consulted, the new men insisted on their right to representation' (ibid., pp 120-1). At the local level in relation to employers, therefore, house unions became viable organisations which had successfully earned the right to consultation (typified in the establishment of Joint Industrial Councils within each establishment), established job security (daily-paid jobs were more the norm previously) and gained wage increases.

On charges of corruption by some union officials, Peace has an interesting observation: 'particularly in the period 1964 to around 1967, most union leaders seem to have spent a good deal of time accusing one another of corruption and nepotism as well as the personalizing of union offices' (ibid., 14). The reasons are not far to seek, one of which Peace himself identifies, namely 'constant jostlings for union control within elected house union executives (ibid., 114). This was the crucial transition period, at the local level, between the old and the new men. It took place against the background of political leaders hanging desperately onto power despite denunciation for blatant corruption, nepotism and general indifference to the plight of the general population.

Such charges were also being used in a different sense and context: some union officers were deeply involved in the rivalries of competing central labour organizations (in this case, NTUC, LUF, ULCN and NWC), bodies that had access to considerable sums of money furnished by the International Confederation of Free Trade Unions, the World Federation of Trade Unions, the American AFL-CIO, the British TUC and other foreign labour organizations. The rank and file of most house unions viewed such leaders with suspicion, particularly as such close contacts with central bodies tended to make them progressively relegate local functions to a secondary position.

The 1949 Fitzgerald Commission of Enquiry appointed to probe the circumstances surrounding the killing of 29 striking miners and the wounding of 55 others at the coalmines near Enugu was not satisfied with the explanations offered by the Secretary of the Colliery Workers Union on how he spent £1,500 out of the £2,000 levy money in his care. The point was originally made by Hodgkin (1956,137), that the lack of a clear-distinction between trade union funds and private funds might have less to do with intention to embezzle than to the patriarchal and traditional style of leadership characteristic of this period. Such a union leader might even feel very insulted at any suggestion of misuse of union funds, most probably protesting that he had stuck out his neck and used both union and his own personal resources to protect his members' interests. A review of existing studies has shown that most observers have confused the administration of house unions with that of central bodies. Even if it is conceded that some officials misused funds, as the Adebiyi Tribunal Report (1977) persuasively argued, these monies were really not 'union funds' and could hardly be regarded as such. Special financial provisions, along with scholarships and material aid, were provided by competing foreign interests with the clear intention of influencing the Nigerian labour movement. They were controlled by representatives of foreign donors. Not all members of the executives of respective central bodies knew how much was involved or how such monies were disbursed (Otobo, 1979). Indeed, in the case of direct aid to house unions, which was mostly in kind, such funds were subject to even greater control. Charges of corruption therefore had little to do with misuse of central bodies' funds because this could not be done without the connivance of representatives of the donor, and if his tacit approval was secured, financial impropriety could not be said to have occurred. Such charges could, however, rightly be directed at the officials of central bodies who decamped to rival centres upon the offer of substantial financial inducement and who in turn attempted to bribe house union officials with scholarships and money to affiliate their organisations to their centre.

By the 1970s, as Adrian Peace (1979)[12] perceptively observes, the house union system, however effective it had been as a response to local exigencies, had reached its limit of development. It was unequal to the influence of external factors as these now affected the local situation (*op. cit.*, 127). The reasons were clear. The tremendous changes which took place between 1970 and 1976 have already been mentioned, especially the almost overnight expansion of the private sector that had its roots in the war effort, the quadrupling of crude oil prices in 1973-4 that enabled the state to embark on an ambitious development programme and the indigenisation drive which followed. The scale of activities, an influx of subsidiaries of multinational companies and the increasing complexity of economic organisations, made it awkward and costly for both managements and workers alike to depend on the house union system to deal with the rising level of conflict, to ensure reasonable levels of income in the face of escalating cost of living, and to cope with mounting labour costs.

In this period too, the competing labour centres were suffering from a shortage of funds, experiencing a groundswell of workers' disenchantment aggravated by war-time constraints and truly galloping inflation and being forced to take notice of the more devastating tactics of government and private employers. They had little choice but to form the all-embracing NLC in 1975 in order to stay relevant to a rapidly changing situation. This state of mounting expectations and cross-pressures of employers and organised labour, compounded by internal problems within the state structure, accounts for the promulgation of various decrees dealing with most aspects of union government and administration, industrial conflict, and the use of incomes policies and wage tribunals.

How have these decrees influenced union-membership relations? More rationalised union administrative structures are fine recipes for extensive bureaucratisation and the creation of a stratum of full-time paid officials with token elected positions of President and vice presidents, the latter drawn from within the ranks of workers. The rank and file were beginning to experience a new form of labour management which demanded loyalty and accountability, and required explanations for every projected move by union

---

[12] PEACE, A., *Choice, Class and Conflict: A Study of Southern Nigerian Factory Workers*, Harvester Press, 1979

officials. Many began to speak with pride about their unions, sustained by funds regularly generated through the compulsory check-off system, and were quick to remind full-time staffs that 'we pay your salaries.' Astute leadership of the NLC under the presidency of Hassan Sunmonu, increased the impression of respectability and confidence of the movement and made possible the successful prosecution of the 1981 general strike.

The new union structure has not been without problems of its own. Officially designated 'industrial unions', they remain essentially 'national', with federations organising workers in related activities. Since each industrial union spans the length and breadth of the country, its administration is perforce decentralised, with branch unions in individual establishments or plants enjoying a measure of autonomy. For the national union official, the job involves constant travelling. Except for the annual conference which two or three officials of each branch attend as delegates, he remains the main, if not the only link between national organisations and rank and file. Parallels can be drawn between this and the former house union system. Plant organisation, for example still remains the basis of the unions and the frontier of conflict. Here the similarity ends. Management can no longer argue or insist that national union officials are 'outsiders'. The tendency has rather been the opposite, individual employers appealing to national officers to intervene in local disputes to avoid issues being referred to the Industrial Arbitration Panel.

As in the case of other 'collective goods', it is far from easy to quantify the material benefits derivable by individual workers from union membership. Unions, in varying degrees, have financially assisted members in such personal matters as marriages and funerals, and become involved in the celebration of acquired chieftaincy titles. Between 1960 and 1967 'workers education' was mostly in the form of seminars, workshops, short-term courses in labour institutes managed by the ILO, the British TUC, the American AF of L-CIO, the Israeli Histadrut, the West German DGB, the ICFTU, the WFTU and by other institutions of higher learning located in Africa and western and communist countries. Scholarships and grants were offered by external benefactors, the union meeting part of the costs in some cases. Apart from the courses organised by individual trade unions, two of the competing centres had permanent training schools, - the NTUC's Patrice Lumumba Labour Academy and ULCN's Trade Union Institute for Economic and Social Development, each funded by rival external interests. The NLC, like the new unions, is required by its constitution to spend at least ten per cent of its income on workers' education. In this regard, several workshops have been organised at the NLC headquarters in Lagos, the latest a two-day workshop on the lessons to be drawn from the 1981 General

Strike. More workshops and seminars are expected to be organised across the country.

The more effective articulation of workers' demands has played some part in the dramatic establishment since 1960 of six wage tribunals which have produced wage increases. Other material achievements include the upward review and establishment of a national minimum wage, the review of pensions and fringe benefits in the public sector (the latter also affecting lower paid workers in the private sector), the virtual elimination of the category of the daily-paid worker with its built-in job insecurity and irregular earnings, the government acceptance of May I (May Day) as a public holiday, the direct allocation of imported scarce food items to individual unions and the NLC by the current military administration for consumption by their members, and the successful pressure by labour on the military to compel the trading subsidiaries, of multinational companies to bypass 'middlemen' and sell commodities directly to consumers.

Limitation of space precludes a fuller discussion of union membership relations, especially the importance of separating union administration as a set of technical and administrative activities from tactics and strategies adopted by union officers and membership in response to specific developments in both industry and wider society. Most of the studies earlier referred to have posed to union members the question 'how often do you participate in union affairs' with an eye on re-discovering the Michelsian 'iron law of oligarchy'? The assumption seems to be that unions' affairs are distinct from what union members think and do in relation to their collective interests as organizationally represented by the union.

The present union structure could certainly promote the feeling by a sizeable proportion of union members that it remains 'unaware of union decisions.' Some disputes only affect particular establishments and hence only particular groups of union members. If after inconclusive or unsatisfactory discussions with the employers' organisations and managements involved, the national union declares a 'go-slow' or embarks on strike action, the member in an establishment hitherto unaffected is bound to feel 'dragged in' and 'not consulted'. To counter this, many union officials have recently resorted to sending circulars and bulletins to branch unions apprising them of important developments and of ongoing negotiations while clearly requesting them to be prepared to be called out at very short notice. This seems hardly sufficient to cope with rapidly developing situations or 'perishable issues' requiring only a few hours before decisions have to be taken. But there are no union structures without complications which present challenges to both employers and workers.

Chapter 5

THE TRADE UNION STRUCTURE AFTER 1977-78 RESTRUCTURING

INTRODUCTION

In this chapter we examine some aspects of the new trade union structure in Nigeria, especially some of the implications of those changes brought about since 1976 when the Federal Military government successfully initiated what has come to be described as 're-structuring' or 're-organization' exercise. The re-structuring exercise involved legally reducing 721 'house unions' (936 organizations were registered) to a mere 70, forty-two of which were designated 'industrial unions' organizing 'junior workers'; fifteen senior staff associations; four so-called professional unions; and nine employers' associations.[1] These changes are important and need to be properly understood because union structure has industrial consequences and other implications for industrial relations in general, some of which are touched upon here. Before this is done, we shall first critically review dominant views on previous trade union structure in order to correct certain misrepresentations some of which might have unfortunately achieved a measure of orthodoxy, and in the process highlighting factors, such as nature of the state and of economy, which have hitherto received insufficient attention.

Probably the first thing that we ought to understand is what the term 'union structure' means. The term 'structure' as used in the study of organizations is usually taken to mean the relationship between constituent parts of an organization. But in labour studies and related fields, it is used to isolate and identify the distinguishing characteristics of any wage-earning population, particularly wage earners that have organised themselves in protection of their interests and rights. Rather than offer one precise definition of the term, it might be more profitable to see structure, in this context, as representing many variables which operate at different levels, notably distribution of organized labour along such criteria as age, sex, skills and according to industry. At the micro or narrower level, union structure

---

[1] Abiodun, M.O. *Restructuring of Trade Unions in Nigeria,* 1976-1978, p. 11.

could also mean the type and size of labour organizations, their distribution according to geographical zones and industry, and how they relate to each other. The way some of these characteristics have been combined would normally distinguish the structure of one labour movement from another.

FACTORS WHICH HAVE INFLUENCED THE TRADE UNION STRUCTURE

For a fuller understanding of the present structure, it is important to undertake a review of the factors that have so far influenced trade union structure in Nigeria because the dramatic way in which the reorganization was undertaken and the fanfare which accompanied it, (not to mention the familiar immediate historical antecedents which included official probe of rival central labour organizations), seem to have created an impression of a clean break from the past. It is here contended that this would, undoubtedly, remain an inaccurate and static conception of a dynamic situation, because the nature and structure of any labour movement are constantly evolving; therefore implying that factors which hitherto had had substantial impact on the trade union structure might lose their saliency as others, or a combination of others, supersede them. Like the present embodying some past, it also suggests that some factors of old might still be in operation if only in an attenuated and less significant form: which has remained the case in this situation as will soon become obvious. We might also at this point like to sound a precautionary note to the effect that some of the factors as discussed immediately below are difficult in practice to separate one from the other, and our doing so here is merely designed hopefully to facilitate easier comprehension of a far more complex situation.

The first of these factors has been the type and nature of the national economy. The economy is a capitalist one, with a larger public sector but more powerful private sector. This is more popularly referred to as a 'mixed economy'. Whatever the changing ratio between 'public' and 'private' sectors of the economy, because it is a capitalist economy, a significant proportion of means of production and distribution remains privately-owned or controlled. Little confusion should derive from the logic of 'mixed economy' which some observers and conservative politicians would seem to have misleadingly labelled 'socialist' or 'welfarise', thereby implying a qualitative movement away from a presumably pure capitalist economy. Ralph Miliband (1969)[2] and Baran, P. (1957),[3] among others, have pointed out the positive relationship between a growing public sector and increasing economic needs and socio-political requirements of the private sector, indicating a symbiosis even where specific legislation might be considered

---

[2] Miliband, R., *The State* in *Capitalist Society*, Quartet, 1969;

[3] Baran, P., *The Political Economy of Growth*, Pelican, 1976

constraining on activities of businessmen and of the business community in general.

If the whole of the public sector remains geared to servicing the private sector by providing 'basic infrastructure' and creating 'favourable climate for investors and investments,' the size of the public sector hardly detracts from the essentially capitalist nature of the economy. Indeed, Miliband (1969:69) reckons from this 'bias of the system' how frighteningly easy it is that governments in such economies would wish to help 'business' and 'industry' in *every* possible way, and yet do not feel that this entails any degree of bias towards particular classes, interest and groups. For, 'if the national interest is in fact inextricably bound up with the fortunes of capitalist enterprise, apparent partiality towards it is not really partiality at all,' and 'on the contrary, in serving the interests of business and in helping capitalist enterprise to thrive, governments are really fulfilling their exalted role as guardians of the good of all' (ibid). We know from our own experience and examples of other countries that the protection of private economic interests is not the same thing as protecting 'national interests', however defined; it is often at the expense of the latter which, in fact, draws attention to the role of the state in society, an issue referred to again below.

Despite sprawling public sector therefore, such private control as exercised over means of production and distribution system is done by one-man enterprises, from fairly small to medium-sized businesses and by large and complex companies. What is relevant to our purpose is that the 'mixed economy' ensures that labour is employed by both the state and private employers, and workers therein are sometimes forced to, and at other times do voluntarily and correspondingly organize themselves into public and private sector unions, creating a lasting feature of current and past trade union structures. And this, as we all know, would tend to create differentials in pay, fringe benefits, capacity to organize (private employers are far more ready to resist trade unionism, though equally matched by state authorities, in those establishments designated 'essential services' and like statuses) and general expectations of wage-earners in respective sectors.

Intertwined with the type of economy is the nature of the economy itself, which also goes some way in determining trade union structure. The nature of the economy has to do with the kind of economic activities carried out and thus consequent division of labour at workplace and skills that may be encouraged to emerge in response to demands of controllers or owners of economic and industrial organizations. Among development economists still rages a general contention as to whether these types of economies found in most of Africa, Asia and South America can be more accurately described as 'developing' or 'underdeveloped'; others also wonder whether they could really be referred to as 'capitalist' or just plain 'dependent capitalist economies.'[4] What has remained indisputable is the fact that most of these economies are still inextricably bound up with advanced capitalist economies of Western Europe, Japan and North American subcontinent; they are suppliers of basic agricultural and mineral produce for processing elsewhere; and they stand little chance of being able to alter this historically enforced international division of labour if they persist on current lines of 'development'.

Thus, despite iron and steel and petroleum industries in Nigeria, major industrial and economic activities revolve around trading or commerce: that is, the buying and selling of largely imported and smuggled goods. The other activities of some importance are construction and transportation and the assembly of finished products ironically described as 'manufacturing'. A consequence for trade union structure is that one tends to find, outside of the main bureaucracy, that major unions organize workers in transportation field (sea, land, air) and commerce (retail, wholesale) and assembly plants (vehicles and electronics).

Similarly for the public sector where the state, till only recently, has primarily been involved in the provision of supportive infrastructure (roads, railways, air and sea transport, housing, etc.), training and development of manpower (provision and funding of institutions of higher learning and creation of the Industrial Training Fund and like institutions), formulation and implementation of social and economic policies (hence bureaucracy and parastatals such as the Central Bank, Nigerian Industrial Development Bank, various Insurance companies and other financial institutions), and provision of basic utilities (water, electricity, postal services and so forth), unions have sprung up in these areas of activities. Naturally the main unions would be those organizing civil servants (technical and non-technical), employees in transport (docks, air, sea, railway), teachers and local government employees.

It would have sufficiently become clear that the type and nature of economy would serve to dictate the following: (a) types of economic organizations (indigenous one-man businesses, parastatals, large indigenous companies to subsidiaries of multinational companies); (b) type of skills required and developed; and (c) distribution of workers and their organization among industries and sectors. In this context, trade union structure is bound to be less complex, closely approximating the structure of economy and constituent economic and industrial organizations.

A second important factor is the geography of the country, where this is taken to mean geographical size and natural endowments combined. As has been identified by most observers of the Nigerian trade union scene, notably

---

[4] Roxborough, Iain, *Theories of Underdevelopment*, Heinemann, London.

Yesufu (1962), Davies (1966), Kilby (1967), and Cohen (1974),[5] the large size of the country would partly explain the wide dispersal of commercial and industrial establishments, and along with poor state of communications (which have only marginally improved over the last decade), most probably ensured that workers and their organizations are dispersed accordingly. This would be another way of saying that the large size of the country and distribution of towns and cities have themselves influenced the structure of respective companies and hence of unions too. It would seem to be the case that because branches of the same company have tended to retain a measure of autonomy as a result of distance from headquarters (some, in fact, functioning as autonomous units in various geographical areas), most managements have tended to encourage their employees to form unions and staff associations around them—hence the notorious 'house unions' of pre-1973 era. To a large extent therefore, both multiplicity and smallness of trade unions, which was characteristic of the period 1943-76, could be regarded as inevitable consequence of distribution and structure of industrial and commercial organizations brought about by vastness of territory, poor communications and other historical factors some of which are discussed immediately below.

As for natural endowments, we refer to topography, soil, mineral deposits, and rock formations of some economic and industrial use. For example, ports and docks may only be developed on the coast or where there are navigable stretches of rivers; plantations where required crops and trees can grow; minerals (crude oil, coal, columbite and tin) can only be mined where they are found; quarrying undertaken where such rock formations as marble, granite and limestone are located. Secondary and tertiary economic activities (service organizations or industries utilising outputs of these economic activities as inputs in their own production processes) are consequently generated, leading to some concentration of allied industries and sub-sectoral interdependence due to attempts at backward and forward integration. The larger point is that certain economic activities would be restricted to certain geographical areas and so would be resultant workers' and employers' organizations themselves. This partly explains why a greater percentage of the wage-earning population is concentrated around Lagos-Ibadan zone, Enugu-Port Harcourt-Warri axis and Kano-Kaduna-Jos axis.

[5] Yesufu, T.M., *An Introduction to Industrial Relations in Nigeria*, OUP/NISER, 1962; Davies, I., *African Trade Unions*, Penguin, 1966; Kilby, P., 'Industrial Relations and Wage Determination: Failure of the Anglo-Saxon Model' in *Journal of Developing Areas*, Vol. I (4), July 1967, 489-520; Cohen, R., *Labour and Politics*, Heinemann, 1974.

Legal Provisions

The other group of factors of note are legal provisions as they affect the formation and functioning of workers' and employers' organizations. It has generally been pointed out, with Yesufu (1962:78-88) and Cohen (1974:112) being most emphatic, that one of the reasons for smallness and numerous number of house unions in pre-1977 period was the provision as contained in the 1938 Trade Union Ordinance which permitted as few as five persons to form a union. And that because a minimum of five persons could form a union, another by-product that has also been suggested was the multiplicity of unions due to factionalisation as any disgruntled faction of either leadership or rank-and-file could legally constitute itself into a union. The state authorities could be said to have taken note of these two possible permissive implications of the original Ordinance as the Trade Union Decree 31 of 1973 increased the minimum number of persons that could form a union to fifty (50). This provision did not seem to have made any difference since most of the house unions still remained small, more so as this decree did nothing about those existing house unions which had less than fifty members. If it did, this could have led to extensive re-organization of the union structure at the time. This job was finally done in 1976-7 with the re-organization and consequent creation of the now very familiar forty-two industrial unions.

One is here inclined to agree with Peter Kilby (1967: 493) that not only is the number of unions slightly overstated but so is the preponderance of small unions. For one, as at 1967 Kilby found that some 20 per cent of the organizations registered as unions under the liberal and broad definition of 'trade union' contained in the Ordinance were in fact not labour unions at all but associations of self-employed and of independent Nigerian businessmen in such fields as carpentry, tailoring, fishing, building, baking, truck-pushing, timber selling and transportation. It is in this unusual and most inappropriate sense that some observers, such as Fashoyin (1981:21), have had surprising little difficulty in describing Chief Awolowo as a former trade unionist simply on account of being involved in an organization of motor transport owners, an investment from which attendant accumulated economic resources enabled the latter to successfully launch his person in colonial politics.[6] In 1976, there were 936 registered organizations and of which 721 were labour organizations: nearly 25 per cent of these organizations were not labour organizations, 56 of them were 'connected with supervisory/management staff associations', 44 'relating to Employers' Associations' and the 'remainder representing associations of self-employed persons or individual owners of various businesses' (Amalgamation Report,

[6] See his "Industrial Relations and the Political Process in Nigeria", Research Series No. 69, International Institute for Labour Studies, Geneva, 1981.

op. cit., 11).

Secondly, there is hardly any hard evidence to indicate a direct relationship between smallness and numerosity of unions and the said provision: for that matter there were no unions with membership of five persons. Rather, as further discussed below, the state of affairs seemed more a reflection of size of commercial and industrial establishments than wilful exploitation of legal provisions by presumably unscrupulous or ambitious union members. This should not be taken as a denial of the possibility of factionalisation of unions through dissensions: this was always a constant factor but like strikes, such threats of factionalism and recourse to the said provision of the law would seem to have been *temporary* phenomena, consistently invoked and used by employers, managements and dissenting union members alike depending on issues. A good many labour officers had frustrating times mending organizational fences and sorting out disputes of this kind. On the whole, it would seem that the impact of the Ordinance on the smallness and numerosity of house unions, if it had any, has been unduly impressionistic and thus exaggerated.

Factionalization was perhaps more dramatically the case at the level of central trade unionism where a motley selection of internal and external factors had come into full play. The first central labour organization in the country had been formed in November 1942 as Federated Trades Unions of Nigeria but changed its name to the Trades Union Congress at its 1943 annual conference. After the first general strike in 1945, the 'TUC leadership was divided over several issues, including affiliating with the political party: the National Council for Nigeria and the Cameroons (later National Convention of Nigerian Citizens), and compounded by divisive activities of international labour organizations, political pres are mounted by western European governments (including the United States of America), and personality and political differences Among leading labour leaders, it was exceedingly difficult to have only one central labour organization in spite of the brief existence of the first Nigerian Labour Congress in 1950 and of the All Nigeria Trade Union Federation from 1953 to early 1956. All that most Nigerian governments and political parties did, including respective colonial administrations since 1945, was merely to exploit the situation by playing off all the rivals against one other, although one centre usually emerged as a favoured one.

It was not until 1973 that the first legislation dealing with federations of anions and of central labour organizations was brought out, although this in itself did not appreciably help matters much. The more decisive step was taken in 1976 by the relevant state authorities when the Trade Union Central Labour Organizations (Special Provisions) Decree No. 44 formally dissolved existing four rival central labour organizations, impounded their assets, appointed an 'Administrator of Trade Union Affairs', followed by the reorganization exercise and the re-constitution and inauguration of the Nigerian Labour Congress (NLC) on 28 February 1978 as the only central labour organization to which the industrial unions must be affiliated. We find, from this brief account, how the structure of the labour movement has changed from that of several central labour organizations at the top with hundreds of small house unions below and a few large unions in the middle to that of one central body and forty-four industrial unions. In this re-structuring, the enormous powers of the state have been deployed against, generally and in questions of detail, preferences of unionists and employers, workers consistently expressing a desire to amalgamate and form industrial unions themselves while most private employers would prefer to retain house unions as they were.

The fact that laws and other national economic and social policies do not enact themselves into being brings us to the next very important factor, namely: the nature of the state. By 'state' we mean the government as formed by representatives of a political party or of parties in case of coalition or 'accord' (as was the case between the National Party of Nigeria and Nigeria People's Party during Shagari's administration), or commander-in-chief and council of ministers or commissioners in case of military regimes, the legislature (comprising Senate and House of Representatives in case of civil rule or Armed Forces Ruling Council or Supreme Military Council for military regimes), the bureaucracy (including parastatals and local government), judiciary, and law enforcement agencies (armed forces, police, intelligence and security organizations, etc.) All these institutions are the main organs of the state, forming what Miliband (1969) calls the 'state system' and the relatively few persons who occupy positions of power in these institutions and who take crucial decisions may also be referred to as 'state elites' or elites of the state system.

That the *government* is not the same as *the state* is a distinction worth bearing in mind constantly, particularly in industrial relations where problems always seem to crop up and state elites, whether in police or cabinet or arbitration panel or main bureaucracy, might disagree over appropriate response or new policy. For example, agreements arising out of discussions or negotiations between representatives of workers and politicians or the president and his men (as occurs during and after major strikes) could be modified or dropped altogether if top bureaucrats (from cabinet office and ministries of finance, establishment, and employment, labour and productivity), other advisers and the Nigerian Security Organization (NSO) considered them against 'national security' or 'national interest'. The government usually announces most policies but this does not mean that politicians always decide on industrial relations issues and on other policies alone. In fact, the bureaucracy and law enforcement agencies and the judiciary usually implement laws and official policies in ways that might not have been originally intended by legislators or the government of the day.

The importance that should be attached to the nature of the state can therefore be hardly overstated. The nature and future of the state in areas more recently decolonized has been subject of considerable controversy, the more interesting views being those of Fanon (1967), Gunder Frank (1969) and Alavi (1974) just to name a few.[7] Despite differences in emphasis, there seems little disagreement over the less complex and fragile nature of post-colonial economies and states, largely attributable, in their view, to external control exercised over such economies and essentially parasitic political class that is sustained by shifting and unstable internal alliances and backed by subsidiaries of multinational companies and western governments with considerable strategic and economic interests in such countries.

Aside from the economy, the nature of the state has a good deal to do with the kinds of people who occupy positions of power in its various organs. This is quite crucial because both political and economic systems, holding constant other historical determinants and economic elites outside of the state system, would largely depend on the preferences of such persons. If they prefer, for instance, communism to capitalism, they might be tempted to change the system and by so doing private employers might well disappear from the Nigerian economy with obvious consequences for organized labour that would now have to directly contend with the state as in communist Eastern Europe and Soviet Union. Should they harbour intense dislike for trade unions, then attempts might be made to suppress unionism, with likely consequent killing, or jailing or general harassment of workers who attempt to unionize the labour force. If they do not mind having unions around so long as such unions remain weak, as has been the case in this country for the past fifty years, either specific laws further weakening the labour movement might be deliberately passed (like Decrees 27 and 53 of 1968 and 1969 respectively that banned strikes and imposed a wage freeze), or laws that could stimulate more effective unionism, such as check-off and compulsory recognition, would not be passed until workers' protests and other circumstances compel state elites to do so.

Another aspect is that the nature of any political regime, again holding as constant resistance by other interest and pressure groups in society, would largely dictate its policies towards organized labour. The colonial state, in

[7] Fanon, F., *The Wretched of the Earth*, Penguin, 1973 edn.; Gunder Frank, A. *Capitalism and Underdevelopment in Latin America*, Monthly Review Press, New York & London, 19n; Alavi, H., 'The State in Post-colonial Societies', *New Left Review*, 1974.

view of colonial military conquest, racial differences, and unremitting resistance offered by the colonised, would pass laws affecting the structure of the labour movement quite differently from a post-colonial government. The same would hold good for a military regime *vis-a-vis a* civil rule, the former holding every chance, at least in this country, for more dictatorial and arbitrary industrial relations policies.

In more practical terms, whatever the regime or political ideology, all state functionaries attempt to control or influence organized labour and in the course of so doing pass laws that determine the structure of the labour movement. In the case of Nigeria, it must have seemed obvious to many that the desire on the part of state authorities to influence the leadership of the NLC would easily account for the military government's refusal to extend recognition to the organization when it was first formed in December 1975, and also its consequent re-constitution in 1978 as the only central body. It might also be observed that the official fear of more powerful unions could be seen behind the decision to legalize separate unions for so-called 'junior workers' although the Administrator of Trade Union Affairs let it be known that employers' representatives demanded same (Report, 1978:10).

This is not to imply that had junior workers belonged to same unions as the so-called senior staff, problems of sorts might not have arisen. On the other hand, such problems might not have been any worse than those now experienced in industrial unions of junior workers or in senior staff associations themselves, particularly as the boundaries between junior and senior staff have largely been arbitrarily fixed by the relevant state authorities. Whatever the case might have been, by the stroke of the pen, as it were, the structure of the labour movement currently includes a division of workers into two categories of senior and junior and separate organizations legalized for them, while senior staff associations are being prevented by the Registrar of Trade Unions from becoming affiliates of the NLC.

Another aspect of this factor concerns political arrangements that the elites have been able to fashion out for themselves. Up till 1951, Nigeria was a unitary state but was at this point constitutionally divided into three political regions of East, North and West with Lagos as federal territory. By 1954 when internal self-government was granted by Britain, the nationalist political parties sought to neutralize all opposition within the regions over which they had political control.

Many trade unions also broke into three main factions or branches. The same seemed to have been repeated in 1967 when twelve states were created out of former regions but to a lesser extent because of the civil war that in fact led to the demise of many unions and the collapse of some companies. Since nineteen states were delimited out of the twelve in 1976, most trade unions have had branches in all nineteen states, perhaps more so in the public than private sector and nor has the existence of industrial unions eliminated this situation. If tomorrow more states are created or dismantled, the trade union structure and union administrative arrangements would most likely also change again.

The attitudes of private employers to workers and other organizations has been another influential factor to date in the development of trade union structure in Nigeria. Like has been mentioned in passing, most employers, when they could not prevent unionism, encouraged their employees to form unions around branches of their companies. With such large companies as the United African Company (UAC) and John Holt Ltd., even when only one union has been organizing their respective employees (as the Amalgamated Union of UAC African Workers did late 1940s for UAC workers), internal reorganization into several divisions and establishment of new branches would almost inevitably compel unions to do likewise, sometimes reverting to smaller and numerous house unions. In the case of the UAC and the Amalgamated Union of UAC workers, this union was killed upon de-registration by the Department of Labour late December 1950 after embarking on a series of strikes. The company refused the formation of any union until 1957 (Kilby, 1969: 292). Conversely, a large company might prefer to deal with only one union leadership and would deliberately set out to prevent splintering process by denying recognition to factions, while some others might connive at or tacitly agree to a closed-shop situation.

And most certainly, this tended also to proceed *pari passu* with applying enormous amount of pressure on individual members of middle and upper management to prevent unionization, and when not preventable have made sure 'senior staff associations' were formed in an attempt to separate them from other lower placed workers. Some reference has been made to employers' objections to unions embracing all employees, a position strongly maintained by delegation of NECA to the then Administrator of Trade Union Affairs. In a reaction to this, the Administrator noted that 'the point made by NECA is well taken' and 'my Consultative Committee had previously concluded that it would be best to create separate unions for senior staff in various organizations on lines parallel to the industrial unions covering the junior and subordinate workers' (Report, *op. cit.,* 10).

Another significant factor of note has been the activities of the so-called international labour organizations and of foreign labour centres. Such international labour organizations include the International Confederation of Free Trade Unions (ICFTU), the World Federation of Trade Unions (WFTU), and World Confederation of Labour (formerly International Federation of Christian Trade Unions), while foreign labour centres include the British TUC, the French multiple labour centres (CGT, CGT-FO, and CFTC), West German DGB, Israeli Histadrut, American AFL-CLO and its African-American Labour Centre, and, in fact, all central labour organizations in Western Europe. Others include central labour organizations in all communist countries, the more important ones being those of the Soviet Union, Yugoslavia, Czechoslovakia, East Germany, Bulgaria and China. The older of these organizations, subsequently joined by others, have since the 1950s financially, materially and ideologically kept alive mutually hostile central labour organizations in Nigeria.

This form of international trade union 'aid' and solidarity had several important consequences, of which two have affected the trade union structure. One, it served to maintain a structure of multiple national labour centres, individual trade unions accordingly divided into five groups as affiliates of such centres and one broad 'independent' group respectively. Some recognition should be paid to the fact that, and whatever one's objections to the activities of these foreign bodies might have been, they only succeeded that much because elites of the system did not really mind for a long time, and even actively participated in keeping the labour movement divided. Two, it led, in several cases, to both disintegration of some house unions, and factionalism for others as rival central labour organizations made inroads into same union and resulting in confusion, quarrels and splitting into factions for the union executive in question.

Another important factor has been the prevailing type of union leadership, a handful of trade unionists who have borne the brunt of much of the criticisms of a great majority of observers of the Nigerian trade union scene, with Kilby (1967, 1969) and Robin Cohen (1974) bordering on the excessive. It has commonly been charged that the habit of pre-1977 union secretaries of organising more than one union at a time served to perpetuate the existence of small and numerous house unions because such 'general secretaries' tended to resist amalgamations. They are thought to have resisted amalgamations and growth of larger unions because fewer unions would have led to shrinking personal income and possible displacement of the less efficient of them (Cohen, 1974:117).

There is some truth in all of these claims but not only has this phenomenon been exaggerated, most critics would seem in addition to have missed out on the intricacies of the situation. The very obvious fact is that most of these house unions would not have existed in the first instance if the 'general secretaries', in their rivalry and bid to 'create' as many unions as possible and have them affiliated to a central labour organisation of their choice, had not moved into unorganised establishments to 'organize', with or without permission of affected employers. To this extent, they could rightly be accused of increasing the number of house unions, not that this was necessarily detrimental to interests of the newly-organized or that workers involved would have preferred remaining unorganized. Secondly, these general secretaries could only amalgamate house unions that were affiliated to same central body, and not without the permission of the Registrar of Trade Unions and consent of employer or employers. Such permission was hardly granted because: (a) despite general condemnation of smallness and numerous numbers of house unions, both private employers and state authorities have in practice been very comfortable in the situation, making for easier control, the state only being pushed in 1973 into providing guidelines that could facilitate amalgamation process, almost four decades after its spokesmen first acknowledged the problem; (b) employers themselves resisted many attempts by unions at amalgamating, consistently opposing over the years workers' demands before all wages tribunals for the creation of industrial unions, a fear of bigger unions that also would account for employers' resistance to the 1976-77 reorganisation exercise itself; (c) since all Nigerian governments had shown preference for one central body at any one time, it stayed unlikely that permission for merger would be granted to unions not affiliated to that centre, more so as security agents and officials of Ministry of Labour always sought to prevent labour leaders from the other central bodies from leaving the country to attend international conferences and from even holding rallies for their members. Moreover, there is enough evidence to show that employers did not want much to do with these general secretaries whom they considered to be 'outsiders'. It was unlikely, as the case of UNAMAG and UAC has clearly shown, that private employers would even contemplate encouraging such relative outsiders to achieve bigger federations of unions when for existing large unions, Cohen (1974: 116-7) observed, 'many managements have been less than enthusiastic in recognising large unions whose officials would be likely to have greater independence from management pressures.' In sum, the logic of private enterprise would ensure that employers and the state could nearly always prevent amalgamations or formations of large unions if such were viewed to be too threatening. Not to put too fine a point to it, hardly in any capitalist country can workers on their own achieve considerable re-ordering of structure of labour movement without active involvement of both the state and employers, except in a revolutionary situation in which both are being destroyed or reconstituted.

The other factor of note but which is of little relevance nowadays has been the ethnic one. Peter Kilby (1967:494) would seem to have made heavy weather of this factor, quite unable to disentangle it from any and all developments within the labour movement. He has written about 'tribal rivalry inherent in any larger grouping' and 'rarely does union dissension or disintegration not involve either tribalism or personal competition among paid officials' (ibid.) There appears to be no significant historical evidence to support the claim of 'union dissension or disintegration involving tribalism': to the contrary, going by Kilby's parlance, a substantial number of prominent labour leaders (including Michael Imoudu) come from minority ethnic groups and, surely, there were hardly enough Hausas, for example, to have elected Kaltungo as President of the United Labour Congress in 1969. Individual house unions and central labour organizations, unionists have tended to shun ethnicity and if anything, they have been most successful in Nigeria in managing a multi-ethnic organization, an example that politicians and economic elites might well be encouraged to emulate.

This is not the same thing as saying that some unions did not draw the bulk of their members from a particular ethnic group or combination of ethnic groups. If the operations of a company are restricted to a particular locality and given great distances, poor communications and relative immobility of labour, this was bound to happen. Bill Freund (1980)[8] and Cohen (1974) have discussed intense rivalry among multi-ethnic labour force in the tin mines, Bukuru, near Jos, citing instances of rival unions drawing their membership from different ethnic groups, namely local Berom people and migrant Hausa, respectively. Both observers perceptively chronicled how rival northern-based political parties sought to influence existing unions, and given political passions of the time, pro-NPC workers flocked into a particular union while those against moved into the two other main unions. Cohen *(op. cit.* 115) rightly concluded, from such a complex situation, that Jos provides a unique case of congruence of ethnic rivalries, political tensions, and differing levels of skill. Even if other examples of ethnicity intruding into union affairs, as Cohen (1974, ibid.) put it, can be given, the ethnic factor could not be claimed in any meaningful sense to have played a part in influencing trade union structure in Nigeria like, for example, one could claim for that of the United States of America where specific racial groups dominate particular industries or unions and racism is rife. Against the foregoing background, the general implications for industrial relations of new trade union structure will be briefly examined.

SOME IMPLICATIONS OF NEW TRADE UNION STRUCTURE

Some of the more general implications of the new trade union structure might be better examined at three levels, namely union government administration, relationship between industrial unions and the Nigerian Labour Congress, and collective relations in industry.

Union Government and Administration

The implications for union government and administration might be more

[8] Freund, B., *Labour and Capital in Nigerian Tin Mines*, Longman, 1981, 174ff.

fruitfully looked at under two broad aspects: the nature of the structure of a typical industrial union and then consequences of such a structure for effective management of the organization. Relating to structure of any of the new unions, the label 'industrial union' hardly imparts any true meaning of the situation because of the rather loose usage of the term 'industry' in the Nigerian economy, plus the fact that even by standards of such less rigorous usage unions do straddle several industries. The standard definition of an industrial union has been given as 'a trade union whose membership is organized on the basis of representing all grades of workers in a particular industry, and hence includes unskilled, semi-skilled, skilled and sometimes non-manual employee.'[9] In its historical usage, as can be seen from the definition, industrial unions only rarely include 'non-manual workers' among their membership, and it would seem in the case of the Nigerian Union of Teachers, for example, that 'profession' has been regarded as synonymous with 'industry'. And not all teachers are even members of the NUT as University teachers have their own union, the Academic Staff Union of Universities (ASUU)—perhaps university teachers are 'senior staff' while all other categories of teachers are 'junior workers' although several categories of the latter earn higher salaries than the bulk of the former!

Equally confusing and hardly explicated upon, it has remained unclear how the Administrator of Trade Union Affairs and his team managed to demarcate boundaries of an 'industry' in the public sector. It is more likely that strong consideration might have been given to existing structure of the bureaucracy itself, including a measure of recognition extended to distribution of skills or functional specialization within individual ministries. This would probably explain why 'technical' workers belong to the Civil Service Technical Workers Union (CSTWU) and 'clerical' to the Civil Service Union. This grouping has inexplicably excluded 'clerical' and 'technical' workers who abound in numerous parastatals if skills or job specialization is the only criterion. It is not as if such technical workers are absent from refineries and exploration departments managed by the Nigerian National Petroleum Corporation or might not be found at the state-owned Delta Steel Company, Aladja, employees who respectively belong to National Union of Petroleum and Natural Gas Workers and Iron and Steel Workers' Union of Nigeria.

Such inconsistencies in grouping of workers is also evidenced in some unions organizing private sector employees, where the general tendency, it would appear, has been to include all workers in companies with diversified economic interests or activities in one industrial union. Fashoyin (1980:33-

[9] Marsh, A., *Concise .Encyclopaedia of Industrial Relations*, Gower Press, 1979, 1st edn., 154.

4) discusses the case of Leventis Motors Company whose employees are being claimed by two industrial unions, the National Union of Shop and Distributive Employees (NUSDE) and the Automobile, Boatyards, Transport Equipment and Allied Workers' Union (ABTEAWU). The company specializes in distributing vehicles manufactured by two well-known European car manufacturers but also provides extensive maintenance services. Whereas the Administrator of Trade Union. Affairs originally placed these employees under the jurisdiction of NUSDE, ABTEAWU regards them as rightly belonging to it, the workers themselves opting for membership of ABTEAWU. The solution proffered by Fashoyin *(op. cit.,* 34) is that of the employees belonging to both unions, a solution that might in fact provide no remedy because such criteria for determining which of the workers could come under which union have not been specified. However, a visit to any garage or motor company that also offers maintenance services would reveal an insignificant administrative component (many of whom are 'technical' in any case), the bulk of employees carrying out very obvious semi-skilled and skilled jobs. If these workers were legally offered to ABTEAWU, the authorities might come closer to adopting 'product market' rather than 'labour market' consideration, a 'principle' strongly advocated by Fashoyin himself (ibid.).

Similar problems have confronted both Iron and Steel Workers Union of Nigeria and other unions organizing workers in mining and metallic industries. Fashoyin *(op. cit.,* 34) strangely disputes the right of the Iron and Steel Workers Union to exist because, according to him, 'it does not have bona fide membership base, for in Nigeria today there are only one or two medium-size steel companies.' It may well be that at the time Fashoyin wrote, the steel rolling mills at Oshogbo, Jos, Katsina and more complex plants at Aladja and Ajaokuta had not become operational but he ought to have noticed that the *Official Gazette* of 8 February, 1978, which gave details about the industrial unions, listed 17 steel companies whose employees and their unions constituted the said union. In the absence of an unstated standard, one might not be able to confirm or otherwise whether most of them are smaller than a 'medium-size' steel company. Other than this, there are areas where iron and steel and other workers engaged in some form of metal fabrication carry out quite similar tasks despite official distinction between 'extraction' of metalliferous ores (excepting coal and petroleum) for potential and actual members of the Metallic and Non-Metallic Mines Workers' Union and 'manufacture' of basic iron and steel products for members of Iron and Steel Workers Union of Nigeria.

What we have here is not merely the case of bungling officials and wrong nomenclature but more of constraining impact of structure of economy and nature of economic activities (in this case, largely trading) earlier discussed.

As the union's name indicates, NUDSE is meant to organise all employees in shop and distributive trade and practically everything is under wholesale and retail trade in Nigeria. But since workers in garages or Leventis workshops also dismantle cars and put them back together as do employees in car assembly plants, then logically nothing should prevent both sets of workers from belonging to the same union! Whereas a slightly different situation prevails among semi-skilled and skilled men of the metalliferous business, a category of them across board are engaged in foundry work and actual fabrication of iron and steel products. Indeed, the fabrication of metal products from scrap metal and making of a limited range of iron ingots and products have been carried on side by side, often by the same company (or traditional blacksmiths or ironmongers). When interviewed, officials of both unions claimed to have arrived at a 'compromise' yet to be divulged but it looks increasingly more likely that respect for wishes of private employers and desire to separate public and private sector employees (who have different rates of pay) might account for such untidy jurisdictional boundaries: self-interest of the state remains a potent factor, officials eager to avoid dramatic increase in labour costs by being unexpectedly and unwittingly saddled with private sector pay levels and other terms of employment.

Another development of some consequence is that each industrial union is a federation of many house unions, criss-crossing several industries (not applicable to public sector unions) held together by an over-arching national executive and following the traditional divide of public and private sector. In most instances, industrial unions are made up of previous house unions but now referred to as 'branches' or 'units', while making allowance for creation of newer branches and units from more recently established industrial and commercial enterprises and a growing number of parastatals at both federal and state levels.

This federal structure would seem to have encapsulated some of the pre-1976 dissensions among union leaders and 'general secretaries' as house unions affiliated in the past to rival central bodies are now grouped under one or the other 'industrial union'. Several conclusions might reasonably be drawn from this:

(a) each industrial union, with the possible exceptions of the Nigerian Union of Teachers, Nigerian Union of Civil Service and Stenographic and Allied Staff and Civil Service Technical Workers Union, and Nigerian Coal Miners Union, have fossilized, as it were, antagonistic factions;

(b) going by analogous example of an American union cited by Lipset, Trow & Coleman (1962) in their study,'[10] emergent industrial unions would be

[10] . Lipet S.M. Trow M. & Coleman J.S., *Union Democracy*, Achor Books, Garden City, New York, 1956.

more democratic because of existence of these ever-watchful vocal groups;

(c) by the same token, internal administration would be a far more difficult and complex process than prevailed under house unions and to which we now turn.

One of the more serious consequences of structure of typical industrial union for effective administration is geographical spread, the vastness of territory coming into play again. Out of 44 industrial unions, only nine have their headquarters outside of metropolitan Lagos,'[11] and irrespective of location of headquarters an overwhelming majority have branches flung and scattered around the country. Some of the organizational consequences are:

(a) *de facto* decentralization of union administration as branches or units enjoy considerable measure of autonomy;

(b) branches or units remain the hub of each industrial union, as frontiers of control and conflict;

(c) there is minimal contact between national union officials and individual managements save for exceptional or heightened conflict situations embroiling the former; and

(d) increased pressure on both executives of branches and respective managements to make things work.

As for the national union officials, the keeping abreast of developments in various branches becomes almost a nightmare, spending a good deal of the time on the road. Quite apart from the time taken up by preparations against meetings of national executive committee or council and attendance at one conference or the other and innumerable and often unscheduled meetings with state functionaries, general secretaries and presidents of industrial unions can hardly be found at union headquarters. A good many of them have remained overworked, fleeting from meeting to meeting and, oftentimes, creating the largely uncharitable and unjustified impression of not being 'prepared' — they always seem to be in such a hurry! The paradox is that these itinerant officials, between meetings of union's national executive committee and annual or biennial conferences, crucially link up all branches.

Union administration is thus handled by three different sets of people, those in branches or units, those at zonal or state levels and then national union secretariat with small full-time professional staff. Union business at the level of branch or unit would be the most immediate and turbulent dealing with day to day mutations in labour—management relations. In relation to this, Fashoyin's (1984) study of six industrial unions, as the most

---

[11] For a good discussion of union government and administration under house unions system see Peace, A., *Choice, Class & Conflict: A Study of Southern Nigeria Factory Workers*, Harvester, 1979.

recent study of 'attitudes of the rank and file towards their unions and to determine the extent of the former's involvement in policy-making functions of unions', sheds little light on union government and attitudes of rank and file because that has more to do with very close imitation of studies carried out by Warmington (1960), Smock (1969), Cohen (1974) and Peace (1979)[12] For one, the study was said to have been carried out in 1977 when the industrial unions were in the process of being constituted and thus could not really be accurately presented as representative or immediately relevant to our purpose, save as a study of transitional phase and which it is regrettably not. Secondly, given the structure of a typical industrial union as previously outlined, the discussion of 'union affairs' in terms of 'attendance at union meetings' can hardly be representative of reality because a sufficient number of branches have to be included in the survey (branches run into hundreds in most industrial unions and yet only four were selected in the above study) as union meetings cannot be called at the national level. Thirdly, and more importantly, because Fashoyin had borrowed so heavily from the older studies, to all intents and purposes he could have been talking about house unions instead of branches of relatively new industrial unions: it is as if things were as they were before the reorganization exercise and whatever prevailed then (attitudes to union officials, reasons for joining unions, etc.) and now are perfect substitutes despite his acknowledging that the 'Nigerian industrial relations system' has recently undergone fundamental changes... *(op. cit.,* 3)

The dimension of practical difficulties created by union structure might have been explored with more fruitful results if Fashoyin was not so keen on reproducing 'findings' of these earlier studies. Because national union officials are always on the move, as it were, and branches are so many and scattered around, it is possible for a typical branch member to experience 'distance' between himself or herself, the branch union on the one hand, and the national secretariat in spite of flow of written communication between the latter and former. If general secretaries had great difficulty 'managing' three, four or more pre-1976 house unions, such difficulty could now be multiplied by multiple factor.

Take the example of union finance, the erstwhile problem of desultory and voluntary payment of membership dues has been eliminated since 1976 by legislation guaranteeing compulsory union recognition and introduction of automatic check-off system for deriving union dues. Different sorts of

---

[12] The older and dated studies of house unions are Warmington, W.A., *A West African Trade Union,* OUP, London, 1960; Smock, D.R., *Conflict and Control in an African Trade Union: A Study of the Nigerian Coal Miners' Union* Hoover Institution Press, Stanford, 1969; and Cohen, R., *Labour and Politics in Nigeria,* Heinemann, London, 1974; and Peace', A. *Choice, Class and Conflict; A Study of Southern Nigerian Factory Workers,* Harvester, 1979.

problems are generated by this new situation, potentially the more worrying is how large union funds are spent. So when Fashoyin (1984:11) imaginatively suggests that 'the above findings clearly reveal the token nature of the dues paid by union members, which demonstrates why union centres, unable to attract adequate funds from their affiliated unions, usually turn to the more affluent international unions thus incurring the attendant dependency,' he could not possibly be talking about any of the forty-two industrial unions from which the sample of six was supposed to have been drawn. There are here the twin problems of periodisation and conflation. Financial aid from external sources had largely dried up by late 1974, while such international labour organizations had themselves been banned by the Federal Military Government from operating in the country in 1975. The issue of 'dependency' did not arise in 1977: it did not exist at all.[13]

The size of union funds is directly related to membership figure and yet in a survey of all industrial unions conducted by this writer between May 1985 and May 1986, it was discovered that precise and accurate membership figures were not available for any of the industrial unions. A good many union officials thought it an impossible task to furnish such information in view of on-going retrenchments and prevailing economic slump and unwillingness of managements to co-operate in the compilation of membership list. Membership dues deducted at source by employers and handed over to unions are not constant amounts, some national union officials cynically suggesting 'collusion' between, and 'financial impropriety' on the part of branch officials and some members of management! While several officials of the NLC remain convinced that national union officials deliberately underestimate their membership in order to remit smaller amounts as affiliation fees and monthly dues!

The constitution imposed by the state on respective industrial unions compels them to spend at least 10 per cent of their revenue on workers' education, aside from bearing administrative costs, setting aside funds for investments, financing the provision of other services to members (including grants and loans), and organization research and development. These various functions have in practice been carried out with varied seriousness, some unions still experiencing some difficulty in arriving at what constitutes 'workers education', not to speak of their organising workshops or seminars and other short-term courses for officials and selected members. To date, the Civil Service Union has not spent anything on workers education and there are rumours about amounts earmarked for such purpose being expended on non-union business or unapproved projects.

The heart of union administration is the growing corpus of professional

---

[13] Fashoyin, T. "Internal Dynamics in Nigerian Unions: A Survey," Working Paper Series, No. 1, Department of Industrial Relations and Personnel Management, University of Lagos, 1984.

administrators as distinct from part-time union leaders holding such positions as president and vice-president. Mostly graduates with social science and legal background, they comprise the 'bureaucracy', generating memoranda containing opposing policy options to those of government and employers, aside from tackling routine chores and presenting papers at workshops, seminars and like forums. It is not uncommon, in certain unions, to find them and the general secretary sharing common views and holding their own against part-time union leaders and other members of the executive. The incidence of arbitrariness and high-handedness of union leaders as claimed to be common in pre-1976 period is nearly absent, partly checked by union bureaucracy and by more stringent implementation of, and compliance with provisions of union constitution. But the ultimate check remains the refusal of branches and units to remit necessary membership dues to national secretariat and declining to send representatives to annual delegates' conferences. This is done either in protest against a specific policy adopted by national executive or to force a particular line of action. Very seldomly, such dues may be held on to for branch or unit purposes to the obvious annoyance of national secretariat. Union government and administration has become far more complex business since the re-organization exercise.

Industrial Unions and the NLC

Such relationship as exist between executives of industrial unions and of the NLC would seem to be coloured by three not wholly unrelated factors, namely: (a) residual animosities from pre-1976 era; (b) differential reactions among union leaders to general developments; and (c) financial links. As for residual animosities, differences in personality, conduct, and general outlook have tended over the decades to 'stabilize' among the older and second generation of trade unionists; some prejudices held by the younger and middle level union leadership calcifying into 'world view' as transmitted by the older generation (and influenced by foreign sponsors of international labour organizations to which they had been exposed) who largely groomed the current crop of union leaders. As already indicated, each industrial union contains many house unions which had been affiliated to rival labour centres and as such, internal decision-making process might be plagued by obstructive tactics of some branches, including withholding of membership dues mentioned earlier. This attritive process would in many be a constant reminder of 'ideological' differences of the past, reinforcing present disagreement as relevant official of the NLC could attempt to exploit such differences in the union in order to make life a bit more difficult for a general secretary or president considered 'too hostile' to the NLC leadership. This is the case between the NLC leadership today and leadership of the Civil Service Union where David Ojeli and his successor as president have consistently opposed the former's leadership, since Hassan Sunmonu, for being 'too left-wing'. Such hostility becomes exaggerated when compounded by rivalry and ambition, as was the case with Ojeli and his friends in the labour movement who have been seeking to make him president of the NLC.

A subsidiary consequence, and which brings us to the second factor, is a seemingly in-built propensity on the part of various factions of labour leadership to represent contradictory and opposing positions over issues and strategies. Discordant noises have been made over such dissimilar issues as car loans, pensions, abuse of import licences, retrenchments, social welfare schemes, compulsory salary cuts, general economic policy, the state of the national economy, military rule, and return to civil rule. The prime motive, as it would seem to an impartial observer, appears to be a persistent urge to either upstage or undermine the NLC leadership, or faction of labour movement thought to back the organization. A better perspective of the situation might be achieved when it is realized that 'leadership of the labour movement' is less than three hundred critical actors if one were to restrict oneself to president, vice-president, general secretary, deputy secretary and treasurer of the forty-two industrial unions, and from among whom officials of the NLC are elected. A significant number of these same persons are members of various organs of the NLC, and it would therefore be difficult to argue the case of any industrial union executive being kept in the dark or of imagined 'undemocratic' inclinations of the NLC leadership. The most dramatic manifestation of oppositional activity was that of a group of eight industrial unions, led by the Civil Service Union under David Ojeli, who sought to break the 1981 general strike by denouncing and boycotting it although a resolution calling for a general strike had been unanimously adopted at the Kano Conference of the NLC where Ojeli contested and lost the position of president.[14]

The state of financial links between unions and the NLC have naturally been affected by personal rivalries and animosities and fluctuations in union membership on account of seemingly interminable lay-offs, ostensibly due to the depressed state of the economy although there is some evidence to suggest cynical exploitation of the situation by many a company. Out of what could only qualify to be called vindictiveness, there are industrial unions (including the Civil Service Union and Agricultural and Allied Workers Union of Nigeria) which deliberately withhold their contribution to the NLC coffers; there is the category of those which fall back on their

[14] For more details see Otobo, D. The 1981 Nigerian General Strike, *Review of African Political Economy*, Vol. 22, 1981. In the years 1981-3 the Registrar of Trade Unions refused to accept NLC's audited accounts on the grounds that he did not choose the auditor. The same situation existed for some industrial unions and they took the matter to court. These cases were pending when the military overthrew Shagari and his men.

dues, sometimes owing up to nine months' dues without offering any explanations or apologies (the Non-Academic Staff Union of Educational and Associated Institutions and the Nigerian Union of Teachers belong to this group); there are unions which pay regularly but are held by NLC officials to understate their membership so as to reduce their contribution (which comprise the bulk); and there are unions which remit their contributions promptly and pay extra as 'levies', a group of which the Civil Service Technical Workers Union is representative.

Some of the union leaders interviewed have sought refuge in the allegation that the NLC officials have not held themselves financially accountable to industrial unions. In all this would seem a rather lame excuse because in between quadrennial (formerly triennial) Congress-in-Session of the NLC, the organization's National Executive Council (NEC) which manages its affairs, has as sitting members presidents and general secretaries of all affiliated industrial unions. It has proved exceedingly difficult, if not impossible, in practice for the NLC executive officials to by-pass this body, aside from the fact that the NLC submits copies of its yearly audited accounts (after approval of the NEC) to the Registrar of Trade Unions. Such charges might more justifiably be thrown at such industrial unions themselves as individual union members are more likely to claim ignorance of what their executive officials are up to.

It would no longer seem a problem of reluctance of union members to pay dues (since automatic check-off obviates this despite provision enabling any union member to contract out of such an arrangement) but more of a state of social relations among members of union bureaucracies, including the NLC. Even so, this is a partial picture that hardly reflects divisive moves and tactics of private employers and of state functionaries alike, some union officials succumbing to all manner of pressures. In other words, one might all too easily exaggerate the degree of prevailing animosity, which in itself is largely a by-product of labour control strategies deployed with devastating effect by the Federal Ministry of Employment, Labour and Productivity, Cabinet Office and intelligence and security organizations and by powerful subsidiaries of multinational companies. But at the end of the day, union leaders are responsible for the views that they espouse and their choice of strategies. So said, there remains the untold story of union officials, within and outside of the NLC, putting heads together in spite of differing shades of opinions to work out proposals and other policy documents and options, and carry out the generally thankless job of sustaining the labour movement.

Collective Relations in Industry

Collective relations in both public and private sectors have greatly been influenced in many ways by the re-organization exercise, two important developments being formal approval given for the first time to associations of 'senior staff' in the public sector, and consequent rationalization of their organizations and of employers organizations generally. The Nigeria Employers Consultative Association (NECA) is still primarily concerned with industrial relations issues and the Manufacturers Association of Nigeria (MAN) and Nigerian Association of Chambers of Commerce, Industry, Mines and Agricultural (NACCIMA) playing complementary roles in the business of applying enormous pressure on both state authorities and organized labour.

The regrouping of employers and workers organizations has served to create a multi-employer bargaining situation, compelling most employers in various industries to break out of their individualist posturing to compare notes and arrive at terms that could apply to all or selected categories of employees in their own particular industry. This tendency is greatly encouraged by prevailing fringe benefits and wages awards in public sector to which private employers have had to react to. A case in point would be those tripartite discussions on rent and transport allowances, and pensions that accompanied the 1981 general strike. And, of course, the upward and unilateral revision of the national monthly minimum wage from ₦60 to ₦100 by the Shagari administration, and its eventual determination at ₦125 by the national assembly also galvanized employers and their organizations into a common approach to industrial relations developments.

This, however, is not to suggest complete unanimity of views among employers. These general terms of employment have only been mandatory for employers employing fifty or more workers and over ninety percent of industrial and commercial establishments have fewer employees. And since establishments operate in different product markets, experience differing advantages and disadvantages in production costs, profit margins, size, and degree to which their activities depend on import licences, state patronage, and so forth, many employers have in fact seen little need in belonging to an employers' organization, not to talk of adopting common policies. Indeed, many of the smaller establishments 'managements' have no 'labour problems' and pay and other conditions of employment are mostly subject to whims and caprices of employers. Lastly, in a competitive market some employers have struck deals with their employees much to the chagrin of rivals and of NECA, particularly in the back-dating of awards and range of fringe benefits offered.

A more comprehensive review of the implications of the new trade union structure should rightly include an examination of post-1976 labour legislation, especially the 1976 Trade Disputes Act, which are designed to regulate collective relations in industry. But this would be outside the immediate concern of this chapter. We might nevertheless observe that the new trade union structure has increased interdependence among employers and increased the likelihood of conflict in one or groups of industries affecting others. The same could be said for industrial unions where disputes affecting only a handful of branches or which might not even be acquainted with issues at stake at the time. In this sense, most branches or units, once thoroughly briefed by national union officials and excepting industry-wide problems or issues, routinely embark on what would really amount to 'sympathy' strikes to back affected branches. The degree of mobilization involved and complexity of the situation can hardly be exaggerated: it gives the lie to easy charges of 'instigation' commonly thrown at labour leaders. Things have changed a great deal and more research needs to be done.

By way of conclusion, we might reiterate earlier assertion about the constantly changing nature of trade union structure, buffeted on all sides by state authorities, private employers and counteracting activities of workers themselves. What has been discussed above should be regarded as preliminary impressions about the new trade union structure in the country, more specific and detailed studies of various aspects would be required to provide a fuller and more rewarding picture.

Chapter 6

RISE AND DEVELOPMENT OF CENTRAL LABOUR ORGANIZATIONS

THE COLD WAR AND THE GOWTH OF NIGERIAN CENRAL LABOUR ORGANIZATIONS

In order to put developments in Nigerian central trade union scene into proper perspective, it is essential to take into consideration the continental context.

It is difficult to estimate or quantify the catalytic role of the feared or actual presence of communists among Nigerian politicians and trade unionists in the decolonization process. But it is essential to recognize, however, that the growth of Nigerian central labour organizations was bound with two forces that inevitably left their mark - the Cold War and Pan-Africanism. Decolonization and the Cold War were mutually reinforcing to the extent that as the Americans and communist-bloc countries constantly denounced 'colonialism', a faster rate of decolonization also heightened and widened the scope of the ideological conflict.

The now seemingly all pervasive ideological struggle and decolonization gave birth to two political movements or tendencies- 'non-alignment' and 'Pan-Africanism'. These two developments portended serious consequences for all parties in the 'game' because the upshot of decolonisation was the emergence of countries[1] whose leaders, highly suspicious of (or perceptive about) the cold war situation, maintained a neutral political stance with respect to both blocs. The terms 'non-alignment' and 'positive neutrality' lack precision but have been closely associated with Nehru of India, Nasser of Egypt, Marshal Tito of Yugoslavia, the latter term being especially associated with Nkrumah of Ghana. Generally, the terms denote, in a bi-polar conflict situation, the desire of the Afro-Asian countries to avoid military alliances with either

[1] India and China had become 'independent' by 1948 as Marshal Tito was loosening ties with the Soviet Union. The leaders of these countries were to spearhead the 'Nonalignment' movement.

side along Cold War lines.[2]

The import of non-alignment was two-fold. First, it tended to jeopardise the results or goals the power blocs had hoped to achieve as it represented a deliberate attempt on the part of the Afro-Asian leaders to exclude their areas from the so-called conflict. Secondly, being 'neutral' was logically interpreted as 'anti-West' and implied a diminution of Western influence in areas in which, until few years ago, Western powers had had absolute sway. The letter view was so strong and widely believed in Western circles that even George Meany of the AFL-CIO came out with his remark about there being no 'neutrals' in the 'struggle between communism and democracy.'[3]

Pan-Africanism represents the movement for some form of an all-embracing (continental government for Africa.[4] Pan-Africanism has itself aroused a great deal of emotion not only because of its general appeal but also because practically every African leader has tended to present his own blueprint for the ultimate union of African countries. Such differences in approach have also affected the development of central labour organizations in Nigeria and in other African countries too. These numerous approaches soon coalesced into two recognizable forms - the gradualists and the revolutionaries. The gradualists argued that regional economic groupings (such as the East African Community and ECOWAS of recent origin) should be used as springboards for eventual continental unity. The revolutionaries, on the other hand recommend more or less immediate political unity on a continental scale. The countries that favoured both a gradual approach with economic emphasis became referred to as 'Monrovia Bloc' and the other 'Casablanca Bloc"[5] Both camps met subsequently in 1963, at Addis Ababa, Ethiopia, to create the Organization of African Unity (OAU).[6]

Ignoring for a moment the bickering that surfaced over Pan-Africanism, what is of direct relevance to this study and also had implications for Nigerian central labour organizations was the unanimous

---

[2] President Nehru of India, Report of the Conference of Non-Aligned Countries, National Publishing House Press, Belgrade, 1961, p. 125. Earlier conferences had been held in Bandung (Indonesia) and Cairo in 1955 and 1957 respectively.

[3] Windmuller, J.P., 'Foreign Policy and the AFL-CIO', *op. cit., p.* 419.

[4] For a systematic treatment of the subject, see Legum, C., *Pan-Africanism,* Pall Mall, London, 1962 and Padmore, G., *Pan-Africanism or Communism,* Dennis Dobson, London, 1956, especially pp. 105-175.

[5] "MONROVIA STATES" included Nigeria, Ethiopia, Somalia, Libiya, Togo, Sierra Leone, Upper Volta, Dahomey, Ivory Coast, Gabon, the Camerouns, Congo (Brazzaville), Central Africa Republic and Madagascar. "CASABLANCA STATES" were Ghana, Guinea, Mali, Egypt and Algeria (provisional government).

[6] Members of the Pan-African Movement for East, Central and Southern Africa (PAFMESCA) also participated. These included Kenya, Uganda, Tanganyika, Zanzibar, Northern Rhodesia, Mozambique and Ruanda-Burundi.

acceptance, at least in words, of the ideals of non-alignment in politics. Tremendously important was the equation of non-alignment in politics with non-alignment in international trade union matters. This disposition led to the formation of the CGTA in 1956 by Sekou Toure, an obvious attempt to *afrizcanise* the CGT in French West Africa.[7] As many workers defected from the Catholic CFTC and FO, the former reacted by transforming itself into the Confederation Africaine des Travailleurs (CATC) - thus ostensibly *africanising.*[8] By January 1957 Sekou Toure was able to persuade Diallo (who led the rump CGT) and David Soumah (of the CATC) into a new body, Union Generaly des Travailleurs d'Afrique Noire (UGTAN).[9] The UGTAN initially provided the catalyst needed for the launching of a pan-African trade union movement because it emphasized its neutrality by not formally affiliating to either the ICFTU or WFTU, and also robbed the CGT of most of its African members in the process. The UGTAN was effectively neutralized by both the French Government's offer of 'independence within the community' to be determined by a referendum in French West Africa, and the consequent upwelling of nationalism within individual French West African countries. Some French West African leaders such as Senghor and Boigny not only had political disagreements with Sekou Toure but associated UGTAN with his political designs and sought to suppress its branches in their territories. Diallo of Guinea then joined hands with John Tettegah of Ghana TUC to campaign for an independent African federation of trade unions.

Nkrumah soon shot into prominence (on continental scale) after Ghana gained her independence in 1957. His political and pan-African ambitions were usually faithfully echoed by the Ghana TUC. When Nkrumah desired to increase his 'respectability and reliability in the eyes of the British' in the early 1950s (like most African leaders of that period) he had purged the TUC of its militant and left-wing officials and affiliated it to the ICFTU.[10] The Ghana TUC has since then disaffiliated from the ICFTU, re-affiliated and finally disaffiliated in 1959 to spearhead the drive for a pan-African trade union organization. With the assistance of Diallo and other trade unionists from Mali, Sudan, Morocco and Tunisia the Ghana TUC arranged a conference that paved the way for the formation

[7] *Sekou Toure*, Panaf, London, 1978, p. 59. For more details see Allen, C., unionParty Relationships in Francophone West Africa; a Critique of Telequidage Interpretations, in Sandbrook, R. & Cohen, R. (eds), *The Development of an African Development...op cit.*

[8] Ibid., p.59.

[9] Sekou Toure.

[10] Jeffries, R., *Class Power and Ideology in Ghana: The Railwaymen of Sekondi*, Cambridge University Press, Cambridge, 1978, p.62; also his 'Populist Tendencies in the Ghanaian Trade Union Movement' in Sandbrook, R., *African Working Class, op.cit.*, for recent activities of the Ghana TUC.

of an All-African Trade Union Federation which was finally launched in May 1961.

The All-Africa Trade Union Federation (AATUF) faced immediate hostility from both the ICFTU and the WFTU, although the WFTU quickly changed its attitude. Such hostility to the fledgling AATUF, especially from the ICFTU, was not unrelated to the anticipated loss of affiliates consequent upon the decision of the AATUF to deny membership to any African central labour organization that maintained its external affiliation. Under colonial rule the WFTU had very little access to trade unions and so by design or force of circumstances most of the trade unions affiliated to the ICFTU. The exceptions were those unions in French-speaking areas where such an alignment was neither automatic nor assured due to the possibly combined effects of French colonial intransigence (Algeria, for example) and the activities of the CGT, a member of the WFTU. The CGT had trade union members or branches in some of the French colonies, notably in North and West Africa, and was thus the possible source of considerable in-roads by the WFTU.

Another thing to note was the ICFTU's tendency, correctly or incorrectly, to regard increased aggregate number of affiliates as an index of the success of its crusade against the WFTU. En masse disaffiliation by African trade unions would thus logically, from this perspective, represent a setback and hence the hostility to the idea of 'neutrality'. Neutrals were consequently seen, following Aristotelian logic, not only 'anti-West' but positively 'communist-influenced':

> ...the communists do not appear to be embarrassed by scarcity of official WFTU affiliations in Africa, and are busily promoting local "united fronts" activities and even international groupings including free trade unions. An example of this is the continuing drive for an Afro-Asian grouping of unions, without respect to present affiliations. It is clear that the ultimate purpose is to bring African and Asian labour under communist influence and direction...

And with reference to the AATUF, another observer has noted that 'what is not in doubt is that Moscow today has an invaluable tool in the AATUF which enables it to exert influence in almost every town and city in Africa...'[11] Such distorted views are commonplace among those that strive to influence organizations in other areas, if only to reap propaganda gains and to enable them to secure more funds for their 'operations'.

In view of the above orientation, ICFTU's reaction was thus predictable. Its regional organization, AFRO, previously based in Accra

[11] Scatterthwaite, J.C., 'Labor in Africa: An American Appraisal,' *Africa Special Report*, vol. 4 (4), 1959.

and which had been evicted as the drive for formation of AATUF gained momentum, was strengthened and re-established in Lagos (Nigeria) to prop up its multi-pronged campaign against both the AATUF and the WFTU. The ICFTU in attempting to influence the AATUF and vaguely sensing a change in the tide of events held its Third African Regional Conference in Tunis in 1960, at which it was decided that all members of the African Regional Organisation (AFRO) - which embraced all ICFTU affiliates in Africa - should participate in the AATUF to fight demands for disaffiliation as a condition of membership.[12] When members of AFRO failed to accomplish this, the ICFTU sponsored the setting up of a rival organization known as the African Trades Union Confederation (ATUC).

The launching conference of the AATUF in Casablanca in May 1961 was stage-managed by John Tettegah and his associates and the disaffiliation clause was not rescinded. After the conference, prominent unionists in the AFRO, such as Tom Mboya of Kenya and Ahmed Tlili of Tunisia, issued statements denouncing the disaffiliation clause and tried to defend continued affiliation to the ICFTU.[13] The ICFTU affiliates had earlier put their case in a document published at the annual congress of the Kenyan Federation of Labour (KFL),[14] held in Nairobi from 17 to 19 June, 1960. They not only stated their reasons for supporting the ICFTU but also attacked the attempts of 'one or two countries' (Ghana and Guinea) to dominate trade unions in other countries and called for the non-recognition of the provisional secretariat of the AATUF which, they alleged, had been constituted in an 'authoritarian' manner, without proper consultation with all the organizations involved.[15]

For its part the ICFTU which was invited to Casablanca as observer, rejected the conference's decision on disaffiliation. It also claimed that the

---

[12] Lessing, P., *Africa's Red Harvest,* Michael Joseph, London, 1962, p.4

[13] LICHTBLAU, G.E., 'The Communist Labour Offensive in Former Colonial Countries,' *ILRR,* April 1962, p. 399.

[14] AFL-CIO, 'Free Trade Union News', New York, June 1961.

[15] The history of Kenyan's central trade unionism stretches as far back as 1931, when a workers Protective Society of Kenya was formed. This was followed by the Labour Trade Union of Kenya (later Labour Trade Union of East Africa) in 1935 which was complemented by the African Workers Federation that emerged in 1947 to prosecute the 'Mombasa General Strike'. The Labour Trade Union of East Africa transformed itself into the East African Trade Unions Congress (EATUC) in 1949 and received immediate attention from both the WFTU and ICFTU but declined to affiliate to either one of them. A year later the EATUC was banned by the Colonial Administration, its leaders arrested and which triggered off a general strike, among other reasons. The Kenyan Federation of Registered Trade .Unions, (KFRTU) that emerged in 1952 was to be recognized by the Colonial Administration on condition that it affiliated to the ICFTU, which it did. The Kenyan Federation of Labour (KFL) that succeeded the KFRTU survived largely on the financial support it got from the ICFTU and American sources. For these and other details see Singh, M., History of *Kenya's Trade Union Movement,* East African Publishing House, Nairobi, 1969; Lubembe, C.K., *Labour Movement in Kenya,* Equatorial Publishers, Nairobi, 1968; and Stichler, S., 'The Formation of a Working Class in Kenya, in Sandbrook, R. & Cohen, R. (eds), *African Working Class, op. cit.*

conference was not 'regularly constituted' as the organisers had invited 'trade union groupings which they themselves had created,' and that they refused to admit 'representative trade union movements.' Finally, the ICFTU emphasized that the discussions had scarcely been held in 'democratic circumstances' and that the 'conference organisers deliberately created a split by introducing the extraneous subject of affiliation to international organizations.' [16]

In reply, the Secretary-General of AATUF, John Tettegah, declared that 'the AATUF (is) willing to co-operate with other trade union internationals, but only on the basis of equality. If they (external interests) use money to divide us then there will be no basis for co-operation.'[17] Commenting on the statements issued by Tom Mboya and Ahmed Tlili, John Tettegah dismissed them as 'imperialist stooges'. Referring to 'dissident' unions (ICFTU affiliates) he said, 'we shall isolate them and enter their countries and form unions there. It is as simple as that - total war.'[18] These threats did not prevent the ICFTU affiliates from assembling in Dakar on 9 January, 1962 to inaugurate the rival ATUC.

The reaction of the ICFTU (or WCL) to the pan-African labour movement followed the same pattern. It first tried to pre-empt the UGTAN as the first pan-West African labour organization by forming a regional branch in Africa, the All-African: Union of Christian Trade Unions (AAUCTU), a few days before UGTAN was to be launched. It cynically invited UGTAN to participate in its deliberations fully cognizant of the latter's objection to formal external affiliations. When a tottering UGTAN joined in the formation of the AATUF, the AAUCTU joined ICFTU affiliates to form the ATUC.

In contradistinction, the WFTU's reaction was of a very different kind. It was hostile at first then changed rather quickly. It should be recalled that Formation of the UGTAN had deprived the WFTU of its affiliates in Africa. Executing a *volte-face* with remarkable ease, the WFTU now incessantly denounced colonialism and the 'imperialists' in Africa. British, European American employers were condemned as 'monopoly capitalists' and the TU along with its affiliates were described as the 'willing tools of these agents of imperialism.'[19] Referring to the AATUF the organization announced that:

---

[16] Meynaud, J.S. & Salah-Bey, A., *Trade Unionism in Africa*, op. *cit., p.* 133. For instance the Nigerian delegation claimed it was kept out of the Preparatory Committee by 'a clique formed by certain West African countries' - "*West Africa* ", 13 February, 1960. 17. Meynaud, J.S., Salah-Bey, *op.cit.*, p.133; *Bulletin CISL*, June, 15, 1961., p 166. 18.'West Africa', June 1961. p. 639.

[17] Meynaud, J.S., Salah-Bey, A., *Trade Unionism in Africa*, *op. cit.*, p. 133; Bulletin CISL, June, 15, 161., p 166.

[18] *West Africa*, June 1961, p. 339.

[19] Ibid., p.639.

> ... the WFTU considers the creation of AATUF as a great victory of the forces fighting for unity of the African trade union movement. The fight for unity of the African trade unions, based on anti-colonialism, against the new forms of colonial oppression, against imperialism, feudalism and reaction, deals severe blows to the splitting elements represented by imperialism and the ICFTU.[20]

As Pan-Africanism and decolonization became more topical, the ICFTU experienced increasing strains as national interests of constituent members were threatened. The British TUC, for example, became alarmed at the activities of the American AFL-CIO inside and outside the framework of the ICFTU. Americans, apart from trying to gain control of the pan-African trade in movement, made robust attacks at their European partners. The AFL in its publications and at congresses of the ICFTU spared no pains in attacking the British TUC and linking it with British colonial domination. 'It was essential,' it declared, 'that free trade unions should view Pan-Africanism in its true light, as a movement which developed against the colonialism of European powers.'[21] The AFL-CIO also maintained that colonial labour advisers were saboteurs of trade union development because acted as spies for the colonial administration and thus hindered union growth.[22] A beleaguered British TUC deplored 'a growing tendency for can trade unions to be subordinated to aims of political Pan-Africanism, to the detriment of genuine trade union activity; and this tendency for African unions to be subordinated to aims of political Pan-Africanism, is being wittingly or unwittingly encouraged by some non-African trade union organizations.'[23] The predicament of the British TUC was obvious. Moral condemnation of colonialism was fine but still left untouched the main problem of colonization. It could not at the same time complement attempts by the colonial administration to take the teeth out of militant trade unionism (in lame of non-political unionism), help the Colonial Office formulate colonial labour policies and supply the men (labour officers and the lot) to implement them, and yet spearhead an anti-colonial crusade under the banner of democracy.[24] Given this situation, it apparently did not seem odd for the British TUC to insist on 'non-political' unionism in areas that have been continuously embroiled in violence and where demand for political independence had grown considerably.

---

[20] Roberts, B.C., Labour in the Tropical, *op. cit.*, *p.* 163.
[21] Report of Activities of WFTU, 1961-1965, April, p.23.
[22] American Federationist, March, 1960.
[23] '*International Free Trade Union News*', AFL-CIO Publications, New York, August, 1958.
[24] TUC CONGRESS REPORT, Blackpool, 1959, p.209.

THE EARLY NIGERIAN CENTRAL LABOUR ORGANISATIONS

The Trades Union Congress

The Nigerian Civil Service Union was formed in 1912. A breakaway from it, the Railway Workers Union followed in 1931, together with the Nigerian Union of Teachers (NUT). The Marine Daily Paid Workers' Union (later Nigeria Marine African Workers' Union) dated from 1936. The 1938 Trades Union Ordinance which legalized union organization and the economic difficulties unleashed by the Second World War sparked off a series of workers' protest marches and the formation of more unions. Forty-three were formed between 1940 and 1942 alone.[25] Problems of co-ordination led to the formation of the first federation of unions in the public service, the African Civil Servants Technical Workers' Union (ACSTWU), in 1941. The ACSTWU had twelve affiliated unions in 1942.[26] The unions retained their autonomy and the federated body having 'control over trade union questions including communication with Government over bargaining points.'[27] The ACSTWU was managed by Nkediwe (as President), Imoudu (as Vice President) and Enitan Brown (as General Secretary) with the help of ex-officio, and executive members.'[28]

The ACSTWU organised a meeting in Lagos in November 1942 which inaugurated a more comprehensive body, the Federated Trades Union of Nigeria (FTUN) with T. A. Bankole as Chairman and M. A. Tokunboh as Secretary-General.[29] At its July 1943 Conference the FTUN changed its name to the Trades Union Congress of Nigeria (TUC). Its declared aims included:

a) to unite all trade unions into one organized body;
b) to deal with the general labour problems affecting workers in the country;
c) to protect the legal status and his of trade union organizations;
d) to see to the proper organization of trade unions;
e) to establish a workers' newspaper;
f) to establish a trade union secretariat;
g) to establish a Nigerian Labour College; and
h) to promote scholarship for trade unionists to study abroad.[30]

Among others, two resolutions called on the Administration to nationalize all mining industries and demanded workers' representation

---

[25] One of the greater ironies of the colonial situation was the insistence, on the part of both colonial administration and colonizing powers, on the adoption by trade unions and nationalist political parties of 'democratic', 'constitutional' and 'responsible' means in achieving their aims - in a polity that was set up by military conquest in the first place and maintained by coercion.

[26] Department of Labour Annual Report, Nigeria, 1949-50, para. 80.

[27] Ministry of Labour Quarterly Review, Lagos, March, 1,960, p. 39.

[28] Akpala, A., The Prospects of Small Trade Unions,' *ENPC.*, Enugu, 1963, p.18.

[29] Other members were Bankole, T.A., Adenekan, S.O., Coker, 3.0. and Eluaka, F.O.

[30] Other officials were Chief A. Soyemi-Coker (Vice-President) Shonekan, S.M.O. (Under- Secretary), Kofi Austin, Ogunbajo, F.O., Taiwo, F.S. (Treasurer), Awolowo, O. (Editor and Secretary).

on the Legislative Council.[31] Cohen suggests that the latter demand was 'perhaps as a counterweight to the representation of shipping, banking and mining interests.'[32]

This epoch-making organization was accorded immediate recognition by the Administration and it seems to be *agreed* that mutual and very cordial relationship was struck up between it and the Administration.[33] A system of monthly meetings between the Working Committee of the TUC and the Trade Union Officer of the Department of Labour was formally instituted. The effectiveness of the TUC was duly acknowledged by the Administration when it announced that 'the TUC has rendered considerable assistance to the Department of Labour in settlement of disputes and the general application of labour standards.'[34]

The TUC's conference of 1944 has been described as 'remarkable for its representative character, the high quality of its debates and the wide range of subjects discussed.'[35] Some of the resolutions adopted concerned:

(i) the resettlement and rehabilitation of ex-servicemen;
(ii) scholarships for training Nigerians for responsible positions in the public service and industry;
(iii) social security schemes;
(iv) labour participation in schemes for achieving good industrial relations;
(v) revision of wages and salaries;
(vi) the introduction of a minimum wage of two shillings and six pence per diem;
(vii) slum clearance;
(viii) provision of adequate dwelling houses for workers;
(ix) effective rent control and the amendment of the Workmen's Compensation Ordinance to provide improved rates of compensation for industrial and occupational accidents and to cover cases of industrial and occupational diseases which were outside the scope of the existing Ordinance.[36]

The TUC's influence on labour legislation is instanced by the postponement, at its request of a proposed law that would have increased the powers of the Registrar of Trade Unions to ensure the proper and punctual submission of financial returns.[37] Paradoxically, a note of

---

[31] Akpala, *op. cit.*, p. 19; there were 200 delegates representing 56 trade unions.
[32] This body comprised handpicked men from among Police, European firms, traditional rulers, who 'advised' the Governor.
[33] Cohen, R., *Labour and Politics in Nigeria*, Heinemann, London, 1974. p.72.
[34] Ibid., p.72; Ananaba, *op. cit.*, p.41 and Uvieghara, E. E:, *Trade Union Law in Nigeria*, Ethiope, Benin City, p.30.
[35] Department of Labour Annual Report, Nigeria, 1943, p.18.
[36] Ananaba, *op. cit.*, p.4.
[37] Ananaba, *op. cit.*, p.42.

apprehension was being sounded in official quarters because of the perceived effectiveness of the TUC, especially over the impact of the *Nigerian Worker*, the organization's newspaper that had reached a circulation of about 10,000. The Administration subsequently imposed censorship upon the paper claiming that it 'contained incorrect statements or allegations of fact and has repeatedly contained unfair and unjustified comments...such statements, allegations and criticisms are likely to excite disaffection and create or encourage discontent against the Government of Nigeria.'[38]

Other developments also threw doubts on the otherwise praiseworthy activities of the TUC. Some large unions stayed outside it, a notable example being the Nigerian Union of Teachers (NUT). The NUT which was affiliated to the British National Union of Teachers opted out upon the 'advice' of the latter.[39] Thereafter, its General Secretary was only authorized to attend the meetings of the TUC 'on the understanding that such attendance did not commit the union thereby to membership in the Federation.[40]

A major development affecting workers' attitudes and the welfare of the Nigerian population was the economic hardship and pressures brought about by the Second World War. There was scarcity of essential food items including salt, and the prices of the food available rose astronomically, so much so that a wave of cost-of-living-allowance agitations broke out. In one such march to Governor Bourdillon's residence, Michael Imoudu was arrested and banished to Auchi, his hometown, for 'threatening the peace of the Colony'![41]

The Administration opposed another round of wage increase in spite of real wages in 1941 having fallen to sixty-eight per cent of their 1939 level.[42] It was not until the marches and agitations had become widespread and labour in Lagos was desperately scarce that the Administration acceded to the demands of the workers and granted increase[43] appropriately termed 'cost of-living-awards' (COLA) with a promise to review them according to movements in the cost-of-living index.[44] In 1942 the index figure stood at 154 (base year 1939 = 100). It rose to 174 by October 1943 with no signs of slowing down. By 1945 the

[38] Uvieghara, *op. cit.* p. 32.
[39] Ananaba, *op. cit.*,p.41-42
[40] Uvieghara, *op. cit.*, p.34.
[41] ibid, p.3. This was an unwholesome development, an early indication of the future pattern of the activities of external interests.
[42] Cohen, R., Labour and Politics, *op. cit.*, p.71.
[43] Weeks, J., 'The Impact of Economic Conditions and Institutional Forces on Urban Real Wages in Nigeria,' *NJESS*, vol.13 (3), November 1971, p.323.
[44] ibid, p.324

situation had deteriorated considerably and subsequent exchanges between the workers and government simply served to increase hostility. The official response being to declare that 'unless the public is willing to do without or reduce their consumption of commodities which are scarce, or to substitute other commodities for them. . .no benefit will result from increasing COLA. . .'[45] Workers replied in the form of a general strike on June 22, 1945.

The Administration declared the general strike illegal on the ground that it violated the Nigerian General Defence Regulations. The banning order shattered the unity of TUC's leadership. One section of the leadership wanted the strike called off while another wanted it to run its full course until demands were met.[46] The latter had its way and the strike dragged on for six weeks before the Administration agreed to negotiate. Although not all workers were solidly behind the strike, its general impact on the Colonial Office; especially as a result of its wide coverage by the British media, was such that the Secretary of State for the Colonies instituted a commission of enquiry to look into the situation.

The appointment of the Tudor Davis Commission in October 1945 had two immediate consequences: first, the near-unilateral determination of wages and salaries by employers seemed finally to have been ended. Arising- from this, workers felt sufficiently confident to regroup within and without the TUC to present well-reasoned memoranda to the Commission. It was in this connection that the Federation of Nigeria Civil Service Union, the Nigerian Union of Teachers and the Federated Union of Native Administration Staff established the Supreme Council of Nigerian Workers (SCNW), a body hastily recognised by the Tudor Davies Commission as 'sufficiently rational and sufficiently responsible to voice the opinions of Nigerian Labour-as a whole....'[47] in the private sector not only to voice their opinions for the first time but also to amalgamate to form country-wide trade unions, e.g. UNAMAG.

The TUC and Post-General Strike Period

In spite of the disagreements and tensions generated by the strike, the TUC survived and progressively took over 'the functions of various mushroom and rival bodies which grew up as a result of the 1945 General Strike and the presence of the Tudor Davies Commission. . .[48] Fifty out of a total of ninety-seven registered trade unions remained affiliated to it[49] and the Supreme Council of Nigerian Workers, which apparently was

---

[45] Ananaba,*op.cit.*, p.44

[46] Quoted in Cohen, *op. cit.*, p.160.

[47] Ibid., p.72.

[48] Dept. of Labour Annual Report; Nigeria, 1946; Cohen, R., *op. cit.* p.73.

[49] Annual Report, 1946, par.6.

being promoted as a rival and substitute to TUC by a section of the business community was frustrated when the Commission firmly concluded that 'such a body should not attempted to usurp the functions of the Nigerian TUC.'[50] The TUC consequently maintained undisturbed relations with the Labour Department, and at its Annual Conference on 14 December, 1945, 'fraternal' delegates from Ghana (Gold Coast) and Sierra Leone attended. It was at this conference that the establishment of a West African Federation of Trades Union was agreed upon in principle.[51] With the assistance of the Administration, the TUC was able to send delegates to the founding conference of the World Federation of Trade Unions in London that same year,[52] and M.A. Tokunboh (the TUC's General Secretary) proceeded to Ruskin College, Oxford for a course under the sponsorship of the Labour Department.

Political developments in this period broadened the horizons of trade unionists and most certainly broke into the routines of clashes with law enforcement agencies, courts, imprisonments and strikes. The first political party, the National Congress of Nigeria and Cameroons (NCNC), had been formed in 1944.[53] Thereafter, there grew up a number of quasi-pressure groups and voluntary associations. The most important ones were the Nigerian Youth Movement (NYM), and Egbe Omo Oduduwa. The possibility of self-rule appears to have sparked off, within the NCNC, competitive theorizing on strategies and best form of government for Nigeria. The Zikists, 'some Fabian Socialists, some communist, some racialist'[54] were most vociferous: drawing from all sections of the literate population and criticizing all and sundry was the 'Marxist Group'. Trade unionists were to be found within the ranks of some of these groups both inside and outside the NCNC. These were often antagonistic and mutually hostile. A trade unionist might be both a Zikist and a member of the Marxist Group; another, might be a member of NYM, NCNC and an implacable foe of Zikists.

The presence of trade unionists in mutually hostile groups (the NCNC and NYM for example), the ethnic character of much of the political argument and the differential political socialization and consciousness of the elements that comprised TUC leadership soon took their toll. The TUC foundered on the issue of political affiliation to the NCNC. There had for some time been a running controversy within the TUC over the nature of links with the NCNC to which it had affiliated on 30 November,

---

[50] Uvieghara, *op. cit.*, p.32.
[51] Akpala, *op. cit.*, p.33.
[52] Uvieghara, *op. cit.*, p.33.
[53] Ibid., p.33; the 'educational training programmes for trade unionists had just been initiated.
[54] For further details see Sklar, R., Nigerian Political Parties, Princeton, 1963; Coleman, J.S., Nigeria Background to Nationalism, Berkeley, University of California Press, 1965.

1947. Some opponents of continued affiliation to the NCNC argued that overt political links were incompatible with 'trade union principles; and that the organization should 'steer clear of anything whatever that might tend to jeopardize the interest of its members.'[55] Others who were members of opposing political groups and who tended to associate the NCNC with a specific ethnic group (Igbo) thought that 'tribalism, a feature of the existing politics in Nigeria was being allowed to overshadow industrial issues.'[56] A substantial number thought that political affiliation should be left to the individual member to decide as continued affiliation of TUC to the NCNC might preclude flexibility in negotiations. After much recriminations and talks of forming a Labour Party by elements thoroughly disgusted with the NCNC and Colonial Administration, the issue was finally settled against continued affiliation by 32 votes to 8 at the TUC's General Council meeting in Lagos on 28 December, 1948.[57]

Twelve leading trade unionists disagreed with the decision to disaffiliate with the NCNC, among them Imoudu, F.O. Coker, P.O. Balonwu, Ralph Aniedobe, Richard Aghedo and Nduka Eze, who together formed a Committee of Trade Unionists 'to destroy the present Congress if the set-up were not reshuffled and if its policies were being controlled by nihilist Lagos Aristocrats of intelligence and friends of the Government House.'[58] When the TUC failed to reverse its decision, a mass withdrawal of unions including that of the General Secretary's himself, (the Nigerian Union of Nurses),[59] was organized by the Committee. The Committee of Trade Unionists and like-minded trade unionists founded a rival central labour organization, the Nigerian National Federation of Labour (NNFL).

Nigerian National Federation of Labour (NNFL)

The Nigerian National Federation of Labour (NNFL) was formally launched in March, 1946 and Imoudu emerged as its President, Nduka Eze as General Secretary and Aghedo as Treasurer.[60] The declared aims and objectives of the new body included:

a) to assist by practical efforts the attainment of the objects of member-unions in the Federation;
b) foster a spirit of working-class consciousness among all the workers of Nigeria and Cameroons;
c) to fight for the realisation of the social and economic security of workers and to advance their educational and political aspirations by imparting

---

[55] Cohen, R., *Labour and Politics, op. cit.,* p. 73.
[56] 'The West African Pilot,' Lagos, 24 February, 1949.
[57] Ibid.
[58] Ibid., *West African Pilot,* Lagos, 24 February, 1949
[59] Ibid, 5 February, 1949.
[60] Ananaba, *op. cit.* p.95.

political knowledge to the workers;

d) to press for the socialisation of important industries in the country with a view to realising a socialist government where identity of the working class would not be lost; and
e) to cooperate with all democratic federations of trade unions the world over in order to make possible the clarion call of "Workers of the World, Unite" for the triumphant emergence of a World Parliament of the working class.[61]

This split in the Nigerian labour movement coincided with the rift in the so-called international labour movement. By December 1949, the ideological squabbles within the newly formed World Federation of Trade Unions (WFTU) climaxed in 'Western' countries breaking away to form a rival International Confederation of Free Trade Unions (ICFTU). It should be noted that this development tended to accentuate the anxieties of various colonial administrations over possible 'communist infiltration' of labour movements and of the nascent political parties.

Under the circumstances the colonial administration viewed the NNFL with some misgiving not only because of the organization's continued interest in the political future of Nigeria but also because of its talk of 'imparting political knowledge to the workers', of 'a socialist government' and of encouraging the 'emergence of a World Parliament of the working class.' The NNFL not only formed an alliance with the NCNC, it constantly denounced the rump TUC as a 'government-sponsored centre'.[62] Its newspaper, *Labour Champion*, not only had 'toward the creation of the Socialist Republic' as its motto, 'it showed a strong political interest, notably in communism, and carried on for some weeks without carrying any advertisements.'[63] By 31 March 1950 the majority of registered trade unions were outside both organizations,[64] with the NNFL drawing most of its support from the bigger unions among which were the ACSTWU, the Civil Service Union, the Nigerian Union of Railwaymen and UNAMAG.

The continued loss of affiliates to the NNFL[65] and the desire for a united labour movement propelled the TUC into seeking a unification of the two organizations. Both were brought together by the miners' strike at Enugu in which twenty-one miners were shot and killed by the police and fifty-one others had gunshot wounds. The quarrelling labour leaders formed the National Labour Committee in November 1949 to 'see that

---

[61] Balonwu, P.O., Assistant Secretary; Olatokunboh; Permanent Under-Secretary; Omjioba, K.O.K., as Field Secretary; Ibid., p.96.

[62] Ananaba, *op. cit.* p.96

[63] Ibid., p.96.

[64] Annual Report, 1949-50., p.15.

[65] Ibid., p.12.

justice was done.[66] This newfound spirit of cooperation and unity was a boost to reconciliation and in April 1950, with the co-operation of neutral unions such as the Federation of Government and the Municipal Non-Clerical Workers' Union, both organizations formed a caretaker committee to work for unification.[67] This mediation led to the formation of an all-embracing central labour organization, the Nigerian Labour Congress (NLC), on 25 May, 1950 at a public meeting in the Glover Memorial Hall, Lagos.

Nigerian Labour Congress (NLC)

A quick glance at the leadership of the Nigerian Labour Congress (NLC), and at its later subsequent policies, leads inevitably to the conclusion that the substantially defunct TUC was simply absorbed. Imoudu, Coker and Nduka Eze (all former leaders of NNFL)' became President, Deputy President and Secretary-General respectively. N.A. Cole, ex-President of TUC in its after stages, became Information and Publicity Secretary of the new body. Of the six departments created within the Secretariat, four were headed by ex-NNFL personnel.[68] A few weeks later, the NLC established formal political links with the NCNC and announced lists affiliation to the communist-controlled WFTU.[69]

The NLC was full involved in the politics of the day. It 'took considerable interest in the elections held in September for the new Lagos Town Council and allied itself with certain political groups, and the alliance secured eighteen of the twenty-four seats.'[70] Although there has been a tendency to link NLC's affiliation to the WFTU with the 'left-leaning' image of Imoudu and Nduka Eze (the former being a member of the Marxist Group),[71] Nduka Eze himself traced the derision to the 'conduct' of the ICFTU during the Enugu Coal mine episode. Only the WFTU was vocal in its expression of sympathy or support while the ICFTU was either apathetic or silent.[72] ICFTU's orientation could only be understood, according to Nduka Eze, as representing the 'imperialist bloc',[73] and in any case, 'there was a massive Nigerian Congress vote for the WFTU in 1950.'[74] The pro-ICFTU faction within the NLC muted their protest as it was difficult to defend ICFTU's stance during the shooting,

[66] Annual Report, 1949-50., p. 15.

[67] Ananaba, *op. cit.,* p.109.

[68] Members were Coker, F.O., Cole, N.A., Okpareke, T.O.E., Offiom, E.O., and Aghedo, R.

[69] Secretaries were: Ikoro, A.N., Asemota, S.M.V., Balonwu, P.O., Oduleye, J.O., Ogonsi, L.U., and Adio-Moses, A.A.

[70] Ibid., p. 12; Nduka Eze, NLC's Secretary-General, contested and won his seat.

[71] Cohen, R., Labour, p.74-76; Ananaba, *op. cit.*, pp. 96-97.

[72] 'West Africa', September 1, 1962.

[73] Ibid.

[74] Ibid.

an episode Sklar described as 'no previous event ever evoked a manifestation of national consciousness comparable to the indignation generated by this tragedy.'[75]

The NLC ran into increasing difficulties and was especially frustrated by lack of funds brought about partly by the refusal of two of the contracting parties (TUC and the Federation of Government and Municipal, Non-Clerical Workers Union - FGMNWU) to the merger to transfer to it their assets. The refusal of the TUC and the FGMNWU to pool their resources as agreed upon would seem not unconnected with what has been described as the 'unhappiness' of the ex-TUC officials over their under-representation in the new leadership, affiliation of NLC to WFTU and the mounting political involvement of the new leadership as instanced by the participation of Eze and others in the Lagos Municipal elections.[76] This course of action was bound to be counter-productive as the consequent dependence on the obviously lean resources of the former NNFL could only tend to increase the dominance of ex-NNFL elements in the NLC.

Be that as it may, the NLC's stature was eroded by three apparently unconnected developments. Firstly, a labourer who was said to have claimed allegiance to the Zikists attempted to assassinate Sir Hugh Foot, the Chief Secretary of the Colonial Administration; known Zikists (not including Eze) were thereupon arrested and the organization proscribed by the Administration. Secondly, the Amalgamated union of UAC African Workers (UNAMAG) went on a countrywide strike upon the refusal of management to pay a 12s cost-of-living award won by workers and effective from April 1, 1950 (the date of original dispute) instead of November 10, 1950 as held by management (the date of the award). The strike failed, according to the Department of Labour 'owing to intimidation and the fear of intimidation', and that most of the firms concerned had forewarned their employees that by participating in this strike they would render themselves liable to dismissal.[77] The prestige of NLC and Nduka Eze (who was the Secretary of UNAMAG) became tarnished especially as the organization could not alleviate the hardship imposed on workers who had lost their jobs.[78] Lastly, as decolonization progressed with internal devolution of power (self-government) and projected constitutional talks, trade union-political party ties were

---

[75] Sklar, R., Nigeiran Political Parties, op. cit., p. 77.

[76] Cohen, R., *op. cit.,* p. 75; Cohen, however, erroneously attributes the distribution of the tract 'CALL FOR REVOLUTION' to Eze. The speech was delivered by O.C. Agwuna at a Zikist meeting in October 1948 and tract was officially distributed by the Zikist organization. See Sklar, *op. cit.,* p. 126 footnote.

[77] Annual Report. 1905—1, p. 34.

[78] Ibid., pp. 33-4.

transformed. Nationalist politicians could hardly ignore the fact that political gains now depended on their own activities (apart from the blunders of the colonial administration) and the willingness of the British Government to relinquish political control. A consequence was the almost total exclusion of trade unionists, as from 1950, from political spoils and office. All trade unionists became an embarrassment to politicians:

> Had the NCNC/NNDP politicians been willing to share their leadership with the Labourites, a leftist mass party might have merged and the ensuring ineffectual, sectarian radicalism of the isolated labour left might have been averted. When the NLC was staggered by defeat in the mercantile strike of December 1950, radical labour leaders, including Nduka Eze, wee swiftly excluded from positions of control in the 'triple Alliance' (NNDP, NLC and Lagos Market Women's Guild).[79]

The fortunes of NLC plummeted after the abortive UNAMAG strike, and its operational capability was weakened by a pro-ICFRTU faction which exploited the creeping unpopularity of NLC to oppose the leadership and maintain open links with the ICFTU.[80] The rift became public in March 1951 when the NLC expressed is opposition to the visit of ICFTU delegates to Nigeria. The pro-ICFTU faction clashed with NLC's demonstrators who arrived at Ikeja airport to ask ICFTU delegates to 'go home'.[81] The rift became public in March 1951 when he NLC expressed its opposition to the visit of ICFTU delegates to Nigeria. The pro-ICFTU faction clashed with NLC's demonstrators who arrived at Ikeja airport to ask ICFTU delegates to 'go home'.[82] A disillusioned Eze, who was being 'hounded'[83] by the Administration, resigned from the NLC, UNAMAG and Freedom Movement. The NLC disaffiliated from the WFTU in September 1951 and was subsequently noted to be 'dead and buried' early in 1952.[84] Thereafter, the pro-ICFTU faction maintained an autonomous existence, and for practical purposes there was no all-embracing central labour organization. The importation of 'divisions within the European trade union movement'[85] into Nigeria had grown and was to take on greater significance as political independent loomed larger.

In the interim, the imposition of the so-called McPherson Constitution

---

[79] Ibid., p. 33

[80] Sklar. *op. cit.*, p. 85.

[81] Cohen, *op. cit.*, p. 76; Ananaba, *op. cit.*, p. 123-4.

[82] Anababa, p. 123.

[83] Melson, R. 'The Political Dilemmas of the Nigerian Labour Movement' in Damachi, U.K., Seibel, D.H., (eds), *Social Change and Economic Development in Nigeria*, Praeger, New York, 1973, p. 126.

[84] Annual Report. 1951-2, p. 7.

[85] Hodgkin, T., *Nationalism in Colonial Africa*, Frederick Muller, London, 1956, p. 128.

of Nigeria generated a lot of heat as it created three political units (regions) within a federal structure. The problem of political affiliation facing labour leaders at the centre was compounded by the injection of regional political loyalties. As the three main political parties (Northern People's Congress, Action Group and the NCNC) consolidated their hold in their respective regions (North, West and East) and co-opted most organized groups the rein, it was difficult for trade union leaders to reach common ground over specific and controversial issues of national importance – especially as they appeared in the ranks of different political parties. Albeit, in July 1952, Lewis Agonsi, Acting General Secretary of the Railway Workers Union convened a meeting of all trade unions to consider the formation of a central organization. A Committee led by Imoudu and Agonsi was appointed to 'work out details of a new organization.'[86] The new organization was finally launched at a conference in August 1953 in Lagos.

All-Nigeria Trade Union Federation (ANTUF)

The All-Nigeria Trade Union Federation (ANTUF), which embraced all factions, was launched at a conference to which twenty-nine trade unions sent representatives. Imoudu was elected President and Gogo Chu Nzeribe the Secretary-General. The aims of the organization were:

a) to improve the position and living conditions of the workers of Nigeria and to unite them in the realisation of all objectives common to the interests of the working class;
b) to organise and unite the trade unions of Nigeria irrespective of creed, nationality, region, sex and political conceptions;
c) to encourage the spirit of oneness and collective security among all working peoples and establish Trades Council all over the country;
d) to lead the struggle of trade unions against influences which oppose their democratic rights and liberties by striving to obtain for them social and economic security;
e) to secure improvements in wages and service conditions, to obtain full employment, to encourage the introduction of, and watch developments in labour and social legislations;
f) to plan and provide for the education of trade union members and to awaken them to realise their real functions in the state;
g) to seek for the state ownership of major industries in the country;
h) to cooperate with democratic federations of trade unions or other organisations whose aims Are acceptable to the Federation;
i) to undertake or participate in the printing and publishing of

[86] Ministry of Labour, Quarterly Review, March 1960, p. 41. Other members were Ayo Ogunsheye, H.P. Adebola, N.A. Cole, Gogo Nzeribe, M.I. Ujegbor, E.U. Ijeh and O. Egwunwoke.

newspapers and other literature in the interest of the Federation and of trade unionism generally; and

j) to establish and support the political wing of the workers' movement (political party) with a view to realising a socialist government.[87]

Nduka Eze and two of his friends (S. G. Ikoku and E. A. Cowan) who turned up for the inaugural conference were expelled on the ground that they were neither duly appointed officials of a trade union nor accredited to the conference by any registered trade union.[88] Two unions took exception to the exclusion of the three men and withdrew their delegates. Along with other sympathisers, they formed the Committee of Trade unions (COTU).[89]

The Administration procrastinated over according ANTUF recognition. Recognition came after a month but withdrawn six months later (February 17, 1954) ostensibly on the grounds that COTU had challenged its representativeness. Recognition was restored after seven months when it became impossible to continue with such a policy in face of contradictory evidence. ANTUF had submitted a declaration from twenty-seven unions representing 63,000 workers,[90] roughly fifty per cent of total trade union members. The rest were grouped as 'independent' unions such as the Nigerian Union of Teachers and the UAC workers which had since 1950 not been able to muster enough courage and strength to form an all-embracing trade union. The ANTUF resolved not to affiliate externally with ICFTU or WFTU. This decision seems to have increased its popularity and by the end of 1955 it had thirty-nine affiliated unions with a membership roll of 95,000.[91] It was consulted from time to time by the Administration on industrial matters and it provided observer delegates to the 39th session of the International Labour Organisation's (ILO) conference in January 1956.[92] At the end of 1956, ANTUF had within its fold forty-nine trade unions[93] that organized some 181,000 workers out of a total labour force of 200,000.[94] In spite of its immense popularity, by April 1957 a rival body was created in the form of the National Council of Trade Unions in Nigeria (NCTUN).

The immediate cause of the split within ANTUF appears to have been the decision of the leadership not to affiliate the organization either to the

[87] Ananaba, *op. cit.*, pp. 141-2

[88] Eze's trade union had been de-registered in 1950, part-penalty for UNAMAG's strike.

[89] Ananaba, op. cit., p. 143; A cynical manoeuvre by the Administration while hounding Eze.

[90] Ibid., p. 144.

[91] Annual Report, 1954-5, par. 92

[92] Uvieghara, *op. cit.*, p. 18

[93] Annual Report, 1955-6, p. 18.

[94] Cohen, R., Labour; *op. cit.*, p. 79

ICFTU or WFTU.[95] There were others within and without the organization who desired affiliation to the ICFTU. At ANTUF's second annual conference, the 'government tried to infuse moderate elements into the leadership.'[96] When this failed, some trade unionists set up in April 1956 a Council of ICFTU-Affiliated Unions although most of them still retained their positions in ANTUF.[97] Within ANTUF itself, pro-ICFTU elements led by L.L. Borha (General Secretary of the Locomotive Drivers Union), N.A. Cole (President of the Nigerian Union of Nurses) and H. P. Adebola sought to persuade the organization to affiliate to the ICFTU. When a motion to this effect was not carried, they demanded that the General-Secretary, Gogo Chu Nzeribe, should be removed from office on the charge of being 'communist-inclined'.[98] When this demand was rejected, pro-ICFTU elements withdrew their trade unions from ANTUF and along with other members of ICFTU-Affiliated Unions they formed, in April 1957, the National Council of Trade Unions in Nigeria (NCTUN) which 'looked to the ICFTU for leadership.'[99]

National Council of Trade Unions of Nigeria (NCTUN)

The National Council of Trade Unions of Nigeria (NCTUN) had N.A. Cole as President, Adebola as Vice-President and Borha as General Secretary.[100] Considering the circumstances that led to the creation of the NCTUN some of its aims are somewhat puzzling:

a) to provide a powerful and effective central trade union body independent of any ideological influences and pledged to the task of promoting the interests of working people in the country...;
b) to cooperate in whatever manner it is deemed fit with free and democratic international trade union federations whose aims are acceptable to the council;
c) to establish a political committee to promote political action in support of the above aims and objectives;
d) to seek for state ownership of major industries in the country;
e) to encourage the organising of workers in free and democratic trade unions; to unite them towards their common objectives regardless of sex, tribe and differences of political views, and to afford them a

[95] Yesufu, *op. cit.*, p. 46; Ananaba *op. cit.*, p. 147; Cohen, *op. cit.*, p. 79.
[96] Cohen, Ibid., p. 78.
[97] *Ibid.*, pp. 78-79.
[98] Cohen, *Labour and Politics*, p. 79
[99] Akpala, *op. cit.*, p. 38
[100] Others were Miriki, F.W. Okei-Achamba, E.C., and Oluebake, F., as Vice Presidents; Agonsi, L.U., Gbadamosi, R.O., and Anunobi, N., as Assistant General Secretaries; and Ogunwoke, O., the Treasurer.

furtherance of their genuine interests....[101]

ANTUF claimed thirty-nine unions with 57,000 members while the NCTUN claimed twenty-four unions with 50,000 members. About 100,000 trade unionists were organised in some 270 additional unions outside both bodies.[102] The NCTUN formally affiliated to the ICFTU and was accorded official recognition by the Administration, upon which both organizations castigated each other publicly. The NCTUN customarily accused ANTUF of being 'under veiled Communist control'[103] and the latter's reaction was described thus:

> ANTUF saw conspiracy at, work from four directions; First, from the government whose Minister of Social Welfare and Labour, Chief Festus Okotie-Eboh granted immediate recognition to the new body without ascertaining its representativeness. Secondly, from the Commissioner of Labour, George Foggon, and British TUC advisers who had influenced the Ministry decision. Thirdly, from the leadership of the NCNC. A subcommittee of ANTUF meeting in 1955 whose membership included Imoudu, S.U. Bassey and Wahab Goodluck...had recommended the formation of a Nigerian Labour Party. The party was duly formed in March 1956, and its leaders argued that the NCNC were anxious to thwart any attempt by the new party to gain a mass-based body of support. Finally, the machinations of the ICFTU were seen to be at work.[104]

As the acrimony between the organizations increased, ANTUF applied to the ICFTU for an affiliate status but was turned down,[105] a decision that Proehl has argued, 'must be seen as a fundamental error, the results of which should have been startlingly clear even then.'[106] ANTUF's officials have pointed out that ICFTU was more interested in 'divide and rule' than in the unity of the labour movement.[107] In 1958, the General Secretary of ANTUF, S.U. Bassey, was prevented by immigration authorities from attending the ILO conference in Geneva as 'the Ministry felt obliged to accept the nominee of the NCTUN, L.L. Borha, as the workers' delegate.'[108] ANTUF sent a petition to the ILO on June 4, 1958 in which it sought the rejection of Borha's credentials. The petition is quoted

---

101 See Ananaba, *op. cit.*, pp. 151-2 for all NCTUN's aims.

102 Proehl, P.O., *Foreign Enterprises in Nigeria*, University of N. Caroline & OUP, Chapel Hill, London and Ibadan, 1965, p. 112.

103 'West Africa', December 24, 1960.

104 Cohen, *Labour*, pp. 78-79

105 Ananaba, *op. cit.*, p. 78-79

106 PROEHL, Ibid., p. 112.

107 Imoudu, Bassey, Interviews, Lagos, 1977.

108 Yesufu, *op. cit.*, p. 150

extensively here as it gives the possible range of the activities of all external interests:

> ...It becomes necessary to state briefly the role of the ICFTU in Nigerian Trade Union movement. For a long time now the ICFTU has been coercing trade unions in Nigeria to affiliate to it and its trade departments. In order to accomplish this it has procured some trade unionists in Nigeria by award of scholarships, pleasure trips, agencies, commissions, monetary gifts, etc., to destroy such trade unions and their leaders who are imagined to constitute an obstacle to the affiliation. By these subtle methods and mercenary means, the ICFTU has become an antithesis of freedom and democracy, and has been responsible in the main for the diabolical activities of the few dissident elements known as the NCTUN. It is therefore the general impression of Nigerian workers that the ICFTU is an imperialist-international organisation purposely designed to serve the material interest of Colonial possessing-Countries, and that its main policy is to mislead colonial workers in their fight against Colonialism, industrial and economic oppression.[109]

The bickering went on for three years until efforts at reconciling the organizations took concrete form in 1958 when some labour leaders led by Ayodele Adeleke (Chairman, Enugu Labour Council) and A.U.D. Mba (General Secretary, Shell-BP Workers Union) founded the National Labour Peace Committee. The Committee was able to announce on 21 January 1959 an agreement to a merger by ANTUF and NCTUN. Both bodies supposed to have agreed, among other things, that 'in the interest of permanent unity, communism, fascism, and national political partisanship should not be projected in the Nigerian Labour Movement' while recognising the right of the individual to 'believe in any brand of political ideology.'[110] At the same time, paradoxically, it was also agreed that 'the assets and liabilities of the two organisations, including the existing international affiliation of either ANTUF or NCTUN be taken over by the new organisation.'[111]

After a series of meetings a new body, the Trades Union Congress of Nigeria (TUCN) was formally launched on 7 March, 1959 at the 'Dayspring Hotel', Enugu. Imoudu was elected President and L.L. Borha General Secretary. But the TUC(N) practically broke up before it could even stand on its feet. Imoudu, ANTUF's nominee for the presidency

---

[109] Quoted in Yesufu, *op. cit.*, p. 150

[110] Anannaba, *op. cit.*, p. 154.

[111] Ibid., p. 154. If the issue of international affiliation kept both sides apart, one wonders why it should form basis for a new body.

easily defeated N.A. Cole, NCTUN's nominee. But Borha, NCTUN's candidate for General Secretary defeated S.U. Bassey, ANTUF's nominee. As soon as the results were announced ANTUF's delegates swept out of the conference hall in anger, suspecting the organizers of having rigged the elections - ANTUF as the organization with the largest membership had more delegates and did not expect to lose. While ANTUF's delegates gathered together in consultation outside the conference hall, NCTUN delegates proceeded to elect members of the new Central Working Committee, the executive organ, from among themselves, delivering the *coup de grace.* NCTUN's delegates⁻ were apparently keener on gaining control of the new executive than forging the united body.

The denouement was an organization completely dominated by ex-NCTUN elements with ANTUF's members not forming a rival body outright because of mounting pressure on all sides to present a united front before the Mbanefo and Morgan Commissions.[112] Complementing this was Imoudu's public confirmation of an unblemished electoral process during the conference. Such a declaration seems to have been made because Imoudu hoped his own influence could be set against the rest of the new executive.[113] The issue of international affiliation was suspended until the first annual conference of TUCN which was to take place in March 1959.[114]

Trades Union Congress of Nigeria (TUCN)

The Trades Union Congress of Nigeria (TUCN) was beset with problems from the outset. ANTUF, following a well-worn path, withheld its assets at the same time presenting formidable opposition from within the new body. ANTUF elements published a booklet entitled 'The Case of Overhaul of the TUC' which in many parts urged the 'overthrow'[115] of the leadership, and maintained strong links with the Ghana TUC. The leadership also showed divergent tendencies. Imoudu as President embarked on a countrywide political tour with Dr. Azikiwe and other NCNC officials, and also took off on a tour of Europe, including Moscow where he made a broadcast over the radio lashing out at 'imperialists' and the ICFTU.[116] The rest of the executive (including the Central Working Committee) thought differently and affiliated the organization to the ICFTU in April 1959 before the proposed annual conference of TUCN could even

[112] Appointed in 1959 by Federal Government and other regions/Western Region respectively to review wages.
[113] Cohen, *op. cit.*, p. 182.
[114] Akpala, *op. cit.*, pp. 35-6.
[115] Ananaba, *op. cit.*, p. 181.
[116] Imoudu, Interview, La gos, 1977; Ananaba, op. cit., p. 176

be held.[117]

The affiliation was kept secret because of its controversial nature[118] and not until 12 November 1959 when the ICFTU gave TUCN £4,000 and 'Opel' car was there formal and open acknowledgement of TUCN links.[119] Formal affiliation sparked off another round of invectives and recrimination between ex-ANTUF elements and pro-ICFTU members of TUCN. The pro-ICFTU faction argued that the instrument of merger which contained t inheritance of 'existing international affiliations' had automatically affiliated TUCN to the ICFTU as ANTUF had no formal external links. The timing of any announcement was thus irrelevant.

The visit of a Ghana TUC delegation to Nigeria on 21 August, 1 appears to have exacerbated the acrimony between the factions. The for was in Lagos to discuss the formation of an All-African Trade Union Federation (ANTUF) and in the process had discussions with both TU officials and ANTUF faction. This caused a great deal of resentment as TU officials interpreted this as a *de facto* recognition of their opponents. Their fears were confirmed when later in the year TUCN's delegation to the preparatory conference of the All-African Trade Union Federation (AATUF) was displaced by ANTUF's elements with the active collaboration of Ghana TUC.[120]

The creation of a rival central labour organization was finally precipitated in the following many events or developments. Firstly, the ICFTU had stepped up its activities 1n Africa with the formation of an African Regional Organization (AFRO) which was to hold its meeting in Lagos in November. This annoyed anti-ICFTU trade unionists. Secondly, the first federal elections which were to usher in the first elected government of an independent Nigeria were to be held in December 1959. Political preferences, therefore, gave room to partisanship which in turn reinforced other disagreements. Thirdly, the Ghana TUC had left the ICFTU and under the leadership of John Tettegah was seeking a Pan-African Trade Union body in line with the political tendencies of Dr. Nkrumah's and those of the prevailing pan-African movement. It now opposed the ICFTU vigorously, seeing it as an organization of essentially European character having as one object the recruitment of African workers exclusively for anti-WFTU general 'Cold War' purposes.[121] Its opposition to the ICFTU was clearly shown when the former arranged a conference of

[117] Akpala, *op. cit.*, p. 36.

[118] Ananaba, *op. cit.*, pp. 181-2.

[119] Ibid., p.182.

[120] ANTUF's elements were Wahab Goodluck, Oduleye, S.O., and Egbuna Ifedira.

[121] Ghana became 'independent' in 1957 and its TUC was ICFTU's staunchest ally. A possible comment on how seriously colonial trade union alignments should be taken.

the All-African Trade Union Federation (AATUF), which took place in Accra (Ghana) from 4-8 November, 1959, to *coincide* with ICFTU's own conference in Lagos. The meeting of most African trade unionists in neighbouring Ghana not only overshadowed and dampened the intended impact of ICFTU's conference, the virtual expulsion of the TUCN official delegation (replaced by ANTUF elements) made matters worse especially with 'Radio Ghana' and Ghanaian newspapers denouncing the TUCN delegation as 'imperialist stooges' and describing the Lagos conference as 'imperialist organised and inspired.'[122] To cap it all, AATIUF insisted on disaffiliation from all external bodies as a condition of membership for any African central labour organization.

The last straw, however, soon appeared in the form of an open break between Imoudu and the rest of TUCN executive. Stung by talks of 'puppet' and 'powerless', provoked by an undercurrent of rumours about a mysterious flow of money from Brussels into the bank accounts of TUCN, Imoudu demanded an audit and a personal scrutiny of the financial dealings of both his Deputy and the General Secretary.[123] This request was refused, whereupon Imoudu persuaded two-thirds of affiliated trade unions to call a conference to be held in Lagos. The rest of the executive (through the Central Working Committee) pre-empted this move by suspending Imoudu from office. Imoudu then announced the dissolution of the Central Working Committee and fixed a conference for 21 April in Lagos.[124] His opponents in turn fixed their conference for 20 April, to take place in Kano, 500 miles away from Lagos.

Both sides campaigned hard in the interim to get trade unionists to attend their respective conferences. Other 'independent' labour bodies, like the Enugu and Aba Councils of Labour, were split into two camps which supported different factions.[125] The Lagos conference convened by Imoudu duly opened on 21 April, 1960. Delegates from fifty-five trade unions representing 184,612 workers attended.[126] The emergent central organization was named the Nigerian Trades Union Congress (NTUC) with Imoudu as President and Gogo Chu Nzeribe as its General Secretary. The NTUC shunned the ICFTU, WFTU and ICFTU (later WCL) and affiliated to the All-African Trade Union Federation (AATUF).

The Kano conference organized by the Central Working Committee (CWC) opened at the 'International Hotel' on 20 April as scheduled. It was attended by 351 delegates from ninety-eight affiliated trade unions

---

[122] Ananaba, *op. cit.,* 181
[123] Cohen, *op. cit.,* p. 81.
[124] No provisions in the Constitution empower the President to dissolve the CWC.
[125] No provision in the Constitution empowers the President to dissolve the CWC.
[126] Ministry of Labour, *Quarterly Review,* September 1960, p.71.

representing 98,000 members.[127] Imoudu was expelled and Alhaji Adebola elected in his place while there was a massive vote of confidence in the General Secretary Borha, who quickly reaffirmed TUCN's affiliation to the ICFTU. Among others, goodwill messages came from the ICFTU headquarters in Brussels, the British TUC and MacDonald Moses, ICFTU representative in Nigeria.[128]

As usual, both TUCN and NTUC attacked each other and the usual expletives were dutifully utilised. TUCN accused Imoudu of being a 'splitter' and apart from being 'communist-inclined' the NTUC was additionally accused of being 'teleguided' from Ghana - an obvious reference to its affiliation to Ghana-based AATUF. For its part, NTUC had described Borha and Adebola as 'imperialist stooges' and argued that the TUCN had split the labour movement in preference to its links with the ICFTU. 'For good measure, it demanded 'the immediate introduction of a unitary constitution, the resignation of British personnel employed in the Army and police force, the nationalisation of the major industries and the creation of an African Liberation Fund.'[129] The AATUF's General Secretary, Tettegah, chipped in and said NTUC was the only central body recognized by the organization. This infuriated the TUCN leaders.[130]

Several attempts were made to reconcile the two organizations. The first was undertaken by three former trade unionists, R.B.K. Okafor, A.U.D. Ubah and P.E. Ekanem, who were now Members of Parliament, but their efforts came to nought. Another attempt was made by the executive of the Eastern Nigeria Development Corporation and Allied Workers Union in July 1960 when both sides were invited to 'peace talks' at Aba but NTUC representatives failed to show up.[131] Yet another attempt was made by a Labour Solidarity Committee formed in August 1960 to devise ways and means of healing the rift. In spite of the Committee's enlistment of the services of the Oba of Lagos, His Highness Adeniyi Adele II, and two meetings of all parties at his palace, the two sides remained apart. On 3 December, 1960, the Prime Minister, Sir Abubakar Tafawa Balewa intervened (Nigeria had become independent on 1 October, 1960). A series of meetings of both parties including the Prime Minister with the Honourable Minister of Labour, J.M. Johnson in

[127] Ananaba, *op. cit.*, p.186.

[128] Ananaba, *op. cit.*, p.185.

[129] Ibid., p.185.

[130] Tettegah's remark should be seen in light of AATUF's insistence on non-affiliation to external bodies as condition of membership. AATUF in fact urged all trade unionists to sink their differences and form only one body, as only one central labour organization from each country could become members.

[131] Ananaba, *op. cit.*, p.187.

attendance[132] failed to resolve outstanding differences.

The continuing bickering at the centre made it impossible for the leaders to reach an agreement on a workers' delegation to the 1960 ILO conference. The Ministry of Labour showed its own preference when it appointed Borha as delegate with eleven other nominees of TUCN as his advisers.[133] The NTUC's protests were ignored but at the conference in Geneva copies of a document captioned 'The Great Conspiracy against Africa' (its Foreword written by Gogo Nzeribe, NTUC's General Secretary), issued by AATUF Secretariat, were found in the, pigeonholes of all delegates. It was claimed to be an annexe to a British Government Cabinet paper on policy in Africa, and in the main reviewed the state of relations between ICFTU members, conflicts of national interests and strategies, and the acrimonious atmosphere at the ICFTU Sixth World Congress in 1959. It generously explained that:

> The gradual abdication of direct British and other European rule in favour of measures to establish local independence makes it all the more necessary to maintain our African connections by the development of non-political means. In these conditions the role of trade unionism and therefore the role of ICFTU have acquired a new and vital importance for us. This had been only partially foreseen as regards Africa when ICFTU was founded. Recent developments there have greatly increased the importance of the unions as an alternative instrument of Western influence and especially as a brake on unchecked political and national movements. Since it is difficult to accuse trade unions of serving colonial ends, with their aid it should be possible to establish harmonious relations with the new social and political institutions in Africa now being created and with the administration of industrial and agricultural interests, which we hope to maintain after any political changes. Trade unions will be needed to check irresponsible nationalisation and to maintain control in the key sectors of the economy in the newly created African states. The principal aim should be the development in Africa of genuine trade unions movement as we know it in Britain and on the Continent. This must be done with our help and under our influence from the start...[134]

Referring to American trade unions, the document warned that,

[132] Cohen erroneously names Dr. K.O. Mbadiwe as Minister of Labour, *op. cit*

[133] Ananaba, *op. cit.,* p.188.

[134] Cited in Ananaba, *op. cit.*, p. 189

> We need unfortunately to realise that this American policy has little or nothing in common with our aims in ICFTU or indeed with our policy in Africa. On the contrary the aim seems to be to take advantage of the difficult situation in themselves and to replace our influence and interests by direct U.S. penetration of Africa, using the machinery of ICFTU and American contacts that have been built up with African leaders for this purpose.[135]

Although the contents of the document accurately reflected the state of relations between American trade unions and their European counterparts and bore British Cabinet Office letterheads and official insignia, the British delegate denounced it as a 'forgery'.[136]

The Ibadan Merger Conference (3 May 1962.)

The All-Nigeria Peoples Conference, masterminded by Dr. Mbadiwe as Personal Adviser on African Affairs to the Prime Minister and held in Lagos on 19 August 1961, appointed a Labour Reconciliation Committee, with Alhaji Jalo Waziri (Speaker of the House of Representatives) as chairman, to resolve all disagreements in the labour movement.[137] After intensive discussions and a study of memoranda submitted by interested parties, a decision in principle was apparently reached to unite. A caretaker committee comprising twenty men drawn equally from both TUCN and NTUC was formed to set about organizing a conference for the launching of a new organization.[138] On the issue of international affiliation it was agreed that joint unity conference' be held and the issue submitted to the vote by secret ballot.[139] After initial disagreement over the system of representation a compromise arrived at stipulated that all registered trade unions affiliated both bodies would participate with registered non-affiliates attending only observers.[140] The conference was then fixed for 3 - 5 May 1962 at Ibadan.

The few months before the conference witnessed intense canvassing for support by both factions and further attempts by each to discredit the other to TUCN proposed to retire Imoudu on the score that he had become 'a capillary attraction for dissensions and splits in the labour

---

[135] Ibid., p.189.

[136] Ibid., p.189.

[137] Other members were Dr. S.O. Aluko, (Secretary), C.C. Mojekwu, Chief Kola Balogun, Dr. Otegbeye, Reverend (Dr.) J.O. Lucas and E.T. Orodi.

[138] For TUCN: H.P.-Adebola, N.A. Cole, Fagbenro Beyioku, L.L. Borha, A. Adeleke, Y. Kaile, E.U. Ijeh, O. Zudonu, Wogu Ananaba and N.F. Pepple; NTUC: Imoudu, S.U. Bassey, S.O. Khayam, P.B. Olanrewaju; V.I. Oshinaga, P.I. Okoye, Ibrahim Nock, Wahab Goodluck, S.O. Oduleye and A. Ikoro.

[139] Ananaba, *op. cit.,* pp.215-216.

[140] Affiliates with over 1000 members would have *five* delegates each while those with under 1000 members were to have *three* delegates.

movement.'[141] Imoudu replied at a press conference on 30 January, 1962 flourishing a letter from Irvin Brown of American AFL-CIO to George McRay - another American trade unionist at the Lagos offices of TUCN - as evidence of American machinations and alleged that the organization had been infiltrated by the Central Intelligence Agency (CIA).[142] Even as late as the eve of the conference, TUCN's Ene Henshaw, alleged in a telegram to the Inspector General of Police that AATUF's General Secretary, John Tettegah, had brought fifty armed thugs from Ghana to sabotage the conference.[143]

As the conference day drew nearer, representatives of external interests, mostly from Western Europe and the United States of America, converged on Lagos.[144] More embarrassing to TUCN, it was rocked by internal disagreements that found coverage in the front pages of newspapers. Nnaemaka Chukwurah, an Assistant General Secretary, accused the leadership of 'maladministration, fraud, squandermania, nepotism, favouritism, misappropriation of funds, unauthorized reversion of Executive Council decisions and non-rendition of accounts.'[145] He further pointed out that 'in the past and under the traditional pretext and guise of "prestige fight" and "ideology", "scientific crooks and swindlers" have cleverly bulldozed and defrauded us.'[146] However, the Central Executive Council was reported to have passed a vote of confidence in the leadership when the allegations could not be substantiated.[147] On top of this the NTUC demanded the expulsion, of Irving Brown and George McRay before it was prepared to take part in the conference, but was talked back into it by the Committee.

The conference opened on 3 May 1962 in the Trenchard Hall of the University of lbadan. Apart from Dr. J.O. Lucas, the organizers and presiding officials were drawn from the parties that formed the Federal Government (NPC and NCNC).[148] The conference unanimously adopted a draft constitution of which clause 15, Article I clearly stated 'only maintenance of fraternal relationships with international trade union organisations as shall be determined by Congress in accordance with its constitution,'[149] thus apparently ruling out formal affiliations. Even

---

[141] Cohen, *op. cit.*, p. 85.
[142] Ibid., p.85. Irvin Brown later became the Director of the AALC.
[143] As it turned out, there was no truth in the allegation.
[144] Namely, the ICFTU, the British TUC and American AFL-CIO.
[145] He also sought explanation for the disbursement of £8,000 given to the TUCN by the ICFTU in previous three months; Cohen op. cit., p.85; Ananaba, *op. cit.*, p.218.
[146] Cohen, Ibid., p-85.
[147] Ananaba, *op. cit.*, p.218; 'Voice of Labour', Lagos, Feb. 1962.
[148] Alhaji Jalo Waziri (Chairman), Dr. Mbadiwe (Deputy Chairman), Alhaji A.A. Koguma (Chief of Credentials), A.K. Balogun (Electoral Officer) and O.Okarevu (African Affaors Officer of the NCNC).
[149] Ananaba, *op. cit.*, p.224.

before officials of the new organization could be elected, the Chairman brought forward the issue of international affiliation and asked for a vote to be taken. The NTUC representatives opposed the move and pointed to clause 15 Article I. It appeared that the Chairman interpreted 'fraternal relations' to mean 'affiliation' and the vote was proceeded with. A majority seemed to be in favour but the situation remained confused:

> Delegates from moribund and non-existent unions dutifully lined up for each vote. When the votes were counted...the number of voting delegates had swollen to 1,025, the majority of whom came out in favour of affiliation with the ICFTU...About 400 extra unionists had apparently appeared since the conference opened. Who had allowed them admission? Or had the voting figures been rigged?...[150]

The NTUC representatives demanded that the figure be checked against the number of delegates actually present in the hall. The Chairman refused on the grounds that some delegates might already have left the Conference: he was then accused of collaborating with TUCN and of being under the influence of the Americans.[151] On this note the conference adjourned for lunch recess. When it reconvened at 2.30 p.m. NTUC delegates remained absent from the hall. After a delay reminiscent of that in the Enugu episode, the conference went ahead and elected officers. Alhaji Adebola became President, Borha and others were elected 'unanimously' to their respective positions and the organization adopted a name appropriate for an all-embracing body, the United Labour Congress of Nigeria (ULCN). Soon afterwards NTUC delegates headed by Imoudu trooped in chanting 'freedom' and other songs to present a petition to the Chairman which reaffirmed their refusal to join the new organization so long as it remained affiliated externally. They then abandoned the conference to demonstrate around the university campus, after which they formed a rival body, the Independent United Labour Congress (IULC) with Imoudu as President, Amaefule Ikoro as General Secretary and Anunobi as Treasurer (the latter was at the same time IFCTU or WCL representative in Nigeria).

Reaction to the apparent failure of the conference was universally unfavourable. The press unanimously condemned the way the conference had been handled and blamed both the Chairman and Dr. Mbadiwe. In a front page comment one of the newspapers declared that:

---

[150] Cohen, *op. cit.*, p. 86.

[151] *Ibid.*, p.86; for NTUC accusations see also 'West Africa, 17 February, 1962 where U.S.A., Britain and West Germany were specifically mentioned.

> Alhaji Adebola rode some of his human horses last week. So did Mr. Michael Imoudu. And I am tempted to suggest that the "riding in majesty" will continue for some time because the Nigerian worker prefers to he ridden to riding, to be exploited mentally and physically by the secretaries he pays. Alhaji Adebola has won no victory; let him be told that. Imoudu is right on this occasion, if he sincerely meant that the Nigerian Trades Union Congress should not be affiliated to any foreign body...It would be unfair and unreasonable for the government to take sides by giving recognition to the Adebola faction when all that faction has succeeded in doing is in gathering a motley crowd whose votes are suspicious as those of the Imoudu crowd...[152]

Another newspaper was even more scathing:

> The Ibadan peace talks ended in a disastrous failure...The cause of the strife all these years had been the question of foreign link. Adebola supports foreign affiliation, Imoudu does not...We agree with Imoudu that tying our trade union movement to the chariot of alien bodies is not only inconsistent with our foreign policy but also on our domestic affairs. The saying that he who pays the pipers dictates the tune is true even in trade union movements. It would have occurred to those who voted for foreign affiliation that those alien bodies are not charitable or philanthropic organisations. They must have a purpose for what they are doing...[153]

The IULC, for its part, issued an 800-word statement that was prominently carried by all the major newspapers. Among others, the Chairman and Dr. Mbadiwe were blamed for mismanagement and partisanship which had led to its failure. The statement claimed that representatives of de-registered unions were admitted and allowed to participate; that some trade unions with fewer than 300 members had as many as five delegates rather than three, that there had been large-scale impersonation; and their voting on international affiliation was a violation of Article 1, section 15 of the Constitution.[154] Whichever way the Chairman's interpretation of the phrase 'fraternal relations' is regarded, it seems evident that the procedure adopted was unconstitutional. It is doubtful whether without the prior election of officers and the establishment of other vital organs the organization could be said to have existed when the affiliation vote was taken. It seems that the organizers were attempting to commit an unborn organization to a

[152] *Nigerian Morning Post*, Lagos, May 7, 1962.
[153] *West African Pilot*, Lagos, May 7, 1962.
[154] Ananaba, *op. cit.*, pp. 223-4

position on the issue before the leadership was elected, and before anyone could be sure. of the colour of the leadership that might emerge. If the *raison d'etre* of the conference was the establishment of a *united* central labour organization, other means might have been found for defusing so divisive an issue, reference, for example, to a sub-committee or a deferral to some other time. In any case, why were elections held at all in the absence of NTUC delegates?

The dissension in the labour movement mounted sharply as a result of the acknowledged partial attitude of the Ministry of Labour which manifested itself in the exclusive-recognition accorded the ULCN in June 1962. To dampen criticism, the government reiterated its previous stance:

> The Government is not at present considering the advisability of prohibiting Nigerian trade unions and their leaders from having foreign assistance and affiliation. It is the declared policy of the Government to foster and encourage the development of sound and independent and responsible trade unions oil democratic lines. The Government wishes to preserve the rights of the trade union movement to develop freely, and any restrictions placed on these rights will infringe the freedom of association which the Government seeks to preserve.[155]

By pitching its tent openly on the side of the ULCN the Government forced all other trade union leaders into hostile camps and contributed in no small measure to the deepening rifts between and within sections of the Nigerian labour movement.

In June 1962, the ULCN workers' delegation to the International Labour Organization (ILO) conference was vigorously but vainly opposed by the IULC in a telegram to ILO in Geneva.[156] The stage was now set for another round of vitriolic and vituperative press warfare and thinly disguised efforts at eliciting sympathy and workers' loyalties. The government fanned the flames by banning the Secretary-General of AATUF, John Tettegah, from entering Nigeria, a move ULCN had consistently advocated.[157] The ULCN made heavy weather of the 'communist threat': it alleged that IULC was 'communist-led, communist-inspired and communist-directed'[158] an allegation a jittery, hard-pressed and heavily anti-communist government was not disposed to ignore. The IULC, for its part, played on the former's links with American trade unions and claimed it had proof of AFL-CIO's

---

155 Dept. of Labour Annual Report, Lagos, 1960-1, p.27.
156 Ananaba, *op. cit.* , p.223.
157 Cohen, *op. cit.*, p.86-7.
158 Ibid., p.86.

sponsorship of the organization through George Meany, its president,[159] and generally drew attention to its unrepresentative nature.

Be that as it may, the struggle between the two organizations spawned new splinter groups. In December 1962, Anunobi (IFCTU or WCL representative in Nigeria), cast adrift by developments within the IULC, joined Chukwurah (who in turn had abandoned the ULCN) to form another central organization, the Nigerian Workers Council (NWC) which immediately affiliated to IFCTU or WCL - 'Anunobi and Chukwurah can be thought of as being "in the market" for a split. When the IFCTU was forthcoming with promises of aid and support, it made their break from the ULC possible.[160] On 28 December 1962, Ibrahim Nock left the IULC to set up the Northern Federation of Labour (NFL) and allocated the post of General Secretary to himself. It is thought that the prime motivation for the birth of the latter was 'the desire to move closer to the locus of regional power.'[161] The NFL subsequently affiliated to the International Confederation of Arab Trade Unions (IFATU),[162] and thereafter its main preoccupation appeared to be 'the undermining of the ULC and the political promotion of Ibrahim Nock.'[163] A fifth central organisation was created by Imoudu and Ikoro in 1963 after they had apparently been displaced from office by Wahab Goodluck, S.U. Bassey and Sidi Khayam in an internal power struggle,[164] The Labour Unity Front (LUF), as it was called, insisted that its sole business was to achieve unity of all central bodies, which probably explains its nature, 'it was a conglomeration of unions with various political and ideological inclinations which detached themselves from both the ULC and the NTUC.'[165]

To put all these developments into proper perspective, the following ought to be noted. Firstly, there had been increased rivalry between Nigeria and Ghana since the former gained her independence in 1960. Ghana's pan-Africanist inclinations met with hostile reactions from governmental circles in Nigeria, and some of the differences between them manifested themselves in their foreign policy.[166] At the continental level, while Nigeria led the African states grouped under the so-called

---

[159] Cohen, *op. cit.*, pp.86-7.
[160] Ibid., p.88.
[161] Ibid., p.88.
[162] Lynd, G. E., *The Politics of African Trade Unionism*, *op. cit.*, p.127.
[163] Ibid., p.127.
[164] *op. cit.*, p.227; Cohen, *op. cit.*, pp. 88-9.
[165] Lynd, G.E., *op .cit.*, p.129; For similar view see Report of the Enquiry into the Activities of Trade Unions, Federal Ministry of Information: Lagos, 1977. p.59.
[166] Ghana had diplomatic relations with both East and West whereas Nigeria remained firmly tied to the West in spite of its 'non-alignment policy'. For a review of Ghana-Nigeria relations see Aluko, *Ghana-Nigeria Relations: A Study in Intra-African Discord*

'Monrovia bloc', Ghana led the rival 'Casablanca group'.[167] The Nigerian government thus looked with the utmost disfavour at the activities of the Ghana TUC and the AATUF, if only because the latter was based in Ghana.

Secondly, the Federal Government (formed by the NPC and NCNC) had by late 1961 begun a crackdown on political opposition. The leaders of the opposition party were by mid-1962 under trial for allegedly planning to overthrow the government.[168] Most top members of ULCN (or TUCN) were also members of the ruling parties. NTUC and LUF showed their distaste for the major political parties in the formation of two labour-based parties, the Socialist Workers' and Farmers' party (SWAFP) and the Nigerian Labour Party (NLP) in 1963 and 1964 respectively. The government's decisions could therefore be said to have been coloured by political considerations.

The Joint Action Committee (JAC), 1963-4

The Joint Action Committee (JAC) was formed by the existing five central labour organizations - ULCN, IULC, NWC, NFL and LUF - in face of government's reluctance to review wages - each central body having submitted a memorandum on the state of the economy and on living standards and demanded an increase in wages. The Government called in ULCN delegates on 20 August, 1963 for discussions but with no positive results. The other organizations being without official recognition were ignored but allowed their affiliates to register their protest against a fall in real wages. The National Council of Dockworkers and Seamen, an affiliate of IULC, led the way with a lightning strike which eventually involved the police as dockworkers tried to stop the use of strike-breakers by stevedoring contractors. The consequent national dockworkers strike and a rash of other strikes tended to show up ULCN in a bad light as it was in a position to monitor neither workers activities nor demands. The ULCN was thus practically forced by circumstances to propose the co-ordination of activities, an invitation other central bodies eagerly accepted. On 12 September, 1963 all registered trade unions met in Lagos to form the Joint Action Committee (JAC) specifically to prosecute the wage demand. The meeting also decided on a general strike by 27 September if their demands were not met.

The government sat out the deadline and workers went on a one-day

---

[167] For details see Legum, C. *Pan-Africanism, op. cit.*

[168] Further details in Sklar, 'Nigerian Politics: the Ordeal of Chief Awolowo 1960-1965' in Carter, G. (ed.) *Politics in Africa: Seven Cases*, Harcourt Brace & World, New York, 1966; Jakande, L.K., *The Trial of Obafemi Awolowo*, John West, London, 1966; For a general view see Dudley, B.J. *Instability and Political Order: Politics and Crisis in Nigeria*, Ibadan University Press, Ibadan, 1973,

strike as a warning. To defuse the situation a Commission of Enquiry headed by Justice Morgan (referred to henceforth as the Morgan Commission) was appointed by the government to review the situation and make recommendations.[169] The Morgan Commission wound up its activities in April 1964 and the government only published its findings when the JAC threatened another general strike. It did so simultaneously with a White Paper rejecting and diluting most of its findings and recommendations.[170] The JAC organized a demonstration in protest in the course of which demonstrators clashed with police. The fracas that ensued left hundreds injured and Adebola with a fractured arm and battered head. Two days later the general strike,[171] began which was to last for fourteen days before the government agreed to negotiate.

The negotiations were very successful. The government seemed to have conceded to JAC on most points raised by workers. The leaders of JAC were flushed with success and basked in the attendant publicity and limelight. Indeed, the 'result of the strike meant that JAC was held in such high regard by wage earners that it was difficult for any union leaders to withdraw.'[172] For all that, the JAC collapsed six months later. To some labour leaders it was an ad hoc committee which some believed might presage a permanent central organization. When Imoudu advocated the formation of such a body under the umbrella of JAC, V.M.I. Jack on behalf of the ULCN publicly upbraided him and dissociated his organization from such a move.[173] Prior to this, one Mr. Durosomo of Joint Commercial and Industrial Workers Council had, at a press conference, deplored the tendency within JAC for 'everybody to use the organization to feather his nest. Today the ULC will send a protest, tomorrow the NTUC will attack the previous statement all in the name of JAC'.

The position of the NWC was clearly spelt out by Chukwurah at a press conference at which he attacked NTUC and the labour-based parties in these terms:

> ...we know for certain that there are some workers and even leaders of the JAC who are members of a so-called Socialist Party which claims

[169] Terms of reference were: to investigate the existing wage structure, remuneration, and conditions of service in wage-earning, employments in the country and to make recommendations concerning a suitable new structure, as well as adequate machinery for a wages review on a continuing basis; examine the need for a general upward revision of salaries and wages of junior employees in both government and private establishments and the introduction of a national minimum wage.

[170]See Ananaba *op. cit.*, pp.241-8 for comparison and analysis.

[171] For some political implications see: Melson, R., 'Nigerian Politics and the General Strike of 1964 in Rotberg and Mazrui, A, (eds): *Protest and Power in Black Africa*, OUP, New York, 1970

[172] Cohen, *op. cit.*, p.92.

[173] *West African Pilot*, Lagos, 7 July, 1964.

> to espouse and cater for the interests of the workers. As far as we are concerned we are not opposed to these persons for they are perfectly entitled to identify themselves with any political party of their choice. But confusion is bound to arise when certain leaders of the JAC begin to use the platform of the JAC for membership drive of their so-called socialist workers party...[174]

The collapse of the JAC arose mainly from political factors, and from ULCN's *de facto loss* of its 'recognized' status. 1963 saw a poorly organized and hotly disputed census,[175] and the hacking off of Midwest Region from Western Region. 1964 witnessed the controversial federal elections which resulted in a constitutional crisis when the President declined to invite the leader of the coalition of parties that had majority of seats to form a cabinet.[176] Although the crisis was to be resolved after a few days, wide-spread riots, looting and arson continued unabated in Western Region after subsequent regional elections were blatantly rigged in favour of Chief Akintola's party.[177]

The labour leaders struck discordant notes over the elections and other political developments. Ibrahim Nock whose organization, NFL, had achieved an umbilical union with the northern-based party (NPC), welcomed the results of both the census and the 1964 elections. Borha was delighted at the creation of the Midwest Region where he contested, and won his seat on the NCNC platform in 1964. Adebola was drawn into the partisan politics of the West and jettisoned the NCNC for the NNDP. Chief Fagbenro-Beyioku of the ULC became an NCNC Senator while S.U. Bassey ignored the Socialist Workers and Farmers Party (SWAFP), contested and won his seat as an NCNC candidate. Imoudu and Gogo Chu Nzeribe contested at the election but lost as candidates of the newly created Nigerian Labour Party. Such criss-crossing loyalties made consensus on most issues by labour leaders a difficult business.[178]

The JAC condemned the rising political violence and urged .the

---

[174] *West African Pilot*, 7 August, 1964, p.8.

[175] *West African Pilot*, 13 July, 1964, p.5.

[176] Revenue allocation for The regions and delimitation of constituencies depended on size of population, thus censuses took on great political significance. In this case, apart from the NPC or 'the North', most political parties or regions found the census figures 'unacceptable' largely because the former region emerged as having over 51 % of Nigeria's total population (this implied 'perpetual Northern domination'). A 'revised' set of figures were then adopted for 'administrative purposes' but which did not alter both political and other implications.

[177] All parties were grouped under two umbrella organizations, Nigerian National Alliance (NNA) and United Progressive Grand Alliance (UPGA), to contest the elections - which UPGA later boycotted. There were widespread election irregularities notwithstanding .

[178] The Nigerian National Democratic Party (NNDP), Chief Akintola's Party, broke away from the AG and formed an alliance with the NPC, the senior coalitional party forming the Federal government in Lagos.

Federal Government to postpone the 1964 elections. When it declined and went ahead with them, the JAC condemned the result and called a strike in protest. The strike failed largely because of the workers' well-founded fear of political thuggery and Adebola's 'timely dissociation from it.'[179] Both the ULCN and NWC seized this opportunity to withdraw from the JAC to form a rival Supreme Council of Trade Unions (SCTU). 'Its formation can be regarded as a defensive gesture by Chukwurah and Adebola in case the NTUC-controlled JAC revealed some hidden teeth'[180] wrote one observer. Be that may, the Eastern Nigeria branch of ULCN refused to withdraw from AC for a long time while the Western Region branch accused Adebola straying Nigerian workers by resigning his post of Joint Chairman of JAC and withdrawing the ULC from the JAC.[181] It said it would continue to play an active role in the affairs of the JAC until the Morgan recommendations were implemented. Only the Northern branch, predictably, went along with Adebola's directives when it announced its boycott of JAC conference scheduled for March 1965 in Kaduna.[181]

Adebola was later to say that the ULCN left JAC because 'the NTUC took opportunity to advocate and further interest of the Socialist Workers and Farmers Party' and 'the NTUC...wrote a letter without our knowledge urging the Federal Government to withdraw the recognition accorded to the ULC.'[182] For the NWC it was 'certain irresponsible and politically ambitious leaders of the JAC who used the platform to promote their individual personal political aims arid ambitions' and 'declared the JAC's support for the Socialist Workers and Farmers Party...and it was this imposition of political ideology which caused the dissolution of the JAC...'[183] The ephemeral nature of the JAC is perhaps best reflected in the fact that it conducted-daily business without a programme (as decisions were predicated on Government's reaction), with no minutes, no records, no constitution and no permanent secretariat.[184] The only 'coming together' was between handpicked leaders of respective central bodies that ran the JAC: the 'organising secretaries' went about their business of 'winning' affiliates.

MILITARY RULE AND CENTRAL LABOUR ORGANIZATIONS: 1966-75

The deteriorating political situation was eventually ended in a military *coup d'etat* on 15 January, 1966. The military presence *per se* did not

[179] For a discussion along these lines, see Melson, R. 'Ideology and Inconsistency: the Cross-pressured Nigerian Workers', American Political Science Review LXV (i), 1971.
[180] Cohen, *op-cit.*, p. 93.
[181] Cohen, p. 93.
[182] *Daily Times*, 19 January, 1965.
[183] Ibid.
[184] *Daily Times*, 8 February, 1965.

visibly alter the peculiar nature of central trade unionism in Nigeria. External interests still gained easy access and labour leaders were still unable to bury the hatchet. But the military's obsession with 'law and order' and its unending quest for legitimacy in the face of latent civil hostility to its continued monopoly of political power clearly dictated the way in which it dealt with other organized groups in the country.[185] One of Major-General Aguiyi-Ironsi's first act as Head of State was to urge labour leaders not to organize strikes as these might disturb the prevailing 'peaceful and orderly atmosphere.'[186] He also sought assurances from employers that they would refrain from steps that could lead to strikes or lockouts.

Wartime exigencies saw the introduction of somewhat draconian measures: decree 53 banned strikes and other related activities; there was a wage freeze; and an 'Emergency' decree gave the police and government almost unlimited powers.[187] The ULCN, in spite of its abandonment of the JAC, never regained its favoured status. The military consulted all the central labour organizations. Taking advantage of this more even-handed approach the NWC offered to give up its affiliation to the IFCTU or WLC if other central labour organizations would agree to, a merger. The NTUC and LUF were favourably disposed and the three organizations formed a new body called the Nigerian Trade Union Federation (NTUF) - the constituent bodies remaining relatively autonomous.

The ULCN, which declined to join the new body, denounced it in a press release on February 17, 1966:

> The presence of the Labour Party and SWAFP representatives in the so-called exploratory meeting summoned on the platform of the NWC furnishes an absolute proof that the meeting which ought to be an industrial one was used by some politicians for the political manoeuvres in complete disregard and violation of the undertaking given to the Supreme Commander and Head of the Federal Military Government in a meeting with labour leaders. The ULC is purely an industrial and not a political organisation...[188]

If the ULC was striving to make capital out of the fact that some members of NTUC and LUF were members of the Labour Party and SWAFP it was evidently hypocritical since most members of the ULCN

---

[185] *Daily Times*, 8 February, 1965.

[186] Secretary General's Report to the Bi-Annual Delegates Conference of the NUC, Report Activities of Trade Unions, Federal Ministry of Information, Lagos, 1977, pp. 4-5.

[187] Cohen, *op. cit.*, p.92.

[188] For an overview: Dare, L.O. 'Nigeria Military Governments and the Quest for reconstituted NLC), S.O. Sonubi, (Acting Head of Dept. of Adult Education, University Legitimacy, Jan. 1966 to July 1975 *NJESS*, vol. 17(2), July 1975.

were also prominent members of banned NCNC and NNDP,[189] though there is no need to spell out the military's possible reaction to any form of political opposition at this time.

If the military ignored the bait thrown by ULCN, the Federal Ministry of Labour did not and struck with decisive effect. It refused to give NTUF permission to function as a central labour organization.[190] Here a distinction has to be made between *permission* to function and *recognition* as a central labour organization.[191] Permission is a necessary and sufficient condition to existence as a central labour organization; recognition carried with it extra advantages such as visits abroad, delegation to ILO conferences, appointment to arbitration and labour advisory boards and the like - the ULCN enjoyed the latter from 1962 to 1965. This apparent disjunction between the military and the 'deviationist' goals of the civil servant could be accounted for in terms of the former's need for specialized knowledge and guidance, a tendency which Gavin Williams has noted:

> In 1966 the overthrow of the politician's Government forced the new military rulers to turn to civil servants for advice and direction...State policy was to be directed by 'statement', committed in principle to the national interest as institutionalised in the Federal Government.

This general tendency has been described by Finer as 'the technical inadequacy of the Armed Forces.'[192]

At the same time, the NTUC suggests that the ULCN applied indirect pressure on NWC by contacting IFCTU or WCL, to which NWC was affiliated, revealing that the latter was cooperating with the 'communist section' of the labour movement. And it was only when the WCL threatened to cut off its aid and scholarship programmes that the NWC withdrew from NTUF.[193]

The riots and killings (popularly referred to as 'pogroms') that preceded and occurred after the 'July Coup' that brought General Gowon to power in 1966[194] led to a mass exodus of 'southerners' from Northern Nigeria and the death of many trade unions.[195] All central labour organizations lost affiliates in the process, and were to lose more when the

---

[189] 'West Africa', 12 February, 1966, p.19.

[190] Ibid., p.19; these measures were to outlive the war. The obnoxious 'Emergency' decree 'Daily Times', Lagos, 3 April, 1978, p.21. was only repealed in September 1978'.

[191] Quoted in Cohen, *op. cit.* , p.94.

[192] All political activities and parties had been banned.

[193] Report of the Tribunal of Inquiry into the Activities of the Trade unions (Adebiyi Report) *op. cit.*, p.49.

[194] Explained to me by Mr. Okogwu, Director of Labour at the Federal Ministry of Labour, Lagos.

[195] Williams, G. (ed), *Nigeria : Economy and Society*, Rex Collins, 1976, p.44.

Eastern Region seceded on 30 May, 1967 to declare itself the 'Republic of Biafra' within which all trade unions formed the 'Biafran Trade Union Confederation' (BTUC) with Udokporo (ex-ULCN) as its General Secretary.[196]

Throughout the war the five central bodies retained their autonomy and their mutual hostility remained unabated. But in January 1968, the LUF merged with the NFL (now Northern States Federation of Labour-NSFL in line with creation of states to replace regions) as a prelude to further merger with NTUC. The ULCN shunned these merger moves but the proposed union Failed to materialise largely as a result of the failure of the constituent organisations to reach agreement on: (i) the allocation of posts (which were not decided by voting); (ii) the constitution; and (iii) as a result of the refusal of LUF to accept the Nigerian Youth Thinkers as a part of NTUC.[197] In the game year, following disagreements within NTUC, one of its Assistant secretaries, Etienam Bassey, broke away to form the Nigerian Federation of Labour but was denied permission to function by the Federal Ministry of Labour.[198]

With the collapse of 'Biafra' both militarily and as a viable political unit on 15 January 1970, the 'Biafran Trade Union Confederation' disappeared leaving the central bodies to resuscitate unions and scramble for affiliates. The ravages of the war, inflation and shortages of some foodstuffs alongside wages led to demands for wage increases and widespread militancy among workers.[199] Partly in response to those conditions and in keeping with its promise of review of wages 'after the war', the government set up the 'Adebo Wages Commission'[200] Again, to present a common front and coordinate workers' demands the labour leaders formed a United Committee of Central Labour Organizations (UCCLO) which drew its representation equally from all the central bodies. After the Adebo Commission had published its report and the government its White Paper, followed as usual by a spate of strikes and further conciliatory moves by government, the UCCLO came apart. Despite Imoudu's intervention in the form of Nigerian Workers' Unity Committee, the labour leaders were of the mind that the Committee had done its task and duly reverted to their bickering factions.

An upshot of the sizable monetary surplus gained by the government

---

[196] Finer, S.E., *Man on Horseback: The Role of Military in Politics*, Penguin, Harmondsworth, 2nd enlarged edn., 1976, p. 14.

[197] 'Advance', May 1966; Cohen, *op. cit.*, p.94.

[198] Details in Dudley, *Instability*, op. cit., Kirk-Green, A.H.M., *Crisis and Conflict in Nigeria : A Documentary Source book*, vols. 1 & 2 OUP, London, 1971 - to mention but two.

[199] Ananaba, *op. cit.* , p.225

[200] The BTUC was preceded by the Eastern Nigerian Council of Trade Unions, formed on 8 October, 1966 as Eastern Nigeria began the move towards secession.

from the quadrupling of crude oil prices in 1973 and of its attendant ambitious development plan was the abandonment of its officially neutral attitude to developments in the labour movement. Sensitized to international intrigues and intervention in the course of war, it produced a decree on central labour organizations. Decree 31 listed conditions for the formation and registration of any new central body. It also stipulated that the 'total membership of all trade unions concerned is at least 40 per cent of all the trade unions for the time being registered under this decree.[201] This marked the watershed in central trade unionism in Nigeria as central bodies came for the first time fully under legal control and regulation.

In practical terms, the decree marked an end to the creation of new central labour organizations. It was manifestly impossible for any *new* centre to win the allegiance of forty per cent of registered trade unions. The decree also sought to regulate 'admission of further trade unions to membership of registered federations,' declared that 'no person to hold office in more than one federation of trade unions at the same time,' and regulated 'the admission of further bodies to membership of central labour organisations and the amalgamation of central labour organisations.'[202] Drawing attention to our earlier distinction between permission and recognition, the decree emphasized that 'the registration of any central labour organisation under section 33 or 37 of this decree shall not be construed as entitling such central labour organisation to any form of recognition by the Federal Military Government.'[203]

Nigerian Labour Congress (NLC)

Sensing the changing and more interventionist mood of the government, the leaders put out feelers, sounding each other out on the prospects of establishing an all-embracing central body. This cautious approach was transformed into precipitate action by a rather curious incident. All the labour leaders were brought together at the cemetery by the death of one of their colleagues, J.A. Oduleye of ULCN (his brother, S.O. Oduleye was General Secretary of LUF). As it happened:

> It was during that moment of mourning at the cemetery that Mr. Okon Eshiett...drafted the unity document, which later became known as Apena Cemetery Declaration, that led to a meeting of the union leaders in Lagos on October 1, 1974 at which it was decided to merge all four central bodies under the name the Nigerian Labour

[201] Goodluck, interview, Lagos, 1977.
[202] Adebiyi Report, p.49.
[203] *West Africa*, 12 November, 1971, p.1337; Cohen, *op. cit.*, pp. 225-229 for details.

Congress NLC). It was also agreed that the house unions should be restructured on industrial case after the central body had been inaugurated.[204]

After about thirty years of dissension and squabbling at the centre, it took about ten minutes and the sobering presence of a corpse for Nigerian trade union leaders to finally bury the hatchet. Whether this reflects the superficial nature of the schisms and issues dividing them remains a matter of opinion. What is certain is that the 1974-75 period coincided with the termination of financial and other forms of aid from external sources, which can itself be represented as a 'push' factor toward unity. The Nigerian Labour Congress was finally launched on 18 December 1975.

On the day the NLC was to be launched, the Commissioner for Labour[205] raced at a press conference that certain international labour organizations would be proscribed so as to remove complet ely 'ideological or external influences which have plagued Nigerian trade union unity for more than a quarter of a century.'[206] During the previous night, police had occupied the offices of the four centres, removed documents and files and arrested about 100 trade unionists - including all top labour leaders - who were released soon afterwards.[207]

Amidst fanfares and handshakes, the NLC was formally launched on 18 December, 1975 with Wahab Goodluck as President and Chief Odeyemi as General Secretary. Signatories to the merger could not append their signatures on the merger instrument because 'vital documents were for the moment inaccessible, having been kept at the ULC's Trade Union Institute which had just been raided by the police'.[208] Signing was not done till the next day, and for added measure Wahab Goodluck (the new president of NLC), along with Dr. Tunji Otegbeye and Kunle Oyero, was arraigned before a Lagos magistrate's court on charges of transacting activities of a banned political party and remanded in custody until 30 January, 1976.[209] The case was later thrown out for want of evidence. It would appear that the authorities were trying to intimidate the new leadership of NLC for reasons not unconnected with the fact that the President was the President of NTUC, a centre clearly not liked by the

[204] It had the long-term job of recommending a system of periodic review of official pay scales and for harmonizing these with those in the private sector.

[205] Decree 31, 1973; Federal Ministry of Information, Lagos, p. A562. For details see *Official Gazette*, No. 38, vol. 6., 24 July, 1973.

[206] Federal Government of Nigeria Official Gazette, vol.6 (38), pp. A562-A567.

[207] Gazette, vol. 6. (38), op. cit., section 38, p. A566.

[208] Unoh, J.U., Mixed Reception for Amalgamation in Nigeria's Trade Union Movement. *New African* June 1977, p.533.

[209] Brigadier (now Major-General, retired) Adefope.

Federal Ministry of Labour.

However, before the excitement over the elections of NLC's officers could die down, the Commissioner for Labour (representing the government at the inauguration) announced that all international labour organizations operating in Nigeria had been banned with the exception of ILO and the Organisation of African Trade Union Unity (an arm of the Organization of African Unity). Expatiating on his earlier remarks, the Commissioner declared that under the government's new labour policy, a national institute for labour studies would be established and trade unions would be formed along industrial lines to accelerate the formation of bigger and more viable amalgamations and federations of registered trade unions.[210] He then startled all present by announcing the institution of a judicial tribunal to investigate the activities, finances and administration of the four central bodies. 'It is sad', he opined, 'to observe that the trade union movement has in recent past become a haven for ill-informed and ill-motivated persons masquerading as trade union leaders.'[211]

The Commissioner also thought that labour leaders had

> engaged in unwholesome rivalry, based upon foreign ideology and inspired by the lust for financial and material reward which foreign governments and their agents are prepared to offer for the sake of establishing their influence over the social, economic and political policies in Nigeria.[212]

The government later annulled the elections as trade union leaders became preoccupied with preparations against the impending probe.

It is essential to see government's actions against the following background so as not to get a misleading picture. The drive towards unity among top labour leaders generated opposition from within labour movement itself. A group of younger men, mostly located in middle rungs of the leadership of all central labour centres, took strong objection to the way and manner in which the top leaders literally shared out the top positions among themselves. In order to accommodate every one of their colleagues in the executive of the new NLC, there were five deputy presidents, twenty-five vice-presidents, four deputy secretary-generals, and thirty-one assistant secretary-generals.[213] These dissenting young men formed two organizations: the Progressive Front for the Labour Movement (which was centred around Pascal Bafyau of ULCN) and the Committee of Trade Unions in Defence of Trade Union Rights (centred

[210] *West Africa*, 15 December, 1975.
[211] *West Africa*, 5 January, 1976, p.3.
[212] *West Africa*, 5 January, 1976, p.3.
[213] Ibid., p.22.

around Hudson Momodu of the NTUC).

Both the Progressive Front for the Labour Movement and the Committee of Trade Union inundated the Federal Ministry of Labour with petitions and 'evidence' to prove 'foreign intervention' in the labour movement.[214] The former, in a press release on 15 December 1976, called for an investigation of the affairs of the central labour organizations and the assets of their leaders. It also alleged that the positions in the new organization had been 'slated' and that the impending elections at the inauguration were thus a farce as all leaders had agreed beforehand on who was to occupy what positions.[215] The government took advantage of potential or expressed support within the labour movement and the confusion which reigned in trade union circles to appoint the Commission of Inquiry into the activities of the central bodies with Mr. Justice Adebiyi, the Lagos High Court Judge, as the chairman henceforth referred to as Adebiyi Tribunal).[216]

The Adebiyi Tribunal sat for eighty days in Lagos during the period 3 March to 17 August 1976 and sat in Brussels, Belgium from 2 to 4 August, 1976. A total of 495 exhibits were received and evidence heard from 71 witnesses.[217] Ironically most of the witnesses were top labour leaders who accused each other of abuse of office, mismanagement of funds and so forth. It also presented the younger trade unionists the golden opportunity on which to get even with their leaders. Abuses and insults were traded so liberally that the chairman of the Tribunal had to intervene on innumerable occasions to remind everyone that this was neither the time nor place for character assassination - and that the intention of the government was not the 'witch hunting' of trade unionists.[218]

The government in its White Paper accepting the recommendations of the tribunal *banned* eleven top leaders (Imoudu, Odeyemi, S.U. Bassey, J.U. Akpan, R.A. Isagua, J.O. Orotunde, S.O. Odeniran, P.A. Nwaneri, N.J. Sule and Wahab Goodluck) from further engaging in trade union activities. Conspicuously absent from the list of banned names was Alhaji Adebola. The White Paper concluded rather punctiliously:

> The Federal Government therefore has responsibility to take reasonable measures not only to enforce the fiduciary duties of trade union officials and ensure internal trade union democracy, but also to strike at the source of untrammelled power exercised by trade union leaders and submit their power to reasonable and civilised regulation

---

[214] Ibid., 15 December, 1975.
[215] *New African*, June 1977, p.533.
[216] *West Africa*. 5 January, 1976, p.22.
[217] List of Officers of the NLC 1975; document in my possession.
[218] Mr. X, top official of Federal Ministry of Labour, Lagos. Momodu, interview, Lagos, 1977.

> ... To this end, Government intends to stop the activities of criminal elements who force their way into the trade union movement and exploit the workers whom they pretend to serve. Racketeering, abuse of office, personality cult, politicisation, corruption, conflicts of interests and similar malpractices will be stamped out through appropriate legislation in the trade union movement...[219]

In pursuance of other aims and showing renewed interest in the labour movement, the Government in September 1976 appointed one Michael Abiodun, former senior official of the Ministry of Labour, as 'Administrator Trade Union Affairs'. He was saddled with the responsibility of appointing union delegates to seminars and conferences abroad, drawing up a code of induct for trade unionists, supervising the restructuring of the 'house unions' to industrial unions and drawing up a model constitution for the projected trade unions.[220] By February 1978, the Administrator of Trade Union Affairs had created a total of seventy industrial trade unions, forty-three for junior staff, eighteen for senior staff and nine for employers.[221] The government was to get involved in the appointment of full-time officials for the unions top labour leaders argued against the exclusive determination of such an exercise by a panel of trade unionists 'as trade unionists so appointed would have ambitions, it would be unfair to appoint them to preside over the fate of their colleagues – some of whom were openly not on good terms.'[222]

The NLC was re-inaugurated on 18 February, 1978. At the ceremony the government representative, Brigadier Yar'Adua announced that the Congress would be provided with necessary financial support 'in the form that would not prejudice the independence of the organisation.'[223] It was difficult to see how this could be achieved though technically possible for government influence to taper off as a compulsory check-off system gained ground and as the NLC depended on workers' contributions for its survival. One was hardly left in doubt in the end as to the government's definition of NLC's future role:

> ...the relationship between the Federal Military Government and the NLC should be one of partnership in progress, without prejudice to the overriding responsibility of the Government to preserve the security and peace of the nation...The Congress should adopt a

[219] Progressive Front for the Labour Movement Press Release, Lagos. 15 December, 1975, p. 1.

[220] Other members were Dr. A.A. Adeogun (Associate Professor of Law at Lagos University), C.O. Spiropoulous (Chartered Accountant) and Alhaji Dan Madami (Commissioner of Police).

[221] Adebiyi Report, *op. cit.*, p.8.

[222] Adebiyi Proceedings, vo l.7., p.20.

[223] Federal Military Government's Views on Report of the Tribunal of Inquiry into the Activities of Trade Unions, Federal Ministry of Information, Lagos, 1977, pp. 4-5.

> rational and conciliatory approach in industrial disputes. Conflicts should not be resolved either by "artificially imposed conditions or by free play of economic forces"... and ... union leaders are warned against "unrestrained use of economic power, and exhibitions of intransigence, violence and blackmail in the conduct of trade disputes..."[224]

As of March 1978, the NLC started out with a projected budget of 5 million for its first year with each of its forty-two unions receiving ₦50,000 for salaries, education and vehicles for full-time officials.[225] After twenty-eight years, Nigeria now boasts of an all-embracing central labour organization and a new phase has begun in the chequered history of the Nigerian trade union movement.

Summary Chart of Factionalisation

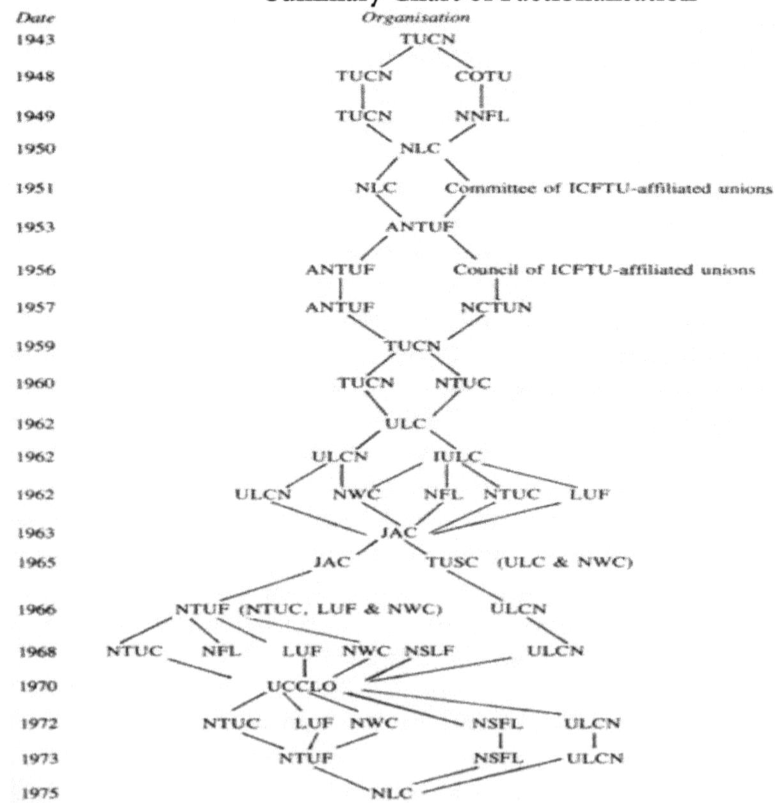

---

[224] *'New African'*, June 1977, p.531. He was assisted by Alhaji A. Dangiwa (a lecturer at Ahmadu Bello University who later became the first General Secretary of the reconstituted NLC), S.O. Sonubi, (Acting head of Dept. of Adult Education, University of Ibadan) Alhaji B. Daroda.

[225] *West Africa*, 13 March, 1978, p.493.

UNITED LABOUR CONGRESS (ULC)

Like in most labour movements, membership of one or two central labour organisations hardly eliminates differences in orientation, political preferences and strategies. On 18 December 2016, the NLC broke into two factions; its twenty-five affiliates, including some of the Trade Union Congress (TUC) declared themselves affiliates of a rival United Labour Congress (ULC).[226] Among other issues, apparently Ajaero had refused to step down for Ayuba Wabba in the wake of the disputed outcome of the March 2015 NLC's National Delegates Conference in Abuja. A good deal of altercations went on between both sides on several socio-political issues and several prominent labour leaders, including Governor Adams Oshiomhole, tried to reconcile both parties but to no avail. It was generally held that the ULC was more receptive to the federal government's approach to solving the petroleum subsidy and economic challenges, while Ayuba Wabba and NLC opted for a nationwide, not so successful, strike in respect of the subsidy issue. Both sides seemed quite unable to fully and effectively mobilise workers and trades unions for nearly five years during which the rift subsisted. However and finally in July 2020, an agreement was brokered that brought back the twenty-five affiliates to the NLC with Joe Ajaero, its President, appointed Deputy-President of the NLC. In 2023, Joe Ajaero become the President of the NLC

THE SENIOR STAFF CONSULTATIVE ASSOCIATION OF NIGERIA

Introduction

We here tell the story of the rise, formation and development of a central body specially meant to watch over the interests of a stratum of white-collar employees, the senior staff. Before we do so, however, the narration should rightly be prefaced by some general remarks on the historical antecedents, no matter how sketchy, as not everyone might be familiar with early Nigerian labour history.

Workers organizations had been in existence in the public sector since the mid-1870s in the Crown Colony of Lagos which was occupied and ruled

---

226 Academic Staff Union of Research Institutions (ASURI), Association of Nigeria Aviation Professionals (ANAP) Chemical and Non-Metallic Products Senior Staff Association of Nigeria (CANMPSSAN), Fitters Senior Staff Association of Nigeria (FISSAN), Iron and Steel Senior Staff Association of Nigeria (ISSSAN), Metal Products Senior Staff Association of Nigeria (MEPROSSAN), National Association of Aircraft Pilots and Engineers (NAAPE), National Union of Banks, Insurance and Financial Institutions Employees (NUBIFIE), National Union of Electricity Employees (NUEE), Nigeria Union of Mine Workers (NUMW), Nigeria Union of Petroleum and Natural Gas Worker (NUPENG), Nigeria Union of Railwaymen (NUR), National Union of Shop and Distributive Employees (NUSDE), Precision, Electrical and Related Equipment Senior Staff Association (PRESESSA), Steel and Engineering Workers' Union of Nigeria (SEWUN)

by Britain from 1862. But most of these organizations were short-lived, small and not well-managed on a regular basis, and did not receive much official encouragement either till early 1930s when Britain had begun to colonize Nigeria as a whole and a sizeable wage labour force had emerged.[227] In the early 1930s, the more militant and better organized 'technical' workers in railways and marine had broken away from the Civil Service Union, inaugurated in 1912, to form separate unions in 1931 and 1936 respectively. There seemed to have been three main sources of tension at the time within the budding labour movement, and around which disagreements eventually coalesced. The first was an uneasy state of relations between largely 'clerical' group on the one hand, and artisans or 'technical'. The latter group included in its ranks plumbers, electricians, masons, welders, fitters, drivers, apprentices in various trades, and suchlike 'skilled and semi-skilled' persons. Differences between the two groups were reflected in general outlook and perception of social status and place within the colonial order, relative willingness or unwillingness to embark upon direct industrial action, negotiating technique, internal cohesion, and leadership style. As can be expected, the clerical group saw itself in superior terms, both socially and economically and mostly preferred writing petitions to other forms of protests.[228]

The second cleavage was between employees in the main civil service proper and those gainfully employed in the periphery of it and some of whom sometimes straddled the private sector. The teachers were representative of the latter, mainly employed in schools established by various Christian and Islamic religious organizations as state owned or 'government colleges' and primary schools constituted a small percentage. They formed the Nigerian Union of Teachers in 1931 which retained its autonomy and relative inactivity till only recently.

The third cleavage was between the top and better placed African employees and the bulk of the lower paid and occasional or daily-paid employees. Right through 1900 to mid-1930s, the better-placed African employees dominated the leadership of the labour movement, which was still mainly a public sector affair, until those in marine, railways, and teachers formed their separate organizations as earlier remarked. Petitions, aside from demonstrations over 'war bonus' during the First World War (1914-1919), were the preferred mode of protest by this leadership, and 'on-

---

[227] Some details in Cohen, R. & Hughes, A., 'Towards the emergence of a Nigerian Working Class, 1897-1939', Occasional Paper Series D, No.7, Faculty of Commerce and Social Science, University of Birmingham, 1971. An abridged version is contained in R. Cohen *et al* (eds.) *Peasants and Proletarians,* Hutchinson University Library, 1979.

[228] This was how the leadership of the Civil Service Union was characterized. See Yesufu, T.M., *An Introduction to Industrial Relations in Nigeria,* OUP/NISER, 1962 and Ananaba, W., *The Trade Union Movement in Nigeria,* Ethiope, Benin City, 1969.

strike' pledges were faithfully met for most of the time. Obviously, such a situation could not last for too long as younger and more aggressive men swelled the ranks of the employed (and of the unemployed) between 1930s and 1950s.

Perhaps not too surprising, the first central labour organisation was formed by 'technical' workers. Against a background of severe economic difficulties which accompanied the outbreak of the Second World War, and because of increasing problems of co-ordination, the more active 'technical' workers formed the first federation of unions in the public service called the African Civil Servants Technical Workers' Union (ACSTWU) in 1941 and which had twelve affiliated unions in 1942. Akpala (1963) observed that the ACSTWU had 'control over trade union questions including communication with Government over bargaining points.'[229] The ACSTWU organized a meeting in Lagos in November 19542 at which a more comprehensive body, the Federated Trades Unions of Nigeria (FTUN) was inaugurated, and which changed its name at the July 1943 conference to the Trades Union Congress of Nigeria (TUC). A few large unions, including the Nigerian Union of Teachers, did not become members of the TUC. The NUT preferred to 'affiliate' to the British National Union of Teachers instead, having been 'advised' by the latter to stay out of the TUC.[230]

Senior staff associations themselves emerged in large numbers in the 1950s and 1960s since not many Nigerian employees had been became 'senior staff' in any great numbers in the 1930s and 1940s in both the private and public sectors. Indeed, the public utilities or 'parastatals' themselves did not fully come on their own till early 1960s, only established in late 1950s. The rapid 'Nigerianisation' of positions in public sector through the politics of decolonization (internal self-government, regionalism, and all that), actual political independence, and the dramatic expansion of both public and private sectors of the economy in the 1970s contributed in no small measure to the growth of senior staff associations. Line 'house unions' of lower paid employees which were formed around branches of companies, the senior staff associations which existed in this period were mostly under the influence and outright control, in many instances, of respective managements where they were allowed to exist. Not much evidence has been found to support the incidence of active unionism on the part of any of the senior staff associations. They seemed to be mostly petition writing organizations and tended to focus their attention on eradicating or minimizing discrimination in remuneration on racial grounds, improving on their situations within the establishment, and on increasing the number of Nigerians in more responsible positions.

---

[229] Akpala, A., *Prospects of Small Trade Unions*, Eastern Nigeria Publishing Corporation, Enugu, 1963, p.18.
[230] Ananaba, W., *The Trade Union Movement in Nigeria*, *op. cit.*, p.41-42.

Their focus was to change somewhat in the 1970s due to many factors, including: (a) rapid expansion in white collar jobs and thus dilution of this class of labour with attendant concern for differentials and other status attributes; (b) a decade of relative economic boom which ironically brought about dramatic diminution of both status and earnings of salaried persons as compared to the emergent commercial, trading and contractor-dominated values in society; (c) two decades of unparalleled corruption in the body politic, the 1980s being further complicated by national economic mismanagement, economic depression, equally dramatic loss of civil rights and liberties under military regimes, were all factors which served to heighten protest potential and criticisms. Two immediate consequences were (i) increased organization among white collar workers of all grades, and (ii) more outspokenness even on the part of such groups as medical doctors, nurses, teachers, lawyers, and their organizations, persons who have been used to being regarded as 'conservative'; and (d) the Trade Unions (Amendment) Decree No. 17 of 1978 which gave official recognition to senior staff and professional associations but prevented them from affiliating to the Nigerian Labour Congress (NLC), a central labour organization whose membership was thereby legally restricted to the 42 industrial unions of 'junior workers'. This being the case, it was only a matter of time before senior staff associations formed their own central body. Some of the reasons offered by the president of the Senior Staff Consultative Association of Nigeria (SESCAN) for the growth of senior staff associations are revealing in themselves and substantially agree with what we have observed above:

> Let me reiterate the fact that the emergence of senior staff unionism was dictated by the expediency of individual development. Faced like any other worker with the problems of rapid changes in their positions at the workplace and affected by organizational, technological changes with the attendant problems of mounting pressure of work; loss of responsibility and authority, retrenchments and an erosion of their living standards, the senior staff unions emerged to defend their members' rights as workers and to improve on their terms and conditions of employment. It is also a major objective of the senior staff enhance the practice of industrial democracy through the evolution of a genuine culture of trade unionism.[231]

The Formation of SESCAN

Despite the provisions of the 1978 Trade Unions (Amendment) Decree No. 17 which sought to prevent senior staff associations from affiliating to the

[231] Address delivered by Engr. Femi Kila, President-General of SESCAN at the 1st triennial delegates' conference on Thursday 22 September, 1988 at the Durbar Hotel, Badagry Expressway, Lagos, p.5.

NLC, several attempts were made by officials of many of such associations to disregard the said provisions. Although there seemed to be other reasons for the late formation of SESCAN, this disposition served to delay its formation. But in the end only two associations, one of which was the Academic Staff Union of Universities (ASUU), formally announced their decision to affiliate to the NLC, a decision that was partly responsible for the proscription of ASUU by the government in 1987.

Given the legal and administrative difficulties in the way of senior staff associations affiliating to the NLC, views were divided among executive committees of the various senior staff associations on how to surmount such problems and thus on the issue of affiliation itself. The attempt in 1978 to form the Federation of Senior Staff Associations of Nigeria (FESSAN) failed largely on account of this or, according to the organization, 'due to personal differences and aspirations.'[232]

By 1985 a good many of these associations had begun reconciling themselves to the possibility of affiliating to the NLC being a long-term goal, and began serious moves towards forming their own central organization. To this end a conciliatory meeting of most of the factions took place on 4 February, 1985 at the secretariat of the Construction and Civil Engineering Senior Staff Association at 79 Tejuosho Street in Surulere, Lagos. A seven-man steering committee was elected and charged with the responsibility of (a) preparatory work against formal launching and inaugural Delegates Conference with a target date; (b) the furtherance of efforts at registration; (c) raising funds for an effective take-off of the proposed Federation of Senior Staff Association of Nigeria (FESSAN); and (d) make contact with other groups or associations which should be in the fold, and also contact the Federal Ministry of Employment, Labour and Productivity.[233]

The inaugural Delegates Conference was eventually held on Thursday, 2 May, 1985 at the Federal Palace Hotel, Victoria Island, Lagos and chaired by Chief J. Adelusi, the proprietor of a chain of pharmacy shops. An executive committee and a central working committee of FESSAN were duly democratically elected.[234]

---

[232] *Secretariat Report on the Activities of SESCAN 1985-1988,* 1988, p.1.

[233] Ibid. Members of the steering committee were Engr. Femi Kila as president, Mr. A.D. Okutade as secretary, and Chief A.B.O. Oga, Dr. Femi Oladimeji, Mr. J.O. Akintola, Mr. H.E.R. Ozegbe, and Mr. Olawole Adewuyi as members.

[234] The elected members of the executive committee and of the central working committee were Engr. Femi Kila as president-general, Chubby Nwagbara as 1st deputy president-general, J.D. Arogundade as 2nd deputy president-general, Femi Oladimeji as 3rd deputy president, Dele Ariyo as assistant secretary-general (organization), Lola Olanipekun as assistant secretary-general (publicity), S.A.O. Sokeyo as assistant secretary-general (education and industrial relations), M.A. Babayemi as National Treasurer, Prince M.A.O Adejiyan as Financial Secretary, Mr. E.A.E. Bassey as Internal Auditor, Messrs. Tunde Oyelola, M.O. Agboola and V.O. Omoare as Trustees, and Messrs. H.E.R. Ozegbe and

The Politics of Registration

About the first step the organization took was to apply for registration with the Registrar of Trade Unions but who seemed unable or unwilling to either reach a decision or convey one. An apprehensive FESSAN then established 'a registration committee', comprising the seven members of the former steering committee, the secretary-general, an assistant secretary and a trustee, to pursue the matter more vigorously. After several meetings with the Registrar of Trade Unions, all the Registration Committee got was that 'the matter was still being looked into', and with such a vague reply the Committee lobbied most top officials of the Federal Ministry of Employment, Labour and Productivity, particularly the Assistant Director Trade Union Services, and the Director of Industrial Relations but to no avail.[235] When the Committee sought a meeting with the Minister himself, hoping to pass on to him their own document which contained what was though to be reasoned and convincing argument on why the body should be registered, the minister declined it audience on the ground that the FESSAN was not 'a registered body'. Fortunately, the permanent secretary at the time, Mr. Chikelu, met with the Committee on Tuesday, 15 April, 1986 and made it abundantly clear that existing laws could not permit the registration of another central labour organization in the country since the NLC was the only such legal body. And should FESSAN still wished to be registered at all, it would only be possible under the Land Perpetual Act Cap. 98 of 1958 but with the Ministry of Internal Affairs, and that FESSAN would have to change its name to the Senior Staff Consultative Association of Nigerian (SESCAN)! This suggestion was accepted by the Committee and at the meeting of the national executive council meeting of FESSAN on 24 April, 1986, a resolution to that effect was passed and SESCAN was duly registered on 12 December, 1986. Needless mentioning that this mode of registration has been considered most unsatisfactory by SESCAN. In the view of the organization, it has been a 'temporary evolution of FESSAN to SESCAN', and that 'this evolution is regarded as temporary since it is considered a stop-gap in our bid to get a Central Body for all the registered senior staff associations officially recognised and registered under the labour statutes.'[236]

The official aims and objects of SESCAN, which remained the same as those of its predecessor, FESSAN, were (a) to organise and unite all registered senior staff associations in Nigeria into a single entity; (b) to promote and safeguard the economic and social welfare of its members, preserving and extending their civic rights and liberties within a free and

---

A.O. Aigbe as Ex-Officio members.

235 Ibid., p.4.

236 Ibid., p.5.

democratic society; (c) to establish a common front on all matters affecting all the registered senior staff associations in Nigeria; (d) to secure an equitable observance of all agreements reached between SESCAN and all employers of labour, and among themselves; (e) to promote and support legislations in the interest of the senior staff associations in Nigeria; (f) to render such assistance as shall be consistent with members' interests; (g) to encourage the participation of members in commerce, industry, mines, agriculture and labour at national and international levels, including the printing and publishing of the Association's newspapers, journals, books or any other undertaking, industrial or otherwise, with the sole purpose of furthering the interests and welfare of all the registered senior staff associations in Nigeria; (h) to render all possible contributions to the well-being of the government, all employers of labour, and therefore ensure maximum productivity and economic sufficiency; (i) to promote and establish cultural, co-operative, and social activities; and (j) such other objects as are lawful and are not inconsistent with the spirit and practice of trade unionism in Nigeria.

Structure, Government and Administration

The structure of SESCAN follows closely that of the NLC but with some modifications. According to its constitution, the government of the organization is vested in the (a) national delegates conference, (b) the national executive council, (c) the central working committee, and (d) the secretariat. The delegates conference is supposed to hold every three years, and delegates are drawn from constituent members. The body lays down policies and elects the national executive committee. The first triennial delegates conference took place in Lagos on 22 September, 1988 at which a new executive committee was elected.[237]

The President-General, assisted by three deputies, heads the National Executive Council, the other national officers (treasurer, financial secretary, secretary-general, deputy secretary-general, and the three assistant secretary-generals) making up the rest of the team. This team guides the organization in-between triennial delegates' conferences and executes policies approved there.

Immediately below comes the Central Working Committee which includes, along with members of the executive committee, the three trustees, two ex-officio members, the internal auditor, financial secretary, national

[237] The new executive comprised Engr. Femi Kila as President-General, Mr. C.O. Nwagbara, Dr. Femi Oladimeji, and Mr. S.A.O. Sowemimo as 1st, 2nd and 3rd Deputy President-Generals, Comrade Sole Iji as Secretary-General, Mr. Lola Olanipekun as Deputy Secretary-General, Messrs. M. Lawal, J.A. Kolawole and B.O. Adewunmi as Assistant Secretary-Generals for organization, education/training, and research/industrial relations respectively.

treasurer and the secretariat. The secretariat itself revolves around the secretary-general with his three assistants in charge of the departments of organization, publicity, and education and industrial relations respectively.

Membership

The membership of SESCAN is voluntary and open to all the registered senior staff associations. There is also provision for 'associate member' status for non-affiliates who may be corporate bodies or individuals. At formation some 18 senior staff associations were members, two others joining since then to bring the grand total to 20 by 1991. The members were:

- National Association of Aircraft Pilots and Engineers
- Nigerian Merchant Navy Officers' and Water Transport Senior Staff Association
- Association of Senior Civil Servants of Nigeria
- Association of Senior Staff of Banks, Insurance and Financial Institutions
- Food, Beverage and Tobacco Senior Staff Association
- Shop and Distributive Trade Senior Staff Association
- Construction and Civil Engineering Senior Staff Association
- Petroleum and Natural Gas Senior Staff Association
- Chemical and Non-metallic Products Senior Staff Association
- Footwear, Leather and Rubber Products Senior Staff Association
- Textile, Garment and Tailoring Senior Staff Association
- Automobile, Boatyard, Transport Equipment and Allied Senior Staff Association
- Senior Staff Association of Statutory Corporations and Government Owned Companies
- Senior Staff Association of Universities, Teaching Hospitals, Research Institutes and Associated Institutions
- Metal Products Senior Staff Association of Nigeria
- Precision, Electrical and Related Equipment Senior Staff Association
- Hotel and Personal Services Senior Staff Association
- Agricultural and Allied Senior Staff Association
- Electricity and Gas Senior Staff Association
- Metallic and Non-metallic Mines Senior Staff Association

The four organisations which are yet to take up their membership of SESCAN are the Senior Staff Association of Shipping, Clearing and Forwarding Agencies, the Academic Staff Union of Universities, the Paper and Paper Products Senior Staff Association, and the Nigerian Union of Pharmacists, Medical Technologists and Professions Allied to Medicine. But a newly formed Air Transport Services Senior Staff Association is likely to become a member once it is duly registered. Even then, considerable loss in membership by affiliates has occurred due to continuous massive retrenchments in both private and public sectors since 1982.

Finances

SESCAN, like most other trades unions and the NLC, derives most of its funds from membership application fees, membership dues, levies and from other special contributions. Application fee is ₦500, and members should pay monthly dues of 10% of their own respective monthly subscriptions to SESCAN. Associate members may themselves also pay any subscriptions and levies that might be required of them. But the initial attempt to make affiliates pay a monthly contribution of between ₦250 and ₦500 according to respective sizes and financial strength yielded poor results because 'of inability to define or identify which are the large Associations and principally because of the general wish to maintain a uniform rate which would be affordable by all the affiliates irrespective of size.'[238] The monthly contribution by affiliates was then fixed at ₦150 with effect from 1 July, 1987.

Despite this, things were a bit difficult financially for most of the time, SESCAN relying on special levies and on one or two of its affiliates to meet some of its obligations. The first reason to account for this state of affairs was that most affiliates were in arrears of their payments because: (a) they were having financial problems themselves as a result of massive layoffs of their members, thus dwindling resources with which to run their own organizations and programmes; and (b) the government's decision in 1986 to make the check-off system of collecting membership dues voluntary for senior staff associations made matters much worse, some affiliates taking full advantage of this legislation not to pay anything.

SESCAN IN ACTION

We take a closer look at SESCAN in respect of some of its activities and actual policies to permit us a clearer understanding of its effectiveness and general position and relevance in the Nigerian labour movement. Largely for convenience we proceed in the following manner: (a) internal working; (b) relations with affiliates; (c) relations with rest of the organized labour movement; and (d) relations with the State.

Internal Workings

The membership of the major organs of SESCAN was unusual in some respects, the national executive council (NEC) being an integral part of the central working committee (CWC). It meant that the CWC could not really act as a check against the national executive as it in reality turned out to a

[238] *Secretariat Report, op. cit.*, p.8.

slightly expanded version of the latter. Perhaps the CWC was never intended to act as a watchdog because the meetings of both organs were merged and both organs now met monthly as one body, the National Executive Council.

Secondly, the composition of both organs seemed designed not to encourage effective participation by affiliates since the principal officers of individual senior staff associations were neither members of the NEC nor of the CWC. The only forum left open to them was thus the triennial delegates' conference, although the NEC's meeting were after some time 'open to national presidents and general secretaries of affiliates'. The absence of their *institutionalized* attendance left such much to their personal preferences and convenience. It was not surprising therefore that many affiliates did not show much interest and poor attendance became such a problem that the secretariat was forced to propose to the first triennial delegates' conference in 1988 that: (a) the attendance at NEC meetings include the national presidents and general secretaries of affiliates or their representatives; (b) and failure by any affiliate to attend such meetings should attract a fine; and (c) the CWC meetings be held at least twice a month, and as the exigency may dictate.

The Secretariat functioned as it best could under difficult conditions. Two out of the three assistant secretary-generals, for organization and education and industrial relations left their respective senior staff associations and their positions with SESCAN, a situation which obviously affected the growth and development of administrative procedures and hampered effective co-ordination and monitoring of activities. Second, 'problem of communication arising mainly from the locations of the offices of the secretary-general, the deputy secretary-general, and the assistant secretary-general (publicity).'[239]

And, third, 'the non-availability of the officers at times when they were mostly required for consultation and urgent assignments.'[240] A situation in which the crucial officers of a 'secretariat' have different offices located in different parts of a city and who were personally very busy on their jobs and professions could not be the best of circumstances for any organization. Indeed, the facilities and support staff were not readily available, including full-time secretary/typist, typewriter and 'minor office equipments.' The secretary-general fell back on the facilities provided by some of its affiliates, particularly the Food, Beverage and Tobacco Senior Staff Association and those of the Construction and Civil Engineering Senior Staff Association.

---

[239] *Secretariat Report*, p.7.
[240] Ibid., p.7.

SESCAN and Affiliates

It was indicated earlier how the membership of the CWC of SESCAN did not formally include the leadership of individual senior staff associations and this tended to weaken the CWC and the national executive council in respect of their affiliates. As far as SESCAN's secretariat was concerned,

> the above categorization of affiliates of SESCAN are by no means true reflection of members' commitment to the organization. Some affiliates have failed to address themselves diligently to their obligations toward SESCAN. This is reflected in their non-attendance of SESCAN meetings and conference, as well as non-regular payment of monthly contributions and levies.[241]

Be that as it may, there has been a 'growing spirit of brotherhood and comradeship among its affiliates and their leadership.'[242]

By and large SESCAN appeared not all the time that successful in sorting out problems and differences within and between some of its affiliates. Two prominent cases were the report by the Nigerian Merchant Navy Officers and Water Transport Senior Staff Association on the refusal of the Nigeria Ports Authority (NPA) to allow it organise its members, and the conflict between the national president and the general secretary of the Agriculture and Allied Senior Staff Association. Apparently in both instances, enough information was not given to SESCAN officials and according to them there was not given to SESCAN officials and according to them there was 'non-co-operation from the parties concerned.' As can be expected, the affiliates sought to guard their autonomy, a predictable development that nevertheless did not go down well with SESCAN. Its secretariat again observed in this regard that 'as an umbrella organization SESCAN has a constitutional duty to ensure not only its cohesion, but also that of its affiliates without interfering with their internal operations. There is, however, the need to overcome the underlying suspicion that SESCAN would want to interfere with the internal affairs of affiliates.'[243]

SESCAN and Organized Labour

The official policies of SESCAN towards the so-called industrial unions of junior workers and to the NLC show a high degree of ambiguity, embodying both rivalry and complementarity. On the one hand, SESCAN officials seemed unhappy over several developments, namely: (a) that industrial unions were duly recognized in law to be trade unions of workers as if members of senior staff associations were not; (b) that the NLC is recognized

---

241 *Secretariat Report, op. cit.*, p.6.
242 Ibid.
243 Ibid., p.13.

in law as the only central labour organisation; (c) that the industrial unions could affiliate with the NLC and senior staff associations could not; (d) that the federal government uneven-handedly gave financial assistance to industrial unions to enable them meet their initial administrative and other obligations in 1977-78; (e) that the government has tended to invite persons from industrial unions and the NLC to participate in many tripartite bodies, including the Industrial Arbitration Panel, the National Labour Advisory Council, the Nigerian delegation to the ILO Annual Conference in Geneva, and the National Institute for Labour Studies in Ilorin; and (f) that the Federal Government made a refund to junior workers alone of monies deducted compulsorily from wages of all wage earners under the provisions of the Economic Recovery Emergency Decree;[244] and (g) only industrial unions of junior workers are legally entitled to utilize the automatic check-off system for deriving union dues and also enjoy compulsory membership.

On the other hand, officials of SESCAN sought strenuously to have senior staff associations affiliate with the NLC despite Section 33 (2) of the Trades Unions (Amendment) Act No. 22 of 1978 which expressly forbade it. An impressive delegation of the organisation was always sent to the Delegates Conference of the NLC, showed solidarity in many little ways, aside from denouncing the government when it temporarily proscribed the NLC in 1988 and imposed a Sole Administrator of Trades Unions, Michael Ogunkoya, to manage its affairs until fresh elections could be held, and generally encouraged its affiliates to achieve closer ties with industrial unions of junior workers.

It is not difficult to see the predicament in which the SESCAN has been caught. The effectiveness of the various legislations aimed at separating senior staff from junior workers cannot be denied, and they seem to have created a situation for SESCAN where demands become sectional and remain distinguishable from general grievances, and certain demands can only be justified by stressing differences between it, the NLC, and the rest of organized labour. For example, it was contented that 'mature and well articulated contributions have characterised the trade union activities of the senior staff associations', and that 'the incidence of man-hours lost as a result of strike actions, if any, by the senior staff associations, and carried out jointly or individually from 1978 to date, could be counted on the finger tips.'[245] This is, as can be seen, then leads sometimes to invidious

[244] The Babangida administration declared a 15-month State of Economic Emergency in 1986, and one of the attendant measures was compulsory deductions of varying proportions from employees' wage towards an Economic Recovery Fund. All importers were also required to pay 15 per cent of the value of imports into this Fund. At the end of the period, industrial unions of junior workers mounted protests against lack of movement in wages, and to which the government responded by refunding all monies deducted in the 15-month period.

[245] President-General Address, *op.cit.*, p.6.

comparisons in order to establish government's partiality in favour of the NLC and of industrial unions. These issues are brought out more clearly in our discussion of the relations between SESCAN and the State.

SESCAN and the State

Relations between SESCAN and agencies of the State would seem to have been coloured by the inherited policies or prejudices of public sector elites and of the political class itself. The official policy of separating white collar or senior staff from the other employees was first institutionalised in the public sector with the establishment of different Whitley Councils or committees for them in 1947. Hitherto the distinction was first between 'European' and 'African' positions, and subsequently 'established' as against 'unestablished' or daily-paid African workers.

Private colonial employers did not have much problem in this regard as only a handful of their employees earned the status of 'senior staff' even in the 1950s. Members of management were expatriates and the differential use of or access to company welfare and recreational facilities in and outside of premises was on that basis too. When a sufficient number of indigenous senior staff began to emerge, created by departing expatriates in a somewhat enlightened but self-serving gradual indigenization policy, the first generation of those that made that status imitated their European predecessors and behaved likewise by discriminating against the rest of the workforce. The first set of senior staff associations therefore turned out to be very exclusive bodies of some Africans that rose through the ranks and supervised by the few remaining expatriates.

Those senior staff associations which emerged in the late sixties and seventies were of a different sort due to economic, social, and political changes brought about by the Civil War, oil boom and the dramatic expansion of the public sector as a result of massive investments, official indigenisation policy on ownership and management structure, an unprecedented purge of public servants who ended up in the private sector, the rapid growth of the private sector itself and increased competition within it, and the influx of young graduates into both public and private sectors.

The upshot was that public and private employers were faced with more restive and, later, much more active senior staff associations, whose members were better educated, more articulate and more assertive, more politically aware, who were in the policy-generating (if not actual policy-making) group, and more likely to experience relative deprivation and loss of status, and were thus the most devastating critics of any management and government.

One initial step taken by public and private employers was to seek to contain this category of labour by institutionally isolating them from junior workers. Within private enterprises, managements insisted that any employee promoted into the supervisory and high positions could not belong to house unions, bodies which were themselves small and weak and unable to stand up to a determined management. State authorities formally reinforced this policy in 1971, against a background of fairly widespread post-Adebo labour protests, by stating categorically that 'no member of the staff above the rank of supervisor may join a trade union of any of the junior staff or participate either directly or indirectly in the activities of such a union. Senior staff, in their own right, may form an association or a trade union of their own to protect their right.'[246]

The State next turn its attention to central trade unionism where there were four competing organizations. Decree 31 of 1973 listed conditions for the formation and registration of any new central body, and such a projected body must have at least 40 per cent total membership of all registered trades unions. The decree also sought to regulate admission of further trades unions to membership of registered federation of trades unions at the same time', and regulated the further admission of labour unions to membership of central labour organizations and as well as their amalgamation.[247] This marked a watershed in central trade unionism in Nigeria because such bodies for the first time came fully under legal control and regulation, the main object being to influence the structure and functions of such organisations and not a reduction in their numbers since the latter made for easier control as any could be played against the other despite the official recognition extended to one of them.

Having separate organizations for white-collar workers or senior staff is not new, practised for many decades in Sweden, Britain and several other countries. The difference here, like the two-party system for politicians, was that state authorities, set out deliberately to create such more as a divisive and labour control measure. Section I (i) (a) of the Trades Unions (Amendment) Decree No. 22 of 1978 says that 'for any avoidance of doubt, no executive or senior staff shall be a member of or hold office in a trade union whose members are workers of a rank junior to his own, but such executive or senior staff may form and be members of or hold office in a trade union workers of equal or higher rank than his own.' Another clause then specified twenty-four (24) senior staff associations which could neither affiliate with the NLC nor form their own over-arching central body although the Michael Abiodun Commission which restructured the trades unions in 1977 had recommended such a body.

Despite the earlier provision, ASUU, legally described as a senior staff association, was predisposed in the early 1980s to affiliating with the NLC, a

---

[246] *Trade Disputes (Central Bank of Nigeria Arbitration Award) Confirmation Order* 1971, *Supplement to the Official Gazette* No. 3, Vol. 58, dated 21 January, 1971.

[247] For details, Federal Ministry of Information, *Official Gazette*, No. 38, Vol. 6, 24 July, 1973.

decision that did not go down well with the military government. Largely to frustrate this decision, to discourage other senior staff associations that might have been toying with the same idea, and to punish ASUU, the military government came out with the Trades Unions (Miscellaneous Provisions) Decree No. 17 in 1986 which (a) barred senior staff associations from utilizing the automatic check-off system for deriving union dues; (b) re-emphasized the provisions of the Trades Unions (Amendment) Act that the senior staff associations could not affiliate with the NLC; and (c) made membership of senior staff associations voluntary.

The logic behind this legislation was quite simple: if membership was voluntary and members paid their dues voluntarily, membership would be reduced and dues collected were therefore likely to be less than what were hitherto deducted by employers and handed over to the respective associations. Financially weaker senior staff associations would thus be less active, less efficiently organized and presumably less threatening.

Several senior staff associations did have some problems with collecting dues as a consequence of the decree, although many of them attempted to circumvent the decree by getting their members to sign documents giving the associations the powers to deduct and receive their dues at source. But more damage was done to their finances and administration, including that of SESCAN, by the deepening economic recession and the structural adjustment programme adopted by the Babangida regime in 1986. The loss of thousands of jobs through layoffs and redundancies left both SESCAN and many senior staff associations much the poorer, even if it were possible to collect dues with ease and which was not so either.

Predictably, SESCAN took a very dim view of Decree 17, enough for its national executive council to set up a committee to work out the legislation's likely adverse implications for the organization. The committee's report, accompanied by a protest letter, was then sent to General Babangida, and copies sent to both the members of the Armed Forces Ruling Council and Council of Ministers, and also to 'other well meaning Nigerians having sympathy towards the cause of SESCAN.'[248] Requests to see General Babangida were denied but audience was granted by the Minister of Employment, Labour and Productivity on December, 1986 to a delegation of SESCAN. At this meeting, the Minister promised vainly, among many other promises, to look into the possibility of restoring the automatic check-off system.

The other state functionaries lobbied between 1986 and 1988 by SESCAN delegation were the Chief of General Staff, the Minister of Education, the Secretary to the Government, and the Minister of Justice and Attorney

[248] Secretariat Report on the Activities of SESCAN for the period 1985-1988, 22 September 1988, p. 10.

General of the Federation. These attempts failed to produce the desire results despite promises made by the public officials concerned, particularly those of the Minister of Justice who at two meetings held on 3 February and 12 June 1988 respectively reassured SESCAN that not only would the issue of restoration of the automatic check-off system be reviewed, but also that a government decision would soon be taken on whether senior staff associations be allowed to affiliate with the NLC or be allowed to have an officially recognized central body.[249] As at February 1992, none of these promises has been kept by state authorities.

One of the commendable rituals performed by various organized interests and voluntary groups at their important or annual or biennial conferences is to publicly undertake extensive review of prevailing economic, social and industrial policies, and ending with recommendations of sorts for official consideration. The harsh economic realities and official policies in response undoubtedly provoked critical comments from many quarters, including SESCAN.

The government's structural adjustment programmes SESCAN thought was clearly unpopular, and 'cost of living has risen disproportionately to the level of incomes; the rate of unemployment has grown at an unprecedented rate in the history of this nation; and the daily or even hourly threat to life and property by men of the underworld has become commonplace ...SESCAN believes that mere existence is not enough!'[250] And that even if the structural adjustment programme was well conceived, 'its implementation has continued to unleash untold hardships on the average citizen' (ibid.) In a wholesale critique of official economic policies at its 1988 Delegates Conference, SESCAN noted that:

> The premature outright ban imposed on the importation of certain essential raw materials has led to shortfalls in production capacity utilisations, and in more cases to outright closures of business concerns arising from the ever-increasing cost of doing business in the country, and inevitably...manifested in the wave of retrenchment exercises which have continued unabated. Even governments (state and federal) have continued to retrench workers in their hundreds and thousands!

Of serious concern to us is the continuous but largely unprecedented decline in the exchange value of the Naira since the inception of the Structural Adjustment Programme. Much as SESCAN identifies itself with the broad aspects of the SAP of the Federal Military Administration, the

---

[249] *Secretariat Report,* p.11.

[250] President-General Address of Engr. Femi Kila at SESCAN's 1st Triennial Delegates Conference, 22 September, 1988, p. 10.

SFEM (now IFEM) component has further worsened the economic fortunes this nation, thus leading to the highly unprecedented level of hardship... The general imports which by implication account for the increasing value of general imports which by implication account for the increasing cost of doing business in Nigeria—the end result of which is the ever increasing level of prices, both of general goods and services within the country.

According to the Federal Office of Statistics, the Composite Consumer Price Index rose by 8.1% (or 53.6 points) between March and April, 1988 to 715.6, using 1975 as base year. The report also indicated that the average percentage increase in the Composite Consumer Index (CCI) for the two months ended April, 1988 stood at 12.6%. Realistically and evidently, from what obtains at the marketplace, the situation is much worse.[251]

The organization's communiqué at the end of the delegates' conference speaks for itself and is reproduced immediately below:

1. that rather than the consistent and deliberate policy of neglecting the Senior Staff in labour matters, the Federal Government should allow the existing senior staff associations to be properly integrated into the Nigerian industrial relations system like their junior counterparts as the activities of these senior staff associations have been characterized by peaceful, mature and well-meaning trade union practices;
2. that the Federal Government should either abrogate the Trades Unions (Miscellaneous Provisions) Decree No. 17 of 1986 which discriminates against the trades unions of senior staff or remove the provisions of part II of the Decree and in its place provide expressly for automatic check-off system in clear terms to enable the senior staff associations functions as veritable social institutions;
3. that short of allowing the senior staff associations to be affiliated to the NLC, the Federal Government should register SESCAN under the Trades Unions Decree as a rallying point for the existing senior staff associations in the same manner as the NLC does make room for a well articulate, mature and purposeful trade unionism much needed in the nation's developmental aspirations;
4. that since the Emergency Economic Recovery deductions aimed at ameliorating the economic plight of the nation had already been refunded to the junior employees and it is apparent that the senior staff are not being held responsible for the nation's plight, SESCAN hereby calls on the Federal Government to refund the deductions to them in order to ensure fair play and justice;
5. that since the economic activities of the country revolve around the value of the Naira and the high exchange rates which have led to the current

[251] President-General Address, p. 12.

high prices of general goods and services, SESCAN therefore calls on the Federal Government to intervene in the foreign exchange market by fixing or standardising the exchange rate of the Naira to ₦2 to $1 (US), such that the prices of goods and services could be brought within the reach of average Nigerians;

6. that SESCAN appeals to the Federal Government to desist from incurring further international debts as the nation is still experiencing untold hardship in servicing its current loans;
7. Finally, SESCAN calls on all Nigerians to eschew all forms of corruption, and mismanagement of our meagre national resources; and to rededicate ourselves to the return-to-civil rule programme of the Federal Military Government so as to ensure the emplacement of a fair, just and more enduring political structure for Nigeria of tomorrow.

For a regime that has shown little appetite and patience for criticism and most unforgiving of critics, SESCAN was unlikely to be endeared to it by such observations. It represented the interests of senior staff associations in Nigeria despite the fact that the government did not recognize it officially. To the officials of the organization itself, the 1977 restructuring exercise was incomplete to the extent that senior staff associations could neither affiliate with the NLC nor create an officially recognised central body of their own. This unfortunate situation, from SESCAN's point of view, has been made worse by government's decision to literally harass senior staff associations. These decisions and the massive retrenchment brought about by the economic recession at the time tended to reduce membership strength, and made for less administratively effective and financially poorer senior staff associations, and which imposed additional constraints on the operations and activities of SESCAN.

THE TRADE UNION CONGRESS OF NIGERIA (TUCN)

A lot of political waters flowed under the bridge between 1985 and 2005, and under President Obasanjo, with increasing pressure from organised labour and political rivals and opponents and also part of political strategy, the federal government allowed the Trade Union Act to be amended to permit the formation of multiple national trade union federations, and for senior staff unions to join any federation of their choice. SESCAN was dissolved, with most of its affiliates forming a new Trade Union Congress of Nigeria, with Peace Obiajulu emerging as President, succeeded by Peter Esele (2007), Bobboi Bala Kaigame (2013), Quadri Olaleye (2019) and Festus Osifo (2022). General Secretaries have been John Kolawole (2005), Musa-Lawal Ozigi (2012) and Nuhu Toro (2022). The TUCN in its external affiliation move became in 2006 a founding affiliate of the International Trade Union Confederation. As at 2020, it had twenty-nine affiliates.[252] Apparently, the TUCN and NLC were the main backers of the Labour Party and its presidential candidate, Peter Obi, in the 2023 Nigerian General Election.

[252] Anacowa Motorcycle Owners' and Riders' Association, Academic Staff Union of Secondary Schools (ASUSS), Association of Freight and Heavy Goods Carriers of Nigeria (AFHGCN), Association of Senior Civil Servants of Nigeria (ASCSN) Association of Senior Staff of Banks, Insurance and Financial Institutions (ASSBIFI), Automobile, Boatyard, Transport, Equipment and Allied Senior Staff Association of Nigeria (AUTOBATE), Bus Conductors' Association of Nigeria (BCAN), Chemical and Non-Metallic Products Senior Staff Association (CANMPSSA), Construction and Civil Engineering Senior Staff Association (CCESSA), Food, Beverage and Tobacco Senior Staff Association (FOBTOB), Footwear, Leather and Rubber Products Senior Staff Association of Nigeria (FWLRPSSA0, Hotel and Personal Services Senior Staff Association of Nigeria (HAPSSSA), National Association of Community Health Practitioners (NACHPN), National Association of Nigerian Professional Footballers (NANPF), National Towing Vehicle Owners' Association (NTVOA), Nigeria Merchant Navy Officer and Water Transport Senior Staff Association (NMNOWTSSA), Nigeria Union of Allied Health Professions (NUAHP), Petroleum and Natural Gas Senior Staff Association of Nigeria (PENGASSAN), Precision Electrical and Related Equipment Senior Staff Association (PERESSA), Pulp, Paper and Paper Products, Printing and Publishing Senior Staff Association of Nigeria (PPAPPPPSSA), Shop and Distributive Trade Senior Staff Association (SHOPDIS), Senior Staff Association of Electricity and Allied Companies (SSEA&AC), Senior Staff Association of Statutory Corporations Government Owned Companies (SSASSCGOC), Senior Staff Association of Shipping, Clearing and Forwarding Agencies (SSASCFA), Senior Staff Association of Universities, Teaching Hospitals, Research, and Associated Institutions (SSAUTHRIAI), Textiles, Garments and Tailoring Senior Staff Association of Nigeria (TGTSSAN), Tricycle Owners' Association of Nigeria (TOAN), Union of Tipper and Quarry Employers of Nigeria (UTQEN)

Chapter 7

THE PARADOXES OF INTERNATIONAL SOLIDARITY IN TRADE UNIONISM 1950-1975

The goals of external interests in trade union activity in the Third World have already been identified as the propagation of models, the infusion of suitable ideological orientations and the creation of technically proficient organisations. To this must be added the concern of employers, like governments, with control of labour and reduction of labour costs.

PROPAGATION OF MODELS

The organizational models external interests held up for adoption by Nigerian ventral labour organizations have, depending on source, been remarkably similar in format to those in Britain, North America and Eastern Europe. The ULCN, NTUC and NWC were fashioned with structural forms displaying he usual hierarchical systems of authority, functions and rules and other regulations. In all three organizations, power was largely concentrated in few hands which in turn were accountable to representatives of vernal interests. Personal relations governed rules and patterns of interaction just is the needs of external interests continuously modified both rules and goals.

In contrast, for example, the Secretary-General of the British TUC is elected by Congress and 'remains in office as long as his work gives satisfaction.'[1] He is assisted by an Assistant General Secretary and coordinates the work of specialist departments, which include Economic, Education, International, organization, Production and Social Insurance. In addition, standing committees are concerned with examining a range of subjects such as incomes policy and other specific developments. These are drawn from a General Council that meets at least once a month. Complementing the above are a number of joint committees which habitually co-opt experts in various fields, enabling the TUC to present alternative policies to either CBI or Government it any point in time.

On paper the Secretariats of all Nigerian central labour organizations have departments and their constitutions make provisions for various committees, though these are rarely set up except when needed to justify an

---

[1] British TUC, *Trade Unionism*, Congress House, London, 1966, p. 7.

unpopular decision. The external factor itself did not actively seek the establishment of competent bureaucracies. These might have made the maintenance of control more difficult, and there were in any case enough funds to pay for services of foreign experts. In addition, labour leaders and staff of congress secretariats were poorly educated (see table below). Trade union education as envisaged by the external factor entailed imparting the essentials about its own system of industrial relations. ULCN and NWC officials were mostly exposed to 'collective bargaining' and the 'role' of trade unions 'in a democratic society', while NTUC, though it participated in a 'collective bargaining' regarded it a device for justifying inherently unfair wages. And there was a tendency for trade unionists who had acquired some training to abandon the labour movement for better-paid jobs in both private and public sectors.[2]

Educational Levels of Central Leadership 1976-77

	ULCN	NTUC	NWC
Graduates	-	-	-
Others & Teachers'	3	7	5
Certificate	2	4	3
G.C.E. A/L	10	15	12
G.C.E. O/L	15	4	10
Primary School			
N =	30	30	30

Source: Survey carried out in 1976/77. All top labour leaders had G.C.E. O/L apart from Imoudu who never completed primary school education. They all attended some courses abroad.

The practice of paying large sums of money into the personal accounts of top officers was less in accord with organizational traditions in Europe, America or Soviet Union, and it tempted the leadership into not accounting for its financial transactions because knowledge of movement of money was monopolized by a few. At any rate, the occasional usurpation of some functions by representatives of external interests clearly distorted the organizations and negated any behavioural norms and practices expected to be transmitted.

Perhaps the saddest comment on activities of external interests is the unwitting transmission of anti-democratic norms or behaviour. Their attempts at maintaining in power some individuals necessarily subverted organizational rules and democratic electoral processes as they had recourse

[2] Out of six persons offered scholarships in 1950, three took up appointments with the government, two were employed by firms and remained in Britain to read Law; Annual Report, 1951/52, par. 129. Of recent times, union officials (e.g. Adio Moses) have been appointed as 'personnel officers' in private firms.

to the 'buying' of delegates, the offering of bribes to opposing candidates to stand down; the encouragement of incumbents to cultivate the art of discrediting opponents by use of unsigned leaflets carrying malicious and unfounded allegations; and the distorting of voting procedure as well as the unilateral alteration of parts of the constitutions of bodies with which they became involved. The effect was to distort choice and dissent which are essential to the democratic process and to weaken the legitimacy of both formal and informal 'rules' that regulate behaviour. Rules and the constitutional provisions came to be invoked only in bids to unseat rivals, and thus Cohen's belief that the 'challenge' presented to the authority of the 'Lagos Leaders' by the middle-rung leadership (regional and district secretaries and assistant general secretaries) could be regarded as some measure of the 'ethic of efficient and rational organisation'[3] can hardly be sustained. Successful 'coups', especially by the NWC's young revolutionaries in 1973, led to no improvements in administration and as soon as financial aid was assured the new incumbents proceed to build up clientele relations and cliques very much as their predecessors had done.

Where external interest attempts also to export organizational arrangements, they commonly succeeded in transferring the form rather than the substance (socio-historical determinants and a whole cultural milieu can hardly be transferred). The apparent 'inability' of the recipients of their attentions to operate such 'institutional transfers' may be related less to the 'sophistication' of models than had hitherto been recognized. This most certainly has little to do with the presumed fact of such institutions requiring centuries to mature, as Peter Kilby believes,[4] in the case of Nigerian trade unions. The 'untransferability' of trade union models (leadership qualities, entrepreneurial ability, effective management, and so forth) from one country to another is reflected in the fact that unionism (organization, structure, and practice) in North America, New Zealand and Australia do not approximate to that of metropolitan Britain, despite movement of people from Britain to these areas. The presence of multinational companies and trade union 'experts' abroad is no transfer of 'technology' or 'organizational structures': only extension of control. In Nigeria, warped end products (central labour organizations) testify also to the expedient and extensive modifications to which external interests resorted as strategies and tactics demanded. Such constraints and contrivances imposed by donors render 'received' organizational forms totally unworkable and totally dependent on external interests to function.

Infusion of a Suitable Ideology

Ideology in this situation should be understood simply in terms of the

---

[3] Cohen, R., *Labour and Politics in Nigeria*, London, 1975., *op. cit.*, p. 125-6

[4] Kilby P., *Industrialisation in an Open Economy: Nigeria 1945-66*, Cambridge, 1969, p. 302.

adoption by labour leaders and their organizations of the definition adopted by external interests to describe certain social phenomena and concepts such as 'economic development', the 'nature of society and social order', the 'role of trade unions in society' and perhaps also 'the alignment of forces in the conflict between East and West.'[5]

The ULCN and NWC themselves could be said to have adopted similar views about Nigeria. Nigeria was regarded as a developing country with a mixed economy. The aims of the labour movement were to 'improve the working and living conditions of workers' and to 'establish an egalitarian society.'[6] The best means to achieve these ends appeared to be 'rapid industrialisation' through 'State ownership of major industries and a properly planned national economy.' It was accepted that Nigeria would need 'considerable foreign capital to augment what we save locally, and this can only be possible if there is no fear of any kind.'[7]

Relationship with and nature of government were described thus:

> The United Labour Congress of Nigeria does not organise to create problems for the country, rather -we are organising to assist in solving most of our problems. Consequently, we do not consider harmonious relationship with our Government something outside the ordinary. The Government of this country is an indigenous one run by our own sons and daughters. The aims and objects of our governments are to find solutions to our social and economic problems. The government as of now is not oppressive in spite of its being a military regime and often is in constant touch with the people. We have never experienced an unnecessary protocol, nor have we experienced any ugly incident on any levels against our membership or leadership. Therefore our decision to co-operate with and participate in government's programmes both at the national and State levels is a wise decision. . .[8]

This contrasted strongly with the NWC's view of political leaders between 1960 and 1965, a view not shared by the ULCN because most of its leaders were prominent members of the NPC, NCNC and NNDP:

> 'Mr. Chukwurah however lashed out at our national leaders and top civil servants. He attacked what he described as "revolting aspect of their behaviour and attitude" and referred to their "apparent levity, hypocrisy and indifference with which they treat the long-standing

[5] Windmuller, J. P., 'External Influences on Labour Organizations in Underdeveloped Countries', *Industrial and Labour Relations Review*, vol. 16, July 1963. 569-70.

[6] Brother Odeyemi's Report of Activities to 4th Biennial, *op. cit.*, p. 3.

[7] Ibid., pp. 3 and 20.

[8] Brother Odeyemi's Report to 4th Biennial, p. 18.

> and widespread complaints, groaning and sufferings of their poor . . . workers and . . . proletariat of the land. . .[9]

At its 1969 Zaria Conference the ULCN declared, 'we shall support without reservation or equivocation the effort of the Federal Military Government to crush the rebellion and to preserve the territorial integrity of Nigeria.'[10]

Organizational strategies for accomplishing goals were to culminate in 'peaceful transition' to an enviable egalitarian society. There was to be avoidance of strikes and other acts that might weaken the war effort; Decree 21 was to be used as a guide in processing trade disputes; workers have to be represented on all nationalized agencies and statutory bodies; and consulted by State and Federal Governments in respect of proposed labour legislation; collective bargaining was to be encouraged because ULCN is 'a free and independent labour movement' that enables workers to demand for higher wages and rising living standards…as much recognition is given to employers' demand for profits.'[11] In 1964 and as Joint Chairman of the Joint Action Committee (JAC), Chukwurah declared the new slogan for workers to be 'productivity'.[12]

Politically, the organization subscribed to 'pragmatic socialism',[13] and 'a democratic and free' society through 'democratic parliamentary measures supported by free and dynamic trade union action.'[14] Essential to its policy was the prevention of trade union leaders from setting up independent political parties based on the working population as recommended by the ICFTU and AFL-CIO. In the end both organizations became involved in the partisan politics of the 'First Republic', a government heralded in the West as a show place of democracy in Africa which was in fact infamous within Nigeria for oppression, thuggery and blatant corruption.

NTUC

The NTUC considered itself a socialist organization and this governed its rhetoric. It saw Nigeria as a 'neo-colony' controlled from outside; 'But the masses of the Nigerian people know. . . that behind the paraphernalia of Nigerian Administrators are unseen foreign hands - British and American -

---

9 *West African Pilot*, Lagos, 7 July, 1964, p. 8.
10 Odeyemi, Report 4th Biennial, p. 4.
11 Ibid., p. 5.
12 *West African Pilot*, July 7 1964, p. 8.
13 Odeyemi, Report 4th Biennial, p. 4.
14 ibid., p. 4.

that control the life of every Nigerian.[15] It identified multi-national companies and Nigerian middlemen as 'exploiters' and saw the polity as riddled with class conflicts and exploitation of peasants and workers. As Peter Waterman16 noted, the NTUC's view and analysis of Nigeria was often inconsistent, especially after General Gowon came to power. Its views could often hardly be distinguished from those of the ULCN. The reason for this apparent convergence lay in the fact of increasing contacts between Nigeria and the Soviet Union especially after the latter sold to it jet planes and arms and threw its weight behind Gowon during the early phase of the war when international support was thought to be crucial, but which was not readily offered by *Western* countries. The NTUC declared its support for the 'crushing of the rebellion' and later commended the government for its victories over the 'forces of neo-colonialism headed by U.S. imperialism.'[17]

Politically, the NTUC declared its support for 'Marxist-Leninist principles' and brought reality to the long-standing threat of the NNFL and ANTUF to join in the formation of a 'workers party', SWAFP, that turned out to be specifically communist. Although its leadership and that of SWAFP did 'coincide' - which generated problems - the NTUC nevertheless declared its preference for union-party relations along the lines of those showed by the British Labour Party and the British TUC.[18] In such circumstances its members could stand for elections, join in partisan politics not necessarily by contesting on the platform of SWAFP and still remain 'Marxist-Leninists' at the end of the day.

The NTUC deplored the breaking of strikes by law-enforcement agencies, the ban imposed on strikes had related activities by Decree 53, and the banning of mass meetings and demonstrations under the 'Emergency Decree'. All these it described as attempts to further weaken workers who were already suffering intolerable 'exploitation'. Collective bargaining was a temporary measure designed to keep the enterprise going and to exact attractive wages. The ultimate solution lay in political action and it is thought that Wahab Goodluck may really have believed that workers could govern Nigeria after the 1964 general strike.[19]

Technical Competence

Technical competence is understood to mean the general capacity of the

---

[15] For a useful critique of NTUC see, Waterman, P., 'Neo-colonialism, Communism and the Nigerian Trade Union Congress' M. Soc. Sci., Dissertation, Centre of West African Studies, Birmingham University, 1972.

[16] Waterman, P., Communist Theory, p. 11.

[17] Cited in Waterman, P., Communist Theory in the Nigerian Trade Union Movement,' *Politics and Society* (1973). p. 6.

[18] ibid., p. 6.

[19] Waterman, Communist Theory, p. 10.

central labour organizations to establish basic administrative procedures, to negotiate (collective agreements, to mediate between the conflicting aspirations of different groups of workers and to compete successfully for control over organized expression of worker aspirations.

Central Bodies-Unions Relations

Minimal contact seems to have existed between central labour organizations and individual trade unions. The only link between any central body and any such union was the union secretary who was invariably a 'professional' and might be serving in that capacity to three or four other unions - his 'portfolios'. The secretary's office was usually far removed from the place of work. He could, therefore, be hardly abreast with shop-floor developments and maintain contacts with members of the union through work place representation. Secretaries were as a result either briefed by other 'ex-officio' members of his executive or by delegations sent by each union. When, as often happened, the delegation or officials were victimized by management or 'rewarded' by promotion, the secretary was faced with two options, should he co-opt new members to his 'executive' or in the former case, should he declare a dispute alleging 'unfair dismissal' or absorb the victims into the administrative machinery of central body?

In view of the practical difficulties of work place action, there was a noticeable tendency on the part of union members to regard both secretary and central bodies as agents to handle their 'foreign affairs'; that is, the negotiations with management and contacts with government. Negotiations within individual enterprises tended to take on the character of a meeting of two Heads of State, each accompanied by a retinue of experts. The secretary is 'advised' on shop-floor developments and converts these into bargains because he is literate and has been taught how to draw up collective agreements either by the Labour Department, the ICFTU, the AFL-CIO or the WFTU. Where 'perishable issues' (such as assault by a member of management) were concerned workers were often on strike for hours before the secretary got to know. Workers on the shop-floor receive little reinforcement from leaders so far removed from their immediate circumstances.

A distorting element was the use of 'scholarships, trips abroad and patronage' by central leadership as rewards to trade unions that paid at least some dues. According to Odeyemi of ULCN, 'those who do not pay should not enjoy these privileges.'[20] Some secretaries were able to attract workers in an establishment to be their 'organisers' by dangling such bait before their eyes. Scholarships and other courses were avenues for social mobility and greater security if they resulted in the acquisition of greater skills or

---

[20] Odeyemi, Report 4th Biennial, p. 16.

bargaining power. Paul Lubeck, in a study of some establishments in Kano, came across two such ULCN organisers each of whom was anxiously awaiting an opportunity to receive advanced training . . . at institutes in Israel, Western Europe or the United States'. One did receive such a scholarship.[21]

If the Union secretary was in a position to dispense patronage, members could then seek 'privileges' without paying dues. This further reinforces the dominant position of the official and had the effect of weakening union democracy. As Paul Lubeck further observed, 'the union organiser is assumed (by members) to be corrupt, or generally suspected of being corrupt'. 'They took our money', declared one worker, 'and did not even work in our factory. Our heads were in darkness (i.e., ignorant) as they took our money but never told us how they were elected as our leaders or when the elections would take place.'[22]

Interesting complications often arose when the secretary either 'defected' on his own accord to a rival centre but was opposed by elements within the union (encouraged by infuriated central leadership) or when a rival 'organiser' secured the allegiance of some union members and formed a rival union within the same establishment. Generally, the rank and file members did not even realize their union had changed hands. It was management which was confronted with a problem of recognition. Both 'unions' usually appealed to the Federal Ministry of Labour when recognition was denied and after workers had gone on strike in support of one union and against management's refusal to countenance their demands in respect of changes in job content and other shop developments. In the last six months of 1974 the Ministry intervened in no fewer than thirty such cases.[23] The writer personally witnessed two such cases in Benin City in 1975 and was told the situation had been thus for six months because neither management nor the Ministry could determine which union was the more representative. Factionalisation has been a direct consequence of the quest of external interests for affiliates and of the centres competitive 'winning' of affiliates internally.

Paradoxically, over ninety per cent of trade unions which have come into existence since 1960 have resulted from the competitive 'winning' of affiliates by rival central bodies.[24] In their bid to outshine each other in the 'numbers game' several secretaries and 'cadres' have been forced to move into previously unorganized sectors to form unions. This partly accounts for

---

[21] Lubeck, P., 'Unions, Workers and Consciousness in Kano, Nigeria: a View from Below', in Sandbrook, B., & Cohen. R., (eds), the *Development of an African Working*, London, 1976.
[22] ibid., p. 144.
[23] Director of Labour, Federal Ministry of Labour, Lagos, 1976.
[24] The Registrar of Trade Unions, interview, Lagos, 1976/77.

the number of 'portfolios' or unions handled by some secretaries and their relative unconcern about details of union-management relations especially where management has connived at the organizing' of its workforce. Even in cases where 'house unions' had been sponsored by employer, it was still essential to beat a rival to it by co-opting its executive and having it registered at the Ministry (there is no legal existence without registration), often to the chagrin of management. Good as this may, seem, central bodies have often discovered that many such unions have not only refused to pay dues but often demanded 'gratification' for remaining affiliated.[25]

Inter-Centres Relations

Much has already been said in this regard but two developments should be mentioned. Apart from the abusive nature of the verbal relations between fie central bodies, they have also tended to function like rival intelligence organizations and tended to be immersed in self-validated values. A prime consideration was how to get members of the opposition to 'defect' and how to make things generally difficult for one another. Means used included bribes (cash, cars, jobs, etc.), inciting individuals against each other by spreading rumours and issuing defamatory and libellous press releases, bribing landlords to evict opponents and the use of 'goon squad' or 'thugs' to break into offices to remove vital documents. All these tactics were developed in close collaboration with representatives of external interests who funded the 'projects'. The ULCN and NWC used 'special organizers' while the NTUC used some of its 'cadres'. For example, when the Independent ULC broke away in 1971, its offices were broken, the perpetrators of the offence were defectors to the ULC and the former sued for damages and illegal entry.[26]

Having cooperated briefly in NNFL, ANTUF and TUCN most top labour leaders had become acquainted with each other and differences between them had 'stabilized'. But younger leaders followed their 'principles' and moved on to more promising pastures: Borha moved into limelight after he had left the 'Marxist Group' for NCTUN through ANTUF and ICFTU-Affiliated Trade Unions Committee; Anunobi and Chukwurah passed through the NTUC (IULC), and the TUCN to NWC; Ijeh passed through all three and ended up in ULCN while Olanrewaju deserted the NTUC for the NWC as a sacked Agbator surfaced in Benin as NTUC's state official. Many others can be quoted. This 'reshuffling' of personnel involved, in many cases, a settling of personal scores in the name of organizational goals and an animosity which only served to hinder cooperation at a practical level and to obstruct ultimate unity of all factions. Flowing from this was a reaction to

[25] All labour leaders interviewed confirm this as their greatest 'headache'.

[26] James, Interview, Ibadan, 1977.

industrial developments - the deregistration of union, strikes, the arrest of unionists or workers, and so on - depending on which section of the labour movement was most affected. For example, Odeyemi announced in 1971 that 'quite a number of unions have been newly registered whilst others have been removed from the register of Trade Unions. I am happy to report that most of the unions, removed...are not affiliates of the ULC.'[27] This enabled both management and government to exploit specific situations to the detriment of a continuously weakening labour movement. When the Northern premier, Sir Ahmadu Bello, announced increases in wage rates on 14 September 1964. Adebola thanked time publicly while he NTUC denounced the, as 'political manoeuvre'[28] although both factions were members of the JAC.

The ideological conversion hoped for by external interests failed to occur. Instead, there was 'a cynical attempt to exploit the apparent naivetй of American, Russian, East European and Chinese donors who actually interpreted…trade union conflict in terms of East-West rivalry.'[29] This occurred in Nigeria encouraged by the fact that that the activities and facilities provided by donors (equally matched by recipients' expectations) increased in proportion to the activity of rival organizations. Thus the NTUC established a Labour Academy in 1963 and ULCN pressed or and got one in 1965, while the NWC waned one 'as soon as possible' in December 1962. The arrival of cars from Eastern Europe for NTUC officials led to the officials of other centres spending valuable funds on obtaining cars also. Even in proven cases of misadministration and embezzlement, there was of intense pressure both from within and from representatives of external interests against sanctions in order to maintain a favourable public image. It was in this regard that Etienam and Chukwurah denounced both the NTUC and ULCN in 1968 and 1962 respectively for condoning unacceptable practices in the name of 'prestige' and 'ideological' fights. The need to demonstrate fidelity to external sponsor pushed labour leaders into uttering phrases which encapsulated one ideological predilection or another while being essentially meaningless in themselves. The NTUC elements addressed one another as 'comrades', talked about being 'representatives of the masses' and of 'leading workers and poor farmers to victory over their class enemies.' ULCN elements called each other 'brother' and declared they believed in 'free and democratic trade unionism' and 'democracy' for Nigeria. The NWC talked vaguely of 'social democracy' and of the 'brotherhood of man'. Most press releases and directives to affiliates were punctuated with such

---

[27] Odeyemi, Report 4th Biennial, p. 32.

[28] *West African Pilot*, Sept. 17 and 10, 1964, pp. 2 and 1 respectively.

[29] Sandbrook, R., 'Patrons, Clients and Unions: the Labour Movement and Political Conflicts in Kenya', *Journal of Commonwealth Political Studies*, vol. 10 (1), 1972, p.

words and phrases accompanied by favourable references to whichever external contacts seemed to be involved.

Centre-Government Relations

Until workers' grievances became generalised by means of strikes, he established pattern of interaction between the central bodies sand government was mostly indirect, through newspaper reports where even a recognized centre was involved. As must have become clear by now both colonial and post-independence political; authorities developed policies in which interest affected would appeal for a hearing of its grievances. The centres customarily appealed to the government over issues such as union recognition, the introduction of check-off system, the restructuring of house unions into industrial ones, the release of arrested or detained leaders (neither court injunctions nor habeas-corpus was ever asked for), and so on. Such arrangements could have been said to reflect a realistic appraisal of power-relations since only the government could compel some employers to, say, recognize unions.[30]

The government as a major employer tended naturally to lean towards any centre whose memorandum and recommendations would most ease its problems in relation to wage bill and incomes policy. Partly because of this and also of schisms in central leadership, appointment to bodies (such as Wages Board, Labour Advisory Board, Administration Board and other relevant commissions) become a privilege instead of right. The appointment of persons to these bodies, and especially to delegations to ILO conferences in Geneva, because a 'goal' and measure of 'success' to be flaunted before rivals, hence the intense lobbying of officials of the Ministry of Labour for recognition. The effective performance o any 'appointee' became compromised in the process, exceptionally as when a general strike placed a government on the defensive and face-to-face negotiations took place. Even then the government usually announced he increases it considered adequate, rather than seeking mutual agreement. Wages Commissions would then recommend independent awards which strikes by workers would compel government and private employers to implement. As an index of 'technical incompetence', neither the Ministry of Labour nor central bodies has reliable statistics on strikes or union membership. In 1971 official membership of all registered trade unions was put at 655,215; yet, ULCN claimed a membership of 626,859 in 1967 (as against 530,000 for all unions in the same year). All central bodies, like their external benefactors, inflated membership figures.

---

[30] Individual unions often went on strike over 'recognition issue'.

Centre-Management Relations

Employers did not deem it necessary to form an organization until 1957 when it had become clear that political independence was only a few years away and thus industrial developments might not be very predictable thereafter. But the delay in forming such a body should also be attributed to the fact that the UAC and its subsidiaries easily comprised over fifty per cent of employer-element in the private sector, excluding indigenous employers. Internal consultation with the UAC as a 'prize' leader appeared for long time thought to be sufficient in itself. Labour Officers and Police Commissioners usually mediated between management and union centre. Some of the large private enterprises formed the Nigerian employers' Consultative Association (NECA). Though this could not speak 'with authority and conviction for its members' and was 'not a negotiating body and cannot commit its members on economic matters,'[31] it nevertheless 'supported collective bargaining unequivocally and emphatically for private industry.'[32] Both parties were brought together with the government in the National Labour Advisory Council in 1965. This body advised the later on the application and operation of existing or proposed labour and social-security legislation and the application of ILO conventions and recommendations. It was also expected periodically to review labour legislation relating to wages and other conditions of employment. This apart, all communication between employers and union centres was conducted through the news media. Generally, NECA frowned on the 'existence' of an all-embracing labour organization. Cooperation between central bodies (such as the JAC and UCCLO) occurred in fits and starts and NECA sought to 'neutralise' them by challenging their legal status. In 1964, during negotiations between the JAC and Government, for example, in a secret memo to its members that was leaked to the newspapers, NECA argued that 'the JAC is not a legal body and cannot legally as JAC, claim to attend or participate in negotiations.'[33] The reluctance of individual employers to recognize trade unions was paralleled by NECA's reluctance to recognize central labour organizations. Clearly, this was not the best combination of ingredients for collective bargaining.

COMMENT

International aid or solidarity as presently practised is unlikely to significantly contribute to the strengthening of labour movements in Nigeria and other underdeveloped countries. It is instructive in the case of Nigeria that all unions drawn from establishments or companies owned or

---

[31] Nigerian Employers Consultative Association, *NECA News*, Lagos, Feb. 1965, p.
[32] Ibid., p. 3.
[33] *NECA News* April 1965, p. 5.

controlled by British, American and West German investors were affiliated to the pro-ICFTU United Labour Congress of Nigeria (ULCN): leaving public sector unions as open targets.

The 'aid' programmes seem to revolve around projected 'role' of trade unions and their leadership in the political and economic development of target countries. The general idea being that, at best, external interests' definition of social reality should prevail. Usually, such descriptions include a 'mixed economy' (which explicitly recognizes private investments and repatriation of profits abroad while advocating severe limitations on government's economic activities) and 'collective bargaining' being the best and democratic method for tackling industrial matters. Collective bargaining in this sense excludes a challenge to foreign ownership of enterprises while it paradoxically includes a push for legislation inimical to trade unions, a situation that is passed off rather glibly as part of the bargaining strategies.

But the fact of foreign ownership and racially stratified managements (with Europeans, Asians and Levantines occupying higher positions) is so striking that most strikes tend to have a nationalist tinge to them as some of workers' demands routinely including a change of ownership and removal of certain members of management.[34] Two related implications are that attention paid to racial composition of management draws attention away from the fact of any incumbent playing similar roles so long as the enterprises stay privately owned and respond to the dictates of the 'market'. Secondly, as racial preferences are clearly discernible and not subject to rational criteria, part of the myth of institutional transfers explodes revealing links between ownership, policies and organizational structure. That 'standard' organizational practices have not been transferred and that no foreign trade union is in a position to either export 'collective bargaining' or introduce 'industrial democracy' elsewhere are not too difficult conclusions to reach. These are not exportable commodities that call for 'experts' and 'aid'.

Typologies on 'role' of unions in Africa are replete, the commonest being 'productionist' as against 'consumptionist'. Along another dimension, using political party-unions relationship as criterion, others are 'integrated' versus 'opposition' or 'independent'.[35] The 'independence' of Nigerian unions as identified along the latter dimension by Robin Cohen[36] needs -several qualifications. Firstly, top trade union leaders have always belonged to

---

[34] *West African Pilot*, Lagos, July 17, 1964, p. l; memorandum was signed by a D. Borrie, Ref. 146/64/6, NECA, 47 Marina, P.M.B. 2237, Lagos.

[35] This point was overly exaggerated by Kerr et al. in their asserting that the protest by indigenous workers is generally organized around the principle of anti-colonialism and independence in *Industrialism and Industrial man*, Pelican, 1964, p. 215.

[36] See Davies, I., *African Trade Unions*; Bates, R. H., Unions, Parties ... *op. cit.* Cohen, R., *Labour and Politics in Nigeria, op. cit.*

different political parties and with a divided central leadership in the form of numerous central labour organizations, the unions have often been pulled in different directions. Secondly, trade union members, like most other literate and semiliterate Nigerians, have fully participated in sectional politics of the day; some of them assuming prominent positions in erstwhile ethnic or 'tribal' associations.[37] Thirdly, external interests themselves have influenced various factions of the labour movement, and often in tune with their preferences for or against certain political parties. Much aware of what he calls 'negative aspect' of affiliation of national centres to the international bodies, Robin Cohen strangely argues that 'it is possible that in some cases the support that the international bodies have given to the individual centres has allowed them to stand out against governmental control and direction of their activities.'[38] This is a rather curious definition of independence, quite uncomfortably close to arguments representatives of international labour organizations have variously put before the writer.

If at the enterprise level the emphasis of unionism is on better conditions of service, conversion of daily-paid workers into permanent category and a change in racial and national composition of managements (which, at any rate is partly what the indigenization decrees are aimed at especially with provisions for 'expatriate quota'), the institutional isolation of trade unions has not been as great as some observers imagine. Most labour leaders, from available evidence, seem fairly nationalistic and tend to accept government's budgets and do subscribe to the whole and quite untenable belief in 'catching up with the developed countries' - and the national sacrifices that go with it. That most of them are galvanized into more intransigent posturing by activities of workers has been proved again and again, activities themselves that are predicated upon issues clearly delineated by respective wages commissions. What all this amounts to is that if trade unions in socialist oriented countries in Africa and elsewhere are described as 'integrated', trade unions in capitalist countries, neo-colonial or not, can hardly escape the label of 'collaborationist' - notwithstanding the presence of a very vocal section. That any labour organization can criticize the government and indeed offer alternative set of programmes may be a reflection of prevailing democratic situation and not necessarily an index of independence. That the established channels of communication, including the lobbying of members of parliament, are utilised and deference to constituted authorities still prevail, not to mention a general concern over the declining British or American or Nigerian economic standing, do suggest a degree of interdependence and compatible 'ideologies' that the pluralist

---

[37] Cohen, R., *Labour and Politics in Nigeria*, *op. cit.*, p. 255.

[38] In fact, Cohen approvingly cites Yesufu's perceptive observation on workers adherence to tribal associations than trade unions; p. 132-3.

ideologues are not tired of pointing out. Having said this one should also recognise that some workers are dedicated to the establishment of an alternative kind of society; the only problem seems to be the number imbued with such a vision.[39]

The constellation of international economic forces into two main ideological camps undoubtedly represented the transnational character of both capitalism and communism. These are tactically manifested in trade union matters in the form of the ICFTU-AFL-CIO-ITSs axis and the WFTU. The point seems to be that there are national units within these camps that are in a constant state of rivalry even if overshadowed by the great ideological divide. National capitalisms and National socialisms have their peculiarities just as national labour movements. Despite internationalism national preferences sometimes take precedence. In this light a trade union centre that is funded from abroad though 'independent' in the Cohen's sense of it may actually be branded 'imperialist stooge' and like invectives by both trade unionists and government alike. Apart from the American AFL-CIO it seems no happenstance that the British TUC, French and Belgian national union centres channel most of their 'aid' to the unions of their former colonies. National sentiments partly explain, as this study shows, why leaders of union centres fall out with their foreign sponsors. Retorts such as 'Americans can spend their money the way they want' may not only reflect passive acceptance of dominant position of foreign sponsor but also indicate cognizance of national origin of funds and national interests involved. And when some activities are considered inimical to perceived national interests, often usually complicated by internal power tussles, reports have promptly been made to both government and police - hence the commonplace habit of branding some unionists as 'dissidents', 'renegades' and 'traitors' in trade union circles.

Given the nature of a capitalist neo-colonial economy, the ideological coloration of the trade union movement may not be as problematic as made out to be. Nigeria, for example, has no historical experience of truly revolutionary movements, no radical intellectual activity and cultural expectations have been distorted by the Western-educated elite that confusedly associate 'consumerism' and mimicry of European ways with 'modernity' and 'development'. The acceptance of wealth as a success symbol and acquisition of electronic gadgets and other consumer items which has spread across all social classes, workers and trade unionists not excepted, tend to create an environment most unconducive to critical appraisal of the economic set up. Recent studies of Nigerian workers, though establishing workers' capacity to organise in protection of their corporate interest, reveal the ultimate ambition of the low-paid worker is 'self-employment' (an understandable

[39] Ibid., p. 250.

reaction to economic insecurity with preferred occupations as petty trading and some form of 'business' requiring small initial capital outlay) and not the replacement of the capitalist system.[40] Radicalism is in this sense related to the readiness to resort to the strike weapon over issues already determined by the various wages commissions - indeed quite reminiscent of the often violent reaction of British workers to the government's five and ten per cent pay guidelines of the 1977-78 period. In the Nigerian case the degree of violence involved may only be inversely related to the intransigence of various managements (including the government as an employer) in meeting officially announced awards and gradings, and not 'threats' to the power-structure. This is not to suggest an unchanging situation: the lesson remains that inaccurate diagnosis, especially tainted by observer's own predilections, may be more harmful to workers themselves.

Like nationalism, 'ethnicism' - a factor which cuts across social classes - has been inadequately dealt with by both Marxism and orthodox analysis. Both analytical approaches not only view ethnicism as primordial sentiments and historically 'archaic' but also imply that its consequences could be nothing as great as those of inter-class conflict. Along with religious and other community conflicts, ethnic conflict is viewed as irrational, a state that would be overwhelmed by proletarianisation and its accompanying class consciousness. Liberal or bourgeois political theory pretends that a constituency is populated by persons of similar social needs and thus any chosen representative would be quite effective. Whereas, the supposedly socialist Soviet Union has taken greater care to devise a constitution that not only makes movement between each of the internal republics a difficult business but also provides for the representation of all racial and other minority groups. Even if not carried out to the letter in practice, such constitutional provisions do represent a greater sensitivity to racial and other ethnic problems and less dependence on the magic of proletarian consciousness.

In this regard European trade unionism may provide little guidance to Nigerian trade union leaders faced with a multi-ethnic situation. To deprecate 'tribalism' or 'ethnic chauvinism' in the Nigerian labour movement hardly sheds light on the problems accompanying the organizing of a multi-ethnic labour force. To dismiss ethnic consciousness as a hindrance to the emergence of workers' class-consciousness may even be a poor conception of social reality and an inadequate grasp of the problems associated with self-identity. If only to misquote Frank Parkin and parody Karl Marx, it seems quite possible for a man to think of himself as an

---

[40] Such workers are more in evidence in Italy, France and Britain than in West Germany, United States of America or Canada. It is probably not an exaggeration to assert that they are more in Nigeria than West Germany and the United States of America!

industrial worker in the morning, an Ibo or Urhobo in the afternoon, and a Nigerian in the evening without any difficulty.[41] In short, that class and ethnic identities can simultaneously be held and activated hardly signifies less proletarianisation. It stays unlikely that a student of the working classes in Northern Ireland (where the Irish are at loggerheads with descendants of English settlers), Belgium (where the Flemings and Walloons are implacably opposed), and the United States of America (where the tendency is for specific racial groups to dominate unionism in certain industries) would be that myopic. The overwhelming numerical dominance of the English over the Scots, Welsh, Irish, Asians and West Indians in Britain, and near homogeneity of the French, German and Italian populations may have clouded this issue in the realm of unionism. That ethnic separatist movements have become serious political issues in some European countries cannot be denied and it is certainly self-delusory to imagine that such inclinations may only be found among the non-working classes of such ethnic groups.

The point of all this is that there is nothing peculiarly African or Nigerian about a member of the proletarian class displaying some other form of consciousness considered less rational or scientific. The peculiarly European reaction has been, so it seems from historical evidence, to exclusively organize either along racial or religious lines: there never seems to have been any serious attempts on multi-racial or multi-religious basis without the unwritten understanding of the dominance of a particular group or religion. There thus seems to be no sufficient grounds for the widely-held assumption of the 'homogenizing influence of the modern industrial state would be too powerful to allow the survival of traditionalistic and narrower tribal loyalties that flourished under agrarian systems.'[42] In spite of the long history of industrial work and unionism, recourse has frequently been taken to ethnic-racial and religious sympathies in times of union elections in some European and North American countries. Nigerian unionists have not been remarkably different.

One may, of course, foresee the possibility of the emergence of a less

---

[41] Adrian Peace has convincingly demonstrated the ability of Nigerian workers to organise in protection of their corporate interests in two of his papers, namely, 'Industrial Protest in Nigeria' (in Kadt, de E. & Williams (eds) Sociology and Development) and the Lagos Proletariat: Labour Aristocrats or Populist Militants' in Sandbrook & Cohen (eds.) The Development of An African Working Class. Although workers are seen to correctly identify exploiting elites, their activities are hardly geared toward the search for an alternative system thus reinforcing Lenin's view on the limitations inherent to 'trade union consciousness' - the improvement of working conditions within existing order. Peace himself confirms this when he points out that 'the aspiration to become self-employed is a near-universal one on the shopfloor of the Ikeja factories', a theme that runs through the study; see his *Choice, Class and Conflict*, Harvester, 1979, p. 13.

[42] See Parkin, F., *Marxism and Class Theory: A Bourgeois Critique*, Tavistock London 1979, pp. 29-43 for a rather intriguing commentary.

efficient, or even corrupt, labour leader because of blatant exploitation of these sympathies, but the tactics adopted for maintaining or assuming-positions of power have not been famous for their technical, ethical or moral purity - not even in proletarian organizations.[43] But in the Nigerian experience, a significant proportion of the top labour leaders (including Michael Imoudu) have come from the so-called minority ethnic groups; a fact that suggests considerable success in organising across ethnic lines and which is also reflected in the careful attention paid to ethnic composition of executives of the various central labour organizations.

Except one is still strongly wedded to an imperial view of international relations, it does seem difficult to justify the formal subordination of African, Asian and Latin American labour organizations to the ICFTU, WFTU and the American AFL-CIO. To be an 'affiliate' incorporates a subordinate status and an acceptance of the ideological differences presumed to exist between both ideological camps. That Nigeria has a capitalist economic system may not be taken to automatically imply a natural affinity between the trade unions and the ICFTU. The average trade union official is aware of the fact that companies owned by member nations of the ICFTU, along with those of the United States of America, dominate the Nigerian economy. He hardly expects the ICFTU to impart knowledge as to how best to tackle and dispossess them. He might seek information and other relevant documentation on their activities elsewhere, especially on payment systems and degree of consultation as reflected in the disclosure of information, in order to devise a most effective strategy for dealing with management of such multinational companies within the constraints imposed by a neo-colonial economic structure. It seems perfectly logical and reasonable to expect that the maintenance of relations of some sort with all international labour organizations may offer wider exposure to essential practices and viewpoints than a partisan affiliate status.

One of the criticisms of this study in its original form by Robin Cohen was 'the little discussion of the ITSs' which he considered to be 'one of the most important forms of international trade unionism' in Europe.[44] It has been established above that in terms of the preservation of the capitalist world system and thus the partisan business of 'recruiting' non-European trade unionists as ideological bedmates, the ITSs have synchronized their activities with those of the ICFTU and AFL-CIO, their institutional autonomy notwithstanding. The same may not be said of the ILO because of its membership that cuts across ideological blocs and in spite of its model of

---

[43] Parkin, F., *Marxism and Class Theory: A Bourgeois Critique*, Tavistock, London, 1979, p. 31.

[44] In the United States of America, some union leaders habitually harrass opponents during elections; in fact, some opponents have been known to disappear without a trace in spite of the investigative efforts of the FBI.

industrial relations bearing a strong similarity to a general Western model with its recognition of private employer and primacy of status accorded to 'collective bargaining'. The crux of the matter lies in the historically different role played by the ITSs in the Third World which no amount of great detailing of their activities in Europe can alter. Some of the ITSs not only contributed funds to the 'Solidarity Fund' with which the ICFTU 'won' unions in the Third World, they also organised talks, seminars and offered scholarships to members of their affiliates in Nigeria, all who happened to belong to the central body affiliated to the ICFTU. The possibility of a Nigerian unionist viewing the ITSs in a light quite different from Cohen's should not be taken lightly. The President of the Nigerian Labour Congress has bitterly complained about the 'obstructionist role' of the organisations, and most especially their repeated attempts at undercutting the African equivalents under the control of the pan-African OATUU (an arm of the OAU). In his own words, 'the European ITSs are spending a lot of money to prevent the taking off of their African counterparts.'[45]

GENERAL IMPACT OF EXTERNAL INFLUENCES ON THE NIGERIAN LABOUR MOVEMENT

Occupational and Social Distinctions

Both union organization and the outlook of workers towards it were influenced by a very early distinction made between manual workers and white-collar employees. Emphasis on the ability to read and write in English, the status and jobs that went with it and the underlying assumption of cultural superiority and acceptability of the literate and adaptee made the distinction more invidious than it might otherwise have been. Clerks and artisans thus earned early leadership of workers' organizations. The dislike of this leadership largely accounts for the emergence of Imoudu in the 1930s. His splinter union was disposed to represent the less literate segment of railway workers. As the literacy factor per se carried differentials in income, status and other privileges, productivity and the idea of a 'fair day's pay for a fair day's work' became relatively divorced from wage settlement, the more so when illiterate members of the various communities were the main victims of forced labour policy.

Allied to this was the unusual lack of concern for training of labour and the absence of manpower development schemes. During almost a century of effective colonial occupation the Administration had built only ten secondary schools[46] and established only one institution, Yaba Higher College (which awarded diplomas in forestry, teaching, science, etc.) by 1934 to train a 'body of men and women who can perform some of the tasks in

[45] Private communication dated 13 December, 1979 and not meant for publication.

[46] Interview, Lagos, February 1981.

the Government work and private enterprises.'[47] Education was restricted both in scope and quality to the base-level requirements of the colonial regime and it was not until 1948 with mounting pressure from all sides that a university, University College, Ibadan, was established. Secondary school education was mostly left in the hands of missionaries who set up self-supporting schools with fees which few could afford to pay. The table below shows the number of scholarships awarded by the Administration for overseas training and it was only after 1945 that individuals who could afford it were allowed to go abroad.[48] In all, the celebrated 'training programmes' of the Department of Labour and those of institutes of external interests, secondary school and university education was somehow omitted. Even 40 years later most top labour leaders had no G.C.E. O/Levels. A diploma in trade union studies from Ruskin College, from the London School of Economics, or from Harvard, or Patrice Lumumba in Moscow remained the upper limit of academic qualifications for trade unionists. In fact, the Federal Ministry of Labour carried on the traditions of the colonial Department of Labour in its approach to 'trade union education' and adopted external interests' view of the Nigerian trade union scene: namely, that if trade union leaders were taught how to draw up collective agreements 'labour relations' will automatically. Apart from looking upon the various 'trade union institutes' set up by external interests with an approving eye, the Ministry organized occasional seminars and proposed the establishment of a National Labour College. The important thing, however, is that high value attached to academic qualifications in Nigeria necessarily contributed towards a loss of social status by trade union leaders, and the desire on their part to seek other status-yielding activities such as business and political positions to the detriment of unionism.

Overseas Training Scholarship Awards

Year	Men	Women
1938-9	1	-
1940	1	-
1941	-	-
1942	-	-
1943	2	-
1944	11	-
1945	19	6
1946	21	6
1947	19	11
1948	34	6
	108	29

[47] Dudley, B. J., *Instability and Political Order- Politics and Crisis in Nigeria*, Ibadan, 1973, . p. 26.
[48] Colonial Annual Reports, Nigeria, 1931, p. 39.

Structural Characteristics

The dominant role played by some groups of workers in Nigerian trade unionism is attributable to the conduct of the external factor, especially where the manner and mode of exploitation of natural and human resources are concerned. The concentration of commercial activities in the coastal ports and areas and the necessity to construct roads and railways to link up mining areas in the interior and to evacuate agricultural produce for exportation enabled transport workers and government employees to form the earliest unions: the Nigerian Civil Service Union emerged in 1912; the Nigerian Railway Workers' Union in 1932 and the Marine Daily Paid Workers Union (later Nigerian Marine African Workers Union) in 1936.

The Administration's preference for clerks and other white-collar workers clearly dictated the early recognition accorded to the Civil Service Union while the extensive use of forced labour at the ports and in constructing railway lines and roads bred militancy and delayed the recognition of the ports/railway workers organizations. But it is the sheer weight of number employed in the transport industry, its strategic importance and the specific historic form of its organizations has resulted in the dominating role of these industries in the Nigerian labour movement even to this day. And the dominance of government employees has also been a reflection of the scope of governmental activities, considerably widened in recent times by the Indigenization Decree.[49]

The smallness of unions, the preponderance of 'house unions' and their late emergence in the private sector in no small way reflect the structure of individual firms, the intense hostility and dominant position of both private and public employers. Employers opposed the introduction of the check-off system successfully throughout the colonial period in spite of the recommendations of various commissions and the laments of the Department of Labour about the 'weaknesses' of unions and the intense desire which labour officers were supposed to have had for 'properly-organized' unions. The postcolonial government saw the usefulness of compulsory registration of unions and absence of a check-off system for deriving union funds and hedged on its introduction. When it finally came in 1961 it was made voluntary and dependent on agreement by both employer and unions; any union that attempted to introduce it (or compelled an employer to do so) without official permission of the Ministry was liable and could be prosecuted. The emergence of financially strong unions seemed to have raised strong apprehension in the authorities and private employers.

Although most observers habitually identify 'political attitudes' of Nigerian workers, it is too easily forgotten that colonial administration and

[49] Akpala, A.,, 'Industrial Relations Policies in Nigeria,' *Genieve Afrique*, vol. 10(1), 1971, p. 24.

military governments in Nigeria have been authoritarian and that the country has only had a five-year spell of civilian government by 1975. Demographic changes have ensured that few workers have experienced the three phases nor can one assume literacy and political socialization (or consciousness) have enabled most people to become aware of political 'alternatives'. The only measure of continuity is provided by an elite, which still in its formative stages, has been recruiting from all segments of the population - teachers, professionals and intellectuals, businessmen, failures in all walks of life (especially business) and trade unionists.

The relevance of the above can be seen in respect of the ultimate career goals of labour leaders: of the 90 labour leaders interviewed 75 expected to end up in 'business' or 'politics', 50 of which admitted to having 'laid the foundation' (meaning that they had investments and were also involved in clandestine political groupings).[50] Their conception of authority and leadership, it also appeared, was derived from two mutually reinforcing factors: of being the 'early leaders', 'those who fought for independence' (thus quite paternalistic) and the colonial-style (and authoritarian) total control of subordinates which left no room for opposition. These tendencies were reinforced by the then existing Nigerian political parties which made impossible political activities outside their framework. The reference group of labour leaders became their 'counterparts' in politics (who gained power because of being 'early leaders'), a category that was still recruiting and labour leaders were logically qualified candidates. Having been deprived access to the general population by '-politicians', it could be said that most labour leaders regarded the labour movement as their 'constituency', a card up their sleeves with which to command access to political office and to respect from their 'counterparts' in politics. The labour movement was thus simply used as a vehicle for upward mobility as neither labour leaders educational attainments nor the scope and direction of external interests' 'educational activities' appreciably enhanced their statuses. Indeed labour leaders, thanks to external interests, acquired cars and paraded around like their 'counterparts' - cars are a status symbol in Nigeria - and tended to supplicate for traditional titles and chieftaincies (again like their 'counterparts') by virtue of the fact of being 'leaders' and of being 'important sons' of their communities or hometowns.

These tendencies have necessarily affected the affairs of individual trade unions and workers' activities. As previously mentioned, labour leaders sitting on Arbitration and Labour Advisory Boards have, for all these reasons, tended to promote ideas and policies workers have had to reject. But more crucial has been the general adverse effect on organizational

---

[50] Imoudu, Etienam. Wahab Goodluck, Adebola and others are fully involved in the formation of recent political parties (1978) in Nigeria.

strategies. Adrian Peace in his excellent participant observation study of the strikes over 'Adebo' awards in 1970 in the Ikeja industrial estate (suburb of Lagos), has provided the most direct evidence that Nigerian workers have developed a fairly explicit consciousness of their class position vis-a-vis others and evolved tactics to deal with their environment.[51] Paul Lubeck in another fascinating study of unorganized workers in three enterprises in Kano has shown the ability of workers to develop strategies and cope with management's tactics while substituting 'class-based loyalties' for 'communal loyalties'. But, the upper limits of this consciousness have been set, among other reasons, by the disjunction between central leadership's aims and goals and those of unions and by the lack of opportunity for leaders thrown up by workers at the plant level to move into central leadership. These limitations have then been reinforced by the imposed choice of issues as set by the relevant wages tribunal or commission. Simplified almost to the absurd, it is all similar to a common practice in various African communities whereby for a specified period during some festive occasions all taboos are, as it were, suspended. On these occasions outrageous and anti-social behaviour takes place - but at the end of the festival everyone behaved as if nothing had happened. In this sense, most workers' protests have been 'enacted' for the commissions have clearly set limits and issues in dispute whatever 'threats to the power structure' any observer may have noted on these occasions. From the 'structure of the situation' and from the writer's own experience at Ibadan in respect of 'Adebo' awards, even participants themselves (workers, government officials and management) realized their temporariness, with the exception of the Udoji awards which involved many other factors as previously indicated. Such transience has been confirmed by the inability of central leadership to tap workers' consciousness and provide it with a coherent and systematic ideological position. Explicit worker class consciousness has thus occurred in starts and has not, so far as the observer can judge, brought any meaningful challenge to managerial authority in respect of workload or job content such as which has arisen in Britain, the United States of America and in Europe generally.

CONCLUDING REMARKS

In spite of the negative aspects of the activities of external interests as they affect central trade unionism in Nigeria, it could also be maintained that there were some beneficial results. Many trade unionists have become exposed to unionism as practised in Britain, Europe and elsewhere; knowledge that is sometimes used to evaluate policies of multinational and

---

[51] Peace, A.J., 'Industrial Protest at Ikeja Nigeria' in Kadt de, E. & Williams, G. P., (eds), Sociology *and Development*, Tavistock Publications London, 1974.

other foreign firms. This could be termed the 'demonstration effect' factor.

Even if the 'educational programmes' of external interests had their shortcomings, it has increasingly dawned on several trade unionists that the 'asset' of having been around during colonial times would not sustain a labour movement. Better trained leadership is required and schemes to provide university education to workers who would lead the labour movement are seriously being considered.[52] Indeed, many trade unions and the NLC and TUCN today have officials who are graduates. University education may be of considerable use to a bureaucratizing labour movement but can hardly be an effective substitute for more thorough-going organization and activity towards eliminating factors that make both economy and political decision-making mostly governed by external constraints.[53]

Although it is evident that the form of 'aid' offered by external interests to central labour organizations in Nigeria since colonial times has served to weaken the labour movement and substantially produced a divided central leadership, external aid may still be needed. Such aid should include exchange of information on the activities of multinational companies, international sympathy strikes and boycotts of firms whose activities are seen as threatening to workers of a particular region or industry and worsening effects of climate change. Having said this, it must be emphasized that continuation of 'aid' programmes in the form which they assumed since colonial times and made more sinister by Cold War complications should cease. Such 'aid' allows trade unionism to degenerate into the murky and dangerous games of espionage and counter-espionage, by drawing in government's intelligence services with talks of 'destabilisation' and the like. If the so-called international labour organisations wish to provide 'legitimate cover' for European and American and Communist governments with which to gain control over non-European trade unions for strategic and economic reasons, they should be quite prepared to face up to the consequences of such activities instead of raising a hue and cry over 'attacks' on 'free trade unionism' or 'revolutionary unionism'.

[52] Lubeck, P., 'Unions, Workers and Consciousness in Kano, Nigeria: A View from Below' in Sandbrook, R. & Cohen, R., (eds). *The Development of an African Working Class*, London, 1975, p. 156.

[53] The forty-two industrial unions are obliged by their own constitutional provisions to spend not less than ten per cent of their annual income on workers' education training.

STATE, LABOUR AND SOCIETY

Chapter 8

THE COLONIAL STATE AND EMPLOYMENT RELATIONS

The term 'industrial relations policy' usually implies an attempt to regulate employment relationships or to establish 'control over work processes' (Hyman, 1975, 45)[1] in an industrial environment by all affected groups. In the colonial situation what Vic Allen (1971, 222)[2] has described as the 'buying and selling of labour power' was also of considerable importance. The creation of a wage-labour force to meet the commercial needs of both local and European companies, in this case, was sufficient to trigger a proletarianisation process which the imposition of taxes and structural economic change served to reinforce (Allen, 1971; Sandbrook & Cohen, 1975).[3] On the other hand, the economic and financial complications of administering a colonial territory, the reactions of 'labour' and of indigenous various communities to official policies, and the activities of private employers, quite apart from pressures from Whitehall, meant that sooner or later the colonial administration had to formulate policies for dealing with employers operating in various communities and hence towards the development of industrial relations policies. We turn our attention first to labour.

COLONIAL LABOUR POLICIES

Wage labour in the form of porterage followed the footsteps of the itinerant European trader, slaver, missionary and adventurer. It was a personal service that required no institutional response and pre-dated colonial status in a formal sense. Despite this, the bases of the colonial State and of subsequent industrial relations policies (more' accurately, 'labour policy') were laid after Lagos became a Crown Colony and before 1900. Labour became a 'problem' to the Colonial Office in several ways: widespread slave trading made it manifestly difficult: a) to create a labour market; and b) to develop a stable

---

[1] Hyman, R., *Strikes*, Fontana, 1972

[2] Allen, V. L., *The Sociology of Industrial Relations*, Longman, London, 1971;

[3] Allen, V. L., *The* Sociology *of Industrial Relations, op cit.;* Sandbrook, R. & Cohen, R. (eds) *The Development of An African Working Class*, Longman, London, 1975.

labour force; c) ensure a ready market for imported consumer goods and wares; and d) to generate conditions favourable for 'legitimate trade' and other commercial activities of increasing importance both to metropolitan business circles and to European national rivalries. Colonial military conquest, 'penetration of the interior' and 'pacification' thus became inevitable.[4]

Labour policy in the period 1862 to 1900 was directed at achieving conditions a) to d) above. In practice, a military approach seems to have been adopted, with conscription of people into labour gangs and army platoons and battalions, the immediate objective of which was the construction of roads and railway lines. This class of labour was officially regarded as temporary and treated as such: no wages were paid, nor was provided accommodation, 'work' was regarded as a civic duty despite an element of compulsion in recruiting and labourers were expected to go back to their homes at the end of the day. Such a system could not cope with the laying of lines for tens of miles through uninhabited country, and mass desertions forced the introduction of wages. Such wages were very low but upsetting for colonial officials who had grown used to utilizing forced labour without pay.

Another aspect of the situation has been examined by Hopkins (1966) and Hughes & Cohen (1971) who sketched out the emergence of a working class in the Lagos Crown Colony.[5] The institution of an urban administration and the creation of public utilities generated a standing corpus of officials, artisans, and other categories of labour. The willingness of successive governors to involve an increasing number of the locally literate population, indigenous political authorities and emergent commercial interests in government so as to promote and protect British imperial interests, created a vigorous political community where free rein could be given to individual aspirations. Subject to budgetary and other overriding political constraints and developments both within the colony and metropolis, the basis was thus laid for a social policy directed at meeting the resultant expectations. Enlightened self-interest on the part of colonial officials, the torrent of criticism of official policies poured out by nationalist politicians, a vigorous and often libellous press, combined with bouts of economic depressions and boom and the many grievances of 'public servants' to set the stage for an increasingly systematic processing of

---

[4] It would also be true that 'suppression of the slave trade' was oftentimes a convenient screen for elimination of rival indigenous and European commercial interests.

[5] HOPKINS, A.G., 'The Lagos Strike of 1897: An Exploration in Nigerian Labour History', *Past and Present*, 35, 1966; HUGHES, A. & COHEN, R., *Towards the Emergence of a Nigerian Working Class, 1897-1939, Occasional* Papers Series D, No. 7, Faculty of Commerce & Social Science, University of Birmingham, 1971. An abridged version may be found in GUTKIND, P.C.W., COHEN, R., & COPANS, J. (eds.), *African Labour History*, Sage, Beverly Hills & London, 1978.

problems and claims against the colonial administration.

This administration comprised some technical and professional departments and a central core of 'general' civil service. The departments concerned were Customs, Medical, Constabulary (a division of it was converted to a civil police force in 1896), Sanitary, Public Works, the Post Office, the Surveyor-General, the Lagos Railway, the Harbour, Engineering, and Education. While the governor was technically at the head of the civil service, day-to-day service was provided by the colonial Secretariat to other central organs of government, including the 'advisory' Nigerian Legislative Council to which prominent members of the business community (mostly expatriates), representatives of the indigenous professional classes and rulers were appointed. The nature of the skills required implied the existence of persons and work groups who possessed relatively scarce expertise, who were strategically placed and who therefore enjoyed considerable bargaining leverage. With a status in the colonial pecking order and in the activities of political officers, such men were even more likely to feel relative deprivation when this impinged on their situation.

Little is known about specific policies on 'Consultation' or 'negotiation' inside the public administration of the time. Such processes as existed seem to have related to European officers whose terms and conditions of service were settled by the Colonial Office in London. From Nicholson's account (1969, 57),[6] these numbered 'less than ninety' by 1897, including the governor himself, and were a mixed bag of Irish, Scots, Welsh and West Indians. Office hours were from 8 a.m. to 11 a.m. and 1 p.m. to 4 p.m. on weekdays and 8 a.m. to noon on Saturdays, arranged to suit the business hours of the Bank of West Africa (the only bank) into which the chief revenue collecting officers (e.g. the Collector of Customs and the Postmaster) paid the day's revenue at 4 p.m. each day (ibid.). Many of the officials were housed individually in standard one-bedroom flats, and proceeded to their offices by rickshaw or bicycle. Outside Lagos, however, touring officers went by launch, hammock, canoe, on foot, and occasionally on horseback wearing rubber wellingtons. This contrasted sharply with officers of the Niger Coast Protectorate who, having spent most of their time in the subjugation of various local communities, lived after the fashion of soldiers, eating and drinking in communal messes, and living under canvas or in makeshift huts of wood, mud or metal.

As for indigenous public servants, Nicholson (1969) reckoned the procedures adopted 'surprisingly sophisticated' and the colony 'quite intensively administered with more of the apparatus of the modern European state than could have been found in some of the states of Europe

[6] NICHOLSON, I.F. *The Administration of Nigeria 1900-1960: Men, Methods, and Myths*, Clarendon Press, Oxford, 1969.

at the time' (1969, 54-55). Entrance to the lowest clerical grade was by competitive examination in arithmetic, handwriting, English composition, dictation, conversation, and knowledge of Yoruba. To obtain promotion to senior grade, middle grade clerks had to undergo a further examination in the government system of accounting, in the drafting of letters, and in the docketing and scheduling of dispatches and documents, and local Ordinances and Orders in Council. They were required to interpret to and from Yoruba, and to write shorthand at the rate of eighty words per minute.

All promotions were centrally regulated by 'merit and ability, and not necessarily by seniority nor length of service', leaving a great deal of discretionary power in the hands of expatriate superiors in spite of the use of annual confidential reports which included such details as the African's 'endeavours after self-improvement since joining the service' (Nicholson, 1969, 56). A junior clerk earned £54 per annum while middle clerk earned £96. Senior grade clerks' salaries ranged between £108 and £300 per annum, the lowest in this category (2nd class clerk) earning £105-£150, 1st class clerk £168- £204 and a chief clerk £240-J300. Salaries in the technical and professional departments were less, an inevitable cause of dissatisfaction. Most chief clerks earned more than several categories of European officers, including the foremen of works, the assistant commissioners of police and officer in charge of the prison (ibid.).

Chief clerks were, however, very rare and it took a long time for Africans to rise to such positions. In any case, the range of other financial and non-monetary benefits enjoyed by expatriate personnel far outstripped differences in pay between chief clerks and the relevant categories of Europeans. All in all, the general population lived in squalid slums, including all African civil servants with the exception of 'about twenty Africans' in senior positions at the time.[7] Both the distribution of personnel in positions of authority and differences in housing policy and fringe benefits provided strong grounds for criticism by the press, by the professional classes and by nationalists of every kind.

For a cost-conscious governor, labour costs could only be reduced in many of the technical departments which utilised daily-paid workers and other seasonal or temporary labourers. This partly explains why most industrial protests in this period came from artisans and labourers engaged in construction, building and engineering, the most celebrated case being the 1897 strike by staff of the Public Works Department (PWD) whose salaries were unceremoniously slashed overnight by Governor McCallum who

[7] Sir Henry Carr, an African, in fact was the head of the Department of Education. Nicholson reckoned that more than twenty Africans could have held senior positions at the time. The prevalence of European names among Africans has made it difficult to ascertain their true number since there was no separation by race in the lists (1969, 57).

considered the existing low wages still too high.[8]

The period 1900 to 1939 witnessed a coalescence of ideas and a more stereotyped approach to 'labour problems'. Colonel Lugard became Governor of Nigeria in 1900 and he had 'pacified' the last of the Hausa-Fulani emirates in 1906, creating the opportunity for the formulation of policies that could cover the whole country. The major reason why this had not happened earlier lay in Lugard's orientation and prejudices, and in the dissenting activities of provincial lieutenant-governors and their men. An important element in all of this was Lugard's intention to turn back the clock, as it were, regarding 'experiments' in the Crown Colony of Lagos as essentially misguided; the creation of a black Englishman was total anathema to him, a possibility that would considerably undermine the underlying assumptions of indirect rule and gradualness of 'development' for 'natives'.

Social and labour policies can hardly be divorced from the dispositions of the principal actors. Racial discrimination became institutionalized under Lugardian 'principles', the more unscrupulous of the colonial officials invoking the racial attitudes which had dominated social intercourse in slave-trading European and North American communities since the sixteenth century. The 'native' was now officially viewed as 'lazy', 'unintelligent', a 'primitive', to be chastised, educated and civilized. Happenings in Lagos since 1862 were regarded as an 'aberration' that had to be stopped. If not they were to be restricted to Lagos or the southern provinces.[9]

The use of forced and convict labour had become increasingly institutionalized and widespread. In 1900 only the Lagos-Ibadan rail line had been completed in the south, with plans to extend it to Shaki. The line from Baro did not reach Kano till 1911 and during the next fifteen years an additional 600 miles of line were laid connecting Kano with Port Harcourt. By 1936 a rail network of 2,178 miles of track covered Nigeria (Coleman, 1958, 55). The 'chiefs' and 'emirs' were the main recruiting agents in this intensified construction programme and were well paid for the privilege. The demand for forced labour grew sharply as tin and coal mines were opened in 1902 and 1915 at Jos and Enugu respectively. Thousands more were conscripted into the armed forces at the outbreak of the First World War in 1914, most of whom were demobilized in 1919. A low-wage policy for this class of labour continued until the 1940s.

This low-wage policy was systematically rationalised in respect of labourers and forced labour when mass desertions compelled private and

[8] Details in HOPKINS, A. .G., 'The Lagos Strike of 1897'.

[9] Coleman, J. .S. devotes a section of a chapter to the attitudes of expatriates to educated elites in particular - *Nigeria: Background to Nationalism;* University of California Press, Berkeley & Los Angeles, 1958, 145-153.

State authorities to pay token wages. One of the outstanding merits of forced labour, according to Lugard, was that it represented 'an educative process to remove fear and suspicion among primitive tribes' (1919, 243). In the burgeoning public administration system, positions were now clearly designated 'European' and 'African', the former attracting higher pay and fringe benefits. At the initial stages of colonial administration in Lagos, the problem seemed to be the dearth of qualified Africans. Racial prejudices now became institutionalised, the first three decades of this century being taken up by official attempts to preserve positions for European personnel in the face of an increasingly large number of qualified indigenes. Ananaba (1969, 13)[10] has written about the palpably absurd situation of fully qualified African doctors of medicine being allowed to occupy 'European' posts on the understanding that they earned only 75 per cent of European salaries.

By and large, therefore, two civil services existed, the African and European, with parallel career structures. Coleman (1958, 155) noted the two contrasting terms of employment in the African clerical service where salary scales ranged from £36 to £400 a year, the highest salary accruing to the oldest and most senior African chief clerks who were no more than twenty-five in number, and the European where an official fresh from university started at £450 a year, and within seventeen years could top the £1,000 mark. On top of this, in the African civil service only 185 out of 5,841 positions (3%) were classified as 'senior' (that is, with a salary above £100 a year) by 1936, a frustrating situation given the very slow turnover and the fact that most of the senior positions were held by Africans who were not Nigerians and who therefore 'had no bonds or feeling of identity with thousands of Africans in the junior service' (Coleman, 1958, 155).

That European civil servants enjoyed better terms of service did not mean their satisfaction was such as to exclude grievances. As Nicholson (1969, 223-225) has so convincingly shown, most were quite unable to meet their social and family obligations both in Nigeria and in England. The state of morale and living condition were described as 'frankly disgraceful' by the 1919 Cameron Committee Report (ibid.). Living standards had been severely affected by soaring inflation, conscriptions and shortages brought about by military hostilities and insufficient public revenue. The first two decades of the century prepared the ground for more active unionism in the public services as a result of widespread disenchantment, 'the African juniors expressing their discontent in open strikes, and European seniors openly disaffected' (*op. cit.*, 223-25).

This did not prevent Lugard at amalgamation in 1914 from proposing augmented salaries for himself and the upper echelons of his team:

---

[10] Anababa, W., *The Trade Union Movement in Nigeria*, Ethiope, Benin, 1969.

Governor-General £6,857 per annum; £2,000 plus duty pay of £600 in the south and £400 in the north for the two lieutenant-governors; £1,500 plus J300 duty pay for the Administrator (governor) of Lagos; £1,600 plus £320 duty pay for the Chief justice; £1,400 and £280 for the Attorney General; £1,000-£1,200 and £200 for the Treasurer; £900-£1,100 and £180 for head of Customs; and £1,000-£1,200 and £200 duty pay for head of Marine (Nicholson, 192). These officials also occupied the biggest and most comfortable mansions.

What could be described as the 'official response' largely depended on the personalities of governors and lieutenant-governors in office at any particular time and their relative success in misrepresenting the situation on the ground to the Colonial Office. Financial resources were chronically insufficient so that from the time of Lugard until 1919 when Clifford took over, little concern was shown about expatriate conditions of service, while Africans were said to be too 'expensive', both in and outside of the service. It was erroneously held that there was a backward sloping supply curve for native workers' who had limited needs that could easily be met by low wages. Indeed, as soon as these needs and wants were met, the workers disappeared. Very low wages were therefore advantageous to all as workers would ultimately satisfy their wants while their services would be available for a much longer time.[11]

Outside the public services the 'disappearance' of labour had little to do with so-called limited wants. It was rather the combined harshness of forced labour and low wages which militated against the retention of a stable labour force. Hopkins noted in this regard that between June 1900 and January 1902 approximately 6,500 labourers left Lagos to work on the Sekondi railway and in the gold mines of the Gold Coast where pay was much higher, and that by 1909 labour shortage in Lagos was acute enough for the authorities to give serious consideration to the possibility of importing Indian labour into West Africa (1966, 147 & 149).[12] After Lugard resigned in 1906 to become governor of Hong Kong, it was possible to institute an internal administrative review by a committee headed by Cameron (Central Secretary) and Carr. Their report was largely ignored by Lugard and his men after he had come back to Nigeria in 1913 with an express mandate to

---

[11] The 'target-earning' hypothesis or 'backward-bending supply curve effort' has been debunked. See BERG, E.G., 'Backward-sloping Labour Supply Functions in Dual Economies: the African Case', *The Quarterly Journal of Economics*, Cambridge (Mass.), LXXV, 1961; VATTER, H.G., 'On the Folklore of the Backward-sloping Supply Curve', *Industrial & Labour Relations Review, vol.* XIV, 1961.

[12] Lugard had moved to Nigeria from Uganda where he had taken to the relatively hardworking but 'docile' Indian and Asian labour in general. And as made clear by Nicholson (1969) throughout his whole book, there were, not far from the surface, constant disagreements over introducing indentured labour from Asia, especially Ceylonese, Malaysians and Indians, into West African economies. The economic and political uses of such a move are pretty obvious.

amalgamate Southern and Northern Nigeria.

This review was, it appears, the first to be originated in Nigeria itself and was the progenitor of so many wage tribunals that they became almost a habit in the public sector. All classes of public servants shared the dissatisfactions arising from the economic difficulties caused by inflation and other shortages brought about by the military hostilities that had broken out in Europe in 1914. Even when the report was eventually made public in 1919 (Lugard had again left in 1918), the inadequacy of its recommendations was readily acknowledged by members of the committee themselves. Within a few days of the arrival of the new governor (Sir Hugh Clifford), he was asked to receive a delegation of senior European civil servants, which included Cameron himself, to protest against general conditions. A few days later, a similar deputation of African civil servants (Civil Service Union) argued before the new governor that 'proposals recently made for the improvement of African salaries did not meet their needs' (Nicholson, *op. cit.*, 221-222).

As from this point the chronology of events becomes a little less clear. Nicholson (1969, 222) gives the impression that another Cameron-Carr Committee was appointed by Clifford, while Ananaba (1969, 12) mentions a Bratt Committee. Since only one Cameron-Carr report is in existence and since Bratt was the Treasurer to the government, and given the financial straits of the colonial administration which was bound to keep any treasurer sleepless and busy, Ananaba's account is more likely the accurate one. The Bratt Committee's report is little known, the mystery arising from nothing more than official concealment of the new terms of employment for European staff contained in it. With strikes by African civil servants on the increase, a new committee headed by Dr. Rice, Director of Medical Services, was appointed, which also included representatives of the Civil Service Union, to revise African salaries. According to Nicholson (1969, 222) 'the case of the African civil service was met within a few weeks, by doubling of an existing 30 per cent War bonus, after emergency Executive Council meetings and telegrams to the Secretary of State, followed by a more complete overhaul of salary structure.

These initial stirrings within the upper echelons of the public service against the terms of employment, and attempts by residents and governors to pre-empt possible political repercussions from the use of forced labour in mines and construction were the origin of an industrial relations institutional framework in Nigeria. At least in the public sector, internal reviews in the form of wage commissions became routine, some of which had consequences for labour and employers in the private sector, particularly from the 1950s when both politicians and bureaucratic elites began to show more than a passing interest in prevailing pay rates.[13]

Major commissions, tribunals and committees from 1920 till the eve of political independence in 1959 include the Hunt Committee (1934), the Bridges Committee (1941), the Harragin Commission (1945 which published its report in 1947), the Tudor Davies Commission (1946), the Miller Committee (1947), the Cowan Enquiry (1948), the Gorsuch Commission (1954) the Mbanefo Commission (1958), and the Morgan Commission (1959).[14] These Committees and Commissions, including those such as the Fitzgerald Commission (1949) appointed to examine the peculiar circumstances leading to violent protests and deaths such as those at the Enugu' coalmines in 1949, were representative of the significant twists and turns of public sector industrial relations over the four decades ending in 1960. Very brief comments on the more important ones may provide a useful overview of the events and issues to which both political authorities and bureaucrats felt compelled to address themselves.

After the war bonus granted in 1914 and the appointment both the Cameron-Carr and Rice Committees, there was no wage review until 1937 when the administration reinstated levels of wages that had been cut in 1929. The Hunt Committee was charged with the task of reviewing the wages of unskilled workers and of determining a reasonable standard of living for a labourer. Wartime shortages and spiralling prices occasioned further workers' protests, to which the administration responded in 1941 with the Bridges Committee which reviewed wages of African government workers in Lagos and recommended compensatory increases, subsequently called 'cost-of-living awards' (COLA), Governor Bourdillon subsequently promising to review COLA according to movements in the cost-of-living index (Yesufu, 1962, 44).[15] Although the index rose from 147 to 174 in October 1943, the new governor, Sir Frederick Richards, did not consider himself bound by the undertakings of his predecessor, and failed to keep the promise of a review. Subsequent exchanges between the unions and the administration only served to increase bad feelings on both sides, a condition hardly helped by worsening shortages and ever-rising prices that rationing and efforts at price control proved unable to moderate. Workers went out on a general strike on 21 June, 1945. The Tudor Davies Commission appointed in the wake of the general strike granted all the workers' demands. Some workers received increases ranging from 50 to 75 per cent. It also recommended that a special *ad hoc* committee called the National Negotiating Committee should be set

[13] This is discussed in greater detail in OTOBO, D., 'Bureaucratic Elites and Public Sector Wage Bargain in Nigeria', *Journal of Modern African Studies*, 24 (1), 1986.

[14] These committees and commissions have been designated after respective chairman. For full official titles see section on 'references' and 'bibliography'.

[15] Yesufu, T.M. *An Introduction to Industrial Relations in Nigeria*, OUP for NISER, 1962.

up, consisting of representatives of various government departments and trade unions, and that provision be made for machinery for settlement of disputes by arbitration.[16]

Political developments, including direct rule, the adoption of a ministerial system, the formation of a new crop of modern political parties and constitutional developments with a view to internal self-government and political independence, an officially espoused policy of rapid 'Nigerianisation' of civil service and more effective trade unionism, hurried the pace at which a loose institutional framework was being erected. In 1946, the Harragin Commission reviewed salaries of 'established' government staff while the Miller Committee looked into wage rates of daily-paid labourers. As a follow up to the Harragin recommendations, the Cowan Enquiry of 1948 investigated and reported on methods of negotiation between government and employees in state-owned industrial establishments. It introduced 'Whitley Councils': a Junior Whitley Council (A) for clerical and other office employees, and Junior Whitley Council (B) for industrial or manual workers. The devolution of power to the political regions in 1954 gave rise to the Gorsuch Commission which largely sought to reconcile the salaries and other fringe benefits of federal and regional civil servants. Lastly, political differences and competition among political parties, partly manifested in competitive wage increase against a background of workers' agitation, led to the establishment of the Mbanefo Commission by the Federal, Eastern, and Northern Regional Governments, with the Western Region Government appointing its own Morgan Commission in 1959.

Some of these developments are commented upon later in a general review of the role of the State in industrial relations. Failing a detailed study of public sector industrial relations, which is not a subject of our immediate concern, this section ends with the observation that the decisive impact of rivalries between State elites, or the teething problems of budding bureaucracies, and of self-interest among dominant political figures and groups, on industrial relations in Nigeria is yet to be fully appreciated. This theme is also explored later.

UNION POLICY

Union policy is here taken to describe attempts on the part of various arms of the State to cope with the organization of workers as legal entities, and to responses by the State to the social, economic and political effects of such organizations within the political economy of a colonial state. Such a policy is typically concerned with the regulation of the external and internal affairs

[16] Further details in Report of the Tudor Davies Commission into the Cost of Living in the Colony and Protectorate of Nigeria, HMSO, No. 204, London, 1946.

of workers' organizations, an exercise that involves various State agencies. It is usual to find the police, intelligence officers, and the armed forces concerning themselves with open and/or widespread industrial conflict; the Department of Labour, though primarily relating to general policy guidelines, is directly involved in mediation, conciliation and arbitration; the Ministry of Justice and the Department of Labour are responsible for the legal prosecution of workers and union officials on behalf of government and the state; the law courts (sometimes), and the registrar of trade unions (along with the police) handle litigation, and the governors, lieutenant-governors, various grades of residents and administrators, chiefs and emirs and *obas* and their hierarchy of officials routinely attempting to neutralize social and political fallout from the activities of workers and their organizations. Such attempts are often badly co-ordinated and provide new sets of grievances or grounds for more protests. We shall now add some flesh to this skeletal structure.

The first problem, from the point of view of colonial governors, political officers and relevant sections of the bureaucracy, seems to be the fact of collective organization by workers itself. Strike action presumes a measure of conscious organization and the deliberate intent to change an offending situation, if not the actual formation of trade unions. The background against which trade unions emerged among public servants has earlier been explained and only a few observations need be made here. *Tout court,* it was difficult to manage a colony when 'the public service was at loggerheads with itself, with the public, with traders, with miners, with everybody and everything' (Nicholson, *op. cit.,* 223). Such a general malaise seemed to have been complicated by institutionalised racial separatism under Lugardian influence:

> in part cause and in part effect of hardening of the divisions between black and white in the official hierarchy, with Nigerians relegated more and more to the lower rungs of the ladder as the older men who had won distinctions in earlier days retired, as civil service became more of a pioneer, frontier service in the unrulier parts of the protectorate, and as civil service came, in these hard conditions, to resemble military discipline, with an almost exclusively European officer caste often too hard-pressed in their ordinary duties to pay sufficient attention to the welfare of their staff (Nicholson, *op. cit.*, 78)

Though the Southern Nigerian Civil Service Union (which changed its name to Civil Service Union when amalgamation was achieved in 1914) was inaugurated in 1912, European civil servants were organised under a separate body. In view of what has been said above, it seems remarkable that Yesufu (1962, 34) could claim that 'the Union was thus not formed by a group of dissatisfied workers, who wanted a platform from which to fight amelioration of grievances or for the improvement of specific conditions of employment,' but that 'it would appear that the main reason for its formation was merely to match the existence of such institutions elsewhere.' The formation of a trade union in any country or context is not usually an act performed at leisure or for amusement: when formed, it immediately invites the not altogether friendly attention of employers and the wrath of State authorities on most occasions. The idea that mere imitation alone was involved seems totally inappropriate to explain the formation of the Nigerian Civil Service Union of 1912. It also seems to be completely at variance with historical facts.[17]

Be that as it may, our concern here is less with the rise and development of trade unionism than with official policy at the time. All governors after Lugard, whatever their personal inclinations, saw the sense in maintaining a virile and co-operative public service without which their own careers might be jeopardized. Having granted audience and formally had dealings with delegations of European civil servants, Clifford eventually even-handedly extended similar recognition to the Civil Service Union whose membership's 'nuisance' potential might be disturbing when supported by vocal elements among professionals and nationalist politicians. Divisions among occupational groups within the Civil Service Union led to teachers, marine and railway workers to form separate organizations in the 1930s. The changing character of the private sector in the Nigerian economy due to amalgamations and collapse of many companies [well discussed by Perham (1948) and Hopkins (1973)][18] and labour revolts in most British colonies in the late 1920s and in the 1930s, caused enough concern internally and in England for the administration and Colonial Office to set out broad guidelines for dealing with unionism and trade unions. It may also be recalled that the so-called 'tax riots' had occurred in Warri in 1927 and in Aba in 1929.

As outlined in the introductory sections of this essay, law enforcement agencies and political officers saw little distinction between workers' and community protests: both were violently put down. To the control of labour by Residents, by personnel in the native administration, and by troops and police was now added that of relevant civil servants who began systematically to apply a growing body of regulations and guidelines laid down in London. To ensure the existence of 'safety valves' and to assuage the fear that 'the

[17] Of course, it does not prevent union officials from referring to the prior existence of a similar combination in Freetown, Sierra Leone, but this should be recognized for what it is — namely one of the protective arguments presented to prevent suppression of their union. Within civil service practice, precedence is the universally recognized policy-guiding principle.

[18] 23. Perham, M. (ed.), Mining, Commerce, and Finance in Nigeria, Faber & Faber, London, 1948; HOPKINS, A.G., *An Economic History of West Africa*, Longman, London, 1973.

prohibition of trade unions might well give rise to "extremist organizations" which might become politically active' (Roberts, 1964, 183),[19] the Colonial Office sought to apply pressure on all colonial administrations, by building on the famous 'Passfield Memorandum' and successive Colonial Welfare and Development Acts.

The Colonial Secretary, Lord Passfield (formerly Sidney Webb), in a dispatch to all colonial governors, urged them to see the growth of trade unions as a natural and legitimate development, advocating the enacting of trade union legislation along the lines of the United Kingdom Trade Union Act of 1871. All colonial administrations resisted or delayed the passing of such legislation; Yesufu (1962, 29-30)[20] has noted how it was only conceded in Nigeria under great pressure from the Colonial Office. This and other developments I have more comprehensively discussed elsewhere, but the general argument presented by the government and by private European employers was that such statutory provision was too sophisticated for African conditions, and had only been adopted by the 'civilised world' after a considerable period of time (ibid., 29-30).[21]

The first in the series of Colonial Development and Welfare Acts appeared in 1929 and the last in 1946. Taken together they were designed to achieve three main objectives. Two objectives were officially described as being 'to promote commerce with, relieve economic depression in the United Kingdom and stimulate agricultural activity in the colonial territories' (cited in Ekundare, 1973, 121).[22] The third objective was simply to cajole and persuade colonial administrations to pass the necessary legislation to formalize union activities, establish machinery for labour inspection, and initiate collective methods for processing grievances and bargaining, thereby providing such long overdue 'safety valves'. The Secretary of State for the Colonies had also, in several dispatches, later incorporated in the Colonial Development and Welfare Act of 1940 (and its 1945 additions), requested that economic surpluses derived from colonies should be passed on to colonial workers in the form of improved social services. More important, for our purposes, he also required from any colony desiring to benefit from funds set aside by these Acts, to pass laws facilitating the establishment and functioning of trade unions and to ensure that wages were reasonable.

It was a tempting offer, particularly for financially hard-pressed colonial administrations of which Nigeria was one. We have seen how efforts to increase internally derived revenue through the imposition of taxes resulted

[19] Roberts, B. C., *Trade Unions in A Free Society*, Institute of Economic Affairs, London, 1959.

[20] Yesufu, T. M., *An Introduction to Industrial Relations in Nigeria*, OUP for NISER, 1962.

[21] See Otobo, D., *The Role of Trade Unions in Nigerian Industrial Relations*, Malthouse Press, Oxford, 1986.

[22] Ekundare, R. O., *An Economic History of Nigeria, 1860-1960*, Methuen, London, 1973.

in riots during the late 1920s and how wages were cut in 1927. We also know that during this period, 'native administration' was collapsing and social protests and political ferment were on the increase, creating anxious moments internally and in London. Against great opposition from employers, the administration passed a Trade Union Ordinance in 1938 which came into force in April 1939, and was quickly followed by the creation of a labour inspectorate which became the Department of Labour in 1942. The administration also enacted a Trade Disputes (Arbitration and Inquiry) Ordinance in 1941. Akpala (1971, 23)[23] records that the colonial administration was rewarded to the tune of £23 million which it used in financing its 1945 Ten-Year Development Plan.

Details of the Trade Union Ordinance may be found in Ordinance No. 44 of 1938 but a far more readily available source is Yesufu (1962) who gives a good summary of its contents.[24] The definition of a trade union adopted in the Ordinance was British, embracing organizations of workers and of employers. It was:

> any combination, whether temporary or permanent, the principal purposes of which are the regulation of the relations between workmen and workmen, or between masters and masters whether such combination would or would not, if this Ordinance had not been enacted, have been deemed to have been unlawful combination by reason of some, one or more its purposes, being in restraint of trade.

Following the British tradition, members of the prison service and the police were barred from forming or belonging to a trade union.

As may be expected, the ordinance placed much emphasis on 'duties' and 'obligations', hardly any on benefits or rights. Every trade union had to be registered within three months of formation or disbanded, and if the Registrar of Trade Unions so declined to register any union, or cancelled previous registration, the union had to be disbanded within three months of such refusal or cancellation. Two copies of union rules or constitutions and a list of officers were required to be given to the Registrar at registration, and any other information concerning registered office and address, rate of contributions and use to which union funds were to be put. Trade union membership was restricted to persons above the age of sixteen and as few as five persons could form a union, but neither a minor nor an illiterate would be allowed to hold positions of treasurer, secretary and president. It was obligatory for a union to keep comprehensive membership list, indicating members' occupations, trade and names of employers, and for these and

[23] Akpala, A. 'Industrial Relations Policies in Nigeria', *Genieve Afrique*, vol. 10(1), 1971

[24] Yesufu, T.M., *An Introduction to Industrial Relations in Nigeria*, OUP for NISER, Ibadan, 1962, pp. 30-32

other records be open to inspection by any persons having an interest in the funds of the union. Accounts were required to be kept and audited annually by a person approved by the Registrar of Trade Unions. A copy of the accounts were to be submitted to him within a month, and a general statement of account be rendered every year before 1st of June of the following year, accompanied by a copy of all alterations to union rules and changes in union leadership. The Registrar also had general powers to call for special returns and, if any statutory requirement was transgressed, empowered to institute criminal or civil proceedings.

Many of these provisions have an air restrictive of the workers' point of view. Compulsory registration, which had no precedent in the United Kingdom and was in fact recommended for inclusion in these labour ordinances by the Secretary of State for the Colonies, represented a formidable weapon in the selective harassment of union leadership, particularly in the turbulent forties when colonial officialdom strenuously sought to drive a wedge between nationalist politicians and union leaders. Second, decisions not to register caused a not inconsiderable number of strikes and compelled, in some instances, employers to intervene in favour of their employees, thus forcing registration, (especially in the public sector). Third, cancellation or de-registration was persistently used in the 1940s and 1950s to extinguish many trade unions for a variety of reasons, ranging from direct employer pressure to dissatisfaction with union leadership through 'political involvement', ideological orientation, the nature of demands made, and/or engaging in strike action. Fourth, the registration process seems to have been deliberately protracted, both to keep numbers down and as a source of pressure on potential union members and leadership. For example, every application for registration had first be announced in the official *Gazette*, the length of time involved in doing this depending on the priorities set by the publication itself. And even when an announcement could be made, a further six months was allowed for any objections to a proposed registration to be filed (Yesufu, *op. cit.*, 31). It was not really surprising that strikes over union recognition were frequent right up to the 1960s.

The provision of the ordinance that a minimum of five persons could legally form a union has also been criticized. It has been largely held responsible for the multiplicity and small size of unions. In this there may be some truth though the divisive tactics of some union officers and employers alike who, at various times, have fomented crises and instigated factionalism may have contributed even more. It may be that the colonial administration favoured small unions, as making official control easier while making union coordination for union leaders more difficult. As it turned out clusters of power within the labour movement did make it weaker. Ironically, they also made it more democratic even if the colonial administration remained blatantly authoritarian! The attention of private and official employers could only but be fixed on the leadership of central labour organizations, the only concentration of power representing the interests of organised labour.

Nevertheless, the Trade Union Ordinance was an important piece of legislation. Tayo Fashoyin (1980, 91)[25] is of the view that 'technically speaking, unions organised before 1938 were illegal associations formed in constraint (restraint?) of trade, following the British pattern.' This was certainly not the case. The device of British courts in declaring the very act of combining to be illegal (and hence also lobbying by unionists for repeal of the 1799-1800 Combination Acts) was never used in Nigeria. Second, the absence of legal protection against tortious and criminal actions arising from union activities did not mean that unions themselves were illegal. They were simply more vulnerable to the hostile and, sometimes damaging, tactics of employers and of state officials. If representatives of the colonial administration bargained with officials of pre-1938 unions and even appointed some of them as members of the Cameron-Carr and Bratt Committees, such a situation was (and is) somewhat preferable to one in which a union is duly registered and yet management refused to deal with it, the situation which applied in the 1940s and 1950s. Although the latter is a different sort of argument, the fact remains that neither the Civil Service Union, nor the Nigerian Union of Teachers, nor the Marine Workers Union, all formed before 1938, were deemed to be illegal, nor did private employers who fiercely resisted unionisation of their establishments so describe them. In the main, private employers argued in terms of modern trade unions being 'too sophisticated' for these parts or, conversely, that workers were too 'primitive' to understand the essentials of trade unionism. Ironically the labels 'illegal' and 'legal' as applied to unions was introduced by the ordinance, in remarkable contrast with the experience in the United Kingdom where unions not registered with the Registrar of Friendly Societies had never been seen nor described 'illegal'. Nevertheless, and with some element of exaggeration and not discounting the workers' protests, it could be said of the ordinance that 'without it workers were largely impotent to act on their own account, and had to depend upon the grace of the state, or of employers, to ensure that working conditions were tolerable' (Yesufu, 1962, 32).

The Department of Labour established in Lagos in 1942 had become a full-fledged federal ministry by 1951, with a minister at the top and the usual hierarchy of officials. The functions of its specialized sections and of its major officers are well described in Yesufu (*op. cit.*, 22-28) and need not detain us here. It is sufficient for our purpose to recognize its central role in administering laws and regulations pertaining to organised labour and

[25] Fashoyin, T., *Industrial Relations in Nigeria*, Longman, London, 1980

providing such services as conciliation, arbitration, and supervision of the provisions of the Factories Act that periodically involve employers. Moreover, its very existence and the functions of its staff were all products of a specific philosophy underlying the labour policy adopted by the state.

It is perhaps important to point out that anxieties over 'safety valves' and 'politically active unions' related not only to colonial experience, and the scares created by labour rebellions in British colonies. The Bolshevik Revolution occurred in 1917-18 and the subsequent two decades were a period of ideological and political ferment in Europe and North America. In the latter, ideological conflicts in the labour movement were only successfully contained in favour of non-socialist groups in the 1950s.[26] Ideological divisions among unionists still persist in more conspicuous fashion in British and most European labour movements to the present day, just as the world has remained divided into two main ideological blocs. In short, the *policy of containment of socialism by conservative and right-wing governments was actively pursued by both metropolitan and colonial governments at the time.*

Thus, the political and ideological preferences contained in the Passfield Memoranda re-surfaced in the 1946 Tudor Davies Commission, with the Commission noting that the 'real issue' was not the destruction of unions, which seem to have become a matter of routine, 'but how they are to be directed into right paths', and how if not given 'help and encouragement by Great Britain to develop along proper trade union lines, they might be swallowed up and converted to political uses in the wider demands for self-government and independence, that is, their drifting finally and irrevocably into the hands of politicians' (*Report*, 1946, paras. 88 and 27).

Four observations seem proper. 'Proper trade union lines' could hardly be said to exist in Britain at the time. There was still a good deal of confusion over the proper limits to trade union activities and the most appropriate methods to be adopted in connection therewith (a situation which persists to this day), even if the Colonial Office had its own conception of what unions should do in the colonies. This, along with provisions of the ordinance, such as compulsory registration, the use to which they were put and the conduct of state officials in respect of union officers and members suggests the conclusion that commitment to 'proper trade union lines' was little more than a facade, behind which a many activities that had little to do with proper unionism were carried out. It was a position that had great tactical advantage, for it had enormous appeal to critics and to the business

[26] 26. For details see, GUERIN, D., *100 Years of Labour in the USA*, Ink Links, London, 1979; EDWARDS, R., *Contested Terrain: The Trans formation of the Workplace in the Twentieth Century*, Heinemann, London, 1979; and GROB, G.N., *Workers and Utopia: A study of Ideological Conflict in the American Labour Movement 1865-1900*, Quadrangle Books, Chicago, 1961.

community, both internally and in the United Kingdom, when officials were perchance forced to defend some excesses. Secondly, it provided, of course, ready grounds for direct official involvement in the affairs of unions in excess of that provided for under the ordinance, thereby in practice eroding whatever measure of legal protection was afforded to them.[27] Thirdly, it represented a strategy to achieve the twin objectives of: a) weakening the 'independence movement' by counter-posing the more cooperative sections of the labour leadership to nationalist politicians (which perhaps partly explains why nationalist politicians largely ignored the former since the late 1940s because many of them were regarded as too close to the colonial administration); and b) influencing political events and political actors alike in relation to various British interests since there were hardly any guarantees as to what nationalist politicians, as emergent political superiors, could do with unions and the economy. Fourthly, it formed part of a strategy of slowing down the spread of communist or socialist ideas in the colony by reserving the right to determine methods to be adopted by organised labour, and the ends to which organised labour and other interest groups could be directed. All of these sub-goals were intertwined, reinforcing each other.

The proclaimed aim of the State's trade union policy was the creation of 'non-political unionism', carefully defined to exclude any form of contact with nationalist politicians and political parties. According to Davies (1958, 32),[28] there had slowly evolved between the Colonial Office and the British Trades Union Congress 'a theory of the role of trade unions (in the colonies) which stresses the importance of effective democracy within trade union movements and seeks to maintain independence of trade unionists from government control.' This policy was to be adopted, in respect of labour movements in Africa, Asia and South America, by the International Confederation of Free Trade Unions (ICFTU) founded in 1949 by representatives of Western labour movements who abandoned the World Federation of Trade Unions to the communists because of irreconcilable ideological and political differences.[29]

Apart from those agencies of the State identified with 'labour policy', the additional instruments introduced for effective and sophisticated implementation were 'labour officers' and 'trade union officers' supplied by the British TUC to the Department of Labour on the request of the Colonial Office. Their role was, according to Tayo Fashoyin (1980, 92) who borrowed heavily from Yesufu (1962), 'to assist in the formation of new unions, to advise existing ones on their administrative problems and to conduct various

---

[27] At any rate, General Defence (Emergency) Provisions Decree of 1941 suspended all human and political rights of the Nigerian population and of organized groups therein.

[28] *African Trade Unions, Penguin*, Hammondsworth, 1966.

[29] See Otobo, D., *Foreign Interests and Nigerian Trade Unions*, Heinemann, Ibadan, 1986

programmes of trade union education.' In this bland and misleading view of the duties performed by trade union and labour officers (the title of 'trade union officer' was dropped in 1954), it may be discerned that 'programmes of trade union education' had to do with imparting their own peculiar model of unionism to their students. It may be an interesting coincidence that the General Secretary of the Nigerian Trades Union Congress (1943) was a recipient of a British TUC scholarship to study at Ruskin College, Oxford, at a time when the colonial administration had no scholarships scheme for academic studies abroad (the first University at Ibadan was established only in 1948) and was not even persuaded to allow those who could privately afford them to leave the country until 1945.[30]

There were a host of problems associated with 'formation of new unions', but these had more to do with official procedures for doing so and to the refusal of employers to recognize unions or their officials for bargaining purposes. Trade union officers and labour officers were involved in the process of determining which of the unions should be registered or de-registered. Similarly, there were 'administrative problems' which derived largely from the factionalisation brought about by the divisive tactics of employers, the small size of unions and paucity of funds largely because official and private employers preferred these situations as being helpful to their retention of control. As early as 1944 (when there were only 91 registered trade unions), union leaders began to press, unsuccessfully, for the reorganization along industrial lines. Other factors were the poor state of communications, the vast territory to be covered, and style of management adopted. This is not to imply that workers and union officials were without blemish. The point is that there was very little that they could do as regards the size of unions in the light of fierce employers' resistance to unionism in the first place, and the insistence, much later, by employers on formation of 'house unions' in branches of their companies, and, of course, the colonial administration's full sympathy with them. It is important to emphasise this point because most observers since Yesufu (1962), who showed some insight, and particularly Ananaba (1969), Cohen (1974), Fashoyin (1980) and Ubeku (1983),[31] have appeared to attribute lack of movement toward amalgamations and reorganization of small unions solely to the self-aggrandizement of union leaders in maintaining little empires and the financial rewards obtainable by managing several unions at the same time.

The overwhelming role of both State and employers in substantially

---

30 The generation of Nigerians that studied abroad after 1900 till 1948 did so illegally by sneaking out of the country. This was inclusive of prominent professionals and politicians such as Dr. Nnamdi Azikiwe.

31 Ubeku, A.K., *Industrial Relations in Developing Countries: The Case of Nigeria*, Macmillan, London & Basingstoke, 1983

determining union structure can be illustrated by two examples. First there was the case of the United African Company (UAC) which led an oligopoly since 1930. When its workers, under the aegis of the union UNAMAG, embarked upon a series of strikes in 1949 and 1950, the union was promptly de-registered. The company prevented the formation of any union till 1955 when it recognized one UAC house union in Lagos. A company-wide union, organising all of its workforce nationally was allowed only in 1957 after its prospective general secretary 'requested and was granted permission' by management (Kilby, 1969, 292).[32] The union concerned, the Associated Companies African Workers' Union, thereafter negotiated eight national agreements with the UAC from 1959 to 1962 at which point the company unilaterally decentralized and 'negotiated' fifty-five individual site agreements (ibid.). The union had no choice but to adapt its own structure into fifty-five autonomous units to enable it to continue to function within the parameters established by the company.

The second example has to do with the 1976-77 reorganization of nearly a thousand Nigerian unions into 42 so-called industrial unions. All central labour organizations since 1943 and all wage commissions since 1946 recommended a streamlining of union structure along industrial lines, a suggestion both government and private employers successfully resisted. For a variety of reasons which have been discussed elsewhere, and which are touched upon later, the military government under General Murtala Mohammed, with the cooperation of union leaders and much against employers' opposition, undertook this particular union reorganization. For once, the interests of the State conspicuously diverged from those of private employers and produced decisive action. It was the same story with the national minimum wage legislation finally passed in 1981 under President Shagari's administration.[33]

It seems likely that the provision of a minimum of five persons to form a union was designed to accommodate the smallness of commercial establishments and therefore the wishes of employers. Despite much decrying of this provision, there were no unions which had actually a membership of five persons. If the Trade Union Ordinance had required a minimum of fifty persons, as is now the case, this would have meant a multi-employer bargaining situation and formation of industrial and general unions spanning numerous establishments, a possibility that private employers would have vehemently opposed. The representativeness of emergent unions was an issue labour officers, employers and State officials

---

[32] *Industrialization in an Open Economy: Nigeria 1944-1966*, Cambridge University Press, 1969

[33] For details on the national minimum wage issue, see OTOBO, D., 'The Nigerian General Strike of 1981', Review of African Political Economy, 22, 1981.

were only too willing to determine, hence the innumerable protests over non-recognition in spite of the ordinance.

The lack of realism of Fashoyin (1980) and others in their views of labour and trade union officers and the intimate involvement of the State in industrial and social matters can also be exemplified from the coal industry in which, in 1944, the Colliery Workers' Union declared a dispute over cost-of-living allowances. After an unsuccessful arbitration attempt at a meeting held at the Government Lodge on 19 April, 1945, the administration decided that the union did not enjoy the full support of its members and had thus forfeited the right of recognition by management. To seal the fate of the union, a labour officer in his report advised that 'if a strike does occur, if conciliation breaks down, there can be no doubt that it will have been engendered and fostered entirely by the union officials and I shall watch their activities closely, as I consider that their dismissal from the colliery would in the event of a strike, have a most salutary effect.' The strike broke out and his advice was taken (cited in Akpala, 1984, 109).[34] The conduct and views of this labour officer were by no means exceptional. Labour officers were primarily expected to gather as much information as possible on unions and unionists with a view to pre-empting protests and undermining potential claims and demands made by workers, and on the basis of both to decide upon de-registration and choice of model of 'responsible' union and unionists.

Since union members and officers were no less literate than the typical European, Levantine and Asian traders that dominated the economic landscape of the 1940s and 1950s, and since it is a well-established historical fact that employers and managements were generally reluctant to countenance unions, reluctant to negotiate, and that the brutality of law enforcement agencies served to dominate the conduct of industrial relations, it is an odd thing that most observers and official spokesmen have turned the picture upside down and consistently tended to portray a picture of ignorant unionists who required remedial 'courses', 'seminars' and the like to remove deficiencies to ensure 'proper unionism'. It is ironical that even trade unionist themselves seem unwittingly to have adopted this view, hence the great emphasis placed by them on 'trade union education', their acceptance of the approaches adopted by the Department of Labour (now Ministry of Employment, Labour and Productivity), the ICFTU, the WFTU, and other foreign national labour centres such as the British TUC, the American AFL-CIO, the West German DGB, and their equivalents in Eastern Europe, the Soviet Union and China.

A new element in the equation in the 1940s and 1950s was the changing

[34] Managing Industrial Relations in' Nigeria: A Case Study the Nigerian Coal Industry, Dept. of Management of Univ: of Nigeria, Nsukka, 1984

complexion of the driving force of the State system, the government. Nationalist political parties had developed mass appeal and by way of successive constitutional talks and the adoption of new constitutions their leaders were gradually being eased into positions of power within the colonial order. The 'internal self-government' arrangements effected in 1954, which included direct popular elections based on universal adult suffrage, signalled the ever weakening positions of expatriate colonial governors and civil servants. Indeed, the end of the Second Would War may be said to mark a turning point, providing powerful arguments for political independence and democracy and the wholesale 'Nigerianisation' of positions in all arms of the State.

The relations between trade unions and political parties in Nigeria have been extensively commented upon, especially by Hodgkin (1956, 1961), Coleman (1958), Ezera (1960), Sklar (1963), Berg & Butler (1965), Davies (1966), and Dudley (1968), we content ourselves with a few pertinent remarks.[35] In the fight for political positions and social placing within the colonial polity, nationalist politicians sought closer links with trade unions, violent suppression of workers' protests often providing ready ammunition for the politicians' own remonstrations. Institutional links were developed between the NCNC and the TUC, the latter having been represented at the inaugural conference of the political party to which it subsequently affiliated. This formal affiliation was preceded by seven out of seventeen members of the party's national executive committee being drawn from the ranks of trade unionists, some of whom, such as Imoudu and Aghedo, were important officials of the TUC. Another group of younger unionists, who clustered around Nduka Eze and Lawrence Borha, were heavily involved in both the militant Zikist Movement and its protagonist the Nigerian Youth Movement. These and other developments are well discussed in Coleman (1958) and Sklar (1963), and we merely note that the issues of the TUC's affiliation with the NCNC was largely responsible for the breakup of the former in 1948, when, after disaffiliating, many unions abandoned it to form a rival body.

By contrast, between 1948 and 1951 when nationalist politicians were engrossed in the constitutional mechanics for sharing power among themselves and between themselves and expatriate colonial officials and the metropolitan government, they had less need of unions for applying pressure for political concessions. If anything, politicians now adopted the

[35] Hodgkin, T., *Nationalism in Colonial Africa*, Frederick Muller, London, 1956; *African Political Parties*, Penguin, 1961; Coleman, J.S., *Nigeria: Background to Nationalism*; Ezera, K., *Constitutional Developments in Nigeria*, CUP, London, 1960; Sklar, R., *Nigerian Political Parties*, Princeton Univ. Press,1963; Berg. E. & Butler, J., 'Trade Unions' in Coleman, J.S. & Rosberg, C.G. (eds.), *Political Parties and National Integration in Tropical Africa*, Univ. of California Press, Berkeley & Los Angeles, 1965; Davies, I., *African Trade Unions* Penguin, 1966; Dudley, B. J., *Parties and Politics in Northern Nigeria*, Frank Cass, London, 1968

perspectives of the colonial political authorities and saw many unions and unionists as 'obstacles', as too articulate and demanding. Dr. Azikiwe personally denounced the activities of the Zikist Movement which he thought too militant and radical, and the years 1950 to 1955 saw combined efforts by both the NCNC and the colonial administration in Lagos to suppress the organization. It is instructive that nationalist politicians (and most post-colonial governments for that matter) co-operated with trade union and labour officers and other relevant state organs to undermine unions, unionists and officials of central labour organizations known to have dealings of any sort with communist countries. It was this combined pressure, in addition to those of private employers and of international labour organizations representing the two main ideological camps (the Western having unrestricted access till they were prevented in 1975), which were largely responsible for producing a factionalized labour movement from the late 1940s to the 1960s rather than ideological and personal differences among trade unionists as has generally been argued.[36]

Other than the above, hardly any nationalist political party had a coherent policy toward organised labour and the welfare of workers save in the context of rivalries engendered by regionalism and the projected 1959 federal elections which would usher in Independence and the political basis for the first directly elected federal cabinet and government. In 1954, the Western Region government established a five-shilling minimum wage, a move that was matched by both the Eastern and Northern Region governments in 1955. As we have already seen, against a background of workers' protests, the Mbanefo and Morgan Commissions were established in 1959 to review wages and conditions of service. This Yesufu (1962, 142) dismissed as 'political wage fixing'. The economic situation appeared nevertheless to justify a minimum wage, and the problem of daily-paid employees (a cost-saving and labour control device adopted as it became legally and practically impossible to continue with the forced labour policy) which the Eastern Region government tackled by transferring all such categories of labour into permanent establishment, did exist and such transfer had been among organised labour's demands for the previous three decades. The timing of the two wage commissions may have been politically

[36] In the light of this it is perhaps easier to comprehend why unionists could not do much about union structure, 'administrative problems' of which these pressures were a large component, and other issues discussed in this chapter. Interestingly when, in 1974 foreign financial aid to mutually hostile central bodies in Nigeria started tapering off with government interference and final proscription of such aid in 1975, these same 'ideologically-divided' labour leaders were able to form an all-embracing body, the Nigerian Labour Congress, which a frightened government quickly banned and proceeded to reconstitute under its direct supervision. Details may be found in Otobo, D,, Foreign Interests and Nigerian Trade Unions and Otobo, D., The Nigerian General Strike of 1981, *Review of African Economy*, Vol. 22, 1982

astute, but it was hardly plausible to maintain that the 1955 wage increases were solely designed to win votes from daily-paid labourers, since they comprised, at that time, and indeed still do, such an insignificant proportion of the electorate at the 1959 elections. Such intense conflicts and disagreements existed among politicians, including numerous threats to secede, that it would be very surprising if such medium to long-term electoral calculations formed part of their thinking; neither workers nor unions were so politically important.[37] One possibility, however, that can sustain Yesufu's position but not in the sense intended by him would be if both governments or political parties, in seeking to outflank and undermine a prospective Labour Party, deliberately courted the section of organised labour not predisposed to direct political action. The Labour Party was, indeed, formed in 1956, much to the annoyance of many a nationalist politician, but failed to gain any wide following, even among working people.

The economic justification of such awards was recognised in April 1950 when the colonial administration increased wages by administrative fiat because of an increased cost of living resulting from inflation. The administration noted that no general review of salaries and wages had taken place since the 1947 Harragin Commission and asked the private sector to follow its example (Cohen, 1974, 75). The issues of daily-paid labourers and geographical differentials remained unresolved between 1951 and 1953 because it was a period of transition to both ministerial and regional systems of government. It was a fluid and unsettling time of a kind which led bureaucrats to procrastinate and shy away from serious policy decisions. Whatever the shortcomings of the nationalist politicians, the general goal of betterment of conditions was initially shared by all. Operating within the ambit of prior selection of problems and labour policy after they were firmly in the saddle could only be unfairly and injudiciously dismissed as 'political'.

The penchant for dismissing certain policies and actions as 'political' is unhelpful because it has tended to draw attention away from serious underlying economic and social difficulties which have industrial relations impacts at the time and in the post-colonial period. Such difficulties have also immeasurably contributed to the fragility of the State and the vicious struggles and rivalries among State elites. Again, according to Yesufu (1962, 142), the 1959 missions were appointed because 'the labour movement that it was not altogether incapable of exploiting the political situation; and the TUC spearheaded a general demand for wage increase using the workers' votes in the pending federal elections as reward for various political parties,

[37] Ezera, K., *Constitutional Developments in Nigeria*, CUP, London, 1960; Dudley, BJ., *Instability and Political Order: Politics and Crisis in Nigeria* for more details.

which the parties greedily swallowed.'

Such monocausal explanations are at best superficial and leave a host of questions. For example, statistics supplied (1962, 57) himself confirm a worsening strike situation, the officially recorded figure jumping from 30 in 1956-57 to 49 and 53 for 1958-59 period, with corresponding increase in disputes involving stoppages of work. In the period 1955-56, during which 'political wage fixing' was said to have taken place, 45 strikes with a consequent 901,000 lost man-days, a record for that decade; the nearest was 73,095 in 1958-59! On the basis of such figures, unreliable and conservative as most official are, Yesufu somewhat tortuously and uncomfortably noted 'although providing no firm evidence for any particular...the state of industrial relations in Nigeria has worsened, within the last few years' (1969, 57).

A second point relates to the basis for mobilizing workers in The central trade union leadership was factionalised at this substantial number of trade union leaders were allied to political parties, a situation exacerbated by the prominent lie or tribal associations in colonial urban society and the concomitant centripetal forces unleashed by ethnic chauvinism and regionalism which largely formed the basis for political mobilisation and socialisation. That trade union leaders successfully mobilised workers for strikes and other forms of industrial conflict to persuade governments to undertake a general review can only be attributed to the existence of widespread and sufficiently serious grievances. It is doubtful whether any of the political parties required the political gesture of a wage commission to secure so few votes. Given regional, ethnic and political differences among workers and union leaders (differences that were actively exploited by both politicians and employers and some of whom had been incorporated into the party leadership structure at local, regional and federal levels and were campaigning on behalf of respective parties), and the general excitement generated by approaching Independence, was there sufficient social consciousness to permit a great many workers to individually attach such great importance to a 'workers vote'.[38]

The third factor has to do with pay levels and low standards of living. African workers were generally poorly paid in relation to expatriates, depressed levels of wages being much worse in private establishments in which pay rates only caught up with so-called government rates in the public sector in the mid-1960s. Lower wage levels in private establishments were partly a reflection of a lower degree of unionisation in this sector, a situation that was rapidly reversed between 1960 and 1970, which accounted for the

[38] But there have always been some sections of the labour movement that have developed such a consciousness. In fact, a Labour Party was formed by some trade unionists as earlier indicated. As already noted, colonial resistance among the Tivs persisted throughout the colonial period.

greater frequency and intensity of strikes in the immediate post-colonial period. The improved chances for unionization in the private sector may be attributed to the dilemma in which Balewa's government found itself. Caught between organised labour and conspicuously foreign private employers, and the necessity to maintain a stable political order (which had begun deteriorating sharply by 1961) it was forced to scrutinize certain industrial practices (or malpractices?) and to appear nationalistic. On the other hand, aggrieved groups of workers no doubt reckoned that an indigenous government was bound to experience greater difficulty in justifying to itself and the public the suppression of unionism in the private sector in light of recently won political independence. Although the 1959 Morgan Commission published its findings by mid-1960, by late 1961 comprehensive demands were already being made. These mounted as inflation rose in 1962 and 1963 and finally culminated in a series of national stoppages and a general strike in 1963. We may note for the moment that workers in the private sector had such importance for the 1963/64 Morgan Commission that it dramatically departed from all preceding wage commissions in being specifically required to look into pay conditions in private establishments. We now take a look at State policies towards employers.

THE COLONIAL STATE AND EMPLOYERS

An industrializing Britain required both markets and raw materials for its industries; hence the emphasis from the late 1700s on 'legitimate trade' and suppression of the trans-Atlantic slave trade. The traders and merchants had had commercial contacts for centuries with areas that were later to be colonized. Such commercial activities of pioneer individual traders and of limited liability companies in the nineteenth century formed, as we have already seen, the basis of territorial claims made by European colonial powers, the better known occasion being the 1884-85 Berlin West African Conference, where rival European countries literally shared out African territories into spheres of influence as potential dependencies.

In tune with this development, over much of Africa (especially the Congo, now Zaire) several colonial monopoly companies actually traded in and governed large tracts of territory for many years before formal colonial rule was militarily imposed. As already noted, the Royal Niger Company (RNC) was the main vehicle in Nigeria. One relevant consequence was that both trading companies and business communities in metropolitan countries had considerable influence over colonial policies, even to the point of choice of colonial governors and other important appointees. It was earlier indicated how Lugard himself was an employee of the RNC; nor was he the last of such company-influenced appointments in Nigeria.

The predominant position of merchant and industrial groups in Europe resulted from the prevailing capitalist ideology of *laissez-faire* which in the main argued against government intervention in economic matters, thus giving such groups of individuals an unlimited degree of freedom. Such unfettered freedom could neither be complete, nor could it last forever. It was, for example, slightly curtailed when State authorities required legal registration of limited liability companies, tax obligations, and custom duties, thus producing legislation that has been codified as commercial and company law. The *laissez faire* doctrine was, however, only substantially modified in the light of the difficulties experienced during the 1930s economic depression. It is against a background of the above factors that State policy toward employers may be viewed.

ORGANIZATIONAL AND PERSONNEL POLICIES

In respect of the organizational and personnel policies of private companies, the colonial State was both aloof and intimately involved. How private economic organizations were established in the United Kingdom and how such organizations were managed did not concern colonial governors, residents and other officials for many years. Owners were seen as having the right to manage their property as they saw fit. Individualism and the right to own property and manage it accordingly were the underlying philosophical bases of the *laissez faire* doctrine. In the protectorate of Northern Nigeria (established in 1906), the trading community was hardly liked by Lugard. To him it seemed to consist of 'undesirables', with "i fondness for litigation' and of agents of 'modernization', whose activities in several important ways served to undermine native administration and indirect rule (Nicholson, 1969). This attitude contrasted sharply with the situation in the Southern Protectorate of Nigeria where the operations of traders and companies were more openly accepted.

Much as he personally disliked the trading and business communities, Lugard shared with them the overriding goal of exploitation of both human and material resources for the profit and growth of British Empire. For this, and for much of the colonial period, State authorities furnished for the use of private companies both convict and forced labour. Aside from crucial expatriate personnel and insignificant numbers of African clerks, State authorities in the 1940s and 1950s could rightly be said to have assumed many personnel functions for private firms, particularly in the 'recruitment', 'motivation' and 'discipline' of the workforce. The use to which forced and convict labour were put differed with historical periods. Earlier periods coincided with massive construction programmes (road, rail lines, public buildings); later forced labour was used in mines and subsequently in the construction of ports and military bases, and in the armed forces and agricultural plantations.

The importance of this phenomenon for colonial labour-management relations can hardly be overstated. This may be pertinently illustrated by the mining industry which was jointly dominated by both the colonial administration and the Niger Company, the predecessor of the UAC. The Niger Company, as part compensation for losing its official charter in 1899, became entitled to fifty per cent of all proceeds from mining. In the Plateau tin mines, forced labour was obtained via direct raiding of various communities by troops and through the 'co-operation of the Native Authority system which was decisive for rounding up and holding labour on the minefields' (Freund, 1981, 141).[39] With the exception of the Emir of Katsina, other emirs were engaged in this exercise, the Emir of Jemaa organizing 'recruitment himself' (ibid.). In 1943 at Bisichi, a group of recruits was reported to have been locked overnight in the UAC canteen at Maidobi and then packed off for the Plateau (ibid.). And as desertion increased, the Native Authority system was 'enlisted to seek out deserters' as mine managers took to bribing chiefs to provide more recruits. In this regard, J. J. Emberton, the administrative director of mineral production and the central figure in the forced labour programme, wryly noted at the end of 1942 that 'many a pagan chief was to be seen wearing splendid new outfits on the proceeds of his take in this labour trafficking' (ibid.). Managers of the few mining companies supplemented 'recruitment' by State authorities, some procuring large numbers of recruits through direct arrangements with political district officers (ibid.).

One attendant problem was the feeding of thousands of men concentrated in a relatively small area which was itself being ecologically destroyed through open cast mining and loss of farmland to prospectors. Combined with the social disorganization caused by mass 'recruitment' exercises and the consequent neglect of traditional agricultural activities, food was always in short supply. The colonial administration reacted by establishing a Purchase Board for foodstuffs, which entered into negotiations with private contractors, notably John Holt and UAC, to procure and supply food for mine workers. Mining companies were themselves obliged to store eight months' supply of grain and to provide both food and firewood at official subsidized prices for workers (Freund, 1981, 140).

The motivation and discipline of mineworkers were equally intricate and elaborate affairs. The ultimate official goal was the creation of 'voluntary' labour, since a forced labour policy only met with limited success because of mass desertion and there was a dearth of European supervisory staff and inadequate number of troops to guard conscripted labour due to the diversion of troops for war purposes. The colonial administration therefore

[39] Freund, B., *Capital and Labour in Nigerian Tin Mines*, Univ. of Ibadan Press, Ibadan, 1981

sought the introduction of a wage· system. To begin with, the colonial administration compelled all companies to pay for the transport of forced recruits to the mines, subsistence en route and the cost of the first week's food for conscripts. Bill Freund (1981, 138) notes that conscripts were promised 3s. 6d.- 4s. a week but on arrival at the minefields after a long rail journey and an initial stay in the reception centre at Kuru (Jos), they were paid 2s. 3d. and less, sometimes under 2s. a week. By 1944 the colonial administration imposed a minimum wage of 4s. a week, pick-and-shovel men earning most at 4s. 6d. A more benevolent item was the provision by Emberton of blankets for mine workers against very cold nights at the colonial administration's expense, but this was only to reduce the alarming number of deaths due to exposure in order to maintain high output levels.

The colonial administration most probably excelled in matters of 'discipline', the administrative director for minerals production, J. J. Emberton, thinking it might be more appropriate to refer to conscripts as 'National Service Workers'. As Freund (1981, 140) aptly observed, the colonial bureaucracy favoured military-style labour corps in principle. The Resident of Plateau Province, L. H. Goble, proposed that deserters could and should be searched for and recaptured through the use of the Native Authority system and, if caught, be liable to two weeks imprisonment and a full sixteen weeks' labour service on the Plateau (ibid.). Fines, corporal punishment and labour service (working without pay) seemed to have been standard disciplinary measures. Armed troops or guards, provided by the administration continually watched over the toiling mine workers.

Many of these measures invoked resistance and protests from within and among socialists and liberals in the United Kingdom. Forced labour was a constant object of attack, with a campaign against this obnoxious practice gaining momentum in the metropolis around 1919. When Lugard's thesis of an 'educative process' wore very thin, the colonial administration sought to pass off most of these conscripts as 'volunteers'. The first Colonial Development and Welfare Act had been passed in 1929, representing further pressure by the Colonial Office on colonial administrations to dispense with the more unsavoury aspects of their 'labour policy'. Coupled with mounting pressure within England and the moral and political necessity of complying with the International Labour Organization's recommendation on forced labour, the Nigerian colonial regime was made to pass a Forced Labour Ordinance in 1933 which banned its use except for works of public importance and of national defence.

This caveat enabled native administrations and the central colonial administration to continue with the forced labour policy, particularly in the tin mines, although its use in the service of profit-making private enterprise was now strictly illegal. By 1942, Freund (1981, 137) noted that Harold

Macmillan, then Parliamentary Under Secretary of State for the Colonies, defended forced labour in the British House of Commons on grounds of overriding needs of the Supply Ministry for tin. Of more interest perhaps, since it indicates the forces which fashioned policy at the Colonial Office, Frederick J. Pedler of the Colonial Office wrote a memo in which he observed that 'this conscription of African labour for work in European enterprises which are making private profits is a measure open to attacks from many directions and very likely the attack will develop in Parliament and the Press. I think that the measure may be defended on grounds of wartime necessity (ibid., 137). Sir Frederick Pedler (as he later became), moved from the Colonial Office to become an employee of the UAC! Indeed, the exigencies of 'wartime necessity' were ever more firmly established when the Japanese overran the Malayan tin mines which had hitherto supplied the bulk of British requirements. Major Orde-Brown, thy Colonial Office specialist on African 'labour problems', thought that the whole situation might induce fewer protests if it were 'understood in Britain that in reality, the work around Jos is much more akin to agriculture (than underground mining), being merely the shifting of soil' (ibid., 137). Here one sees at work not only the symbiotic and interdependent activities of the State and private employers but also the full involvement of all arms of the State, along with metropolitan political and bureaucratic personalities, in the process of labour control in a colony. The UAC finally relinquished its right to fifty per cent of royalties from tin mining in 1950, marking a direct and an unique exercise of State control over labour.

Whatever was true of the tin mines also applied to commercial establishments with only slight variations. Both the UAC and John Holt owned and operated all ports in Nigeria, for whose construction the colonial administration had happily supplied convict and forced labour. As main entreports and outlets for imported consumer goods and exported mineral and agricultural produce, aside from the military uses to which they were constantly put, industrial organizational arrangements for the motivation and control of the workforce were brushed aside in preference to police, administrative and military surveillance of employees and their organizations. Every trading post up and down the River Niger was a port of *a* sort and major trading stations or branches located in Warri, Forcados, Burutu, Koko and Calabar also doubled as seaports. Since all ports and trading stations were garrisoned and had an ample supply of residents, 'chiefs' and other colonial officials of lesser rank, agents of the State constantly supervised and protected the operations of companies from the presumably dangerous activities of employees.

We may recall at this juncture those 1927 'tax riots' in Warri, Burutu, and other delta areas of the southern provinces. These first began as strikes, escalated into general boycotts of goods sold and services offered by European companies, and eventually exploded in violent communal protests. According to Okonjo (1974, 185),[40] the colonial administration was so shaken that the whole of Warri province was declared a 'proclaimed area' under the Peace Preservation Ordinance and Mr. William E. Hunt, a senior resident, was given extraordinary powers under this ordinance to 'pacify' the province. It was manifestly difficult to separate the 'law and order' preoccupations of colonial officialdom from the private employers' own real or imagined organizational difficulties.

Such a marriage of private economic interests and the political objectives of colonial officialdom obliterated the importance of the *laissez faire* doctrine as an operating principle as the State apparatus was brought to the full service of private employers. There is no moral judgement here concerning the ultimate coincidence of the interests of the state and economic elite in such a primitive capitalist economy: only that considerable caution has to be exercised in attempting to discuss the role of the Nigerian state in industrial relations within the framework of 'voluntarism', where this it taken to mean lack of involvement or interest by the State in the actions of employers and workers. In this connection, not even the faint re-cognition of the implausibility of such a position is to be found in the analyses of Yesufu (1962, 1980), Fashoyin (1980) and Ubeku (1983), an issue that is taken up later.

The ascent of nationalist politicians to positions of power in the colonial political apparatus did not appreciably alter the situation. Such criticisms as were directed at employers concerned the scant African representation in management, and the generally slow pace of Africanization of all ranks. As junior partners to expatriate colonial governors and metropolitan politicians in the decolonization process, nationalist politicians were unlikely to initiate dramatically new policies, save in the public sector. Existing policies were routinely executed by both bureaucrats and law enforcement agencies, labour officers going about their business of creating 'non-political' unionism in the face of a vigorous groundswell of nationalist fervour.

It may also be pointed out that some nationalist politicians, professionals, and ex-employees and agents of UAC, John Holt Ltd. and other companies, including such resilient indigenous businessmen as Odutola, had at this time developed extensive business interests of their own. Thus, apart from growing relations between political parties and private employers, it was also the case that as from the late 1940s most Nigerian politicians sought to use political office not just for self-enrichment but also to create an indigenous capitalist class, the prospects of which had been blighted by the

[40] Okonjo, I.M. *British Administration in Nigeria: A Nigerian View*, Nok Publishers, New York, 1974.

discriminatory policies of the metropolis and of expatriate colonial officials.[41] This policy was continued in the post-colonial period in the form of various indigenization decrees that sought to achieve a greater degree of Nigerian ownership of enterprises, a subject of later discussion. The growth of the private sector and of its indigenous component, and the self-seeking activity of the political class were to guarantee hostile labour legislation and push Nigerian State elites into playing a confused role in industrial relations. Before this can be discussed, we may briefly examine the processes of collective bargaining and industrial conflict and the part played by the colonial State, and the impact of its policies on employers and workers alike.

COLLECTIVE BARGAINING, INDUSTRIAL CONFLICT AND THE COLONIAL STATE

At the micro-level or in the context of individual economic organizations, collective bargaining is usually taken to describe collective on part of both employees and management to sort out ;sues arising from the work situation. This, though commonly accepted, is as simplistic as it is partial since social existence and other developments outside the work situation impinge on the content of collective bargaining and the conduct of the parties.[42] Inasmuch as some issues emanating from production or work procedures may be resolved within the organizations, notions of 'fairness' and 'proper conduct' which guide behaviour largely derive from prevailing norms in the greater society and the ideas and practices which this encourages and perpetuates. The State has always played a leading role in the generation and continuation of values, often modifying the socializing role of the which is itself located in some substratum of a social class) through the pervasive information media and the curricula of institutions of formal instruction.[43]

Collective bargaining presumes mutual recognition by each representative interest. This, in turn, assumes a measure of autonomy and the right of such interests to be protected against encroachments. The protection of interest assumes a capacity to do so, namely, an element of power, which is assumed to be fairly distributed, hence making possible a bargaining situation. All this seems to imply that collective bargaining is more than a mechanism or method for resolving disputes; it is also 'conflict-in-progress' Nor is it a polar opposite of industrial conflict as John Dunlop

[41] This is the main theme in Akeredolu-Ale, E.O., *Underdevelopment of Indigenous Entrepreneurship in Nigeria*, Ibadan Univ. Press, 1975.

[42] For a comprehensive treatment of the concept of collective bargaining, see Flanders, A. (ed.), *Collective Bargaining*, Penguin, 1969 and Chamberlain, W., *Collective Bargaining*, McGraw-Hill, 1958.

[43] Three relevant studies that immediately come to mind are Marcuse, H., *One Dimensional Man*, Abacus, 1972; Habermas, J., *Toward a Rational Society*, Heinemann, London, 1971, and *Legitimation Crisis*, Heinemann, London, 1976

(1958), among others, has implicitly argued.[44] Collective bargaining includes third party intervention as in conciliation and arbitration since these processes are activated by disputes or strikes over new demands and/or developments on the shop floor and divergent interpretations of clauses in, and manner of implementation of, previously negotiated collective agreements.

The following observations may be made on the role of the colonial State. The colonial State (and private employers) by use of convict and forced labour sought for a long time to deny the individual worker a right to the job. As the need for a wage earning and a permanent labour force became imperative, there prevailed in both State and private establishments what Alan Fox (1966) has labelled a 'unitary ideology'- an essentially paternalist and patronizing outlook that enabled employers and managements to see their employees as part of the 'family', a 'team', sharing common goals and destiny.[45]

With all the myths surrounding the 'white man' and social and political relations arising out of colonial domination, 'labour' could hardly be seen as representing any legitimate interests. In fact, it was the case, as has been amply demonstrated earlier, that while colonial governors and their native administrations denied indigenous communities political rights and political representation of their own choosing, workers and their organizations were initially correspondingly thought not to possess any legitimate rights in the workplace. The State and private employers therefore largely unilaterally determined the terms of employment, an early phase of the process of establishing contractual relationships.

In the example of tin mining discussed above, a rudimentary contract of employment could be said to have existed at the point at which conscript labour accepted the offer of 3s. 6d., although it is more usual to view a contract as freely entered into by two or more consenting parties. Whether in practice employers kept their own side of the 'bargain' (which they did not) and mine workers insisted on those terms and on improvements on physical and other conditions of employment is germane to processes of industrial conflict and collective bargaining. Until unions were formed, 'bargaining' on the side of conscript labour was through desertions, sabotage, theft, mostly unorganized strikes, communal petitions and physical protests.

Colonial governors, residents, bureaucrats and law enforcement agents

---

[44] See his *Industrial Relations System*, S. Illinois University Press, Carbons-dale & Edwardsville, 1958.

[45] Fox, A., *Industrial Sociology and Industrial Relations*, Royal Commission on Trade Unions and Employers Association, Research Paper No. 3, HMSO, 1966; 'Managerial Ideology and Labour Relations,' *British Journal of Industrial Relations*, 4, 1966, For a later recanting also his 'Industrial Relations: A Social Critique of Pluralist Ideology', in CHILD, J. (ed.), *Man and Organization*, George Allen & Unwin, London, 1973.

undoubtedly took their time about extending bargaining status to workers and their organizations because the use of forced and convict labour reduced costs and increased profits. By creating a situation in which labour remained semi-permanent and casual, daily-paid workers were preponderant, thereby considerably reducing the basis for, and scope of bargaining. The obverse side of the coin was the situations are of a small permanent wage labour force made possible because of the large numbers of forced and convict labourers. Both conditions are themselves a reflection of the nature and scope of economic activities and the control strategies adopted by employers.

An overriding consideration was the poor financial state of the Nigerian colony which colonial officialdom sought to improve by imposing all manner of taxes. A more extensive money economy and payment of money wages was in this context indispensable and inevitable. The pay levels of expatriate personnel in State administrative and commercial establishments tended to serve as reference points for Africans employed by them, just as meagre cash payments given to conscript labour formed the lowest levels upon which improvements were sought (Yesufu, 1962; Ananaba, 1969; Freund, 1981).

Long-running financial crises and attempts by the colonial administration to control wages and prices in the face of inflation and shortages created by war situations, mounting protests by communities and workers alike, the pressure brought to bear by the Colonial Office in pursuance of political and economic interests of metropolis, all served to dictate institutional responses. Cost of living allowances were *ad hoc* measures. The first serious measure was taken only in 1938 with the enactment of the Trade Union Ordinance. As regards collective bargaining, the ordinance was silent, Akpala (1982, 76) sarcastically noting that 'it seemed to have been assumed that the passing of the Trade Union Ordinance would by itself generate collective bargaining'. Nor was there provision for the recognition of unions by employers, an issue which in practice was left to be handled by trial of strength. Employers could and did ignore unions at their leisure or peril, depending on the size and effectiveness of such unions. It would be reasonably accurate to conclude as Akpala (1982, 75, 77) has done, that the ordinance 'was not helpful to either the development of effective or meaningful collective bargaining or the use of voluntary settlement of industrial disputes in the private sectors,' and that the law therefore gives room for frustrating the real objective of trade unionism which is strength for collective function of workers.

As previously indicated, the 1933 Forced Labour Ordinance which banned the use of forced labour was a much needed step toward the effective organization and formal representation of labour. This was improved upon in the 1943 Labour (Wage Fixing and Regulation) Ordinance No. 40.

Though this was a somewhat feeble attempt at price control it fortunately succeeded in establishing a higher minimum wage in the tin mines, an achievement Freund (1981, 151) described as 'unprecedented for Northern Nigeria labour in the private sector'. The more important legislation in terms of potential for regulating collective relations in industry at the time was the Labour Code Ordinance 1945 which sought to protect workers from more serious abuses. It reiterated the prohibition of forced labour, regulated the employment of young persons and women at night, spelt out the manner of payment of wages, concerned itself with other non-monetary benefits and entitlements such as maternity leave for female workers, with apprenticeship systems, and specifically required written contracts of employment.

It should be pointed out that the Labour Code Ordinance owed little to the generosity or paternalism of the colonial administration. It was enacted in the aftermath of the 1945 General Strike. The Tudor Davies Commission appointed in its wake deplored both the relative absence of official direction in matters of collective bargaining and disputes and the ineffectiveness of the Department of Labour. Aside from recommending the establishment of an *ad hoc* National Negotiating committee comprising representatives of State, private employers and workers, the commission additionally recommended that 'matters of wages and conditions of employment should entirely be the responsibility of a reconstituted Labour Department, and all stages from conciliation to final enforcement should be in its hands' (Report, 26, para. 93).

Be that as it may, labour advisory boards were established by the Labour (Wage Fixing and Regulation) Ordinance of 1943, bringing to fruition one of the recommendations of the 1941 Bridges Committee. Although section 6 of the Ordinance empowered the boards to *make* inquiries into conditions of service and wages in any trade referred to them by the colonial authorities and to make recommendations for fixing the statutory minimum wage, this was hardly ever, done. In 1944 when E. A. Miller, the Commissioner of Labour, proposed the formation of a permanent Labour Advisory Board (LAB) in the Plateau in view of persistent labour protests, he was not only opposed by private employers who considered it 'undue interference', but a fellow bureaucrat and Minerals Administrator in charge of tin production, Emberton, was not too keen either, seeing the board as 'a stage for agitators' (Freund, 1981, 180). When the board finally came into being in July 1946, the Jos Resident felt that 'he or some other provincial officer was far more suited to represent labourers than any trades union members.' (ibid.).

It is fairly easy to establish the relative ineffectiveness of these boards since they hardly made any impact on those 'sweated' occupations where workers were persistently underpaid, a situation they were supposed to correct. In the main, despite their tripartite r" nature, they, would seem to have confined themselves to the general function of advising the colonial administration on labour questions in general. This may not have been entirely unexpected since labour officers were generally encouraged by employers to choose 'responsible' union officials organising workers in their establishments to represent all sections of the labour movement, such appointments leading to sponsored trips abroad and to attend ILO Annual Conferences in Geneva took on added importance as interested labour leaders of divided central labour organisations competed for such 'prizes'. The chances were that the Lieutenant-Governor might be more inclined to listen to any of his residents than members of the board, whose recommendations were rejected, modified and implemented without further reference to them.

The Wages Board was established by the Wages Board Ordinance of 1957 as a successor to, and to offset the inadequacies of the Labour Advisory Boards. It had the same powers to look into industries or occupations where wages were observed to be unusually low and to make recommendations. Unlike the *ad hoc* Labour Advisory Boards it was permanent. Despite the equal representation of both employers and workers and not more than three so-called independent persons, the Wages Board suffered the singular weakness of being dependent on the whims of the Minister of Labour. If the minister did not feel like calling a meeting on receipt, for example, of the recommendations of a Commission of Inquiry, precious little could be done about it, especially in private establishments where employers and managements routinely insisted on 'private and voluntary collective bargaining', as if prevailing low wages owed nothing to their anti-unionism and brand of 'bargaining'. With a touch of irony, a defence offered in parliament argued that 'although the Minister is responsible for initiating action in underpaid occupations and responsible also for making an Order fixing minimum wages, etc., the responsibility for determining those wages and conditions of employment rests squarely on the shoulders of the members of the Wages Board. In this way it is hoped that this will promote the rise of and growth of voluntary collective bargaining' (cited in Akpala, 1982, 81). The Wage Board system fell into disuse in 1966 when political crises came to a head and the country rapidly plunged into a three-year civil war.

Enough has been said in the earlier about successive Nigerian governments' continuous use of salaries and wages commissions since the 1930s to permit of only a few closing remarks. Perhaps the commission or committee with by far the most enduring consequences was the 1946 Miller Committee which established the principle of payment on a geographical basis for unestablished (daily-paid) workers. It made a simple distinction between general labour, on the one hand, and special and semiskilled on the other, dividing the country into six geographical zones with differentials in pay for these two groups of labour. The basic assumption was that cost of living was highest in Lagos and its immediate environs, and that wages should be progressively (regressively?) lower the farther away from Lagos a worker was employed.

The colonial administration, in line with this recommendation established Provincial Wage Committees, which were joined in 1951 by Regional Wage Committee to reflect the new political structure of three regions. Akpala (1982, 106-107) has a brief but useful description of the workings of these committees. The main gist of this is they met infrequently, were not bargaining bodies, and functioned against the opposition of trade unions which deprecated the administration's attempts to entrench a geographical wage structure, a policy that had enormous appeal to provincial residents and native administrations who were most unlikely to overlook any opportunity to save on labour costs, having grown used to utilizing forced labour which they could no longer legally do. The unions understandably asked for uniform rates for daily-paid workers everywhere while at the same time refusing to take up their membership in the Central Committee set up by the central government to reconcile their own views with those of the Regional Committees which favoured geographical disparities in wages.

The upshot was that against a background of workers' protests co-ordinated by the All Nigeria Trade Union Federation (ANTUF), the Western and Eastern Region governments disbanded the Provincial Wages Committees. The dissenting northern residents and administrations retained theirs, while the Federal Government itself settled wages in Lagos (Akpala, 1982, 106-107). In such an uncertain and conflict laden situation the Federal Government was obliged to establish a Minimum Wage Fact-Finding Committee comprising three of its own officials. In its representations before this committee the ANTUF made short shrift of a geographical wage structure, demanded a national minimum wage, and further pointed out that wage committees had hardly been in the interest of workers since they were not fully represented on them; administration and employers' representatives dominated them, using their majority vote in arriving at decisions against workers' interests (Akpala, 1982, 107).

Nothing of an innovative nature could be expected from the Minimum Wage Fact-Finding Committee in view of its composition. Akpala (1982, 107) pertinently observed that the committee's recommendation was nothing but an 'adoption of the thinking of Council of Ministers which seemed to have made up its mind before the appointment of the Committee that provincial wage bodies and therefore the Miller scheme of wages should remain.' A minimum wage as claimed by the committee would create difficulties' and undermine the effectiveness of the contemplated incentive bonus scheme! After its recommendations were made public, the 'federal government did not see fit to meet the unions for discussion'. It was against this background that both Western and Eastern Region governments took the more decisive, self-serving but positive step of paying a uniform wage and transferring all daily-paid workers to permanent employment respectively as discussed earlier.

As wage committees were not bargaining bodies, such unpleasant decisions could only be reversed by confrontation at the workplace, and to strike action, thus accounting for the higher incidence of recorded strikes in the period 1953 to 1959. Yesufu's (1962) wholesale dismissal of these pre-emptive moves by the regional governments as 'political wage fixing', does not do justice to the facts on the ground. His assessment fails to reflect the intense union pressures against geographical wage structure and the confusion and acrimony generated by the desultory operating style and very limited impact of these wage committees. More important, the Federal Government was only too pleased to pass on the problems of daily-paid workers and a minimum wage to the regional governments as soon as the latter came into being in 1951, the former having, in fact, increased wages across the board by administrative fiat in 1949/50. It was extremely unlikely in view of the administrative and political arrangements at the time that the Federal Government would initiate the establishment of any minimum wage or wage rates that it could not uniformly enforce across the country. At any rate, the battle by political parties over control of the Federal Government was already on, and could only encourage the governor-general and his men routinely to reiterate existing policy on geographical wage structures and wages boards.

We might also recall the three 'Whitley Councils' established in 1948 by the Cowan Committees, one for 'senior staff' and two for 'junior staff'. These were a dismal failure by 1949 because as Yesufu (1962, 52) correctly observed, they had become consultative instead of negotiating bodies, suffered difficulties over representation, and 'broke down completely because of staff side dissatisfaction over progress in negotiation.' They were also undermined by frequent use of salary and wages commissions. Akpala (1982, 78) additionally noted that 'the structural relationship between the two junior Whitley Councils could not be reconciled with the structure of the trades unions of the government employees.' Despite their reconstitution along lines proposed by Mr. Carruthers, sent by the United Kingdom Ministry of Labour, no visible improvements were observed operation, Fashoyin (1980, 106) suggesting continued failure as the reason for the 1974 Udoji Commission's preference for a National Public Service Negotiating Council, a body which itself has made little impact to date.

Yesufu (1962, 52-54) discusses parallel developments in private establishments, where labour officers had joined employees and unions in cajoling and coercing employers into establishing more permanent negotiating structures in the form of joint consultative committees. These Joint Industrial Councils (JICs) or Joint Consultative Committees (JCC) were also adopted in public corporations and utilities (later called parastatals), many of which carried on business in partnership with foreign and indigenous investors, financial institutions such as the World Bank, and agencies of the United Nations Organization (UNO). Yesufu's position on the workings of these committees has remained ambivalent, sometimes implying a respectable degree of 'joint consultation' and 'collective bargaining', and sometimes not. Citing official figures of a total of 212 of such committees in the country as at 1957 and nominally covering an aggregate of 207,582 employees, he concludes that 'between 25 per cent, and 30 per cent, of the estimated wage-earning population come under a system of joint consultation, or collective bargaining' and that 'such machinery is widely diffused in the various sectors of the economy, although usually confined to expatriate firms, apart from government departments and public corporations' (1962, 52-54).

A few clues to their real effectiveness as provided by Yesufu (1962) include the fact that these committees were 'used to deal with both negotiation and consultation', that employers refused to establish separate bodies for both 'consultation' and 'collective bargaining' on grounds of likely 'duplication', that there was an 'absence of formal trade union organisations', and that there was 'sheer ignorance not exclusively on the part of workers, as to the nature of the difference between joint consultation and collective bargaining' (ibid.). His claim that 'under Nigerian conditions it has not often proved possible to effect in practice the distinction between joint consultation and collective bargaining is both refutable and unnecessary for, on the whole, private employers sought to do without either consultation or collective bargaining throughout the sixty odd years of direct colonial rule. It has also been mentioned how most of the institutions established by the State and private employers were inevitably turned into forums for merely informing employees about policies. If anything, the insistence of trade unions and workers on a collective approach to the tackling of industrial issues and protests in pursuance of that demand, and the resistance of employers to unionism and collective bargaining seem to have been the distinguishing characteristics of colonial industrial relations practice. In practice both parties seemed to have understood the distinctions between unilateral action and joint consultation and between joint consultation and collective bargaining well enough.

Indeed, Yesufu (1962, 57) later concedes that 'workers accused management of bad faith and of attempts, which were justified in some cases, to use the committee against the recognition of a trade union'.

Moreover, besides he claims some of these committees never met and for met less frequently than they were expected, 'neither management nor the workers had faith in the machinery' and 'in the case of one committee the workers were able to provide examples where management had victimised worker representatives by transfer, change of job, or withholding of an increment because those representatives expressed views which were considered "dangerous" or distasteful to, or did so in a manner that did not show respect for, the management.' His unhappiness over the apparent 'failure' of workers to recognise a distinction between 'joint consultation' and 'collective bargaining' may be detected in Yesufu's further observation that 'the workers regarded the committees solely as avenues for demanding increased wages and for airing grievances, and hardly gave thought to matters such as productivity and safety, to which management attached great importance.' This is then followed by a somewhat curious but revealing comment to the effect that 'the Department of Labour has put on record that the main instances where success of joint committee is found have usually been only in those establishments where there had been a history of industrial disturbance which apparently made the employers anxious to maintain contact at all levels with workers' (1962, 58). So, only conflict could compel private employers to use 'joint consultation' machinery!

If these committees remained the only institutional avenues open to workers, it is puzzling that Yesufu would expect them not to 'air their grievances' and concentrate on issues they considered more important to their well-being. Inasmuch as one might admire Yesufu's attempt at even-handedness in allocating blame, especially when he talks about the 'overbearing attitude on the part of employers' and the 'irresponsible methods of approach by union officials, or other workers' representatives, ignorance, and exaggerated expectations on the part of the generality of workers' (ibid.), such evidence as he has himself provided would tend toward the conclusion that it was the employers that were largely to blame for the failure of these joint industrial committees (as also happened in Britain). Nowhere have employers willingly shared decision-making power with trade unions and workers, and as such the tendency on the part of the former to reduce bipartite or tripartite bodies to mere talk shops and media for announcing managements' policies may be said to be inherent and predictable if, in the first place, the formation of such bodies could not be avoided or prevented.

Incontrovertible evidence to support the above position was provided by the 1957 Sofola Commission of Inquiry into retail and ancillary trade in Lagos, the only such body instituted to examine this thriving section of the private sector.[46] The Sofola Report (1957, 4) cryptically stated that 'we are

[46] The official title is Commission of Inquiry into the Retail and Ancillary Trades in the Federal Territory

informed that most of these unions are neither given recognition nor encouragement by the employers', and that 'some employers treat with the unions on sufferance than as of right.' In general, it further noted, 'we are satisfied that there at present exists no machinery for the regulation of wages and conditions of employment of workers employed in the retail and ancillary trades and, in fact, that there does not exist an organization of the employers on one side and of the workers on the other side through which such a machinery can evolve on a voluntary basis' (p.5). Indeed, it concluded, 'a voluntary machinery would be difficult, if not impossible, to secure because of the special problems connected with the scattered nature of the industry, the weak position of the unions and the uncooperative attitude of certain employers (ibid.).

The Sofola Report, however, noted the existence of 'informal arrangements' in some establishments which, in the main, amounted to employers and the union executive (where they exist) getting together at 'short notice' to 'discuss' matters relating to the welfare of workers including 'wages and conditions' (1957, 5). It was only in one large retail house, employing over 800 workers, that a Joint Consultative Committee OCC) was found to exist, and both employers and workers confirmed that in the light of the prevailing conditions in the industry, the JCC could not be 'restricted only to matters properly belonging to such a body'. It was also the case that 'in answer to the question put to .other employers visited or who gave evidence before us as to the means of consultation in matters of common interest to both sides, we were told that they were open at all times to approaches by their workers'. In view of this, 'we are not impressed by this answer which, expressed as the sole means of management-labour relations, reveals a paternalistic outlook which is not conducive to the development of sound labour relations' (ibid., 5). The workers' view, as contained in the Report, was that 'the informal arrangement, where it exists, is unsatisfactory in that it places the workers at the mercy of the, employers', the commission tortuously concluding that 'we do not necessarily share this view but it is our view that these arrangements are ineffectual and cannot be regarded as machinery for the fixing of wages and conditions' (ibid.).

As regards the process of wage fixing itself, employers were found unilaterally and arbitrarily to reach decisions on basic rates and increments. Such arbitrariness seemed to have been facilitated by two tactics, namely secrecy over individual incremental rates (thus absence of a wage scale) and cultivation of personal relations in the smaller establishments, the latter

of Lagos, under the chairmanship of Kehinde Sofola, Esq., LL. B. Independent Members were Mrs. Aduke Moore and Chief Imam Y.P.O. Shodeinde; members representing employers were J.A. Tuyo and R.A. Clarke; for workers were H.P. Adebola and S.O. Oduleye; Assessors R.O. Gbadamosi and H. Monsour.

usually 'directed against union solidarity' (ibid., 6). One employer was found to have 'abolished the salary scale previously in his establishment and he now awards increase at random' (p.6.). A consequence was that wages were considerably lower than anywhere else, ranging between 2s. and 3s. per day as compared with the minimum wage of 4s. 8d. per day paid to the lowest employee in the public sector. The commission was forced to conclude that 'we do not consider the prevailing practice among the majority of employers of awarding increases in wages as and when they like to be in the best interest of labour' (p.6). And, after noting relative absence of machinery for determining wages and other conditions of employment, it deprecated the 'unreasonably low wages and prevalence of long hours as a result of the inadequacy of the machinery (if we might so call the present various arrangements) for regulating the wages and conditions of employment of workers engaged in the trade' (p.6). Worse still, the report pointed out, 'the informal machinery at present existing in a negligible number of the firms engaged in the Retail and Ancillary Trades is unsatisfactory and is not likely to develop to a point where normal collective bargaining could be possible and may even with a set-back cease to exist'. We have quoted at length from the Sofola Commission Report simply to establish the reluctance of private employers to encourage collective bargaining processes or to facilitate the evolution of institutions tending in that direction. We may at this point consider in greater depth colonial State policies and reactions to industrial conflict processes.

COLONIAL STATE AND INDUSTRIAL CONFLICT

What has emerged from an analysis of colonial industrial relations so far is the near impossibility of separating industrial from other forms of social conflict. Colonial resistance was sporadic in nature and, depending on areas, dragged on into the 1940s and 1950s. It may be necessary to distinguish resistance to military conquests *per se* from continual resistance to political and administrative changes introduced by colonial officialdom, the latter type being of greater relevance since political and administrative arrangements were designed to facilitate economic exploitation of human and material resources while state agencies attempted keeping a lid on the social and political consequences most threatening to this goal. The so-called 'tax riots' of 1927 and 1929 in many parts of the southern provinces fall into this class; they were directed at corrupt 'chiefs', native administration and colonial social policies in general.

It is also true that an innumerable number of communal protests first began as temporary stoppages of work embarked upon by identifiable groups of workers. As Eliot Berg pertinently noted, these strikes were later escalated and 'generalised' into African protests against colonial administration and European private employers (in Galenson, 1964, 226).[47] That the colonial administration .generally oversaw the operations of private employers and actively participated in the 'recruitment' and 'disciplining' of personnel as outlined above, made the 'institutional isolation of industrial from political conflict' along the lines adumbrated by Ralf Dahrendorf (1959, 171)[48] exceedingly difficult to achieve. The 1947 strike by UAC employees in Burutu and the 1949 coal miners' protests at Enugu come under this head; a majority of strike, whether in the public or private sector, belong to this category.

Then, there were also those limited stoppages directed at aspects of the wage or union policy of private or public employers, say, the award of a cost of living allowances, or the implementation of increases made by an arbitration or wage commission, or the elimination of differentials based on racial and ethnic differences among employees, or the pursuit of union recognition. These were likely to be the most frequently occurring strikes and characterized the period under consideration. In some instances, they became more widespread, developing into community protests and inviting brutal suppression by police and troops.

Finally, another type of conflict, restricted or widespread, resulting from the nature of the work, the manner of 'recruitment' of labour, the high-handedness of management, or the harshness of physical supervision can be identified. Such conflicts were generally induced by the forced labour policy all over the colony at centres of labour concentration for long periods of time, such as mining activities near Enugu and in the Plateau, and on plantations in Southern Cameroons and parts of the southern provinces (Sapele). Akpala (1982. 81), for example, wrote in respect of coal mining areas that the 'forced labour policy was breaking the spirit of the people and by 1919 they were coming out in open revolt'. Moreover, 'in 1920 the Akpugo people marched down to Enugu for the purpose of stopping their men from working in the mines, and clearly popular feelings everywhere were bitter against the Chiefs because of their role in recruiting forced labour.'

It is perhaps difficult to exaggerate the extent of social dislocation wrought by the forced labour policy and the imposition of all manner of taxes on different Nigerian communities. Such administrative and other social policies could only be implemented at gunpoint until such a time as an extensive coercive apparatus could be established. Given the expanse of the territory and the relative dearth of administrative personnel, this could not readily be achieved, as a result leading to a fragmented authority

[47] GALENSON, W., *Labour in Developing Countries*, Univ. of California Press, Berkeley & Los Angeles, 1963.

[48] DAHRENDORF, R., *Class and Class Conflict in Industrial Society*, Routledge & Kegan Paul, London, 1959

structure with provincial residents, chiefs, emirs and district police officers wielding enormous discretionary powers. All industrial or commercial establishments were routinely protected or guarded by troops and police, particularly where forced and convict labour had to be used. Lugard had himself in 1903 appropriately described railway construction labour as 'forced levies of carriers guarded by bayonets' (Freund, 1981, 51). Political and judicial powers could not be separated under colonial, authority relations with residents, chiefs and emirs and governor embodying both. The same could be said of the private economic activities of companies which remained inextricably bound with the colonial administration. The implications of this for the role of the State in colonial industrial relations are only too apparent.

Against a background of widespread social protests in Nigeria and labour rebellions in all British colonies in the late 1920s and 1930s, the Colonial Office was sufficiently disturbed to take a closer look at the 'labour policies' of respective colonial administrations. The upshot, as earlier indicated, was the Passfield Memorandum and the passing of a series of Colonial Welfare and Development Acts which were designed to minimise social and political unrest, induce colonial administrations both to enact laws, and to establish negotiating and conflict regulating machinery. The colonial administration was itself finally forced to promulgate the 1933 Forced Labour Ordinance which declared this form of labour illegal.

In terms of institutional development and official attempts to provide neutralising 'escape valves', the most relevant legislation was the Trade Disputes (Arbitration and Inquiry) Ordinance of 1941. It took away some *de facto* powers from Residents and the like in matters of 'dispute settlement' and vested these in the Commissioner of Labour, who could undertake preliminary administrative inquiry into the causes and circumstances of a dispute. A nominee of the Commissioner would carry out conciliation if either of the parties so formally requested, and if this failed a dispute would be reported to the Governor. The Governor was required to refer the matter to an arbitration tribunal with the consent of both parties, a tribunal that could consist of a sole arbitrator, with or without assessors, or comprise several members under an 'independent' chairman nominated by the Governor on behalf of the parties to the dispute.

It may seem surprising that the ordinance failed to reduce the frequency of disputes or to increase the readiness of employers to take fuller advantage of some of its procedures. For one thing, much depended on the idiosyncrasies of both the Commissioner of Labour whose attitudes and behaviour, as we have seen, were not all favourable to organised indigenous protest groups. Similarly, the 'neutrality' of arbitrators and assessors appointed by the Governor and corresponding confidence in their performance on the part of disputants could not necessarily be assumed. For example, employees of the UAC embarked on the nationwide stoppage when they feared collusion between the company and the Baramain Arbitration panel on the issue of backdating awards, even though such awards favoured them (Ananaba, 1969, 122). The perception of a possible bias on the part of the arbitrators by either of the parties seemed more than sufficient to render the whole exercise futile. Prevailing political and social circumstances made it easy for workers and union officials in particular to be suspicious of officially appointed arbitrators and assessors. Yesufu (1962, 140) has written of workers being 'extremely distrustful of the government' (which was itself overwhelmingly the largest employer) and 'of the intentions and the much proclaimed "independence" of the Labour Department which was supposed to be the mediator in disputes between the two sides of industry'.

To the extent that the machinery for conciliation and arbitration could only be voluntarily activated, this meant lack of cooperation by one party reducing its effectiveness. Employers were generally reluctant to utilise the facilities, claiming instead the necessity for the colonial administration to deal firmly with 'trouble-makers', 'political activists' and 'communists' among their employees. Since this view of unionism and workers' demand was, to a large measure, shared by colonial political and administrative officers, 'it seemed therefore that behind every disturbance that occurred or was threatened, the Administrative Officers could hardly see anything but the hands of nationalist agitators goading the nation into revolt' (Yesufu, 1962, 140). He was not exaggerating!

For all that, the Trade Disputes (Arbitration and Inquiry) Ordinance of 1941 was a useful piece of legislation. Akpala (1982, 84) rightly criticized those that enacted it for supposing that 'there existed some collective bargaining machinery and an adequate internal arrangement within each affected industry, trade or establishment,' a supposition for which there was almost empirical evidence. Although the legislation was expected to encourage the emergence of such arrangements by providing some degree of legal guidance and support, the constant attempts by one party to invoke conciliation and arbitration would no doubt over a period of time weaken the resistance of the other and lead to discussion and the eventual institution of more formal and lasting collective bargaining machinery. Akpala (1982) admits of this possibility while discussing a provision under this act enabling the Governor to set up a Board of Inquiry to investigate any incident without reference to or the consent of the affected parties. Although the Board of Inquiry was principally 'for purposes of information to the Governor and the Public', he recognised that 'an inquiry would, however, influence settlement because its processes might afford the disputing parties the opportunity to further air their grievances, see the other's point of view and cool down their emotion for a future re-opening of negotiation' (ibid., 84).

The importance of this should not, however, be exaggerated. Such externalization of organizational problems in practice worked against the evolution of effective internal grievance procedures and other conflict-regulating institutions and practices. A consequence was therefore increasing development and perfection of labour control strategies on the part of relevant State agencies, and conversely an increasing tendency on the part of organised labour to reach above the heads of management to the State authorities, where ultimate political power resided, for meaningful solutions. This mode of interaction between organised labour and the State inevitably politicized industrial relations problems, quite apart from the deleterious and amplifying effects of the episodic and floundering incomes policies of respective administrations or regimes and of tensions arising out of the politics of decolonization. It also made it a little more difficult for the relevant State agencies to lay any serious claim to 'neutrality' or 'umpireship' as generally presumed by Dunlop (1958), Dahl (1966), and others,[49] so much so that even the most compromising of Nigerian unionists would habitually group the State and private employers in one camp *vis-a-vis* the working classes.

We may also point out that wartime exigencies and provisions as contained in the 1942 General Defence Regulations served to undermine the legal intentions of the ordinance. For the duration of the Second World War, strikes and lockouts were made illegal, and governors had emergency powers of arrest and detention without trial and the use of conscript labour for both military and economic purposes. Food was rationed in Lagos and other parts of the country and demonstrating workers were severely put down by troops in several instances. The immediate post-war situation was, in fact, more volatile because of the activities of ex-service men, of nationalist politicians, and of protesting workers as previously discussed.

[49] See Dunlop's *Industrial Relations System*, 1958. 'Others' here refer to the orthodox view of industrial relations 'actors' as may be read in standard texts, more so with 'pluralists' such as Hugh Clegg and Robert Dahl. - Dunlop, J.T. *Industrial Relations System*, Southern Illinois Univ. Press, Carbonsdale & Edwardsville, 1958; Dahl, R. *Preface to Democratic Theory*, Chicago University Press, 1956

Chapter 9

TRADE UNIONS AND THE DEVELOPMENT PROCESS IN NIGERIA: AN OVERVIEW

INTRODUCTION

In this chapter we try to achieve two interrelated goals. The first is to present a general review of the part played by organized labour in Nigeria's development process. The second is to outline the political economy of the development crisis in Nigeria, especially the 1970s which mark three decades of post-Independence 'management', by its political and economic elites, of an undoubtedly larger and more complex economy, but which has left the way of life and standard of living of an overwhelming majority of Nigerians relatively unaffected, wallowing in poverty and relative ignorance.

Four reasons account for our focus. The first is that the Nigerian economy has been in unprecedented dire straits since 1982, and those most adversely affected have been workers. The second reason is that representatives of organized labour, along with the various factions of the political class, have disclaimed responsibility for the parlous state of affairs. The third is that three decades after political independence, a review of dominant views on the role of organised labour in the development process in Nigeria seems overdue in the light of more evidence.

The fourth reason, and which has misled more than a few observers, is that in general some surprise is still expressed in several quarters about linking trade unions with the development process in African countries in particular, for the process is generally presented as originally initiated by colonial European companies and the various colonial administrations, and now directed and sustained by the economic activities of both post-colonial state and those of subsidiaries of multinational companies, with some agencies of the United Nations Organisation (UNO) and such other institutions as the International Monetary Fund (IMF) and the World Bank playing useful but supplementary roles. Trade unions are, after all, just trades unions, it is frequently contended, organizing a not too impressive percentage of the wage earning labour force, which itself represents an insignificant proportion of the total active labour force, not to say of the total population. Trade union leadership, it is further pointed out, is preoccupied with personal gain, and leading by the nose a mass of apathetic and equally half-literate workers.

This characterisation of the development process which emphasises the role of the "organiser" or "leadership" or "regime" has a long history which stretches back to classical economists' disagreements over the status of labour as a factor of production *vis-a-vis* capital or entrepreneurship in the production of values.[11] And its more modern version and in relation to Africa or Nigeria may be said to derive from the overwhelming publicity given to the "role" of the State and of political and economic elites in the general development process, and which has had the largely unintended consequence of drawing attention away from the critical part played by organised labour in the national development effort.

We start by first taking a brief look at such terms as "development" and other subsidiary concepts as 'participation', since trade unions and rural populations are officially enjoined and said to participate in development as conceived from above, to enable us clearly delineate limits to this discussion. Then an overview of views proffered in the dominant studies or literature in respect of the role of trade unions would be presented and which is intended to serve as a background for further general analysis. The general analysis of the participation of trade unions in development then necessarily involves a brief review of the history of the development effort itself. The conclusion then distils the main arguments, ending on a plea for critical appraisal of the development effort itself.

SOME PROBLEMS OF DEFINITION

Before any review of both theoretical and practical considerations on the participation of organized labour in the development process in Nigeria is undertaken, it is imperative for us to enter a few caveats in order to prevent the discussion from ending in a quagmire of definitional problems and relativism of meaning. Rather than reproduce here existing controversy surrounding the terms "development" and "economic development" or "economic growth', our immediate requirements would more than satisfied by some of Gunnar Myrdal's (1968) cautionary statements in his somewhat controversial book.[2] As he soberly noted, it is difficult to give one precise meaning to the term "economic development', and perhaps easier to say what it is *not!* For one, Myrdal points out, economic development is not equivalent to the total development of society: it is only a part or one dimension of general development.

Second, since the unit of analysis is often the "nation-state', the notion of

---

[1] For an informative collection of papers on this see Steedman, I. *et al.*, *The Value Controversy*, Verso & New Left Books, London, 1981.

[2] Details in his *Asian Drama*, New York, 1968.

"national development" tends to embrace more than economic development to include social and political development as well. To this extent, it is equally relevant to talk in terms of legal or administrative or some other type of institutional development, the interrelationships of these various types of development being of critical importance to general development. One implication is the likelihood that not everything in "economic development" is "economic', indicating as it does that social-cultural and political development are usually inextricably intertwined with economic development.

By way of definition, Gunnar Myrdal (1968,53) sees economic development as *"the process* whereby the *real per capita income* of a country increases over a *long period* of time- subject to the *stipulations* that the number below an "absolute poverty line" does not increase, and that the distribution of income does not become more equal. Thus economic development transcends mere economic growth since the former represents the "upward movement of the entire social system" (ibid., p.1869). Equally important, given the general thrust of economic policies in Africa, he further warns that economic development is much more than the mere acquisition of industries nor is it to be equated with industrialisation, noting that industrialization everywhere is dependent upon agriculture or the primary sector. Consequently, from his point of view, the concentration of a large percentage of production in the primary sector is in itself not a cause of poverty: the cause is the low productivity in agriculture.

And perhaps more contentiously, Myrdal is much against equating economic development with "economic independence', a habit he thinks that most African, Asian and Latin American countries, those decolonised since the Second World War in particular, are most prone to. In what he calls the "economics of discontent', many of these poor countries in the flush of their recently acquired political independence have begun reacting against their "dependence" on export markets and foreign capital, usually seen as "exploitation" and "foreign domination'. Import-substitution as a consequent policy is thus designed to minimise such dependence, including other "inward-looking" policies which, according to him, are most likely to run counter to economic development in the end - especially where they restrict the inflow of foreign capital.

Naturally, many have disagreed with several strands of Gunnar Myrdal's views. What has sometimes been described as economic development in some countries has led neither to economic progress nor to an increase in economic welfare. Indeed, an increase in real per capita income is not in itself necessarily a sufficient condition for economic development if, for example, population growth rate far outstrips the percentage increase in the former. Even where populations are small but are said to have a high statistical per capita income, the highly skewed income distribution conveys a somewhat different picture of the welfare of the general population.

Furthermore, foreign domination of an economy does exist, a phenomenon that is hardly restricted to Africa, Asia and Latin America either. Dependence on foreign imports seems to be deplored by most governments, employers and trade unions, more so in Western Europe and North America where restrictive and protectionist policies have been most pronounced in more recent times despite the various rounds of talks under the auspices of the Council for General Agreements on Tariff and Trade (GATT). In point of fact, it would seem to have been the case that the "economics of discontent" have been a common feature or stimulant in the development process of most countries in modern times. Be that as it may, Myrdal's position, as summarised above, can still provide a useful backdrop to our analysis.

The other concept which requires brief comment is the notion of "participation" by any one group of persons in economic development. Participation, in its ordinary usage, simply means "taking part in'. One could take part in a process without establishing the ground rules, so to speak, and such a mode of participation is unlikely to be the same with the other parties who initially conceive of and then implement an idea albeit with the assistance or "participation" of some others. Participation is therefore a *power relationship,* encompassing rules anti activities which impose limits on the degree of participation by each and everyone of the parties involved. This being so, participation may theoretically be voluntary or involuntary, but the sheer necessity of material survival and other social responsibilities for the individual in a market or "free" economy rule out abstention or voluntary participation as a realistic option. This best explains why participation in the development process shall also include involvement in the determination of some of the fundamental rules for participation to be really meaningful.

SOME ORTHODOXIES ON UNIONS AND DEVELOPMENT

Such early concern about the "role" of organised labour in Africa or Nigeria as betrayed by such observers as Lugard (1919), Lord Hailey (1938), Orde-Brown (1940) and Roper (1958) was directed more at its nuisance value, "labour problems" as they militated against the flow of minerals and other raw materials to European industries, and hindered the more effective and thorough establishment of colonial rule.[33] Subsequent preoccupation by Western scholars and politicians alike with decolonisation, the spread of

[3] LUGARD, Sir F.D., *Political Memoranda,* HMSO, 1919; Bailey, Lord, *An African Survey, OUP,* 1938; Orde-Brown, G. Sul Major, *The African Labourer, Frank* Cass, 1967; Roper, J. J., *Labour Problems in West Africa,* London, 1958

communism, and shaky post-colonial state apparatus and the sometimes dramatic failure of such economies to substantially increase aggregate standard of living tended to shift the emphasis of many observers to the "political role" of labour in "nation-building', "union-party relationships', "productivity of labour', and thus whether trade unions were largely "consumptionist" or "productionist" and, of course, assessing their "revolutionary potential" in light of independence and liberation struggles and mass poverty in these areas.[4] With the exceptions of such studies as Berg & Butler (1964), Davies (1966), Cohen (1974) and Sandbrook & Cohen (1975), Gavin Williams (1976), in assessing these poor economies and their performance in the last two to three decades, organised labour has largely been regarded as incidental to the whole developmental process, sometimes as an obstacle. We now take a closer look at the Nigerian situation.

The Development Environment in Nigeria

It is perhaps appropriate at this point to sketch out the sort of environment under which Nigerian trade unions have had to operate. Environment in this context refers to, among others, the state and its agencies, politicians and governments, other voluntary organizations (educational, religious, and cultural), private development agencies, private and public financial and commercial institutions, non-human resources and the dominant web of rules and conventions in existence within and without industry and the economy. This should render it much easier for us to situate the activities and policies of workers and their organizations. We start with the international context of the environment

As Paul Streeten (1972,5)[5] so well puts it, "the fact that advanced industrial societies already exist when countries embark on development,

[4] SUFFRIN, G.C., *Unions in Emerging Societies,* Syracuse University Press, Syracuse, New York, 1964; KILBY, P., "African Labour Productivity Reconsidered', *Economic Journal,* vol. 71, 2, June 1961 and *Industrialization in an Open Economy: Nigeria 1945.1960,* CUP, 1969; GALENSON, W. (ed.), *Labour and Economic Development,* Wiley, New York, 1959 and *Labour in Developing Countries,* Univ. of California Press, Berkeley & Los Angeles, 1963; MILLEN, B., *The Political Role of Labor in Developing Countries,* The Brookings Institution, Washington DC, 1963; MOORE, W.E. & FELDMAN, A.S., *Labour Commitment and Social Change in Developing Areas,* Social Science Research Council, New York, 1960; KERR, C., DUNLOP, J.T., HARBISON, R., & MYERS, C.A., *Industrialism and Industrial Man, Heinemann,* London, 1960; BELING, W.A. (ed.), *The Role of Labour in African Nation-Building,* Praeger, New York. 1968; BERG. E. & BUTLER, J., 'Trade Unions* in COLEMAN, J.S. & ROSBERG, C.O. (cds.), *Political Parties and National Integration in Tropical Africa,* Univ. of California Press, 13erkeley & Los Angeles, 1964; DAVIES, I., *African Trade Unions,* Penguin, Hammondsworth, 1966; BATES, R.H., *Unions, Parties, and Political Development,* Yale Univ. Press, New Haven, 1971; COHEN, R., *Labour and Politics in Nigeria,* Heinemann, London, 1974; SANDBROOK, R. & COHEN, R. (eds.), *The Development of an African Working Class,* Longman, London, 1975; WILLIAMS, G. (ed.), *Nigeria: Economy & Society,* Rex Collins, 1976.

[5] STREETEN, P., *Frontiers of Development Studies,* Macmillan, 1972.

makes a number of important differences to the development prospects of underdeveloped societies." These differences have both positive and negative consequences, and the positive include: a) a growing stock of scientific, technical and organizational knowledge accumulated and on which developing countries can draw and thus avoid obvious pitfalls; b) the higher level of income in advanced industrial countries and its continued growth create demand for the products of the former and enable them benefit from wider international specialization than was possible for the pioneers; c) private investment, financial aid and technical assistance contribute to the transfer of resources and skills from the rich countries to the poor and thus enable these to draw on a bigger pool of resources; d) and the progress achieved in centres of economic advancement over time diffuse to the poorer areas.

The negative consequences resulting from the coexistence of rich and poor countries and from the policies pursued by the economically advanced countries include:

a) the advanced state of medical knowledge with consequent reduction in mortality rates without a corresponding decrease in birth rates has led to accelerating rates of population growth in developing countries which lack the wherewithal to cope - more difficult obstacles, Paul Streeten (1972, 6) admits, than those the now economically advanced Western countries faced in their pre-industrial phase when the rate of population growth was considerably less and was partly the *result* of successful development and rising levels of living;
b) despite the stock of scientific and technical knowledge to which developing countries could have access, most modern technology is ill-adapted to the conditions and the factor endowments of the developing countries. In any case, modern technology has tended to discourage labour-intensive methods of production and where imported indiscriminately has tended to aggravate the gross under-utilization of labour already prevalent in developing countries;
c) that for a number of reasons, capital and skilled men are attracted to the richest industrial societies, consequently capital flight has peen substantial, attracted by higher rates of return and greater political security, while emigration of professionals and skilled persons has been on the *increase;*
d) that, as Dudley Seers has shown, high levels of remuneration for professional skills in advanced countries raise obstacles to development in developing countries which go beyond the losses through emigration. By the creation of an international market in these skills, not only are internal inequalities without functional justification increased in underdeveloped countries, but obstacles are put into the path of devel-

opment. International inequality has an impact on internal income distribution in these countries which, like the impact of modern technology and modern institutions, impedes development;

e) that systematic research and institutionally built-in innovation, which are reflected in the annual growth of productivity which is characteristic of rich economies, have not only been heavily biased towards products which are not suited for production in underdeveloped countries, but they have, in some cases, also led to a reduction in the demand for the traditional primary exports of underdeveloped countries. Technical progress has reduced the need for the imports of the staple products of developing countries because: i) synthetics have been substituted for natural products; ii) there has been increasing the progress achieved in centres of economic advancement over time diffuse to the poorer areas.

The negative consequences resulting from the coexistence of rich and poor countries and from the policies pursued by the economically advanced countries include:

a) the advanced state of medical knowledge with consequent reduction in mortality rates without a corresponding decrease in birth rates has led to accelerating rates of population growth in developing countries which lack the wherewithal to cope- more difficult obstacles, Paul Streeten (1972, 6) admits, than those the now economically advanced western countries faced in their pre-industrial phase when the rate of population growth was considerably less and was partly the *result* of successful development and rising levels of living;

b) despite the stock of scientific and technical knowledge to which developing countries could have access, most modern technology is ill-adapted to the conditions and the factor endowments of the developing countries. In any case, modern technology has tended to discourage labour-intensive methods of production and where imported indiscriminately has tended to aggravate the gross under-utilization of labour already prevalent in developing countries;

c) that for a number of reasons, capital and skilled men are attracted to the richest industrial societies, consequently capital flight has peen substantial, attracted by higher rates of return and greater political security, while emigration of professionals and skilled persons has been on the *increase;*

d) that, as Dudley Seers has shown, high levels of remuneration for professional skills in advanced countries raise obstacles to development in developing countries which go beyond the losses through emigration. By the creation of an international market in these skills, not only are internal inequalities without functional justification increased in underdeveloped countries, but obstacles are put into the path of development. International inequality has an impact on internal income distribution in these countries which, like the impact of modern technology and modern institutions, impedes development;

e) that systematic research and institutionally built-in innovation, which are reflected in the annual growth of productivity which is characteristic of rich economies, have not only been heavily biased towards products which are not suited for production in underdeveloped countries, but they have, in some cases, also led to a reduction in the demand for the traditional primary exports of underdeveloped countries. Technical progress has reduced the need for the imports of the staple products of developing countries because: i) synthetics have been substituted for natural products; ii) there has been increasing economy in the use of raw materials; and iii) demand has shifted towards services and products with low primary import content. Thus, for such reasons, as well as because of protectionist policies, and in particular tariffs, rising with the stage in processing, the trade opportunities for primary products of underdeveloped countries have been reduced and their ability to diversify and industrialize has been hampered, though their incentive to do so has been increased. These obstacles go beyond worsening terms of trade for they are themselves the expression of a desire to insulate a rich and comfortable society from the disturbance of change, even at the cost of some reduction in the benefits derived from international specialization;

f) that while it is true that foreign private enterprise can help to transfer material resources and human skills from rich to poor countries, it also creates greater difficulties than did borrowing from abroad by industrialized countries in their pre-industrial phase. Unlike then when interest rates were fixed between 5% and 6% and default was uncommon, interest rates are now much higher even allowing for inflation. Moreover, default on loans, whether private or official, is hardly ever allowed to occur. Remitting profits, interest and dividends creates or aggravates the balance of payments problems of developing countries, partly because of their height compared with early nineteenth century, and partly because of inadequate reinvestment;

g) that some people have argued that foreign aid to many developing countries has obstructed progress towards development by supporting and upholding feudal or conservative regimes which are unwilling to carry out the social and political reforms necessary for progress. Aid policies directed at investments and neglecting social reforms are encouraged by powerful vested interests on both the donor's and the recipients' side (And I wish to add that a larger component of this aid is in the form of military hardware and training which contribute little to the building of a strong productive economic base); and i) such internal developments within economically advanced countries as the desire to maintain full employment, desire to maintain and raise wages and the need to mobilise savings for domestic objectives have provided pressing grounds for most governments therein to check immigration and impose severe limits on the export of capital and aid to the poorer economies aside from other economic and political considerations which already work in favour of transfer and movement of same to the economically advanced countries as earlier enumerated. All the points above may be said to capture the essential gist of the so-called North-South debate and calls for a new international economic order.

The other side of the coin, of course, is the coexistence of poor and poor countries, South-South relations in modern parlance. In this regard, Paul Streeten (1972, 11, f.n.1) again sums up beautifully and concisely much of what we already know thus: the treatment of the Third World as if it is a homogeneous group and the interests of each member in harmony with those of others is misleading. Competition in exports of a narrow range of primary and manufactured goods, competition for a limited amount of capital and skilled services, competitive nationalism and the refusal to sacrifice sovereignty for gains in production, beggar-my-neighbour tax concessions, tariffs and other import restrictions have led to the mutual impoverishment of a group of countries which should set an example in mutual help.

By the time one combines the effects of the coexistence both of poor and poor countries and of rich and poor countries, the net result is a rigid and constraining international economic specialisation and order which Nigerian trade unions can do little about on their own except with a little help from other groups in society, including trades unions in other countries.

THE NATIONAL CONTEXT OF THE ENVIRONMENT

The State

An important part of the national environment is the State and its organs. Institutionally these include the government, federal and state civil services (including parastatals), local government, the judiciary, police and security agencies, and the armed forces. All of these, in varying degrees, are involved in the setting of economic priorities and goals and thus influence the size and direction of public expenditure and investments. The persons occupying the policy-making positions or strata in these organs are themselves members of particular social classes, ethnic groups, clubs, secret societies, cults and mason lodges and of political parties and are partisan, subjective factors which have objective consequences in the realm of development policies and the implementation of development plans or projects. The important point to note here is the lack of unanimity in respect of which economic policy or measure is in the national interest or can best foster more rapid economic development, with various factions of the public sector elite pulling in different directions in line with their own preferences.[6] Often, therefore, what emerges in the end as a specific goal or policy is the result of internal trade-offs or the imposition of certain policies and projects by more powerful groups who also draw support from without. The choice and location of such projects as iron and steel rolling mills, refineries, airports, vehicle assembly plants, small scale industries, for example, are the fruits of power-play and conflict which characterize policy making itself, while minimal cost-effectiveness and irrelevance to genuine national development efforts and thus numerous "white elephant" projects the principal side-effects.

Fully involved in some of these projects and schemes are international organizations, foreign governments, foreign private development agencies and financial institutions, and some agencies of the United Nations Organisation (UNO). Some, for mostly ideological reasons and a few out of conviction, evolve and participate in schemes designed to encourage the growth of and reinforce private entrepreneurship by providing "technical assistance" and funds to finance "cottage or small scale industries'. The same sort of thing has been going on for decades over "rural development" and special schemes to extend credit facilities to peasant farmers. In a majority of cases, by the time the *politics* of choice and location runs its full course within the bureaucracy and with enormous pressure mounted by potential benefactors in individual states or regional administrative units who are usually menthe u. of the elite (all retired- generals, politicians, members of the bench, and bureaucrats- or some local traditional ruler and frontmen for serving public official), a "peasant farmer" can be anyone and cottage or small scale industry be anything and rural development an elusive mirage. Here the international and national contexts of the environment remain inextricably bound up with each other.

Some remarks are in order here so as not to perpetuate a seemingly one-sided picture. One, the issue is not whether the representatives of all parties to the scenario are inherently corrupt and collude to create the conditions as outlined immediately above. The fact is, whether sponsored by non-profit making body or by a commercial financial institution, the situation has a logic of its own quite independently of the original intentions of some of the parties (one cannot vouchsafe for all!). Some international banks (particularly in the mid- to late twenties when petrodollars were bursting in

---

6 On rivalries among the factions of public sector elites see OTOBO, D., "Bureaucratic Elites and Public Sector Wage Bargain in Nigeria', *Journal of Modern African Studies*, 24, 1, 1986.

their vaults and banks were falling over each other to advance loans) do not care much about how a loan is utilised in developing countries: their only concern is with the repayment of the principal along with periodic interests accruing. While for international development agencies, the need to justify their own existence makes them generate projects and programmes: once stuck with one they tend to accommodate "local circumstances" and which in turn provide grounds for obtaining more funds to enable them complete the programme or project. As for foreign governments, mostly for political and diplomatic reasons and partly for domestic reasons where a powerful lobby or movement exists, most have an aid programme for developing countries. A more cynical view shall he that in more recent times less and less amount of concern is shown about how well such aid contributes to the recipient's development requirements, especially in Latin America and Asia where most of it is in the form of military assistance. Whatever form the aid programme takes, a combination of the above reasons ensures its continuance until funds dry up or project is completed.

Two, obvious from the above is that the politics of choice and location of projects or programmes within developing countries also involves the representatives of foreign donors of aid, whether government, private or an agency of the UNO. This implies that such politics commences from the point of conception, through inception, implementation to termination, and this suggests further that such charges as "internal mismanagement" and "corruption" often hurled at governments and public officials in developing countries do not truly reflect the dynamics of the situation. Much as this is so, the latter are not being exonerated for they nevertheless bear ultimate responsibility for the plight of their respective economies and societies.

Three, aside from the strings attached to some aid and technical assistance programmes, much of these grants and loans are expected to be repaid at some future date. When projects and programmes fall behind schedule and many of the former do not begin to generate revenue on time, if at all, the repayment periods are overshot and compounded by dramatic fall in crude oil prices, general adverse terms of trade, and public sector overspending, all serve to bring about balance of payment difficulties as is currently being experienced.[7] This is partly why, along with the manner in which many international financial institutions extended easy credit in the seventies and the crushing burden of debt servicing on debtor countries, that demands for outright cancellation of most debts and blame to be extended

[7] Two typical examples are the Iwopin Paper and Pulp factory and the Ajaokuta Steel Plant which are many years behind completion and yet the financing has a large foreign exchange component whose interests have been mounting staggeringly, aside from the huge principal sums involved.

to creditors equally are on the upswing and the legitimacy of such demands being, in fact, accepted by many western creditors countries themselves.

Socio-economic Organisations

It is sometimes possible to view any society as comprising a multiplicity of social and formal organisations, their membership being voluntary or involuntary and whose activities by accident or design influence the course of general development. Typical examples are political parties, business or commercial organizations, religious and other socio-cultural organisations, students', farmers', consumers' and labour organizations. Of these and in relation to the environment under which trade unions operate, only business organizations and political parties are discussed. There are a variety of business or commercial organizations, ranging from the family-type, small, and medium to large-scale organizations, just as there is increasing complexity of structure and activities to match type. The ownership or form of control is also varied, parastatals (state-owned utilities or commercial enterprises), a few large indigenously operated and subsidiaries of multinational companies as largest and most complex.

Taking any of the organizations as a single unit, at the point of commencement of operations its goals would have been chosen by the owners or controllers and, in the relative absence of a closed shop situation in Nigeria, it goes without saying therefore that trade unions come after the essential parameters have been laid down. The only option this leaves open to workers within the enterprise is the possibility of influencing company policies subsequently. But what remains instructive here is that company *policies relate more to profitability and avenues for ensuring it, rather than a response to the general developmental needs or the deliberate attempt at increasing the productive capacity of the economy.* For example, a number of companies may well import second-hand clothing in one year worth US$100 million, and not only find a ready market but also obtain necessary funds to finance such imports from the international finance institutions. Thus, by and large, government's developmental objectives are usually *incidental* to the operations of a company.

But government's economic and industrial policies are of tremendous interest to the companies in two main senses: one, how they are likely to effect operating costs and, two, how they are likely to affect profitability and what can be done with profits. Incomes and wages policies, social legislation, tax laws, manpower development and training, employment policies, and industrial safety legislation come under the first category, while investments incentives, policy on capital transfers or remittances, budgets and contents of development plans relate to the second sense. The mode of compliance with legislation and manner of involvement in such development projects as approved in plans and actually implemented by the government, as alluded to earlier, are all part and parcel of the development process.

Trade Unions as Participants in Development

For analytical purposes the resources available to trade unions can be classified into three, namely human, financial and socio-political. Human resources refer to the productive economic activities of the millions of workers organized by trade unions as a contribution to development, financial resources referring to the funds and investments available to workers organizations, and socio-political resources include general influence wielded by organised labour in society, particularly the demonstration effect of their activities, views and demands and their capacity to mobilise other dissenting groups. These three resources of organized labour are not treated separately in our analysis here because they often are so difficult to separate in practice, apart from the fact that only scanty funds and other financial resources are general available to unions, while "influence" in particular is difficult to quantify.

We delineate three broad historical periods for convenience and examine the use to which these resources have been deployed by organized labour, The first period is the "pre-war period" ending in 1939, the second "the decolonization period" ending about 1960 and the third "post-independence period', representing 1960 till now.

Trade Unions in the Pre-war Period

European rivalries before and after the 1884-85 Berlin West African Conference led to the well-known scramble for African territories. Between 1860 and 1910 (Lagos was seized by Britain in 1862) most of Africa and Nigeria was militarily occupied following the so-called "pacification" exercises as a result of which all indigenous political authorities lost their sovereignties. The establishment of a rudimentary colonial administration greatly accelerated the creation of a Nigerian wage labour force because of its infrastructural activities, mostly in the building of houses, construction of roads, bridges, ports, railways, and other works of public importance.

The nature of the international environment helped to fashion the character of the state itself, which was at the time volatile and tense as Germany, the United States of America, France especially were mounting an increasingly devastating challenge to British world domination.[7] The shaky colonial administration was essentially a military regime, deriving immediate support from the West African Frontier Force and the British government: it was thus authoritarian and dictatorial. The period also coincided with the military conquest of Nigeria which formally ended with the sacking of the Hausa-Fulani emirates and the declaration in 1906 that they constituted the

"Protectorate of Northern Nigeria" and with the amalgamation of the Southern and Northern Protectorates in 1914. And following from the above reasons was that in a new political order largely based on force, and thus lacking political legitimacy, organized interest groups, particularly trade unions, bore the brunt of government hostility, their activities being regarded as destabilizing of the colonial regime whose prime interest lay in the rapid exploitation of minerals and its supply of raw materials to European industries.[8] But more importantly in relation to the focus here, the colonial administration at this point made no pretence that it was governing in the interest of the citizen. Welfare schemes and social legislation were of little interest to it, and thus workers and their organizations (as well as nationalist politicians) had to fight for the establishment of a basic floor of industrial and human rights, payment of wages (the administration preferred to use forced labour right into the 1950s), the elimination of racial discrimination, and provision of amenities.[9]

We note also that workers and their organizations at this time were striving to assert their presence against employer resistance which was equally fierce. It was a volatile political situation; "firms" were often no more than armed gangs or groups. It was only in 1930 that an oligopoly dominated by the United African Company (UAC) was formed from a merger of three powerful companies.[10] Furthermore, the colonial administration was also in the process of imposing its rule and administrative machinery on a countrywide basis. It therefore paid no respect to the rights of indigenous political authorities or workers' organizations. All protests groups and communities were ruthlessly dealt with, as firms did what pleased them in the private sector in tune with the prevailing ideology of *laissez faire* which stood for minimum government interference in economic matters- though widespread protests in the 1930s in all British colonies and the mass suffering engendered by the economic depression of the 1930s led to the official abandonment of this doctrine and

---

[8] The numerous German principalities had united under the Emperor and Otto von Bismarck in the 1860s to crush the French in the 1870 Franco-Prussian war, a development which launched the Germans, to join the British, French, Portuguese and Spanish, into colonial ventures in Africa and elsewhere. The European rivalries escalated and exploded in 1914 as the First World War, a scenario that was re-enacted on a more destructive scale in 1939 as the Second World War, the equation changing in the end because of the emergence of Soviet Union and Japan and the United States of America as world powers.

[9] For more details sec ANANABA, W., *The Trade Union Movement in Nigeria*, Ethiope, Benin City, 1969; COHEN, R., *Labour and Politics in Nigeria*, Heinemann, London, 1974; and OTOBO, D., *Tice Role of Trade Unions in Nigerian Industrial Relations*, Malthouse, Oxford, 1986

[10] The Niger Company was bought in 1920 by W.H. Lever, the soap magnate, whilst the African Association merged with Miller Bros. and F. & A. Swanzy to form the African & Eastern Trade Corporation Ltd. in 1919. In 1929 the African & Eastern came to an agreement with Lever Bros, to form a gigantic UAC. See HOPKINS, A.G., *An Economic history of West Africa*, Longman, 1973 for more details.

encouraged direct state intervention. Certainly, "development" in this period stood for the more effective exploitation of human and material resources for the benefit of metropolitan industry. What trade unions did in the pre-war period therefore was to attempt to force the state to define "development" to include the economic welfare of indigenous wage labour in the first instance, and of the population in general. That they met with little success was a reflection of the unconducive and hostile state of the international and national environments.

Trade Unions in the Decolonization Period

As John Mars (1948, 68),[11] and Peter Kilby (1969, 59-60) have chronicled, following trade wars and consolidations of the 1920s, the Nigerian economy came to be dominated by a relatively small number of large, highly integrated merchant firms. These were the United African Company-UAC-(a Unilever affiliate), John Holt, Paterson Zochonis (PZ), Compagnie Francaise de l'Afrique Occidentale (CFAO), Societe Commerciale de L'Ouest Africain (SCOA) and the Swiss Union Trading Company (UTC).[12] The two largest firms, UAC and John Holt, in addition to commercial activities, operated ocean shipping companies and inland water transport services for evacuating the country's export product which they purchased and bringing in the country's imports which they sold. In all, the merchants were not only importers and carriers, they operated as wholesalers, as providers of credit and were influential in the retail trade (Kilby, ibid.). Given "their reluctance to harm home manufacturers and home processors with whom they have contractual relations or in whose property they are financially interested'[13] the merchant firms were both unwilling and "ill-prepared to take leading roles in the country's industrialization.'[14]

The posture of organized labour on development issues was quite different. In 1943, at the Trades Union Congress (TUC) inaugural conference there were calls for the nationalisation of the mining industry (coal and tin) which was dominated by the UAC and the colonial administration, and the Africanisation of prominent positions in government and industry and demands for workers' representation on the Legislative Council - a body comprising of handpicked men from among police, European firms and traditional rulers which the colonial governor. At the 1944 TUC's annual conference, some of the resolutions adopted

[11] MARS, J., 'Extra-territorial Enterprises' in M. PERHAM (ed.), *Mining, Commerce and Finance in Nigeria*, London, 1948.

[12] Details in Mars, J., Extra-territorial Enterprises', in Perham, M. *(cd.),Mining, Commerce and Finance in Nigeria*, London, 1948; and Kilhy, P., *Industrialization in an Open Economy: Nigeria 1945-1960*, CUP, 1969.

[13] Mars, *op. cit.*, p. 68.

[14] Kilby, ibid, p.61.

concerned the resettlement and rehabilitation of ex-servicemen, scholarships for training Nigerians for responsible positions in the public service and industry, social security schemes, the revision of minimum daily wage rates, slum clearance, the provision of adequate housing for workers, effective rent control and the amendment of the Workmen's Compensation Ordinance to provide improved rates of compensation for industrial and occupational accidents and to cover cases of industrial and occupational diseases which were outside the scope of the existing ordinance.[15]

It may be counterposed that these were mere resolutions and therefore made little impact on colonial development policies as such. Such a position would be misleading. What can be disputed would correctly be the extent of such impact and not its absence, for certainly all the labour protests in the 1920s earlier mentioned (along with the intensification of European rivalries) compelled the Colonial Office in London to pass a series of Colonial Development and Welfare Acts, the first in 1929 which sought to interest respective colonial administrations in their own economies as they were "to promote commerce with, and to relieve economic depression in the United Kingdom and to stimulate agricultural and industrial activity in the colonial territories" (cited in Ekundare, 1973, 121).[16] This was quickly followed by a dispatch of the Secretary of State for the Colonies, Lord Passfield (formerly known as Sidney Webb), to all colonial governors which requested that economic surpluses derived from colonies be passed on to the colonial workers in the form of improved social services.

It may be recalled that workers and their organizations had spearheaded demonstrations across the Southern provinces in the late 1920s, protests which also involved respective communities. Some of these began as protest against wage cuts and the economic monopoly exercised by foreign firms but later escalated into general protests against the colonial administration and its agents proper (Berg in Galenson, 1964, 226). Indeed, the Colonial Development and Welfare Act of 1940 (as amended in 1945) elaborated on this dispatch and required that any colony desiring to benefit from UK funds should enact laws to facilitate the establishment and functioning of trade unions and ensure that wage levels were reasonable. In Nigeria a Trade Union Ordinance was enacted in 1938, followed by the establishment of a labour inspectorate in October 1939 and a Trade Disputes (Arbitration and Inquiry) Ordinance in 1941. The colonial administration benefited to the extent of £23 million for financing its Ten Year Development Plan in 1945, a sum it attracted by expanding its organization for labour inspection (Akpala, 1971, 23).[17]

---

[15] Ananaba, W., *The Trade Union Movement in Nigeria*, Ethiope, Benin City, 1969, p. 42.
[16] Ekundare, R.O. *An Economic History of Nigeria, 1860-1960*, Methuen, London, 1973
[17] Akpala, A. 'Industrial Relations Policies in Nigeria', *Genieve Afrique*, vol. 10(1), 1971

The international and national environments were at this time also undergoing rapid economic and political changes as a result of the Second World War (the rise of the American economy to a pre-eminent position, the economic weakening of Britain and the rest of Europe, the intensification of ideological differences with an emerging Eastern bloc of countries under the leadership of the Soviet Union as from 1946), and the activities of nationalist political parties. The American-sponsored Marshall Plan which resuscitated British and West European war-ravaged economies was not extended to the colonies, but the political turmoil in the colonies and the possibility of radical or communist regimes therein made the Americans put pressure on Britain and France in particular to reach some political accommodation with nationalist politicians: these gave birth to a series of constitutional talks from the late 1940s, internal self-government, and eventual political independence.[18]

Correspondingly, the economic situation in Nigeria, according to Peter Kilby (1969, 61) was transformed during the latter part of the 1950s. The rapid post-War growth in imports (from £20 million to £166 million) attracted many new sellers of merchant firms, manufacturer's sales agencies and indigenous traders. The UAC, John Holt and other large companies began diversifying, moving into brewing, cosmetics, meat products, ice-cream, packaging materials, tobacco growing and cigarette manufacture, and construction. The period 1946-1956 also witnessed the beginnings of unionism in the private sector which was as a result plagued by various forms of industrial protests as workers met with fierce employer resistance. These protests in the mid-forties were first in support of the demand for compensatory cost of living allowances (COLA) for African employees, and then against the administration's economic and social policies: they reached their flashpoint in the 1945 general strike. Emboldened by the relative success of this big strike, employees of the UAC and John Holt, among others, undertook series of protests from the late 1940s till 1954 against general policies of the companies. In the case of UAC, the company and the colonial administration combined to kill the workers' union, the Amalgamated Union of UAC African Workers (UNAMAG) after the 1950 strike, by having the organization de-registered and its officials declared *persona non grata* within company premises- aside from the fact that many workers were also dismissed for engaging in strike action.

The emergent Nigerian businesspersons, who were largely tied to foreign firms as distributors and agents, were also heavily involved in partisan political activities and along with the bulk of nationalist politicians and their

[18] This did not stop the French, smarting from the humiliation of German occupation, from hanging on to their colonies with greater tenacity; their defeat by the Vietnamese at Dien Bien Phu in 1954 and a ferocious twelve year-long colonial war in Algeria finally changed this policy.

political parties, began to regard organized labour as too loud-mouthed, too "radical", a nuisance. By 1954, all the political parties had literally ostracized prominent leaders of organized labour, so much so that *a* section of the labour movement was sufficiently alienated to form an ineffectual Labour Party in 1956 with the obvious intention of influencing the state apparatus, the driving force of the national environment.[19] The close of the decade ending 1960 represented a period during which departing European bureaucrats and nationalists politicians and the Colonial Office in London haggled over terms for the devolution of power and political independence.

Aside from some reserves built up from the post-Korean war boom in exports of primary products and some social welfare initiatives of the Western Region government, the economy was actually in a bad shape as we see below. Trade unions' contribution to development at this time was not in the form of quantifiable physical investments which generated both profits and employment opportunities, but in resisting the erosion of living standards and of workers' purchasing power, denouncing the violation of human rights and civil liberties, mounting a campaign against company policies perceived to be detrimental to the national interest, while protesting against the colonial administration's own social welfare, economic and industrial policies.

Trade Unions in the Post-Colonial Period

The series of political crises which rocked Nigeria between 1961 and 1965 have been so well documented that such details need not detain us. In economic matters, "the lack of impact of the 1962-68 and earlier plans could be traced to overspending on administration, under-spending on directly productive projects for lack of executive capacity, and investing in prestige projects not included in the plan." Moreover, the 1962-68 Plan overestimated the availability of foreign aid and underestimated imports. While economic planning as such has had little effect upon the course of events, government policies and public investment have been of critical importance in determining both the path and the speed of economic development" (Kilby, 1969, 23). Thus until 1962, plans were primarily collections of infrastructure investments and government-sponsored development schemes; the document for the 1962-68 period included macroeconomic projections, sectoral targets, resource and foreign exchange requirements, and policy implications.

Kilby *(op. cit.,* p.15) further observed that since the start of the first five-year development plan in 1955 (and the end of the abnormally high export prices of the Korean War period), Nigeria's merchandise imports have surpassed her exports every year until 1966, reaching a cumulative balance-

[19] For details see Sklar, R., *Nigerian Political Parties,* Princeton University Press, 1963.

of-payments deficit on current account of £621 million by the end of that year. This deficit has been financed by the drawing down of accumulated reserves, private foreign investment, receipt of grant foreign aid, and external borrowing (£227m. as of April 1965). In response to increasing balance-of-payment pressure as a result of the growing burden of debt servicing and the continuation of aggregate investments at a higher level than domestic savings, tariffs have been progressively raised to curtail imports and to increase public saving.

It was not that the federal and regional governments and their agencies did not undertake investments at all and that they did not create institutional bodies for such purposes: how and what they invested in and therefore their own *definition* of development were what constituted a problem- with the advantage of hindsight. Between 1960 and 1966, for example, they provided over 90 per cent of the capital in establishing such projects as a fruit cannery, four cement mills, two large sack factories, a paper mill, two breweries, an integrated textile mill, two soft drink bottling plants, a ceramic factory, a mint, a glass factory, and four oil-seed crushing plants. Outside of the industrial sector, these governments and their agencies also invested in a five-ship merchant marine, an international airline, three Olympic-sized sport stadia, four television-broadcasting stations and five luxury hotels. Of these latter investments, only the merchant fleet operated at a profit, none of the industrial investments had proved profitable as at 1966 (Kilby, *op. cit.,* 24).

These were the days of promoter-entrepreneurs and what Kilby (1969, 77) called "machinery-sale public investment" projects. Many of these private entrepreneurs "have proved to be swindlers', some shipping "crates of junked equipment" and others passing off overvalued antiquated machinery (Kilby, ibid.). The machinery-sale public investment projects were usually turnkey projects, where the supplier was also the financier, designer, builder, and consultant, a situation Allison Ayida (1965), a federal permanent secretary at the time, critiqued in a devastating fashion.[20] We quote Kilby (1969, 78) extensively again for a good summation:

> The explanation for the rash of "machinery-sale public-investment" project is political: prestigious capital-intensive projects can be achieved quickly, they provide well paid directorships for politicians as well as jobs for the unemployed, they are an important source of party finance via the "kick-back', and they do not require any money down—t hey are financed on the basis of supplier credit. The

[20] Ayida, A.A., "Contractor Finance and Supplier Credit in Economic Growth,' *Nigerian Journal of Economic and Social Studies,* Ibadan, July 1965; and his *Reflections on Nigerian Development,* Malthouse Press & Heinemann, Lagos and Ibadan, 1987.

drawbacks of this type of public investment are the extensive promotion of political and personal corruption, inflated capital costs (100% or more), serious external debt servicing problems, and money-losing investments. The reasons for this last and economically most damning fault are i) that both the selection of the industry and its location are based upon political grounds and can seldom pass the test of economic viability, and ii) the machinery merchants' method for providing managerial staff to the projects they commission is inadequate to ensure efficient operation.

As a consequence Nigeria's external debt, which stood at about 482.4 million in 1960, had risen to ₦435.2 million in 1965. The debt management burden during this period was 1.1% in 1960, 3.7% in 1965 and 3.5% in 1970. And measured in terms of the ratio of debt service to the gross domestic product (GDP), it jumped from 3.4% in 1960 to 12.5% in 1965.[21]

The three-year long civil war absorbed a lot of resources which would otherwise have been put to more profitable use if the political class and the military had not factionalized into bitter warring factions at the time. The immediate post-Civil War period coincided with the rise of crude oil receipts to an unassailable position in contributions to public revenues, and a boom in the price of the commodity as a result of the 1973-74 Arab-Israeli crisis. The quadrupling of crude oil prices enabled various Nigerian governments to embark on fairly ambitious development programmes, while initiating an indigenization drive of managerial positions and of economic ownership structure. This unexpected boost in external reserves led to a considerable improvement in the country's balance of payments position and reduced drastically the debt service ratio from 3.5% in 1970 to 0.7% in 1975, 0.5% in 1976 and 0.4% in 1977, and the total outstanding debt decreased from ₦488.8 million in 1970 to ₦374.6 million in 1976.

But this buoyancy was within three years transformed into an unprecedented level of external indebtedness. What the oil boom did for Nigeria was, among other things, to encourage indiscriminate and large-scale importation of consumer goods, and the unrestrained growth of "industries', with little local value added, many of which specialized in and siphoned monies abroad through very brisk trade in imported "raw materials", fake spare parts and oftentimes wholly unsuited machinery and fertilizers for the industrial and agricultural sectors. Not surprisingly, the Nigerian federal government's planned expenditure increased staggeringly from ₦8.258 billion in 1975 to ₦23.695 billion in 1980.[22]

---

[21] Bangura, Y., "The Politics of Nigeria's Debt Crisis', in Okello Oculi (ed.), *Nigerian Alternatives*, Dept. of Pol. Science, Ahmadu Bello University, Zaria, 1987, p.94.

[22] One of the worst affected sectors was the trade in motor vehicle parts: not only were most spare parts fake, badly reconditioned tyres that flooded the market led to numerous fatal road accidents so

The bottom began to fall out in 1977 following an equally *dramatic* fall in oil revenues as overproduction all round and energy-saving measures of Western countries combined to create a glut in the international oil market. Although average crude oil production marginally increased from 2.071 million barrels per day in 1976 to 2.104 barrels a day in Nigeria, revenue from this source declined from ₦7 billion to ₦5.001 billion at the end of 1977, of which the external debt component also increased from ₦378.6 million in 1976 to ₦496.9 in 1977, just as the balance of payments position deteriorated from an estimated deficit of 1339.9 million in 1976 to ₦447 million in 1977.[23] Following the worrying shortfall in revenue, the Obasanjo military regime obtained a "jumbo" Eurodollar loan of US$1 billion which it used to finance such projects as the laying of oil pipelines, the construction of storage facilities for refined and imported petroleum products, the construction of two refineries at Kaduna and Ekpan-Warri, pulp and paper mills at Jebba, Calabar and Iwopin, steel plants at Ajaokuta and Aladja-Ovwian, sugar refining and cubing factories at Lafiaji and Gongola State, and for port development (Bangura, *op. cit.,* 97).

The important considerations here were not only the size of the loan, but also the fact that most of these projects were not completed on schedule, and those which were finally completed years behind schedule generated little revenue. Consequently, the massive loan was not disbursed to finance those projects which could ensure its repayment within the contractual period. Despite this, the Obasanjo regime obtained a second Eurodollar loan of US$1.145 billion on terms similar to the first jumbo loan and for basically similar projects. But the crunch did not come in 1979 because oil prices had again picked up, reaching an all-time high of US$40 a barrel in 1980-81. Shehu Shagari's civilian administration, which assumed the reins of government from the military on 1 October, 1979, was gravely taken in by the illusion of affluence generated by the spurt in oil prices.

Between 1980 and 1982, the federal and state governments embarked upon an amazing borrowing spree which brought the economy very close to total collapse by 1983. As Olukoshi (1988, 8) put it graphically, "foreign financiers, various export credit guarantee agencies and the federal and state authorities bent or disregarded all manner of rules to facilitate long-term borrowing by the country."

Ordinarily, the act of borrowing should not on its own create economic and social problems of such magnitude as Nigeria has been experiencing

---

much so that tyre manufacturing companies and the police from time to time placed advertisements in the newspapers to warn buyers. It was usual to find in abundance of tyres meant for wintry and snowy conditions.

[23] Olukoshi, Adebayo, *Nigerian Erternal Debt (this: Management and Problems,* Malthouse Press and NIIA, Lagos & Oxford, 1990.

since 1982. The sad fact was that no one knew exactly how much was really borrowed and how much found its way to the country: millions were diverted abroad through deliberate over-costing of projects and the inflation of management fees by public officials, by politicians, and by political party bureaucracies; a great many importers and suppliers within and outside Nigeria engaged in such fraudulent practices as over-invoicing and claiming payments for goods not shipped; and, indeed, foreign banks, suppliers, several multinational companies, local companies, and officials of the central and commercial banks and the customs department colluded to transfer huge sums of money abroad, a situation that was brought into the open by the collapse of the London-based Johnson Matthey Bank (JMB) in 1984.[24] Given the outrageous scale of fraud in the external loan procurement and disbursement process, the exact amount owed by Nigerian importers became a contentious and controversial issue as a gap of some US$4 billion still existed in 1989 between what creditors claimed and what Nigerian importers actually received as loans, goods and services! In addition, in the interim the debt service ratio hit an all-time high of 44 per cent in 1985 under the Buhari Administration which overthrew Shehu Shagari's administration on 31 December, 1983, the figure currently oscillating between 25 and 30 per cent.

The act of managing external indebtedness has given birth to a set of policies that are meant to improve the overall performance of the economy, generate external reserves so as to meet financial obligations, and persuade creditors to both reschedule loans and payments due and extend new lines of credit. The broad outlines of the structural adjustment programme for Nigeria seemed to have been delineated in 1983 when the Shagari administration sought a tiding over loan of US$2.7 billion from the IMF. The main policy changes demanded of the Nigerian government by the IMF before it could advance such funds concerned the three broad areas of: i) public expenditure, ii) the structure and operational efficiency of the economy; and iii) fiscal and trade policies. Prominent among such IMF-approved policies were: a) trade liberalisation; b) the devaluation of the currency; c) review of federal government expenditure; d) pruning down of grants, loans and other subventions to parastatals (public utilities); e) the reduction and ultimate elimination of non-statutory transfers to the 21 state governments; f) improving on the effectiveness of internal revenue collection agencies; g) the rationalization and simplification of customs and tariff structure and codes; h) the review of industrial policies; i) export promotion; j) producer prices to be dictated by the forces of demand and supply; and I) the adoption of a coherent and consistent external debt management programme.

[24] See *West Africa*, London, 7.13 November, 1988, p.2106 for details.

Although the Shagari administration resisted the demand for the devaluation of the Nigerian currency, the *naira,* the removal of petroleum subsidies, and the privatization/commercialization of public enterprises, its April 1982 Economic Stabilisation Act was in fact the beginning of the structural adjustment programme which sought a cutback on government expenditure, a reduction in imports by reclassifying several items and commodities as requiring special import licences while prohibiting the importation of an increasing number of others. These measures were supplemented by an incomes and wages policy which soon ran into problems as both the National Supply Company and the Pay, Prices and Incomes Board (PPIB) performed poorly.

The succeeding Buhari administration implemented the Act with greater single-mindedness and successfully reduced the budget deficit by some forty per cent to ₦3.5 billion. But it continued to resist the IMF demand for devaluation, the elimination of subsidies, privatisation and the liberalisation of trade. It then sought to outflank the IMF by seeking a loan from the Saudi Arabian government but which was not granted. The alternative option preferred by the Buhari administration for overcoming the continuing shortage of foreign exchange and for financing imports was a series of counter-trade or barter arrangements with such countries as Brazil, France, and Austria. This latter action was also a sequel to the mounting international financial squeeze on the regime as foreign banks and other finance houses and institutions refused both to confirm letters of credit opened by Nigerian banks and to extend new lines of credit respectively as that country's short-term debts piled up — in spite of the fact that the government had on its own increased the debt service ratio to 44 per cent. This was the state of affairs when General Babangida and his men took power on 27 August, 1985.

The Babangida regime, despite the public debate over and the official rejection of the IMF loan, sought to implement practically every policy recommendation of the Washington-based IMF, the major planks of its structural adjustment programme being the substitution of the Second Tier Foreign Exchange Market (SFEM), later Foreign Exchange Market (FEM), for the import licensing system of allocating foreign exchange and a general deregulation of the economy. Privatisation/commercialisation, removal of subsidies, export promotion, rationalisation of the tariff regime, and the reduction of public expenditure were logical consequences. Thus by 1987 the government had through the backdoor granted the IMF a higher surveillance role over the Nigerian economy, thereby obtaining considerable foreign exchange from the World Bank, the IMF and a few other creditors, to fund the operations of FEM to date.

A few remarks seem in order here. First, there were also several companies in the private sector which invested wisely, as the saying goes, created employment opportunities thereby, reaped profits and reinvested. Second, whatever the external linkages of subsidiaries of multinational companies, the private sector has remained heavily dependent on the public domain and has not created that kind of economy where production and investments and therefore supply are in response to domestically derived demand: rather, it has always stayed a sellers' market with the bigger companies procuring goods and services of their own choice, and on whom thousands of the smaller firms are dependent as distributors and agents, from their principals abroad for domestic consumption and distribution. It has widely been acknowledged for sometime now that this hardly represented the most appropriate recipe for rapid economic growth not to mention general development of resources for the benefit of the mass of the citizenry, and this course has been charted in Nigeria by the active participation of the state, of private economic organizations and of private development agencies.

What part has been played by organised labour in this post-colonial period? The general tendency among bureaucrats, politicians, and a bulk of academicians and the mass media has been to view trade unions and workers, as earlier observed, in terms of how many "obstacles" they have managed to put in the way of managements, governments and politicians. There has thus been that persistent but erroneous notion that everyone else in society "builds" and workers and students '"disrupt" with their protests and wide-ranging criticisms: the implication being that those who disrupt production processes and constitute "a threat to public order", as the police and members of the judiciary would like to put it, could hardly contribute much, if anything, to the development process.

The truer situation, of course, has been that workers and their organisations most often than not *reacted* to the policies and actions of managements and of governments. Therefore during the period 1960-1965, the economic and social problems that workers and their organizations had to come to grips with were those generated by managements and governments before and during the period in question — that is, the configuration of both the national and international environments in the colonial and post-colonial periods.

These included widespread political violence perpetrated by political parties and their supporters, law enforcement agencies and governments and the feeling of insecurity this bred, the drastic erosion of purchasing power through inflation, inadequate urban housing and transport facilities, a shocking degree of corruption, unviable economic projects, the relative absence of social and welfare amenities, unemployment, and manpower development. Methods used included the condemnation and denunciation through press releases and press conferences of various aspects of official economic and social policies, and writing of petitions, presentation of counter-proposals to official economic policies in written and verbal forms, demonstrations and strike actions including a general strike in 1963 to which the 1964 Morgan Wages Commission was a response, the formation of a political party by a section of the labour movement (as was the case in 1956) and the involvement of prominent labour leaders in all other political parties, and demands for wage increases and formal negotiation of collective agreements.

In the Civil War years, a majority of workers, especially in those areas closest to the war front, was part of civil defence groups at night, as members of respective communities donated various sums and food items towards the war effort, had to give up part of their pay packets as compulsory loans to the government, faced official wage freeze in the face of galloping inflation and of shortages, and had to put up with the general hardships imposed by the war which included the severe curtailment of civil liberties and frequent use of armed police and troops on strikers.

In the immediate post-Civil War years, partly due to workers struggles, the Gowon administration was constrained to establish a series of wages Commissions (1970 Adebo Commission, 1973 Udoji Commission, and 1975 Williams Commission) which undertook a review of wages and salaries and comprehensive regrading of skills and jobs.[25] The mid-seventies were turbulent years as a petrodollar-fuelled boom encouraged rising social expectations as General Gowon seemed to lose effective control over his military governors and other officials. Trade unions, along with other social groups, led the attack on official corruption, against the unsatisfactory manner in which indigenisation of enterprises was being effected, the relative lack of political direction, and what was described in union circles as the "plundering of the economy."

The overthrow of General Gowon by General Murtala and his men did not alter the above situation appreciably, except for decisive changes in foreign policy, as such grandiose schemes as the Second All Black World Festival of Arts and Culture (FESTAC) managed to take place. While the Obasanjo regime was characterised by a morale-breaking and institutionally damaging mass purge of public servants, repressive labour legislation as workers' opposition to various official economic and social policies intensified, complemented by consequent official direct involvement in the government and administration of trade unions,[26] the Shehu Shagari

[25] For details see Otobo, D., *State and Industrial Relations in Nigeria*, Malthouse Press, Lagos & Oxford, 1988.

[26] The Trade Disputes Act 1976 (as amended in 1977) created both the Industrial Arbitration Panel (AIP) and the National Industrial Court (NIC) and banned strikes and related activities; the federal

administration re-enacted whatever transpired under the Gowon administration (with the conspicuous exception of the massive construction programme and investments in the petrochemical industry and capital investment of any sort) on a much larger and shocking scale which, as earlier indicated, almost ruined the economy.

Beginning from early 1979, the tail end of Obasanjo's administration, organised labour clashed with the federal government over its budget and, most economic and political matters. Under Shagari administration, the contentious economic issues came down to a national minimum wage, review of pensions, fringe benefits (rent, housing and transport), overhauling of pay structure in the public sector, absence of a coherent industrial policy, corruption in and delays over the issuance of import licences particularly as bankruptcies and collapse of many companies increased (closures and rationalizations exacerbated unemployment condition) because party faithfuls, politicians, and frontmen became main recipients of such licences, and a seemingly out of control or bloated public expenditure despite the fact that several parastatals and state governments owed workers arrears of salaries sometimes up to nine months!

Till the Shagari administration was overthrown on 31 December, 1983 not much was done about most of these issues, except for the eventual fixing of the national monthly minimum wage at ₦125 and the institution of the Onosode Commission (1980), the Cookey Commission (1981) and the Adamolekun Commission (1982) which looked into the terms of employment in the parastatals, universities, and other federally funded post-primary institutions respectively. And despite the absence of reliable official statistics on strikes, it was fairly clear that the years 1980-82 featured not just far many more strikes than before but also major strikes which cut across both public and private sectors of the economy.

In the Buhari-Idiaghon years (1984-1985 August) the opposition to the very rapid erosion of civil liberties was reasonably general but organized labour still, by and large, bore the brunt of official reaction: many trade unions and other voluntary associations were banned and their leaders detained. What transpired was not just mere opposition to an increasingly dictatorial regime: opposition largely concerned the *direction* in which society was seen to be moving. It was fairly certain that the public was unlikely for much longer period of time to tolerate the spending of 44 per cent of its GDP in the servicing of external debts in the face of obvious

---

government denied recognition to the Nigerian Labour Congress (NLC) formed by workers in December 1975, reorganized the about 800 trade unions; with the consent and active participation of labour leaders themselves, in forty-two industrial unions; and reconstituted the NLC in February 1978 after getting the Adebiyi Tribunal to probe the four defunct central labour organizations. For a useful coverage see Otobo, D., *Foreign Interests and Nigerian Trade Unions*, Heinemann, 1986.

general immiseration and mass unemployment.

The main issue, under the Buhari and Babangida regimes, has always remained that of hard political and economic choices to be made, and aside from the famous "IMF Debate" in which all sides took some comfort and read their own meanings, little "participation" and consultation seemed to have occurred over very weighty decisions. This perhaps would explain why in the end and in spite of the "IMF debate", the economic policies of the Babangida regime seem indistinguishable from those recommended by the much-maligned IMF and why two years after so much monies have changed hands between the World Bank, the IMF, some western governments and the federal government of Nigeria to enable one wonder about the nature of, and "consensus" of opinion at the end of the debate.

Of course, on the structural adjustment programme itself and the over-valuation of the Naira, trade unions and most workers have steered a diametrically opposed course to that of the federal government, hence protests and protests over the removal of petroleum and other subsidies, wage freeze, rampant inflation, defence expenditure, retrenchments, and shortages.

CONCLUDING ISSUES

In concluding this chapter, the salient points and arguments are summarised as follows:

a) development from above, as reflected in "economic" or "development" plans and location of consequent projects, is a contested terrain, the state and other components of the international environment as identified above being the dominant forces;
b) in view of the largely negative implications of the politics of choice and location of projects, and after almost four decades of this *modus operandi* with mostly unsatisfactory outcomes, a change in direction is most desirable;
c) trade unions and other groups in society, aside from the state and public sector elites, may be more correctly and usefully conceived as being the objects of the development process itself rather than being participants in a disembodied and distant 'development';
d) this being so and granted all of the above, it is clear that a decentralization in planning for development would be desirable, projects in agro-allied sector (including, cultivation of selected crops, processing, storage, package and distribution) and meeting obvious community needs given pride of place;
e) that workers and trade unions have contributed much more to the national development effort than is realized, and it is suggested that viewing their contributions only in terms of their readiness to participate in bilateral and trilateral institutions established by the state and

employers organizations and how well they accept official policies and management objectives are narrow and misleading approaches. As indicated above, not all official policies and management objectives are themselves in the national interest given the attendant politics of choice and location of projects and preoccupation with profitability; and

f) that workers and trade unions have tended, above all, to fight against capital flight in all of it forms (over-invoicing, illegal transfers, etc.), the dumping of inferior goods, foreign domination of the economy and of managements, inefficient import licensing system, the erosion of purchasing power and living standards, national economic mismanagement, and political corruption. If all social classes and organized interest groups have been doing *as* much, the Nigerian economy and standards of living therein would be enviable.

Chapter 10

ORGANISED LABOUR AND THE POLITICAL PROCESS UNDER MILITARY REGIMES

INTRODUCTION

We discuss labour and the political process in Nigeria in the contexts of our historical experience, the current political transition programme of the Babangida regime, and of the Third Republic. We do not here offer definitions of 'democracy', which I believe have been competently done by others. Rather we restrict ourselves to the parameters as laid down by the military government and as embodied in the transition programme itself. In the main, these consist of two political parties, a national electoral commission which vets and approves candidates for various elected positions aside from organising the elections themselves, the federal military government's own regulations on public servants and others who may qualify to run for various positions, the 1988 Nigerian Constitution and the constitutions of the unions and of the NLC.

We begin by stating the seeming obvious, namely what trade unions are by law, followed by a presentation of contrasting views on the role of trade unions in society, then a brief examination of the political roles trade unions played in Nigeria since colonial times, and ending with general remarks on what role trade unions are likely to play in the Third Republic.

WHAT ARE TRADE UNIONS?

Obviously, from common usage, a trade union is an organization of workers, and which follows the classical definition offered by Sidney and Beatrice Webb almost a century ago that 'it is a continuous association of wage earners for the purpose of maintaining or improving the conditions of their working lives.' But in many countries, including Nigeria and Britain, the legal definition of 'trade union' includes employers' organisations too. The legal definition of a trade union in Nigeria, which draws heavily on the British definition is:

> any combination, whether temporary or permanent, the principal purposes of which are the regulation of relations between workmen and workmen, or between workmen and masters, or between masters

and masters, whether such combination would or would not, if this Ordinance had not been enacted, have been deemed to have been unlawful combination by reason of some, one or more of its purposes, being in restraint of trade.[1]

In this chapter, however, we shall take the term trade union as referring to organisation of workers. It is evident that the above definition of trade union contains a prescription of what such organisations should be doing in the society. That definition then contains the preferences or biases of whoever imposed it, and opposition in words and deeds is to be expected from those who do not agree with it. This is why it is important that we take a brief look at the likely implications of similar definitions.

PRESCRIBED UNION ROLES IN SOCIETY

Interestingly, it is almost impossible to separate an examination of the place of trade unions in any society from looking at the nature of that particular society. Since the two World Wars, the 'role' of trade unions has been more explicitly spelt out by both communist and non-communist writers and propagandists. This has not been unconnected with: a) the fact of post-war economic recovery in western Europe and its attendant rise in the standard of living of a great many workers; b) with the division of the world into two ideologically hostile camps; c) with the collapse of Nazism and consequent official denunciation of authoritarianism in European political affairs; d) with political upheavals in the colonies and subsequent decolonization of most of them; and e) that international trade union diplomacy been deployed to complement traditional instruments for achieving foreign policy goals. Attention must also be drawn to the fact of unlike the utopian scholars and writers of the eighteenth and early nineteenth century (Karl Marx, Webbs, Lenin, Trotsky, Kautsky, etc.), post-war theoreticians and propagandists have become engrossed in somewhat self-conscious and systematic attempts to rationalize their own ideological preferences (contained in their respective models), citing these with elaborate attempts to disseminate and propagate such viewpoints.

Western View

We discuss only the Western world for three main reasons: a) we are more exposed to it (culturally, politically and economically), and b) many observers and writers in Nigeria and in much of the developing world seem not to have tried hard enough to separate the model from reality, hence faulty diagnosis and ineffective policies. For our purposes, an examination of only the views of a few representative writers and scholars would suffice; and

[1] Uvieghara, E.E., *Trade Union Law in Nigeria*, Ethiope, 1969

c) the communist world seems to prefer capitalism in recent times and tremendous changes are going on there, the residuals being China and Cuba. If Eastern Europeans have abandoned their own views, and none is communist today, there would be not much point bothering you with them either.

Western social scientists between the two World Wars found themselves particularly concerned with the growth of fascism in pre-war Germany and Italy. The search for social and political institutions which would he both *democratic* and stable took on an increasing note of urgency as European ideological tensions mounted, producing a major theoretical and ideological by-product which is commonly described as *pluralist doctrine* or *pluralism.*

Although there are variants on the theme, all draw heavily from the view of a society comprising functional and interdependent parts. In the main, the political theory of pluralism supposes the existence of numerous sectional interest groups in society, all organizing within mutually acceptable guidelines in protection and pursuit of their members' interests. Society therefore becomes democratic as power is diffused through a multiplicity of agencies or centres of power. Some of these 'centres of power' include political parties, trade unions, employers' organizations, consumer associations, students' organizations, government, and peasant organizations.

Given the 'diffusion of power' principle, the role of trade unions or of any other interest group therefore relates to the *distribution of power in society at any particular time.* In this vein, Professor J. T. Dunlop (1958)[2] has discussed an 'industrial relations system' in terms set of three actors and their representatives, namely: a) hierarchy of management; b) hierarchy of workers' organizations; and c) public or private agencies concerned with the regulation of the affairs of the other two. How these actors operate would be influenced, according to him, by i) locus and distribution of power in society, ii) market and budgetary constraints, iii) the respective ideologies of the actors, and iv) the rules and regulations which are generated to govern conduct of all parties. And very central to his analysis and ideological preferences, Dunlop insisted that "each of the actors...may be said to have its own ideology. The notion of a pluralist industrial relations system simply requires that these ideologies be sufficiently compatible and consistent to permit a common set of ideas which recognizes an acceptable role for each actor- an appropriate set of shared understandings" (1958,7,17).

As Hugh Clegg (1960, 21)[3] himself sees it, an assured place for trade unions in society depends on three conditions: a) that trade unions should be independent both of the State and management; b) that unions alone are

[2] Dunlop, J .T., *Industrial Relations System*, S. Illinois University Press, Carbondale & Edwardsville, 1958.
[3] Clegg, H.A., *Industrial Democracy and Nationalisation*, Blackwell, 1951.

seen as representing the industrial interests of workers; and c) that unions should not concern themselves with such considerations as the ownership of industry for this has no relevance to good industrial relations. Indeed, for him, 'trade unions are an opposition that can never become government' (1951, 19-36).

In plainer language, trade unions should neither take over the role of management nor seek political power to overthrow the capitalist State, but concentrate on are compatible with their proper function, ale lobbying of legislators, and government to pass protective legislation, the undertaking of strikes in a 'responsible' fashion and, above all, the practice of collective bargaining, where this represents the union role in settling terms and conditions of work and problems arising out of employment.

When dissenting parties or actors regularly sit down to thrash out points in dispute, conflict in this sense becomes routine, predictable and less dangerous to the political order. In this respect, 'routinisation of conflict' is made possible with the establishment of 'parliamentary' negotiating bodies in which actors in industrial relations meet, namely the institutions of mediation and arbitration; the formal representation of labour within the individual enterprise; and the tendency towards an institutionalization of workers' participation in industrial management (Dahrendorf, 1959, 257).[4] Logically, since interdependence generates co-operation and multilateral discussion of problems and discourages extreme and violent reaction, collective bargaining is thus expected, by giving it a substantial role in the social process, to take the edge off any labour protest of a revolutionary kind.

Critique of the Western Model

Such an analysis of the model and of the political process has not gone unchallenged, even within Europe and North America. There have been many objections to the basic premises of the pluralist doctrine. It may be misleading, to say the least, to present either political parties or government as being in the same position as other interest groups in society. The State appears to be cast in the role of a disinterested umpire or referee preoccupied merely with reconciling conflicting interests. Ralph Miliband (1969),[5] by contrast, dismisses the notion of State impartiality or neutrality, basing his objections on two grounds which appear to be highly realistic: a) that in spite of a plurality of associations and sometimes overlapping memberships, some groups in society seem persistently to exercise disproportionate influence over the government and other arms of the State; and b) that as a general proposition, the 'bias of the system' continuously favours certain groups in society.

---

[4] Dahrendorf, R. *Class and Class Conflict in Industrial Society*, Routledge & Kegan Paul, London, 1959

[5] Miliband, R., *The State in Capitalist Society*, Quartet, 1969

Expanding on the second point immediately above, Miliband (1969, 74) and Galbraith (1967, ch.5)[6] observe that for a capitalist economy to survive, it needs profits for investment and reinvestment. Theoretically, investment ought to generate further income, job opportunities, and profits for further and more extensive investment, thus maintaining the system. With governments, under the welfare capitalist states especially, defining 'a buoyant economy', 'higher standard of living' and 'national interest', among others, as their objectives, management and business groups possess a clear advantage over labour. The government usually attempts to 'create' a 'healthy' climate for investors and investment, while the discouragement and suppression of strikes by law-enforcement agencies in the name of 'national security' or the 'poor state of the economy' or to 'safeguard the public interest' can hardly conceal the fact that management and business groups gain from such a situation.

Equally critical, as Alan Fox (1973, 185ff)[7] points out, groups cannot all possess equal bargaining power and resources, and there is no guarantee that initial advantages gained by any of the more powerful groups will not be perpetuated, In sum, the distribution of power is skewed in favour of political parties, government, and the business community, sectional groups which all seek to limit the economic and political aspirations of workers and their organisations.

As for Professor Hugh Clegg, the attempt to rationalise the 'permanent opposition' role of trade unions by comparing it with parliamentary democracy has serious deficiencies in an industrial context. In industry, no elections are held to select members of management, nor are managerial or worker roles or wages and salaries democratically determined. Moreover, if unions constitute an 'opposition that can never become a government', we can hardly speak in terms of 'parliamentary democracy' at all, but rather of an autocracy moderated by limited dissent.

In such a situation, Dunlop's notion of 'compatibility of ideologies' also becomes suspect, especially if such ideologies differ over the issue of relative distribution of power and income in society. It is possible for politicians, the business community, workers and other groups in society to sustain a capitalist economy and yet vehemently disagree over who gets and owns what. To claim otherwise would be to deviate from a truly pluralistic model in the direction of authoritarianism.

With respect to collective bargaining and routinisation of conflict to which Dahrendorf refers, a preoccupation with the 'institutional isolation of industrial conflict from political conflict' follows both from the context of

[6] Galbraith, K., *The New Industrial State*, Houghton Mifflin, 1967

[7] 'Industrial Relations: A Social Critique of Pluralist Ideology' in J. Child (ed.), *Man and Organisation*, George Allen 8; Unwin, London, 1973

European history since the last century and from rest-war ideological and technological developments. However, while collective bargaining has become a social device for addressing the less intractable industry, the collapse of *laissez faire* economics and emergence of the welfare state has unwittingly ensured the non-separation of politics from economics. The use of incomes policies and fiscal measures as a means of achieving some goals of governments has increasingly forced workers and the business community to scrutinize such policies carefully and often unfavourably. Moreover the State itself has become a major employer and industrialist, thereby blurring the distinction between politics and economics. Indeed, the politicization of economic policies may be said to have brought about, in several instances, the superimposition of industrial on political conflict.

Following this line of thought, Allan Flanders (1970, 41)8 cautions that trade unions, like any other interest group, exist to 'promote the sectional interests of the section of the population they happen to organize, as do professional associations and many other bodies. There is nothing selfish or slightly disreputable about this: it is an essential part of the democratic process.' He concludes, rather provocatively, that 'the first and over-riding responsibility of all trade unions is to the welfare of their own members, not to a firm, not to an industry, not to the nation' (ibid., 40).

Allan Flanders's conclusion above will no doubt inflame many passions in Nigeria, particularly in official circles. In sympathy with such concerns, a plausible argument in opposition to Flanders's position may be that *limits* must be imposed on the pursuit of sectional goals of any kind, thus subjugating them to national interests in certain respects at least. Such an argument, unfortunately, opens up a veritable Pandora Box. First, if applied to unions only, it assumes that other sectional interest groups pursue their interests with less determination. Second, that the ruling group which imposes such limits on interest groups generally has no interests of its own. Third, that such a limit can be imposed on all sectional groups with equal force (no double standards). And, four, that there is a common definition of what comprises 'national interest'. On this last point, even assuming that a common definition of 'national interest' is possible (e.g. an aggregate increase in the standard of living), this still leaves much room for disagreement over how the specified end can best be achieved.

What turns out to be a 'Western' view is a generalised model, hardly approximating reality, and from which deviations can readily be found not only by comparing various European countries but also within individual Western European countries themselves where factions of the labour movements behave in a fashion far removed from that suggested by the model. Western brand of unionism, if there is indeed such a thing, has

[8] Flanders, A., *Management and Unions*, Faber & Faber, 1970

generally been described by the International Confederation of Free Trade Unions (ICFTU) and the American AFL-CIO as 'free and independent trade unionism.' As defined by Bruce Millen (1963, 5) in relation to the United States of America:

> The term 'free and independent trade unionism' which thereafter became the policy beacon for both government and organised labour assistance to labour movements abroad has never been precisely defined, except as expressed in the Benton amendment. But in general, it seems to imply a model of unionism that a) is primarily, if not exclusively, concerned with economic function of collective bargaining to win benefits for workers, b) not linked with or/and controlled by a government or political party, c) has no communist connections.[9]

Unionism not complying with the above conditions is then negatively labelled 'political unionism', a term that has been used in a biased fashion to describe trade unionism in developing countries since the sixties and which has since proved to be both misleading and meaningless at best, especially in view of the nature of unionism in Western Europe.

The naked fact is that trade unions in Western Europe cannot be separated institutionally from the political parties therein, whether conservative, religious, socialist or communist. In France and Italy, all trade unions are heavily involved in the affairs of all political parties, and vice versa, in line with their ideological and political persuasions. One cannot distinguish between the Labour Party and the Histadrut (the central labour organization) in Israel. In Norway, the Labour Party (DNA) and the federation of trade unions, Landsorganisasjon (LO), as pointed out by Martin (1974-5,76), 'are dual arms of a single labour movement' and the 'basic premise of a unified and integrated labour movement has never been seriously questioned.' And that the DNA and LO have a joint committee, Samarbeidskomite, comprising three members each from both organizations including their respective chairmen, which meets regularly to discuss such issues as collective and home insurance, union-political committee, Scandinavian co-operation, tax, and parliamentary elections. Virtually all the members of the LO Secretariat are members of the DNA Central Committee.

Furthermore, the West German DGB (central labour organization) closely co-operates with and gives direct and large-scale financial support to the Social Democratic Party (SDP). Indeed, there is joint-membership in the unions and the party, and as Wiley (1974, 40) observed,

[9] Millen, B., *The Political Role of Labour in Developing Countries*, The Brookings Institution, 1963.

> regarding the recruitment of parliamentarians, salaried union officials constitute the second largest occupational group in the SDP (17.3% in 1969)...Similarly, union officials were found to be the second largest occupational group among SDP Landtag and Bundestag members from Schleswig-Holstein in the years 1947-58. Well under one-half of the 110,000 CDU/CSU (Christian Democratic Party) Social Committee members are also DGB members.[10]

As for Britain, Professor Ben Roberts (1964, 85)[11] has pointed out that 'British trade unions were involved in the struggle to reform Parliament in the nineteenth century, since it was a necessary prerequisite to securing the legislative changes the unions required.' And that 'in practice the Labour Party has not only been the direct agency of the Trades Unions Congress's political expression' and 'born out of the trade unions,' but also that 'its early development was such that the industrial and political freedom of trade unionism and the survival of the party were closely intertwined.' The Labour Party and the Trades Unions Congress (TUC) used to share a national headquarters and are equally represented in the National Joint Council (later National Council of Labour), quite apart from exchanging co-opted subcommittee representative and *ad hoc* representation on joint committees. The sovereign body of the party, the Annual Conference, has always been dominated by trade unions: in 1953, for example, the trade unions had 5,086,000 votes out of a total of 6,417,000 and effectively controlled a majority of seats in the party's administrative council, the National Executive Committee (NEC). Between 1945 and 1970 the numbers of parliamentary candidates sponsored by the trade unions varied from 30 to 39 per cent of the Parliamentary Party, and the party had relied upon unions for the upkeep of its national organization and election funds- total financial contribution to the party varying from 40 to 70 per cent. It was only recently that Neil Kinnock, the leader of the Labour Party, sought to introduce changes that could reduce the numerical influence of trade unions, and even in this he has been meeting stiff resistance.

In concluding this section, we should note the following: a) all the European countries discussed above are members of the ICFTU; b) that Western trade unions are deeply involved with the political parties and in the political process itself; c) the constitutions of trade unions do not prevent them from either funding political parties or sponsoring candidates for elections; d) there is nothing that stops trade unionists or labour leaders from contesting elections as union candidates within a political party; e) that political parties themselves do not have a monopoly in the selection of

---

[10] Wiley, R.J., 'Trade Unions and Political Parties in the Federal Republic of Germany,' *ILRR*, 1974

[11] Roberts, B.C., *Labour in the Tropical Territories of the Commonwealth*, Bell, 1964.

candidates to run for elective positions; and f) the model of unionism where trade unions should not be actively and directly involved in the political process, except as pressure groups to lobby politicians, bureaucrats, etc. for favourable legislation is *peculiarly* American and politicians and trade unionists in Europe do not accept it in theory and in practice - hence they are divided along ideological and religious lines to the point of the presence of socialist and communist unionists and politicians all over western Europe and who enjoy civil and political liberties like anyone else (which has not been the case in the United States of America).

TRADE UNIONS AND THE POLITICAL PROCESS

For ease of analysis and to reflect points at which roles of organized labour in the political process changed somewhat we break our historical experience into three, namely early colonial period (1900-1946), decolonisation period (1947-1960) and the post-Independence period (1961 to date). We assume a basic familiarity with our colonial history and the development of a wage labour force, and so all we do below is a sketchy presentation which highlights those facts and developments of relevance to our focus.

Early Colonial Period

Although Lagos was occupied and ruled as a Crown Colony since 1862, the rest of Nigeria was not successfully colonised till 1906 when the last of the Hausa-Fulani emirates was militarily subdued and both Southern and Northern Protectorates amalgamated in 1914. The period between 1906 and 1939 was taken up by attempts to a) build infrastructure (roads, rail, ports, buildings, etc.); b) erect a rudimentary administrative structure; c) and organize the exploitation of mineral, agricultural and human resources. All three sets of activities led to the growth and development of a wage labour force in both the private and public sectors.

The political process was severely restricted for most of the time. With a few exceptions, all indigenous political authorities were victims of military action, Lugard having deposed and replaced most of the emirs in the north and *obas* in the Yoruba states and Bini kingdom. The *modus operandi* was first adopted in 1862 in the Lagos Colony where the governors became embroiled in a vicious cycle of deposition, replacement, protests against official nominees, reinstatement of previous rulers, and re-deposition. Military subjugation and disruption of traditional authority systems had predictable consequences: both British colonial conquerors and their appointees lacked political legitimacy and a garrison was required to protect each emir from his own 'subjects'. New emirs or *obas* who drew their political and military support from colonial authorities tended towards oppressive tactics which were denounced by deposed local rulers and their supporters, thus ensuring widespread disturbances and equally brutal and violent repression by the colonial law enforcement agencies. If these were sufficiently well publicized, the Colonial Office would establish a commission of inquiry and whose report would recommend some cosmetic changes, and the cycle of events would repeat itself at a lower or higher intensity depending on issues and local circumstances.

The policy as applied to the 'segmentary' societies of the southern provinces was equally unsettling, and perhaps even more destructive of their social structures. Here Lord Lugard, in his wisdom, sought to create the equivalent of emirs and *obas* in order to apply his principle of indirect rule. The 'warrant chiefs', so-called because they were issued with certificates of recognition by the colonial authorities, were appointed to fulfil that role, furnished with police, native courts, powers to impose and collect taxes, and vested with the management of all matters relating to the peace, order, and good government of the designated area.

By 1927, this system had begun to collapse as a result of widespread corruption by the chiefs, miscarriages of justice, and widespread social protests against the 'native administration' and against taxes. These protests, during which chiefs were physically attacked, and courts, prisons, and public buildings destroyed, also involving trade boycotts in several instances, were designed to bring pressure to bear on commercial firms and thus on the colonial administration to abolish taxes and purge the chiefs.

Things were not this bad until Lugard showed up, for a substantial number of indigenes in the Lagos Crown Colony attained enviable heights both in the colonial political apparatus and other walks of life. Right up to 1900, the institution of an urban administration and the creation of public utilities generated a standing corpus of white-collar officials, artisans, and other categories of labour. The willingness of successive governors to involve an increasing number of the locally literate population, indigenous political authorities and emergent commercial interests in government by creating the Nigerian Legislative Council so as to promote and protect British imperial interests, created a vigorous political community where free rein could be given to individual aspirations. Enlightened self-interest on the part of colonial officials, the torrent of criticism of official policies poured out by nationalist politicians, a vigorous and often libellous press, combined with bouts of economic depressions and boom and the many grievances of 'public servants' to set the stage for an increasingly systematic processing of problems and claims against the colonial administration.

What Lugard did was to attempt to turn back the hands of the clock, as it were, by excluding western-educated and urban-based indigenous elements from the mainstream of colonial administration, until the 1940s, by imposing his indirect rule and native administration. In particular, Lugard chose to muzzle the Nigerian Legislative Council that comprised chosen indigenous and expatriate representatives and the western-style legal system. In 1923, for example, a small number of taxpayers were accorded the right to elect only three representatives to the Council, against which Herbert Macaulay organized his Nigerian National Democratic Party to contest the election. As Robin Cohen (1974, 1) perceptively observed, 'political parties' of that era should 'more properly be considered political movements than parties.'[12]

That said, the stilling of the operations of the Western-style legal system, with consequent restrictions on the activities of lawyers, was even more evident in the workings of the provincial and native courts where lawyers were kept out by the transparent device of denying accused persons and other litigants legal representation. The undermining of these institutions brought into question the quality of justice dispensed in *obas*, chiefs, emirs, and residents-supervised courts, and provided more grounds for protests and petitions from lawyers and other vocal nationalist politicians, resulting in judicial reforms in late 1930s after the dramatic collapse of 'native administration', and the introduction of a ministerial and federal political system. Only then were Nigerian lawyers and other professionals able to practice their profession and make their presence felt in the newer political parties of the late 1940s.

What part did trade unions play in all these? The paramount consideration here was the economic exploitation of the colonies, which put organized labour on the centre stage of colonial development policies and politics. True, trade unionism in private sector at this time was practically non-existent, but not so in the public sector where the colonial administration had to depend on employees for construction and maintaining infrastructure, public utilities (water, electricity, transport, etc.), law and order (troops, police, etc.), general maintenance (artisans), and administration (civil servants and other officials). Although the Southern Nigeria Civil Service Union (which changed its name to the Civil Service Union in 1914 at amalgamation) was inaugurated in 1912, other labour organizations had been in existence and actively so since the 1880s.

The activities and demands of these workers' organizations, be they temporary or more permanent ones, were directed at a) improving physical conditions at the workplace; b) improved conditions of employment and payment of regular wages; c) the minimization and eventual elimination of the use of forced and convict labour, the former which affected various Nigerian communities that were regularly raided and forced to provide such labour; d) the provision by the colonial administration of health, education and social welfare facilities; e) legislation to protect women and children at

---

[12] *Labour and Politics in Nigeria*, Heinemann, 1974.

work, particularly in the coal and tin mines; 1) provision of grievance processing procedures within industrial and commercial establishments; g) indigenisation of top positions; h) representation of labour on the Nigerian Legislative Council to counterbalance those of mining and commercial interests; i) nationalisation of mining and other sensitive sectors of the economy; and j) wider political representation or process.

So, one finds that although most labour economists and industrial relations experts have tended to concentrate on narrower issues of collective bargaining and on whether and how trade unions succeeded or not in providing a range of services to their members, their activities undeniably had more to do with *the democratization of the authoritarian colonial political order* and this explains, apart from slowing down the rate at which human, mineral and other resources were being exploited, why their protests and strikes were met with such great ferocity by colonial authorities.

Second, flowing from this, this helps to explain why both colonial administrations and metropolitan governments sought very strenuously to regulate, if not control, the formation and administration of trade unions.

Third, the political process, as far as colonial authorities were concerned and as we indicated above, revolved around the Nigerian Legislative Council to which the members were official appointees *and* representatives of European business interests, native authorities, chiefs, *obas*, emirs and various categories of residents, all supervised by colonial governors. There was thus no place for political parties in the scheme of things, and trade unions turned out to be the only organized group (no students' organizations either) in colonial society with any voice and which could not be ignored because of both its strategic position and legal place in society, and which a foolhardy administration could only suppress at very great economic and political cost. Trade unions, with nationalist politicians in the background, talked and protested about everything.

Fourth, the situation was not peculiar to Nigeria alone. With remarkable timing and coincidence, labour rebellions broke out in all British colonies in the late 1920s, particularly violent in the Caribbean, in reaction to taxes, labour policies, and general injustices associated with colonial domination. Here we had our own Warri, Burutu and Aba protests with some loss of lives. The result was a series of measures, including labour and trade union ordinances and Colonial Development and Welfare Acts and constitutional arrangements, meant to contain and direct the social and political consequences, and introduce some semblance of a colonial development strategy or policy.

Towards the end of the Second World War, the British hold over most of its colonies was weakened considerably, morally, militarily and politically, and independence movements gained strength. In the intervening period the

1938 Trade Union Ordinance had given some legal backbone to the trade unions and the Trades Union Congress (TUC) had emerged in 1942-3 to co-ordinate the activities of organized labour nationally. The National Congress of Nigeria and Cameroons (NCNC) had been formed in 1944, and thereafter there grew up a number of quasi-pressure groups and voluntary associations of which the most important were the Nigerian Youth Movement (NYM), and the Egbe Omo Oduduwa. The possibility of self-rule sparked off within the NCNC competitive theories on strategies and best form of government for Nigeria. The Zikists, described by Robin Cohen (1974, 73) as 'some Fabian Socialists, some communists, some racialist', were the most vociferous. Drawing from all sections of the literate population and criticizing all and sundry was the 'Marxist Group'. The important fact, from our point of view, was that *trade unionists were to be found within the ranks of some of these groups, both inside and outside the NCNC.* These groups were often antagonistic and mutually hostile. A trade unionist might be both a Zikist and a member of the Marxist Group; another, might be a member of NYM, NCNC and an unrepentant foe of the Zikists. All these were opposed by many members of the Egbe Omo Oduduwa. This was the prevailing situation in Lagos and a few other cities before other political parties were formed.

The Decolonization Period (1947-1960)

The beginning of the decolonization period also coincided with the intensification of ideological rivalries in Europe, which understandably reinforced the determination of metropolitan governments to prevent the spread of socialist and communist ideas in the colonies. It is difficult to estimate or quantify the catalytic role of the feared or actual presence of communists among Nigerian politicians and trade unionists in the decolonization process. But decolonization and the Cold War, as the ideological rivalry which divided the world into two ideological blocs was dubbed by Winston Churchill, were mutually reinforcing to the extent that as the Americans and communist-bloc countries constantly denounced colonialism, a faster rate of decolonization also heightened and widened the scope of the ideological conflict.

In Nigeria, as in other British colonies, the British government , through the colonial administration, began to advocate 'proper trade unionism', a form of unionism which, among other stipulations, required *minimum contact between trade unionists and nationalist politicians, and excluding alliance of any sort between the two or union involvement in political affairs!*

But the TUC had affiliated to the NCNC on 30 November, 1947, seven members of its own executive becoming members of the national executive of the NCNC. And given the official policy on 'proper trade unionism', there developed a running controversy within and outside the TUC over the issue of political affiliation. Some opponents of continued affiliation argued that overt political links were incompatible with 'trade union principles' and that the organization should 'steer clear of anything whatever that might tend to jeopardize the interest of its members.' Others who were members of opposing political groups and who tended to associate the NCNC with a specific ethnic group thought that 'tribalism, a feature of the existing politics in Nigeria was being allowed to overshadow industrial issues.' A substantial number thought that political affiliation should be left to the individual member to decide as continued affiliation of the TUC to the NCNC might preclude flexibility in negotiations. After a protracted debate the TUC ended its affiliation on 28 December, 1948.

Those who disagreed with the decision to disaffiliate, which included some of the more prominent labour leaders, formed a Committee of Trade Unionists that later became the Nigerian National Federation of Labour (NNFL), a rival central labour organization to the rump TUC and to which a majority of registered trade unions subsequently affiliated. The NNFL was, as can be imagined, viewed with some misgiving by the colonial administration, employers and British officials, not only because of the organization's continued interest in the political future of Nigeria, but also because of its talk of 'imparting political knowledge to workers', of 'socialist government' and its encouragement 'of a World Parliament of the working class'. Its newspaper, *Labour Champion,* not only had 'Toward the creation of the Socialist Republic' as its motto, it also, according to official sources, 'showed strong political interest, notably in communism, and carried on for weeks without any advertisements' (Annual Report, 1950-1, para. 36).

The official unpopularity of the NNFL did not prevent it from being very popular among the trade unions, and in the end the TUC saw the need to merge with it to form the Nigerian Labour Congress (NLC) on 25 May, 1950 which now represented all trade unions. The NLC wasted no time in establishing political links with the NCNC and affiliated internationally to the communist-controlled World Federation of Trade Unions (WFTU), a body West European trade unions left in 1949 to form a rival International Confederation of Free Trade Unions (ICFTU). The metropolitan goal of divorcing union leaders from politicians was totally disregarded when some members of the NLC leadership stood and won seats at the 1950 Lagos municipal elections. This, as it turned out marked the height of union-political party co-operation in Nigerian political history, and to which we now turn.

By 1951 the NLC had collapsed from the combined onslaught of the colonial administration and the United African Company (UAC), and from ensuing internal problems. Nduka Eze, the general secretary of the NLC was also the secretary of the union organizing UAC African workers. When workers embarked on a nation-wide strike late 1950 in UAC establishments, the strike was successfully broken by the company, Nduka Eze declared *persona non grata* and the union de-registered by the colonial administration through the Department of Labour. The NLC disaffiliated from the WFTU in September 1951 after Nduka Eze resigned his position.

The McPherson Constitution of 1951 which created three political and administrative unit went a long way in driving a wedge between trade unionists and nationalist politicians. The problem of political affiliation facing labour leaders was now compounded by the injection of regional political loyalties. As the three main political parties (the NCNC, AG and NPC) consolidated their hold in their respective regions (East, West and North) and co-opted most organized groups therein, it was manifestly more difficult for trade union leaders to reach common ground over specific and controversial issues of national importance - especially as they themselves appeared in the ranks of different political parties.

Furthermore; internal self-government marked a major step in the decolonization process, and with the projected constitutional talks, trade union-political party ties were necessarily transformed. Nationalist politicians could hardly ignore the fact that *political gains now depended on their own activities, the blunders of the colonial administration, and the willingness of the British government to relinquish direct political control.* A consequence was the almost total institutional exclusion of trade unions, as from 1950, from political spoils and office. Vocal trade unionists became an embarrassment to politicians who just beginning to enjoy the perquisites of power. As the NCNC fell out with the Zikists and other radical labour leaders, so did other political parties isolate 'unruly' unionists and Marxists. Nationalist politicians began to insist on 'constitutional means' for resolving problems and 'proper unionism' meaning politics should be left to the politician. It was against this distressing situation, for trade unionists, that a faction of the labour movement formed a Labour Party in 1956 but which did not make much impact.

Of course, the formation of the Labour Party only served to antagonize nationalist politicians the more and who reacted in two ways: first, unionists could only contest elections under the umbrella of the political parties as individuals; second, the federal and regional governments gave official recognition to one central labour organization, a faction which also happened to be affiliated to the ICFTU, thereby further dividing the labour movement. Thus since the formation in 1956 of the All Nigeria Trade Union Federation (ANTUF), trade unionists have had problems forming one embracing central body because of government's policies, the activities of foreign and international labour organizations (WFTU, ICFTU, WCL, etc.), discounting personal differences among major actors, till December 1975 when they inaugurated the second NLC that the federal government refused to recognize. The concluding point is that by the time political independence came on 1 October 1991, it was reasonably clear that trade unions were not expected by the politicians, and officials of the Ministry of Labour to form political parties, fund candidates at elections, nor directly involve themselves in the political process.

Post-Independence Period (1960-1991)

One of the fascinating things about the First Republic and its constitution was its liberal nature: there was no limit imposed on the number of political parties, nor on who could form one. Given the facts of regional and ethnic politics, and the thorough manner in which the dominant parties set about monopolizing political power in their respective regions, those in the labour movement who felt sufficiently denied or deprived of opportunity to contribute in a different manner formed the Socialist Workers and Farmers Party (SWAFP), a political party that had umbilical union with the Nigerian Trade Union Congress (NTUC), one of the central bodies. The Trade Union Congress of Nigeria (TUCN) which after the abortive 1962 Ibadan merger conference became the United Labour Congress of Nigeria (ULCN) was recognized by the federal government and many of its leading figures were members of the federal ruling coalition parties of the NPC and NCNC. The Northern Federation of Labour (NFL), another labour centre and which was largely a one-man band, disappeared into the NPC. Imoudu of the Labour Unity Front (LUF) and Eskor Toyo formed the Nigerian Labour Party in 1964 to contest seats in the controversial federal elections.

The point we are trying to bring out here is that the *political process and the relationship between political parties and trade unions in the First Republic was no different from that of most Western European countries.*

Unfortunately, more doctrinaire and illiberal changes actually began with the military regimes, especially from 1975. It is worth noting in this regard that the Commissioner for Labour in his speech denouncing the NLC (1975) and establishing the Adebiyi Tribunal to probe the four central bodies, which had incidentally dissolved themselves since April 1975, and Adebiyi Tribunal itself seemed preoccupied by 'politics', 'foreign ideologies', 'ideological struggles' and 'misuse of funds'. Combined with the restructuring exercise carried out by the Administrator of Trade Union Affairs appointed by the government too, these two measures were largely meant to 'purge' and 'purify' the labour movement of any lingering ideological and political pollutants.

One now entered a stage in the country's history where a regime, for a short while and for the first time, behaved as though it knew what was best for everybody. The industrial unions and the re-inaugurated NLC of 1978 had constitutions imposed on them which reduced their political role, if it could be so called, to mere lobbyists: they could not form a political party, nor fund one nor sponsor any candidate. Nor could senior staff associations he affiliates of the NLC. The politicians themselves could not form more than four 'national' parties, no independent candidates, and freedom to change one's membership of a party within the life of a parliament (carpet-crossing) was severely curtailed.

For the duration of the Second Republic (October 1979-December 1983) therefore, whatever links prominent union leaders and the leadership of the NLC developed with any political party, legislator or politician, was done purely at the personal level, since neither the 1979 Constitution, nor the constitutions of the unions provided institutional avenues for such. For example, if there was constitutional provision for *proportional representation* of major interest groups in society, the representation of students, trade unions, women, pensioners, ex-servicemen and other minority groups in parliament and other appointments or positions would have been taken for granted and the 'politics' of Nigeria might have been different, Indeed, a few former trade unionists won their seats as party members and politicians, some of whom proved useful to the labour movement at various times just as some, to Bassey Etienam, made things difficult for the NLC as members of the Parliamentary Labour Committee.

Organized labour thus lobbied, issued threats and ultimatums over national minimum wage and pensions, protested about salary arrears, went on a general strike in 1981, pleaded, wrote petitions, and presented counter-proposals to official economic, industrial and social policies for the duration of the Second Republic. Only once did the National Party of Nigeria (NPN) attempt openly but unsuccessfully to interfere in union affairs by sponsoring a rival road and transport workers union in Lagos. As a watch-dog and critic of government and of politicians, and a check against some excesses of private employers, seemed to be the main service organized labour could offer in the further democratization of the Nigerian political process in this period.

What is remarkable and strangely ironically about it all *is the return to, or the adoption in the 1970s and 1980s of the colonial administration's view in the early colonial period, by Nigerian political and economic elites of today, of the role trade unions should play in society.* For a while in 1989 when 13 so-called political associations were formed, inclusive of the Labour Party formed by sections of organized labour in conjunction with some left-wing' theoreticians, it seemed there was a movement back to what prevailed during the liberal First Republic in terms of pluralism. The Babangida regime's decision to create its own two political parties put paid to that possibility.

From the current transition programme, therefore, the 1990s promise not to be any different in terms of perpetuating a tendency to virtual elimination of trades unions' direct involvement in the political process, with the political parties even reduced to two in number, and while a good number of members of the political and business classes have themselves been banned from participating in the political process.

The Third Republic and Organized Labour

From all that has been said, it is obvious that the 1988 Constitution as well as the constitutions of individual industrial unions and of the NLC have indicated broadly the sort of role organized labour is expected to play now, during the transition, and later when the two political parties have won and lost. The main lesson to be learned here is that the formulation of the Constitution is the first battle ground for all vested interest groups, for the document stipulates positions, manner and institutions fur electing persons to such positions, who may qualify to he elected, and what sort of legal bodies could participate in the process. **In** this organized labour has lost out already.

It is possible, however, to argue that industrial unions and the NLC could formally change the relevant provisions in their constitutions and opt for more meaningful and direct involvement with a political party of their choice. One suspects that the impact of such a move would be insignificant so long as these bodies still have to account to the Registrar of Trade Unions on how their monies have been spent and, in any case, most unions do not have enough funds with which to operate with, not to speak of funding expensive political activities.

On the other hand, within the constraints imposed externally and internally on organized labour, no law or constitutional provision can stop trades unions and the NLC from declaring sympathy with and support for the policies of any of the two parties. How closely such a party and the NLC, for example, co-ordinate their activities and policies would strictly be their business. Logically, like political parties and other voluntary or interest groups in society, organized labour should be able to raise funds voluntarily (not from union or affiliation dues) for many purposes, including the political without violating any constitutional provision.

One more thing, though. It is neither honest nor sensible for anyone to keep suggesting that organized labour should be 'neutral'. None of the political parties nor interest groups in society is neutral, which is the doubt raised earlier about 'double standards' and the inability to apply rules and regulations with equal force on all groups. There is not much to confirm, in light of our historical experience, that the activities of business persons, of employers, of political parties, governments, legislators, immigration and customs, law enforcement agencies, and other interest groups, are all in the national interest, and any more so than those of workers or organised labour. On many occasions therefore, including the incidence of arrears of salaries for months as occurred in the Second Republic, 'neutrality' in that context easily translates into attempting suicide: nobody protects your life better than yourself even where law enforcement agencies arc very active and efficient, and governments socially responsive to citizenry.

CONCLUDING REMARKS

The current official conception of the role of organised labour in the political process, upon examination, seems to be in the same mould as the colonial mode of the 1940s, and the only one close to it today is that of the United States of America, which is the only one out of tune with all Western countries where organised labour and various political parties have joint programmes, policies, and political candidates. Their situations evolved and emerged over time, but the Nigerian experiment has been imposed. Being imposed does not necessarily mean that it might not work, at least to the benefit of some: it just that we may not lay any serious claim to being liberal and democratic, and it might take us a while longer to develop that competence to resolve conflicts and disagreements more democratically. For the Third Republic to be more meaningful and to survive in a better form, we suggest that organized labour and other interest groups should contribute their share more relevantly than now. Of course, there is always that possibility of politicians in power being forced to realise this and pass relevant laws.

Chapter 11

THE STATE TACTICS AND STRATEGIES PRE-1985 PERIOD: SOME CONSIDERATIONS

Before we indulge in speculation about the likely directions of State involvement in industrial relations in Nigeria in the future, a recapitulation of why and how it had been intimately embroiled might prove useful, if only to distil the essentials of what has so far been said and written. Some of the reasons for this Yesufu (1984, 33)[1] has, most fortunately for us, conveniently grouped under four broad categories, economic, historical and international imperatives, its status as the dominant employer, and political and social. A brief comment on some of the arguments provided by Yesufu and subsumed under the above headings is in order, not because the classification itself is defective but because he has imputed certain 'intentions' of the State and made some assertions about industrial relations practices which require a critical second look. Some do, indeed, seem difficult to sustain both historically and empirically. More important, Yesufu has consistently presented one of the most influential and sophisticated analyses of industrial relations processes in Nigeria and should therefore be taken seriously.

Under the group of 'economic' reasons, Yesufu (1984, 33) observes that 'the state acquires a vested interest in the industrialisation process, the success of which...depends to an incalculable extent upon the skills, attitudes and efficiency of the industrial labour force and it relations with management.' Furthermore, that 'industrial strife even in one major enterprise or industry could cause economic chaos or stagnation through linkage effects. In these circumstances, governments feel the compulsion to be specially concerned with industrial relations, because of the extent to which these relations determine the levels of productivity and the effective utilization of scarce capital and other resources.'

The issue raised here goes beyond our immediate interest and the confines of industrial relations proper, having more to do with development strategies. However, in relation to the political economy of industrial

[1] Yesufu, T.M. , *The Dynamics of Industrial Relations: The Nigerian Experience*, University Press Limited, Ibadan, 1984.

relations, it maybe that rapid expansion in public investments has sharpened the manipulative instincts of those public servants who manage these portfolios for greater returns. This may explain their interest in the restive nature of organized labour and in the latter's attempts to resist offers of 'special inducements' to foreign financial sources and technical partners as indicated by Yesufu himself. If so, it has to be said that large-scale investments by the State only recently (i.e. in the 1970s), became a feature of the situation and can hardly account for the deep involvement of the State in industrial affairs throughout much of our earlier history. Secondly, much of the 'general economic chaos or stagnation through linkage effects' that have occurred have directly been attributable to the nature of the international capitalist system itself (cyclical 'booms' and 'depressions') and the dependent nature of the Nigerian economy with its highly inflated and expensive 'development projects'. The irrelevance of some of these 'white elephants' to meaningful national development, brazen official corruption and the general mismanagement by state elites of 'scarce capital and other resources' form another element of the situation. This, unfortunately, does not vitiate Yesufu's second point: governmental fear of the possibility of industrial strife resulting in chaos. But such a fear can only be in relation to the conduct of, and the social and economic policies adopted by government and state elites themselves. The greater such fears the more ineffective and bankrupt such policies are. This aside, rivalry between state elites and within the political class itself has contributed in no small way to the very odd geographical siting or location of these 'project', often against the recommendations of consultants and experts as contained in feasibility reports. This has not only escalated costs but also created all manner of problems for respective labour forces which are sometimes forced to work in areas devoid of housing, water, food, and facilities of any kind, much like building a settlement from scratch. Such workers, understandably, ask for somewhat different terms or allowances from other public employees, differentials which 'government' refuses to entertain, thus leading to strikes, followed by charges or 'economic sabotage' from State functionaries, detentions and summary dismissals.

The consolation perhaps is that it has never been contended that three general strikes since 1945 and an untold number of strikes in both public and private establishments have led to 'general economic chaos or stagnation through linkage effects.' This said 'fear' of government and of State elites should, perhaps, be more appropriately seen as part and parcel of rationalising and 'selling' to all concerned an essentially anti-labour policy, and to reflect the composition of the state rather than an objective assessment of the situation on the ground.

Under 'historical and international imperatives', Yesufu has drawn attention to those pressures, whether political, moral or otherwise, brought to bear by reformers, politicians, metropolitan governments, on colonial administrations and post-colonial governments to fulfil certain international obligations, whether to the United Nations (or League of Nations before it) or to conventions of the International Labour Office (now Organization), in so far as they relate to labour or industrial relations 'actors'. Such pressures have served as an impetus for State intervention in the form of specific legislation. We have already noted, in this regard, the resistance of various colonial administrations to passing legislation recognizing the right of workers to organize and form trade unions, and the ultimate prohibition, after considerable pressure from the Colonial Office and protests by communities and conscript labour, of the use of forced labour. These are forms of State intervention. They also include the legal enactment and enforcement of the length of the working day and week, of contracts of employment, legislation on safety and injury at work, and attempts to establish minimum wage rates in 'sweated' trades, some of which were the subject of investigation by the Sofola Commission (1957).

But Yesufu (1984, 33) moves on to very uncertain ground when he claims that 'before independence the colonial powers in Africa intervened in industrial relations to implement certain labour policies which were developed and tested in their home countries, and which had become an inseparable adjunct of their social and political philosophy and systems of government', and contends that 'such intervention appears to have been regarded as part of the civilizing mission of the colonial administration.'[2] Aside from low wages which prevailed in industrializing Britain for centuries, it is difficult to find equivalents of these 'well tested' labour policies as applied in the colonies. During centuries of slave trading abroad, for instance, slaves were legally free in Britain itself. In Britain there was no precedent for the use of forced labour, nor of compulsory registration of unions. Indeed, even right up to the first decade of the twentieth century when employment of children and women was rampant in Britain, the United States of America and the rest of Europe, only able-bodied men were forcibly recruited in Nigeria although legislation was later to be passed prohibiting this method of recruitment.

It may be that Yesufu has in mind other institutional arrangements and legislation such as the Whitley Councils and Trade Union Ordinances. Whitley Councils themselves were not introduced in Britain till 1917 and, as Arthur Marsh, OBE,[3] has pointed out to me in one of his several comments

[2] Yesufu, T.M., *The Dynamics of Industrial Relations: The Nigerian Experience,* University Press Limited, Ibadan, 1984.

[3] Marsh, A., OBE, Director of Industrial Relations Unit, St. Edmund Hall, University of Oxford. He has published extensively and is the author of several books including the *Concise Encyclopaedia of*

on this chapter, joint machinery for negotiation and participation was widely developed in Britain during the First World War of 1914-18, but when formally advocated by government after the war found employers unwilling to share control with their employees. Such councils were introduced into Nigeria's public sector about thirty years later with equally dismal results. The 1938 Trade Union Ordinance was supposed to have been modelled along the lines of the United Kingdom Trade Unions Act of 1871 but, as already indicated, its crucial provisions on compulsory registration (and legal and other consequences of de-registration), compulsory yearly returns, and the categories of persons who could hold union jobs, were not contained in the 'parent' Act. The only common denominator was 'voluntary' recognition of unions by private employers with both parties committed to collective bargaining. The latter, as earlier discussed, was rendered largely ineffectual by the 1941 Trade Disputes (Arbitration & Inquiry) Ordinance, the authoritarian and undemocratic nature of colonial political order, the Nigerian General Defence Regulations which institutionalized forced labour, not to speak of the liberal use of police and soldiers on protesting workers and communities and to provide coercive support for rationing and a crude incomes policy. The point, of course, is that the 1938 Nigerian Trade Union Ordinance was a far cry from the British Act, both in content and intent, and operated differently and under different cultural, political and social circumstances.

On the 'civilising mission' argument of Yesufu (1984), it has earlier been established that most colonial officials, staff of the Colonial Office, and spokesmen of British business circles were largely aware of the reprehensive nature both of forced labour and the brutal killings of striking workers and of protesting members of various communities and other unwholesome aspects of colonial 'labour policy'. The 'civilising mission' presentation was directed at minimising the outrage felt by the British public at large and reformist groups in particular. We have also shown how the anti-unionism of colonial employers was often disguised by statements claiming either 'over-sophistication' of unionism *per se* or the 'primitivism' of colonised workers struggling to develop their own forms and concepts of trade unionism in African conditions. There is thus little to support the conclusion that colonial labour policy was in the main used as an instrument for civilising the 'native', an exercise missionaries thought they were doing unusually well at through the spread of formal Western education and religious beliefs. The economic advantages for colonial employers and metropolitan industry were clear. The potentially frightening political repercussions within the colony forced substantial modification of 'labour policy', particularly in the 1940s and 1950s. Following this argument, Lord

---

Industrial Relations, Gower, 1977

Passfield, specifically cited by Yesufu (1984, 33) and under whose secretaryship of the Colonial Office a flurry of despatches suffused with the civilising mission syndrome are supposed to have appeared, was, undeniably a reformer and an astute political animal. He was, perhaps, more preoccupied with the provision of political 'safety valves' in the colonies and preventing colonial trade unions and other protest movements from falling into 'wrong' hands than with any civilising mission. This is not to deny the presence of racialists and the occurrence of racism. Some colonial officials pursued racism single-mindedly and encouraged official resistance to much-needed changes in this regard.

More surprisingly, Yesufu (1984, 33-34) has precious little to say about the consequences for all parties and the general tenor and drift of industrial relations of the policies adopted by relevant State authorities as the major employer. He does mention that the State's example 'becomes the standard for the regulation of employer and employee relations in other sectors of the economy,' but fails to examine the said 'example', an exercise that might have thrown more light on the role of the State in industrial relations in Nigeria. Instead, he takes off at a tangent with a broad criticism of trade unions: 'Thus, the nascent trade unions, because of their inability seriously to negotiate with employers, tend generally to adopt the apparently easier but, perhaps, more compelling political strategy and battle cry for their employers to conform with government wage rates, labour standards and conditions of employment' (p. 34). Yesufu seems not to approve of the tendency of trade unions and their members to compel private employers, by declaring trade disputes and embarking on strikes, to conform with 'government wage rates, labour standards and conditions of employment.' Implicit in this position is that these government wage rates, labour standards and conditions of employment are either in themselves to be condemned or, that they are not in the interest of private employers who would seek to keep down labour and other operational costs in the quest for higher profits. Although some of these concerns are not the immediate focus here, it may be observed in passing that the labour standards and conditions of employment prevailing in most of the private (the handful of medium and large companies probably accounted for over seventy per cent of employed hands in this sector) have since the early 1970s been superior to those of the public sector. The pertinent question, from the private employer's point of view, might be what the ultimate objective of the numerous wages and salaries tribunals was in establishing minimum wage rates for low-paid employees along with a basic floor of non-wage (fringe) benefits (transport and rent allowance and so forth). Ubeku (1983, 105), who incidentally was president of NECA and managing director of Guinness Nigeria Limited, categorically states that 'for years the Association (NECA) fought to prevent the introduction of a housing allowance and transport allowance for workers.'[4]

The ways of achieving these ends would of necessity admit of conflicting views because of partisanship and self-interest. This is precisely why such policies as adopted by the State as the largest employer of labour, its underlying considerations and philosophy, and their implications for workers and private employers should have been thoroughly examined by Yesufu. A final observation on this account is that the Nigerian State and private employers are as 'nascent' as trade unions. If umbrage is taken against the *modus operandi* of the trade unions which Yesufu has seen in terms of 'nascency' and an 'inability seriously to negotiate with employers' with a consequent 'compelling political strategy', he is taking us back to the so-called Kilby/Weeks debate of the late 1960s which, in the main, sought to establish the primacy of 'political' as against 'economic' factors in the wage bargain situation in Nigeria.[5] I have since pointed out that the distinction between 'economic' and 'political' in bargaining relationships remains at best dubious, whether within the enterprise, the industry or nationwide, both remain inseparable in practice.[6] For much of the history of industrial relations in Nigeria, the matter for concern since colonial times, as we now know, has been the employers' reluctance seriously to negotiate unless compelled by circumstances generated by workers, the State, or increased competition in the product market, rather than the incapacity or unwillingness of the unions.

Concerning the last group of factors Yesufu (1984, 34) labelled 'political and social', he pertinently observes that 'poor industrial relations', including strikes, which lower or suspend production, cut into incomes and welfare of workers and their dependents, will generally affect the conditions of work and life of a substantial section of the population'. His more illuminating observation is on the nature of the salaried and wage-earning populations which, he has rightly noted, 'constitute (particularly in developing countries) the best educated, the most articulate, highly organised and vocal elements in society, who therefore wield tremendous political influence, not only in urban areas where they reside, but also in villages.' We may note in this regard that: a) an overwhelming majority of the salaried and wage-earning population is employed by the State; b) their preferences and rivalries influence the character and composition of the State; c) such power and influence as they wield within the State system is used in challenging the

---

[4] Ubeku, A.K. *Industrial Relations in Developing Countries: The Case of Nigeria*, Macmillan, London & Basingstoke, 1983.

[5] KILBY, P., 'Wage Determination in Nigeria: Failure of the Anglo-Saxon Model', *op. cit.;* and JOHN WEEKS' replies in Journal of Developing Areas, 5 (2), 1971

[6] See Otobo, D. 'Bureaucratic Elites and Public Sector Wage Bargaining in Nigeria', *Journal of Modern African Studies*, 24 (1), 1986

counterclaims of those in the private sector, either as members of management or shareholders of a sort; d) industrial relations policies therefore simultaneously project certain sectional interests and attempt to reconcile conflicting interests, outcomes largely dependent on the constellation of forces and issues at stake.

The two 'political and social' reasons adduced by Yesufu in explaining State intervention in industrial relations are that 'the state, as a guardian of the social conscience and welfare, feels compelled to ensure that working conditions are humane, fair and reasonable' and in the ex-colonial territories, the working class was often a strong ally in the nationalist struggle, and the post-independence governments have accordingly generally felt committed to assuring progressively better conditions of employment for the workers' (1984, 34). Little comfort can be drawn from the notion of the Nigerian State as 'guardian of the social conscience and welfare', even if successive 'development plans' have contained state intentions to create a better tomorrow. In view of our history and the conduct of our elites, one would like to believe that what Yesufu has in mind is what the State ought to become. Similarly, if the supposed commitment of post-colonial governments to progressively better conditions of employment for workers derives from the need to compensate the latter for their role in the nationalist struggle, there may exist the twin problems of faulty diagnosis and insufficient appreciation of historical antecedents. For one thing, not all current politicians and workers were involved in the 'nationalist struggle' and such lingering sentiments and nostalgia are unlikely to be pervasive. The bulk of the people comprising the wage labour force today were only born since the 1940s; most have only read about nationalist struggles. Second, the nationalist struggle itself was only partially an issue of 'self-determination' and termination of alien colonial rule; it was also primarily a struggle and competition among and between various components of indigenous elites for position and privilege within the colonial structure proper, with the workers and their organizations largely relegated to the sidelines and excluded from the spoils and perks of office since the 1950s. There has been little -remotely to suggest, from all the political mayhem, arson, thuggery, corruption and suppression of political dissent which characterized immediate post-colonial politics that 'progressively better conditions of employment of workers' could have been a preoccupation of anyone. The rest of the first decade (1966-70) was taken up by more heartrending social crises, culminating in a civil war. Water of sorts has undoubtedly passed under the undeniably shaky bridge since 1970 and a consensus is by no means assured over a) whether there has been an improvement, relative to inflation and standards of living, in conditions of employment, and b) whether any observable improvements enjoyed by a limited number of wage earners (managerial groups in particular) have been due to direct government policy or worker activity, or business profitability. If the intention to improve the general conditions of workers has been existing, this has been amazingly been at variance with the process whereby each concession has been achieved by organized labour at considerable personal cost and conflict and against the opposition of employers and the political class. Not even in communist countries is 'government' commitment to progressively better conditions of employment for workers assured; there are always conflicting priorities and interests, mediated only by power relations between classes and groups. This fact alone is reason enough for close scrutiny of proposed and current 'government' policies, particularly in such political environments as prevail in Nigeria, where serious decisions and policies are decided upon with little discussion or consultation and in which regional and ethnic interests appear to loom very large. What the 'national interest' is therefore remains perpetually problematic no matter how strongly the observer believes, like Ubeku (1982), in the right of government to legislate and make laws.

THE LOGIC OF STATE INVOLVEMENT IN INDUSTRIAL RELATIONS

In the context of an underdeveloped capitalist economy, the logic governing the involvement of the State in industrial relations is, as aptly summed by Yesufu (1984, 34), 'rooted in economic, social and political foundations and has both national and international dimensions.' On the whole, repressive governments care very little about such 'international dimensions' and even countries like the United States of America, Britain and most Western European countries which loudly proclaim their democratic virtues, have found reasons not to ratify various conventions and recommendations of the ILO and resolutions of the UNO. There are other important aspects which surprisingly did not catch Yesufu's attention as they remain crucial to any meaningful discussion of both politics and role of the State in underdeveloped economies.

One such missing international dimension is the position of the Nigerian economy in the 'world economy' or world capitalist system. Whether as a producer or as a consuming unit, the economic relations of Nigeria are predominantly and firmly with Western capitalist countries. Hence on strategic (military), economic and ideological grounds, the maintenance of 'political stability', the safety of 'foreign investments', and the availability of institutional avenues for transferring profits abroad remain important goals for which the affected Western countries, particularly the United States of America, Japan, West Germany, Britain and France, would do much to achieve. Likely 'threats' to these goals could come from a) the elites (political, economic, cultural, etc.); and b) organized labour and the peasantry.

From all that has been said so far, bearing in mind the fusion of politics and business, widespread official corruption, the extensive personal economic interests of powerful factions of elites of the State system, the dependence of indigenous economic elites on subsidiaries of multinational companies and on Western financial institutions, the relative absence of revolutionary intellectual activity, the general predatory activities and disposition of this class of Nigerians, it seems doubtful whether any serious threat could possibly emanate from the elites. The profits remitted abroad by subsidiaries of multinational companies would compare favourably with the amounts siphoned out by various factions of the elites. But there remains that possibility, that remote chance, identified by Andre Gunder Frank (1969)[7] in respect of certain regimes in nineteenth century Latin America, that 'nationalist' political classes could develop independent and self-generating economies to replace dependence on primary production and dependence on the import of a wide range of consumer items. In the case of Nigeria, the post-civil war indigenization drive that might have been a 'patriotic' and 'nationalistic' act if it had been carefully implemented turned out, as earlier noted, to have the rather limited objective of creating a small indigenous capitalist class which still fronted for foreign investors, increasing the number of elites in nominal managerial positions, and opening up positions of authority for competing State elites in a much expanded public sector.[8] Nor could the more recent military interventions into politics and successive coups be represented as shifts in the ideological positions of the political class. Economic development is still largely seen in terms of an 'import substitution strategy', 'transfer of technology' in the forms of assembly plants and 'industries' that require imported 'raw materials'. Presumably, as it is officially argued, more prudent management of scarce foreign exchange by adopting a 'fairer' system of allocating import licences and foreign exchange among 'genuine' importers and 'respectable' companies might get better results.

This leaves organized labour and the peasantry as the more likely threats to private profits and foreign investments. The political class itself would induce these threats by its consistent show of an embarrassing capacity to generate political instability by its own clumsiness and general incompetence at resolving internal contradictions and rivalries— consequently jeopardizing the *status quo* itself. The activities of organized labour and of peasantry need have no original intention to restrict private profits and

---

[7] Frank, A.G. *Capitalist Underdevelopment in Latin America*, Monthly Review Press, New York, 1969

[8] Part of the profits 'earned' by subsidiaries of multinational companies actually go to some members of the elite, and are usually built into the highly inflated costs of projects, as commissions, or as outright bribes in many cases.

throw out foreign investments, for this suggests to an inherent revolutionary quality to their activities which is not necessarily the case.

However, both intended and unintended radical repercussions appear from protests and other activities of these classes of Nigerians. These include the continuous impoverishment of rural populations as a result of largely urban-centred 'development' policies, an almost suicidal neglect of agriculture in preference to 'industrialisation' (a misnomer and euphemism for indiscriminate importation of consumer goods and assembling of an assortment of electronic goods and of motor vehicles), the general mismanagement of the economy as urban populations have great difficulty in making ends meet as a result of inflation and scarcity of imported food items (most ironically and tragically dubbed 'essential commodities'), and the demonstration effect of conspicuous consumption and life-styles of the elites and of open abuse of office and official corruption.

Thus more than ever before, the wage-earning population, peasant farmers and the mass of the unemployed and urban poor have begun to relate their worsening economic plight directly to the woeful failure and inadequacies of government economic and social policies and operations, or to the activities of 'middlemen' and the business community in general. The latter includes the trading subsidiaries of multinational companies and the consortia of Western financial institutions which are held to collude with political and bureaucratic elites in 'generating and financing highly inflated 'contracts' and 'projects' that have only a marginal impact on their marginalized existence. Growing demands for 'better leadership', food, housing, higher wages, social amenities, a more effective distribution system without middlemen, less imports and the abandonment of import licences, the establishment of industries that utilise local raw materials, curtailment of the activities of multinational companies and a greater say in governance and formulation of national policies by representatives of workers, students, peasants, and other groups considered deprived in this process, all portend fairly serious consequences for elites and the *status quo.*

The relevance of all this is shown in the exertion of constant pressure on the State authorities by Western governments, with the intention of influencing various policies, especially those relating to industry and labour. These pressures take various forms, overt or covert, diplomatic, economic and political (withholding of aid, grants, loans, refusal to reschedule debts, etc.) and military in a few instances. The character of elites, and particularly their internal cohesion and vision, substantially determines resistance or acceptance of such routine pressures. Sometimes such pressures may, in the short term, be in the interest of the general population, especially when they result in the overthrow or rejection of a particularly corrupt regime or leadership. But this may also be a rearguard action on the part of foreign interests and other alarmed factions or sections of the elite in protecting their economic and political investments. In all, it is a dialectical relationship which removes the possibility of a passive role for elites and other groups, thus engendering volatile political conditions and a fragile State.

Industrial relations issues themselves inevitably become politicized, relating as they do to differentials in pay, fringe benefits, status at work, control over work processes, living standards and attendant disputes and conflicts. The nature of elites, both internal and external to the State system, their rivalry and competition, the politics of the political class, the abuse of the sovereign status of the State, the logic of the State as the largest employer of labour, and constraints imposed by the dependent nature of the economy even, at the best of times, render suspect industrial and labour policies presented as being in the 'national interest'. Industrial relations practices are therefore 'negotiated', labour laws governing collective bargaining and disputes, for example, are constantly themselves in dispute and become modified in an interactive process. Compulsory registration and the submission of annual returns by trade unions, restrictions on the right to strike and pursue lock outs, compulsory recognition by employers of workers organizations, the 're-organisation' of trade unions, the provision of conflict-regulating institutions, use of troops and police in breaking strikes and other forms of industrial conflict, demonstrations, and other forms of social protests, are some of the weapons deployed by all parties in staking out their own *claims,* while countering those of others. The obvious fact is that the State enjoys disproportionate power in relation to employers and organized labour, and that such power has been used more often in support of the business community and to protect the equally narrow interests of factions of state elites than for any other purpose.

In attempting to capture, in a single phrase, the role of the Nigerian state in industrial relations, the utmost caution should be exercised therefore in applying such concepts as 'voluntarism'.[9]5 In this connection, Tayo Fashoyin (1980, 92)[10] simply asserts that '...the basic characteristic of the British industrial relations system, i.e., the doctrine of voluntarism, was entrenched in Nigeria's industrial relations....and it is important, therefore, to point out at this initial stage that voluntarism is another term for abstentionism.' Ubeku (1983, 1)[11] in the opening paragraph of his book

[9] For a good discussion of the concept and its relevance to the conduct of industrial relations in Britain and the United States of America see FLANDERS, A., 'The Tradition of Voluntarism', *British Journal of Industrial Relations* (BJIR), XII (3), Nov. 1974; ROGIN, M., 'Voluntarism: The Political Foundation of an Anti-political Doctrine', *Industrial and Labour Relations Review,* July 1962; FINK, GM., 'The Rejection of Voluntarism', *Industrial and Labour Relations Review,* January 1973.

[10] FASHOYIN, T., *Industrial Relations in Nigeria*, Longman, London, 1980

[11] UBEKU, A.K., *Industrial Relations in Developing Countries: The Case of Nigeria*, Macmillan, London & Basingstoke, 1983.

makes a similar claim, noting that since Independence and the first military regime, 'Nigeria has moved away from the voluntary ethic in industrial relations into one of government involvement and intervention.' Yesufu (1984, 39)[12] espouses a similar thesis, while Peter Kilby (1967) assumes such a transfer of institutions, norms, etc., to enable him to lament the 'failure' of an Anglo-Saxon model of industrial relations in Nigeria.

Some of these writers have failed to separate official pronouncements, designed, in large measure, to win support while disarming potential critics inside and outside the colony, from the actual tactics and methods employed. The very claim that the British system, no matter how vulgarised, was, in the first instance, transplanted in Nigeria is simply misplaced, and contrary to historical facts. It is not a question of racial and cultural differences alone; there were also qualitative differences. The proletarianisation process in Britain was a product of an overwhelming industrial and social transformation which marked the crucial watershed in the transition of a feudal society to a capitalist one. In Colonial Nigeria by contrast, the economic activities which prevailed were restricted in the main to construction, mining and trading, and involved only a small fraction of the total population. Less than fifty years ago, Major Orde Brown noted in this regard that he had 'been somewhat surprised to find that the situation in Nigeria differs in one respect from that of most African countries, with certain exceptions there are few clearly defined areas where large numbers of men are regularly employed (1941, 67).'[13] The only common denominator in both situations was the existence of conditions permitting the creation of wage labour, the responsible factors differing in type, scope, time, space and role, as their results have been starkly different too. Historical experiences can hardly be recreated within the same cultural area in a different time period in view of differential intergenerational socialisation and social change, not to speak of transfer to totally different continents and races. This is, indeed, why British industrial relations, institutions, processes and practices have not been transferred to the United States of America, Canada, New Zealand and Australia, countries which were at one time British colonies and whose populations even share a common racial stock.

In the light of colonial realities in Nigeria, with colonial governors, residents and other officials combining judicial and political functions, and the intimate involvement of the State in the 'recruitment', 'motivation' and 'disciplining' of the labour force, Fashoyin's equating of 'voluntarism' in the Nigerian context with the 'abstention' of the State from industrial relations is really inexcusable. The move away from voluntarism to greater intervention

---

[12] YESUFU, T.M., *The Dynamics of Industrial Relations: The Nigerian Experience*, University Press Limited, Ibadan, 1984.

[13] ORDE—BROWN, G.M., *Labour Conditions in West Africa*, HMSO, Cmd, 6227, 1941

is also a mirage, a misrepresentation of the process of formalising constant State involvement. Subsequent legislation since the 1938 Trade Unions Ordinance represents an attempt to codify the bases of action and the activities of various State agencies and colonial officials, a formerly personalised system that had gone awry and become obsolete and could no longer withstand the passions, pressures and ideas of more recent years. *A fragmented political authority system had become increasingly centralised, pockets of intense economic activities have broadened into a national economy, concomitantly creating a national labour market and labour movement. A situation of two or more major private employers has given way to variety and larger numbers, including subsidiaries of multinational companies. In short, the crude colonial economy had progressively been overtaken by a more rationalised, albeit dependent, capitalist system, boasting more sophisticated 'sets of actors' who now operate at the national level and make demands on the total system. Thus relations have become more contractual in response. In Weberian terms, it has been a transition from a paternalist context to a legal-rational one. At no period, then or now, has State involvement in industrial relations been less. It was certainly never absent.*

Employers and employees do enjoy a measure of autonomy in settling internal problems within their establishments without the intervention of the law courts and the State. If this is what voluntarism is taken to mean, by many of these writers, in the Nigerian context, then there is hardly anything peculiarly British or Anglo-Saxon about it, because such autonomy is necessarily enjoyed wherever the rights of private ownership of property and the means of production are recognized. But by no stretch of the imagination can such autonomy be taken to mean the abstention of the State from industrial affairs. There has been no great erosion of the voluntary principle in recent times. Despite a flourish of legislation to govern the conduct of the parties in industrial relations, managements have been allowed by the State to manage their private empires, collective bargaining has only been marginally affected by growing attempts to establish minimum wages rates and a basic floor of non-wage (fringe) benefits for lowly paid workers in both the public and private sectors of the economy. It is too easily forgotten that minimum wage legislation and other relevant industrial relations policies only apply to establishments of fifty employees and more, an overwhelming majority of employers thus remain unaffected and able unilaterally to determine terms and conditions of employment, subject only to limited checks imposed by aggrieved workers in the form of rapid personnel turnover or individual acts of sabotage.

It is commonplace to cite legislation governing the contract of employment, workmen's compensation, safety, health and social security as evidence of State intervention in the labour market and industrial relations in general. The relevant legislation in Nigeria includes the Labour Decree No. 21 of 1974 (as amended by Decree. No. 21 of 1978), the Wages Boards and Industrial Councils Decree No. 1 of 1973, Factories Act No. 33 of 1955, Workmen's Compensation Act No. 51 of 1941, and the National Provident Fund Act No. 20 of 1961. The inadequacies of the first two decrees have been discussed and it would take very little effort to show the minimal impact of the last three Acts, the compensation and benefits offered being laughable and a source of immense anguish for affected workers and pensioners. Of course, there are no unemployment benefits or comprehensive social security schemes and the bulk of employees have no retirement benefits.

Such shortcomings in the implementation of the said Acts and Decrees do not explain why they were enacted in the first place. We have noted that mass desertions, incessant strikes and an alarming number of deaths among conscript labourers in the tin and coal mines, and appalling conditions were condemned both by nationalists and informed critics in the metropolis. More important, from the metropolitan government's point of view, the situation had begun to affect production and compelled the colonial administration to create 'health areas' where certain minimum standards of safety and hygiene should be maintained by employers. Similarly, mass desertions with attendant periodic labour shortages, community protests, innumerable strikes, international pressures as identified by Yesufu (1984) and those applied by the Colonial Office in response to social and political protests within Britain, led to the legal prohibition of the forced labour policy and the introduction of wages and contracts of employment.

In this regard, an important sociological insight into the rationalization process in an increasingly complex capitalist society was offered by the French sociologist Emile Durkheim over a century ago. He noted in his studies how a situation characterized by undifferentiated economic activities and regulated by communal norms would give way to greater specialization of functions and greater division of labour. He also noted how this would in turn lead to the breakdown of communal standards, and to complex social relations requiring external regulation and contractual regulation to maintain a new form of social order.[14] The Nigerian situation has not been remarkably different and there are good grounds for arguing that such a rationalization process might have provided *greater room within which organized labour and some employers could manoeuvre. This might have resulted in less not greater state intervention, because avenues developed whereby any of the parties could formally challenge state policies and the claims made by the other.* This could hardly be said of the situation prevailing between 1862 and 1947 when the State forcibly 'recruited',

[14] Durkheim, E., *The Division of Labour in Society,* The Free Press of Glencoe, New York, 1951.

'motivated', and 'disciplined' labour while physically policing all commercial and industrial establishments, and enacting largely politically expedient laws.

THE FUTURE

Predicting the future is always a hazardous affair in view of constantly changing parameters. Where the role of the Nigerian State in industrial relations is concerned, however, it may still be possible to map out general outlines because of the structure of the economy and nature of elites, both of which are unlikely to change much in the immediate future. An import substitution strategy of industrialization is unlikely to be abandoned. The revamped policy, one is informed at the time of writing, is to persuade Nigerian industry progressively to substitute domestic raw materials for imported ones, to de-regulate the economy by discontinuing the use of import licences as the principal means of allocating 'scarce' foreign exchange, to encourage a 'second tier' system (now merged with the first tier, the official rate) whereby the forces of demand and supply would establish a market exchange rate for Nigerian currency *vis-a-vis* major trading currencies; to increase the scope for private enterprise by 'privatizing' many of the state-controlled parastatals, to develop agriculture, to encourage exports, and to promote reduced dependence on crude oil as the major source of state revenue.

The economy will most likely be in a depressed state for a considerable period of time. There is little hope of oil prices recovering to their previous high levels, organized labour has been weakened by continuous retrenchments, lay-offs, and other labour cost-saving methods adopted by employers and the State. Employers themselves will come under increasing pressure to comply, with 'national economic recovery' policies, such as payment of 30 per cent of the current value of imports toward the national economic recovery fund. Many companies will collapse and there will be a growth of mass unemployment, inflation and economic hardship which will increase social tensions.

The political situation is also ominous since the political class is more divided than ever before. In general, the military faction is becoming more and more authoritarian and would seem to have alienated a powerful segment of the population by prohibiting all those who held political office during the period 1960 to 1983, at state (or regional) and federal levels, from holding public office. In alliance with sections of the economic and administrative elite, this amorphous civilian segment of the political class (which also forms part of the economic elite) could present a formidable opposition both to the military dispensation and new crop of political office holders. These intra-elite realignments and a depressed economy could further enfeeble a battered and rickety State, as no cohesive group may now easily emerge successfully to implement some of the controversial policies designed to redress the increasingly unbearable economic situation. Politically, the flash point may come anytime between 1989 and 1992 when a return to constitutionally elected government is envisaged and political elites sort themselves out in what promises to be a bitter tussle, assuming the military does not develop an insatiable taste for political power and hang on to it for a while longer.

In the short term therefore, both private employers and organised labour may be forced by circumstances into accepting unpalatable 'economic emergency' policies. The former is already on the defensive for being held responsible by the general public for high prices of goods and services and the siphoning abroad, through over-invoicing and phantom transactions, of considerable sums of money. In spite of this, the elite preference for free capitalist enterprise and the package of economic policies already contemplated, with approving nods from the International Monetary Fund (IMF), the World Bank, and Western creditors (Club of Paris, London Club, and so on), will inevitably involve the business community in more direct policy making and implementation. In fact, it is already indirectly represented in the informal Presidential Advisory Committee (PAC).[15]

In the medium to long run, organized labour, peasants and the general population are bound to react negatively to the not inconsiderable loss of purchasing power that is bound to accompany the devaluation of the currency (euphemistically described by State officials as 'downward floating') and other inflation-fuelling complications that are likely to arise from the adoption of the so-called second-tier foreign exchange market (SFEM). This may be compounded by the continuing destruction of peasant farming as the official agricultural policy seems to veer increasingly toward creation of a few large farms to be owned by retired members of the State elites, subsidiaries of multinational companies and private investors. Should the products of these farms manage to meet the requirements of the general population and of industry, which is unlikely, it remains unclear what the

---

[15] The PAC, headed by Professor Ojetunji Aboyade, with Professor Akin Mabogunje and Mr. Michael Omolayole as prominent members, has remained shadowy, taking on the role of 'economic adviser' to the President. Aside from the fact that Omolayole was the former managing director of Lever Bros (Nigeria) Ltd. and is actively involved in the activities of both the Manufacturers Association of Nigeria and Nigeria Employers Consultative Association, various committees of the Chambers of Commerce and of employers associations also prepare numerous memoranda on policy options for the PAC. I was informed by Prof. Aboyade that the PAC has sought to counterbalance any undue influence exercised by the business groups by taking oral as well as written evidence from representatives of organized labour, from the universities, and from any other interested parties (Interview, June 1986). Furthermore, since the military seized power on 31 December, 1983, various groups of employers and 'industrialists' have organized and hosted a series of seminars on policy options, with ministers and members of the Armed Forces Ruling Council (including the President himself) either in attendance or delivering the 'key note' address.

source of livelihood of millions of rural peasant farmers is to be.

For organized labour, its ranks are likely to be continuously thinned by redundancies and retrenchments, but demands for a general upward review of salaries and wages, backed by strikes and mass protests, should not easily be discounted. Joined with tensions and conflict the political class itself will most likely generate, and unless crude oil prices dramatically recover, or massive job-creating public investment is undertaken to pull the economy out of the recession, there are likely to be some very trying times ahead, with the Ministry of Employment, Labour and Productivity, other state agencies, the IAP, the NIC, police and security organisations ever so fully preoccupied with the business of "regulating" industrial relations.

Chapter 12

ORGANISED LABOUR AND STRUCTURAL ADJUSTMENT POLICIES IN NIGERIA

INTRODUCTION

In this chapter we present a largely impressionistic overview of the structural adjustment policy in Nigeria, and of its implications for the parties to industrial relations. We begin by identifying those sets of policies which have been described officially as the 'structural adjustment programme', followed by an examination of the general consequences or impact of such policies, and ending with remarks on the likely drift of industrial relations policies and the effectiveness of relevant industrial relations institutions in light of recent developments in the economy.

THE STRUCTURAL ADJUSTMENT PROGRAMME

Structural adjustment programmes are said to address 'structural imbalances' in the economy, resulting in marked shifts towards a desired direction. Here 'structural problems' have to do with the respective sizes and efficiency of the public and private sectors, the pattern of public expenditure, sources and size of revenue accruing to the government, employment opportunities and unemployment, terms of trade, and the ratio between gross earnings and expenditure and thus the capacity to meet international financial obligations arising out of trade and other economic transactions.

Structural adjustment programmes have therefore usually been brought about by severe economic and financial difficulties, especially those that are likely to lead to either a default in the payment of interest rates on external debts or principals as at when they fall due, or insufficient foreign exchange to sustain even current or diminished levels of imports and other capital expenditure. A typical situation is thus often characterised by a marked deterioration in the aggregate performance of the productive sectors of the economy, a chronic balance of payments deficit, the collapse and/or deterioration of social services and infrastructure, an escalating level of inflation, an acute shortage of basic consumer goods, a sharp decline in living standards due to severe reduction in the quantum and value of external financial assets.

In the context of developing (or underdeveloped) countries, for an economy to be in such dire straits, all or most of the following would most likely have taken place: extensive external borrowing, embarking on largely unviable economic projects, massive importation of consumer goods (including arms and munitions) in place of capital goods, fairly widespread official corruption with minimal accountability, large public expenditure, the existence of a private industrial sector that has little value added because a high proportion of raw materials and partially finished goods are imported, some degree of national economic mismanagement, and adverse terms of trade for mostly agricultural exports and/or one or two minerals.

The Origins and Growth of the Debt Crisis in Nigeria

In order to achieve a fuller understanding of the structural adjustment programme in Nigeria and its import for industrial relations, it would be necessary to provide a fuller backdrop against which subsequent analysis is undertaken. In this wise, a discussion of the origins and growth of Nigeria's external indebtedness remains a minimum requirement since the management of external debts has given rise to and, in fact, dominates the structural adjustment programme itself.[1]

According to Olukoshi (1988, 1),[2] Nigeria experienced its first debt crisis soon after independence in 1960, though at a less severe level. Nigeria's external debt, which stood at about ₦82.4 million in 1960, had risen to ₦435.2 million in 1965 and by 1970 was put at some ₦489 million. At the time, the debt consisted mainly of long-term loans from the World Bank, the United States of America, Britain, West Germany, Holland and Italy. The interests on such loans were as low as two per cent with grace periods of ten and forty years. The country's debt management burden during this period was therefore minimal, with debt service ratio standing at a mere 1.1% in 1960, 3.7% in 1965 and 3.5% in 1970. And measured in terms of the ratio of debt service to the gross domestic national product (GNP), Nigeria's economic burden was not critical, fluctuating from 3.4% in 1960 to 12.5% in 1965 and 8.2% in 1970.

This debt profile underwent a dramatic change in the 1970s through a combination of factors. A major factor was the deepening global economic crisis of the early 1970s which tended to discourage fresh or new investments, reduced profit levels to precarious proportions, and led to the collapse of many a company. Such bankruptcies, mergers, and failures were greatly accelerated by the 1973/74 Arab-Israeli crisis and its accompanying

---

1 Bangura, Y., 'The Politics of Nigeria's Debt Crisis', in Okello Oculi (ed.), *Nigerian Alternatives,* Dept. of Political Science, Ahmadu Bello University, Zaria, 1987, p.94

2 Olukoshi, Adebayo, *Nigerian External Debt Crises: Management and Problems,* Malthouse Press and NIIA, Lagos & Oxford, 1990; 'Economic Crisis, Structural Adjustment and the Coping Strategies of Manufacturers in Kano, Nigeria,' United Nations Institute for Social Development, DP 77, 1996.

oil crisis and much increased costs of operations which reduced profit margins further.

Close to being the other side of the coin were the huge external reserves with which most members of the Organization of Petroleum Exporting Countries (OPEC), particularly Saudi Arabia, Kuwait, the United Arab Emirates, and other Gulf States, found themselves as a result of the quadrupling of crude oil prices. Since their respective internal banking systems were unable to cope with such a deluge of funds, vast amounts were then recycled through the international capital market. Investment funds were now available and the next problem for bankers was how to find borrowers in the face of stagflation.

Nigeria as a member of the OPEC also experienced its version of an oil boom in the same period. As Olukoshi (1988, 4) correctly observed, the quadrupling of oil prices led to a considerable improvement in Nigeria's balance of payments position and reduced drastically the country's debt service ratio from 3.5% in 1970 to 0.7% in 1975, 0.5% in 1976 and 0.4% in 1977. This unexpected boost in external reserves made it possible for the Nigerian federal and state governments to execute major capital projects without recourse to external loans, and the country's total outstanding debt decreased from ₦488.8 million in 1970 to ₦374.6 million in 1976.

But this buoyancy was within three years transformed into an unprecedented level of external indebtedness. What the oil boom did for Nigeria, among other things, was to encourage indiscriminate and large-scale importation of consumer goods, and the unrestrained growth of 'industries', with little local value added, which specialized in and siphoned monies abroad through very brisk trade in imported 'raw materials', spare parts and oftentimes wholly unsuited machinery and fertilizers for the industrial and agricultural sectors. A a result, the Nigerian federal government's planned expenditure increased staggeringly from ₦8.258 billion in 1975 to ₦23.695 billion in 1980. The bottom fell out in 1977 following an equally dramatic fall in oil revenues as overproduction and energy-saving measures of western countries combined to create a glut in the international oil market. Although average crude oil production in Nigeria marginally increased from 2.071 million barrels per day in 1976 to 2.104 million barrels a day, revenue from this source plummeted from ₦7 billion to ₦5.9 billion in 1978.2 Concomitantly, the public debt increased by 66.4 per cent to ₦5.001 billion at the end of 1977, of which the external debt component jumped from ₦378.6 million in 1976 to ₦496.9 in 1977, just as the balance of payments position deteriorated from an estimated deficit of ₦339.9 million in 1976 to ₦447 million in 1977.[3]

Before 1978, the impressive looking Nigeria's external reserves enabled

[3] Central Bank of Nigeria, *Annual Report and Statement of Accounts*, Lagos, 1977 and 1978

government officials resist pressures in support of obtaining loans of any sort, especially from the international capital market. The only loan of note was the US$80 million from the World Bank and was for general post-civil war economic reconstruction, rehabilitation and resettlement. Following the worrying shortfall in revenue, the Obasanjo regime obtained a Eurodollar loan of US$1 billion which it used to finance such projects as laying of oil pipelines, the construction of storage facilities for refined and imported petroleum products, the construction of two refineries at Kaduna and Ekpan-Warri, pulp and paper mills at Jebba, Calabar and Iwopin, steel plants at Ajaokuta and Aladja, sugar refining and cubing factories at Lafiaji and Gongola State, and for port development.[4]

The critical developments here were not only the size of the loan, but also the fact that most of these projects were not completed on schedule, and those which were finally completed years behind schedule generated little revenue. Consequently, the massive loan was not disbursed to finance those projects which could ensure its repayment within the contractual period. Despite this, the Obasanjo regime obtained a second Eurodollar loan of US$1.145 billion on terms similar to the first loan and for basically similar projects. These loans, it should be pointed out, had nothing to do with ameliorating the balance of payments problems which persisted; rather the administration was either most gullible to, or for undisclosed reasons went with along the propositions of overly anxious international bankers who were only too eager to find borrowers for the mounting billions of dollars in their vaults.

The crunch for Nigeria did not come in 1979 because oil prices had again picked up, reaching an all-time high of US$40 a barrel in 1980/81. Shehu Shagari's civilian administration, which assumed the reins of government from the military on 1 October, 1979, was gravely taken in by the illusion of affluence generated by this spurt in oil prices. Between 1980 and 1982, the federal and state governments embarked upon an amazing borrowing spree which brought the economy very-close to ruin by 1983. As Olukoshi (1988, 8) put it graphically, 'foreign financiers, various export credit guarantee agencies and the federal and state authorities bent or disregarded all manner of rules to facilitate long-term borrowing by the country.'

Ordinarily the act of borrowing should not on its own create economic and social problems of such magnitude as Nigeria has been experiencing since 1982. The sad fact was that no one knew exactly how much was really borrowed and how much found its way to the country: millions were diverted into personal accounts abroad through deliberate over-costing of projects and inflation of management fees by public officials, by politicians, and by political party bureaucracies; a great many importers and suppliers

[4] Bangura, *op. cit*, p.97

within and outside Nigeria engaged in such fraudulent practices as over-invoicing and claiming payments for goods not shipped; and, indeed, foreign banks, suppliers, several multinational companies, local companies, and officials of the central and commercial banks and the customs department colluded to transfer huge sums of money abroad, a situation that was starkly brought out in the open by the collapse of the London-based Johnson Matthey Bank (JMB) in 1984.[5] Given the outrageous scale of fraud in the external loan procurement and disbursement process, the exact amount owed by Nigerian importers became a contentious and controversial issue as a gap of some US$4 billion still existed in 1988 between what creditors have claimed and what Nigerian importers actually received as loans and goods!

Structural Adjustment Programme in Nigeria

The act of managing external indebtedness, as indicated above, gave birth to a set of policies that were meant to improve the overall performance of the economy, generate external reserves so as to meet financial obligations, and persuade creditors to both reschedule loans and payments due and extend new lines of credit. Creditors would always wait to see some policies implemented before even agreeing to discuss such rescheduling or making fresh funds available. At this point, external regulation or demands and internal or domestic economic policies tend to merge, creating a delicate balancing act for domestic political leadership which has to face the sometimes hostile reaction of the populace subjected to some deprivations.

However, the broad outlines of the structural adjustment programme for Nigeria seemed to have been delineated in 1983 when the Shagari administration sought a tidying over loan of US$2.7 billion from the International Monetary Fund (IMF). The main policy changes demanded of the Nigerian government by the IMF before it could advance such funds concerned the three broad areas of i) public expenditure, ii) the structure and operational efficiency of the economy; iii) fiscal and trade policies. Prominent among such IMF-approved policies were: a) trade liberalization; b) the devaluation of the currency; c) review of federal government expenditure; d) pruning down of grants, loans and other subventions to parastatals (the very many utilities and state-owned companies); e) the reduction and ultimate elimination of non-statutory transfers to the twenty-one state governments; f) improving on the effectiveness of internal revenue collection agencies; g) the rationalization and simplification of customs and tariff structure and codes; h) the review of industrial policies; i) export promotion; j) producer prices to be dictated by the forces of demand and

[5] See *West Africa*, 7-13 November, 1988, p.2106 for more details

supply; k) interest rates to be established through demand and supply; and I) the adoption of a coherent and consistent external debt management programme.

But the government resisted pressure from foreign creditors and a section of the local business community to devalue the Naira, deregulate the economy and remove subsidies from petroleum products, rice, fertilisers and the parastatals. Olukoshi (1988, 14) has suggested that such reluctance to remove subsidies and privatize/commercialize public enterprises was not unconnected with the fact that 'many stalwarts of the ruling National Party of Nigeria (NPN) owed their enormous wealth to the direct control which they exercised over the parastatals and the marketing of rice, fertilizer and petroleum and its products.' And that negotiations between the Shagari administration and the IMF were therefore not very smooth even though the regime was very reluctant to enter into open confrontation with the Fund. Negotiations with the IMF were stalled at the time the Shagari administration was overthrown by the military on 31 December, 1983, although some trade debts were converted in July 1983 to medium-term debts repayable within three years, with a grace period of five and half months at 1.5-1.37% above the LIBOR-US prime interest rate, and an agreement concluded with some creditors in September 1983 involving the refinancing of US$480 million with 25-26 years of maturity, three and half months grace period and the same level of interest as the July agreement.

The succeeding Buhari regime laid a firmer basis for the structural adjustment programme despite the fact that it had its differences with the IMF. The regime implemented the 1982 Economic Stabilization Act with greater simple-mindedness and successfully reduced the budget deficit by some forty per cent to ₦3.5 billion. But it continued to resist the IMF demand for devaluation, the elimination of subsidies from internally consumed petroleum products, the privatization of public enterprises and the liberalization of trade. The Buhari administration sought to outflank the IMF by seeking to obtain a loan from the Saudi Arabian government. But when this failed, it then sought to overcome its shortage of foreign exchange and ensure a continued inflow of imports, by engaging in a series of counter-trade or barter arrangements with such countries as Brazil, France and Austria. This latter action was also a sequel to the mounting international financial squeeze on the regime as foreign banks and other finance houses and institutions refused to confirm letters of credit opened by Nigerian banks and to extend new lines of credit respectively as the country's short-term debts mounted.

At this point in 1984, Nigeria's debt service ratio had jumped from 19.9% in 1983 to 30.3%: the country was beginning to spend one-third of its earnings on servicing debts alone, and it was the intention of the Buhari administration to push the ratio on to 40 per cent! All that the administration could do in respect of industry was to throw many more items into the prohibited or special licence list or category and issue import licences to those segments of industry and agriculture it thought more important. The dearth of foreign exchange rendered most of these import licences superfluous and, at any rate, sustaining industry had assumed second position to debt servicing. For example, ₦1.2 billions worth of import licences were allocated to industry at a time when US$3.54 billion were devoted to servicing external debts and interest payments alone for 1984 was a handsome US$1.248 billion, an amount that equalled what was made available to industry.

As the IMF stuck to its demand for a more comprehensive structural adjustment programme, the more desperate Buhari's administration became and it cleverly sought to drive a wedge between the IMF and international financiers and creditors by raising the debt service ratio to forty-four per cent in 1985, in the hope that it could achieve a rescheduling of the country's debts without recourse to a full dose of the former's economic recipe. However, despite the absence of complete unanimity among creditors and international financiers, those with greater clout, such as the United States of America, Britain, Japan, and the London and Paris Clubs, insisted on a meeting of views between the Nigerian government and the IMF. This was the state of affairs when the Buhari regime was overthrown by General Babangida on 27 August, 1985. What proved eventually to be an albatross on the neck of the Babangida's regime was the widespread domestic opposition to the IMF and whatever the organisation stood for. In the end, the administration rejected the IMF standby credit facilities after a well orchestrated national 'debate' on the issue. Although the Babangida administration rejected the IMF loan, it nevertheless began to implement all other policy recommendations of the Washington-based organisation. The government's brand of structural adjustment programme was: a) to restructure and diversify the productive base of the economy in order to *reduce* dependence on the oil sector and imports; b) to achieve fiscal and balance of payments viability over the period; c) to lay the basis for a sustainable non-inflationary or minimal inflationary growth; and d) to reduce the dominance of unproductive investments in the public sector, improve the sector's efficiency and enhance the growth potential of the private sector.

A major plank of the structural adjustment programme was the Second Tier Foreign Exchange Market (SFEM), which came into force in September, 1986. Hitherto foreign exchange was literally allocated through import licences, classified as 'valid for foreign exchange', for pre-selected range of capital and consumer goods thought to be necessary for improved productive industrial and agricultural capacity. Such administrative delays and corruption surrounding the issuance of such import licences led to scarcity, high prices, sporadic and thus inadequate supply of raw materials and of other goods. SFEM was thus presented as part of a general 'deregulation' of the economy, the creation of a partially free market for foreign exchange: import licences were abolished and the exchange rate of the Naira against such major international trading currencies as the US dollar and pound sterling established at weekly, later fortnightly, open bidding sessions by representatives of commercial and merchant banks with officials of the central bank presiding.

As comprehensive as the government's 1986 budget was in terms of laying the foundation for a structural adjustment programme, it nevertheless was a statement of intention and thereby did not receive the IMF's official approval. Intention became action in 1987 with a creeping privatisation and liberalisation programme, beginning with an increase in the prices of petroleum products as some percentage of 'subsidy' was removed across board and a drastic reduction in the budgets of respective parastatals and other state-owned social and educational institutions, such as the universities, teaching hospitals, and research institutes. Thus by 1987 the government had through the backdoor granted the, IMF a higher surveillance role over the Nigerian economy and considerable amount of foreign exchange was obtained as a result from the World Bank, the IMF and a few other creditors, to fund the operations of SFEM and projects on small scale industries. In this way, the Babangida administration was able to conclude a 'letter of intent' with the Fund, after which a standby credit facility of US$600 million was made available although the Nigerian government indicated publicly that it did not intend to draw on the funds- such a stance had more to do with the fear of reaction than to the lack of need as there still prevailed a generally negative image of, and resentment against the IMF.

Structural Adjustment Programme and Wage Bargain

The structural adjustment programme had its immediate impact on the business community and the employees therein. Part of the problem here, of course, was that it was exceedingly difficult in the beginning and in practice to separate the autonomous impact of the programme from the general consequences of the worldwide economic recession. The Shagari administration had found itself gliding into recession mostly not of its own making, but this did not alter the fact of increasing incidence of unemployment that was dramatically worsened by bankruptcies and many manufacturing companies' inability to secure import licences to bring in raw materials to keep production going.

Second, many aspects of the administration's industrial relations policies were simply scandalous: for example, the federal government, state governments and a majority of the parastatals were in arrears of workers' salaries for months, and non-wage or fringe benefits were either unilaterally revised downward or scrapped altogether- and yet legislators and ministers drew their salaries regularly and voted higher salaries and allowances for themselves. But it must be pointed out that in 1980 President Shagari had increased the minimum monthly wage from ₦60 to ₦100, a figure which eventually rose to ₦125 by the grace of the national assembly and workers' pressure in the form of a general strike early May 1981.[6] The 1981 general strike and the rash of strikes which plagued industry and the public sector were to force President Shagari into establishing three wage tribunals, the Onosode Commission to look into the conditions of service of employees in the parastatals, the Cookey Commission for university employees, and the Adamolekun Commission for teachers in federally-funded institutions of higher learning.[7]

Such difficulties confronting economic organizations and thus employers were predictably compounded by the structural adjustment policies of successive military regimes since December, 1983. The more important developments, from our point of view, were that SAP not only considerably eroded the ability of respective employers to absorb production costs and maintain existing levels of employment but also created conditions which made it difficult for most of them to stay in business, the critical variable being the continuous devaluation of the Nigerian naira. The scrapping of the import licensing system of allocating foreign exchange among competing interests did not ameliorate the problem of the scarcity of foreign exchange, both in terms of the quantum earned by the government through the sale of crude oil in the international market and of what could be made available to all through the fortnightly FEM bidding sessions. The 'downward floating' of the naira or 'the naira finding its true level' through FEM meant that more naira was now required to even obtain current low levels of imports and raw materials as the exchange rate appreciated in favour of the United States dollar (and other major inter national trading currencies such as the British pound sterling, Deutschmark, the Yen, Swiss franc and the French franc) from a 0.6:1 in 1983 to 1:4.5 in 1987 and 1:7.5 in 1989.

An immediate impact was a cash squeeze and a liquidity crisis experienced by many employers and companies, and bearing the brunt were

[6] Details may be found in Otobo, D., The Nigerian General Strike of 1981', *Review of African Political Economy*, vol.22, 1981; Otobo, D. & Omole, M. (eds.), *Readings in Industrial Relations in Nigeria*, Malthouse Press, Lagos & Oxford, 1987

[7] Official titles were the Presidential Commission on Parastatals, Presidential Commission on Salary and Conditions of Service of University Staff and the Presidential Commission on Conditions of Service of Federal Polytechnics, Colleges of Technology, Advanced Teachers Colleges and National Teachers Colleges.

those who already had excess capacity by way of low capacity utilization and whose imported raw material inputs constituted a high proportion of their total cost of production. There was thus a sharp rise in interest rates and a rapid escalation in the prices of imported goods as well as for locally assembled and/or manufactured goods. The other side of the coin was the creation of a largely buyer's market, although when there was shortage or scarcity in respect of soap detergent and a few other items, the consumer was obliged to scramble for whatever was available. By and large, therefore, there was a strong consumer resistance to suiting in low effective demand for many goods and services and a large stock of unsold goods in warehouses, more so as the many and cheaper smuggled goods often found ready market.

At the same time, official fiscal and monetary policies seemed directed at reducing the purchasing power of the general population, while for the organized private sector it was an exercise in 'mopping up excess liquidity' in the system, the latter presumed to have been caused by an indeterminate inflow of privately held foreign exchange. Drawing legal support from its own 1985 National Economic Recovery Fund (NERF), in November 1985 the federal government announced compulsory deductions of varying percentages from all salaries without notice or previous discussion with affected workers or unions. The central labour organization, the Nigerian Labour Congress (NLC), was obliged to issue an ultimatum to the government demanding that it should rescind the decision. By mid-1987, with protests from unions in the face of rapidly falling standards of living, the government undertook a refund of monies deducted but only to 'junior workers', the likely group to begin a demonstration which could generalize by drawing in the urban poor and other disaffected groups.

This was a remarkable departure from the practice in the period 1979-1984 when the Productivity, Prices and Incomes Board (PPIB) issued 'incomes and wages guidelines' which established upper limit of fifteen per cent wage increases and five per cent for prices. If any management sought such increases more than once in a year, it was obliged to obtain the permission of the Minister of Employment, Labour and Productivity-though the guidelines applied more to the private sector. However, following hard on the heels of wage refunds to junior workers was a decree which was designed to win back what the government seemed to have lost. The States (Special Development Levies) Decree No. 37 of 1936 had as its first clause:

> the Governor of a State shall have power to levy and deduct monies from the salary earnings and wages of any person employed in the public service of a State, civil service, judiciary and other government statutory corporations, commissions, authorities or other agencies or group of persons employed in the private sector of the State, or authorize any person appointed by

> him to deduct from an employee's salary or wages such other levies as may be deemed necessary to furtherance of the development of the State.

It was backdated and thereby deemed to have come into force on 11 November, 1985! For peace time collective bargaining, it was an incredible piece of social legislation which was roundly denounced by all sides of industry.

As for prospective importers, they were now subjected to Advanced Import Duty Payment Scheme which compelled all importers to deposit with the relevant state agency thirty per cent of the duty due on goods to be ordered in advance. And, on top of this, companies had to forgo about 15 per cent of their income until the economy recovered (requirement of NERF) but this was stopped in 1988 after much protests from the business community and pressure from the IMF concerning liberalization of the economy. This state of affairs, including such other complicating factors thrown up by the economic recession had several consequences for labour-management relations within individual enterprises, the most obvious being a striking lopsided distribution of bargaining power in favour of managements and of employers.

Mass retrenchments and layoffs became routine, and those workers and unions who had the courage and strength to protest could only direct their attention to the adoption of a more orderly and systematic retrenchment policy and not the principle itself. And in several instances retrenchment was often traded against *a* reduction in basic wage rates and fringe benefits, while there was *a* noticeable increase in the number of dismissals or sackings on patently flimsy grounds. Of course, in many establishments all this went hand-in-hand with barely disguised victimization of union officials. This sort of situation served to undermine the legitimacy of union leadership and the cohesion of union members, especially in negotiations with management: it was often the case that managements used such reasons as poor sales, high cost of raw materials and thus low profits (if at all) to abandon ongoing renegotiations of collective agreements upon expiration and reneging on earlier understandings and agreements.

In January 1988 General Babangida announced what was said to be a reflationary budget, finally accepting a basic truth Keynes established over four decades ago about the futility of dampening demand and further reducing purchasing power during a depression. The seventeen salary grade structure for the public sector created by the 1974 Udoji Commission was reviewed by administrative fiat with basic rates increased by as much as 50 per cent. But within a month the government retraced its step under pressure from the IMF as an across the board wage increase violated that aspect of the SAP which required a drastic cut in public expenditure: it resorted to nominal increases and actually spread out the deductions of the difference between the new and old scales that had been paid out over three months!

Equally surprising and without consulting organized labour nor employers and their organizations, the government in late 1988 amended the section of National Minimum Wage Act which made it mandatory for establishments employing more than fifty workers to pay the minimum rates to read five hundred employees instead! As an overwhelming majority of private establishments was already outside the purview of this legislation because of their small size, the amendment was intended not only to further decrease the number of affected establishments but also to reduce labour costs by making it the minimum wage itself subject to negotiations. The latter would not have been a bad idea in itself if both sides could freely negotiate: the fact was that it represented a one-sided deregulation since salaries and wages could not be increased and consequently any 'negotiations' could only but be a downward review of wages. And as the government made quite clear, because of consumer resistance and lower profits and thus reduced capacity of employers to meet their wage bills and other fixed costs, those workers who were unprepared to accept cuts in their pay should go to the rural areas where they might be equally useful as lowly paid staff.[8]

The protests from all sides of industry were so loud and angry that the government was forced to withdraw its amendment even before it had a chance of being implemented. Employers rightfully argued that such a measure would upset understandings and co-operation in industry and further denude them of productive capacity (which was already so low, in any case) and loss of production time through strikes and acts of sabotage, and that further erosion of purchasing power was bound to be counterproductive as they would be left with ever-mounting stocks of unsold goods. For workers, it provided that rallying point for, and opportunity with which to engage in a, massive display of their opposition to the structural adjustment programme in its entirety, demonstrations that the government would have found difficult to contain as was the case with protests against the withdrawal of subsidies from petroleum products discussed below.

Conflict and Conflict Regulation

Two caveats which should be entered in discussing conflict and conflict regulation under the structural adjustment programme in Nigeria relate to the basic nature of military regimes and the general impact of economic

---

[8] The official focus at the time was 'rural development' to which two sprawling special parastatals devoted their attention, namely the Directorate of Mass Mobilization for Social Development (MAMSER) and the Directorate of Rural Development, Roads and Infrastructures (DFRRI).

recession on the incidence of strikes and other forms of industrial protests. Military regimes are basically authoritarian and because of the 'chain of command' principle of military organization, plural centres of power or authority have always seemed anathema to the military mind. It means that such protests movements and other organised interests groups as exist in society, even when they support most official economic and social policies, are to a large measure regarded by military governments with some suspicion and are therefore very often suppressed or subjected to rigorous surveillance.

The other is heightened job insecurity during economic recessions because of mounting mass lay offs and redundancies which tend to spread fear among workers, particularly among the unskilled and semi-skilled groups. In a largely undifferentiated and mono-cultural economy and where a majority of enterprises depend on government patronage and on a handful of subsidiaries of multinational companies to obtain contracts, goods and services, job losses are far more numerous and worrying than has generally been recognized. Thus, while on the one hand, a great many of the workers who can still hang on to their jobs seem reluctant to embark on strike action, on the other hand rapidly growing unemployment tends to increase the prevalence of social disenchantment and crimes. This is only a generalized and partial picture because economic depressions do not affect all industries or enterprises equally: some industries or enterprises do in fact grow rapidly. There is theoretically a consequent accretion of some bargaining power to some groups of workers, especially those who are strategically located in the production process or company operations and therefore difficult to replace in the short to medium run.

By 1982 when President Shagari embarked on his Economic Stabilization Programme, most sectors of the economy had been buffeted by strikes, sabotage and absenteeism. Given a more democratic political environment and a multi-party situation with all the dissent and mutual criticism and rivalry, it seemed much easier for the government to reach some accommodation with labour and employers over many issues-the notable exception being the vexed question of arrears of salaries which those parastatals and state governments affected claimed they could do nothing about because of huge deficits they had already accumulated. The pattern of strikes in the public sector, which had been established since the 1940s, was re-enacted faithfully: a spate of strikes before the establishment of, and during the sitting of wage tribunal, and more strikes after the publication of its findings and awards.[9] The private sector was inevitably affected by the

---

[9] See Warren, W.M., 'Urban Real Wages and the Nigerian Trade Union Movement', *Economic Development and Cultural Change (EDCC), 15,1,1966* and 'Urban Real Wages and the Nigerian Trade Union Movement, 1939.1960: a rejoinder', in ibid. 17, 4, 1969; Berg, E., 'Urban Real Wages and the

spill-over or demonstration effect of industrial protests in the public sector, especially over such issues as national monthly minimum wage, rent and transport allowances which applied nationally to all workers.

The processing of workers' grievances took place simultaneously at various levels; within the enterprise, industry-wide, regionally and nationally, depending on issues. The main conflict-regulating institutions were the national assembly, the Federal Ministry of Employment, Labour and Productivity, the Industrial Arbitration Panel (IAP) and the National Industrial Court, of which the last two were established by the 1976 Trade Disputes Decree No. 7. As indicated elsewhere, aside from the active involvement of the Federal Ministry of Employment, Labour and Productivity, the Industrial Arbitration Panel (IAP), and the National Industrial Court, the President, and individual politicians and legislators freely intervened in the process at local and national levels- not to mention the increasingly visible role of the police and intelligence organizations in the apprehension of conflict.[10] The upshot, particularly in times of fairly widespread industrial conflicts, was a rather confusing and conflicting set of policies and results because of overlapping jurisdictions and the often strong temptation on the part of politicians to score political points off each other. One important consideration from the employer and worker point of view would seem to be that disputes were at least resolved, even if not all of time in one's favour. The other, deriving from the situation as outlined immediately above, remained a crying need for a more co-ordinated and comprehensive approach to matters relating to conflict and conflict-regulation in industry.

The sense of direction that seemed lacking in Shagari's civilian administration appeared to have been provided under successive military regimes since December 1983, but with the unfortunate substitution of high-handedness and a large element of arbitrariness for consultation and consensus in industrial relations matters. The worst in this regard was easily the Buhari regime which detained without trial members of management, officials of employers organisations, and workers and trade union officials as a matter of routine. Prominent examples would include striking airline pilots and medical doctors whose leaders were detained and organizations proscribed in 1984. Despite the air of intimidation which pervaded public sector industrial relations, matters were so what different for the private sector where managements still grappled with production and labour problems. The police and security agents, union officials, and top officials of

---

Nigerian Trade Union Movement, 1939-1960: a comment', *EDCC*, 17, 4, 1969; Kilby, P., 'Industrial Relations and Wage Determination: failure of the Anglo-Saxon Model', *The Journal of Developing Areas (JDA)*, 1, 4 July, 1967; Weeks, J., 'A Comment on P. Kilby: industrial Relations and Wage Determination', *JDA*, 3, 1, 1968 and subsequent exchanges in vols. 3, 1, 1968 and 5, 2, 1971.

10 Otobo, D., 'Strikes in Nigeria: some considerations', *Nigerian Journal of Economic and Social Studies*, Ibadan, November 1983.

the Nigerian Labour Congress (NLC) were also actively involved in pre-empting and breaking up strikes (the latter by the police) and other protests for many workers embarked upon industrial action, sometimes violently, against lay-offs and redundancies.[11]

The diplomatic, social and political pressures on the Babangida regime were more varied, persistent and urgent and this predictably influenced its basic orientation to industrial conflict and conflict-regulation. After the alleged but unsuccessful attempt at overthrowing the regime in December 1985 and the official rejection of the IMP economic package and the institution of its own structural adjustment programme, the Babangida administration seemed at pains to convey its determination and capacity to contain any form of social protest. The open use and scale of operations of intelligence and security agencies in this regard has remained unparalleled in the history of the country. It has become commonplace to interrogate and detain individual workers, while locking up the relevant union leaders well beyond the duration of the strike. In the case of workers in some public utilities, legally described as 'essential services' (water, electricity, telecommunications, etc.), industrial protests have been especially hazardous to them because of their being prevented from forming trade unions and going on strike.[12] For example, in February 1989 twelve employees, out of the hundreds involved in the protest, of the Nigeria Electric Power Authority (NEPA) were jailed ten years each under a special military decree for causing irregular power cuts for a few days.[13]

There were, however, two major successful strikes in the public sector, the first was undertaken by most workers in late 1987 over the removal of subsidies from petroleum products. The relatively small increase in the prices of petrol, kerosene and diesel drew very strong reactions from organized labour and the urban poor as transport fares and other prices rose far more than the original increases could justify. Indeed, months before the government announced increases in the prices of petroleum products, the

---

[11] The 1976 Trade Disputes Decree requires employers and workers to report strikes and lockouts promptly to the police upon penalty of a hefty fine and term of imprisonment.

[12] Although the law requires such workers to give fifteen days notice before declaring a trade dispute and embarking upon any other form of industrial action, another clause in the same legislation attaches a penalty of five years imprisonment to such an act. At any rate, Section 13(1) of the Trade Disputes Act (or Decree) 1976 makes it illegal to continue a strike or lockout once the processes of conciliation and arbitration are in progress. This is a roundabout *way* of proscribing strikes and lockouts since such actions would have to *be* suspended as soon as the Ministry of Employment, Labour and Productivity furnishes a mediator/conciliator or the Industrial Arbitration Panel is looking into the case.

[13] There is a vast array of decrees dealing with such diverse issues as economic recovery, national security, economic sabotage, and transition to civil rule in 1992. The provisions of most of these decrees classify the expression of such civil liberties as press criticism and protests of any sort criminal acts, and if they were to be even mildly enforced would make life very difficult for the average citizen.

NLC, along with such unions as the Civil Service Technical Workers Union (CSTWU), was engaged in public campaign against any such increases through posters and leaflets that were distributed all over the country. These were supplemented by similar advertisements in the newspapers. The Babangida regime was forced to abandon temporarily further increases which were due to come into force in another few months, and it is generally thought that the opposition mounted by the NLC against the main policy objectives of the government contributed in no small measure to its eventual proscription in March, 1988.

The other successful public sector strike in recent times occurred in the banking industry where the federal and state governments have controlling shares in most of the commercial banks. When employees of one of the major banks first attempted to go on strike early 1988, a week to the deadline security agents simultaneously in all nineteen states (now twenty-one) detained union officials in all branches. The arrests went unreported in both the electronic and print media because of direct censorship and threats of reprisals.[14] In a repeat performance in January 1989, all bank employees made sure they went on strike at the same time, and despite the detention of their leaders and threats of further reprisals, the government and managements gave in when the public could no longer take the resultant inconvenience and the troops could not be paid their salaries.[15]

Industrial conflicts were still much in evidence in the diminishing organized private sector despite the massive coercive apparatus at the disposal of the state. What, however, remained unclear was how much of such conflicts could be attributed to the impact of the structural adjustment programme itself. As hinted at above, a general and tentative impression would confirm the incidence of industrial protests due to mass sackings and the unilateral extension by managements of the life of expired agreements. On the other hand, along the lines suggested by Walton & McKersie (1965) in their concept of *co-operative bargaining* there were also some establishments in which managements sorted out outstanding differences and issues peaceably and jointly presented memorandum to the relevant state agency on some or other policy, and funding advertisements in the dailies condemning dumping and smugglers perceived as threats to the industry or their range of products.

---

[14] For more a comprehensive coverage see Otobo, D., *State and Industrial Relations in Nigeria*, Malthouse Press, Lagos, 1988.

[15] The banks, almost without exception, had been making whopping profits largely from foreign exchange transactions. But most sought to renege on earlier agreements, taking advantage of the economic recession and the government's policy of reducing public expenditure in line with the structural adjustment programme. The strike was well-timed: it began towards the end of the week and towards the end of the month when wage earners had to be paid.

Union Government and Administration

The area of union government and administration has always been a sensitive one with African governments, especially the one-party states and the military specie. Trades unions have historically turned out to be the only other units of concentration of power or centres of opposition outside of government and of political parties, whatever their ideological leanings. To this extent, state intervention has been constant, its positive or negative impact being largely a function of the issues at stake.[16] As for Nigeria and its governments' structural adjustment programme in recent years, there has been a marked increase in high-handedness, the detention of union members, and some brutality in dealing with some union officials. The main difference between the regimes of Generals Buhari and Babangida in this regard has been more of style rather than of degree: the former was more arbitrary while the latter more systematic.

Ordinarily, the officially approved forty-two industrial unions for so-called junior workers, the fifteen senior staff associations and the nine employers associations have enjoyed enough freedom and individual autonomy to enable them pursue whatever purposes for which they were established. The Federal Ministry of Employment, Labour and Productivity, through its mediation, conciliation services, factory inspectors and the Registrar of Trades Unions usually maintained continuous contacts with officials of the organizations. The regulatory role of the Ministry has undoubtedly been conflictual given the nature of sectional interest groups and the desire of the government to win support for some of its programmes and policies. What the structural adjustment programme seemed to have done has been to heighten the adversarial aspects of such contacts, as most employers and organized labour are opposed to the very many policies associated with the former.

With respect to trades unions, relations with the state have been more overtly conflictual and comprehensive, the former presenting a wide-ranging critique of the government's social, political and economic policies. Mention has been made of the NLC's effort in this connection in 1986 and 1987, reaching its apogee early 1988 in the form of seminars and talks across the country at which practically every aspect of SAP, with the exception of the demise of the import licensing system and the ban imposed on the importation of wheat and maize, came under severe attack, and the nationwide distribution of leaflets and posters denouncing cutback in subsidies, and placing advertisements in the newspapers for the same purpose as earlier mentioned.

The government counter-attacked by asking the Registrar of Trades

[16] For a dated but useful overview see Davies, I., *African Trade Unions;* Penguin, Harmondsworth, 1966.

Unions to query the audited accounts of the NLC which were required to be submitted every year to the former. As the NLC's campaign gained wider sympathy and support, the government intervention in the internal affairs of the organization escalated by the adoption of the patent ruse of sponsoring a rival executive committee against the All Chiroma-led committee at the organization's third quadrennial conference held in Benin in April 987. The government aborted the conference proceedings by proscribing the organization and appointing a 'sole administrator f trade union affairs' to manage the affairs of the central labour organization and organize fresh elections within six months. Official spokesmen, no doubt speaking with tongue-in-cheek, unconvincingly claimed grounds of disunity within the ranks of organized labour and the unsatisfactory state of the NLC's accounts to justify government's action. Happily the elections were duly organized and the NLC reconstituted under the leadership of Pascal Bafyau in December 1988, the interim period witnessing those spontaneous protests against the removal of the petroleum subsidy and the direct intervention of the Organization of Africa Trade Union Unity (OATUU) on behalf of the NLC.

The short-lived proscription of the NLC was just one strand in the government's goal of containing organized labour's opposition to the SAP. By June, 1988 the Sole Administrator of Trade Union Affairs offered a much wider interpretation of his powers to include the reorganization of the forty-two industrial unions themselves, asking their officials to submit copies of all audited accounts and offer suggestions on a new trade union structure with fewer trades unions. The main intention of this move, it seemed generally acknowledged, was to restructure the more vociferous unions out of existence at the worst, or at best dilute their membership considerably. Despite organized labour's misgivings about existing trade union structure which was imposed on them by the Obasanjo's regime in 1978, and have, along with the NLC, often announced their intention to reduce the number of trade unions from forty-two to twenty-five, the unions were strongly opposed to this move and took and Administrator and the government to court. Fearing its legally weak grounds and the fact that it would have taken at least a whole year to restructure the unions (with their consent and active involvement as was the case in 1977-78) and the chaos in industry and social and political climate which was short on patience and sympathy for government's policies, the Administrator was constrained to restrict himself to organizing fresh elections.

The proscription of the NLC was the culmination of the attempts of the government to influence workers' demands, expectations and attitudes to its economic programme. Indeed, much of 1987 was taken up by official attempts to gag the Academic Staff Union of Universities (ASUU) which, along with two other senior staff associations, not only affiliated itself to the NLC (whose membership was open only to the forty-two industrial unions organizing 'junior workers') but was also most critical of both the Minister of Education, Dr. Jubril Aminu, and of the *status quo.* In *response* to this, the government came out with a decree which specifically excluded senior staff associations from affiliating to the NLC. Seeking to weaken senior staff associations in general and ASUU in particular, organizations of those workers or employees commonly identified in most literature on white collar unionism as conservative but which were markedly restless and vocal in Nigeria because of fall in standards of living and decline *in* social status, another section of the legislation provided for voluntary deductions of membership dues instead of the previous legally compulsory method. The senior staff associations neutralized this provision by requesting their members to sign a form empowering their executives to deduct dues at source. When the administration of the University of Benin had problems with the branch of ASUU therein, the government through the Minister of Education, sacked the national president of ASUU, Dr. Festus Iyayi, and four others from their jobs. And when, ultimately, the ASUU called out its members on strike over the deplorable conditions in the universities and the near collapse of the university system itself, the federal -government promptly proscribed the union, held most of its officials in detention for varying lengths of time, but it nevertheless met most of the union's demands. In summary, the period 1979-1988 was characterized by consistent (some would say pernicious) intervention of the state in the government and administration of trades unions in Nigeria. It was the sort of intervention which alternated between accommodation and conflict, sometimes inseparable as conflict situations were accompanied by negotiations and compromises. But in relation to the structural adjustment programmes of the Buhari and Babangida administrations, conflict has been more in evidence as both regimes seemed bent on bending unions and workers to their will, hence greater involvement in union affairs.

A fascinating aspect of Nigerian industrial relations has been the relative paucity of institutional fora for the exchange of information among the parties, except within individual enterprises where joint industrial councils exist. In the fifties and sixties the experiments with wages councils and boards were a dismal failure and contemporary Public Service Negotiating Committees have not made any great impact either. Other than these and the adversarial confrontations at the Industrial Arbitration Panel (IAP) and the National Industrial Court (NIC), and *ad hoc* tripartite meetings during and after widespread conflicts, communication has usually been through and over the pages of newspapers, by way of news conferences, press releases and memoranda and protests letters. The structural adjustment programme has only accentuated this tendency toward mutual exclusivity till conflict erupts, although, as indicated earlier, the Babangida administration has held talks with the representatives of organized labour *over* the 1989 budget proposals and last year feted a cross-section of the business community for three days in Abuja at which the government tried very hard to sell its economic policies.

What flows from this is the largely informal nature of contacts between government officials, employers and trades unions despite such formalized and legalistic institutions as the IAP, NIC, and a formidable body of legislation to regulate industrial behaviour. Indeed, the economic recession and the structural adjustment programme have practically institutionalized informality and the rather unfortunate habit on the part of state officials to either ignore or bypass relevant industrial relations institutions- and some of their own legislation. On balance, the structural adjustment programme in Nigeria has served to weaken the hands of employers and of workers in their dealings with the government and other arms of the state, and workers and trades unions suffering the same fate in relations to managements and employers.

CONCLUDING OBSERVATIONS: THE LIMITS TO TRIPARTISM UNDER SAP

Under the structural adjustment programmes of successive Nigerian governments since 1982, the autonomy and sovereignty of the state *have* proved to be tenuous and illusory. In practical terms, the content of such economic packages have often been imposed from the outside, notably by creditors, the IMF and the World Bank. To that extent, minimum consultation has taken place between government, employers and workers and their organisations. But actual implementation of various policies has provided room for employers and workers to manoeuvre and compel the government, in some instances, to alter the time frames or schedule of such policies.

This may be illustrated by the examples of institution of the structural adjustment programme itself, wage cuts and petroleum subsidies discussed above. It was quite clear that the government did not consult the other two actors in industry over the scrapping of the import licensing system (which a large proportion of the business community still prefer), the introduction of SFEM or FEM, reduction in public expenditure, wage cuts, and removal of petroleum subsidies. Though the government held its own over the major aspects of its SAP, it was forced to make a refund and stop cutting wages and to postpone further increases in prices of petroleum products despite the fact that the IMF was dead set against any postponement.

In light of existing evidence, it would also be reasonable to assert that basic agreement in the community on the essential features of the existing economic and social order has been lacking. There is undisputed general objection to the structural adjustment programme, particularly the drastic erosion of living standards and the quality of life, strong antipathy to military rule and authoritarianism. Furthermore, such objection from a respectable component of organized labour and some intellectuals transcend the material to ideological grounds. They have been demanding a radical restructuring of society, and this would partly explain Babangida regime's obsession with 'radicals' and 'extremists' within the armed forces, students' organizations, labour movement, politicians, and the general population. This government has painstakingly identified these radicals by its own criteria, banning their organizations (ASUU, Chiroma-led NLC, National Association of Nigerian Students) and physically excluding others from the Political Bureau (a body of thirty persons which made recommendations on the political system to be adopted by 1992) and the Constituent Assembly which has been deliberating on a Draft Constitution.

It would hardly be an exaggeration if one maintained that the manner of implementing structural adjustment policies over the said period literally turned unionism into a criminal activity from official point of view, with intelligence and security agencies overtaking the Federal Ministry of Labour as "regulators" and tripartism driven into a state of coma.

Chapter 13

THE 1988 BANNING OF THE NLC

INTRODUCTION

On 29 February, 1988 the executive committee of the Nigerian Labour Congress (NLC), headed by Ali Chiroma, was dissolved in a nation-wide broadcast by Abubakar Umar, the Federal Minister of Employment, Labour and Productivity. In its place, the minister appointed a 'sole administrator' in the person of a Michael Ogunkoya who had the responsibility to manage the affairs of the central body while working towards organizing a delegates' conference that would elect a new executive committee. The special delegates' conference was eventually held on 19 December, 1988 at which the new executive, with Pascal Bafyau as president, was elected.

In this chapter, we document what happened, going behind officially proffered reasons for the banning of the NLC's executive to unmask the forces at play, and which should enable us achieve a better understanding of the relations between the state and organized labour. We then conclude by examining the implications of these types of events or developments for theorizing industrial relations in such countries as Nigeria.

THE BACKGROUND STORY

The Nigerian labour movement has since the mid-1930s been literally divided into two broad rival blocs, the reasons for such varying with the historical period. Between 1931 and 1945, when the teachers, railway and marine workers unions broke away from the Civil Service Union, the first federation of trade unions was formed, and the first general strike took place, it was the 'conservatives', 'white-collar' versus 'nationalists' and 'unestablished workers'. And from 1945 to 1948 during which the political party, the National Convention of Nigerian and the Camerouns (NCNC) was formed and took root, it became for while 'pro-NCNC' and 'pro-nationalists' as against 'anti-NCNC' and 'pro-establishment'. When Europeans and North Americans divided themselves into two ideological blocs and 'Western' trade unionists broke away from the World Federation of Trade Unions (WFTU), formed in 1945, to found a rival International Confederation of Free Trade Unions (ICFTU) in 1949, the divisive activities of these two bodies were mirrored in Nigeria by 'pro-WFTU' or 'Marxists' versus 'pro-ICFTU' and 'free' trade unionists.[1] These last labels seemed to have survived the 1977-78 reorganization exercise, and right through the 1980s with the 'free trade unionists' also calling themselves 'democrats', particularly after the 1981 NLC conference in Kano.

In relation to the banning of the NLC in 1988, a practical starting point would be 1975 as it marked the virtual end to the spectacle of squabbling numerous central labour organizations in the country. In 1974 the Nigerian Trade Union Congress (NTUC) which was affiliated to the WFTU, the United Labour Congress of Nigeria (ULCN), affiliated to the ICFTU, the Nigerian Workers Council, affiliated with the Roman Catholic and Brussels-based World Confederation of Labour (WCL), and the Labour Unity Front (LUF) that was affiliated to neither of the three so-called international labour centres, agreed in principle to come together to form just one body. This famous agreement was dubbed 'Apena Declaration' because it took place in that Lagos cemetery at the funeral of a prominent unionist.

By April 1975, the four central labour organizations successively held their final conventions at which they voluntarily dissolved themselves and handed back to the Registrar of Trade Unions their certificates of registration in compliance with the provisions of the 1973 Trade Union Act or Decree. While doing this, a steering committee was established to work out the details and arrangements for the launching of one all-embracing labour organization, the Nigerian Labour Congress (NLC), in December 1975. The rest is, of course, history: the military government first launched its labour policy of 'limited intervention' or 'guided democracy' a few months before the NLC was inaugurated on 17 December; the government refused to recognize the NLC, while 'banning' the four central labour organizations (which had dissolved themselves!) and instituting the Adebiyi Tribunal to probe their activities; a Trade Union Administrator, Michael Abiodun, was appointed to spearhead a team to 'reorganise' the nearly a thousand trade unions; and the NLC, with official approval and participation, was re-inaugurated in February 1978 as the *only* central labour organization after the 42 industrial unions were themselves formally launched during 1977.

The years 1978-79 were those of uncertainty and consolidation at the centre (NLC) and at the level of industrial unions when unionists and union officials were faced with teething problems thrown up by the new trade union structure, union administration proper, and developments within the economy and polity. Whatever new cleavages that might have emerged in

---

[1] For details see Yesufu, T.M., *An introduction To Industrial Relations in Nigeria*, OUP/IN ISER, 1962; Ananaba, W., *The Trade Union Movement in Nigeria*, Ethiope, 1969; Uvieghara, E.F., *Trade Union Law in Nigeria*, Ethiope, 1970; Cohen, R., *Labour and Politics in Nigeria*, Heinemann, 1974; and Otobo, D., *Foreign Interests and Nigerian Trade Unions*, Heinemann; 1986.

the labour movement were also tempered and muted by the transition to civil rule programme of the Obasanjo regime.

Things began, however, to change somewhat as soon as civilian politicians took over the reins of government on 1 October, 1979. First, the more democratic and less coercive political environment made it much easier for the trade unions to pursue demands (that included national minimum wage, review of pensions and other fringe benefits, and the restoration of car loans to civil servants) which were outstanding from the days of the Obasanjo administration more vigorously. Second, the first triennial conference of the NLC was coining up in 1981 and those unionists who had ambitions and coveted positions began to stake out their claims and court publicity and popularity, the most glaring example being David Ojeli, the NLC's Vice President. Third, the competing five political parties of the Second Republic and whichever state governments, including the federal government, they controlled, also sought to win friends among the leadership of, and influence organized labour. We have documented elsewhere how the unions and the NLC co-ordinated approaches in respect of workers' demands, leaving little room for any unionist to score points against potential or putative rivals.[2] The impending NLC's conference and elections in Kano and the politicians' interest and involvement in the same, accentuated whatever differences that existed among and between prominent union leaders. The federal government even organized a television debate of contestants for the position of NLC's president, between incumbent Hassan Sunmonu and challenger David Ojeli of the Civil Service Union. Sunmonu easily defeated Ojeli at the elections. Thereafter, Ojeli and a few unions that backed him constituted themselves into a vocal opposition to Hassan Sunmonu-led NLC executive.

With the decline of Ojeli's fortunes within his own union, the mantle of opposition was taken up eventually by such figures as Ijeh of the Nan-Academic Staff Union (NASU) and Agbonikhena of the Nigeria Ports Authority Workers Union. But before then, the dissenting activities of about twelve industrial unions in the labour movement, the 'democrats', particularly in the intervening period of 1981-1984 before the next NLC's triennial conference in Enugu, were conspicuous. Such obstructive and divisive activities of these unions were many, beginning with unsuccessful legal attempts at challenging the election of Sunmonu at the Kano Conference. They then mounted enormous pressure on legislators to amend the 1978 decree which made the NLC the only central labour organization to enable them convert their own 'Committee for Democratic Trade Unions' into a second and rival centre. The 'democrats' even sought the termination of the compulsory check-off system; their call for a boycott by workers of the

[2] Otobo, D., 'The Nigerian General Strike of 1981', *Review of African Political Economy*, 22, 1981.

1981 general strike went unheeded; and subsequently the 'democrats' attacked NLC's position on such issues as inflation, state of the economy, relationship with Shagari's government, and the role of organized labour in society.

When all these moves achieved unsatisfactory results, attention was then directed at the NLC itself where union presidents and general secretaries were also members of the organization's national executive council and of the central working committee. The proceedings of these two bodies were marked by disagreements, rancour, and members and voting polarized into two camps. The 'democrats' always came off worse since they were inferior in numbers by a very wide margin. In the end, their presidential candidate at the 1984 Enugu Conference, Aruna Agbonikhena, was badly defeated by Ali Chiroma. Takai Shamang, who was a 'progressive', ran as an independent candidate but also lost.

The 1988 Benin Conference would be the next battle ground, and the lesson drawn from the last three conferences was simple enough, and namely that the 'democrats' could *never win in a free and fair election because they lacked the numbers.* Since the 'democrats' were also close to the political (federal) establishment, only the partisan "involvement of willing organs of the State could possibly swing things their way. Left to their own devices, it was difficult to see how they could legitimately unseat any incumbent NLC president sponsored by all other unions for re-election.

The oppositional activities of the 'democrats' within and outside of the NLC continued unabated, most of the unions under their influence refusing to pay affiliation dues, while those that paid only paid token amounts in a desultory fashion. The only exception was the National Union of Postal and Telecommunications Employees which paid up fully. The NLC thus found itself relying financially more on those industrial unions that paid regularly, and particularly on a few of them such as the Civil Service Technical Workers Union (CSTWU) which paid additional levies. These unions the 'democrats' and government officials called 'Marxists'; but they called themselves 'progressives'.

THE 1988 BENIN CONFERENCE

The build-up to the Benin Conference was largely influenced by developments within the economy, notably the impact of the structural adjustment policy (SAP) on wage earners and citizenry in general, and the reaction of the NLC to these. With the possible exception of the scrapping of the import licensing system, the NLC expressed contrary views to those of government on practically all issues: arbitrary arrests and detention of people under the Buhari regime, unilateral deductions from salaries of public servants in 1987, cost of living indices, the officially trumpeted 'gains' of the structural adjustment policy, exchange rates of the naira, removal of petroleum subsidies, educational policies, human rights record, to political appointments. To say that Chiroma's executive was unpopular with the Babangida's administration would be a gross understatement.

The 'democrats' were themselves divided into two camps, one led by Agbonikhena and the other by Shamang. Shamang had abandoned the 'progressives' after failing to secure their sponsorship against the post of president of the NLC at the 1984 Enugu Conference. Both factions held a series of 'unity talks' in 1985 and by 1986 had achieved a common front. The main grouse at the time was that the 'democrats' were not adequately represented in the executive of the NLC, the principal officers all being 'progressives'. It would appear that Chiroma at some point offered a personal guarantee on some positions being reserved for the 'democrats', particularly in the filling of existing vacancies in state branches of the NLC. He was accused of reneging on this promise as 1987 drew to a close and the Benin Conference loomed round the corner. In protest, the 'democrats' began to boycott the meetings of the organization's NEC, holding numerous press conferences to denounce Chiroma, the NLC and threatening to form a rival centre.

As can be expected, representation at the Benin Conference was uppermost in the minds of those who wished to run for election. The 'democrats' publicly demanded for equal representation of all unions, irrespective of size, a position that was predictably opposed by the NLC and other trade unions. The NEC had in 1980 established representation to the conferences be based on membership strength of union as determined by the dues paid to the Congress. According to Michael Ogunkoya (1988), 'this was a compromise decision to enable unions which had not fully paid up their dues based on NLC estimates, to he represented at the congress.'[33] Every union was required to pay 10 kobo per member per month to the NLC. It is not too difficult to identify which unions would have been falling back on their affiliation dues to the NLC.

As for membership and number of delegates, this worked out as up to 1,000 members 1 delegate, 1,001 to 5,000 3 delegates, 5001 to 10,000 2 additional delegates, and every additional 5,000 after the first 10,000 members would be entitled to one (1) additional delegate up to a maximum of 35 delegates. Having problems ascertaining the numerical size of membership of affiliates, and with some affiliates deliberately understating their membership figures in order to pay less, the NLC in 1984 changed the rate of contribution to 10 per cent of the total check-off dues accruing to industrial unions. By dividing the total annual affiliation dues by ₦1.20 (i.e. 10 kobo per month per member), it was possible to have some idea of the

[3] Report of the Administration of the Nigerian Labour Congress, Lagos, 1989, p. 36

membership strength.

A consequence of this, which was to the mutual advantage of the NLC and the unions concerned, was that those unions whose members paid higher membership dues to them also paid higher affiliation dues to the NLC. Thus for a 5,000-man strong union but whose members paid, say, ₦10 each per month, its 10 per cent dues to the NLC would be more than that of a union with a membership of 10,000 whose members paid ₦4 per month per member.

Whilst minimizing monthly quarrels over membership figures between the NLC and those unions that bothered to pay affiliation dues and actually increasing what came to the NLC for the more effective management of the organization, it was also easy to find fault with the decision. In terms of number of delegates, the smaller union would then end up with more than the larger union! This decision, the Administrator of Trade Unions rightly concluded in his report, meant that 'representation at the Congress was no longer based on numerical strength but on financial strength' and, more controversially, that 'this could lead to financial manipulations for electoral advantage '(ibid., 37).

As was usual and part of preliminary preparations against these triennial (now quadrennial) congresses or conferences, the NLC set up a broad-based accreditation panel and saddled it with the responsibility of going through the financial books very carefully to determine payments of affiliation dues and calculate size of respective union delegates based on same. Obviously realizing their numerical weakness and seeking to pre-empt the work of this panel, the 'democrats' demanded that all unions should have equal number of delegates, thereby rejecting the use of the payment of 10 *kobo* per month per member and 10 per cent total dues formulae as the bases for calculations. When this was rejected by a majority of the National Executive Council, the 'democrats' then claimed that other unions were credited with amounts they had not paid in order to beef up their delegates, and that, in any case, the account of the union to which Shamang belonged, the National Union of Electricity and Gas Workers, was 'under-credited', while that of Chiroma, the Medical and Health Workers Union, was 'over-credited'. A gullible and patently biased Sole Administrator of Trade Unions, fed with these many unsubstantiated and wild allegations, generously offered in his report that 'the "democrats" saw this as a deliberate effort on the part of the Secretariat (of the NLC) to "rig" the election in favour of the "Marxists" ' (p, 40). In their more sober and truthful moments, however, the 'democrats' themselves would be the first to admit that the other unions or the 'progressives' need not have bothered to rig the elections in the first place merely on account of their overwhelming numbers, but particularly because the NLC's constitution clearly stated that three months to the date of the conference, any union still owing affiliation dues would not be entitled to a delegation with voting powers. As at November 1987, the deadline, only a few of the unions under the influence of the 'democrats' had paid up fully. Rather than implement the constitution of the NLC and win the elections hands down, Chiroma and his executive magnanimously, in the quest for a 'united' labour movement, extended the deadline to January 1988 to enable his opponents pay up all their arrears. Not even in the so-called 'civilized' and 'advanced' countries would a threatened incumbent of any position consider doing what Chiroma did here: over there, 'rules are rules'. And talking about stories, a more credible and widely circulating one at the time was that these 'democrat' unions, being broke, were said to have obtained such funds from the political and intelligence sections of the Presidency.[4]

In all, the 'democrats' would seem to have been shopping around for an excuse to either disrupt the conference or abandon it altogether and they found one in the accreditation issue. This done, they raked up all manner of dust and dirt, reaching back to the old allegations that dominated the decades 1950s, 1960s and 1970s which included, among many others, the dissemination of Marxist ideology, running the NLC along 'Marxist lines', the lop-sided sharing of scholarships, the biased selection of worker-members to tripartite and bipartite bodies, representation on state-owned corporations and companies, workers' delegation to the ILO conferences in Geneva, partisan intervention in the internal affairs of member unions, maladministration and mismanagement of NLC funds.

To calm tempers down many veteran trade unionists such as Wahab Goodluck intervened but to no avail. At the last meeting of the NLC's central working committee (CWC) before the Benin Conference, the 'democrats' staged a walk-out, followed by many press conferences at which they repeated most of the above allegations. At this point the Minister of Employment, Labour and Productivity himself invited ostensibly leaders of 21 individual industrial unions, obviously representing the feuding interests, to a meeting, of which 9 were 'democrats' and 12 for 'progressives'. The Minister broached the matter of accreditation at the impending congress, sued for compromise and, interestingly from many points of view, used the analogy of 'elder statesmen' of the First Republic who out of 'national interest' shared out positions. He and his Assistant Director of Industrial Relations, Mrs. Okoronkwo, got into some argument with the 'progressives' over calling them 'Marxist group', much like the 'democrats' always did. The Minister also promised to hold joint talks with Chiroma and Shamang before delegates departed for Benin.

---

[4] When confronted during interviews, this story was denied by the prominent leaders of the 'democrats'. But none could offer an explanation as to how they came by the monies they used in clearing their arrears of dues and in funding their splinter Congress in Benin.

A group of unionists on both sides met to find ways of going round whatever problems there were and proposed a postponement of the congress for a few months to allow frayed nerves to calm down and enough time to work out something.[55] They could not carry a majority of members of the CWC with them and, at any rate, a slightly annoyed Chiroma, who thought he had compromised too much already, refused to buy the idea either. The hope as delegates left for Benin was therefore that the conference environment and behind-the-scene midnight talks would somehow produce a compromise of some sort. But for most delegates, 'let's go to Benin and put democracy to the test.'

The Benin Conference was slated for 24-26 February, 1988, and although most delegates were in town, the last minute indications were that the 'democrats' were up to something, and might even refuse to participate in the proceedings. But, as it turned out to most people's surprise, the 'democrats' announced on the morning of 24 February that they had in fact held their own congress the previous day (23 February) with Shamang emerging as president of the NLC! When the Minister was taken up on the legality of this, he seemed a bit at loss. Rather, he suggested that the main conference could be postponed to give him time to sort matters out! Chiroma and his team, smelling a rat as the saying goes, decided to test the Minister's 'loyalty' by a very simple request. They pretended to go along with the suggestion provided the Minister gave a firm guarantee that the federal government would continue to recognise Chiroma's executive while sorting out Shamang and his gang. This he refused to do, and whether it was an official ploy to smuggle Shamang in through the back-door remains a moot point.

Delegates, however, ignored the 'democrats' and the official conference went ahead as scheduled, attended by the Minister of Employment, Labour and Productivity, his team of top officials, members of diplomatic missions and representatives of foreign and international labour organizations, including Hassan Sunmonu the general secretary of the Organization of African Trade Union Unity (OATUU). Certainly the delegates present exceeded the two-thirds quorum required by the constitution of the NLC. The 10 per cent of total dues formula was adopted for accreditation and which was meticulously implemented. At the elections, Chiroma easily defeated Shamang for the position as his name had not been withdrawn from the ballot. The election results for the principal officers of the NLC may be seen from the following table.

1988 NLC Election Results of Principal Officers

[5] The better known of them were Ejiofoh of CSTWU and Olabode of the nurses and mid-wives' union for the 'progressives', and Oramulu of NULGE and Otikpo, president of NASU for the 'democrats'.

	CONTESTANTS	VOTES
President	Ali Chiroma	280
	Takai Agang Shamang	4
Deputy President	Morrison Mpamugo	255
	John Uduaghan	-
	Jonathan Blonde	244
	Frank Oramulu	10
	Nasir Balogun	4
Vice-President	Paschal Bafyau	263
	Emmanuel Ojeiwa	244
	Adams Oshiomhole	260
	Benedict Aso	6
	Kabir Yar'Adwa	5
	Joshua Ogunleye	8
National Treasurer	Stevenson Osidipe	247
	Adegtmle Sodade	3
Dep. Nat. Treasurer	Adcbisi Adeniran	254
	David Emovon	4
National Trustee	Adedayo Ademoyero	252
	Ahubakar Umar	5

Source: NLC Secretariat document, Ref. No. NIC/GSO/AC 1 dated 26 February, 1988.

When Chiroma, his executives and full-time bureaucrats of the NLC got back to Lagos, they were denied access to the NLC secretariat at 29 Olajuwon Street, Ojuelegba. Prior to his departure to Benin City, Dr. Lasisi Osunde, the General Secretary of the NLC had as was customary requested the Surulere Police Station to provide 'police protection' for the Secretariat for the period 22 to 29 February when all his staff would be down in Benin engrossed with the details of conference organization and proceedings. The police had obliged but would seem subsequently to have taken over the place instead. The police in the days that followed argued that in keeping with the 'neutrality' of the government, it was necessary to keep both 'factions' out. Although the police did prevent Shamang and his men from attempting to forcibly occupy the premises, as we sec later, this was a bogus reason.

Chiroma and Dr. Osunde had each sent in his report on what transpired to the government, through the Minister of Employment, Labour and Productivity on Sunday 28 February and on the evening of the very next day, 29 February, the same Minister announced the banning of the NLC in a television broadcast referred to earlier. In his introductory remarks, the Minister painted a picture of an NLC divided into two irreconcilable ideological factions; that never again 'would the central labour organization be permitted to break up and revert into inconsequential little unions which can be ready tools of manipulation and subversion of industrial peace, harmony and security of the nation'; and that given the 'government's commitment to its programme of economic recovery and its clear perception of the positive role a united labour organization could play and its awareness that a divided labour organization would constitute a stumbling block to national effort', it had to intervene (*Report*, 1988, 12).

The National Economic Emergency Powers (Nigeria Labour Congress) Order 1988, signed by General Babangida and which appeared in the 'Supplement to Official Gazette Extraordinary', No, 16, vol. 25, dated 4 March 1988 repeated and elaborated upon what the Minister of Employment, Labour and Productivity had announced a few days back. It stated that:

i) the two factions of the NLC were illegal and unlawful;
ii) the purported elections of the national executive council (NEC) and the conferences held by the factions of the Congress were null and void and of no effect whatsoever;
iii) the NECs which emerged from the purported elections held at the said conferences dissolved forthwith;
iv) the officers of the factions including the two general secretaries hereby removed from office; v) an Administrator for the Congress be appointed by the Minister of Employment, Labour and Productivity with the approval of the President;
vi) the Administrator shall, after consultation with the Minister, administer and organize the affairs of the Congress and shall manage and protect the funds and properties of the Congress;
vii) the Administrator shall within six months of his appointment organize special delegates conference at which all the industrial unions affiliated to the Congress shall participate and a new NEC elected therefrom;
viii) the Congress or any person holding or having possession of any property or assets of the Congress shall surrender to the Administrator such property or asset including check-off dues; and,
ix) any person who failed to comply with the provisions of this order be liable on conviction to a fine of ₦10,000 or imprisonment for a term not exceeding 2 years or both such fine and imprisonment.

The Minister of Employment, Labour and Productivity in his own letter to the Sole Administrator, Michael Ogunkoya, appointing him to that position, dated 15 March, 1988, ordered that:

1. in order to ensure a peaceful, free and fair election at the NLC

Conferences in future, you are required to look into and examine critically the procedural machinery being adopted by the NLC to conduct its general elections. Consider whether such electoral procedure is sufficiently free and fair as effective machinery; if not, to recommend any other procedure or step that should be taken to ensure such;

2. to enquire into the cause or causes, whether remote or immediate, of the crisis within the NLC that subsequently led to its factionalisation and recommend to the Federal Military Government how best to prevent same in future;
3. whether the issue of scholarships offered to the NLC is connected with the cause of the crisis. If so, inquiry should be made into who were the recipients of these awards and how the scholarships offered were shared among the unions;
4. the audited accounts of the NLC since 1978 have not been approved by the Registrar of Trade Unions. There were many queries raised on the accounts which have remained unanswered by the NLC leadership. The Administrator should investigate and make recommendations;
5. in order to ensure a successful take-off of the then newly-established NLC, the Federal Military Government in 1978 donated to the NLC its present Secretariat. In addition to this, a sum of ₦1,000,000 was also given as a take-off fund which was expected to be shared between the NLC and the industrial unions. You should-ascertain and come out with a clear picture indicating how the take-off fund was actually disbursed; 0 during the period 1982-84, a total of ₦1,270,200 was given to the NLC as subvention for the construction of warehouses in all states of the federation for storage and distribution of essential commodities in order to alleviate the suffering of workers. You should ascertain the physical progress in monetary terms. The extent to which the money has been utilized for the purpose intended should also be investigated, as well as what happened to the interest which accrued to the part of the money which the NLC itself disclosed was put into a fixed deposit account. Officials of the NLC responsible for handling this fund should be identified and the part played by each;
6. since the inception of the NLC, the policy of succeeding governments of the federation have been and still remains that of upholding and maintaining only one strong and virile central labour organization whose concern should be the protection and enhancement of the interest of the ordinary masses of the workers. But somehow ideological pursuits have crept in, to the detriment of the central aim. The Administrator should examine the divisive impact of foreign ideology in the Nigerian trade union movement, and shall inquire into the activities of the incursion by foreign trade union organizations in the NLC, their collaborators in

Nigeria and ascertain to what extent these organizations have, by way of donation, training, international workshops/seminars, promoted ideological differences within the NLC and come out with recommendations aimed at strengthening the central aim of establishing a united NLC;

7. the administrator should examine whether there is need to review the constitutions of the NLC and of the 42 industrial unions to strengthen the democratic spirit and accountability in the movement;
8. at the moment, none of the 42 industrial unions or the NLC has been able to produce a register to show the numerical strength of any of them. The Administrator should ascertain the membership strength of each industrial union and recommend a machinery by which this can be done on continuous basis; and
9. the Administrator should feel free to inquire into and make observations and recommendations on any area not covered by these terms of reference, if in your opinion such can help the cause of workers, the unions and the NLC.

The 'democrats' were on the whole ecstatic, though some of them felt let down by the federal government's failure to recognize their own 'executive' as the true NLC. Ali Chiroma and the rest were shocked, and got three unions, the Iron and Steel Workers Union of Nigeria, the Precision Electrical and Related Equipment Workers Union and the National Association of Nigeria Nurses and Midwives, to take the President, the Minister and the Sole Administrator to court. The Lagos High Court ruled in favour of the government, and upon appeal, the Federal High Court delivered its judgment on 23 June also in the government's favour.

POST-BAN DEVELOPMENTS

The Sole Administrator had a difficult time initially in carrying out his assignment. About the first problem he encountered was what do with the full-time bureaucrats of the NLC who had been sent on compulsory leave. These he recalled and, according to him,

> the democrats were stunned by my action and they did not hide their feelings. Earlier they had sent me a list of staff they had appointed to man the secretariat and state councils of the NLC. They insisted that I should send all the staff away on indefinite leave with pay and start on a clean slate or, in the alternative, invite their staff to assume duty. In the end, wise counsel prevailed and they appreciated my position and respected my decision. *(Report,* p. 16).

The opposition from the 'progressives' was a more determined sort, beginning with the enormous pressure that was brought to bear on Chiroma not to hand over to the Administrator. This, however, only achieved a delay of a few days before Chiroma handed over after bravely telling the 'progressives' at a meeting that he was not a leader of a faction but of the NLC.[6] Greatly disappointed over this, the 'progressives' decided to shun all the overtures made by the Administrator, including invitations to meetings and supply of relevant information and statistics. The Administrator was beginning to get bogged down and frustrated when the government complicated matters for him by announcing the removal of so-called 'petroleum subsidy', an action that 'was a setback to my overtures to the unions that had refused to co-operate with me since my appointment,' he admitted with candour unusual of a government man *(Report,* p. 18).

As even acknowledged by the Administrator, 'it had been rumoured that government intervention in the affairs of the NLC was to enable it remove the subsidy on petroleum without the stiff opposition which the Congress leadership had mounted against the proposal. While this suggestion would appear naive, it was nonetheless held by many people.' (ibid., p. 17). When Jubril Aminu, Minister of Petroleum Resources, eventually announced a modest increase in the price of petrol on 10 April, 1938, students across the country mounted public protests and demonstrations, joined in many places by workers, the aggrieved unemployed and the urban poor. In Benin City, university students in addition to setting official cars, courts and other public buildings ablaze and manhandling police constables (as was the case everywhere) attacked and released prisoners from jails.

A thoroughly rattled government, deprived of the central leadership of the NLC to parley with, as was usual on occasions of nation-wide strikes or protests, engaged in massive arbitrary arrests of students and whomever they found on the streets and flung them into jail. The protests continued unabated until the government shut down practically all educational institutions, from primary to the university level. At this point, some trade unions officially assumed industrial action.

The removal of the petroleum subsidy provided the 'progressives' with the opportunity they had been looking for to *impress* upon the government, as S.O.Z. Ejiofoh of the CSTWU pointed out, that the banning of the NLC would not minimize workers' opposition to the structural adjustment policies and attendant immiseration of wage earners and the general population. Nor would it hinder the organization and co-ordination of such protests. And more importantly, it would show 'where power lies in the labour movement' and 'if the government had any illusions that the Shamang group was the most effective group or they are more in number, the illusion should be erased.'[7] And to make these points, several unions, including the Civil Service Technical Workers Union, the National Union of

[6] Chiroma, interview 1988; Ejiofoh, interview, 1988.

[7] Interview, 1988.

Banks, Insurance and Financial Institutions Employees, the National Association of Nigeria Nurses and Midwives, the Medical and Health Workers Union of Nigeria, and the National Union of Food, Beverages and Tobacco Employees, joined the students and continued with their 'creeping strikes' after the students had stopped theirs, the idea being to catch both the 'democrats' and the government unawares and frustrate whatever counter-measures they might contemplate. The bank workers made sure that they struck at the end of the month when most people, including rank and file soldiers, should be collecting their salaries. With this and food and medical sectors under siege, an exasperated government had to find a quick solution. 'As far as we were concerned, we wanted to make sure the government discussed with us alone and reached an understanding with us', a prominent 'progressive' had said with a grin of satisfaction. And so it was!

On 22 April Jubril Aminu, Minister of Petroleum Resources, along with advisers to the General Babangida and Vice Admiral Aikhomu, held a meeting with union leaders at Dodan Barracks to brief the latter 'on the modalities for the increases'. It was 'statistically demonstrated that the price of petroleum in Nigeria was the lowest among the petroleum-producing countries.' Not surprising, 'the unions were unimpressed since other indices like comparative wages/salaries were not produced' *(Report, op. cit.,* p. 18).

The Administrator was not left out either. After all, he personified the central labour organization. He met representatives of the industrial unions on 26 April to 'give them an opportunity to consider the issue and adopt a mature and constitutional approach in resolving it.' In this pretentious vein, the Administrator seemed persuaded that:

> The meeting served also to debunk the misconception that government intervention in the affairs of the NLC was to deny the unions a forum to articulate their views on national issues affecting workers...I appealed to the unions to appreciate the problems that the government was grappling with through the structural adjustment programme and to co-operate with government in finding an acceptable solution. I drew their attention to the fact that, but for the programme, the economy of the country would have collapsed. I acknowledged the sacrifices already made by the workers but stressed that no sacrifice would be too great for the survival of the country... *(Report,* 18)

The reaction of the captive audience to the pep talk seemed more eloquent despite its brevity, namely 'the unions were annoyed that their earlier views on the issue were not given serious consideration by the government' (ibid.). Aside from workers' threats of mass demonstrations and disquiet when the removal of the 'petroleum subsidy' was first officially floated and their subsequent industrial action over the matter when it was actually implemented, we may recall that the NLC's own opposition included denunciatory pamphlets that were distributed across the country much to the annoyance and embarrassment of the federal authorities. All the same, if the government was prepared to talk, the union leaders were now ready to listen: they thus agreed that: i) an 11-persons delegation representing all the 42 industrial unions should meet General Babangida to discuss the political and social consequences of the recent increases in the prices of refined petroleum products and the effects of the 1988 budget; ii) the government team should include the ministers in charge of finance and economic development, transport and labour matters; and iii) the proposed meeting be arranged within the next seven days!

Two days later, 28 April, the Minister for Employment, Labour and Productivity took his turn and met with the representatives of most of the industrial unions. The meeting was acrimonious with the unionists denouncing official high-handedness in this and other matters. The Minister promised to pass on their views to the appropriate quarters and give them a feedback soon. He, however, appealed to them to plead with the industrial unions that were still out on strike to call off their action. They declined and advised the Minister to appeal to the strikers himself![86]

The meeting with the government side finally took place, lasting from 29 April to 1 May, 1988. General Babangida was not there but the Secretary to the Federal Military Government, the Ministers of Employment, Labour and Productivity, and of Information and Culture, and the Political Adviser to the President, Dr. Tunji Olagunju, joined other government officials for the talks. Agreement was reached on several issues, including the government agreeing to suspend further increases in the prices of refined petroleum products and concession to transporters to import transport vehicles without paying duties, and tyres at low rates.

A follow up to these series of agreements, which made it possible for striking workers and unions to call off strikes, was the establishment by the federal government of a committee of knowledgeable persons and who were also thought to enjoy a measure of respect and goodwill among the leadership of the labour movement, to discuss all grievances with representatives of the unions. Prominent among these were Dr. Michael Omolayole and Professor Nkenna Nzimiro, the former a member of the shadowy Presidential Advisory Committee. The meeting went well in spite of the fact that both the 'progressives' and 'democrats' were meeting for the first time since the Benin Conference.

What struck the union representatives at this meeting was that they were the losers all round, and issues over which they had disagreed did not seem

---

[8] Report, *op. cit.*, 18

that important anymore. Rather, not only had the government dismantled the NLC, there were now talks of 'reorganising' or 'restructuring' the 42 unions to a much smaller number, perhaps 20 or so, a process they might not be able to influence. This contrasted sharply, ironically, with NLC's earlier proposals to reduce through amalgamation the number of unions to 25, a process that they would have had substantial control over. There was considerable unease over all this, and legal action was ultimately threatened and initiated before the government backed down.

In the interim, the Sole Administrator found himself running out of time, 'with the late response of the "Marxists" group' who decided to submit their own memoranda only a few weeks to the deadline of 31 August given to the former to complete his assignment. The government was forced to extend his tenure by another four months, from 31 August to 31 December 1988. It was at this point that the Minister of Employment, Labour and Productivity additionally instructed the Administrator to 'restructure all the existing trade unions into a manageable size, and define clearly their areas of jurisdiction in order to remove all problems of overlapping, duplication, amorphous structures, etc.,' and 'review the constitution of the NLC to ensure that it has a regular source of funds through a provision for the mandatory payment to it of 10 per cent dues by all industrial unions affiliated to it.' As we mentioned immediately above, the unions successfully got the law courts to stop the Administrator from tampering with their structure and numbers. They did not oppose the second proposal since it came originally from them and passed through that committee of knowledgeable men to the government.

The influential members of both the 'progressives' and 'democrats' met at separate times and unofficially to exchange views, views which seemed to converge on most points. The formal intervention came from the Nigerian Union of Teachers (NUT) whose officials appeared to have legs in both camps. The first meeting of both sides under the umpireship of the NUT did not go too well largely because the critical members of both camps stayed away, sending only their subordinates. It is to the eternal credit of such veterans and friends of the labour movement as Wahab Goodluck, Chief E. A. O. Odeyemi, Alaba Kalejaiye who were not only personally present at some of the sessions but also got everyone to attend.

Basically, both sides reached definite decisions on many issues, including the continued existence of only central labour organization, the NLC. Others were that the executive be elected democratically, as it has always been; that positions in the state branches of the NLC could be shared, although how this could be done and in what ratio were not finalized; size of delegates to quadrennial conferences to reflect membership size of union as indicated by fully paid up membership dues; that the full-time staff of the Secretariat had normal contracts of employment with the NLC and would therefore stay on but the Secretariat be 'restructured' for greater effectiveness. On Chiroma and Shamang, the 'progressives' proposed that both men should not be allowed to contest, and at which point the 'democrats' called for a break of thirty minutes for them to consult. The group came back instead after some three hours, accepting the proposal on condition that the General Secretary, Dr. Lasisi Osunde, be added to the list too. The 'progressives' rejected this arguing, quite correctly, that once it was agreed that all full-time staff could stay, it was improper singling out Dr. Osunde. As a concession and compromise, it was then agreed that all full-time staff would be screened to the satisfaction of everyone. While Chiroma accepted this decision, Shamang protested verbally and did not attend subsequent meetings. About the only issue left unresolved was whether the elections for the NLC executive should come before or after those for the state branches of the organization; the 'progressives' wanted those of the state branches first, while the 'democrats' wanted it the other way round. The Administrator in the end had both sets of elections simultaneously.

When all was done, both sides wrote independently to the Administrator, though routed through the President of the NUT, to both inform and request him to pass on to the Minister that the crisis had been voluntarily resolved. According to the Administrator, he himself began a series of meetings with the president and general secretary of each industrial union from 26 October to 18 November, reviewing all problem areas and especially those of election procedures. Based on his own efforts, the agreement between the two camps was not much of a surprise to him, although he did not 'mean to derogate from the efforts made by...NUT and of the two groups, the veteran trade unionists and other well-meaning citizens who in one way or another contributed to the make the accord possible. My role was that of a motivator and a catalyst. I am happy that I showed the light for the people to find the way' *(Report,* 20). For someone who the 'progressives' refused to co-operate with and the 'democrats' later distrusted and disagreed with over restructuring and other matters, one can understand his elation. But as a 'motivator' for both sides, he must have been an incredible one!

These series of meetings by both groups coincided with the absence of the Minister of Employment, Labour and Productivity from Nigeria to attend the African Labour Ministers Conference. He came back to find that an accord had been struck and decided to convince· himself by inviting three persons from both groups to confirm it. Only Ejiofoh showed up for the 'progressives', and the Minister even-handedly suggested they come back the following day. With the Minister and the Administrator in attendance the following day, this small group fixed the Special Delegates Conference for 19 December, 1988. Ijeh of NASU and the 'democrats' proposed that each union's delegation should be of the same size as what they had at the 1984 Enugu Conference, and that the same should apply to the elections for state branches of the NLC too.[9] A pleasantly surprised 'progressives' concurred, having won a majority of positions in those occasions. Mr. R. O. Sanyaolu, also of the 'democrats' further suggested that the government could issue a decree preventing any court from granting any injunction to disturb the conference proceedings. The idea was tossed around and although supported by the Administrator, no firm decision was reached on it.

However, at subsequent meetings with the Administrator, he suggested that both groups could embark on a tour of NLC's state branches, to bring officials and members there round to agreed decisions. The 'progressives' declined but the 'democrats' did. By the close of nominations on 15 December, only the positions of president and vice presidents came up for elections, the others having been returned unopposed. Three unions were disqualified from participating because of internal problems resulting in factions, while a fourth did not attend on its own accord.[10] Out of the 281 accredited delegates, 278 attended representing a 97 per cent attendance rate. Paschal Bafyau defeated George Izobo for the presidency, while Bayo Osidipe and three others emerged as vice presidents. The 12 elected officials were formally sworn in by the Administrator on 30 December, 1988.

CRITIQUE OF EXPLANATIONS AND ACTIONS

The factors which ultimately have a bearing on the banning of the NLC in 1988 easily relate to a) divisions within the labour movement at *all* levels (individual, national unions and within the NLC); b) persistent attempts on the part of the State to influence, if not control, the leadership of organized labour; and c) the economic circumstances of the 1980s. As we see below, and I think it is important to emphasize this, it is simply impossible to separate the factors in practice. We now examine these groups of factors briefly.

Divisions within the labour movement

Divisions within the labour movement have been manifested at the levels of the individual, the union, and the central organization. At the level of the individual have been a handful of persons who have over the decades exercised authority and power in the various positions in the trades unions, whether in the pre- or post-1978 period. The competition, rivalries, animosities and friendship among and between such labour leaders are so

---

9 Ejiofoh, interview, 1988

10 The three unions were the National Union of Banks, Insurance and Financial Institutions Employees, the Agricultural and Allied Workers Union, and the National Union of Paper and Paper Products Workers, whilst the fourth which stayed out was the Metallic and Non-Metallic Mines Workers Union based in Jos.

well known and documented to be taken as axiomatic. It is the same everywhere, typical of all labour and political movements in the world. We should then observe that a) labour leaders and union officials in the pre-1978 period organized different house unions; b) many of these house unions were themselves affiliated to same and/or antagonistic central bodies; and c) three of the four major central bodies since late 1960s[119] were themselves affiliated to rival international and foreign labour organizations. Individual differences and prejudices have thus calcified and, in some instances, transmitted to the next generation of labour leaders by the older ones and external benefactors who groomed them.

Such individual rivalries are best given freer rein in an organizational context, hence the creation of 42 industrial unions in 1977-78 provided ample opportunity for such. For one, as we established elsewhere,[12] several house unions had become constituent members of a new and much larger industrial union respectively, and of which only four or five persons could possibly occupy the four or five sensitive positions in the new industrial union. Not all previous general secretaries and other officials of erstwhile house unions were gallant losers on these occasions. Since the house unions were previously affiliated to competing and often hostile central bodies, the competition was then at once both personal and group in character, with those who belonged to the same central body supporting the same candidates. Each industrial union therefore contained within it oppositional groups or factions which sought to discredit the leadership at every available opportunity. And where the critical positions have been filled by unionists from all the antagonistic groups therein, unanimity in views can hardly be expected from members of the union executive over issues of any importance. Union elections and activities, and reaction to controversial government's economic and political measures (which incidentally might affect different trades unions positively or negatively) have therefore proved to be potentially divisive, and causes of intra-union fracas or conflicts irrespective of the presumed machinations of private employers and of state agencies.

At the central level, that of the NLC, individual and corporate interests seem to merge. The 42 industrial unions are by law affiliates of the NLC, and the presidents and general secretaries of these unions are members of the NLC's policy making organs. The first contest would thus be over the election of the NLC's executive officers, particularly the president. To ensure

---

[11] These were the United Labour Congress of Nigeria (ULCN) that was affiliated to the Brussels-based International Confederation of Free Trade Unions (ICFTU), the Nigerian Trade Union Congress (NTUC) that was affiliated to the communist World Federation of Trade Unions (WFTU) and the Nigerian Workers Council (NWC) which affiliated with the Catholic and Brussels-based World Confederation of Labour (WCL). The Labour Unity Front (LUF) did not affiliate internationally.

[12] Otobo, D. and Omole, O. (eds.), *Readings in Industrial Relations in Nigeria*, Malthouse, 1987

that one's favoured candidate won any of the coveted positions, short of rigging the elections, the sponsoring affiliates (unions) would need to command a simple majority of votes. And since the number of delegates any union could send to such a conference would depend on the numerical strength of its membership, in the short run it was possible to have an informed and often accurate guess about the likely results of the impending elections if one had prior knowledge of preferences of leadership of the 42 industrial unions- assuming there was consensus among members of each delegation on who to back. To avoid the latter, union leaders would try to pick as members of their union's delegates those individuals or middle-rung organizers who were least likely to be persuaded or bought over by the opposition. Given the nature of the typical industrial union as outlined above, and where the union president or general secretary does not have complete control over the process of picking the delegation, one could not predict the voting preferences of such individual members. Even then, a union could still lose the opportunity of sending a voting delegation to this conference if it failed to pay all its affiliation dues regularly to the NLC.

It is easy to see from this that the numerical strength of any industrial union becomes vital in many ways, the three most important being: i) the dues its own members paid through compulsory check-off which should determine its financial strength; b) the amount of affiliation dues that the union in turn paid to the NLC; and c) the size of such affiliation dues which in turn determined the size of its delegation and therefore voting power or leverage at the quadrennial conferences of the NLC. This being so, it would seem self-defeating for any union to withhold affiliation dues from the NLC and yet expect to influence its policies from within. In this regard, the 'democrats' were most unwise and short-sighted and their position would have been much worse if Chiroma had fully implemented the constitutional provision on payment of affiliation dues.

This then brings us to the status of rules and regulations. Rules are meant to guide and regulate conduct and they usually prove to be indispensable yardsticks in times of conflict and tension in particular. If the constitutional provision says '10 per cent of total affiliation dues paid', this should be complied with, just as Chiroma had no business setting aside the provision on cut-off period for determining unions that would have voting rights. The argument that in order to foster unity it may be necessary to bend or disregard basic or fundamental rules or laws is as dangerous as it is inherently counter-productive. It tends to make for a national culture, if it is believed and practised in most organizations, where rules and laws (including the national constitution) are not taken seriously, and incumbents of positions and government officials believe and act on such assumptions and in consequence render organizations and the state fragile structures that are riddled through by arbitrariness and high-handedness. So a union can withhold affiliation dues and expect to have voting rights; a 'democrat' union leader, or the Administrator can say 'I am convinced that any agreement short of sharing of posts would not achieve the desired unity' (Report, 20), or the Minister of Employment, Labour and Productivity can demand for the 'slating' or 'sharing' of positions in preference to free and fair elections and still be quite comfortable in the claim that 'progressives' or 'Marxists' are anti-democratic. It is bound to be a strange morality, which breeds a cynical and mediocre political and organizational culture, and, in the end, most uncertain future through persistent conflict and confusion, and a seemingly habitual disregard of the rational.

State control

The state everywhere never tires of trying to exercise some control over the more important interest groups in society, more especially workers organizations which are particularly vocal and visible. The reasons for this range from the *political, economic* to the *social.* The political and social are usually tied up with all sorts of considerations, beginning with the argument that as the political sovereign the state has a *right* to monitor and regulate all groups for reasons of internal and external security, protection of life and property, and ensuring fair and reasonable social and political competition among individuals and groups.

For the economic, the state itself is the *largest employer* of labour and therefore has a very large wage bill to settle every month. In the case of Nigeria, the state is also the *largest investor.* On top of all this, it also regulates the economy even in these days of deregulation and of allowing market forces to dictate the allocation of resources. From the official point of view, therefore, any groups or individuals who could by their activities adversely affect the state in its multiple roles of employer, investor and regulator of the economy ought to be kept under surveillance and strict check.

All this seem well and proper and to be above board, but not quite so upon closer examination. The two related important points here are: a) the state does not have a monopoly of interpreting what could be in the best interest of everybody, and 1)) neither the government nor the state is itself homogeneous. On these points, different ministries, parastatals, and other organs of the state (judiciary, armed forces, local government, etc.) have different priorities, just as the key individuals who occupy the important positions in these institutions have different views and perceptions based on such factors as contrasting educational backgrounds, experience, ethnic/regional origins, religion, and the membership of cults/mason lodges, just to mention some. More critically, political leaders, whether civilian or military, and top bureaucrats, whether located in the main bureaucracy or parastatals of federal or state governments, certainly have their own favourite advisers and biases.

Thus for those few visionary leaders with a blueprint for the governance and development of the human and material resources of their countries, and of which hardly any of note has passed through our shores or been in control of the central levers of power, the many policies of government and state agencies can only but be based on the views and preferences of the various rival policy-making groups inside and outside of the public sector. Any policy that is defended in public by government officials and held out to be in the *'national* interest' is thus by definition the views of a *sectional group* or coalition of groups with *vested interests within* the policy-making cadres inside, and of interest groups outside the public administration apparatus.

To illustrate the point, the top officials of the Federal Ministry of Employment, Labour and Productivity, for example, were not involved in the decision to ban the NLC. The director-general at the time, S. B. Agodo, insisted that himself and his directors prescribed a different set of policies, and that in the critical period of 28 and 29 February, 1988, the Minister took a typist to his residence from where "he operated and proceeded directly to the television station to make his broadcast."[13] The Minister, as one later found out, liaised with the Presidency through the Political Adviser to the President.

However, there would seem to be two self-correcting or compensatory tendencies in the situation just outlined. The first is the existence of competing and rival policy options. To this extent, the announced policy could be said to be *experimental,* both protagonists and antagonists watching out for general reception to, and full impact of both its intended and unintended consequences. Once sufficiently strong resistance is built up from within and outside to the existing policy, eventually there would most likely be some modifications or complete abandonment of the policy in question.

The second is that, in the end all director-generals, directors of state-owned companies and parastatals, ministers under any administration, and the President himself are concerned about their continued stay in office, and since any of the other officers can be overruled and dropped from office by the President or some higher but intervening authority, there would be continuing pressure, real or imagined, for the modification of practically most policies, particularly when not many of them have been popularly received. A minister or director-general could be made a scapegoat as occasion demands.

But it should be emphasized that the effects of these two tendencies could

---

[13] Interview, Lagos, March 1988.

be delayed for a long while by a largely insensitive and self-opinionated higher authority that places much greater emphasis on stubbornness and interprets any changes in policy as a sign of 'weakness'. It must be pointed out also that because a regime or government considers a particular policy to be in its best interest or necessary for its survival, does *not* mean such a policy is in the *national interest*- particularly where the government itself has not been democratically elected and formal avenues do not exist for a critique of or for opposing such a policy. It is even worse when a government decrees that its policies have 'no alternatives' and persons dreaming up alternatives are 'saboteurs'.

For industrial relations matters, the obvious vested interests are the government, employers/managements and their organizations, and workers and their organizations and the public and families that bear the brunt of the activities and upkeep of the unemployed. As has been indicated elsewhere, the competing policy-making groups within the state apparatus include the Presidency, officials of the Federal Ministry of Employment, Labour and Productivity, the ministries dealing with finance and establishment issues that would be concerned over wage bill, relativities and monetary policy (including the Prices, Productivity and Incomes Board), the industrial arbitration panel and the national industrial court, and the intelligence organizations.[14] We have established above the relative absence of unanimity of views on any policy, as there are competing policy options generated by the different groups, nor is any policy subject to consensus.

With all this in mind, it is reasonably clear that the Presidency exploited latent divisions within the labour movement, literally created its own Shamang faction, to enable it confer some air of legitimacy on its overthrow of Chiroma's executive. Such a conclusion inevitably derives from all the foregoing and may be summarised this way: the constitution of the NLC was imposed by the government (Murtala/Obasanjo regimes) and it was obvious that the NEC of the NLC, duly constituted and which included all 'democrats', approved the Benin Conference and nomination papers were also duly filed by all the parties in conformity with constitutional provisions. The Conference was constitutional and legal and that was why the Minister himself attended.

Second, and following from this, was that not only there was no constitutional or legal basis for Shamang and his gang to pretend to hold an NLC congress, no attempt was made to bring him to book for violating the law as it stood. The law did not permit of a second central labour organization, and the main conference had a quorum, aside from being properly sanctioned. Shamang's sham conference had no quorum, nor were nomination papers filed by anyone else, if at all, than by the 'democrats'

[14] Otobo, D., *State and Industrial Relations in Nigeria*, Malthouse, 1988.

themselves in circumstances that can best be described as secretive. The Minister of Employment, Labour and Productivity had therefore a legal duty to apply the law against Shamang and his gang, rather than violate it.

Third, in any case, if there were truly two hostile groups within the labour movement and one group succeeded in controlling the major elective positions through the ballot box and by rules laid down by both the government itself and the organization as contained in the constitution of the organization, what is wrong with that? There must always be winners in freely and democratically conducted and contested elections: losers in Nigeria must just learn to accept this. Were the elections rigged would be a different matter altogether. Fourth, if there were truly two hostile factions and only in relation to distribution of power within the NLC, the rules for resolving such disputes have been clearly laid out in the constitution. Even if '10 per cent of total affiliation dues' had been changed to '10 per cent of membership dues' and with or without the deadline for fully paid up affiliation dues being enforced, the 'democrats' would still have on the basis of numbers lost anyway. The larger point, however, is that the matter should have remained the *internal problem* of the NLC and of the labour movement. Labour organizations are less influential and less disruptive than political parties, associations of business persons (chambers of commerce, employers' organizations, etc.) and the armed forces. These organizations resolve their internal problems which are often more acute than those in the unions, not to talk of the NLC. There are thus no convincing grounds for applying the consideration of 'public interest' only to labour organizations to justify unwarranted and destructive external intervention, particularly over such relatively trivial matters as once in four years election of officers of the NLC! Organizations in society must be left alone to evolve and manage their own conflict regulating capacity or machinery for the system to be truly pluralistic, democratic and stable. Fifth, from the degree and comprehensiveness of the legal/administrative control of unions and of the NLC, one would think that the *government has always been the main union member or affiliate of the NLC.* The State writes their constitutions, ensures that their provisions are complied with, approves their audited accounts, and arrogates to itself the responsibility of 'protecting' the interests of other union members, whether they like it or not, by weakening those same organizations. It can then also be officially claimed that these workers' organizations 'whose concern should be the protection and enhancement of the interest of the ordinary masses of the workers, but somehow ideological pursuits have crept in, to the detriment of the central aim' *(Report,* 14). The assumption presumably is that SAP has been 'ideology-free' in content, and hence when unionists and NLC officials express dissenting views on official social and economic policies, they would *not* be protecting and enhancing the interests of their members and could be detained without trial and their organizations proscribed. The State in all its wisdom would set the goals, prescribe the methods to be adopted in pursuing them, determine demands and aspirations of its co-union members and decrees whenever that these have been fulfilled or satisfied.

Sixth, it would appear that to sustain control mechanisms and exert constant pressure certain legal provisions would seem to have been deliberately abused or manipulated by public officials, or how else could one explain why the Registrar of Trade Unions managed not to approve any of the NLC's accounts since 1978? Always threats of proscription, fines, etc. for the NLC and industrial unions - all this in a context where neither the federal government, nor state governments, nor most of the parastatals has audited or published their own accounts for many years.

Seventh, assuming the electoral procedures had been perverted by the 'progressives' and the sole concern of the government was for the NLC leadership to be elected democratically, its actions did not so indicate. The Administrator's terms of reference were amazingly sweeping, covering anything the organization has ever done since 1978 when neither the Minister nor General Babangida were directly in government. The 'problem areas' included scholarship awards, audited accounts, general administration, construction of warehouses, the constitution, trade union structure, 'foreign ideologies', investments, and subvention of ₦1,000,000 donated to the NLC in 1978 by the Obasanjo regime - certainly neither Chiroma nor Shamang had anything to do with the last item!

The economic circumstances of the 1980s

Without going into the details of economic policies of successive governments since 1983, it is generally agreed that the economic situation has been a harsh one, characterised by galloping cost of living, rapid inflation, increasing mass unemployment, low capacity utilization in industry, high operating costs, immiseration of wage earners in particular and of the population in general, high external and internal debts, and consequent more intense social and political cleavages/conflicts. The structural adjustment programme (SAP) of the Babangida's regime, adopted in 1986, has been as controversial in conception as in its effects. This regime's *modus operandi,* partly a self-imposed requirement for the implementation of its economic policies and partly part and parcel of its political transition programme, has been to discredit, harass and incarcerate critics.

Some of its most devastating critics have been in the labour movement, and in the NLC, largely because important aspects of SAP have included the holding down of wages whatever the level of inflation, a drastic pruning of the public service, and a massive reduction in social investment (health, education, etc.). Unions have thereby suffered twofold, through loss of membership and dramatic fall in real wages and thus fall in living standards of their members. As a corporate body, the NLC has had to put forward rival policy options, as well as seeking to propagate its viewpoints by means of leaflets, press conferences and press releases, petitions to government officials and to General Babangida himself, and mobilizing workers to go on strikes. Given the indubitable unpopularity of the structural adjustment programme, and the delicate social and political atmosphere left behind by various protests and communal/religious clashes and demonstrations, the regime has found its attention fully engaged in counteracting the actual and potential impact of the opposing activities of all dissenting individuals and groups, especially those of workers, the unions and the NLC. Its main weapon against organizations, whether of students, workers, of so-called professional associations, and any organized group, has been to ban such bodies. Therefore, 'democrats' or no 'democrats', it would have been most surprising and totally out of character if the regime did not find a way to proscribe the NLC.

IMPLICATIONS FOR THEORISING INDUSTRIAL RELATIONS

There may be three 'social actors' in the 'system of industrial relations' but the State seems able to deal ruthlessly and arbitrarily, in the short run, with employers' and workers' organizations at will in Nigeria. Ubeku (1983)[15] and other observers have correctly pointed out the propensity of the government to consistently undermine collective bargaining institutions and processes. This propensity, upon deeper reflection and critical examination of evidence available, would be found to be sustained by a certain attitude that is also reflected in the equally troubling disregard for rules, regulations and laws by those in positions of authority. This attitude appears to be the product of a lack of interest in the democratic and human rights of others. All this business of voluntarism and right of others to organize to protect the interests of their members, for example, are only paid lip-service by both public and private employers.

Indeed, from the degree of legal regulation of trades unions and of the NLC alluded to above, that pervades union government and administration, the classification of the type of unionism here is becoming more and more problematic since the State has little regard for the autonomy of any voluntary association or group in society. One major consequence of this relative lack of institutional autonomy has been the fragility of institutions and thus of the State itself. Industrial relations in an inherently unstable State and where trade unions have little choice but to fiercely contest official

[15] Ubeku, A.K., *Industrial Relations in Developing Countries: the case of Nigeria*, Macmillan, 1983.

social and economic policies all the time, are immediately political however defined. In addition, if the blind cannot lead the blind without ending up in a blind alley, there would certainly be blinding and grave problems where an inherently unstable State that has feuding dominant elites who have no meaningful political and economic agenda and yet attempt to destabilize other voluntary associations and organizations by way of excessive administrative/legal control. In relation to the NLC, if the purpose was merely to get rid of Chiroma, banning the organization seemed to be an awfully expensive way of doing so: the 'progressives' still won the 19 December 1988 elections, *but* with the NLC dragged back to where it started ten years ago- picking up the pieces and going round government-imposed strictures to consolidate!

The other interesting thing which has to be empirically investigated is the precise boundaries of the labour movement. The mass of the urban unemployed, aside from those on the fringes of criminality, tend to depend for survival on some employed unionists. Unionization has itself infected all categories of employees except for the few at the very top. Many petty traders, the magical 'self-employed' of the famous 'informal sector' have largely been squeezed out of business, capital requirement rising beyond their reach with the effects of SAP. And when joined by thousands who crowd the streets hawking one item or the other, victims of 'disguised unemployment', who can be mobilized for protests without notice, the boundaries of the labour movement have become amorphous and expansive than is conventionally assumed.

A last comment concerns the use of 'ideology' both as a source of cleavage in the labour movement, and as an explanation of behaviour of dissenting labour leaders in 1988. The Administrator, in no doubt a moment of inspiration, admitted that

> ...it has to be stressed that it (ideology) has been used as a convenient label by many trade union leaders to disguise their personal ambition. Committed "Marxists" or "democrats" are very few within the trade union movement and this is confirmed by the ease with which they move from one to the other. As Alhaji Chiroma put it in his address..."some leaders who were one thing in Ibadan '78, were another thing in Kano '81, and yet quite something else in Enugu (*Report*, 43).

"State functionaries, along with several observers and academics of sorts, over the years have been 'committed labellists' for spurious reasons, they themselves being neither progressives nor democrats. What does it mean to claim 'the Congress was run along Marxist lines' *(Report,* 40), for an organization whose structure, organs, and constitution were largely determined by a capitalist government and whose staff were drawn from capitalist commercial and industrial establishments, and operating under capitalist 'rule of law'?

CONCLUDING REMARKS

We have attempted above a more credible and comprehensible account of what took place before and after the NLC was banned by General Babangida's regime in 1988. There would always be differences of opinion in any club, political party, trades unions and the labour movement everywhere, and those in Nigeria are no exceptions. The law being what it was, it would be in order to maintain that whatever differences that existed among prominent union leaders, these would not have resulted in the existence of a rival body to the NLC if government officials had not encouraged and exploited them for their own ends. After all, David Ojeli and his friends attempted this in 1981-82, found some support among a few legislators but when the Shagari administration stuck to the law, the former swallowed his pride and sought ways of reaching an accommodation.

No one can claim that because the government was heavily involved in the organization of the Special Delegates Conference of 19 December, 1988, that: i) it now controls the executive of the NLC; and ii) differences of views no longer exist within the organization or the labour movement. It is also true that whenever a government puts a puppet in position of authority in trades unions, workers simply bypass such leadership. Thus whilst governments seek to control or influence the leadership of the labour movement, and may appear to succeed for a while, they should be made aware that workers' own activities impose severe limits. Banning workers, students, and other voluntary organizations therefore provides no solution.

Chapter 14

THE POLITICS OF MINIMUM WAGE IN NIGERIA

INTRODUCTION

The term 'minimum wage' has come under close scrutiny in recent times, acquiring an increasingly but strangely controversial status both in terms of usage and policy objectives especially in the 1980s. After the 1991 federal government's budget, it became clear that the minimum wage issue may yet occupy a centre stage in the 1990s.

For these and other reasons, we examine in this chapter the evolution of the national minimum wage in Nigeria and the uses to which the latter has been put. Some of the factors which seem to have brought the minimum wage issue into sharper focus in recent times have included: i) the current economic depression that became more widely felt as from 1982; ii) the drastic decline in revenues from the sale of crude oil due to a sharp fall in its price since 1982, affecting the capacity of the state as an employer to improve upon the lot of its citizen and of its employees in particular; iii) both aforementioned factors leading to dramatic cutbacks in public expenditure and widespread unemployment in the public and private sectors of the economy; iv) the government's adoption of the International Monetary Fund (IMF) and World Bank-sponsored structural adjustment programme (SAP) in 1986 which, along with the impact of several other developments, has aggravated the unemployment situation; v) the visible general decline in living standards as actual earnings have fallen far behind the rate of inflation, and thus very high cost of living for most people, but more for a majority of wage earners who depend solely on their wages for survival; and vi) the not altogether quiet reaction of organized labour and of other disaffected groups in society to continuing deprivations.

We shall first discuss the concepts of ***minimum wage*** and ***national minimum wage***, so that we know exactly what we are talking about given the amount of confusion that surrounds their meaning at the moment. This is followed by tracing the evolution of national minimum wage policies in Nigeria and the underlying philosophies of the latter, and then closing with some remarks regarding the likely future course of public sector wage bargain in light of our discussion.

MINIMUM WAGE: THE CONCEPT

The term 'minimum wage' is often used in a variety of ways in many countries. It is essentially 'an expression used in a number of circumstances in which a worker's remuneration is not allowed to fall below a given amount.'[1] A publication of the International Labour Organization (ILO) declares that 'the minimum wage is the wage which in each country has the force of law and which is enforceable under threat of penal or other appropriate sanctions.'[2] But, it could also be established 'through the private agreement of those directly concerned, or through dispute settlement procedures, rather than by a statutory process aimed at achieving a more generally applicable lower limit to wages.'[3]

These definitions draw out two aspects of minimum wage, namely *method* and *scope*, which are in fact inseparable in practice. Regarding the method of establishing a minimum wage, it could be done either through the intervention of the state which so enacts one (by decree, or through wages commission or by a tripartite wages board/council, or awards made by arbitration board or industrial/labour courts), or by agreement between affected work groups (which have their own 'custom and practice') and their respective managements in industry (which also have their own notion of what is the 'going rate' for various categories of skills or job specifications). In practice, one finds that what might have been a privately and mutually agreed upon wage rate but once contained in some document, say collective agreement, and deposited with some agency of the state (e.g. Ministry of Labour) may acquire the force of a legally binding document, often similar in effect as an officially enacted rate. Similarly, officially decreed wage rates often become baseline from which private negotiations between unions and managements/employers associations are anchored and built upon.

The *scope* relates to *coverage, that is* the number of workers or categories of workers entitled to such a minimum wage. The definitions reveal that a minimum wage could cover either all wage earners or a group of them, and as such the scope could then be employees of a company or a section thereof, an industry or group of related industries, a geographical region, or all industries.

There are two other things one should note about *scope* or *coverage* of a minimum wage. The first is that often the scope is directly related to the instrument or method for determining such a minimum wage. The smaller

[1] Arthur Marsh (ed.), *Concise Encyclopaedia of Industrial Relations*, Gower Press, 1979, p. 196

[2] ILO, Report VII (1), *Minimum Wage Firing Machinery and Related Problems, with Special Reference to Developing Countries*, Geneva, 1968, p. 8

[3] Starr, G., *Minimum Wage Fixing*, ILO, Geneva, 1981, p. Vii

the group of workers affected, the greater the tendency for the decision to be reached by a small committee which could be in the form of tripartite wages councils or boards (in the public sector in particular) or some such similar body (say, joint industrial council) within the establishment or industry concerned. Conversely, the greater the number of workers or industries affected, the greater the likelihood of such third parties as employers organizations, trades unions, and agencies of the state being involved.

The second factor that is often not sufficiently publicized or recognized is that the fixing of wages at all involves the somewhat technical exercise of grading, that is, of arranging workers in categories according to their job classifications and commensurate skills. Grading therefore turns out to be a form of job evaluation 'in which grades are determined in the light of predetermined definitions of functions, skill and responsibility, and jobs subsequently described and allocated to appropriate grades.'[4]

Having established what a particular group of workers with identifiable skill or peculiar training should earn, other groups with similar or different skills would then expect to earn about the same or more or less, depending on the assessment of each group's position in relation to the first. It is important, of course, that each group and the respective profession to which it belongs tacitly accepts such general ranking-ordering of skills or jobs, and which is not often the case, otherwise a conflict situation would be created over differentials in pay and other benefits. But in general what prevails is a system of series of minimum rates of wages for different jobs in different industries, with workers and their organizations attempting to achieve comparability in pay among jobs and skills within an industry, in the first instance, and across industries subsequently. In this, employers and state agencies are involved, sometimes retarding and at some other facilitating the process.

WHY MINIMUM WAGE?

But why the existence of minimum wages in the first place? Historically it was found in most countries where private employers and trades predominated that some of them paid very low wages, thereby exploiting or 'sweating' such workers or apprentices. And that in many trades or occupations, affected persons were seldom strong enough to compel their employers or masters into joint arrangements for determining terms of employment. Minimum wages have therefore been meant to: a) limit the vulnerability to exploitation of such persons, implicitly encouraging the payment of 'fair' or 'reasonable' wages; b) reduce the level of poverty inflicted upon such groups of persons; and c) correct a situation that is characterised by the absence of machinery for the regulation of wages and

[4] Marsh, A., *Concise Encyclopaedia of Industrial Relations,* Gower Press, 1979, p. 126

other terms of employment by imposing a decentralized system of tripartite wages boards which puts the main responsibility for reaching agreed decisions on representatives of the workers and employers from the industries concerned.

A combination of reasons accounts for the introduction of minimum wages, where such has been done, often depending on the peculiar economic and political circumstances of the country in question. The emphasis on heavy industries and textiles at the beginning of the industrial revolution in Britain, Europe and, later, North America, made it possible for many workpeople, especially women and children, to be badly exploited for a long time. The reasons why minimum wages get introduced usually include social and political protests, labour protests, the ferment and spread of ideas, the activities of reformist movements and of politicians, and the realization of the importance of better-paid workforce to an increasingly consumption-oriented society. The saliency of any of the factors or reasons depended on time and place.

But the criteria for determining the level of minimum wages have changed since the early days of pre-emptive increases designed to ward off more revolutionary or disruptive protests, and of relatively vague notions of 'fair' or 'decent' wages. Such criteria have become more refined in many countries to include: a) the needs of workers and their families; b) the general level of wages in the country; c) the cost of living and changes therein; d) the social security benefits (where they exist); e) the relative standards of other social groups in society; f) economic factors, including the requirements of economic development, levels of productivity and the desirability of attaining and maintaining a high level of employment; and g) the employers' capacity to pay.

NATIONAL MINIMUM WAGE

A national minimum wage is 'a governmental provision whereby wages are not allowed to fall below a national minimum level, thereby relieving poverty among low paid employed workers.'[5] The underlying assumption of a national minimum wage, from this description, is that minimum rates of wages already exist for workers in various categories of trades or occupations and industries, and its prime concern therefore remains the lowest or minimum uniform wage that can be paid to an employed worker, irrespective of trade or occupation, skill or industry.

The important distinction here is that a national minimum wage goes beyond the much narrower concern of employers about ascribing a quantum of wages or salary to a specific job or position. Rather, the objective here would seem to be ensuring that 'a national minimum wage' can enable

---

[5] Marsh. A., *op. cit.*, p. 204

the least paid worker afford the basic necessities of life. In some countries, a national minimum wage would be similar to a 'living wage', as distinct from 'subsistence wage', where the former represents a wage that is sufficient to cover the worker's normal material, moral and cultural needs. As we find out in our subsequent analysis, it is very easy to disagree over what are and the volume of 'normal needs' of an 'average' worker. Despite such difficulties, some notion of relative sufficiency and thus the financial capacity to meet such needs seems implied in the idea of a national minimum wage where workers depend solely on their wages.

THE EVOLUTION OF MINIMUM WAGE IN NIGERIA

The history and course of the evolution of a minimum wage structure in the country is a chequered one. Many reasons account for this state of affairs, and the most important ones include: a) the pattern of colonial conquest and of the consequent administrative arrangements; b) the pattern and development of the public sector; c) the fragmented nature of the private sector; and d) the trade union structure. We make brief comments on each one of these in turn.

Pattern of colonial conquest and administrative arrangements

Till the 1900s, colonial military campaigns against indigenous economic and political authorities were undertaken by private European and British companies, first as measures taken in protection of trading routes and of markets against local and foreign rivals but subsequently for other strategic and political considerations and at which point metropolitan governments took over such direct operations. Thus Lagos stood on its own as a 'crown colony' and was controlled directly from London as from 1862; the Niger Delta and up to Lokoja were conquered and ruled by the Royal Niger Company; just as various trading points up and down the Niger and in various parts of the north were coveted by an assortment of European and Levantine firms; and the Protectorates of Southern Nigeria and of Northern Nigeria were created from conquered territories in 1900 and 1906 respectively by the British government after it took over direct control from the Royal Niger Company in 1900.

Since these areas were conquered at different times and administered separately, the idea of developing systems of pay and wage rates that could be applied uniformly across was not really contemplated at first. But when such a notion was thrown up and rendered necessary by subsequent socioeconomic developments, it predictably met severe resistance from among employers and the colonial administration itself as we see below.

The other subsidiary but important point to be noted in this regard was that the attendant compartmentalization of areas into distinct administrative units thus served to delimit the scope of application of most wages and other conditions of employment for a while longer than would have *been* the case. This tendency was likely to have been encouraged by the disparities in budgets and revenues of these administrative units,[6] the poorer ones hardly considering matching rates elsewhere. It was convenient for private and public employers to make reference, if that could not be avoided, to prevailing terms of employment in their own immediate area of operation, thereby localising wage rates and payment systems. Under such circumstances, it was difficult to have a *national* minimum wage, and what emerged was the coexistence of district, urban, and regional wage rates with criteria for fixing such remaining largely arbitrary for a long time and subject to the whims of employers.[7]

Pattern and Development of the Public Sector

The development of the public sector followed closely the pattern of colonial conquest and the type of economic activities the colonial state was engaged in. The attempt to provide such services as water, transport, electricity, sanitation, housing, and general administration in centres of economic activities in the first instance, and subsequently to provide a general administrative framework, improve upon communications and monitor these and the activities of private employers and of other interest groups in society ultimately generated wage employment, created some skills and bargaining relationships of the sort we are concerned with in industrial relations.

As we have indicated elsewhere,[8] what forms these phenomena took and how complex they were depended largely on the times. From the 1890s and right up to the 1920s, it was a combination of widespread use of forced labour, remuneration in kind and very low wages where paid, a mass of unskilled labour coexisting fitfully with few artisans, and thus the relative absence of rates that could be applied generally. Existing rates of pay and differentials in pay and other terms of employment were first 'European' as against 'African' (and within each category there were variations and different grades), and later among occupational groups, particularly as between skilled and semi-skilled artisans and clerks.[9] The only general item was 'war bonus', a flat sum, which was paid at the onset of the First World War, and even in this that of Europeans was not only higher, Africans were

[6] For a good discussion of this see Nicholson. I.F., *The Administration of Nigeria 19004960: Men, Methods & Myths*, Clarendon Press, Oxford, 1969

[7] For details see Perham, M. (ed.), *Mining Commerce, and Finance in Nigeria.* Faber, London, 1948; Hopkins, A.G., *An Economic History of West Africa,* Longman. London, 1973; Ekundare, R.0, *An Economic History of Nigeria,* Cambridge Univ. Press, 1960

[8] Otobo, D., *The Role of Trade Unions in Nigerian Industrial Relations,* Malthouse, Oxford, 1987; and Otobo, D., *State and Industrial Relations in Nigeria.* Malthouse, 1989

[9] Ananaba, W., *The Trade Union Movement in Nigeria,* Ethiope, Benin City, 1969 *has* a useful account

only paid after protests and strikes.[10]

From the 1930s to the 1950s, what was embryonic in the previous period had become more fully developed, establishing in the process what appeared to be the distinguishing features of wage bargain situation in the public sector and which remained largely unchanged till late 1960s. The use of forced labour was on the decline (abandoned only in late 1950s) and the idea of the payment of regular wages appeared to have been accepted in principle by most employers, terms of employment became largely regionalized, as sharp pay and other economic distinctions emerged between the clerical and non-clerical, among occupational groups, between public and private sector employees, and ethnic and regional particularities and political considerations supplanted racial discrimination.

The way these factors combined with and related to each other produced a complex picture, the more obvious aspect being basic rates for different categories of employees in public utilities (parastatals), local government and main civil service remaining generally applicable only *within* Eastern, Northern, Western regions and Lagos respectively. The comparability of, and thus subsequent changes in terms of employment among the regions became more a question of political considerations, from the employers point of view, especially in the late fifties and early 1960s, than to any great desire on their part to work out a minimum wage or a living wage that would enable the least paid public employee afford more than the basic necessities of life.[11]

The changes in public administration in the 1960s and thereafter were of a fundamental type and made it possible to table the issue of a national minimum wage at different points in time. Hitherto, since the 1920s, the colonial administration merely set up *ad hoc* committees or commissions to look into 'labour problems' or 'wage problems' in designated sections, bodies that were then appointed on regional and federal basis in the 1950s. Although regionalism and ethnic particularities still held considerable sway in political and social matters, in terms of fiscal developments, growth of the monetary system and of financial institutions, there was a swing in favour of a centralised and more co-ordinated approach. This was no doubt reinforced by the fact that 'labours' as a legislative issue was the prerogative of the centre, which also explains why regions (and states) have had no Ministry of Labour.

The factors which accounted for this new tendency were: a) against a background of political upheavals and alliances, it seemed manifestly

[10] Ananaba, 1969, *op. cit.*

[11] Yesufu, T.M., explicitly argues that the 1954-55 upward review of wage rates and including the Mbaaefo (1958) and Morgan (1959) were politically motivated. See his *An Introduction to Industrial Relations in Nigeria*. OUP/Niser, 1962, p.

difficult for regional governments to adopt unilateral measures of the kind experienced in late 1940s and early 1950s. Indeed, we have seen how in 1958 the Federal, Eastern and Northern governments jointly appointed the Mbanefo Wages Commission and the Western region government had its own Morgan Commission in 1959. It stays instructive that when a second Morgan Commission was appointed by the Federal Government in 1963 in the wake of a general strike, no regional government opted out, and wages commissions have since then been either applicable to the public sector as a whole, or to a section of the public sector, or to employees in both public and private sectors of the economy; b) closely related to this was the accretion of fiscal and political power to the centre, especially from 1966 onwards. By the 1970s the states were more dependent on Lagos for funds, the criteria for sharing revenue having been progressively modified in favour of the centre. A logical consequence seemed to be that matters concerning remuneration and scope of rates were handed down from Lagos (through incomes and policy guidelines, awards of wages commissions, Acts of parliament, rulings of both the Industrial Arbitration Panel and the National Industrial Court, the various activities of the Federal Ministry of Employment, Labour and Productivity), financially delinquent states seeking more funds or grants to meet labour costs; c) the public utilities or parastatals had proliferated and grown much bigger and complex than ever before, a large number of them brought into existence by much-expanded economic investments and activities of various state and federal governments and their agencies. These were only made possible by the quadrupling of crude oil prices in 1973/74 and thus receipt of massive revenues, which in turn partly gave rise to an indigenization policy and increased complexity of emerging or reinforced parastatals; and d) the final creation of a national labour market, even for the private sector, and which threw up common personnel issues and problems of comparability in pay and other terms of employment. It was now possible, with all of these developments, for organized labour and social critics to advocate the establishment of a national minimum wage.

The fragmented nature of the private sector

As can be discerned from the pattern of colonial conquests and of consequent administrative arrangements mentioned previously, a good many of the private companies operated in the country long before direct colonial subjugation took place. Most firms or companies carved out various areas, as it were, for themselves and within which they had their own constabulary, troops, well-protected yards and warehouses, distributors, and administrators of a sort.[12] What therefore emerged over time were pockets

---

[12] For more details see Geary, W.N.M. *Nigeria Under Colonial Rule*, Frank Cass, London, 1965.

of intense commercial and military centres which formed the basis of claims to territories by metropolitan governments.

Even after direct colonial domination commenced, the handful of trading and mining companies which survived the depressions of late 1920s and 1930s could be found in a few towns that were flung and scattered across the country. Terms of employment, unions and of conflict regulating machinery and the poor conditions of employment therein, internal self-government and other political and administrative arrangements against political independence in 1960, the dilution of the employer element by the influx of North American, Asian and Levantine companies in the 1960s and 1970s, the emergence of an indigenous commercial and business elite, and massive public investments all presaged a more complex economy and the restructuring of the private sector into one unit albeit with component parts. No subsector or industry could now be relatively insulated from prevailing rates and pay systems in others, and this provided favourable conditions for the evolution of industry-wide, sector-wide, and nation-wide terms of employment.

Trade Union Structure

As may be discerned from the implications of the other three factors as outlined above, the trade union structure was largely influenced by the geographical distribution of companies, the nature of economic activities engaged in by the companies and the colonial administration proper, the poor state of communications, regional and ethnic differences, the activities of employers and their organizations, the activities of international labour organizations (especially from 1949 with the intensification of ideological differences in Europe) and the social consciousness of workers themselves.[13]

The salient points here would seem to have been that: i) forced, convict, and daily-paid or occasional labour far outnumbered fully-employed wage labour, a development that tended to undermine unionism while encouraging and perpetuating haphazard but localised payment systems; ii) unions themselves drew their membership from respective branches of the companies as earlier remarked, making it manifestly easier for employers to discourage workers from comparing their earnings with those of workers in other branches of the same company, not to talk of those in other companies or establishments within the same industry; iii) many union leaders largely accepted jurisdictional boundaries as defined or advocated by companies and, much later, by politicians, with the result that they themselves could not surmount constrictive regional considerations a lot of times and thus helped in no small measure in delaying the emergence of more generalized

[13] Fully discussed in Otobo, D., *The Role of Trade Unions in Nigerian Industrial Relations*, Malthouse, Oxford, 1987

terms of employment; iv) where established, minimum rates were determined without reference to what prevailed in other towns. Indeed, even for such firms as the United Africa Company (UAC) and John Holt Company that created an oligopoly in the export-import trade and in agricultural produce,[14] their branches in various towns operated as independent units. The operations of these units, as we see below, largely accounted for the growth and development of what came to be called 'house unions', namely the tendency for workers to organise autonomous (that is, from other unions) but weak small unions around the branches of the same company.

The main point here is that the combination of geographical dispersion of companies and of distribution of workers would seem to have served to produce and reinforce localised wage rates and payment systems. Allied to this was that such activities as mining of coal in Enugu, of tin and columbite in the Jos plateau, operations of numerous and varied artisans in road, marine and rail transport, just to mention these, were thought not to have much in common and employers enjoyed exploiting highly fragmented and restricted 'labour market' in their areas of operations. And, of course, the primitive state of communications hindered for a long time the spread of common terms for engaging different classes of workers wherever they were be located.

It should also be noted that one other factor which entrenched the fragmented nature of the private sector was the dominant economic ideology of *laissez faire* which the colonial administration fully subscribed to between 1900 and the late 1930s when it had to be modified somewhat in light of the devastation and human misery wrought by the Depression. But in tune with its logic at the time, the colonial administration restricted itself to the provision of forced and convict labour in mines, plantations, construction of roads and rail lines, and to maintaining law and order.[15] Private employers then ran their little kingdoms to suit themselves pretty much of the time.

Much of this was to change in the 1950s and 1960s, the 1940s taken up by Second World War preoccupations of Allied Forces and which manifested themselves in the colonies in the forms of conscriptions, shortages, inflation, rule by decree, extensive use of forced and convict labour on mines and plantations to 'help the war effort', rationing and the rigid regulation of wages. The private sector only began to be opened up in the late forties after the Tudor Davies Report of the post-1945 General Strike queried the absence of attempts at establishing minimum wages or rates.

Simplified considerably, trade unionism *in* Nigeria and the reactions of

---

[14] See Mars in Perham, M., (ed.), 1948 for more details

[15] Comprehensively dealt with in Otobo, D., *State and Industrial Relations in Nigeria*, Malthouse, 1989

public and private employers to it may be said to represent, in a nutshell, attempts at establishing minimum wage rates or wages in various sections of industry - and without implying that unionism has only been concerned with wages. Early attempts at establishing minimum wages as occurred were mostly in the public sector, beginning with the Lagos Crown Colony in respect of which Hughes & Cohen (1971) have recorded how "the institution of an urban administration and the creation of public utilities generated a standing corpus of officials, artisans, and other categories of labour earning different rates of pay.[16] Disagreements over minimum rates led to many strikes, the best documented being the strike by employees of the Public Works Department in 1897 when the governor unilaterally reduced wages which were already too low."[17]

But attempts with longer lasting effects were made in the first two decades of this century, efforts which established wages commissions as the most preferred method of establishing rates in the public sector. As Coleman (1958) observed, two civil services existed, the African and the European, with parallel career structures and the latter enjoying better terms of employment. African terms were determined locally while those of European civil servants cued from London, the former salary scales ranged from J36 to J400 a year while those of Europeans from £450 to over £2000 for the lieutenant governors.[18] Even so, because of widespread disenchantment with prevailing terms of employment and made worse by the hardships caused by the First World War, according to Nicholson (1969), 'the African juniors were expressing their discontent in open strikes, and the European seniors openly disaffected.'[19]

The result was that a series of internal administrative reviews by different committees were instituted, beginning with the Cameron-Carr Committee in 1906, followed by Bratt and Rice Committees in 1919. The other major commissions, tribunals and committees since then have been the Hunt Committee (1934), the Bridges Committee (1941), the Harragin Commission (1945 but published its report in 1947), the Tudor Davies Commission (1946), the Miller Committee (1947), the Cowan Enquiry (1948), the Gorsuch Commission (1954), the Mbanefo Commission (1958),

---

[16] HUGHES, A. and COHEN, R. 'An Emerging Nigerian Working Class: The Lagos Experience, 1897-1939,' in GUTKIND, P., COHEN, R. and COPANS, J, (eds) *African Labour History* (Beverly Hills and London, 1979

[17] HUGHES, A. and COHEN, R. 'An Emerging Nigerian Working Class: The Lagos Experience, 1897-1939,' in GUTKIND, P., COHEN, R. and COPANS, J, (eds) *African Labour History* (Beverly Hills and London, 1979)

[18] COLEMAN, J.S. *Nigeria: Background to Nationalism* (Berkeley, 1958).

[19] NICHOLSON, I. F. *The Administration of Nigeria 1900-1960: Men, Methods, and Myths*, Clarendon Press, Oxford, 1969.

the Morgan Commission (1959), the Morgan Commission (1963), the Adebo Commission (1970), the Udoji Commission (1974), the Williams Committee (1975), the Onosode Commission (1980), the Cookey Commission (1981), and the Adamolekun Commission (1981), National Minimum Wage Act 2000; National Minimum Wage (Amendment) Act, 2011, National Minimum Wage Act 2019, National Minimum Wage (Amendment) Act 2024.

These commissions or committees served two related purposes of establishing minimum rates and of reviewing them at a later date after workers' protests and other conditions make such a review imperative. The Bratt Committee (1919) reviewed the terms of European civil servants but its report was not published. While the Rice Committee (1919), which included representatives of the Civil Service Union, revised African salaries. And, according to Nicholson (1969), 'the case of the African civil service was met within a few weeks, by doubling of an existing 30 per cent War bonus, after emergency Executive Council meetings and telegrams to the Secretary of State, followed by a more complete overhaul of salary structure' (ibid.).

The Hunt Committee (1934) was charged with the task of reviewing the wages of unskilled workers and of determining a reasonable standard of living for a labourer. The Committee noted in its preamble that in computing a 'reasonable standard of living' for a labourer, his wife and children were not taken into account! Given the zeal of the colonial administration in maintaining low wages, following classical *laissez faire* economic doctrine, it actually reduced wages because of the ongoing economic depression. As the depression dragged on and workers protests mounted, the colonial administration established provincial wages committees in 1937 for Eastern, Northern and Western group of Provinces which were the politico-administrative units of the time. Through them the wages that had been cut a few years back were restored.

The Bridges Committee (1941) was a response to wartime shortages and escalating prices. It reviewed the wages of African government workers and also recommended compensatory increases which were subsequently dubbed 'cost-of-living awards' (COLA). But in doing this, it dispensed with the empiricism of the Hunt Committee (which sought to determine the actual costs of basic commodities) and posited its own 'model' diet from which it derived its computations and estimated the wage of the 'average' labourer in Lagos to be two shillings a day!

Equally interesting, in relation to our earlier remarks on fragmented and regionalized wage rates and payment systems, the provincial wages committees and the Bridges Committee made sure that basic pay rates and cost of living allowances throughout the country were not uniform. Towns and areas were classified into categories A, B, and C, areas and towns which had higher rate A inflation and thus higher cost of living falling under the A Category. And within each group, they were subdivisions. Lagos Township and Lagos Colony as a whole came under categories A and B respectively. In the Eastern Province, Port Harcourt, Aba, and Enugu were classified Al, Owerri province, Calabar province, Victoria, Buea, Kumba Township were B, and Cameroon, Onitsha, Ogoja provinces were Cl. As for the Northern Province, Jos, Bukuru, Kaduna, Zaria and Kano Township came under A3, followed by Minna, Lokoja, and Makurdi in B, and florin province, Adamawa province, Bauchi province, Bornu province, Katsina province and Sokoto in C category. While in Western Province, Warri Town and Sapele were in category A2 and A3 respectively, followed by Abeokuta, Benin City, Ibadan Town, and Ijebu province in B, with Ondo province in C category.[20]

Labour advisory boards were established by the Labour (Wage Fixing and Regulation) Ordinance of 1943, implementing one of the recommendations of the Bridges Committee. Although section 6 of the Ordinance empowered the boards to make inquiries into conditions of service and wages in any trade referred to them by the colonial authorities and to make recommendations for fixing the statutory minimum wage, this was hardly ever done. Citing a case in the Plateau where the Commissioner of Labour proposed the formation of a permanent labour advisory board in view of persistent labour protests, Freund (1981) observed that private employers opposed the idea, considering it 'undue interference' and some colonial officials themselves negatively viewing such a board as 'a stage for agitators.'[21]

The Tudor Davies Commission (1946) which was appointed in the wake of the 1945 general strike awarded salary increments ranging from fifty to 75 per cent, while the much-delayed report of the Harragin Commission came out with the salaries of 'established' government staff (as against temporary and daily-paid hands). Indeed, the Miller Committee (1947) reviewed upwards the wage rates of daily-paid labourers but established the principle of payment on a geographical basis, a system that was meant to be less cumbersome than that of the Bridges Committee. The former made a simple distinction between general labour on the one hand, and special and semi-skilled on the other, dividing the country into six geographical zones with differentials in pay of these two groups of labour. The guiding 'principle' was that cost of living was highest in Lagos and in its immediate environs, and that wages should be progressively lower the farther away from Lagos a labourer was.

And in tune with the Harragin recommendations, the Cowan Enquiry

[20] For these awards, a readily available source is Ananaba, W., *The Trade Union Movement in Nigeria*, Ethiope, Benin City, 1969, p. 29

[21] Freund, B., *Capital and Labour in Nigerian Tin Mines*, Univ. of Ibadan Press, Ibadan, 1981

(1948) investigated and reported on methods of negotiation between government and employees in state-owned industrial establishments. It introduced 'Whitley Committee a Junior Whitley Council (A) for clerical and other office employees, and Junior Whitley Council (B) for industrial or manual workers. As Yesufu (1962) confirmed, these were a dismal failure as they had become consultative instead of negotiating bodies, suffered difficulties over representation, and 'broke down completely because of staff side dissatisfaction over progress in negotiation.'[22] Akpala (1982) points out an additional reason for their failure by noting that 'the structural relationship between the two junior Whitley Councils could not be reconciled with the structure of the trades unions.'[23] By 1951 the Provincial Wages Committees were now joined by the government employees Regional Wage Committees to reflect the new national political structure of three regions.

Akpala (1982) in describing these bodies and their operations observed that they met infrequently' were not bargaining bodies, and functioned against the opposition of trades unions which deplored the colonial administration's attempts to entrench a geographical wage structure, a policy that appealed to provincial residents and 'native' administrations who were most unlikely to overlook any opportunity to save on labour costs, having grown used to utilizing forced labour which they could no longer legally do under the 1933 Forced Labour Ordinance. The trades unions demanded uniform rates for daily-paid workers everywhere, and backed this up by refusing to take up their membership in the Central Committee set up by the federal administration to reconcile their own views with those of the Regional Wages Committees which favoured geographical differences or disparities in wages. Against a background of workers' protests, co-ordinated by the All Nigeria Trade Union Federation (ANTUF), the Western and Eastern regional governments disbanded the provincial wages committees, but their northern counterpart retained hers. Given this lack of unanimity in views and of approaches, the federal government constituted Minimum Wage Fact-finding Committee comprising three of its own officials

In its representations before the Minimum Wage Fact-finding Committee, the ANTUF demanded the abolition of the geographical wage structure and the institution of a national minimum wage in their place. The central labour body also argued that the wages committees themselves had not been in the interest of workers since workers were not fully represented on them; the colonial administration and employers' representatives dominated them, using their majority vote in arriving at decisions against

[22] Yesufu, T.M., *An Introduction to Industrial Relations in Nigeria*, OUP/Niser, 1962

[23] Akpala, A. *Industrial Relations Model for Developing Countries: the Nigerian System*, Fourth Dimensions Press, Enugu, 1982

workers' interests. The Minimum Wage Fact-finding Committee in its report thought that the time was 'not ripe' for a national minimum wage system, and if enacted into being would create 'difficulties' and undermine the effectiveness of various incentive and bonus schemes. Akpala (1982,107) pertinently observed that the Committee's recommendation was nothing but an 'adoption of the thinking of Council of Ministers which seemed to have made up its mind before the appointment of the Committee that ...therefore the Miller scheme of wages should be retained.'

The recommendation of the Minimum Wage Fact-finding Committee should not be surprising upon close observation and despite the fact that there were intense union pressures against the geographical wage structure and the confusion and acrimony generated by the desultory operating style and very limited impact of these provincial wages committees. Even with very limited understanding of nationalists' politics of decolonization and of intrigues surrounding those 'constitutional conferences', it was fairly easy to see why the federal administration would only be too pleased to pass on the problems of daily-paid workers and of a national minimum wage to regional governments as soon as the latter came into being in 1951. For, one, it was extremely unlikely that the federal administration would initiate the enactment of any national minimum wage or wage rates that it could not enforce uniformly across the country. Two, the battle by the political parties, which drew most of their support from the regions within which they were based, over the control of the federal administration itself was already on, and could therefore only encourage the Governor-General and his men to routinely reiterate existing policy on geographical wage structures and wage boards. It was against this background that both the Western and Eastern regional governments scrapped provincial wage committees, established their own regional minimum wages, the latter in addition transferring all daily-paid workers to permanent employment as we earlier remarked.

As for the Gorsuch Commission (1954), it attempted to reconcile the salaries and other fringe benefits of federal and regional civil servants, after the regions were created to effect the policy of self-government. The opening salvo was fired by Dr. Azikiwe-led National Council of Nigeria and the Cameroon in 1949 with its call for a five shillings daily minimum wage. But the Western regional government beat all to it by fixing such a wage in 1954, only matched in 1955 by both the Eastern and Northern regional governments.

And political differences and competition among political parties and regional governments, partly manifested in competitive wage increases against a background of workers' agitation, led to the establishment of the Mbanefo Commission in 1958 by the Federal, Eastern and Northern governments, with the Western region government appointing its own Morgan Commission in 1959 as noted above.

The first commission to be established in the post-Independence period was the second Morgan Commission (1963), set up in the wake of another general strike, and it had the unprecedented task of reviewing salaries for both the public and private sectors, at least for those in the lower rungs of the scale, and also to examine the need for the introduction of a national minimum wage. The report of this commission formed the basis for the establishment of the first national minimum wage for the least paid worker even in the private sector. The tripartite negotiations which involved representatives of the state, of employers and of workers reached many decisions but the following are of more relevance to us: a) that the previous classification of labour into general labour, special labour, and skilled artisans be replaced by unskilled, semi-skilled and artisans; the country be divided into six areas, namely: i) Federal Territory of Lagos (including a radius of 16 miles from Tinubu Square, and referring to employees of the federal government and the private sector); ii) Western, Midwestern and Eastern regions; iii) Kaduna and Kano urban areas iv) urban areas of Jos, Zaria, Sokoto, Gusau, Bauchi, Gombe, Lokoja, Katsina province, Benue province, Kano province (excluding urban areas) and Kabba division; v) the provinces of Zaria, Plateau, and Bauchi (excluding their urban areas), Gas-hakal-Mabilla native authority; and vi) the provinces of Kabba (excluding Kabba Division and urban Lokoja), Bornu, Ilorin, Adamawa and Sardauna. The minimum wages applying exclusively within Areas i) to vi) were £10 per month or 75.8d. per day, £8 2s.6d. per month or 65.3d. per day, £6 18s.6d per month or 65.4d. per day, £6 7s.10d. per month or 4s.11d. per day, £5 10s.6. per month or 4s.3d. per day, and £5 4s. per month or 4s. per day respectively; b) the daily wage system be abolished gradually and all skilled workers be transferred to permanent positions or establishment; c) no junior worker in the private sector should earn *less than* the new rates agreed for Area I (i.e. £10 per month); d) the new minimum rates and increases should apply to employees of equivalent status in the public corporations, to nurses, teachers and junior workers in local authorities or government; and new rates and increases equally apply to junior workers in the private sector and legislation be introduced to provide for the machinery for negotiation.[24]

Most of the recommendations of the Morgan Commission would seem to have departed sharply from the expectations of the federal government as enacted in the latter's White Paper. The Commission more than accepted the idea of a national minimum wage which it computed on the basis of 'a

[24] For details see, 1964 Salaries and Wages Revision: Establishment Circular No.7/1964 and Federal Treasury Circular No. A41 1964 and b41 1964, Federal Ministry of Information Printing Division, Lagos, 1964.

living wage', as indicated above (in contrast to the 1934 Hunt Committee which restricted itself to the worker alone) and established different minimum wages for the four zones into which it divided the country. In contrast, the federal government argued against the concept of a 'living wage', noting that the Commission departed from the fundamental concepts and pattern of expenditure in which the existing wages were based. In doing so, the Commission directed its mind to the balanced diet based on local foodstuffs drawn by dieticians. By deriving the new wage structure from its own suggested pattern of living, the Commission has increased the existing minimum wage by 58 per cent in some cases, and in others by 100 per cent, whereas the pattern of the cost of living index would have produced an increase of say 15 to 20 per cent.[25]

In all it would seem that the government was only interested in reducing the size of the new minimum rates and of increases, and in this depended on rather spurious grounds for it did not itself appear to have actually undertaken computations based on some rival criteria. If it did, it would not have been guessing about percentage increases, 'say 15 to 20 per cent', and this explains why the minimum wage finally agreed upon at the tripartite negotiations (£10 per month for Area I) was higher than the original recommended figure of £9 although the government succeeded in increasing the number of zones from four to six as indicated above. The other pertinent point concerns the fact that the tripartite negotiating committee had to agree on new rates applying to junior workers in 'public corporations', nurses, teachers, and local government, apart from the obvious cast of their counterparts in the private sector. The differentials in the public sector were already beginning to constitute a waken even for the period 1963-64, a problem both the Adebo and Udoji Commissions made worse and which had to be addressed by the Onosode, Cookey and Adamolekun Commissions almost seventeen years later.

The Adebo Commission concentrated on the terms of service for public employees (who had suffered enormous deprivations in the civil war years in form of shortages, hyperinflation and thus a fall in real wages and living standards, a ban on wage increases and on strikes) and saw its task mainly in terms of bridging the gap between private and public sector pay, the latter held to be much lower at all levels. The irony was of course that junior workers in the private sector compelled their employers to implement the 'Adebo awards' which they saw as very competitive and more attractive in some respects by embarking upon a series of strike actions.[26] The Udoji Commission (1974) completely overhauled the pay structure in the public

[25] Ananaba, W., *The Trade Union Movement in Nigeria*, Ethiope, Benin City, 1969, p. 241,

[26] Adrian Peace has an excellent piece on these protests. See his, 'Industrial Protest in Ikeja', in de E. Kadt & G.P. Williams (eds.), *Sociology and Development*, Tavistock, London, 1974.

sector by streamlining those of parastatals with rates in the main civil service as well as introducing the unified 17-grade level system. The strikes that followed affected both private and public sectors and most establishments and only ended with the overthrow of General Gowon's government in 1975.

The build-up to the next set of wages commissions covered a period of some six years, from 1975 to 1981, before the Onosode, Cookey and Adamolekun Commissions were established.[27] This was also a period of post-Udoji awards turmoil in the public sector, parastatals expanding very rapidly with grading and differentials constituting aggravated problems, among other developments. The Onosode Commission examined the pay structure and other terms of employment in the parastatals which were all beset by strikes at the time. The employees therein were dissatisfied with their emoluments which were similar to those prevailing in the main civil service. This Commission then erected a new structure for employees in parastatals, they thereafter earning rates that were substantially different from those in the main civil service.

The Cookey Commission did something similar for employees in the universities, establishing a separate University System Scale (USS). The report of the Adamolekun Commission remained unpublished, despite protests from employees in federal polytechnics and the different teachers colleges. However, in 1989 the Babangida regime introduced therein terms of employment closely approximating those of university staff.

The issue of a national minimum wage proper re-surfaced in 1979 in the dying months of Obasanjo's regime when public sector unions, led by the Civil Service Union and the Civil Service Technical Workers Union, sought an improvement on the existing rate of ₦60 a month. The Shagari administration, which eventually inherited the problem along with other grievances of organized labour, was to increase the rate to ₦100 in an unsuccessful effort to stave off a general strike which occurred early May 1981 and lasted only a few days.[28] Thereafter the Nigerian Labour Congress (NLC) on behalf of organized labour asked for a ₦300 monthly minimum wage, pointing accusing fingers at legislators who had unapologetically voted themselves hefty salaries, numerous allowance, fringe benefits and also granted themselves car loans which the government itself had been refusing to give to deserving workers in violation of the ruling of the National Indus-

---

[27] The official titles of these commissions were Presidential Commission on Parastatals, Presidential Commission on Salary and Conditions of Service of University Staff, and Presidential Commission on Conditions of Service of Federal Polytechnics, Colleges of Technology, Advanced Teachers Colleges and National Teachers Colleges respectively.

[28] Details in Otobo, D. 'The Nigerian General Strike of 1981', *Review of African Political Economy*, vol. 22, 1981, and 'The Political Clash in the Aftermath of the 1981 Nigerian General Strike', *Review of African Political Economy*, vol. 25, 1982

trial Court. After tripartite discussions involving the president and his men, employers and organized labour and which were followed by joint session of the Senate and of the House of Representatives, the minimum wage was fixed at ₦125.

Due to successive internal 'reviews', the minimum wage crept up until the economic recession set in proper in 1983, and many state governments and parastatals found themselves owing arrears of salaries upward of six months in several instances. The Buhari/Idiagbon regime, which lasted through 1984 to late August 1985, though cleared arrears of salaries owed to various employees, showed little sympathies for, and no great understanding of, any industrial relations issue, broke all strikes and proscribed affected unions or associations in what appeared to be a single-minded pursuit of 'instilling discipline'. The review of existing rates never arose, especially as the regime had decided on its own to devote as much as 40% of the Gross National Product to servicing external debts,

The minimum wage issue shot to the fore during Babangida's regime because of its adoption of the IMF and World Bank-sponsored structural adjustment programme (SAP), a programme that was instituted in late 1986. Inflation had undermined money wages so badly that even the most conservative of government officials was apprehensive over the possibility of civil unrest. The federal military government in 1989 on its own announced an upward review of wages for the public sector but was forced apparently to abandoned it three months later under pressure from the IMF-increases which had been paid out to workers were recovered through deductions spread over three months.

On 30 January, 1990 General Babangida inaugurated a tripartite minimum wage committee, chaired by Professor Damachi. Its terms of reference were to examine the demand by the NLC for the review of the National Minimum Wage of ₦125 per month laid down in the National Minimum Wage Act No. 6 of 1981, taking into account: i) the provision of the Act; ii) the needs of workers and their families; iii) the effect on employers and high wage/salary earners; iv) the general level **of** wages and salaries in the country, the cost of living and the relative standards of other social groups; v) economic factors, including the requirements of economic development, levels of productivity, related work ethics among workers and the desirability of attaining and maintaining a high level of employment and development; and vi) other options of adjusting minimum wage; vii) to examine any other relevant matters incidental to the Committee's terms of reference; c) arising from a) and b) above, to make appropriate recommendations to the Federal Government for decision to establish a realistic and guaranteed minimum wage.[29]

The chairman presented a 'draft programme of work' before the Committee which was only adopted 'after a critical, protracted and exhaustive exchange of views, comments and amendments (ibid.): These disagreements also plagued the Tripartite Committee's proceedings themselves, almost to a ridiculous extent, throwing serious doubts on whether there was any serious intention to review the minimum wage at all. Incredibly for such a knowledgeable collection of persons and which also drew freely on the services of experts, 'a substantial part of the Committee's time was spent on an attempt to find an acceptable definition or interpretation of *minimum wage* as defined under the National Minimum Wage Act No.6 of 1981' (Report, 6-7). It is worth quoting extensively from the Report:

> There was near impasse in the Committee's proceedings as there was no consensus amongst the three social partners in the Tripartite Committee on the definition or interpretation of minimum wage. The almost total disagreement led to protracted debates. The NLC members of the Committee argued that minimum wage did not include fringe benefits and allowances and emphasized that their understanding of minimum wage under the Act was basic wage and asserted that their definition was consistent with the current practice in Nigeria as no employer paid a worker less than ₦125 per month as basic wage. On the other hand, members on the Employer and Government sides held the view that minimum wage as defined under the Act meant 'total emolument', that is basic wage plus all fringe benefits...(ibid.).

The relevant section of the 1981 Minimum Wage Act says:

> As from the commencement of this Act, it shall be the duty of every employer (except so provided for under this Act) to pay a wage not less than a national minimum wage of ₦125.00 per month to *every* worker under his establishment.

And according to the Report, the NLC delegates thought this section fully coincided with their view that minimum wage excluded fringe benefits and other allowances, and that it also agreed with the current practice as contained in contractual agreements and as reflected in the basic wage paid in the public and private sectors. The 'Labour side, at that juncture,

[29] NLC, *NLC position on Labour Compensation and Collective Bargaining: Minimum Wage, Deregulation of Wages and Collective Bargaining- Aspects of the 1991 Budget Speech*, Lagos, 1991, p. 2. Also confirmed by Bayfau (President of the NLC) and S.O.Z. Ejiofoh: Interviews, March, 1991

challenged NECA, the Government and the Federal Ministry of Employment, Labour and Productivity to produce evidence to the contrary.' (ibid.)

The Government's position was that 'according to the National Minimum Wage Act of 1981, National Minimum Wage means a total emolument of not less than ₦125.00 paid every month to a worker for performing services on the basis of a 40-hour week howsoever the emolument may be defined.' To reconcile both positions, some sought the intervention of the Chairman of the Committee, a suggestion that was rejected by the Labour Side on the ground that 'the Chairman's view/intervention might by opinionated, except it was based on evidence' (ibid., 8-9). A more outrageous suggestion was then offered, and it would not be too difficult to predict which side did:

> a suggestion was made that the Committee should seek for an urgent interpretation of the definition by the Supreme Court through the Federal Ministry of Justice. The view was not acceptable to the Labour Side because it saw the view as a diversionary stance which would waste the Committee's time. Instead, it suggested that the Committees should call for both the Bill and the Hansard containing the records of deliberations on the Act before it was passed by the National Assembly....The Labour Side further proposed that the Committee should fall back on practice if it could not agree on the theoretical definition of minimum wage. NECA and Government members did not accept that suggestion as they argued that *practice* could, and should not be held out as a substitute for the law (ibid., 8).

In the end, 'after protracted arguments and counter-arguments, the issues of definition of minimum wage and of the interpretation of the 1981 Minimum Wage Act were stood down to allow the Committee to move to the next item on its programme...'(ibid., 9). Despite this, there was no consensus either over the quantum of the proposed minimum wage. The NLC had proposed a ₦1400 monthly wage but which it subsequently reduced to ₦450. While NECA, on its part, preferred ₦200.

With no agreement in sight and rumblings from within the ranks of labour over the length of time it was taking the Tripartite Committee to wind up its proceedings and submit a report, reinforced by unfavourable press coverage of the proceedings themselves, General Babangida met with the leadership of the NLC on 4 September, 1990 at which 'Mr. President offered ₦250 basic monthly minimum wage and further stated that this will be in addition to the existing fringe benefits. He also informed the delegation that it is government's intention to add fringe benefits to basic wage/salary in the computation of retirement benefits.'[30] Apparently, Mr. President also insisted on a quick response to his offer.

The President's direct offer to the NLC tended to reduce the influence of officials of the Federal Ministry of Employment, Labour and Productivity, while undermining the Tripartite Committee itself because the latter two had both been displaced or bypassed by bilateral talks. It was therefore not surprising that at its meeting of 7 September, 1990, the other two parties insisted that a) the NLC must channel its reply through the Federal Ministry of Employment, Labour and Productivity, and b) NECA should also submit its own comments on the President's offer to the NLC through the Ministry to Mr. President since the offer was 'aimed at facilitating the work of the Committee!'

The NLC counter proposal of a ₦300 monthly minimum wage was contained in its letter to the President, three days after their bilateral discussions, thereby implicitly rejecting ₦250 offer.[31] The Tripartite Committee clung desperately to the lifeline offered to it by the presidential intervention, being hopelessly deadlocked, and accordingly converted the NLC's reply and that of NECA, which now adopted ₦250 that the NLC had rejected, as part of its recommendations.

And, again, as the NLC correctly indicated, in the Nigerian situation end-of-year or Christmas bonus, other types of bonuses and some other fringe benefits are often a percentage of basic monthly salary or wage. In this wise, claims of minimum wage including fringe benefits can only be made in countries such as Nigeria where low paid workers, especially in the public sector, enjoy very limited range of fringe benefits. In countries where fringe benefits include, apart from holidays with pay, social security benefits, subsidized medical care and health services and housing, educational and recreational facilities, invalidity benefits and family allowances, milk stamps or coupons, such a theoretical and practical misconception would hardly occur.

On the other hand, defining minimum wage to mean ***total emolument*** does no great harm, as long as we are clear in our minds about how much of it is ***basic*** salary/wage. Before the Tripartite Committee was instituted, 'total minimum monthly emolument' for the least paid worker in the public sector was ₦350, made up of ₦125 basic wage/salary, ₦120 housing allowance, ₦30, and ₦60 meal subsidy.[32] Fringe benefits alone come to ₦210, and if as

[30] NLC, *NLC position on Labour Compensation and Collective Bargaining: Minimum Wage, Deregulation of Wages and Collective Bargaining- Aspects of the 1991 Budget Speech*, Lagos, 1991, p. 2. Also confirmed by Bayfau (President of the NLC) and S.O.Z. Ejiofoh: Interviews, March, 1991.

[31] The letter was dated 7 September, 1990, Ref. NLC/NS/E.116/226 and captioned 'Congress Response to the Proposed Basic Minimum Wage of ₦250 per month made by Mr. President and Commander-in-Chief• of the Armed Forces, to Congress Leadership.'

[32] Indeed, all state governments (30 in all) except one have refused to pay the ₦60 meal subsidy,

the President announced, 'accordingly, the federal government has legislated that the National Minimum Wage, understood as total emolument, will as from 1 January 1991 become ₦250 per month,' how much of this is basic salary? It is obvious that what the government has done ten years after is to keep the minimum wage at the 1981 level while drastically reducing fringe benefits. This would be in keeping with the philosophy of SAP and thus with the expectations of the IMF and World Bank. The government could still have achieved the same without creating the not too flattering impression of confusing itself with badly-digested basic industrial relations concepts.

A final point on the total emolument concept is that its prominence in Nigerian industrial relations lexicon and practice would have wide-ranging implications for public and private employers than the delegates seemed to have realized. Total emoluments would be take-home 'pay', in cash and kind, less all deductions.

To review upward simultaneously and periodically these benefits and basic pay, particularly the growing variety of fringe benefits in the private sector and the banking industry, would be moving in the direction of establishing a *living wage* and which might not be a bad thing for workers.

From what has been said so far, the inevitable conclusion would be that neither the government nor its representatives and Committee could not reach a compromise on a particular figure, the Chairman decided to refer the positions of the two parties to the government for a ruling' (para. 11). The government's ruling came three months later when the President in his 1991 budget speech imposed a ₦250 monthly minimum wage, and defined minimum wage as 'total emolument', to include fringe benefits. The ₦250, at least for the public sector, therefore included transport and rent allowances, plus meal subsidy.

Comment

Anyone remotely familiar with industrial relations legislation and practice in Nigeria would have great difficulty in either sympathising or agreeing with the arguments of government's and NECA's representatives on the Tripartite Committee. It is truly remarkable, to put it rather mildly, for these representatives to insist almost ten years after, during which government agencies and private employers that had more 50 employees paid ₦125 as monthly minimum basic salary/wage excluding fringe benefits, that the 1981 Wage Act included fringe benefits in its definition of minimum wage. If their interpretation was correct and that of the NLC wrong, then the ₦125 would have included both transport and rent allowances and which has clearly not been the case since 1981.

As we see below, the original intention might have been to include fringe

resistance which workers are still protesting against

benefits, but once practice deviated from this for whatever reason, NECA attempting to turn back the hands of the clock, as it were, was likely to receive little sympathy in light of current economic circumstances; still much less sympathy for the government's position, being largely responsible for getting employers to follow its decision in this regard.

For another, fringe benefits hardly ever form part of a basic wage or salary as the NLC delegates correctly pointed out. Indeed, as an ILO manual clearly spells out:

> Ordinary wages are those paid regularly, usually at weekly, fortnightly or monthly intervals. They include payments in money and in kind, the amounts earned by piece-workers, earnings under other incentive plans, and regular cost-of-living allowances or bonuses. They also include payments for overtime and work done on Sundays and national holidays. All these payments are generally directly related to work done. ***Fringe benefits are other payments or benefits enjoyed by the workers which are additions to the labour costs of the employers. They are costs borne by employers arising from the employment of workers but for which no specific work is done.***[33]

From this survey of the various attempts that have been made to establish wage rates and minimum wages in Nigeria, it is reasonably apparent that the process has been a chequered one, fraught with conflict, disingenuous arguments, and resistance on the part of the State and of private employers. And almost unfailingly bilateral talks between organised labour and state authorities, after some protests and intense pressure mounted by the former, would seem to achieve quicker results than tripartite discussions involving private employers. Evidence also indicates that the least productive of these tripartite committees has been the 1990 Tripartite Minimum Wage Committee.

Those representatives of private employers on the Tripartite Committee apparently had no intention *to increase the national minimum* wage. From the Committee's terms of reference, that included 'the needs of workers and their families', 'the general level of wages and salaries', 'the cost of living' and 'relative living standards of other social groups', it seems clear that these latter considerations could not have been reflected in the decision to impose ₦250 total monthly emolument. In 1981, at an exchange rate of US$1.25 to 1 Naira, ₦125 monthly minimum wage was the equivalent of US$156.25; ₦250 at 9.98:1 official rate of exchange in 1991 comes to a mere US$25.5. And when you factor into the equation differences in rates of inflation for 1981 and 1991, the result is appalling. In this regard, we have established

[33] ILO, *Wages: A Workers' Educational Manual*, Geneva, 1982 edn., p. 70

how the prices and cost of food, housing, and of inter- and intra-city transport fares increased by anything between 300% and 1000% in the period 1987-1990 alone!

The other evidence pointing to the unserious altitude of the other two parties to the minimum wage could be discerned in their approaches to *notion* of a minimum wage. The chairman and those that represented NECA and the government are experts in their own right. Some of them have been involved in the establishment and workings of the Industrial Arbitration Panel and of the National Industrial Court, the latter being the final arbiter in industrial relations matters. Yet, if the NLC delegation had not strongly resisted, they were to refer the issue to the Supreme Court for *a* ruling! How could there have been a misunderstanding or distortion of the fact that the 1981 Minimum Wage Act as implemented made ₦125 the minimum monthly salary and that fringe benefits are extras? It is no defence at all to say, as NECA and government's delegates argued, that 'practice' could and should not be held out as a substitute for the law. If the practice is based on, and derives from the said Act, and carried out by public and private employers themselves, what distinction is being drawn here? To be fair to private employers and NECA, as alluded to above, it should be pointed out that as originally conceived in 1981, the famous ₦125 monthly wage *was supposed to include fringe benefits.* But the government had enormous problems implementing it in the public sector as differentials between Grade Levels 01 to 06 almost disappeared and workers affected began to protest. In the end, the federal government simply converted the total emolument to monthly basic salary so as to maintain salary differentials among and between the different levels (01- 06). Naturally, NECA likely wanted to avoid repeat performance of 1990 when private sector employers were coerced by government into adopting ₦125 as basic monthly salary.

MINIMUM WAGE DETERMINATION SINCE 1981

Several attempts have been made by parties in the industrial relations system to modify the national minimum wage since 1981, successful outcomes being captured in National Minimum Wage Act 2000; National Minimum Wage (Amendment) Act, 2011, National Minimum Wage Act 2019, and National Minimum Wage (Amendment) Act 2024.

After President Shagari, Nigeria experienced several military coups, with Generals Buhari, Babangida, and Abacha as military dictators, where such demands for wage review were a lot more difficult as already chronicled.

When General Abdulsalami Abubakar became the fort-holding head of state in 1998, the minimum wage for federal workers had become ₦450, and his government announced a move upwards from ₦450 ($5) to ₦5,280 ($60).

In 2000, a year after the return to a democratically elected legislature and government, the Federal Government reviewed the minimum wage upwards to ₦5,500 ($55). As generally known, the economy, which deteriorated during the five years of military rule from 1993-1998, is one of the factors that likely propelled President Olusegun Obasanjo's civilian-led government to pursue economic reforms to combat rising inflation and stabilise the economy. These reforms led the government to increase the minimum wage to ₦7,500 in 2004.

By 2010, just before Goodluck Jonathan became president, the national minimum wage had become ₦7,500 ($50) as noted but his government was able to increase it to ₦18,000 in March 2011, a 140% margin. This situation persisted for another five years despite calls for a review till Buhari became president in 2015. In 2016, the NLC made a formal request to review the wage from ₦18,000 to ₦56,000 and after series of negotiations/meetings, the Buhari administration and the organised labour settled for ₦30,000, an increase by 66.67%.

From 2018, the ₦30,000 was clearly inadequate in the face of inflation and consequent hardships exacerbated by Covid-19 circumstances. More to the point, this upsurge in demand for an increase in the minimum wage intensified after the government's economic policies, such as the removal of some subsidies and the so-called 'unification' of the naira rates (official exchange rates vis-a-vis black market rates) in the closing phase of Buhari's presidency, led to the *de facto* devaluation of the naira and pushed inflation to record levels. Indeed, a mere three days to 2023 presidential elections, Naira notes (cash) were inexplicably and deliberately withdrawn from circulation nationwide, an unprecedented measure in the country's monetary and fiscal history, a move which brought prices of goods and services to such numbing and shocking levels citizens are still battling to comprehend, let alone accept and cope with.[34]

It is with these developments, the widespread consequent social and economic unease and hardship, that organised labour and other civil society organisations began denouncing the state and type of official socioeconomic policies and demanding an upward review of the national minimum for starters, that on 30 January 2024, the federal government inaugurated a 37-member Tripartite Committee on National Minimum Wage, with its secretariat the National Salaries, Incomes and Wages Commission (NSIWC) and its chairman, Ekpo U. O. Nta, as Secretary and Alhaji Bukar Goni Aji, former Head of Civil Service of the Federation as Chairperson, to review the

[34] Equally baffling has been the prosecution of the then Governor of the Central Bank, Emefiele, for that infamous withdrawal of cash from the system, among other charges, as if the Minister of Finance, and President Buhari had nothing to do with it.

National Minimum Wage.[35]

As can be expected and from the moves and counter-moves, formal and informal contacts and negotiations and co-existence of differing claims of organised private sector and organised labour as revealed in our review of previous minimum wage determinations, the 2024 situation was no different. The inaugural meeting of the Tripartite Committee on National Minimum wage was essentially for briefing, its crucial meetings being those after all the Public Hearings organised by the Secretariat in the six geo-political zones for all interested parties to present and defend their respective proposals. Again, what transpired at these zonal public hearings, as was the situation with pre-colonial, colonial and immediate post-Independence geographical and socio-economic differences already discussed, demands by State Governments, branches of NLC and TUCN being influenced more by local circumstances. The Organised Private Sector, represented by NECA, MAN, NACCIMA, other subsectoral employers' organisations, government and regulatory agencies and the state/zonal branches of the NLC and TUC, canvassed various amounts at the hearings, in social and other media. Nor were State Governments and the Federal Government in unison.

---

[35] These are the nominated members, some of who sent representatives, especially on the federal government side. **Federal Government** , Hon. Nkeiruka Onyejeocha, Hon. Minister of State, Labour and Employment (Representing Hon. Minister of Labour and Employment); 2. Mr. Wale Edun, Hon. Minister of Finance & Coordinating Minister of the Economy; 3. Alhaji Atiku Bagudu, Hon. Minister of Budget Economic Planning; 4. Dr. (Mrs) Yemi Esan, Head of the Civil Service of the Federation; 5. Dr. Nnamdi Maurice Mbaeri, Permanent Secretary, GSO. OSGF; 6. Ekpo Nta, Esq, Chairman/CEO, NSIWC – Member/Secretary; **State Government** , 1. Alh. Mohammed Umar Bago, Governor, Niger State- representative from North Central; 2. Sen. Bala Mohammed, Governor Bauchi State- representative from North East; 3. Alh. Umar Dikko Radda, Governor Katsina State-representative from North West; 4. Prof. Charles Soludo, Governor, Anambra State- representative from the South East; 5. Sen. Ademola Adeleke, Governor, Osun State- representative from South West; 6. Mr. Otu Bassey Edet, Governor, Cross River State- representative from South South. **Nigeria Labour Congress (NLC)** 1. Comrade Joe Ajaero, President, NLC; 2. Comrade Emmanuel Ugboaja, mni; 3. Comrade Prince Adeyanju Adewale; 4. Comrade Ambali Akeem Olatunji; 5. Comrade Benjamin Anthony; 6. Prof. Theophilius Ndukuba. **Trade Union Congress of Nigeria (TUC)** 1. Comrade (Engr) Festus Osifo, President, TUC; 2. Comrade Tommy Etim Okon, PhD, Deputy President I, 3. TUC; Comrade Kayode Surajudeen Alakija, 4. Deputy President II; Comrade Jimoh Oyibo, 5. Deputy President. III; Comrade Nuhu A. Toro, Secretary-General 6. Comrade Hafusatu Shuaib, Chairperson, TUC Women Commission Employers' **Consultative Association (NECA)-** 1. Adewale-Smatt Oyerinde, Director-General, NECA; 2. Mr. Chuma Nwankwo; 3. Mr. Thompson Akpabio **Nigeria Association of Chambers of Commerce, Industry, Mines and Agriculture (NACCIMA)** 1. Asiwaju (Dr) Michael Olawale-Cole, National President; 2. Hon. (Dr) Ahmed Rabiu, National Vice President 3. Chief Humphrey Ngonadi (NPOM), National Life President **National Association of Small and Medium Enterprise (NASME)** 1. Dr. Abdulrashid Yerima, President & Chairman of Council; 2. Hon. Theophilus Nnorom Okwuchukwu, **Private Sector representative;** Dr. Muhammed Nura Bello, Zonal Vice President, North West **Manufacturers Association of Nigeria (MAN)** 1. Mrs. Grace Omo-Lamai, Human Resource Director, Nigerian Breweries; 2. Segun Ajayi-Kadir, mni, Director-General, MAN; 3. Lady Ada Chukwudozie, Managing Director, Dozzy Oil and Gas Limited. Professor Dafe Otobo, Comrade Issa Aremu and one other were the main consultants.

At the South-East zonal public hearing in Enugu, the TUC proposed ₦447,000, and the NLC ₦540,000 and none of the Governors was in attendance. For the South-South, both central labour bodies proposed ₦850,000, where the Governors sent respective representatives but expressed their readiness to accept whatever rate that finally emerged. In the North-West, both central labour bodies proposed ₦485,000 in the absence of the Governors, apart from Governor Dikko Radda of Katsina State who sent a representative. For South-West, held in Lagos, Governor Sanwolu hosted and Finance Minister Wale Edun chaired the event, where both the NLC and TUCN proposed ₦450,500 and ₦497,000 respectively and suggested minimum should be being on the Exclusive List, as the Governor with pride drew attention to the fact "that Lagos State has implemented a minimum wage of ₦41,500, surpassing the standards set by many other states in the region."

The respective arguments of various tripartite spokespersons were straightforward. The State Governors, while accepting the need for an upward review of the minimum wage, they claim they cannot afford the rates acceptable to the federal government given less revenue accruing to them by existing revenue allocation formula that is skewed in favour of the federal government. Second, by the same token, each state should be allowed to negotiate with respective workers not only because of peculiarities, but also to conform to a true federal system of governance. Third, given current economic circumstances and deficit financing and state governments' inability to freely obtain foreign loans and engage in income/profit-earning ventures, unlike the federal government, the capacity to bear current costs is limited, and would be much worse by virtue of a new minimum wage. And, for a partly co-ordinated approach among governors, North-West governors shunned the parley with their South-West colleagues, saying it would be hard to sustain higher wages for their workers without a significant adjustment in some of the components of the national fiscal and monetary policies, such as revenue sharing formula.

At the national level, both TUC and NLC advocated ₦615,000 as the new national wage. The Nigerian Governors Forum (NGF) protested, arguing that some states were still struggling to pay the current ₦30,000, not to mention their own proposed ₦60,000. The NGF's proposal of ₦60,000 was instantly rejected by organised labour. The Federal Government proposed ₦62,000 but was rejected by the NLC and TUC, the NLC which having scaled down its own rate to ₦250,000 and demanding a review every two years.

However, after months of back and forth between the federal government, tripartite committee on national minimum wage and labour unions, NLC-TUC representatives accepted the minimum wage of ₦70,000 after a meeting with President Bola Tinubu, the latter who also pledged to review the law every three years. Six months on, in January 2025, since the minimum wage was signed into law, many workers are still being owed arrears, in addition to many apprehensively watching out for full implementation by all state governments. Interestingly, some Governors are touting such figures as ₦75,000 and ₦80,000 as approved rate for their states.

On a more cheerful note, NECA, whose Director General is Adewale Oyerinde, clearly frowned at the notion or suggestion of any state government "not being able to pay" the national minimum wage as is:

> "We have moved away from the context of hope, the reality now is what we should face. The reality for all stakeholders whether at the federal, state or local government is that ₦70,000 has come to stay and everybody should align with the law, except those that are exempted.
>
> "The issue of having funds to pay the ₦70,000 also does not arise because it is no longer hidden that the Federal Government has been consistently supporting the state governments."
>
> "The allocations to state governments have increased proportionately. So, with a little fiscal discipline, no state should complain that they can't pay ₦70,000 as approved by the president."[36]

Some state governments appear to have upped the stakes in the continuing but silent questioning of the sufficiency of the official national minimum wage by approving higher amounts. So far, Akwa Ibom ₦80,000, Delta State ₦77,000 Enugu State ₦80,000, Gombe State ₦71,500, Kebbi State ₦75,000, Kogi State ₦72,000, Lagos State ₦85,000, Niger State ₦80,000, Ogun State ₦77,000, Ondo State ₦73,000, and Rivers State ₦85,000.

Finally, as for state governments and the federal government and their agencies, the implementation of the new minimum wage would inevitably trigger a readjustment of wages and salaries across all levels in the public sector so as to arrive at new differentials within and between salary scales of all positions. This is what led to the inauguration, by the federal government, of a 16-member Committee on Consequential Adjustments in Salaries of Civil Servants, eight members each from the federal government and public sector organised labour.

When the new overall payload is known, given the times, especially general inflation and declining revenue-earning capacity and thus mounting budgeting challenges, it is more than likely that a comprehensive restructuring of pay levels in the public sector will occur soon enough.

---

[36] Leadership News website, 7 January 2024

Chapter 15

THE 2024 NATIONAL MINIMUM WAGE IN NIGERIA – POSITION PAPER

INTRODUCTION

On 30 January 2024, the federal government inaugurated a 37-member Tripartite Committee on National Minimum Wage, with its secretariat the National Salaries, Incomes and Wages Commission (NSIWC) and its chairman, Ekpo U. O. Nta, as Secretary and Alhaji Bukar Goni Aji, former Head of Civil Service of the Federation as Chairperson, to review the National Minimum Wage.[1]

---

[1] These are the nominated members, some of who sent representatives, especially on the federal government side. **Federal Government** , Hon. Nkeiruka Onyejeocha, Hon. Minister of State, Labour and Employment (Representing Hon. Minister of Labour and Employment); 2. Mr. Wale Edun, Hon. Minister of Finance & Coordinating Minister of the Economy; 3. Alhaji Atiku Bagudu, Hon. Minister of Budget Economic Planning; 4. Dr. (Mrs) Yemi Esan, Head of the Civil Service of the Federation; 5. Dr. Nnamdi Maurice Mbaeri, Permanent Secretary, GSO. OSGF; 6. Ekpo Nta, Esq, Chairman/CEO, NSIWC – Member/Secretary; **State Government** , 1. Alh. Mohammed Umar Bago, Governor, Niger State- representative from North Central; 2. Sen. Bala Mohammed, Governor Bauchi State- representative from North East; 3. Alh. Umar Dikko Radda, Governor Katsina State- representative from North West; 4. Prof. Charles Soludo, Governor, Anambra State- representative from the South East; 5. Sen. Ademola Adeleke, Governor, Osun State- representative from South West; 6. Mr. Otu Bassey Edet, Governor, Cross River State- representative from South South. **Nigeria Labour Congress (NLC)** 1. Comrade Joe Ajaero, President, NLC; 2. Comrade Emmanuel Ugboaja, mni; 3. Comrade Prince Adeyanju Adewale; 4. Comrade Ambali Akeem Olatunji; 5. Comrade Benjamin Anthony; 6. Prof. Theophilius Ndukuba. **Trade Union Congress of Nigeria (TUC)** 1. Comrade (Engr) Festus Osifo, President, TUC; 2. Comrade Tommy Etim Okon, PhD, Deputy President I, 3. TUC; Comrade Kayode Surajudeen Alakija, 4. Deputy President II; Comrade Jimoh Oyibo, 5. Deputy President. III; Comrade Nuhu A. Toro, Secretary-General 6. Comrade Hafusatu Shuaib, Chairperson, TUC Women Commission **Employers' Consultative Association (NECA)-** 1. Adewale-Smatt Oyerinde, Director-General, NECA; 2. Mr. Chuma Nwankwo; 3. Mr. Thompson Akpabio **Nigeria Association of Chambers of Commerce, Industry, Mines and Agriculture (NACCIMA)** 1. Asiwaju (Dr) Michael Olawale-Cole, National President; 2. Hon. (Dr) Ahmed Rabiu, National Vice President 3. Chief Humphrey Ngonadi (NPOM), National Life President **National Association of Small and Medium Enterprise (NASME)** 1. Dr. Abdulrashid Yerima, President & Chairman of Council; 2. Hon. Theophilus Nnorom Okwuchukwu, **Private Sector representative;** Dr. Muhammed Nura Bello, Zonal Vice President, North West **Manufacturers Association of Nigeria (MAN)** 1. Mrs. Grace Omo-Lamai, Human Resource Director, Nigerian Breweries; 2. Segun Ajayi-Kadir, mni, Director-General, MAN; 3. Lady Ada Chukwudozie, Managing Director, Dozzy Oil and Gas Limited. Professor Dafe Otobo, Comrade Issa Aremu and one other were the main consultants.

The Committee had the following terms of reference:

i) to consult all stakeholders on the issue of National Minimum Wage;
ii) to consider the National Minimum Wage in the context of the dynamics of the national economy; and
iii) to recommend a realistic and practical National Minimum Wage to the government.

And, as detailed in the chapter on the politics of minimum wage in Nigeria, the Committee also organised Public Hearings in the six geo-political zones of North-West, North-Central, North-East, South-East, South-South and South-West to garner and collate relevant information for its objectives as stated.

The services of some consultants were also engaged, including Professor Dafe Otobo, Issa Aremu, and the Director-General of the Michael Imoudu National Institute for Labour Studies (MINILS) who made presentations at the second sitting of the Committee that of Professor Otobo titled "National Minimum Wage, Living Wage and National Interest."

This chapter, however, is basically the contents of two things: 1) an assignment to me to comment on the terms of reference of the Subcommittee on New National Minimum Wage Recommendation; 2) a commissioned Position Paper on wider issues that may assist in facilitating decision on and implementation processes for the consideration of the Subcommittee. The terms of reference for the Comments were:

1. Recommend an appropriate Minimum Wage amount to the Committee that is equitable, affordable and sustainable;
2. Critically examine all sectors of the economy to identify wage growth trends;
3. Identify minimum and maximum sectoral earnings and establish balance earnings across all sectors; and
4. Identify and analyse various factors affecting minimum wage in the economy and suggest ways to address them.

My indirect apology for providing a not-so-comprehensive version had to do with mostly shortness of time given for its submission, thus observations are largely desk-based review research, while some on evidence-based data.

The salient point, however, is that the Position Paper tries to draw attention away from squabbling over quantum of monies to be approved to the contexts for allocating such amounts in the first place – which give relevant values and expenditure. This way, whatever amount is agreed upon as the new national minimum wage, the context can reveal to anyone, whatever prejudices and preferences harboured, how sensible and meaningful.

COMMENTS ON TERMS OF REFERENCE OF THE SUB-COMMITTEE ON NEW NATIONAL MINIMUM WAGE RECOMMENDATION

TOR 4

IDENTIFY AND ANALYSE VARIOUS FACTORS AFFECTING MINIMUM WAGE IN THE ECONOMY AND SUGGEST WAYS TO ADDRESS THEM

The MINIMUM WAGE IS INSUFFICIENT TO PROVIDE WORKERS WITH NECESSITIES (e.g. food, shelter, transportation, electricity/gas and clothing) they require for a healthy lifestyle. Obviously, minimum wage increases never catch up with REAL COST OF LIVING. Some of the factors that routinely AFFECT ECONOMIC AND SOCIAL EFFECTIVENESS of a MINIMUM WAGE in the economy are now listed immediately below.

HOUSING – rents and housing generally in urban centres have spiked unbelievably high, including price of land, cement, sand and other building construction items and labour. It is strongly recommended that HOUSING BE PROVIDED CLOSE TO PLACES OF WORK at low rent while in service, not for sale. Those for sale should be optional and not take precedence.

TRANSPORTATION – Transportation costs are immediate and daily, whether to and from work or purchase of various personal items and social activities/engagements. Vehicle owners, drivers and their associations and certain regulatory authorities, aside from fuel costs, tend to influence rates which passengers are charged per trip. Official buses to pick up public servants at and return to designated points in the morning and close of work in urban centres comes highly recommended and is practised elsewhere. Fare may be heavily subsidised to buy fuel and pay drivers or free. Same for train services where available and endeavour to provide same in major cities in the medium run.

HEALTH SERVICES – Costs and availability are challenging, a good many more comfortable Nigerians resort to medical services in Dubai, India, European Union, UK, USA and other lands. It is recommended that special subsidised arrangements with all teaching hospitals and suitably located private hospitals and clinics in urban centres for medical services be entered into. If, for example, Constituency Allowances/Projects of legislators include the construction and equipping of a health centre, the country will be in much better position medically, lower costs of medical services in no time at all and attract foreign patients too.

ELECTRICITY – this is indisputably the most shameful national failure where pampered suppliers for a few hours of electricity any day "estimate" charges while refusing to provide meters; and where provided, charge tenants exorbitantly both for pre-paid meters and units of electricity consumed. The concept of categorising consumers and imposing higher rate per unit used on some, frankly not only perverse and reflects the twisted logic of greed, is puzzling and shameful and can only happen in Nigeria. As it were, it is now a favour to have power supply for 20 hours and get penalised for that seeming luxury! The so-called National Grid, like socio-political administration of states, should be DECENTRALISED. And, on the other side of power generation, Generators are now so expensive, as well as diesel and petrol to run them if available! Clearly, effective subsidy regime is here required for working people and to render the Minimum Wage more useful.

FUEL AND OTHER REFINED PETROLEUM PRODUCTS - Once refining and distribution of refined petroleum products, INCLUDING GAS, can emerge from extreme corruption and sabotage in petroleum and related sectors, the immense costs and aggravations associated with 1) transportation; 2) cooking; 3) supply chain and logistics of small and medium scale businesses; 4) improving upon critical power needs of private and public medical facilities; 5) critical power supply requirements of laboratories in training and educational institutions for workers children as pupils and students; and 6) reduced expenses of meals at eateries for the general public, to mention a few, will be diminished considerably. But, in the interim, sanctions have to be deployed swiftly and effectively.

FOOD AT WORK – Either suitable allowance is paid, or heavily subsidised meals and drink at the workplace canteens or both be institutionalised.

MARKETS AND ROAD TRAFFIC ADMINISTRATION – Markets contain most food items workers and the public need and, sadly, the activities of regulatory bodies/agencies and of various private and community-driven persons have impacted adversely on prices of items on sale daily. Simply put, there is too much brazen official and unofficial extortion of money from transporters, market women and men: 1) in course of conveying items to be sold; and 2) random charges for space occupied within the markets – all avoidable extra costs that are passed on to buyers in form of ever-rising prices. Too many agencies, local government and community agents wield too much power here and must be checked.

BANKING SERVICES – Banks have for increased monopoly profits deliberately facilitated "cash scarcity" impression in the economy by:

i) restricting cash available from usual or routine over-the-counter withdrawal to a few thousands, some preventing it altogether;
ii) deliberately underfunding their ATMs where interminably long and rowdy queues and petty crime are the norm; and
iii) literally drowning POS operators with cash, most of whom are agents of and owned by the banks and bank officials.

One sad and immediate consequence has been that most of the petty traders and market women, transporters and other small businesses that patronise POS operators tend to increase prices of their services and items daily, increasing cost of living brazenly without any link to American dollar exchange rate whatsoever. It is now difficult for the price of any commodity or item to remain the same for a few days!

STATE MINISTRY OF LABOUR - States must have their respective Ministry of Labour to create a coordinating council/committee with the Federal Ministry of Labour that will now compare notes with other stakeholders in a Tripartite Panel or Committee. This does not take away the right of Federal Minister of Labour to represent the country at ILO meetings. It certainly is a more sensible and inclusive arrangement for the stakeholders irrespective of geographical location.

MINIMUM WAGE REGULATION CONSTITUTIONAL STATUS - Minimum Wage regulation should be on the Concurrent Legislative List. The cost and standard of living are not the same nationwide and a majority of working people are located in the states. This is why the regulation of minimum wage should not be within the Exclusive Jurisdiction of the Federal Government. The Constitution should be amended to move Item 34 off the Exclusive Legislative List, enabling State Governments, in tripartite mode, legislate minimum wage applicable to their respective employers and workers while ensuring and entrenching True Federalism indisputably best for a multi-ethnic society/country. But, it must be noted that the National Minimum Wage rate must be the lowest that must be paid in ALL STATES.

ENFORCEMENT - The existing statutory provisions for sorting out wage-related disputes need to be revisited, partly for the obvious reason they have not been very effective in application and interpretation, especially speeding up conciliation and adjudication efforts of the IAP and NIC. Both institutions should have a mandatory TRIPARTITE STRUCTURE OF STAKEHOLDERS. Sections 9 and 13 of Minimum Wage Act (2019) should be strengthened.

MINIMUM WAGE AND OUTSOURCING - SECTION 14 provides ready excuse for an employer to subcontract and outsource work in full knowledge the "another person" or "agent" will pay lower rate. This is common practice in the Oil and Gas industry especially. Both the employer and "other person" should be penalised if the Act is contravened, not the latter alone as currently provided for in the Act.

RMAFC AND NSIWC - PUBLIC SECTOR WAGE POLICIES/REGULATION

Even if there is the merger of Revenue Mobilisation Allocation and Fiscal Commission (RMAFC) and of the National Salaries Incomes and Wages Commission (NSIWC), the INTERNAL ARRANGEMENT should be such as to ensure the **NSIWC Division** remains saddled with compensation management of **all public servants, including political office holders**, while the **RMAFC Division** focuses solely on revenue mobilisation and fiscal matters within and between federal and state authorities. A less wieldy and thus more efficient option would be both agencies co-existing, with RMAFC not involved in the regulation of public sector employees' compensation in any form.

RATIO OF FEDERAL AND STATES REVENUE SHARING FORMULA

National Assembly to approve 52.68% for State Governments and 26.72% for Federal Government of federally distributable revenue, since majority of citizens and workers are in the States. The logic of number thus shows that more damage can be and is done to welfare of citizens and of workers by policies of state governments than those of federal – take primary and secondary school education as an example where most workers children are, with thousands of young children in some states on the streets as routine beggars, not to speak of inadequate infrastructure, facilities and funding where educational institutions exist.

TOR 3

IDENTIFY MINIMUM AND MAXIMUM SECTORAL EARNINGS AND ESTABLISH BALANCE EARNINGS ACROSS ALL SECTORS

The major sectors in the Nigerian economy are:

1. Agriculture – Crop Production, Livestock, Forestry and Fishing;

2. Services: Finance and Insurance, Telecommunications, Health, Electricity, Entertainment;
3. Manufacturing: Food, Beverage and Tobacco, Textile, Apparel and Footwear, Oil Refining, Plastic and Rubber Products, Wood and Wood products, Non-Metallic Products, Chemical and Pharmaceutical Products, Basic Metal, Iron and Steel, Other Manufacturing;
4. Construction – Infrastructural (Bridges, Dams, etc.) Roads, Houses, etc.;
5. Mining and Quarrying – Oil & Gas, Other Minerals, etc.;
6. Trade and Retail;
7. Transport, Information and Communication;
8. Other Sectors – Accommodation/Real Estate, ICT, Scientific services

- Not all working persons in the labour market received any of the national minimum wage established so far, especially casual or so-called menial workers. Some of them are in bars, restaurants, makeup parlours and schools and account for nearly 50% of all minimum-wage workers – waiters, waitresses, porters, and bartenders. While others are also salespersons for breweries, shops/stores attendants, security guards, drivers, maintenance crew, bricklayers and labourers in transportation and construction industries.
- Second, accurate records of actual emoluments across sectors have hardly been compiled over the years, particularly in the so-called informal sector where most working persons are found. Whichever the case, formal and informal, such surveys and compilation require time, competent hands and other resources to get done.
- But, the factors that influence basic wages and salaries across sectors, including yearly increments and allowances, are: i) educational qualifications; ii) Sector and Job role/Title; iii) work experience; iv) location; v) financial strength and HRM policies of employing units; and vi) type and origins of business organisation. Of these factors, the attributes or peculiarities of EACH SECTOR, TYPE AND ORIGINS OF BUSINESS ORGANISATION AND JOB ROLES STAY MORE SIGNIFICANT; vii) for example, in the oil and gas industry, some hands located outside cities earn more for the same job role despite higher living costs in urban centres.
- Significantly, also, most of the employment opportunities that exist in the private sector do not have clearly laid out hierarchical positions, offering predictable basic rates and range of allowances, as in the ministries, departments and agencies/parastatals. MOST TERMS ARE SUBJECT TO AD HOC NEGOTIATIONS, WITH TASKS SHARED

BETWEEN AND AMONG SMALL TEAMS TO BE ACCOMPLISHED WITHIN SPECIFIED TIME-FRAME THAT ELIMINATE NOTIONS OF "CAREER" AND CAREER PROGRESSION.

HIGHEST MONTHLY PAYMENTS ACROSS SECTORS

Most rates payable by multinational companies in the oil and gas sector have been deliberately left out since they belong to a class of their own and of little relevance to the National Minimum Wage. Generally, monthly salaries range ₦450,000 and ₦3,500,000 depending role and company.

Banker	₦350,000 - ₦1,450,000
Captains (Airlines)	₦500,000 - ₦3,000, 000
Chartered Accountant	₦150,000 - ₦1,550,000
IT Security Analyst/Ethical Hackers/ Programmers	₦145,000 - ₦600,000
Judges	₦530,000 - ₦1,650,000
Lawyers	₦150,000 - ₦1,330,000
Medical Doctor	₦300,000 - ₦1,500,000
Nurse (middle/matrons)	₦150,000 – ₦250,000
Nurse (Private facilities)	₦150,000 - ₦650,000
Petroleum Engineer	₦200,000 - ₦1,000,000
Pharmacist	₦150,000 - ₦850,000
Pilots (Airlines)	₦200,000 - ₦500,000
Project Manager	₦279,000 - ₦804,000
Sailor	₦220,000 - ₦1,400,000
Software Engineer	₦250,000 - ₦1,600,000
Surgeons	₦630,000 - ₦2,500,000
Telecommunications Engineer	₦220,000 - ₦1,200,000
University Lecturer/Professors/	₦200, 000 – ₦650,000
Senior-level NNPC Staff Salary[2]	₦500,000 – ₦5,000,000
Entry-level NNPC Staff Salary	₦150,000 – ₦300,000
Entry-level Chevron Engineer	₦100,000 – ₦500,000
Senior-Level Chevron Engineer	₦1,000,000 – ₦5,000,000
Entry-Level Chevron Geoscientist	₦100,000 – ₦300,000
Senior-Level Chevron Geoscientist	₦500,000 – ₦3,000,000

[2] The NNPC group includes Nigerian Petroleum Development Company (NPDC), Nigerian Gas Company (NGC), Products and Pipelines Marketing Company (PPMC), Integrated Data Services Limited (IDSL) National Engineering and Technical Company Limited (NETCO), Hydrocarbon Services Nigeria Limited (HYSON), Warri Refinery and Petrochemical Co. Limited (WRPC), Kaduna Refinery and Petrochemical Co. Limited (KRPC), Port Harcourt Refining Co. Limited (PHRC), NNPC Retail.

AVERAGE SALARIES ACROSS SECTORS

Agriculture, Food Industry	₦87,480 - ₦215,412
Administration	₦47,684 - ₦178,720
Banking	₦350,052 - ₦561,377
Finance, Accountancy	₦80,108 - ₦329,934
Car Assembly	₦100,203 - ₦257,074
Chemical Industry	₦105,632 - ₦224,976
Construction & Real Estate	₦67,314 - ₦257,986
Customer Support	₦81,204 - ₦250,582
Drivers (oil and gas)	₦150,000 - N170,000
Drivers (banking and finance)	₦50,000 - ₦100,000
Drivers (commercial) [3]	₦50,000 - ₦70,000
Electrical & Power Engineering	₦88,085 - ₦299,502
Information Technology	₦102,383 - ₦548,130
Insurance	₦85,922 - ₦309,512
Journalism, Printing Arts & Media	₦99,907 - ₦211,950
Nurse (entry) point)	₦130,000
Textile, Leather, Apparel Industry	₦50,000 - ₦60,000

LOWEST MONTHLY WAGES ACROSS SECTORS

Bartender/Waitress	0 - ₦ 50,000
Cafe Attendants	₦ 15,000
Cleaners	₦ 20,000 - ₦ 30,000
Clerk	₦ 32,000
Computer Operator	₦ 15,000 - ₦ 30,000
Factory Odd Jobs	₦ 15,000 - ₦ 35,000
Janitor, Cleaner	₦ 25,000 - ₦ 40,000
Laundry Staff	₦ 25,000 - ₦ 35,000
Lawyer – Entry point	₦ 35,000 – ₦ 45,000
Messenger, Office Assistant	₦ 25,000 - ₦ 40,000

[3] Many commercial drivers get paid per trip, depending on route or destination, ranging ₦20,000 to ₦40,000 of full load (7-40 passengers, depending on type of vehicle). Multiple trips, say 3, in a week earn them between 100,000 and 300,000 and multiply by four to get monthly earnings when vehicles do not break down and not sent for servicing.

Security Guard	₦ 35,000 - ₦ 40,000
Teaching	₦ 35,000 - ₦ 50,000

FEDERAL CIVIL SERVANTS SALARIES

The Consolidated Public Service Salary Structure (CONPSS) is used to determine the salaries of civil servants in Nigeria. The salary structure has 12 grades, ranging from Grade Level 01 (the lowest) to Grade Level 12 (the highest). Other agencies/parastatals have different salary structures, many earning higher than what is available in the main Civil Service or Ministries. The salary scale for each grade level in CONPSS as of 2024 is as follows:

- Grade Level 01: ₦30,000 – ₦33,000 per month
- Grade Level 02: ₦34,000 – ₦38,000 per month
- Grade Level 03: ₦43,000 – ₦54,000 per month
- Grade Level 04: ₦48,000 – ₦63,000 per month
- Grade Level 05: ₦58,000 – ₦77,000 per month
- Grade Level 06: ₦65,000 – ₦87,000 per month
- Grade Level 07: ₦75,000 – ₦100,000 per month
- Grade Level 08: ₦88,000 – ₦148,000 per month
- Grade Level 09: ₦105,000 – ₦170,000 per month
- Grade Level 10: ₦125,000 – ₦210,000 per month
- Grade Level 11: ₦190,000 – ₦290,000 per month
- Grade Level 12: ₦255,000 – ₦700,000 per month

ToR 1

RECOMMEND AN APPROPRIATE MINIMUM WAGE AMOUNT TO THE COMMITTEE THAT IS EQUITABLE, AFFORDABLE AND SUSTAINABLE

- The New National Minimum Wage, based on current cost of living indices, could be anything from ₦200,000 to ₦500,000.
- The National Minimum Wage must apply to All Working Persons in all industries, irrespective of skills and sector. This then means that the power and authority of the Minister of Labour to grant exceptions should be removed.
- A graduated and additional Cost of Living Allowance be given to public servants in designated urban centres (e.g. Lagos, Port Harcourt, Abuja,

Kano) irrespective of Salary Grade Level.

- Funds for salaries, wages and allowances must be LEGALLY AND PROCEDURALLY PROTECTED FROM LEGISLATORS AT FEDERAL, STATE AND LOCAL GOVERNMENT LEVELS. No other project should be a priority over paying public servants, who sustain the system, as at when due.
- SOME STATE GOVERNMENTS claimed INCAPACITY TO PAY MINIMUM WAGE must end OR be ended now. ABILITY TO PAY and AFFORDABILITY indicate enough financial resources and budgetary allocation to cover salaries/wages and allowances for a given period.
- INCAPACITY TO PAY turns out to be REFUSAL TO PAY when salaries/wages become OUTSTANDING in most cases after DIVERSION of earmarked funds to other activities and projects favoured by a few in authority. Or, embezzled via bloated, uncompleted and fake projects and amazing consultancy fees. REFUSAL TO PAY is not only ILLEGAL, also a deliberate violation of contract of employment, salary arrears and underpaid minimum wage frequently occurring consequences.
- The Revenue Allocation and Budgetary processes must be restructured in such a way that wages funds are disbursed timely to public servants at both federal and state levels and cannot legally be diverted into other projects or expenses, even if it means creating a special account for them in the Central Bank.
- The initial reaction by traders, retailers, some companies and service providers to A NEW MINIMUM WAGE would be to INCREASE PRICES, while some may RETRENCH staff despite the fact that current higher prices are attributable mostly to the SUPPLY SIDE (not DEMAND), cross-country transportation and importation and shipping costs especially.
- But incidents of retrenchment are likely to be minimal, if at all, as OUTSOURCING and SUBCONTRACTING have for the last decade drastically reduced the numbers of so-called PERMANENT OR FULL-TIME STAFF and meals and accommodation, and medical services provided for out-of-town operations. Many other companies run PIECE-RATE COMPENSATION SYSTEM UNTOUCHED BY MINIMUM WAGES. In other words, several industries in private sector, particularly manufacturing and oil and gas, OFFER RATES AND COMPENSATION REGIMES THE NEW MINIMUM WAGE CAN HARDLY IMPACT UPON NEGATIVELY.
- Sorting out the oil and gas sector remains the key not only to a more sustainable economy once local refining capacity is restored, kerosene,

diesel and petrol available and electricity generation improved upon, but also to more stable consumer prices, less tense socio-political environment and more decent standard of living.

CROSS-CUTTING ISSUES AND CONCEPTS

MINIMUM WAGE

MINIMUM WAGE/SALARY is the LOWEST TOTAL amount of money/emolument an employed person must be paid, mostly hourly, but can also be daily and monthly depending on nature of task/activity, industry and country as mandated by law.

TOTAL implies that the Minimum Wage consists of BASIC pay/remuneration for the specific tasks/job being performed or carried out, including cost of transportation to and from workplace, housing/accommodation, food, water, education, healthcare, clothing, and other essential needs for living.

Historically, employers in what came to be Nigeria devised ways and means of MINIMISING costs, from the use of slaves, prisoners, forced labour, indentured labour to "free" labour able to negotiate terms. It has never been the intention of employers to pay what can give an employer a decent living standard, hence all the slave riots, community protests, rise of organised labour, rise of indigenous political parties and strikes. Aside from codified personal/individual and human rights, the contents of Labour Law always reflect the social character and outcomes of tussles in employment relations.

As of the commencement of the National Minimum Wage Act 2019, "every employer (except as provided for under this Act) is obligated to pay a wage not less than a national minimum wage…to every worker in their establishment. Any agreement for wages less than the national minimum wage specified in subsection (1) is considered void and ineffective."

SPECIFIC OBSERVATIONS

COVERAGE

Not all working persons in the labour market receive any of the national minimum wage established so far, especially casual or so-called menial workers. Some of them are in bars, restaurants, makeup parlours and schools and account for nearly 50% of all minimum-wage workers – waiters, waitresses, porters, bartenders. While others are also salespersons for breweries, shops/stores attendants, security guards, drivers, maintenance crew, bricklayers and labourers in transportation and construction industries.

Given relatively recent changes in HRM practices and communication technologies, especially information and computer technology, such menial jobs as clerks, typists and messengers are disappearing from the public sector, as the private sector outsourced/subcontracting them even where staff are competent in their usage.

In view of the last two paragraphs, job descriptions and classifications in the Public Sector would relate more to placement of staff on the Salary Structure than to the Minimum Wage as prices are the same for everyone, the difference being some can afford more from current remuneration. However, where the 2024 Minimum Wage exceeds what the least paid public servant earns, an adjustment in all levels or scales would be automatic.

EXEMPTIONS offered in the extant National Minimum Wage Act are:

1. Establishments with fewer than 25 workers;
2. Establishments with workers employed on a part-time basis;
3. Establishments where workers are paid on commission or piece-rate basis;
4. Workers in seasonal employment (such as agriculture);
5. Persons employed in vessels or aircraft regulated by merchant shipping or civil aviation laws;
6. The Minister has the authority to grant other exemptions in the interest of the national economy, based on reports from wages boards or other relevant bodies.

REMARKS

- A national minimum rate must apply to all working persons in all industries, irrespective skills and sector.
- No exceptions, including “where there is no machinery for collective bargaining.”
- This then means the authority of the Minister of Labour to grant exceptions should be removed.

WAGES

‘Wage’ means ‘remuneration or earnings (however designated or calculated) capable of being expressed in terms of money fixed by mutual agreement or by law which is payable by virtue of a contract by an employer for work done or to be done for service rendered.’ It usually refers to pay covering short-term periods, e.g. hourly, daily or weekly.

Minimum wage, as life progressed in work environments, became expected to be a LIVING WAGE. That is, sufficient for an individual to survive on and meet basic needs. Section 16(2)(d) of the Constitution states that the government should provide a reasonable national minimum living wage for its citizens. By Item 34 of the Exclusive Legislative List, Part I, Second Schedule to the Constitution of the Federal Republic of Nigeria, 1999 (as amended), legislation on labour and labour relations is within the exclusive preserve of the Nigerian National Assembly.

REMARKS

I) States must have their own Ministry of Labour to create a coordinating council/committee with the Federal Ministry of Labour that will now compare notes with other stakeholders in a Tripartite Panel or Committee. This does not take away the right of Federal Minister of Labour to represent the country at ILO meetings. It certainly is a more sensible and inclusive arrangement for the stakeholders irrespective of geographical location.

II) Minimum Wage regulation should be on the Concurrent Legislative List. The cost and standard of living are not the same nationwide and a majority of working people are located in the states. This is why the regulation of minimum wage should not be within the Exclusive Jurisdiction of the Federal Government. The Constitution should be amended to move Item 34 off the Exclusive Legislative List, enabling State Governments, in tripartite mode, legislate Minimum Wage applicable to their respective employers and workers while ensuring and entrenching True Federalism indisputably best for a multi-ethnic society/country.

III) Fiscal Federalism should now be the norm, to enhance States' control over own revenue and related activities.

IV) Equally important, as designed by the RMAFC and approved by the National Assembly, the Federal Government takes 52.68% of federally distributable revenue and States, 26.72%. The REVERSE should now be the case.

THE EMPLOYER

Section 17 of the Act defines an 'employer' as 'any person who has entered a contract of employment to employ any other person as a worker either for himself or for the service of any other person, and includes the agent, manager or factor of employer and the personal representative of a deceased employer.

An agent of the employer may be guilty of an offence under section 14 of the Act in the same way that an employer may be guilty of an offence under the Act. Where an action is brought against the employer, he may raise a defence by proving that the offence was due to the act or default of another person, or that he has exercised due diligence to ensure that the Act is complied with. If the authorised officer is satisfied that the offence was due to the act or default of another person and that the employer has established his defence, he may recommend that an action be brought against that other person. Where it is proved in such action that the offence was due to that person's act or default, he shall be convicted for the offence.

REMARK

SECTION 14 provides ready excuse for an employer to subcontract and outsource work in full knowledge the "another person" or "agent" will pay lower rate. This is common practice in the Oil and Gas industry. Both the employer and "other person" should be penalised if the Act is contravened, not the latter alone as currently provided for in the Act.

EMPLOYERS' OBLIGATION

The Act imposes two main obligations on employers:

1. **Payment of Minimum Wage**: Section 9 of the Act places an obligation on employers in establishments covered by the Act, to pay the workers at least ₦30,000 monthly, subject to statutory deductions. Failure to comply with this provision is an offence punishable with a fine not more than 5% of the defaulter's monthly wage, payment of the outstanding monthly wages. For each month the violation continues, the employer is liable to pay an additional penalty of a rate not less than the prevailing CBN lending rate on the wages owed.
2. **Keeping Records of Wages and Conditions of Employment:** By section 10 of the Act, employers have a duty to keep these records to show that they have complied with the provisions of the Act for up to three years after the relevant period. Where the employer does not do so, he is guilty of an offence for which he is liable on conviction to a fine not more than ₦75,000. For each day the violation continues, the employer will pay an additional ₦10,000.

Other offences that an employer may be guilty of are contained in section 15 of the Act:

1. Refusing or neglecting to allow the authorised officer entry to exercise his powers under the Act;
2. Hindering the authorised officer from exercising his powers;
3. Refusing or neglecting to give any document or information to the authorised officer as required by the Act;
4. Making, causing to be made or knowingly allowing to be made any record of wages or conditions of employment that is false;
5. Producing, causing to be produced or knowingly allowing to be produced any wage sheet or record, knowing it to be false; or
6. Giving information to an authorised officer, knowing it to be false.

A person who does any of the above acts is guilty of an offence and liable on conviction to imprisonment for a term not more than six months or a fine not more than ₦250,000.00, or both.

REMARK

SECTION 9 on payment of minimum wages is flagrantly violated by several Governors without legal sanctions or consequences. For that, next statutory allocations may be withheld and/or funds earmarked for salaries and wages be retained in a special account by the Central Bank/RMAFC/Federal Ministry of Finance and in conjunction with relevant State Government Agency paid directly to affected employees.

ENFORCEMENT

Section 13 of the Act empowers the aggrieved worker, trade unions and the Minister to take certain measures to ensure the employer complies with the Act thus:

1. **Worker**: The worker may institute a civil action in the NICN to recover monies due and owing to him/her or file a formal complaint with the Minister.
2. **Trade Unions**: The trade unions have the right to demand that an employer complies with the Act. They can file a claim to the NICN on behalf of their members, demanding that an employer comply with the Act, not more than 30 days after receiving a complaint from the workers.
3. **The Minister**: An authorised officer may serve a notice of enforcement on a defaulting employer directing such person to pay the arrears of wages to the worker whose name is contained in the notice within 30 days. The employer has a right to appeal the notice to the Minister. The Minister is required to resolve the matter within 30 days of receiving the appeal. Section 13(e) sets out the content of the notice of enforcement to include the amount owed to the worker, the relevant period for the payment and the time limit for the payment. If the defaulting employer fails to comply with the notice, the Minister may refer the matter to the National Industrial Court.

REMARKS

The existing statutory provisions for sorting out wage-related disputes need to be revisited, partly for the obvious reason they have not been very effective in application and interpretation. For example, ASUU and the Federal Government case, caught in years of arbitration and adjudication over mere method of paying university academic staff salaries, is more than eloquent testimony and throws up other troubling and totally unnecessary abuse of a procedure and representation rights:

a) University lecturer is employed by a University Council, not by the Federal Government and thus the latter should NEVER have replaced the University Councils for negotiation purposes;
b) the FUNDING OF FEDERAL UNIVERSITIES does not make the Federal Government EMPLOYER AND MANAGEMENT, just as workers and trade unions in the PRIVATE SECTOR do not negotiate with BANKS AND OTHER FINANCIAL INSTITUTIONS THAT FUND COMPANIES' RESPECTIVE PROJECTS AND CERTAIN OPERATIONS – and this despite the fact that the banks and financial institutions own those funds, while those for funding the universities are PUBLIC FUNDS, not Federal Government's funds.

Quite simply, the IAP and NIC must be given shorter periods for processing and adjudicating cases.

Secondly, the structures of the IAP and NIC should be TRIPARTITE. In the case of the IAP, "appointing" persons with relevant expertise in labour and employment relations does not make it Tripartite: other stakeholders should appoint their respective participants or nominee not subject to veto by any other party.

Third, conciliation efforts of the Ministry of Labour should tap into and enrich ADR (Alternative Dispute Resolution) mechanism in the country, with independent Mediators looking into disputes, especially in the public sector where the Minister of Labour wears so many hats in different roles even as a litigant or aggrieved party.

SOME CONCERNS

1. Minimum Wage versus Real Cost of Living.
2. Review of Minimum Wage every 5 years.
3. Omissions and enforcement.
4. Stakeholders involvement and responsibilities.
5. Complying with International Labour Standards.

REMARKS

MINIMUM WAGE versus REAL COST OF LIVING

The minimum wage is insufficient to provide workers with necessities (e.g. food, shelter, transportation, electricity/gas and clothing) they require for a healthy lifestyle. Obviously, minimum wage increases never caught up with real cost of living.

The standard of living in the country is very low, not flattering at all compared to other so-called developing countries, not to mention UK, European Union, USA, Japan and others.

Earning more facilitates a higher standard of living and improved capacity to adapt to periodic increases in the cost of living, and enabling increased productivity of better-motivated workers.

Should a higher minimum wage have the short-term effect of increasing operating costs and the prices of some goods and services, increased purchasing power and thus of demand would also stimulate economic activities and growth in the medium to long run.

Socioeconomic policies changes to render a new Minimum Wage effective for Public Sector employees, at least, include:

HOUSING – housing to be provided close to places of work at low rent while in service, not for sale. Those for sale can come later.

TRANSPORTATION – Buses to pick up public servants at and return to designated points in the morning and close of work in urban centres. Fare may be heavily subsidised to buy fuel and pay drivers or free. Same for train services where available and endeavour to provide same in major cities in the medium run.

HEALTH SERVICES – special subsidised arrangements with all teaching hospitals and suitably located private hospitals and clinics in urban centres for medical services.

ELECTRICITY – this is indisputably the most shameful national failure where pampered suppliers for a few hours of electricity any day 'estimate' charges while refusing to provide meters; and where provided charge tenants exorbitantly both for pre-paid meters and units of electricity consumed. Generators are now so expensive. Once refining and distribution of refined petroleum products can emerge from extreme corruption and sabotage in this, petroleum and related sectors, the sigh of relief will come from all. But, in the interim, sanctions have to be deployed effectively and increased allowance for this for employees.

FOOD AT WORK – Either suitable allowance is paid, or heavily subsidised meals and drink at the workplace canteens or both.

BANKING SERVICES – Banks have for increased monopoly profits deliberately facilitated "cash scarcity" impression in the economy by:

i) restricting cash available from usual or routine over-the-counter withdrawal to a few thousands, some preventing it altogether;
ii) deliberately underfunding their ATMs where interminably long and rowdy queues and petty crime are the norm; and
iii) literally drowning POS operators with cash, most of whom are agents of and owned by the banks and bank officials.

One sad and immediate consequence has been that most of the petty traders and market women, transporters and other small businesses that patronise POS operators tend to increase prices of their services and items daily, increasing cost of living brazenly without any link to American dollar exchange rate whatsoever. It is now difficult for the price of any commodity or item to remain the same for a few days!

FREQUENCY OF REVIEW OF MINIMUM WAGE

Biennial (Every Two Years) Review of Minimum Wage

The Act prescribes a review of the national minimum wage every 5 years. This is GROSSLY MISTAKEN and DANGEROUS economically, politically and security-wise. The periodic review should be biennial basis, coinciding with WHEN ANNUAL BUDGETS ARE PREPARED AND PRESENTED TO LEGISLATIVE HOUSES FOR CONSIDERATION.

Biannual ((Twice A Year) or Yearly Cost of Living Adjustment/Allowance (COLA)

COLA is conventionally taken to be an amount of money that an employee gets IN ADDITION to his or her normal pay, because the cost of living in a particular area is high. Such adjustment is also made to pension payouts.
In this case, aside from statutory yearly increments in the salary structure as captured in various Nigerian salary structures (CONTISS, CONNUAS, CONRAISS, CONTOPSAL, CONPSS, CONMESS, CONHESS, CONJUS, and CONPASS) statistics on inflation as provided by relevant agencies and receiving tripartite acceptance shall then form a basis for adjusting/increasing monthly wages/salaries by a certain percentage – between 5% and 12%.

OMISSIONS AND ENFORCEMENT

- The Act does not prescribe the number of hours that amounts to a full-time work for a month. Some employers tend to exploit this, demanding extra hours of work without extra compensation. The Labour Act, Cap L1, LFN 2004 is also silent on this, leaving the hours of work to be determined by mutual agreement, collective bargaining or an industrial wages board – section 13(1).
- Being compelled to work overtime to earn the legal minimum is a form of non-compliance.
- The number of hours of work that makes up a month's worth of full-time work should be stated. This is often easier to do in the public sector, and it will serve to promote healthier work practices, reduce conflicts while ensuring maximum productivity. The ensuing systemic overtime pay for extra hours worked by employees will promote fair compensation. This practice obtains in the many countries like the EU, UK, USA, etc., where employees working in excess of 40 hours per workweek are entitled to overtime pay.

STAKEHOLDERS INVOLVEMENT AND ACCOUNTABILITY

The names of offending employers and companies should be given publicity in mass media, gazetted and aired over television and radio, after reasonable notice is given for such violation. Offending Employers would have to pay all necessary fines and wages in order to have their names removed from the list. Those on the list should be denied credit facilities by banks and financial institutions as well.

Federal and newly created States' Ministries of Labour, and other tripartite partners should continuously engage attention of employers and working persons covered by the minimum wage provisions on compliance and remedial measures.

COMPLYING WITH INTERNATIONAL LABOUR STANDARDS

Nigeria should ratify and domesticate international conventions and treaties on wage regulation. This would signify the government's willingness to promote fair labour standards.

NATIONAL MINIMUM WAGE AND PUBLIC SECTOR WAGES

The 2024 Minimum Wage, if it exceeds what the currently least paid public servant earns, there would be demand for adjustments in salary structures as contained in CONTISS, CONNUAS, CONRAISS, CONTOPSAL, CONPSS, CONMESS, CONHESS, CONJUS, and CONPASS.

That said, compensation levels are not uniform in the Public Sector as salaries and wages are much higher in some AGENCIES and PARASTATALS. But what I would like to draw attention to here is the remuneration of POLITICAL OFFICE HOLDERS and NEGATIVE DEMONSTRATION EFFECT of their basic pay and allowances on successful implementation of a new National Minimum Wage and civil servants generally.

i) Their salaries and numerous allowances are too high for the public sector and economy. The largely arbitrary approach to public sector compensation began with military regimes whose top officers relied upon and bonded with a handful of permanent secretaries and directors to maintain privileges, in spite of Adebo Commission of 1970-71 and Udoji Commission 1974. For example, in the First Republic (1960 - 1966), a Federal Permanent Secretary earned J3000 a year, and the Professor J3200. The Babangida regime tried unsuccessfully to convert all Permanent Secretaries to Directors whose tenures would end with any military administration/regime that appointed them. By the time of Abacha Regime, the Permanent Secretary was ₦7,800 and Professor ₦7,000. President Obasanjo declared Vice Chancellors and Permanent Secretaries to be "political appointees" to earn between ₦15 million and

₦20 million, and Professors to be equivalent of Directors and Deputy Directors and today top of the range Professors earn around ₦6.7 million a year (₦555, 351.17 gross; ₦414,633.04, Step 10 net monthly in federal universities) and strikes plagued university system since then, bringing a protesting ASUU into existence and another general in mufti, President Buhari, in conflict with it for months on end over the platform for paying lecturers' salaries! NO ONE is talking about ensuring Professors no longer EARN LESS THAN FEDERAL PERMANENT SECRETARIES.

ii) The very heavy load of their salaries and allowances will be drastically reduced by amending relevant sections of the Constitution to have a National Assembly of part-time legislators paid sitting and other relevant allowances only when in session. Same for State Houses of Assembly.

iii) Amend the Constitution to have a Ceremonial President. Such will give room for more inclusiveness in all spheres of policymaking, reducing social tensions and political bickering and instability.

iv) Constitutional changes to ensure that the position of Governor is not pensionable.

v) The GAP between the HIGHEST and LEAST paid Public Servant should be reduced or compressed. In the United Kingdom, USA, Canada, the ratio is between 5.9 and 6 to 1, in Nigeria closer to 1 to 21.

If done, the LOWEST MONTHLY salary in any of Nigerian public sector Salary Scales is ₦33,000, multiplied by 5.8 or 6 gives ₦191,400 or ₦198,000 to the person on the highest Grade Level. For ratio of 1 to 21, however, it would be ₦33,000 x 21, making ₦693,000.

The advantage of compressing the gaps lies in greater COLLECTIVE PURCHASING POWER FOR ALL, holding constant allowances, once the bottom entry points are enhanced and make computation more appealing. Should the monthly minimum wage be ₦150,000, for example, the highest would be ₦870,000 or ₦900,000 multiplied by 5.8 and 6 respectively. So, for those currently earning around ₦700,000 monthly while the least is ₦33,000 and median ₦250,000, satisfaction cannot be widespread, nor collective purchasing power more as there are FEWER PUBLIC SERVANTS in the top rungs or steps. There is no collective economic advantage in this.

Lastly, the Constitution and relevant legislation be amended to remove President Obasanjo's ill-advised involvement of the Revenue Mobilisation Allocation and Fiscal Commission (RMAFC) in compensation management of political office holders. All public sector compensation matters should be processed solely by the National Salaries Incomes and Wages Commission (NSIWC).

REINFORCED RECOMMENDATIONS

SOME STATE GOVERNMENTS claimed INCAPACITY TO PAY MINIMUM WAGE must end OR be ended now. Politicians tend to owe their allegiance to respective political parties and influential ones within them and not to the country or Constitution, apart from a few good ones.

- ABILITY TO PAY and AFFORDABILITY indicate enough financial resources and budgetary allocation to cover salaries/wages and allowances for a given period.
- CAPACITY TO PAY turns out to be REFUSAL TO PAY when salaries/wages become OUTSTANDING in most cases after DIVERSION of earmarked funds to other activities and projects favoured by a few in authority. Or, embezzled via bloated, uncompleted and fake projects and amazing consultancy fees.
- REFUSAL TO PAY is ILLEGAL, a deliberate violation of contract of employment, salary arrears and underpaid minimum wage frequently occurring cases.

The PUBLIC SERVANTS in main Ministries and Parastatals sustain and regulate the fundamental institutional structures of society, hence GOVERNMENTS COME AND GO AFTER OR WITHOUT ELECTIONS but the STATE ORGANS/INSTITUTIONS REMAIN - except where there is secession or internecine civil war and the State reconstitutes into more but smaller STATES.

In fact, the STATE ORGANS regulate SOCIETY in the absence of a government as happened in the first six months of President Buhari's first tenure for health reasons. Send Mr President, Ministers, Governors, Commissioners, Local Government Chairpersons and Councils on leave for the next three months, for example, all hospitals, schools, universities, ministries, agencies, private sector companies, markets, and communities would still go about their activities regularly!

The Government of Nigeria (comprising Mr President and Ministers and assistants, Governors and Commissioners and assistants and Local Governments Chairpersons and Councillors) should not reduce governance and critical socioeconomic issues to selective favours to preferred *public servants* (comprising National Assembly, Civil Service – Ministries, Departments and Agencies – judiciary, military, police and law enforcement and security, local government and municipal authorities), individuals and companies. PUBLIC SERVANTS AND CITIZENS DEVELOP SOCIETY WITH THEIR INVESTMENT ACTIVITIES, PREFERENCES AND LIFESTYLES AND GOVERNMENTS MERELY FACILITATE.

As mentioned earlier, funds for salaries, wages and allowances must be rendered untouchable or inaccessible to any politician and assemblies. The Revenue Allocation and Budgetary processes must be restructured in such a way that wages funds are disbursed timely to public servants at both federal and state levels and cannot legally be diverted into other projects or expenses, even if it means creating a special account for them in the Central Bank.

The simple fact is that many legislators and politicians tend to move funds in the direction of their pet projects, of which a good many are often not of pressing need to respective or targeted communities and economy. The wider the spread of state/government regulation, the more discretion lawmakers and other public servants have at applying the rules. When this happens, it opens the door for dishonest behaviour, including taking bribes.

- Companies and groups may receive government grants and subsidies when they are not the INTENDED recipients – ILLICIT DIVERSION
- Claiming to eliminate foreign competition through trade restrictions, tariffs, and trade barriers, thereby opening up the possibility of a semi-monopoly by domestic players, the DOMESTIC PLAYERS are more likely to resort to CORRUPT BEHAVIOUR to keep restrictions in place, more so where owners and controllers are PROMINENT MEMBERS OF POLITICAL PARTIES AND COMMUNITIES.
- State/Government corruption, as distinct from the Private Sector, thus occurs when a ruling party and critical public servants, jointly or separately, take on a more invasive and pervasive socioeconomic role with VERY FEW CHECKS AND BALANCES.
- Forms include nepotism, bribery, lobbying, embezzlement, inflated contracts, mind-blowing consultancy fees, uncompleted projects, and cronyism. For instance, state/government officials may use their power and influence to grant family members and friends' high-ranking positions and contracts.
- **Oil and Gas Industry** – Location of refineries - Refineries Turn-around Maintenance funds paid and not executed – oil wells – crude oil exports – hijacked refined products importation and distribution – quality of products - Services – NNPC Group and not working refineries workers paid for years, etc.
- **Iron and Steel Industry** - four barely-functioned mills (Itakpe, Jos, Katsina, Osogbo) yet-to-be completed Ajaokuta four decades on, and run-down and privatized Aladja Delta Steel – billions of dollar spent.
- **Physical Infrastructure** – East-West Road and other uncompleted road projects across the country, daily escalating cost of intra- and inter city transportation. Poorly sited, poorly constructed but costly landscape-littering uninhabited housing estates.
- **Education** – Location and Types of Institutions – fees - contracts in agencies (e.g. Lecture theatres, textbooks) – admissions (catchment areas,

zoning, etc.) – curriculum, transportation deficits for school children, recruitment and placement in regulatory agencies

- **Aviation Industry** – Location and construction of airports – purchase and servicing of aircrafts – non-functioning and abandoned ones after billions spent.
- **Financial Institutions** – ownership – shares manipulation -fake accounts – fake schemes - money laundering schemes – foreign currencies exchange rates manipulation – POS manipulation and contrived cash scarcity.
- **Energy Sector** – Location, ownership, epileptic services – meters and arbitrary charges, cost of generators, cost of petrol and diesel
- **General Administration** – ghost workers - arrears of salaries and allowances – career progression games – abuse of Federal Character, ethnicity and nepotism.
- **Pharmaceutical Industry** – low compliance with drug manufacturing specifications – many pharmacies owned and operated by untrained hands – drugs sold without required prescriptions – sloppy regulators – increased drug additions
- **Health Sector** – Fewness and Staffing of Hospitals/Clinics – equipping of and drugs supply to public medical facilities – high cost of treatment - Energy supply – limited Training facilities
- **Nigeria Customs, Industries, and Commerce** – Largely arbitrary charges – bribes - diverted revenues – inferior products – daily increase in prices of consumer goods.
- **Law Enforcement and Regulation** – poor pay – recruitment issues, arbitrary detentions/remands, institutionalized checkpoints extortions, bribes - pro-employers and big people services, inappropriate gifts, brazen disregard of judicial judgements, etc.
- **Judiciary and Justice System** – subjected to immense political and social pressures for favoured outcomes via tainted recruitment, appointment, promotion processes, biased decisions, etc.
- **Elections and Rule/Law making** – main theatre for rival political forces, multi-dimensional impacts on structures and operations of agencies and legislative bodies, costs, unparalleled salaries and allowances, abuse of constituency projects/allowance, etc.

LAW ENFORCEMENT AGENCIES

The maintenance of law and order is certainly very complex and crucial in modern-day societies and does go with information gathering, surveillance of various groups and persons and more.

In relation to push for a NATIONAL MINIMUM WAGE, practice of TRADE UNIONISM and reactions of various groups to HARSH AND DETERIORATING SOCIO-ECONOMIC CONDITIONS, a fuller understanding of CONTEXTS BY SECURITY AND LAW ENFORCEMENT AGENTS WILL PROVE USEFUL TO ALL, especially clashes with protesting students, workers, trade unionists and communities.

Aside from constitutional and legal provisions on individual, human and constitutional rights and liberties, we do have a political system of PRIVATE PERSONS FORMING POLITICAL PARTIES to vie for a place and control of government at the federal, state and local levels and to occupy PUBLIC SPACE AND INFLUENCE, IF NOT DETERMINE, POLICIES for designated periods.

It is a system based on COMPETITION, OPPOSITION, PROMOTION AND PROTECTION OF VESTED LOCAL, REGIONAL AND FOREIGN INTERESTS AND PROTESTS - from ELECTIONS TO APPOINTMENTS AND DECISIONS ON BUDGETARY ALLOCATIONS, PROJECTS, AND MYRIAD POLICIES IMPACTING ALL ASPECTS OF SOCIETY SELECTIVELY – hence those failed and abandoned projects, neglected rail services for transportation of goods by trucks, abandoned refineries for imported refined petroleum products, etc.

1. To arrest, detain, beat, torture and send for trial those protesting against current socioeconomic conditions is neither right nor legal nor in the national interest.
2. To warn and threaten trade unionists for attempting to protest against certain economic and social policies is neither right, nor legal nor in the national interest.
3. IF TRADE UNIONISTS AND OTHERS DID NOT MOUNT PRESSURE VIA STRIKES AND OTHER MEASURES, WE WOULD NOT BE HAVING A NEW NATIONAL MINIMUM WAGE THIS YEAR.
4. For security agencies to announce strikes and protests are being sponsored by certain political forces or persons or groups designed to threaten "peace and order" merely indicates insufficient understanding of their "state protection" roles.
5. The point is, WITHOUT PHYSICALLY, VERBALLY AND OTHER MEANS ADOPTED BY VARIOUS GROUPS IN SOCIETY, INCLUDING SECTIONS OF THE POLITICAL CLASS, TO OPPOSE CERTAIN OFFICIAL POLICIES, POLITICIANS CONTROLLING GOVERNMENT AT FEDERAL, STATE AND LOCAL LEVELS WILL NOT AUTOMATICALLY ADOPT SOUND POLICIES AND MEASURES. That is the system, reality in ALL COUNTRIES. Just worse in some, especially in developing countries. Personal, sectional political

and regional and business interests tend to dominate thinking and dictate tactics.

6. Security and intelligence agencies are designed to protect THE STATE and SOCIETY where GOVERNMENTS are not doing too well in particular. They should not become government's *spokesperson* and *instruments of oppression* in rapidly deteriorating socioeconomic conditions.
7. The governments and political parties have Ministries of Information and spokespersons across the country to disseminate whatever propaganda they prefer. In the absence of this protection and NEGATIVE demonstration effect of methods adopted by security and intelligence agencies themselves, crimes and insecurity increase as more citizen embrace random violent methods to survive and enrich themselves. Everyone is being kidnapped these days, and not only non-indigenes and non-Moslems die from Boko Haram activities, for example.
8. Security and intelligence agents too suffer avoidable deaths. The Police should have their trade union as in the UK, USA, European Union and elsewhere and the Essentials Services Act be amended and made applicable only to the Military as practised in most countries – and the police and other agencies should stop extorting monies at checkpoints nationwide thereby adding to the cost of services and consumer goods as victims recoup expenses via arbitrary price increases.
9. Experts have continued to repeat this: to have a corrupt or inappropriate policy and politician, a public servant perverts the process in the first place. Why? How? Public servants handle the procedure, prepare the documents and oversee implementation. Security and intelligence agencies need to change their current approaches not only to avoid self-created injuries like from the #EndSars incident but also for a better-managed society to emerge. Are we still under military dictatorships that brook no contrary views and demonstrations? No angels are coming to change difficult conditions for us.

COSTING TEMPLATE FOR MINIMUM WAGE

Clearly identifying -

a) job content of relevant positions or roles and numbers;
b) preparing for, going to and returning from work ;
c) Meals at work;
d) The Unmarried;
e) Married and typical family size;
f) Energy (electricity, gas) costs;
g) Food at home;

h) Housing and rent rates;
i) Cost of educational services (kindergarten, primary, secondary, tertiary);
j) Transport;
k) Cost of available medical services in typical cases (childbirth, malaria, infectious diseases, routine medical examination, medicines for typical ailments, more common medical procedures/operations, etc.)
l) Data on those in comparable positions in the Ministries, Parastatals and respective industries in the Private Sector

COMMON FOOD ITEMS - PRICES

Indomitable Indomie	₦500
Indomie belleful	₦1000
Indomie hungry man	₦800
Indomie superpack	₦650
A cup of rice	₦400
Cup of beans	₦350
Bag of Beans (50kg)	₦104,000
Garri (1-2kg)	₦2400
Garri (50kg bag)	₦44,000
A bottle of vegetable oil	₦1,400
A bottle of Palm oil	₦900
A bag of Nigerian rice, different types (50kg)	₦68,000 - ₦70,000
Foreign bag of rice (50kg)	₦78,000 - ₦83,000
Chicken/Fowl – average size	₦7,000
Beef – 1kg	₦4,000
Onions, tomatoes, pepper (5 or 6 pieces)	₦1,000 - ₦2,500
Yam tuber	₦1,000

GOING TO WORK

Transport Mode	
Cab each day	₦3,000 – N10,000
Bus	₦1,000 - ₦2000
Keke	₦600 - N1,600
Fuel - Cars	₦15,000 - ₦25, 000 Weekly
School Runs	Fuel and Transport mode
Lunch (Canteen)	₦500 - ₦1,500
Water	₦10 - ₦20 (sachet)
	₦200 - ₦350 (bottle)
Recharge Cards	₦500 - ₦1,500 daily
Clothing	Different dress/outfit each day

MEDICAL SERVICES

CARD	₦5,000
DEPOSIT	₦50,000
BED	₦6,000 per day
CONSULTATION FEE	₦5000 - ₦10,000 per appointment
SCAN	₦8,000
BLOOD COUNT TEST	₦4,500 – ₦7000
URINE TEST	₦7,000
GENOTYPE	₦5,000
OXYGEN MASK	₦3,000 PER HOUR
SUGAR LEVEL TEST	₦1000 - ₦2000
DRUG PRESCRIPTIONS	₦7,000 – 15,000 for each
APPENDIX	₦150,000 DEPOSIT
CAESARIAN SECTION	₦300,000 DEPOSIT
FIBROIDS	₦500,000 DEPOSIT
MONEY LENDER	2%–3% INTEREST RATE PER DAY

COMPILING A NATIONAL MINIMUM WAGE

CONSUMER PRICE INDEX (CPI)

- Consumer Price Index measures the overall change in consumer prices based on a representative basket of goods and services over time.
- CPI is based on an index covering majority of the population
- CPI is based on wide range of prices collected monthly from representative samples of markets, retail and service establishments as well as different rented housing units.
- House rents are used to estimate the change in shelter costs including owner-occupied housing.

PERSONAL CONSUMPTION EXPENDITURES (PCE) PRICE INDEX

- Measures the prices consumers pay for goods and services and changes in those prices.
- PCE includes how much is spent on goods (durable and non-durable) and services.
- Provides a view of how the economy is faring
- Changes in spending can indicate a growing economy or economic difficulties for households

PERSONAL CONSUMPTION EXPENDITURES (PCE) PRICE INDEX

- DURABLE GOODS: Motor vehicles and parts, furnishings and durable household equipment, recreational goods and vehicles, bikes/*okadas*, *kekes,* computers, mobile phones, etc.
- NON-DURABLE GOODS: Food and beverages purchased for off-premises consumption, clothing and footwear, petrol and other energy goods, and other non-durable goods
- SERVICES: Housing and utilities, healthcare, transportation services, recreation services, food services and accommodations, financial services and insurance, and other services

FARM PRICE INDEX (FPI)

- Farm Price Index is a measure of prices paid to farmers and companies in the agricultural sector.
- Measures price movements for crops, livestock, and livestock-related products
- As with most markets, agricultural prices are subject to natural forces and swings in the economy. People don't stop eating during tough times, but they generally make choices about WHAT they consume, HOW often they eat, and WHEN.

PRODUCER PRICE INDEX (PPI)

- Measures the average change in prices paid to domestic producers for their products and services.
- Represents price movements from the seller's point of view
- Covers all sectors, including retail, manufacturing, food, construction, and agriculture, and every industry

CONCLUDING REMARKS

- The New National Minimum Wage, based on current cost of living indices, could be anything from ₦200,000 to ₦500,000.
- Whatever it turns out to be after surveys and deliberations by the Tripartite Committee on National Minimum Wage, funds for salaries, wages and allowances must be *legally and procedurally protected* from legislators at federal, state and local government levels. No other project should be a priority over paying public servants, who sustain the system, as at when due.
- Where due to a combination of political and other reasons over-employment exists in a Parastatal or Ministry and wage bill has skyrocketed, an audit may be done, in addition to those who fail to pass

statutory tests/examinations but are still retained be released with the excess.

- The initial reaction by traders, retailers, some companies and service providers to a new minimum wage is to increase prices, while some may retrench staff despite the fact that current higher prices are attributable mostly to the supply side, not demand, cross-country transportation and importation and shipping costs especially. Incidents of retrenchment are likely to be minimal, if at all, as outsourcing and subcontracting have for the last decade drastically reduced the numbers of so-called permanent or full-time staff and meals and accommodation, and medical services provided for out-of-town operations. Many other companies run piece-rate compensation system untouched by minimum wages. In other words, several industries in private sector, particularly manufacturing and oil and gas, offer rates and compensation regimes the new minimum wage can hardly influence negatively.
- Sorting out the oil and gas sector remains the key not only to a more sustainable economy once local refining capacity is restored, kerosene, diesel and petrol available and electricity generation improved upon, but also to more stable consumer prices.

APPENDIX: FOREIGN TEMPLATES FOR WAGE RATES

CANADA

Geography3	Canada (map)				
Wages4	Average hourly wage rate				
Type of work	Both full- and part-time employees				
Sex	Both sexes				
Age group	15 years and over				
North American Industry Classification System (NAICS)5	2019	2020	2021	2022	2023
			Current dollars		
Total employees, all industries6	28.32	30.03	30.67	31.96	33.55
Goods-producing sector7	30.27	31.41	31.88	33.44	35.50
Agriculture8	19.83	20.52	20.78	21.75	23.75
Forestry, fishing, mining, quarrying, oil and gas9 10	41.38	42.70	44.16	44.30	47.40
Utilities	43.95	46.44	47.08	47.86	49.41
Construction	30.63	31.39	32.03	33.77	35.46
Manufacturing	27.85	29.11	29.24	31.01	33.13
Services-producing sector11	27.81	29.67	30.36	31.58	33.06
Wholesale and retail trade	22.01	23.03	23.47	24.70	25.94
Transportation and warehousing	27.65	28.90	29.94	30.37	32.10
Finance, insurance, real estate, rental and leasing	33.66	35.94	37.44	38.84	40.93
Professional, scientific and technical services	36.14	37.89	38.47	41.64	44.24
Business, building and other	21.51	22.79	23.53	24.88	25.93

support services12					
Educational services	34.97	36.46	36.70	37.50	38.71
Health care and social assistance	28.08	29.22	29.55	30.70	31.99
Information, culture and recreation	26.47	29.94	31.18	31.23	31.24
Accommodation and food services	16.57	17.02	17.34	18.50	19.68
Other services (except public administration)	24.21	26.32	26.88	27.43	28.83
Public administration	38.26	39.78	39.89	40.79	42.61

2023 Locality Adjustment: --%

Official General Schedule Base Rates
Effective from January 1, 2023 to December 31, 2023.

GS Grade	Step 1	Step 2	Step 3	Step 4	Step 5	Step 6	Step 7	Step 8	Step 9	Step 10
GS-1	$20,999	$21,704	$22,401	$23,097	$23,794	$24,202	$24,893	$25,589	$25,617	$26,273
GS-2	$23,612	$24,174	$24,956	$25,617	$25,906	$26,668	$27,430	$28,192	$28,954	$29,716
GS-3	$25,764	$26,623	$27,482	$28,341	$29,200	$30,059	$30,918	$31,777	$32,636	$33,495
GS-4	$28,921	$29,885	$30,849	$31,813	$32,777	$33,741	$34,705	$35,669	$36,633	$37,597
GS-5	$32,357	$33,436	$34,515	$35,594	$36,673	$37,752	$38,831	$39,910	$40,989	$42,068
GS-6	$36,070	$37,272	$38,474	$39,676	$40,878	$42,080	$43,282	$44,484	$45,686	$46,888
GS-7	$40,082	$41,418	$42,754	$44,090	$45,426	$46,762	$48,098	$49,434	$50,770	$52,106
GS-8	$44,389	$45,869	$47,349	$48,829	$50,309	$51,789	$53,269	$54,749	$56,229	$57,709
GS-9	$49,028	$50,662	$52,296	$53,930	$55,564	$57,198	$58,832	$60,466	$62,100	$63,734
GS-10	$53,990	$55,790	$57,590	$59,390	$61,190	$62,990	$64,790	$66,590	$68,390	$70,190
GS-11	$59,319	$61,296	$63,273	$65,250	$67,227	$69,204	$71,181	$73,158	$75,135	$77,112
GS-12	$71,099	$73,469	$75,839	$78,209	$80,579	$82,949	$85,319	$87,689	$90,059	$92,429
GS-13	$84,546	$87,364	$90,182	$93,000	$95,818	$98,636	$101,454	$104,272	$107,090	$109,908
GS-14	$99,908	$103,238	$106,568	$109,898	$113,228	$116,558	$119,888	$123,218	$126,548	$129,878
GS-15	$117,518	$121,435	$125,352	$129,269	$133,186	$137,103	$141,020	$144,937	$148,854	$152,771

UNITED KINGDOM

PAY ADJUSTED TO REFLECT COST OF LIVING IN LONDON

Treasury pay bands and ranges as of 1 August 2016 are as follows:

Range	London pay range (£)	National pay range (£)
	Min – Max	Min – Max
Range E2 – G6	59,000 – 66,000	56,000 – 63,000
Range E – G7	48,000 – 64,498	45,000 – 61,498
Range D – HEO/SEO	28,003 – 43,124	25,072 – 40,332
Range C – EO	24,000 – 29,650	21,000 – 26,650
Range B - AO	21,000 – 23,913	18,000 – 20,913
Apprentice:		
Range C - EO	22,500	19,103
Range B - AO	18,852	16,715

RECOMMENDATION

Lagos, Port Harcourt, Kano and Abuja should be treated likewise

OVERVIEW

There are around 5.5 million public servants in the UK, but only around 0.5m of these are civil servants. Civil service pay therefore represents only a small fraction of total public sector pay. This chart below shows how much (or little?) they were paid in 2021.

Figure 3.10 **Number of civil servants in each pay range (headcount)**

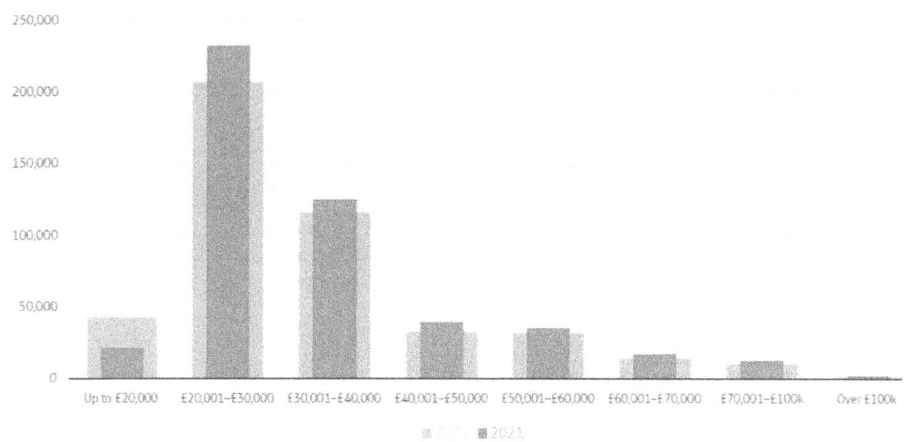

Source: Institute for Government analysis of Cabinet Office, Civil Service Statistics, 2020/21.

Before the early 2000s 'austerity', Brexit and Covid, the vast majority of (relatively junior) civil servants earned pretty much the same as their private sector counterparts. Senior civil servants, however, earned - and still earn - significantly less than their opposite numbers in the private sector. By the early-2000s, though, most civil servants felt badly paid compared with their private sector counterparts. The Home Office, for instance, offered only £21,700 to new Asylum/Protection Officers whilst office managers, working for Directors, could not earn more than £28,000. Their equivalents in the private sector would earn at least £10-£15k more than this. One key grade (Principal/Grade 7) lies around the border between the Senior Civil Service and the majority of the civil service. This chart shows how its pay has declined, decade after decade, compared with wage rates in the wider economy.

Figure 2.7: **Distribution of annual full-time employee pay in public and private sectors**

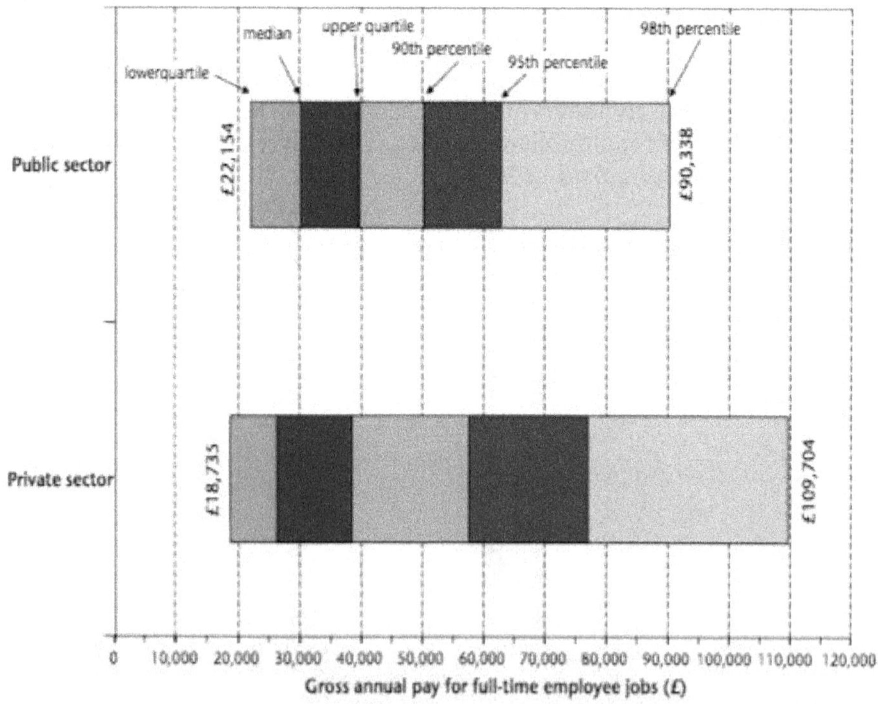

Source: ONS, Annual Survey of Hours and Earnings (ASHE) 2015. Note that source data at the 98th percentile have high coefficients of variation (>5%), meaning that some of the data in this figure should be viewed as illustrating only a broad order of magnitude.

USA -Salary calculation

Salaries under the GS have two components: a base salary and a "locality pay adjustment".

Base salary

The base salary is based on a table compiled by Office of Personnel Management (the 2024 table is shown below).[4] and is used as the baseline for the locality pay adjustment. The increases between steps for Grades GS-1 and GS-2 varies between the steps; for Grades GS-3 through GS-15 the increases between the steps are the same within the grade, but increase as the grade increases. The table is revised effective January of each year to reflect the basic cost of living adjustment (known as the General Schedule Increase).

2024 General Schedule Basic Pay

Grade	Step 1	Step 2	Step 3	Step 4	Step 5	Step 6	Step 7	Step 8	Step 9	Step 10
1	$21,986	$22,724	$23,454	$24,183	$24,912	$25,339	$26,063	$26,792	$26,821	$27,502
2	$24,722	$25,310	$26,129	$26,821	$27,124	$27,922	$28,720	$29,518	$303,164	$31,114
3	$26,975	$27,874	$28,773	$29,672	$30,571	$31,470	$32,369	$33,268	$34,167	$35,066
4	$30,280	$31,289	$32,298	$33,307	$34,316	$35,325	$36,334	$37,343	$38,352	$39,361
5	$33,878	$35,007	$36,136	$37,265	$38,394	$39,523	$40,652	$41,781	$42,910	$44,039
6	$37,765	$39,024	$40,283	$41,542	$42,801	$44,060	$45,319	$46,578	$47,837	$49,096
7	$41,966	$43,365	$44,764	$46,163	$47,562	$48,961	$50,360	$51,759	$53,158	$54,557
8	$46,475	$48,024	$49,573	$51,122	$52,671	$54,220	$55,769	$57,318	$58,867	$60,416
9	$51,332	$53,043	$54,754	$56,465	$58,176	$59,887	$61,598	$63,309	$65,020	$66,731
10	$56,528	$58,412	$60,296	$62,180	$64,064	$65,948	$67,832	$69,716	$71,600	$73,484
11	$62,107	$64,177	$66,247	$68,317	$70,387	$72,457	$74,527	$76,597	$78,667	$80,737
12	$74,441	$76,922	$79,403	$81,884	$84,365	$86,846	$89,327	$91,808	$94,289	$96,770
13	$88,520	$91,471	$94,422	$97,373	$100,324	$103,275	$106,226	$109,177	$112,128	$115,079
14	$104,604	$108,091	$111,578	$115,065	$118,552	$122,039	$125,526	$129,013	$132,500	$135,987
15	$123,041	$127,142	$131,243	$135,344	$139,445	$143,546	$147,647	$151,748	$155,849	$159,950

Some positions have their own unique GS scales. One notable example being patent examiner positions who can receive a supplement of more than 50% from the standard GS scale. Under the laws governing special GS scales, employees whose positions are covered by those scales earn either the special scale salary, or the standard GS scale salary plus a locality adjustment (see below), whichever is higher.[5]

Locality adjustment

The second component of the GS salary, the locality pay adjustment, was introduced in 1994 as part of the Federal Employees Pay Comparability Act of 1990 (FEPCA). Prior to FEPCA, all GS employees received the same salary regardless of location, which failed to reflect both the disparity between public sector and private sector pay as well as differences in cost of living in major metropolitan areas. As noted earlier, an employee in a position with a special GS scale does not receive a locality adjustment unless the pay under the special scale is lower than using the locality pay adjustment.

NIGERIA

SALARIES OF CIVIL SERVANTS FROM LEVEL 1 TO 12 2024
The Consolidated Public Service Salary Structure (CONPSS) is used to determine the salaries of civil servants in Nigeria. The salary structure has 12 grades, ranging from Grade Level 01 (the lowest) to Grade Level 12 (the highest). The salary scale for each grade level as of 2024 is as follows:

- Grade Level 01: ₦30,000 – ₦33,000 per month
- Grade Level 02: ₦34,000 – ₦38,000 per month
- Grade Level 03: ₦43,000 – ₦54,000 per month
- Grade Level 04: ₦48,000 – ₦63,000 per month
- Grade Level 05: ₦58,000 – ₦77,000 per month
- Grade Level 06: ₦65,000 – ₦87,000 per month
- Grade Level 07: ₦75,000 – ₦100,000 per month
- Grade Level 08: ₦88,000 – ₦148,000 per month
- Grade Level 09: ₦105,000 – ₦170,000 per month
- Grade Level 10: ₦125,000 – ₦210,000 per month
- Grade Level 11: ₦190,000 – ₦290,000 per month
- Grade Level 12: ₦255,000 – ₦700,000 per month

Chapter 16

PUBLIC SECTOR COLLECTIVE BARGAINING IN NIGERIA

INTRODUCTION

Since the expression 'collective bargaining' was coined by Beatrice Webb in 1891, it has undergone considerable refinement. Collective bargaining is generally recognised as a central feature of industrial relations systems in Western countries of old as the most desirable means of regulating contracts of employment. At the micro-level or in the context of individual economic organizations, collective bargaining is often used to describe collective attempts on part of both employees and management to sort out specific issues arising from the work situation. Although, this is commonly accepted, it is as simplistic as it is partial since social existence and other developments outside the work situation impinge on the content of collective bargaining and the conduct of the parties generally.[1] In as much as some issues emanating from production processes or work procedures may be resolved within the organization, notions of 'fairness' and 'proper conduct' which guide behaviour at work largely derive from prevailing norms in the larger society and the ideas and practices which these encourage and perpetuate. The State, which is a principal actor in public sector collective bargaining, has always played a leading role in the generation and continuation of values, often modifying the socializing role of the family (which is itself located in some substratum of a social class) through the pervasive information media and the curricula of institutions of formal instruction.[2]

Davey, H.W. (1951, 6) defined collective bargaining as

> "those formal and informal processes of accommodation through which an employer, or a group of employers and their organised workers attempt to establish a mutual set of relationships which will

[1] For a comprehensive treatment of the concept of collective bargaining, see Flanders, A. (ed.), *Collective Bargaining*, Penguin, 1969 and Chamberlain, N.W., *Collective Bargaining*, McGraw-Hill, 1958.

[2] Three relevant studies that immediately come to mind are: Marcuse, H., *One Dimensional Man*, Abacus, 1972; Habermas, J., *Toward a Rational Society*, Heinemann, London, 1971, and *Legitimation Crisis*, Heinemann, London, 1976.

allow them to achieve their respective goals. It involves the formulation of labour agreements (contracts), the application of those agreements to the production processes involved, and the solution of the inevitable differences which arise over their interpretation and application."[3]

We find from Davey's definition that members of management and employees interact with each other both officially and unofficially.

Second, both sides do not have a choice in the matter because they must establish sets of relationships in order to achieve their respective goals. This is a very important point to note, namely a person seeks a job because he/she has some goals to achieve, while an employer offers a job because he/she wishes to use the skills of the person being employed to achieve his/her own goals. So, all the "mission statements", "core values" and "corporate vision", "national survival", "national destiny", "national interest" introduced by management in their companies or public service do not remove the fact that employees have goals of their own they intend to achieve. How and how well both parties achieve their goals are part and parcel of collective bargaining and which brings us to the next important point.

Third, the relationship between the employer or management and the employee begins from the point of recruitment itself, the contract of employment containing the terms of employment. The determination of these terms of employment, which include basic salary and fringe benefits, are supposed to be the main output or results of collective bargaining. How these terms are determined, when and how they can be changed are some of the processes of collective bargaining.

The fourth, after the person has been employed, what he/she experiences at the work place are part of conditions of employment. Thus, conditions of employment include, among others, the physical facilities available, the allocation and nature of tasks to be done, the physical conditions of the workplace (lighting, heat, cold, dust level, noise levels, exposure to chemicals, state of equipment, etc.) that may constitute health hazards, industrial accidents, management style, recognition of and procedures for processing grievances. Both parties, in seeking to address challenges thrown up by some of the conditions of employment are involved in collective bargaining processes and institutions.

Fifth, the challenges thrown up by terms and conditions of employment are either addressed formally or informally. Formally, therefore, both parties create fora or opportunities to meet, and such may be in the form of *ad hoc* bipartite committees, task forces, standing committees or councils and, in

---

[3] *Contemporary Collective Bargaining*, Prentice Hall, NY, 1951.

some cases, tripartite bodies involving representatives of the State or government. All these are collectively referred to as *collective bargaining institutions.*

Sixth, collective bargaining is not restricted to managements and employers alone. In other words, it does not exclude third parties, since external assistance may be required by law and practice to get management and employees to keep their agreements, hence a plethora of labour law. In any case, disputing employers and employees may require a third party assistance to sort out their differences – hence mediation, conciliation and arbitration services provided by the Federal Ministry of Labour and Productivity and private organisations and individuals.

To put everything in proper context and to fully appreciate collective bargaining processes and institutions and their outcomes, and especially collective bargaining in the public sector, we must draw attention to the *distribution of power within the system.* It is an obvious fact that the individual worker or employee has less power than any management, a weak position which a group or collective approach tends to make stronger. From a broad historical perspective, therefore, the terms and conditions of employment may be determined in one of the following ways: a) unilaterally by the state; b) unilaterally by private employers; c) by workers; and d) by combined effort on the part of employers and their organisations, workers and their organisations, and representatives of the state.

Historically there would seem to have been a progressive evolution from situation a) through b) to d), situation c) being attributed to workers' self-managed enterprises that were mostly found in Eastern Europe and other socialist or communist countries. Collective bargaining is collective in the sense of multi-party involvement in forms of decision-making concerning a broad range of issues that affect all parties in industry. In turn, the kinds of issues subject to multi-party attention at any one time would depend on peculiarities of industry involved, a function of dominant norms and social expectations and the relative distribution of power.

Where public and private employers unilaterally determine terms and conditions of employment, collective bargaining cannot be said to exist. This being the case, the following conditions make it possible for collective bargaining to take place:

1) it appears obvious enough that *bargaining* can only occur among and between the parties in the work situation;
2) collective bargaining also implies a negotiating situation among and between groups and organizations (usually workers/trades unions, employers-management and in the case of the public sector - relevant government agencies) otherwise the word 'collective' would not qualify 'bargaining';

3) that all sides (private employer, public employer and workers/their organisations) have *interests* which are *different,* sometimes *conflicting,* sometimes in agreement or congruent;
4) that the interests of all the parties are *recognised by* all to be *legitimate,* and only each of the parties is best placed to represent and defend the interests of its members;
5) the right of workers and their representatives to challenge some management decisions/actions would also be recognised - especially in the public sector where the two interests of the state/government as employer and regulator of the economy - can and do *conflict* and sometimes influence the kind of laws the government passes to regulate the three parties in industrial relations;
6) that industrial harmony and conflict coexist. That is to say that general employment relationships are a mixture of grievances, disagreements and agreements, depending on the issues and contexts.

CONTEXT OF EMPLOYMENT RELATIONS

The framework of employment and labour relations in Nigeria presents two aspects, the *institutional* and the *legal.*

Institutional Framework

Relations that develop from employment, especially where they are structured, lead to the creation of bodies or organs where bilateral or tripartite interactions take place. Such relations represent the *formalisation* of interaction and behaviour governed by rules, understandings, procedures, and social mores. Over time, such arrangements become part of tradition, convention, and practices, and as such the *institutional framework* comprises those institutions through which the social actors engage each other, and those which regulate their conduct. Typical examples include collective bargaining, internal and external disputes settlement mechanisms (DSMs), committees, task forces and suchlike forums.

Legislation may also create institutions or bodies that become part of the institutional framework. For example, the Trade Disputes Act, among other things, defines disputes, strike, and lockouts; stipulates an external dispute settlement mechanism and the powers of the Minister of Employment, Labour and Productivity thereof, while creating the Industrial Arbitration Panel and the National Industrial Court as arbitration bodies. We find in this example the intermingling of both institutional and legal frameworks which, perhaps, explains why many observers lump them together as one – institutional and legal framework.

Legal framework

The *legal framework* is the web of rules and regulations that guide and govern the conduct of the parties. Most often, state authorities lay down such rules or laws, and those directly pertaining to industrial and labour relations matters are collectively known as 'labour law'. Labour law regulates most aspects of collective relations in industry or at work: for example, terms of employment, health and safety standards, determination of wages and salaries, conflict, formation and functioning of workers' and employers' organisations, and types and future of jobs. The sources of these laws include the Common Law of England, statutes enacted/decreed at various times by the Colonial Parliament, the pre-Military Parliament, Military Decrees, and post-Military Elected/Civilian National Assembly. The 1979 and 1999 Constitutions of the Federal Republic of Nigeria provide that only the National Assembly can legislate on "labour, including trade unionism; industrial relations; conditions, safety and welfare of labour; industrial dispute; prescribing a national minimum wage for the federation or any part thereof; and industrial arbitration." This is what is meant by "labour" being "exclusive jurisdiction" of the Federal Government.

Labour law has five main legislative pieces which comprise part of the industrial relations legal framework. These are the Labour or Employment Act, Trade Union Act, Trade Disputes Act, Factory Act, and Workmen's Compensation Act. The Labour or Employment Act concerns itself with the contract of employment, and protection of the job and wages: written terms of employment within three months; withdrawal/termination of service at various notice to be given by both employers and employees, status of collective of agreements, mode of payment of wages/salaries, etc. The Trade Union Act deals with the formation, functioning and administration of trade unions, and spells out the powers of the Minister for Labour and Productivity and of the Registrar of Trade Unions and labour officers regarding these. The Trade Disputes Act contains provisions for internal and external disputes settlement mechanisms: mediation, conciliation and arbitration procedures and processes which revolve around the Minister for Labour and Productivity, and the Industrial Arbitration Panel and the National Industrial Court warehoused by the Federal Ministry of Labour and Productivity. A subsidiary legislation deals with dispute resolution in Essential Services. The Factory Acts attempts to establish health and safety standards in places of work, to be monitored and enforced by Factory Inspectors. While the Workmen's Compensation Act deals with diseases and injuries at work, containing remedies and reliefs entitled to by victims.

But employers also impose rules that are generally referred to as company guidelines or code of conduct or operational rules, etc., which employees are required to abide by. Infractions of such rules may attract negative sanctions, including dismissal. In most cases, upon litigation, courts have generally upheld the binding status of such company regulations, rules, etc., especially when contained in an official handbook or document. It is important, however, to point out that some of such rules and regulations may have been jointly agreed by the parties and included in a collective agreement also. Although, there could be situations where workers and their organisations may unilaterally impose certain conditions (as in closed shop and some custom and work practices), such cases are few and far between under private enterprise economic arrangements and in Nigeria, in particular.

The labour relations system is thus based on a *tripartite* structure or *tripod*: state/government, private (organised) employers and their organisations, and workers and their organisations. These interests are often found and represented at: a) national level; b) industrial level; and c) plant or company level. At the national level for state authorities, the Presidency, Ministry of Establishment and the Ministry of Labour and Productivity play a prominent part, while the Nigeria Employers' Consultative Association (NECA) – complemented by the lobbying activities of the Manufacturers' Association of Nigeria (MAN) and National Association of Chambers of Commerce, Industrial, Mines and Agriculture (NACCIMA) – represents private employers, and the Nigeria Labour Congress (NLC), the Trade Union Congress (TUC) and other federations of trade unions represent workers.

The consequent tripartite relations are both formal and informal but with a tendency toward their institutionalisation. In terms of institutional tripartism, the membership of the National Labour Advisory Board (now, Council), the Industrial Arbitration Panel (IAP), the National Industrial Court (NIC) and appointments to the Boards of many parastatals (such as the National Social Insurance and Trust Fund), *ad hoc* committees on privatisation, deregulation, minimum wage, have tended to be tripartite in nature.

At the industry level, in the Organised Private Sector (OPS), there are employers' organisations for respective industries that are involved in bipartite relations with both senior staff associations and industrial unions which represent the two classes of workers, senior and junior as so defined by law. Aside from resolving challenges facing their respective industries, every two years, both parties embark upon formal negotiations to produce a new collective agreement, modified terms of employment that are meant to be implemented by all employers in the industry concerned.

At the *plant* or *company* level, respective managements are engaged in continuous relations with workers and branches of industrial unions and senior staff associations where they exist. A good many of such managements also engaged themselves in "domestic negotiations" with officials of branch unions and whose outcomes tend to supplement the rates and other conditions agreed at the industry level. More often than not, therefore, collective agreements tend to contain minimum rather than maximum rates and conditions.

PERSPECTIVES ON UNDERLYING ASSUMPTIONS

The industrial relations system in Nigeria was described by Peter Kilby (1967)[4] as the 'Anglo-Saxon Model', giving rise to immediate controversy as to what he meant by that. Peter Kilby's simple assertion was that the Nigerian industrial relations system was 'transferred' by Britain during the colonial period, and he cited the 1938 Trade Union Ordinance, setting up of Whitley Councils, Factories Act and the Department of Labour's frequent reaffirmation of its preference for *voluntary* collective bargaining as evidence of such 'transfer'.

The so-called 'Anglo-Saxon Model' has several assumptions, one of which is the principle of voluntarism. Voluntarism means employers and workers and their organisations on their own reach agreements, just as union membership and recognition are not compulsory.

Another assumption, which is very controversial, is that all colonial powers (Britain, in this case) are said, and do in fact claim, to have 'transmitted' not only certain 'institutional forms' but, in some extravagant cases, the attendant behavioural norms to their former colonies. This "transfer" was supposed to be occurring as the various colonial administrations generated rudimentary social and political institutional framework to enable them to administer their territories for an indefinite period of time, for there was nothing to indicate that their rule would be a short one until China and India became independent in 1945 and 1948 respectively, as well as nationalist protests engulfing all colonies in the same period.

A logical development from the belief in institutional transfers has thus been a tendency on the part of most Western observers to attribute any differences between the principle and practice of transfer either to the intrinsic 'sophistication' of the models offered or to the 'primitivism' or 'backwardness' of recipients or both. The form of trade unionism practised in the underdeveloped parts of the world has thus been loosely referred to as 'political unionism' as against the 'non-political unionism' of the West. Implicit in this 'definition', as in others, is that there exist pure types of union action, 'political' as distinct from 'economic'; clearly a gross simplification of social reality.

It is doubtful whether legislation in the colonies could 'create' same collective behaviour as the one exhibited by British and European unions as implied in the "institutional transfer" thesis, or that employers in Europe

---

[4] Kilby, P. 'Industrial Relations and Wage Determination: Failure of the Anglo-Saxon Model', *Journal of Developing Areas* (JDA)., vol. 1(14), July 1967.

behaved in the same manner as colonial counterparts in their dealings with workers and state authorities. Indeed, such labour legislation in the colonies as existed was largely frustrated by both colonial administrations and colonial European employers - more so as colonial officers combined judicial and executive functions. One does not need a detailed comparative analysis of labour legislation to show significant differences for the example of 'compulsory registration' would suffice. The most troubling feature of the Trades Union Ordinance passed in the colonies in late 1930s was its provision for compulsory registration of trade unions. It enabled the colonial administrations to discriminate against trade unions and often deregistered unions that participated in strikes (like UNAMAG in 1950). This was not the case in Britain itself and this clause has been part of the trade union law since then.

It is therefore mistaken for these observers to maintain that the enactment of a Trade Union Ordinance (while unions were compulsorily registered and struck off at will), ratification of ILO recommendation on collective bargaining (while strikes and check-off were banned with no social security and refusal to recognise unions), the introduction of Whitley Councils (which had failed in Britain - as in Nigeria - because of the uncooperative attitudes of management), a Factories Act (introduced only in 1957 with only three Factory Inspectors for the whole country, and who were opposed by employers because they were thought to act as 'punitive agents and a brake on industry), and other short-term measures adopted by both colonial administration and labour officers amounted to 'institutional transfer'.

In fact, the industrial relations in the European Union in particular are more political than in any other place in the world. There, the emergence of the capitalist welfare state increased the scope of governmental interests and activities and since practically all developments - immigration policy, the educational system, housing, unemployment, nationalisation, deregulation, privatisation, and so on - have become election issues and matters of considerable political interest, any distinction between *political* and *economic* unionism is incorrect and completely misleading – especially as European unions cannot be separated from the political parties. Not even the ascendancy of neo-liberalism in recent times has altered this situation.

Successive Nigerian governments since the 1950s, especially at the centre, proclaimed a policy on industrial relations and trade unionism, different aspects of such a policy receiving greater emphasis in tune with socio-economic developments and preferences of politicians in each decade. Specifically on collective bargaining, in 1954, the Annual Report of the Department of Labour observed thus:

"Government reaffirms its confidence in the effectiveness of voluntary negotiation and collective bargaining for the determination of wages. The long-term interest of government, employers and trade unions alike would seem to rest on the process of consultation and discussion which is the foundation of democracy in industry."[5]

The Annual Report covering the period 1967-69 also noted that:

"The Principle of collective bargaining between employers' associations and the trade unions has been widely accepted in this country as the normal way of settling wages and other conditions of employment."[6]

Then in 1975, under General Gowon military regime, the Commissioner for Labour in his address at the May Day celebrations was quite explicit:

"As you are aware, the pattern of industrial relations has been that of free and voluntary collective bargaining between the employers and the trade unions. Our industrial relations policy is therefore based on the democratic principles which eschew force and upon the firm belief that those directly concerned in the production process are best placed to find satisfactory answers to their problems. Government intervention, a function which my ministry discharges, is only to maintain a balance and ensure that the national interest is safeguarded. Indeed, State intervention becomes the second best."[7]

In 1978, the military regime, represented by Brigadier Shehu Yar'Adua at the inauguration of the Nigerian Labour Congress (NLC) announced its labour policy of 'limited intervention' and of 'guided democracy'. The civilian administration under President Shehu Shagari reverted to a formal position of free and voluntary collective bargaining, while the last crop of military regimes from Buhari in 1984 to Abdusalami Abubakar in 1999, engaged in direct repression of trade unions and largely unilateral determination of terms of employment, especially the national minimum wage, although the Babangida regime talked about decentralization of collective bargaining in the public sector. Till date, the governments of President Obasanjo, Yar'Adua and Jonathan generally talked in terms of voluntary collective bargaining and of decentralisation of collective

[5] Annual Report of the Department of Labour, 1954-55

[6] Annual Report, 1969-71

[7] Cited in Olarewaju Sokunbi, "The Role of the State in Industrial Relations, 11the Advanced Course on Industrial Relations, NECA, 1975 May Day address by the Federal Commissioner for Labour.

bargaining in the public sector, but with practice deviating substantially from posturing.

SOME ASPECTS OF THE LABOUR RELATIONS SYSTEM

The basic labour relations framework today was established under successive military regimes since 1966. The government is both an employer and the body that makes decrees/laws to regulate the activities of everyone else, including those of private employers and workers and their organisations. These two interests, that of employer and regulator, can and do *conflict* and sometimes influence the kind of laws the government passes to regulate the three parties in industrial relations. So, the right of the government to regulate or intervene is accepted in principle by all parties in industry, but how far, where and how frequently are often the problem.

The areas subject to legal regulation are usually: i) union government and administration; ii) employment and manpower development; iii) wages and salaries; iv) collective bargaining; and vi) industrial conflict.

Union government and administration

Out of 29 million wage earners,[8] less than 3 million are organised into trade unions - industrial unions and senior staff associations. Except for the public sector, union coverage in the private sector is less than 50 per cent in each industry because of the prevalence of small and medium scale enterprises where paternalism is the philosophy of management and as such characterised by rabid anti-unionism. Until the 1976-1977 trade union restructuring, both the formation and recognition of trade unions were voluntary, although trade unions were compulsorily registered since the 1939 Trade Union Ordinance.

The Trade Union Act 1973 (and subsequent amendments) concerns itself with the formation and functioning of workers' and employers' organisations, especially union federations. Decree 27 of 1977 specifically recognised separate unions for so-called junior workers (industrial unions) and senior staff (senior staff associations), and the Nigerian Labour Congress (NLC) as the only central labour organisation and to which all industrial unions must affiliate. It also imposed constitutions on all the unions and the NLC. The definition of a trade union also included organisations of employers, as in Britain. In 2005, however, as part of its tactics of undermining the NLC, which was mobilising workers and the general public against President Obasanjo's economic policy and, especially, arbitrary increases in the pump prices of refined petroleum products, the President got the National Assembly to amend the Trade Union Act to permit multiple central labour organisations. The Trade Union Congress (TUC), to which

[8] Federal Office of Statistics.

senior staff associations are affiliated, was successfully registered upon that amendment, after nearly two decades of unsuccessful attempts by its predecessor organisations to do so.

Successive governments since colonial times have routinely targeted the capacity of unions to organise by trying to determine who could be members, who stands for elections and how often union elections can be held, and so forth. Detaining union officials, freezing some bank accounts, dissolving their executives and appointing sole administrators, complemented these objectives. The Registrar of Trade Unions contributes its own part by withdrawing official recognition by deregistration, recognising an unpopular faction of a union, denying some unions permission to amalgamate or federate, extending recognition to only one central labour organisation (pre-1974), insisting on voluntary check-off system for senior staff associations and refusing to accept some union accounts when submitted.

Decrees No. 4, No. 26, No. 29 and the various attempts at restructuring unions (number of industrial unions were reduced to 29 in 1996) are merely specific instances of a continuous policy of intervention in union government and administration. The political climate that prevailed during military rule encouraged anti-union policies in both private and public sectors of the economy. As a result, a good many disputes and strikes were directed against anti-union actions and anti-labour legislation between 1996 and 1998. The state took advantage of moves by unionists to merge some industrial unions to engage in formal restructuring of union structure, a process that was drawn out and deadlock as union leaders opposed the preferences of government officials. In the end and in 1996, Decree No 4 reduced the 41 trade unions to 29, a union structure that is still bedevilled by jurisdictional issues. The regime increased its intervention in the internal affairs of union in the form of Decree No 26 which made a dubious distinction between "card-carrying" members and "non-card carrying" members, allowing only the former to contest union positions. It was a ploy to prevent professional union leaders and bureaucrats from holding critical positions within the industrial unions. This decree was quickly followed by Decree No 29 that prohibited affiliation by Nigerian trades unions with International Labour Organizations, and by the banning of the Academic Staff Union of Universities (ASUU) which was on strike (was later de-proscribed in 1998).

Each industrial union and senior staff association respectively has a branch union in each company where this has become possible by law or tradition: the branch union may thus be regarded as the 'war front' as it is in a position to react to daily developments on the shop floor, while the national headquarters engages in biennial industry-wide negotiations with employers representatives.

Union membership is supposed to be voluntary and a minimum number of 50 workers is required to form a union (at least 2 in the case of employers' union). A union member may also contract out in writing. But there are two important issues here: a) because the Trade Union Act (as amended after subsequent restructuring exercises the last being in 1996)[9] specifically mentions the unions by name, no new union can really be formed; and b) it renders intra-union disputes more intractable as none of the factions can legally constitute itself into a union even where potential and actual members run into thousands (e.g. Dockworkers Union and Maritime Workers Union).

Compulsory registration has remained contentious because: a) an unregistered trade union is an illegal body, while b) it has the effect of workers having to obtain the consent of public authorities, through the office of the Registrar of Trade Unions, for a union to function. All these would seem to go against ILO Convention 87 which recognises the right of workers to form or belong to any union of their choosing and Section 40 of the Constitution that guarantees the right to form or belong to any trade union.

Of similar status are the recognition of a trade union made compulsory, as well as the automatic system of deriving check-off dues at source imposed by law (although a member can also contract out in writing) – except for senior staff associations. Not only do both go against the principle of voluntarism, deliberately denying senior staff associations automatic check-off system for deriving membership dues is indicative of the control function of this provision.

The powers of the Registrar of Trade Unions are overwhelming, including accepting/rejecting audited annual accounts of the trade unions,[10] de-registration of a union, and approving ground rules for mergers. The conditions to be met are so many and demanding to have the net effect of discouraging, if not rendering impossible, voluntary mergers and federations. On the audited accounts, there was a time the Auditor/Accountant was imposed on the unions: now, there is an approved list from which unions should choose. Some trade unions have simply ignored the rejection of their audited accounts by the Registrar of Trade

---

[9] Uba Ahmed, Minister of Employment, Labour & Productivity under the Abacha dictatorship deliberately held on to the registration certificates of the 29 restructured unions right up to when the dictator died in 1998, often describing the unions as 'illegal bodies' on account of not possessing the certificates and thus should not be involved in negotiations of any sort on behalf of 'imaginary' union members.

[10] Aside from having powers to call for accounts of the union at any time, the Registrar may also institute civil or criminal proceedings against the union if not satisfied with the audited accounts!

Unions, and there has been talk over the years of money changing hands for some accounts to be officially accepted.

Most trade union constitutions have been imposed by government authorities, and it is only within the last ten years in particular have some unions been struggling to amend some provisions in their constitutions without any reference to the Registrar of Trade Unions - save to deposit a copy of the amended constitution.

All military regimes have intervened in the internal affairs of some trade unions by dissolving their executive committees and incarcerating their principal officers on undisclosed grounds (e.g. ASUU, PENGASSAN, NUPENG and the NLC).

As part of the consequence of globalisation (mergers, takeovers, etc.), de-unionisation has been on the increase, especially in the banking and manufacturing sectors. In addition, growing unemployment, due to restructuring, downsizing and bankruptcies, is thinning the ranks and membership of trade unions (in the oil and gas sector, outsourcing and subcontracting of 'non-core' jobs could easily lead to the demise of NUPENG in not too distant future, and for the past ten years hundreds of textile mills have closed down).

Collective bargaining and Wage bargain

The Labour Act,[11] aside from defining a worker as any person who has entered into or works under a contract of service or a contract to execute any work or labour in person, concerns itself with written particulars of terms and conditions of employment, protection of wages, recruitment and related miscellaneous matters. In the Organised Private Sector, most employees do have an idea of their terms of employment - an idea, because not all receive personal letters/contract of employment, depending on their level and nature of job. For those organised by trade unions, even where some workers initially received a letter of offer of appointment (which, in most cases, does not go into details of entitlements), whatever terms might have been would be modified by subsequent collective agreements that contain new terms applicable to positions or posts occupied by individual union members. And, it must be observed, most union members have not seen a copy of a collective agreement. This is one reason why the routine implementation of collective agreements and across-the-board awards granted by wages and salaries commissions or by various governments have tended to generate protests and disputes over differentials, many a management taking

[11] This Act which commenced on 1 August 1971 is a consolidation of the laws relating to labour, especially the Labour Code Act (Cap. 91, Laws of the Federation of Nigeria, 1958. The Labour Act is also referred to as Cap. 198, Laws of the Federation of Nigeria 1990.

advantage of the situation to impose their own interpretation of wage levels and entitlements.

As for workers in unorganised establishments, banking and finance, manufacturing and oil and gas sectors, evidence indicates that most managements therein meticulously draft contracts of employment, some so ingeniously so that they often have little regard for human and other rights (e.g. no pregnancy allowed for a number of years; spouses may not work in the same establishment; working hours exceeding 48 hours a week by a wide margin; confirmation of appointment depending on deposits brought in irrespective of job function and performance on that job). Although Section 7 of the Labour Act requires an employer to give a written statement specifying terms of employment within 3 months of such a worker commencing work, in these days of 'casualisation' many employers avoid complying with this provision by dismissing workers within three months - in effect creating a constant stream of workers whose careers in that establishment are just a bit short of three months.[12] Why should an employer be given a whole three months to issue a simple letter after contractual relations have since commenced?

The government is also heavily involved in regulating collective bargaining despite its official position of being fully in support of *free collective bargaining*, a policy it declared publicly in 1954. The government as an employer has been determining public sector terms through the establishment and functioning of wages and salaries commissions (there is now a permanent salaries, incomes and wages commission), and was later to strive to isolate the demonstration effect of private sector terms of employment in order to keep its own wage bill down. It also sought to influence the size of wage settlements and fringe benefits in the private sector in its fight against inflation. But the latter was only a recent development because up till the early 1960s, wages and fringe benefits were higher in the public sector, and this partly explains why incomes policies as a regulatory instrument became widely used by government from the 1970s when rates of compensation in the private sector overtook those in the public. The Labour Act and Workmen's Compensation Act are the main legislation in this respect (the latter focusing more on compensation for industrial injuries), and the government requires copies of collective agreements to be deposited with the Ministry of Employment, Labour & Productivity, and in some cases may actually reject some clauses in the agreements. State authorities have

---

[12] A variation in some of the banks is that of the first four or eight or twelve weeks being regarded as "training period", after which those with "unsatisfactory performance" are not given letters of "final" employment. The successful employees would then commence another six months period of "probation".

continued the habit of unilaterally imposing a national minimum wage in spite of tripartite discussions.

Since the 1980s the dramatically deteriorating standard of living in the face of stagflation and decreasing capacity utilization in many industries has presented problems of sorts for all parties in industry. Not all the problems in the economy and industry have been caused by the bogey of world-wide economic depression. The rate of inflation, monetary and fiscal policy, autonomy and effectiveness of monetary institutions and authorities, extra-budgetary expenditures and budget deficits, official housing, health and educational policies, elite-generated political crises and tensions, sourcing of raw materials, pricing policies of trading and manufacturing industries, activities of middlemen and of market-women and men, just to mention a few, all impact upon the situation. The variety of levies imposed by state and local governments have increased the impoverishment of the general population and of wage earners in particular.

In Nigeria's public sector wages and salaries and grading have been carried out by wages and salaries commission in unionised establishments while national wages board, area minimum wages committees for states and of joint industrial councils for particular industries.[13] The latter-day National Public Service Negotiating Councils do not appear to be central to the processes and procedures for regulating terms and conditions of employment. They seem to have been used in settling controversies over interpretation of specific government measure (e.g. decentralization of collective bargaining) or complications in differentials arising out of across-the-board award.

The International Labour Organisation Convention No. 98 enjoins members of the Organisation to take measures appropriate to national conditions where necessary, to encourage and promote the full development and utilisation of machinery for voluntary negotiation between employers or employers' organization and workers' organisations, with a view to the regulation of terms and conditions of employment by means of collective agreements.[14]

Collective agreements are industry-based, though supplemented by in-plant or domestic negotiations. Domestic negotiations are particularly

[13] Major commissions, tribunals and committees from 1920 till the eve of political independence in 1959 include the Hunt Committee (1934), the Bridges Committee (1941), the Harragin Commission (1945 which published its report in 1947), the Tudor Davies Commission (1946), the Miller Committee (1947), the Cowan Enquiry (1948), the Gorsuch Commission (1954) the Mbanefo Commission (1958), and the Morgan Commission (1959).[13] These Committees and Commissions, including those such as the Fitzgerald Commission (1949) appointed to examine the peculiar circumstances leading to violent protests and deaths such as those at the Enugu coalmines in 1949 were representative of the significant twists and turns of public sector industrial relations over the four decades ending in 1960.

[14] Article 4; Nigeria ratified the Convention on 17th October, 1960.

important in the oil and gas sector, where Shell-BP's rates remain the pace setter to be matched by other companies. Although, employers in this industry do compare notes on terms and conditions of employment, there is some secrecy over certain fringe benefits in order to maintain a competitive edge on this score. This appears to be one of the reasons why employers have seen little need to form a formal association that would make certain conditions binding on all members. In the Food, Beverage and Tobacco sector, the attempt is directed more at achieving uniform rates, narrowing of differences in rates and thus taking labour cost out of competition.

There has always been tension and grievances over disparity in private and public sector rates, especially in the oil and gas industry.

Collective agreements are generally not enforceable in a court of law. Given the increasing incidence of abandonment of agreements by employers, especially in the public sector, the Australian and American-type agreements that are fully justiciable may be more appropriate. Following from the immediate above "bargaining in good faith" has become a problem, and trust is proving to be very elusive. Entering into agreements with the intention not to respect them undermines any system of collective relations.

The monitoring of safety and health standards in industry by the regulatory authorities has been very slack, while compensation rates contained in the Workmen's Compensation Act for injury sustained at work are laughable and provoking.[15]

There is the dominant institutional role of the Minister and of the Federal Ministry of Employment, Labour & Productivity in institutionalised collective bargaining. His powers include, among others, demanding mandatory deposit of copies of collective agreements to rejection of terms already agreed by the parties in industry.

Negotiation processes and procedures are fairly straightforward. Management tends to bear the cost of venue, accommodation, board and allowances. The process is often triggered by workers' side sending a "shopping list" in a booklet or pamphlet dubbed "charter of demand", followed by informal exchanges of views before formal negotiating sessions in an agreed location (usually in an hotel). Each side has a list of issues colloquially referred to as "no-go areas" that the other side may not justifiably make any references to, let alone discuss them. A close study of the "no-go" items would reveal the prevailing power relations: some "no-go" issues a few years ago may become joint issues if in the intervening period the performance of the company and of management has been of a nature to bring into question the legitimacy and wisdom of excluding them from joint-examination.

---

[15] Details are set out in the Second Schedule, especially Sections 7, 8 and 41.

The resulting collective agreement is often in two parts, procedural/disciplinary and substantive. In general, the disciplinary agreement is more extensive, focusing more on employees' responsibilities and management prerogatives. It would be fair to conclude that not much of negotiation takes place since, in most cases, management's offers are on a "take it or leave it" basis, and, as mentioned above, the timing of the implementation of agreed terms (especially fringe benefits) tending to generate more disputes and conflicts. Most management would insist on commencing the implementation of the new terms from the date agreement was signed and not from the date the previous collective agreement expired. While in respect of the payment of certain allowances, management may wish to stagger by commencing payment of some immediately and others six months or so after. And for some strange reasons, management side would neither mention nor discuss these options during negotiations, attempting to pass off such unilateral measures as management prerogative. Needless mentioning that the union side routinely opposes such moves by management.

Only a minority of wage earners are covered by institutionalised collective bargaining, the majority fending as best can for itself.

The management of pension in the public sector seems to have collapsed, state authorities unable to pay pensioners arrears of their entitlements, and this in spite of the tripartite structure of the Nigeria Social Insurance Trust Fund (NSITF). Pensions and their management are likely to prove intractable and conflict-inducing for the near future.

HISTORICAL OVERVIEW OF COLLECTIVE BARGAINING IN THE PUBLIC SECTOR

The development of the public sector in Nigeria followed closely the pattern of colonial conquest and the type of economic activities the colonial state was engaged in. The attempt to provide such services as water, transport, electricity, sanitation, housing, and general ad-ministration in centres of economic activities in the first instance, and subsequently to provide a general administrative framework, improve upon communications and monitor these and the activities of private employers and of other interest groups in society ultimately generated wage employment, created some skills and bargaining relationships of the sort we are concerned with in industrial relations.

What forms these phenomena took and how complex they were depended largely on the times. From the 1890s and right up to the 1920s, it was a combination of widespread use of forced labour, remuneration in kind and very low wages where paid, a mass of unskilled labour coexisting fitfully with few artisans, and thus the relative absence of rates that could be applied generally. Existing rates of pay and differentials in pay and other terms of employment were first 'European' as against 'African' (and within each category there were variations and different grades), and later among occupational groups, particularly as between skilled and semi-skilled artisans and clerks. The only general item was 'war bonus', a flat sum, which was paid at the onset of the First World War, and even in this that of Europeans was not only higher, Africans were only paid after protests and strikes.[16]

From the 1930s to the 1950s, what was embryonic in the previous period had become more fully developed, establishing in the process what appeared to be the distinguishing features of wage bargain situation in the public sector and which remained largely unchanged till late 1960s. The use of forced labour was on the decline (abandoned officially only in late 1950s) and the idea of the payment of regular wages appeared to have been accepted in principle by most employers, terms of employment became largely regionalised, as sharp pay and other economic distinctions emerged between the clerical and non-clerical, among occupational groups, between public and private sector employees, and ethnic and regional particularities and political considerations supplanted racial discrimination.

The way these factors combined with and related to each other produced a complex picture, the more obvious aspect being basic rates for different categories of employees in public utilities (parastatals), local government and main civil service remaining generally applicable only *within* Eastern, Northern, Western Regions and Lagos respectively. The comparability of, and thus subsequent changes in, terms of employment among the regions became more a question of political considerations, from the employers point of view, especially in the late fifties and early 1960s, than to any great desire on their part to work out a minimum wage or a living wage that would enable the least-paid public employee afford more than the basic necessities of life.[17]

The changes in public administration in the 1960s and thereafter were of a fundamental type and made it possible to table the issue of a national minimum wage at different points in time. Hitherto, since the 1920s, the colonial administration merely set up *ad hoc* committees or commissions to look into 'labour problems' or 'wage problems' in designated sections, bodies that were then appointed on regional and federal basis in the 1950s. Although regionalism and ethnic particularities still held considerable sway in political and social matters, in terms of fiscal developments, growth of the monetary system and of financial institutions, there was a swing in favour of

[16] Ananaba, W., *The Trade Union Movement in Nigeria*, Ethiope, 1969.

[17] Yesufu, T.M., explicitly argues that the 1954-55 upward review of wage rates and including the Mbanefo (1958) and Morgan (1959) were politically motivated. See his *An Introduction to Industrial Relations in Nigeria*, OUP/NISER, 1962.

a centralized and more co-ordinated approach. This was no doubt reinforced by the fact that 'labour' as a legislative issue was the prerogative of the centre, which also explains why regions (and states) have had no Ministry of Labour.

The factors which accounted for this new tendency (centralization) were a) against a background of political upheavals and alliances, it seemed manifestly difficult for regional governments to adopt unilateral measures of the kind experienced in late 1940s and early 1950s. Indeed, we have seen how in 1958 the Federal, Eastern and Northern governments jointly appointed the Mbanefo Wages Commission and the Western Region government had its own Morgan Commission in 1959. It stays instructive that when a second Morgan Commission was appointed by the Federal Government in 1963 in the wake of a general strike, no regional government opted out, and wages commissions have since then been either applicable to the public sector as a whole, or to a section of the public sector, or to employees in both public and private sectors of the economy; b) closely related to this was the accretion of fiscal and political power to the centre, especially from 1966 onwards. By the 1970s the states were more dependent on Lagos for funds, the criteria for sharing revenue having been progressively modified in favour of the centre.

A logical consequence seemed to be that matters concerning remuneration and scope of rates were handed down from Lagos (through incomes and policy guidelines, awards of wages commissions, Acts of parliament, rulings of both the Industrial Arbitration Panel and the National Industrial Court, the various activities of the Federal Ministry of Employment, Labour and Productivity) in the age or decades of economic planning and of development plans, financially delinquent states seeking more funds or grants to meet labour costs; c) the public utilities or parastatals had proliferated and grown much bigger and complex than ever before, a large number of them brought into existence by much expanded economic investments and activities of various state and federal governments and their agencies. These were only made possible by the quadrupling of crude oil prices in 1973/74 and thus receipt of massive revenues, which in turn partly gave rise to an indigenization policy and increased complexity of emerging or reinforced parastatals; and, d) the final creation of a national labour market, even for the private sector, and which threw up common personnel issues and problems of comparability in pay and other terms of employment. It was now possible, with all of these developments, for organized labour and social critics to advocate the establishment of a national minimum wage, and a closer examination of the differentials between public sector and private sector pay.

REVIEW OF PREVIOUS COLLECTIVE BARGAINING ISSUES IN THE PUBLIC SECTOR

Simplified considerably, trade unionism in Nigeria and the reactions of public and private employers to it may be said to represent, in a nutshell, attempts at establishing minimum wage rates or wages in various sections of industry - and without implying that unionism has only been concerned with wages. Early attempts at establishing minimum rates of pay has occurred mostly in the public sector, beginning with the Lagos Crown Colony in respect of which Hughes & Cohen (1971) have recorded how the institution of an urban administration and the creation of public utilities generated a standing corpus of officials, artisans, and other categories of labour earning different rates of pay.[18] Disagreements over minimum rates led to many strikes, the best documented being the strike by employees of the Public Works Department in 1897 when the governor unilaterally reduced wages which were already too low.[19]

But attempts with longer lasting effects were made in the first two decades of this century, efforts which established wages commissions as the most preferred method of establishing rates in the public sector. As Coleman (1958) observed, two civil services existed, the African and the European, with parallel career structures and the latter enjoying better terms of employment. African terms were determined locally while those of European civil servants fixed from London, the former salary scales ranged from £36 to £400 a year while those of Europeans from £450 to over £2000 for the Lieutenant Governors.[20] Even so, because of widespread disenchantment with prevailing terms of employment and made worse by the hardships caused by the First World War (1914-1918), according to Nicholson (1969), 'the African juniors were expressing their discontent in open strikes, and the European seniors openly disaffected.'[21]

The result was that a series of internal administrative reviews by different committees were instituted, beginning with the Cameron-Carr Committee in 1906, followed by Bratt and Rice Committees in 1919. The other major commissions, tribunals and committees since then have been the Hunt Committee (1934), the Bridges Committee (1941), the Harragin Commission (1945 but published its report in 1947), the Tudor Davies Commission (1946), the Miller Committee (1947), the Cowan Enquiry

[18] An abridged version of their study may be found in Gutkind, P.C.W., Cohen, R., & Copans, J. (eds.), *African Labor History*, Sage, Beverly Hills & London, 1978.

[19] Hopkins, A.G., 'The Lagos Strike of 1897: an exploration in Nigerian labour history,' *Past and Present*, 35, 1966

[20] Coleman, J.S., *Nigeria: Background to Nationalism*, University of California Press, Berkeley & Los Angeles, 1958, p. 155.

[21] Nicholson, I.F., *The Administration of Nigeria, 1900-1960: Men, Methods and Myths*, Clarendon Press, London, 1969

(1948), the Gorsuch Commission (1954), the Mbanefo Commission (1958), the Morgan Commission (1959), the Morgan Commission (1963), the Adebo Commission (1970), the Udoji Commission (1974), the Williams Committee (1975), the Onosode Commission (1980), the Cookey Commission (1981), and the Adamolekun Commission (1981); National Minimum Wage Act 2000; National Minimum Wage (Amendment) Act, 2011, National Minimum Wage Act 2019, National Minimum Wage (Amendment) Act 2024.

These commissions or committees served two related purposes of establishing minimum rates and of reviewing them at a later date after workers' protests and other conditions make such a review imperative. The Bratt Committee (1919) reviewed the terms of European civil servants but its report was not published. While the Rice Committee (1919), which included representatives of the Civil Service Union, revised African salaries. And, according to Nicholson (1969), "the case of the African civil service was met within a few weeks, by doubling of an existing 30 per cent 'war bonus', after emergency Executive Council meetings and telegrams to the Secretary of State, followed by a more complete overhaul of salary structure."[22]

The Hunt Committee (1934) was charged with the task of reviewing the wages of unskilled workers and of determining a reasonable standard of living for a labourer. The Committee noted in its preamble that in computing a 'reasonable standard of living' for a labourer, his wife and children were not taken into account! Given the zeal of the colonial administration in maintaining low wages, following classical *laissez faire* economic doctrine, it actually reduced wages because of the ongoing economic depression. As the depression dragged on and workers protests mounted, the colonial administration established Provincial Wages Committees in 1937 for Eastern, Northern and Western provinces which were the politico-administrative units of the time. Through them the wages that had been cut a few years back were restored.

The Bridges Committee (1941) was a response to wartime shortages and escalating prices. It reviewed the wages of African government workers and also recommended compensatory increases which were subsequently dubbed 'cost-of-living awards' (COLA). But in doing this, it dispensed with the empiricism of the Hunt Committee (which sought to determine the actual costs of basic commodities) and posited its own 'model' diet from which it derived its computations and estimated the wage of the 'average' labourer in Lagos to be two shillings a day.

Equally interesting, in relation to our earlier remarks on fragmented and regionalized wage rates and payment systems, the Bridges Committee made

[22] Nicholson, I.F., *op. cit.*, p. 222

sure that basic pay rates and cost of living allowances throughout the country were not uniform. Towns and areas were classified into categories A, B, and C, areas and towns which had higher rate of inflation and thus higher cost of living falling under the A category. And within each group, they were subdivisions. Lagos Township and Lagos Colony as a whole came under categories A and B respectively. In the Eastern Province, Port Harcourt, Aba, and Enugu were classified Al, Owerri province, Calabar province, Victoria, Buea, Kumba Township were B, and Cameroon, Onitsha, Ogoja provinces were Cl. As for the Northern Province, Jos, Bukuru, Kaduna, Zaria and Kano Township came under A3, followed by Minna, Lokoja, and Makurdi in B, and Ilorin province, Adamawa province, Bauchi province, Bornu province, Katsina province and Sokoto in C category. While in Western Province, Warri Town and Sapele were in category A2 and A3 respectively, followed by Abeokuta, Benin City, Ibadan Town, and Ijebu province in B, with Ondo province in C category.[23]

Labour Advisory Boards were established by the Labour (Wage Fixing and Regulation) Ordinance of 1943, implementing one of the recommendations of the Bridges Committee. Although section 6 of the Ordinance empowered the boards to make inquiries into conditions of service and wages in any trade referred to them by the colonial authorities and to make recommendations for fixing the statutory minimum wage, this was hardly ever done. In 1944 when E. A. Miller, the Commissioner of Labour, proposed the formation of a permanent Labour Advisory Board (LAB) in the Plateau in view of persistent labour protests, he was not only opposed by private employers who considered it 'undue interference', but a fellow bureaucrat and Minerals Administrator in charge of tin production, Emberton, was not too keen either, seeing the board as 'a stage for agitators.'[24] When the board finally came into being in July 1946, the Jos Resident felt that 'he or some other provincial officer was far more suited to represent labourers than any trades union members.'[25]

The Tudor Davies Commission (1946) appointed in the wake of the 1945 General Strike deplored both the relative absence of official direction in matters of collective bargaining and disputes and the ineffectiveness of the Department of Labour. Aside from recommending the establishment of an *ad hoc* National Negotiating Committee comprising representatives of State, private employers and workers, the Commission additionally recommended that 'matters of wages and conditions of employment should entirely be the responsibility of a reconstituted Labour Department, and all stages from

---

[23] For these awards, a readily available source is Ananaba, W., *The Trade Union Movement in Nigeria, op. cit.*, p. 29

[24] Freund, 1981:180.

[25] Ibid.

conciliation to final enforcement should be in its hands.'[26] The Labour Advisory Board set up to advise government, the Commission found ineffectual as it had no executive powers, and recommended that it be reconstituted under the new name of "Labour, Wages and Conditions of Employment Commission" whose primary function should be to examine the scope and the application of wages and conditions of employment in any industry and make suggestions regarding the establishment of a Wage Council. It also found unsatisfactory the official machinery for and manner of computing cost of living indices (survey based on expenditure pattern of 256 households, rather than on several common items of expenditure preferred and recommended by the Commission, and recommend the Rent Assessment Board be given powers to fix rents); thought official statistics of inflation rate were unreliable; that government advisers themselves were fully aware of the importance of establishing appropriate organisations or even the principle of trade unionism. The Commission awarded salary increments ranging from fifty to seventy-five per cent.

The much-delayed report of the Harragin Commission came out in 1947 with the salaries of 'established' government staff (as against temporary and daily-paid hands). Its terms of reference reflected concerns of the time and the Commission was to review and make recommendations upon the structure and remunerations of the Civil Services (with the exception of unestablished and daily-paid staff) of the four West African colonies with special reference to: a) the general standards of remuneration and superannuation payments; b) the relationship of the salaries and conditions of service of locally recruited and externally recruited officers; c) the machinery for adjusting remuneration to variations in the cost of living; d) the provision of suitable arrangements for consultation between governments and organizations representing the interests of the staff on matters relating to salaries and conditions of service; e) the provision, by means of Public Service Commissions or otherwise, of suitable machinery, where this not already in existence, for regulating the selection and promotion of candidates for posts, the filling of which is not subject to the approval of the Secretary of State (UK). Among its recommendations, aside from substantial wage increases, the introduction of 'expatriation fees' for European officers, and advisory councils modelled along the lines of the Whitley Councils in the UK that should advise the government on all matters of general interest concerning the salaries and conditions of employment of civil servants, was the controversial one of a higher entry point of salary for African technical staff as against white collar workers or clerical jobs – which most of the trade unions rejected.

[26] Report, 26, para. 93.

The Miller Committee (1947) reviewed upwards the wage rates of daily-paid labourers but established the principle of payment on a geographical basis, a system that was meant to be less cumbersome than that of the Bridges Committee. The former made a simple distinction between general labour on the one hand, and special and semi-skilled on the other, dividing the country into six geographical zones with differentials in pay for these two groups of labour. The guiding 'principle' was that cost of living was highest in Lagos and in its immediate environs, and that wages should be progressively lower the farther away from Lagos a labourer was.

And in tune with the Harragin recommendations, the Cowan Enquiry (1948) investigated and reported on methods of negotiation between government and employees in state-owned industrial establishments. It introduced 'Whitley Councils': a Junior Whitley Council (A) for clerical and other office employees, and Junior Whitley Council (B) for industrial or manual workers. As Yesufu (1962) confirmed, these were a dismal failure as they had become consultative instead of negotiating bodies, suffered difficulties over representation, and 'broke down completely because of staff side dissatisfaction over progress in negotiation.'[27] Akpala (1982) points out an additional reason for their failure by noting that 'the structural relationship between the two junior Whitley Councils could not be reconciled with the structure of the trades unions of the government employees.'

The colonial administration, in line with this recommendation established Provincial Wage Committees, which were joined in 1951 by Regional Wage Committee to reflect the new political structure of three regions. Akpala (1982, 106-107) has a brief but useful description of the workings of these committees. The main issue is that they met infrequently, were not bargaining bodies, and functioned against the opposition of trade unions which deprecated the administration's attempts to entrench a geographical wage structure, a policy that had enormous appeal to provincial residents and native administrations who were most unlikely to overlook any opportunity to save on labour costs, having grown used to utilizing forced labour which they could no longer legally do. The unions understandably asked for uniform rates for daily-paid workers everywhere while at the same time refusing to take up their membership in the Central Committee set up by the central government to reconcile their own views with those of the Regional Committees which favoured geographical disparities in wages.

The upshot was that against a background of workers' protests co-ordinated by the central labour organisation, the All Nigeria Trade Union

[27] *Op. cit.*

Federation (ANTUF),[28] the Western and Eastern Region governments disbanded the Provincial Wages Committees, the dissenting northern residents and administrations retained theirs, while the Federal Government itself settled wages in Lagos.[29] In such an uncertain and conflict laden situation the Federal Government was obliged to establish a Minimum Wage Fact-Finding Committee comprising three of its own officials. In its representations before this committee the ANTUF made short shrift of a geographical wage structure, demanded a national minimum wage, and further pointed out that wage committees had hardly been in the interest of workers since they were not fully represented on them; administration and employers' representatives dominated them, using their majority vote in arriving at decisions against workers' interests.[30]

Nothing of an innovative nature could be expected from the Minimum Wage Fact-Finding Committee in view of its composition. As was pertinently observed, the Committee's recommendation was an 'adoption of the thinking of Council of Ministers which seemed to have made up its mind before the appointment of the Committee that provincial wage bodies and therefore the Miller scheme of wages should remain.'[31] A minimum wage as claimed by the committee would create 'difficulties' and undermine the effectiveness of the contemplated incentive bonus scheme! After its recommendations were made public, the 'federal government did not see fit to meet the unions for discussion.' It was against this background that both Western and Eastern Region governments took the more decisive, self-serving but positive step of paying a uniform wage and transferring all daily-paid workers to permanent employment respectively.

As wage committees were not bargaining bodies, such unpleasant decisions could only be reversed by confrontation at the workplace, and to strike action, thus accounting for the higher incidence of recorded strikes in the period 1953 to 1959. Yesufu's (1962) wholesale dismissal of these pre-emptive moves by the regional governments as 'political wage fixing', does not do justice to the facts on the ground. His assessment fails to reflect the intense union pressures against geographical wage structure and the confusion and acrimony generated by the desultory operating style and very limited impact of these wage committees. More importantly, the Federal Government was only too pleased to pass on the problems of daily-paid

[28] Formed in 1953 to embrace all the dissenting union leaders who had formed a rival central body called the Council of ICFTU-Affiliated Unions. However, by 1956 the same labour leaders left the ANTUF to reconstitute the Council of ICFTU-Affiliated Unions and which later metamorphosed into the National Council of Trade Unions of Nigeria (NCTUN) in 1957.

[29] Akpala, A., *Industrial Relations Model for Developing Countries: the Nigerian System*, Fourth Dimensions Press, Enugu, 1981982, 106-107.

[30] Akpala, ibid., p.107.

[31] Akpala, ibid., p. 107

workers and a minimum wage to the regional governments as soon as the latter came into being in 1951, the former having, in fact, increased wages across the board by administrative fiat in 1949/50. It was extremely unlikely in view of the administrative and political arrangements at the time that the Federal Government would initiate the establishment of any minimum wage or wage rates that it could not uniformly enforce across the country. At any rate, the battle by the political parties over control of the Federal Government was already on, and could only encourage the Governor-General and his men to routinely reiterate existing policy on geographical wage structures and wages boards.

We might also recall the three 'Whitley Councils' established in 1948 by the Cowan Committees, one for 'senior staff' and two for 'junior staff'. These were a dismal failure by 1949 because as Yesufu (1962, 52) correctly observed, they had become consultative instead of negotiating bodies, suffered difficulties over representation, and 'broke down completely because of staff side dissatisfaction over progress in negotiation'. They were also undermined by frequent use of salary and wages commissions. Akpala (1982. 78) additionally noted that 'the structural relationship between the two junior Whitley Councils could not be reconciled with the structure of the trades unions of the government employees.' Despite their reconstitution along lines proposed by Mr. Carruthers, sent by the United Kingdom Ministry of Labour, no visible improvements were observed in their operation, Fashoyin (1980, 106)[32] suggesting continued failure as the reason for the 1974 Udoji Commission's preference for a National Public Service Negotiating Council, a body which itself has made little impact to date.

The Wages Board was established by the Wages Board Ordinance of 1957 as a successor to, and to offset the inadequacies of the Labour Advisory Boards. It had the same powers to look into industries or occupations where wages were observed to be unusually low and to make recommendations. Unlike the *ad hoc* Labour Advisory Boards, it was permanent. Despite the equal representation of both employers and workers and not more than three so-called independent persons, the Wages Board suffered the singular weakness of being dependent on the whims of the Minister of Labour. If the Minister did not feel like calling a meeting on receipt, for example, of the recommendations of a Commission of Inquiry, nothing could be done about it, especially in private establishments where employers and managements routinely insisted on 'private and voluntary collective bargaining', as if prevailing low wages owed nothing to their anti-unionism and brand of 'bargaining'. With a touch of irony, a defence offered in parliament argued that 'although the Minister is responsible for initiating action in underpaid

[32] Fashoyin, T., *Industrial Relations in Nigeria*, Longman, 1980

occupations and responsible also for making an Order fixing minimum wages, etc., the responsibility for determining those wages and conditions of employment rests squarely on the shoulders of the members of the Wages Board. In this way, it is hoped that this will promote the rise of and growth of voluntary collective bargaining.'[33] The Wage Board system fell into disuse in 1966 when political crises came to a head and the country rapidly plunged into a three-year Civil War.

Yesufu (1962, 52-54)[34] discusses parallel developments in private establishments, where labour officers had joined employees and unions in cajoling and coercing employers into establishing more permanent negotiating structures in the form of joint consultative committees. These Joint Industrial Councils (JICs) or Joint Consultative Committees (JCC) were also adopted in public corporations and utilities (later called parastatals), many of which carried on business in partnership with foreign and indigenous investors, financial institutions such as the World Bank, and agencies of the United Nations Organization (UNO). Yesufu's position on the workings of these committees has remained ambivalent, sometimes implying a respectable degree of 'joint consultation' and 'collective bargaining', and sometimes not. Citing official figures of a total of 212 of such committees in the country as at 1957 and nominally covering an aggregate of 207,582 employees, he concludes that 'between 25 and 30 per cent of the estimated wage-earning population come under a system of joint consultation, or collective bargaining' and that 'such machinery is widely diffused in the various sectors of the economy, although usually confined to expatriate firms, apart from government departments and public corporations.'[35]

A few clues to their real effectiveness as provided by Yesufu (1962) include the fact that these committees were 'used to deal with both negotiation and consultation', that employers refused to establish separate bodies for both 'consultation' and 'collective bargaining' on grounds of likely 'duplication', that there was an 'absence of formal trade union organizations', and that there was 'sheer ignorance not exclusively on the part of workers, as to the nature of the difference between joint consultation and collective bargaining' (ibid.). His claim that 'under Nigerian conditions it has not often proved possible to effect in practice the distinction between joint consultation and collective bargaining' is both refutable and unnecessary for, on the whole, private employers sought to do without either consultation or collective bargaining throughout the sixty odd years of direct colonial rule. It has also been mentioned how most of the institutions

[33] Cited in Akpala, 1982, 81.
[34] *Op. cit.*
[35] 1962, 52-54.

established by the state and private employers were inevitably turned into fora for merely *informing* employees about policies. If anything, the insistence of trade unions and workers on a collective approach to the tackling of industrial issues and protests in pursuance of that demand, and the resistance of employers to unionism and collective bargaining seem to have been the distinguishing characteristics of colonial industrial relations practice. In practice both parties seemed to have understood the distinctions between unilateral action and joint consultation, and between joint consultation and collective bargaining well enough.

Indeed, Yesufu (1962, 57) later concedes that 'workers accused management of bad faith and of attempts, which were justified in some cases, to use the committee against the recognition of a trade union'. Moreover, besides, he claims some of these committees never met and /or met less frequently than they were expected, 'neither management nor the workers had faith in the machinery' and 'in the case of one committee the workers were able to provide examples where management had victimized worker representatives by transfer, change of job, or withholding of an increment because those representatives expressed views which were considered "dangerous" or distasteful to, or did so in a manner that did not show respect for, the management.' His unhappiness over the apparent 'failure' of workers to recognize a distinction between 'joint consultation' and 'collective bargaining' may be detected in Yesufu's further observation that 'the workers regarded the committees solely as avenues for demanding increased wages and for airing grievances, and hardly gave thought to matters such as productivity and safety, to which management attached great importance.' This is then followed by a somewhat curious but revealing comment to the effect that 'the Department of Labour has put on record that the main instances where success of joint committee is found have usually been only in those establishments where there had been a history of industrial disturbance which apparently made the employers anxious to maintain contact at all levels with workers.'[36] So, only conflict could compel private employers to use joint consultation machinery.

The Sofola Report, however, noted the existence of 'informal arrangements' in some establishments which, in the main, amounted to employers and the union executive (where they exist) getting together at 'short notice' to 'discuss' matters relating to the welfare of workers including 'wages and conditions' (1957, 5). It was only in one large retail house, employing over 800 workers, that a Joint Consultative Committee (JCC) was found to exist, and both employers and workers confirmed that in the light of the prevailing conditions in the industry, the JCC could not be 'restricted

---

[36] Yesufu, *op. cit.*, 1962, 58

only to matters properly belonging to such a body'. It was also the case that 'in answer to the question put to other employers visited or who gave evidence before us as to the means of consultation in matters of common interest to both sides, we were told that *they were open at all times to approaches by their workers*.' In view of this, 'we are not impressed by this answer which, expressed as the sole means of management-labour relations, reveals a paternalistic outlook which is not conducive to the development of sound labour relations.'[37]

The workers' view, as contained in the Report, was that 'the informal arrangement, where it exists, is unsatisfactory in that it places the workers at the mercy of the employers', the Commission tortuously concluding that 'we do not necessarily share this view but it is our view that these arrangements are ineffectual and cannot be regarded as machinery for the fixing of wages and conditions.'[38]

As regards the process of wage fixing itself, employers were found unilaterally and arbitrarily to reach decisions on basic rates and increments. Such arbitrariness seemed to have been facilitated by two tactics, namely secrecy over individual incremental rates (thus absence of a wage scale) and cultivation of personal relations in the smaller establishments, the latter usually 'directed against union solidarity' (ibid., 6). One employer was found to have 'abolished the salary scale previously in his establishment and he now awards increase at random' (p. 6). A consequence was that wages were considerably lower than anywhere else, ranging between 2s. and 3s. per day as compared with the minimum wage of 4s. 8d. per day paid to the lowest employee in the public sector. The Commission was forced to conclude that 'we do not consider the prevailing practice among the majority of employers of awarding increases in wages as and when they like to be in the best interest of labour' (p. 6). And, after noting relative absence of machinery for determining wages and other conditions of employment, it deprecated the 'unreasonably low wages and prevalence of long hours as a result of the inadequacy of the machinery (if we might so call the present various arrangements) for regulating the wages and conditions of employment of workers engaged in the trade' (p.6). Worse still, the Report pointed out, 'the informal machinery at present existing in a negligible number of the firms engaged in the Retail and Ancillary Trades is unsatisfactory and is not likely to develop to a point where normal collective bargaining could be possible and may even with a set-back cease to exist'. We have quoted at length from the Sofola Commission Report simply to establish the reluctance of private employers to encourage collective bargaining processes or to facilitate the evolution of institutions tending in that direction.

---

[37] Report, ibid., 5.
[38] Ibid.

The general thrust of state policy in the early 1960s can easily be seen to have approximated to that of the colonial administration in advocating voluntary collective bargaining for the private sector only, understandable perhaps in the context of the political preference for 'free and private enterprise.' The growing disenchantment of organized labour with Balewa's government in 1961 over the falling purchasing power of wage earners and the lack of institutional avenues for communicating, it seemed logical to expect that sooner or later something had to give. It is also more than likely that the 'demonstration effect' of the general behaviour of politicians, political corruption, and mounting social conflict coloured workers' demands and expectations. The United Labour Congress of Nigeria (ULCN), one of the five central labour organisations but which alone enjoyed government's recognition, for instance, published an open letter in mid-1963 observing, among other things, that the 'splendid prospects that heralded and marked the celebration of Independence were becoming increasingly confused and darkened by the statements and doings of politicians and governments,' and that 'workers are baffled and fearful, disillusioned and frustrated.'[39]

The circumstances leading up to, surrounding, and following the 27 September, 1963 General Strike have been well covered by Ananaba (1969), Melson (1970) and Cohen (1974).[40] Our interest here is in the establishment by government in 1964 of the Morgan Commission to review wages and other conditions of 'junior workers' in both the public and private sectors of the economy. The first post-colonial government not only continued with the bureaucratically-derived and preferred method of tackling such issues in the public sector,[41] its own professed policy of 'voluntary collective bargaining' for the private sector was blatantly violated. The Morgan Commission of 1964 may correctly be regarded as marking the watershed in the wage bargain process in Nigeria, not for its supposedly generous awards (quickly eroded by general price increases) but for making it impossible both then and in the future for private employers to insulate themselves from public sector wage increases. All previous wages commissions had devoted their attention entirely to the various categories of 'government workers'.

---

[39] *West African Pilot*, Lagos, 20 May, 1963 Also cited in COHEN, R., *Labour and Politics in Nigeria*, p. 90. The other central labour organisations were the Nigerian Trade Union Congress (NTUC), the Labour Unity Front (LUF), the Nigerian Workers' Council (NWC), and the Northern Federation of Labour (NFL).

[40] ANANABA, W., *The Trade Union Movement in Nigeria*; MELSON, R., 'Nigerian Politics and the General Strike of 1964' in ROTBERG, RJ. & MAZRUI, A.A. (eds.), *Protest and Power in Black Africa*, OUP, New York, 1970: COHEN, R., *Labour and Politics in Nigeria*, Heinemann, London, 1974.

[41] See Otobo, D., 'Bureaucratic Elites and Public Sector Wage Bargain in Nigeria,' *Journal of Modern African Studies*, Vol. 24(1), 1986 for extensive analysis.

After the Morgan Commission of 1964 and until 1968 there was little evidence of change in official policy towards collective bargaining, with workers in private establishments fending for themselves as well as they could, supported by their respective central labour organizations. In 1968, preoccupied with prosecuting the war against the secessionist forces and demanding co-operation of all organized groups, the Gowon-led military regime passed the Trade Dispute (Emergency Provisions) Decree which, though primarily concerned with procedures for settling disputes, marked the beginning of a 'crude' policy of freezing wages and prices, the latter nonetheless galloping away because of shortages. Its provisions were incorporated and strengthened in the Trade Disputes (Emergency Provision) (Amendment) Decree 53 of 1969, private employers failing this time to bemoan the erosion of 'collective bargaining' processes as they were to do after major wage awards by tribunals.

The hardships imposed by the Civil War, the ban on wage increases, compulsory loans by workers to government to finance the 'war effort', and deferral of all workers' claims until 'after the war', and a rash of strikes through most of 1969 gave birth to the 1970-71 Adebo Wage Commission which started off in grand style with a summary award of a token amount to all workers. The availability of investible funds due to the quadrupling of crude oil prices because of the 1973 Arab-Israeli war and the embargo on oil supplies imposed by OPEC members and, of course, vast expansion in state's economic investments through the implementation of the indigenization decrees generated fears, which were openly expressed by several senior conservative bureaucrats of likely 'shortage of executive capacity' to manage these and other investments as contained in the somewhat ambitious development plan. The anticipated dearth of executive capacity was also interestingly linked with the 'poor' remuneration of senior personnel in the public sector, a class of persons which the Adebo Commission had sought to impress on the general public as requiring motivation like their counterparts in the private sector. It noted that the super scale group of the civil service hierarchy had received no basic increase since 1959 (Mbanefo Commission awards) and that pay differentials between the highest and lowest paid employee in the service had been reduced by this commission from the ratio of 28:1 to a presumably more respectable 16:1! It was therefore important for all to realise that 'while the Federal Government is determined to pursue an enlightened salaries/wages policy, it nonetheless accepts the fact that it is obliged to compete in the world market for skilled manpower without which the development process cannot take place.'[42] The 1973-74 Udoji Commission completed this job by completely overhauling the salary

[42] *West Africa*, 12 November 1971, p. 1337

structure of public servants into a *unified system of seventeen grades*, the highest and lowest positioned civil servant earning ₦15,000 and ₦1,200 per annum respectively.

The very rapid growth of both private and public sectors necessarily threw up problems associated with pay relativities. Such problems were necessarily in the private sector which had finally caught up with and overtaken public sector rates since those heady days of the Sofola Commission, and the emergence of vocal and strategically located groups of workers who would rather look after their own interests, a process Professor Kuhn has described as 'fractional bargaining'.[43] In addition, the abrupt rise in the general level of prices that accompanied the Adebo awards, and subsequently pushed along by the Udoji Commission awards themselves and the high volume of currency in circulation, gave room for more workers' protests and a seemingly anarchic wage bargain situation, with the State's labour costs escalating proportionately. In this disconcerting and fluid situation, the Wages Boards and Industrial Councils Decree No. 1 of 1973 was enacted to give a measure of structure and coherence.

The Wages Board and Industrial Councils Decree is exhaustively examined in Emiola (1980), Uvieghara (2001) and other texts on Nigerian labour law.[44] We therefore restrict ourselves to a few relevant observations. This decree represents the first attempt to provide an institutional avenue for private employers and workers to meet and resolve terms of employment in bodies designated 'joint industrial councils'. The Commissioner of Labour had powers to declare negotiated wages and other terms binding on the workers affected after listening to objections, the life of such terms being extendable upon the request of both parties. An employer subsequently seeking revision of such terms might appeal for exemption to the Commissioner. Altogether, as Akpala (1982, 124)[45] has pointed out, the two provisions, the first making agreements binding on workers and the second allowing employers to apply for exemption permits, appeared to give disproportionate protection in favour of employers. And, as might reasonably be expected, 'this provision of the law would have the effect of watering down the bargaining effect of the workers' union.'[46]

The other section of the Wages Boards and Industrial Councils Decree No. 1 of 1973 repealed the Wages Boards Ordinance of 1957 and established the Industrial Wages Board and National Wages Board for the private and

---

[43] Such workers usually attempt to bargain exclusively for themselves; see KUHN, J. W., *Bargaining in Grievance Settlement: The Power of Industrial Workgroups*, Columbia Univ. Press, New York, 1961.

[44] Emiola, A., *Nigerian Labour Law*, University of Ibadan Press, Ibadan, 1980; Uvieghara, E.E., *Trade Union Law in Nigeria*, Ethiope, Benin City, 1969 and Uvieghara, E.E., *Labour Law in Nigeria*, Malthouse, Lagos, 2001

[45] Op. cit.

[46] *Op. cit.*

public sectors respectively, and the Area Minimum Wages Committees for the states. State Governors could also establish equivalents for local government workers after due consultation with the Commissioner. Akpala (1982, 127)[47] had observed that both the National Wages Board and Area Minimum Wages Committees were a revival of a defunct institution established in 1949 upon the recommendations of the Miller Committee of 1946 which established the controversial geographical wage structure. Under this structure provincial and regional wages committees acted in an advisory capacity to the Chief Commissioners, each of whom combined political and administrative and juridical headship of each group of provinces in Eastern, Northern and Western Nigeria. These committees and boards failed then (as mentioned earlier) and in 1973 for the same reasons: they had no executive power, no bargaining took place, they were largely used by employers as sounding boards for policies and did not succeed in fixing a national minimum wage as required by workers. Akpala (1982, 128) concluded, 'if it is necessary to appoint a minimum wage board at all, setting up of separate machineries for private and public employees would seem not to be desirable.'

If the Whitley Councils met with little success in the public sector, the Joint Industrial Councils, their counterparts in the private sector, were unlikely to fare any better. As Fashoyin (1980, 107) recognised, they 'could easily be manipulated by unscrupulous employers' as was indeed the case. The 1974 Udoji Commission sought to reinforce the flagging machinery for 'negotiation' in the public sector by creating the National Public Service Negotiating Councils, supported by a technical and data-gathering Public Service Review Unit. Following the structure of the civil service, a National Public Service Negotiating Council I concerned itself with problems of the senior administrative and professional classes, Council II with clerical, executive and typists cadres, while Council III dealt with technical cadres. And in line with the existing political and administrative structure of the country, States Public Service Negotiating Councils I, II, III were designed to tackle similar issues for the corresponding classes of public employees in the nineteen states. Although some issues were taken up in these National Public Service Negotiating Councils, they were largely by-passed in tripartite discussions involving representatives of political leadership, of workers, and of employers. They were now saddled with the technical task of reconciling differences in interpretation and problems arising out of implementing agreements reached in such tripartite negotiations. Throughout Shagari's administration, the importance of such 'technical tasks' should, however, be neither underestimated nor ignored because such occasions almost

[47] *Op. cit.*

unfailingly afforded top bureaucrats, drawn from the Ministries of Establishment, Finance, Employment, Labour & Productivity and the Cabinet Office the opportunity for watering down what originally seemed to be cast-iron or binding agreements.[48] Between 1979 and 1982 three salary/wages commissions were set up, the Onosode Commission (1981) for parastatals, the Cookey Commission (1981) for the universities, and the Adamolekun Commission (1981) for federal polytechnics, colleges of technology, advanced teachers and technical colleges.[49]

The Onosode Commission merely laid down guidelines for determining remuneration in parastatals, classified into five groups, in which the upper management of the ostensibly more autonomous could earn a modal salary of ₦17,000 a year. A ceiling of ₦25,000 was fixed for the chairmen and members of the board of directors, usually drawn from the ranks of party faithfuls. Fully cognizant of the likely reaction of top bureaucrats to some of these recommendations, the Commission also suggested that the salary of the head of the civil service could be 'enhanced' to bring him in the ₦17,000 salary bracket. Each parastatal was left to sort out levels of pay for all other categories of employees, thus generating further protests.

The recommendations of the Cookey Commission led to the removal of university staff from the unified salary structure erected by the Udoji Commission for the public sector as a whole, and to the creation of a new and enhanced University System Scale (USS) which, while appreciably increasing basic salaries, ensured a) that professors did not earn more than permanent secretaries, and b) that the salaries of vice-chancellors should not be more than the most senior politicians, and the highest echelons of soldiers, police, and members of the bench. A similar policy position was detectable in the negotiations that went on for some time between the Academic Staff Union of Universities (ASUU) and the Federal Government over recommendations in the Cookey Report concerning the funding and development of the university system. The government negotiators sought to reduce the recommended fringe benefits to those prevailing in the civil service, and bluntly refused to accept a clause which would ensure a minimum differential of 10 per cent between the USS and any future salary scale adopted for the main civil service after a general review. Even before the adoption of 'austerity measures' in early 1983, when oil revenues dramatically declined, the Federal Government sought to suspend the USS and revert to the unified salary structure until 'the economy picked up'. The

[48] This phenomenon is well discussed in OTOBO, D., 'Bureaucratic Elites and Public Sector Wage Bargain in Nigeria', *op. cit*

[49] The official titles were Presidential Commission on Parastatals, Presidential Commission on Salary and Conditions of Service of University Staff and Presidential Commission on Conditions of Service of Federal Polytechnics, Colleges of Technology, Advanced Teachers Colleges and National Teachers Colleges.

Vice-President was reported in the national dailies to have suggested that university staff be paid partly in government bonds if the USS was to be retained in 'the face of austerity measures.'

The report of the Adamolekun Commission (which focused on federal government-owned tertiary educational institutions apart from the universities) has remained unpublished to this day. Apparently, staff of the affected institutions have felt less inclined to agitate under a military dispensation, given especially the current economic downturn and collapse of crude oil prices in the world market. But the comprehensiveness of the control maintained by the Federal Ministry of Education and the National Board for Technical Education over teachers colleges and polytechnics respectively, was bitterly resented by their staff, since even postings and promotions were determined and effected from Lagos at the time. Some polytechnics had a measure of autonomy in the sense of being allowed to recruit temporary staff, and their rectors were permitted to award contracts to the tune of ₦5,000. However, apart from Adeyemi College, Ondo, which has had an umbilical union with the University of Ife, these institutions may rightly be said to be integral parts of the main civil service, a situation that has served to generate protests in the past from their demoralized staff.

By 1982 when President Shagari embarked on his Economic Stabilization Programme, most sectors of the economy had been buffeted by strikes, sabotage and absenteeism. Given a more democratic political environment and a multi-party situation with all the dissent and mutual criticism and rivalry, it seemed much easier for the government to reach some accommodation with labour and employers over many issues - the notable exception being the vexed question of arrears of salaries which those parastatals and state governments affected claimed they could do nothing about because of huge deficits they had already accumulated. The pattern of strikes in the public sector, which had been established since the 1940s,[50] was re-enacted faithfully: a spate of strikes before the establishment of, and during the sitting of wage tribunal, and more strikes after the publication of

[50] On the use of wages and salaries commissions themselves, Bill Warren generated controversy when he argued that trade union pressure was central to the establishment of wages commissions despite their financial and organizational weaknesses. In this he was supported by Peter Kilby. Elliot J. Berg and John Weeks took issue with Warren and Kilby respectively, assigning much reduced importance to union pressure. The ensuing debate also drew some comments from Robin Cohen. For more details, see Warren, B., 'Urban Real Wages and the Nigerian Trade Union Movement, 1939-1960,' *Economic Development and Cultural Change* (*EDCC*), vol. 15(1), Oct. 1966; also *EDCC*, vol. 17(4), 1969; Kilby, P., 'Industrial Relations and Wage Determination: failure of the Anglo-Saxon model', *Journal of Developing* Areas (*JDA*), vol. 3(1), Oct. 1968; 'Further Comment on the Kilby/Weeks Debate: Final Observations,' *JDA*, vol. 5(2), Jan. 1971; Berg, E.G., 'Urban Real Wages and the Nigerian Trade Union Movement, 1939-1960: a Comment,' *EDCC*, vol. 17(4) 1969; Weeks, J., 'A Comment on the P. Kilby Industrial Relations and Wage Determination,' *JDA*, vol. 3(1), 1968; 'Further Comments on the Kilby/Weeks Debate: an Empirical Rejoinder,' *JDA*, vol. 5(2), Jan. 1971; Cohen, R., 'Further Comment on the Kilby/Weeks Debate,' *JDA*, vol. 5(2), 1971.

its findings and awards. The private sector was inevitably affected by the spillover or demonstration effect of industrial protests in the public sector, especially over such issues as national monthly minimum wage, rent and transport allowances which applied nationally to all workers.

The period 1990-2000 was not substantially different in respect of the public sector in particular. It was a period characterized by crisis in public sector compensation, partly as a result of the indifference of military dictators and partly as policy fall-out of SAP which required a cut back on public expenditure, holding down of wages and reducing the size of the work force. The Babangida regime unilaterally slashed wages in 1987, cuts he was forced by protests and strikes to restore in 1988; and even when he attempted to increase wages, he was forced to abandon such moves and recover amounts already paid out by compulsory deductions from wage packets of civil servants under pressure from the IMF, World Bank and other creditors. In other words, a majority of disputes and strikes in the public sector are wage-related: arrears of wages/salaries, stagnant wages/salaries, size of minimum wage, determining differentials arising from across-the-board compensatory increases by successive regimes (dubbed "Babangida award", "Abacha award" and "Abubakar award").

A tripartite committee of the social partners in 1990 failed to agree on a new national minimum wage, thereupon the Babangida regime unilaterally fixed it at ₦250 per month. Protests accompanied its announcement, along with official definition of a monthly minimum wage to include other allowances (rent and transport), fringe benefits: it meant the basic monthly wage was less than the previous ₦125. In September 1998, after some indeterminate discussions with employers and organised labour, General Abubakar announced a "long-awaited, long-deserved revision of salaries of public service employees," and the minimum monthly wage put at some ₦5,238. A circular issued on 2 September 1998 by the National Salaries, Incomes and Wages Commission[51] directed state and local governments to determine their own rates of pay subject to a monthly minimum wage of ₦2,800. The first spate of strikes that broke out was in objection to the unilateral fixing of the amounts for the various categories of workers by the regime. The second round of strikes followed the announcement by all state military administrators of their inability to match the ₦5,238 minimum for federal civil servants, offering figures between ₦2,000 and ₦3,000.

As strikes broke out nationwide and union officials and NLC officers were engaged in continuous negotiations and consultations with state and local government officials, the federal government dramatically and

[51] Inaugurated on 9 October 1992 as a permanent organ in place of the usual ad hoc commissions, this body has made minimal impact on the regulation of wages and salaries and other conditions of employment.

unilaterally reduced its own figure to ₦3,500, Parastatals, state and local governments reluctantly accepted this figure, but commenced retrenchment in order to be able "to cope" with the minimum monthly wage. The strikes as from this point on were directed at both the size of the minimum wage and on-going retrenchment. The police and anti-riot troops attacked striking workers everywhere, leading to injuries, arrests and some deaths.

These disputes dragged in a desultory fashion right into 2000, and President Obasanjo, again following the examples of his predecessors, unilaterally in his May Day address, increased the national minimum monthly wage to ₦5,500. In the controversies and debates that followed, it was then said that the minimum wage for "federal workers" was ₦7,500 and ₦5,500 for state and local government and private sector employees. After initial objections from state governors, at a meeting of the National Council of State (where all state governors, previous heads of government are members), all 36 state governors formally declared support for and acceptance of ₦5,500 for their employees. Even the Central Bank confirmed that "the phenomenal surge in industrial strikes during the year was largely due to the protracted disputes between most state governments and civil servants over the implementation of the new minimum wage in the public sector."[52] In 2011, it was raised during ex-President Goodluck Jonathan's regime from ₦7,500 to ₦18,000, while in 2019, the minimum wage was further increased during the regime of former president, Muhammadu Buhari, from ₦18,000 to ₦30,000 per month. President Tinubu's government opted for ₦70,000, with some State Governments touting figures ranging ₦75,000 to ₦85,000.

CURRENT ISSUES AND PROCESSES IN THE PUBLIC SECTOR

The Public Service or Sector

The public sector as at today may be divided into the following subsectors, and each subsector has its own peculiar characteristics:

- the main civil service;
- public utilities (monopolies and near-monopolies);
- public sector companies operating in near-private sector environment;
- the primary and secondary teaching service;
- higher education and research institutions; and
- local governments.

Main civil service

The consensus among observers and practitioners alike is that of very limited collective bargaining in the main civil service, the dominant method for

[52] CBN *Annual Report and Statement of Account* year ended 31 December 1999, p. 38.

determining terms of employment being *ad hoc* wages and salaries commissions till the National Salaries, Incomes and Wages Commission was created in 1993. This is another way of saying the state or employer has dominated the process, most of the commissions or committees combining the twin tasks of grading and fixing salaries and wages, notwithstanding the activities of public sector trade unions. Despite the tripartite composition of wages commissions, they were not negotiating bodies. Of these the 1974 Udoji Commission left a more enduring impact, merging all salaries in the public sector to create a 17-grade salary structure, each grade level having inbuilt yearly salary increments called "steps". It also described all public servants between grade levels 01 and 06 to be "junior staff", grade levels 07 to 17 to be senior staff. In terms of management structure, those in grade levels 07 were regarded to be supervisory grade, while grade levels 08 to 13 as intermediate group.

It should be noted that hitherto even permanent secretaries did not earn the same salary; some federal ministries (e.g. Foreign Affairs, Finance and Economic Development) were rated higher than all others. Nor was it automatically assumed that federal civil servants or permanent secretaries earned more than their regional counterparts. The accretion of fiscal and political power to the centre under military regimes, especially under the Babangida regime, encouraged the view of so-called deregulation of collective bargaining in the public sector implying less pay packet for state and local government level public servants.

The state's unilateral attempts at determining terms of employment has often met with resistance from organized labour, and ensuing conflict situations appear to have led to the creation of bipartite and tripartite conflict-regulating institutions but often ostensibly officially saddled with the responsibility for negotiations: Whitley Councils from late 1940s, Provincial Wage Committees in the 1950s and Joint Industrial Councils and National Public Service Negotiating Council from mid-1960s.

Originally created upon the recommendation of the 1963/4 Morgan Commission, the current National Public Service Negotiating Councils were revamped by the 1974 Udoji Commission and which remain the main bipartite collective bargaining institution for the main civil service till date.

The Negotiating Councils which were created for federal, state and local government levels had identical constitutions and procedures and were

> "to secure the greatest measure of cooperation between the government in its capacity as employer and the general body of civil servants in matters affecting the civil service with a view to increasing efficiency in the public service combined with the well-being of those employed; to provide machinery for dealing with grievances, and generally to bring together the experience and

different points of view of representatives of the various branches of the civil service combined."

i) have a general responsibility for negotiating all matters affecting the conditions of service of civil servants;
ii) advise the government where necessary of the best means of utilising the ideas and experience of civil servants with a view to improving productivity;
iii) review the general conditions of civil servants, e.g. recruitment, hours of work, promotion, discipline, salary, fringe benefits and superannuation, provided that in matters relating to recruitment, discipline and promotion, the Council shall restrict itself to general principles; and
iv) refer all disputes or differences whatsoever to the Federal Ministry of Employment, Labour & Productivity for settlement in accordance with the Trade Disputes Act No. 7 of 1976 or any statutory modification or re-enactment thereof for the time being in force.

The three sets of negotiating councils are:

National Public Service Negotiating Council I

- Association of Senior Civil Servants of Nigeria

National Public Service Negotiating Council II

- Nigeria Civil Service Union (for intermediate grades and junior non-technical grades, except in Customs and Excise, Immigration Dept)
- Nigeria Union of Civil Service Typists, Stenographic and Allied Staff

National Public Service Negotiating Council III

- Civil Service Technical Workers Union of Nigeria
- Medical and Health Workers Union of Nigeria
- National Association of Nigerian Nurses and Midwives
- Printing and Publishing Workers' Union
- Customs and Excise and Immigration Staff Union (since proscribed)

Although all the governments of the federation are represented at the negotiating table, officials and staff representatives have little or no power to bind their governments regarding the decisions and agreements reached at the negotiating table. These are referred to such higher bodies as the National Council on Establishments (NCE), the Presidency, for ratification before they can be finalized.

By 1998 the Committee on Harmonization of Public Service Remuneration reorganised the thirty-five different salary structures in the public service into five broad salary structures for all ministries, extra-ministerial departments, agencies, military, police and para-military services and parastatals whose personnel costs are fully funded by the federal government. These are:

i. Harmonised Public Service Salary Structure (HAPSS) – for the civil service and extra-ministerial departments, all non-commercialised agencies/organizations which were operating the Unified Grading and Salary Structure (UGSS) in any part of the civil service, medical/dental/veterinary doctors in the civil service currently on Medical Salary Structure (MSS/MSSS), all judicial posts which were formerly on GL12 – 17 before the introduction of Judicial Salary Structure, all non-judicial posts of the judiciary, and all staff of primary schools and federal secondary schools;
ii. Harmonised Tertiary Institutions Salary Structure (HATISS) – for all staff of the federal universities, polytechnics, colleges of education, all research institutes and all institutes and agencies formerly operating the Elongated University Salary Structure (EUSS), and all medical doctors in teaching and specialist hospitals, federal medical centres and health agencies;
iii. Harmonised Police and Para-Military Salary Structure (HAPPSS) – for the Nigeria Police, Customs, Immigration and Prison Services, the National Drug Law Enforcement Agency; and the Security Services. But, within a short period the medical personnel in all these agencies opted out for the HATISS;
iv. Harmonised Armed Forces Salary Structure (HAFSS), for the Army, Navy and Air Force personnel; and
v. Harmonised Top Public Office Holders Salary (TOPSAL) – for the Executive, the Legislative and top judicial personnel.

The period 2013-2016 has been characterised by arrears of salaries for civil servants in most of the thirty-six states of the federation, and this is in spite of special grants from the federal government to state governments. Why? This is largely because succeeding governments in 31 May 2015, after the General Election, inherited not only empty treasuries, but also huge debts arising from recklessly awarded contracts for uncompleted projects to phantom projects, a pervasive corrupt siphoning of public funds by politicians in all political parties since 1999 to compensate themselves just before leaving office. The recent collapse of crude oil prices and drastic drop in foreign exchange earnings did not create that scale of domestic debt, but has been used to rationalise arrears of salaries and justify the disregard for collective agreements and other rights of workers. Probing this huge domestic debt is outside the much-vaunted anti-corruption policy of President Buhari.

Public utilities

Ezeife (1987)[53] has described the prevailing situation among public utilities in the following terms. The facts are that most of the monopolies operate like the Civil Service. There is almost a repugnance to linking input to output, measurement of productivity, development of productivity schemes, etc. Thus, bargaining takes the form of political pressure for increased wages and salaries and better conditions of work — whether or not the operation generates enough funds for meeting the demands. It may not be deliberate, but the effect of the attitude of the workers' union (emphasis on employment as social need and services provided by the monopolies as social or non-commercial) and the performance of management (no regular accounting — even management accounts), is to reduce the situation in the public monopolies to those in the Civil Service. Some weaknesses also exist to a lesser extent with regard to (a) parties to the bargain, (b) distinctiveness of particular interests, (c) intra-group conflict of interest, and (d) competence of the parties to reach and implement an agreement.

Where the management negotiates with the labour unions, the conflict of interest noted in the case of the Civil Service exists. This is even more pronounced as Senior Staff Associations begin to emerge and adopt aggressive postures similar to workers' unions. The winnings of the Senior Staff Association cannot be far removed from the gains of the management staff. The Board members are appointed by the government and while they can be looked upon as the counterparts of the boards in the private sector, this may be correct only in form, as the position of government cannot be likened to the position of private shareholders who intensely guard their interests. The interest of the members of the boards of directors may be mostly to keep their positions and maintain the appearance of industrial peace. It should thus be expected that the position to yield to labour pressures would be quite high.

The competence of the management to negotiate with the unions suffers about the same weakness as in the Civil Service, since, for major decisions, the management would refer to the board which refers to the supervising ministry for possible transmission to the government.

The strengths of the unions lie in: (a) the fact that in most cases (NEPA, now PHCN, for example) they can, by withholding their services, inflict immediate and demonstrably severe damage on the economy or society; (b) they can readily point to comparable conditions of work in not-too-dissimilar environments in the private sector; and (c) by being a little more removed from the government, their actions do not as easily show as political.

---

[53] National Incomes Policy and Bargaining in the Public Sector, in Fashoyin, T. (ed.) *Collective Bargaining in the Public Sector in Nigeria*, Macmillan, Lagos, 1987, pp. 99-104

It should be pointed out that since the structural adjustment programme which commenced earnestly in 1987, and its focus on removal of subsidies and commercialisation, an increasing number of public utilities have achieved near-institutional autonomy from erstwhile 'parent' ministries – a development that encouraged more bilateral negotiations.

The second observation is the attempts on the part of successive military regimes to regulate collective relations in this subsector by increasing the number of parastatals in the "essential services" category, legal constraint that includes the prohibition of strikes while imposing compulsory conciliation and arbitration. By the time the Abacha regime included educational institutions just to combat ASUU, nearly the whole of the public sector had become essential services, including a huge chunk of the private sector (e.g. telecommunications): Nigeria must have the widest definition of essential services in the world.

Third, the main bipartite collective relations institution is the Joint Industrial Committees (JICs) or Joint Consultative Committees (JCCs) which, as has been well documented, have not been negotiating bodies, and in consequence a good deal of management high-handedness and arbitrariness have been evidenced, with strikes leading to summary dismissal of many employees (e.g. the Mint).

Fourth, invoking the sovereignty doctrine or expanding the scope of essential services will not reduce the incidence of strikes and other forms of industrial conflict. If a service is "essential", then the public servants therein should also be treated as "essential" and well remunerated. For example, what does one expect of a poorly paid but armed police who is not allowed to form trades unions, and from the poor salary pays for own boots and uniforms?

Public Sector companies operating in near-private sector environment

In this sector, apart from the weakness associated with the management, party to the bargain (i.e. they do not have keenly interested shareholders looking over their shoulders), the bargaining situation approaches the situation in the private sector. Examples of this sub-sector include the several joint-venture companies in the oil and gas industry (e.g. NLNG), the Nigerian National Petroleum Corporation, many banks and insurance companies till only recently. These companies have conditions of service which should be more related to the private sector business environment in which they operate than with the public sector. For example, an engineer or driller in an NNPC oil-producing subsidiary (e.g. Nigerian Petroleum Development Company -NPDC) sees little justification for differentials between her/his pay and that of her/his counterpart in Shell or Total and, as such, her/his benchmark will always be prevailing rates in the private sector in the oil and gas industry.

However, the bargaining situation is somewhat weakened by state ownership, which deprives management therein of independent financial and other resources as they are firmly tied to the government's budget. Thus the effect of official socio-economic policies on this group is very similar to the effect on the private sector proper, especially commercialisation, deregulation, and privatisation. It would be close to the truth to say that labour relations in this subsector since 1974 has been dominated by attempts by public servants to remove themselves from the unified salary structure erected by the Udoji Commission and imposed by the military regime.

In the NNPC, for example, the structure of bargaining closely approximates the structure of the organization itself. Each subsidiary, though a limited liability company and has its own Board of Directors (with a full complement of executive and non-executive directors) reports to Group Headquarters (GHQ) which appoints a negotiating team. While, on the side of employees, each subsidiary has a branch of NUPENG and PENGASSAN, its executive committee going by the acronym of BEC (Branch Executive Committee). All chairpersons of respective BECs of the subsidiaries meet to prioritise demands after each BEC has collated submissions and demands of members. It is this list that is contained in the "charter of demands" and submitted to "management" at GHQ months before commencement of actual formal negotiations. Respective managements of subsidiaries and of BECs are saddled with the responsibility of implementing subsequent collective agreement, differences in interpretations referred to GHQ for a final position or arbitration. A prominent side-effect of this centralized process is the undermining of the authority of respective managements of subsidiaries before the two trades unions and workers there on residual matters, somewhat akin to that of University Councils and ASUU.

However, negotiations do take place between NUPENG, PENGASSAN and the companies in the oil and gas industry every two years upon the expiration of the collective agreement. In sharp contrast with the rest of the economy, negotiations are company or plant-based, not industry wide since employers therein have refused to form a co-ordinating employers' association or organization to engage the two unions to establish industry-wide minimum rates of pay and types of non-money benefits (i.e. one union versus multiple-employers situation).

Regardless of the above stated issues, respective employers do engage in extensive informal exchange of views and consultations, just as NUPENG and PENGASSAN compare notes. Among employers, the terms negotiated in Shell have become the upper limits against which other employers aim to match or come close enough. None has matched the Shell rates so far. For the unions, it has become almost a ritual for employers to first negotiate with NUPENG and thereafter add a percentage on these for senior staff employees organised by PENGASSAN when they meet at formal negotiations. This means senior staff and PENGASSAN take more than a passing interest in the charter of demands presented by NUPENG as such would form the critical base for their own terms – hence informal and formal exchange of views.

Nonetheless, negotiations appear to be dominated by the following: a) the desire of employees in other companies to narrow the differentials in pay and variety of fringe benefits offered by Shell; b) the ability to pay of companies in exploration and production and those in marketing and services are markedly different, largely because those companies in the services sector, for example, survive on contracts (seismic surveys, supply of rigs, drilling wells, etc.) they can obtain from the exploration and producing companies, while the earnings of the marketing companies depend on the vagaries of importation and epileptic performance of local refineries; and c) the pay and role of expatriates.

Some ostensibly self-funding agencies appear to enjoy a reasonable degree of autonomy and have pay scales much above prevailing rates in the main civil service. By and large, most of the parastatals operating in near-private sector environments have been privatised and/or in the process of being privatised. The dominant issues therein include a) terminal benefits of those staff wishing to leave; b) severance packages for those being disengaged; c) gratuity and pension – especially since the 2014 Pension Reform Act which eliminates gratuity and sets limits to what a pensioner may withdraw.

The Teaching Service, Higher Education, and Others

Labour relations and wage bargaining in these subsectors have also been driven by the desire of teachers at the primary, secondary and, especially tertiary levels, to opt out of the unified salary structure, get employers to pay salaries regularly, and improve upon inadequate and decaying infrastructure. Before the Udoji Commission, *for example, university professors earned higher salary than a federal permanent secretary*, a situation that was reversed under the unified salary structure as they jointly governed the country with dominant military officers.

The National Union of Teachers (NUT) represents the interests of teachers at primary and secondary levels, while the tertiary level has a multiplicity of associations and unions representing the interests of academic and non-academic, with non-academic further split into junior and senior. The polytechnics have separate unions, replicating the situation in the university system. The situation for primary and secondary school teachers and those in the polytechnics is made more complex by the regulatory activities of respective primary school boards and Teachers

Service Commission, and National Board for Technical Education (NBTE). Overseeing all these are respective ministries of education of state governments and the Federal Ministry of Education in the case of federal polytechnics and universities, the National Universities' Commission (NUC) serving as a conduit for channelling funds to the latter. Only a few months ago, the federal government has begun to bypass the NUC in the funding of university system.

The remoteness of and the disconnection between the "employer" and "management" and who to negotiate with as it occurs in the main civil service is more aggravated in the education sector by the lack of mandate of negotiators on employer's side, the proliferation of bodies, and lack of uniformity among the state governments in the use to which such bodies are put. In some states, the Ministry of Education employs teachers for both primary and secondary schools and pays them; in some others, the Primary School Board employs and pays but by way of local government funds; while, in yet some other states, the Teachers Service Commission employs for secondary schools, and Ministry of Education pays; and, there are those states where state governments insist on the responsibility of local governments to employ and pay primary school teachers, a dispute between such state governments and the federal government that has become a constitutional matter in view of the Universal Basic Education (UBE) scheme.

As for tertiary institutions, those owned by state governments negotiate with such state governments, while those funded by the federal government face a more complex set of bodies or institutions, from their governing councils, the NBTE or NUC, the Federal Ministry of Education, to the Presidency and National Assembly. For example, the pretence of academic staff negotiating with individual university councils is gravely undermined by circular to the universities' authorities imposing an upper ceiling on increases and basic salaries; it is still a centralized system, and the respective councils do not have the authority to grant certain concessions. In the end, strikes then compel Presidency to listen, negotiate and implement.

Issues dominating negotiations in this sector are:

a. lack of formal structural negotiating bodies;
b. irregular payment of salaries, unpaid for a few months to a year and longer in some cases. The standing joke is that the National Union of Teachers has given up on applying any pressure or embarking on industrial action after having to call off far too many actions after the employers offered nothing on account of empty treasuries;
c. low basic salaries;
d. stagnation due to lack of promotion;

e. differentials between academic and non-academic in the case of tertiary institutions (in some cases, even among the non-academic, there is a distinction between "admin" and "technical" staff); and
f. decay of and an inadequate facilities due to insufficient funding.

Essential Services

Under the Trade Disputes (Essential Services) Act 1976, a majority of public servants at the federal, state and local government levels are not only legally denied the right to strike, the right to organise and collective bargain is also severely circumscribed. All parastatals (transport, the civil services, law enforcement agencies, the armed forces, etc.) as well as certain private sector establishments (financial institutions, telecommunications), educational institutions are affected by the no-strike law.

Essential services, according to the Trade Disputes Act, means:

a. the public service of the Federation or of a State which shall for the purposes of this Act include service, in a civil capacity, of persons employed in the armed forces of the Federation or any part thereof and also, of persons, employed in an industry or undertaking (corporate or unincorporate) which deals or is connected with the manufacture or production of materials for use in the armed forces of the Federation or any part thereof;
b. any service established, provided or maintained by the government of the Federation or of a State, by a local government council, a town council or any municipal or statutory authority, or by private enterprise -
   (i) for, or in connection with, the supply of electricity, power or water, or fuel of any kind;
   (ii) for or in connection with, sound broadcasting or postal, telegraphic, cable, wireless or telephonic communications;
   (iii) for maintaining ports, harbours, docks or aerodromes, or in connection with, transportation of persons, goods or livestock by road, rail, sea, river or air;
   (iv) for, or in connection with, the burial of the dead, hospitals, the treatment of the sick, the prevention of disease, or any of the following public health matters, namely, sanitation, road-cleansing and the disposal of night-soil and rubbish;
   (v) for dealing with outbreaks of fire;
   (vi) for or in connection with teaching or the provision of educational services at primary, secondary or tertiary institutions.
c. service in any capacity in any of the following organizations -
   (i) the Central Bank of Nigeria;
   (ii) the Nigerian Security, Printing and Minting Company Limited;

(iii) any body corporate licensed to carry on banking business under the Banking Act.

The main aim of the law, it is held, is to ensure that all those who are engaged in essential services follow the procedure laid down by law for the settlement of any differences. Where a particular group of such employees fails to do so, the group may be proscribed. Such a group may also be proscribed where it intentionally disrupts the essential service within which it operates or the national economy.

Any employer or any official of an association of employers or any official of a trade union or any person, not being an official of a trade union, who in any way performs or assumes a leadership role in a trade union or faction of a trade union and either is or has been engaged in acts calculated to disrupt the economy or obstruct or disrupt the smooth running of any essential service or has wilfully failed to comply with the procedure for settling trade disputes laid out in the Trade Disputes Act is guilty of an offence.

It has also been thought necessary to include a power of detention in addition to these powers which appear formidable enough. The Inspector General of Police or Chief of General Staff, if satisfied that any person who was an official or member of a proscribed trade union or association has, subsequent to the proscription, been concerned in acts prejudicial to industrial peace or in acts calculated to obstruct or disrupt the smooth running of any essential services and that it is therefore necessary to exercise control over him, he may by order in writing direct that the person be detained in a civil prison or a police station.

Section 8 suspends the constitutional provisions on fundamental human rights for the purposes of the Act. There is no doubt that sections 5 and 8 must now be regarded as unconstitutional under democratic governance.

The military even often resorted to the promulgation of special Decrees. For example, rather than proscribe the Academic Staff Union of Universities under the Trade Disputes (Essential Services) Act which allows a proscribed union to re-register after six months, it was twice proscribed under a special Decree. Similarly a dissension within the Nigerian Labour Congress was dealt with under the National Economic Emergency Powers Decree 1985.

In addition to the above provisions which apply to all essential services, including the teaching and other educational services, there are provisions which apply especially to teaching and other educational services.

A member of staff, whether teaching or non-teaching, employed in any primary, secondary or tertiary educational institution is prohibited from embarking on an industrial action in the form of a strike, sit-down strike, work-to-rule or any other kind of industrial action which is calculated to disrupt the smooth running of teaching or educational services in any of those institutions. Where such a member of staff continues or persists in any such industrial action for more than one week, he is deemed to have resigned his appointment but without prejudice to any accrued rights.

Also such a member of staff is liable to vacate such accommodation as would have been provided by the institution for him in any part of Nigeria. And every person who is either an ordinary or executive committee member of the trade union or association which embarked on the industrial action is guilty of an offence and liable, on conviction, to imprisonment for a term not exceeding two years. Such an offence is triable in the Federal High Court.

Second, there was no provision for either individual or group bargaining in the parastatals, and the structure of the main civil service did not appear to recognise the possibility of individual and group grievances. The Joint Industrial Councils (JICs), bipartite structures, are weakened by the fact that they are not negotiating bodies; rather, avenues for examining specific government's circulars regarding a variety of fringe benefits and on awards. The issues on such occasions dealt with relativities, timing of implementation and payment of arrears where applicable.

All told, managements of essential services at the federal level have proved more authoritarian but met their commitments more consistently, especially payment of regular wages and salaries, than their counterparts in respective thirty-six states. Privatisation and increasing outsourcing of services have served to reduce the number of workers in this subsector of the public service over the last ten years in particular.

EMERGING GENERAL ISSUES

The challenges and issues that have surfaced in public sector collective bargaining and wage determination include the following:

1. Wage bargaining involves the employer and its representatives on the one hand, and employees and their representatives on the other. In the public sector, the employer is not immediately visible. The Public Service Commission (and the equivalent for the Police, Judiciary, etc.), the Ministry of Establishments, among others, have a hand in the recruitment and disciplining of public servants and yet have nothing to do with day-to-day management of the main civil service and parastatals. The contract of employment is thus not with each ministry, although developments within can lead to the eventual termination of such contract over disciplinary issues.
2. Second, what constitutes "management" in the public sector is also problematic. There seems to exist an amorphous group of public servants seen as "projection of management", usually across ministries and parastatals, and this has several consequences: i) in the main civil service, even if one can identify the civil servants who fall under this

category, no management of a ministry is empowered to negotiate terms and conditions of employment; ii) indeed, staff of the ministry may be transferred to other ministries without any reference to the management of ministry or ministries affected; iii) there is little evidence to suggest that management of each ministry defines its responsibilities to include looking after the welfare and advancement of each civil servant or employee; iv) no management of a ministry thinks its own fortunes might depend on how well it manages its staff, and as such productivity and morale of staff would not loom large in their considerations; v) conversely, each civil servant has no reason to believe the management of his/her ministry has serious regard for his/her progress on the job, thereby encouraging feelings of dissatisfaction, lack of commitment and low productivity.

3. The Udoji Commission sought to eliminate multiple salary and wages systems, which prevailed right up to the Civil War period, by re-arranging basic pay rates and fringe benefits in the whole public sector in a seventeen grade unified salary structure, with no civil servant earning more than the permanent secretary which hitherto was not the case. Even federal permanent secretaries did not earn the same salaries before Adebo and Udoji Commissions' recommendations of 1970-71 and 1974 respectively; those of the ministries of finance, economic development and external affairs earned more. As already mentioned, the interregnum of civilian administration of President Shagari (1979-1983) saw workers in most parastatals attempting to take themselves out of the unified salary structure, and thereby recreating multiple salary and wages systems in the public sector, a phenomenon the Udoji Commission tried to sort out. To complicate things stiff further, the second round of military regimes from 1984 to 1999 (headed by Generals Buhari, Babangida, Abacha and Abubakar respectively) embroiled in heady economic times which gave rise to troubling structural adjustment programme that included frozen wages, stimulated the proliferation of allowances and haphazard compensation systems as bureaucrats manoeuvred to avoid increasing penury and stagnant salaries in the face of ravaging inflation as the naira had been devalued successively from 1986. Confronted by this and while flirting with neo-liberalism policy instruments of privatisation and monetisation, President Obasanjo sought solution in the three tripartite committees appointed by him, namely the Wages, Salaries and Emolument Relativity Panel (Edozien Committee 2005), the Presidential Committee on the Consolidation of Emoluments in the Public Sector (The Shonekan Committee, 2005) and the National Committee of Experts on Parameters for Wage Determination in the Federal Public

Service (2010, chaired by Professor V. P. Diejomaoh). The upshot, despite the splendid job done by the committees, in his selective implementation of recommendations, President Obasanjo ensured that "political appointees" (mostly politicians, legislators and federal permanent secretaries) had RUNAWAY DIFFERENTIALS OR EMOLUMENTS HITHERTO UNIMAGINED IN THE PUBLIC SECTOR, their salaries and allowances well over 300 per cent of the highest earning civil servant, the Director.[54]

The actual roles of the National Salaries, Incomes & Wages Commission (NSIWC) and Revenue Mobilisation, Allocation and Fiscal Commission (RMAFC) are not as straightforward as one would expect. Indeed, the RFMAC should not be involved in labour relations matters, including wage-fixing in the public sector. The issue of mandate for and during negotiations, when they do take place, brings out more clearly the consequences for collective bargaining in the public sector of the questions of who the *employer* and *management* are in day-to-day relations at work. The hierarchy of a chain of decision-makers and approving authorities tends to limit the mandate and empowerment of the negotiator representing the employer and subsequently result in lack of respect for the outcome of the negotiation process by the ultimate employer (or decision-maker). This could undermine goodwill and encourage the growth of distrust and adversarial relations.

4. Related to this is the refusal and/or unwillingness of public sector employers at all levels to negotiate, and when forced by circumstances or out of rational choice to do so, they not only resent the counter-offers and demands of the other parties, but also maintain the right to have a final say as the state/government. This is the so-called *sovereignty doctrine*, and the Morgan Commission (1964, Report, para 103) put it so well: "...it appears that in dealing with their employees, the governments are unduly conscious of their prerogative to determine the levels of remuneration and conditions of service, irrespective of their acceptability to the workers..." Still the same today.
5. For these same reasons, it is much easier for government to renege or go back on agreements without feeling any great sense of responsibility for subsequent conflict situations, or that a breach of agreement is sanctionable. Integrity is a critical element in sustaining collective

---

[54] General Babangida tried but unsuccessfully to re-designate permanent secretaries as "director-generals" and who were to be regarded as "political appointees" and their tenure ending with that of the government or regime that so appointed them! President Obasanjo, a retired general, surreptitiously amended the law to transform permanent secretaries into "political appointees" but remaining silent on their tenure!

relations, and appears not to be taken into sufficient cognisance here. This likely explains why the sanctity of wages are not respected.

6. Following from this is the legal status of collective agreements. Perhaps, like the Australian experience, it is about time we had legally justiciable collective agreements, and all parties might then inculcate the habit of taking their respective contractual obligations seriously. Public sector labour relations that are characterised by blatant disregard for agreements and procedures are dominated by conflicts and low trust relations among and between the parties. If the proposed Financial/Fiscal Responsibility Act that is currently in the National Assembly is passed, this might address the situation somewhat for sums owed to workers and others may be deducted at source and paid directly to those affected.
7. The wage/salary systems are rigid, and there appears to be no real trigger mechanism, except for threats of and actual strikes by public servants and in spite of the existence of the National Public Service Negotiating Councils and other similar mechanisms, for initiating a general review or to respond to devaluation of take home pay by inflation. In fact, it is somehow assumed that the annual increments, represented by the "steps" in each grade level, must be higher than the rate of inflation in each year. Third, and more importantly, there was no institutional trigger mechanism for initiating comprehensive review of wage rates and grading (until 1990 when the National Incomes, Salaries and Wages Commission was created – even this institution did not change the situation) except for mass strikes which the law has sought to prohibit. This has over the years, among other developments, led to demands for "cost of living allowance", "hardship allowance", etc., and actual unilateral grants of "relief measures" on the part of respective federal and state governments. The growth of "hidden allowances" in the public sector may also thus be partly attributed to the rigidity of the grade level system.
8. There was/is the practice of promoting civil servants in sets or groups, such largely determined by date of commencement of employment (also in the military and para-military establishments) without reference to differences in performance levels of individuals.
9. Except a civil servant is skipped in the promotion exercise, it did/does not seem that the possibility of a civil servant disagreeing with quantum of increment or range of fringe benefits available would be regarded as legitimate or expected. This also partly explains the demand for monetary palliatives pending a comprehensive review of salaries and wages as alluded to above.

10. The bases for wages and salaries in the whole public sector remain unclear, of particular concern being pay relativities. Mindful of the complex nature of job analysis and of job evaluation, it should however be remarked that the idea of equal pay for those with "identical skills" and carrying out "identical work" can be misleading in the case of the public sector. Not all who have identical skills carry out identical work in the main civil service and parastatals, even where we can agree on what "identical skills" entail; two persons may have similar or identical formal qualifications but display different skills in performing the job. Not all permanent secretaries, for example, possess identical skills and perform identical work; some are busier than others and the activities of some are more critical or central to the achievement of certain national goals which might be a priority at the point in time.
11. Tied to the above issue of wages and salaries determination basis is the issue of ability to pay. The disparity at the Top (especially Director) level between the state and federal levels could be explained by the scope of responsibilities and span of control; despite that, there might still be some exceptions. Furthermore, in the budgeting process recurrent expenditure is budgeted for, the public servants live in the same towns and cities and barring a dramatic drop in the price of crude oil, there is limited justifiable reason to reduce budgetary allocations to such a level as to affect the salaries of public servants. Even the mismanagement of the budgetary process is no sufficient ground for such, though it might shed light on why some salaries are delayed. The key underlining factor is whether we would like to have a well-remunerated and productive public service. Lastly, to argue that other national priorities take precedence might be inappropriate: without a competent and well-remunerated public service, no country can develop.
12. Deregulation of collective bargaining in the public sector needs to be thought through than has been the case. In fact, there has been no deregulation. As it is, no parastatal and or ministry has the autonomy to negotiate binding terms of employment with employees. For example, the pretence of academic staff negotiating with individual university councils was gravely undermined by circular to the universities' authorities imposing an upper ceiling on increases and basic salaries; it was still a centralized system, and so ASUU opted to negotiate directly with the approving authority! And for another, the NNPC hands over all proceeds from sale of crude oil to the federal government and thus has no independent finances to operate in the manner of Shell or Total or ChevronTexaco.
13. The periodic and arbitrary mass sack of public servants do not appear to be subjected to collective bargaining processes, aside from being an

indication of some form of disregard for civil and human rights, contractual obligations, due process and rule of law. There is not much point in moaning declining morale and productivity, and corruption in the public service when job insecurity is institutionalized.

By way of concluding remarks, collective bargaining and accompanying causes and resolution of industrial disputes in Nigeria are far more complex than is often realised. Indeed, the practices in industry tend to be greatly influenced by socio-political values and practices in the larger society, setting both limits and direction for the social partners. A good deal of social legislation and labour are indicators of underlying assumptions of the status quo. The period 1900–2005 in Nigeria has been that of overwhelming authoritarian rulership notwithstanding it ending in the establishment of democratically elected governments in 1960-1965, 1979-1983 and 1999 till date: the lingering legacy of repressive and authoritarian tendencies still predominates, especially in attitudes to consultation and consensual approach to determine social and other policies.[55]

---

[55] Present immediately below is a list of decrees that would need to be reviewed. Both the Factories Act and Workmen's Compensation Act have recently been reviewed. Those listed below tend to violate some of the rights already enshrined in the Nigerian constitution and various Conventions of the ILO ratified by successive Nigerian governments. Especially coming under attack have been the freedom of association, the right to collective bargain, the right to strike and the right to the due process of law.

Civil Service Commission And Other Statutory Bodies etc. (Removal of Certain Person From Office Decree No. 16 of 1984 — empowers the appropriate authorities (i.e. Head of State, Provisional Ruling Council or Governor of a State) to remove members of the board of any statutory body without recourse to due process. The jurisdiction of the court is ousted in respect of anything done or purported to be done under the Decree.

Trade Disputes (Essential Services) Act (Cap 432) Laws of the Federation of Nigeria, 1990 – empowers the Head of State to proscribe any trade union or association whose members are engaged in any essential service if he is satisfied that the union or association has been engaged in acts calculated to cause industrial unrest or disrupt the smooth running of any essential service. The law further empowers the detention of any official or member of a proscribed union.

Trade Union (Cap 437 Laws of the Federation of Nigeria, 1990 (Section 11 thereof) – precludes members of the Nigerian Armed Forces and the Police, Prisons Department, the Customs Preventive Service, the Nigerian Security and Printing and Minting Company Limited, the Central Bank of Nigeria, the Nigerian Telecommunication Limited, or any state apparatus authorised to bear arms and such other establishments as the Labour Minister may from time to time by order specify, from forming or belonging to any trade union.

Trade Disputes (Emergency Provisions) Decree 21 of 1990 – makes it a criminal offence to embark on any form of industrial action during the period of national emergency.

Teaching, ETC (Essential Services) Decree No. 30 1993 – having declared education as "essential service", it prohibits both teaching and non-teaching members of primary, secondary or tertiary institutions in Nigeria from embarking on an industrial action Section 3 of this Decree completely ousts the jurisdiction of courts, while a breach of its provisions attracts a punishment of 2 years.

Teaching ETC. (Essential Services) Amendment Decree (No. 44) 1993 – The decree amends Decree No 30 of 1993 to prescribe a 2-year imprisonment four any member of staff of any educational institution who persists in industrial action. In addition, the staff shall be liable to forfeit his official accommodation provided by the institution.

Lastly, although successive governments in Nigeria have ratified various ILO conventions, especially those governing the right to strike, freedom of association and effective recognition of the right to collective bargaining, the substance and philosophy underlying them have hardly been reflected in the country's labour law due to some of the reasons and developments outlined above. Even without knowledge of the ILO Core Conventions and the Decent Work Agenda, it would appear that most of the issues dominating collective bargaining and disputes and strikes arising therefrom have to do with achieving decent work and joint approach to solving problems. The complete overhaul of labour law is overdue; many of their provisions violate the right to organize and collective bargain, and the principle of freedom of association, along with the freedom of movement, of speech, of worship and other civil and human rights form the basis of a democratic society.

EMERGING SUBSECTORS-SPECIFIC ISSUES

The existing labour laws contain statutory provisions that are contrary to the fundamental principles of collective bargaining

The relevant portions of the labour laws that regulated the practice of collective bargaining and their related issues are as follows:

1. The "no strike" clause in the Trade Disputes (Essential Services) Act 1976 is a denial of basic rights by majority of public servants at the federal, state and local government levels and all parastatals. Extensive sectors such as transport, the civil services, law enforcement agencies, the armed forces, as well as certain private sector establishments (financial institutions, telecommunications) and educational institutions are affected by the no-strike law. Workers categorised as "essential services" are also too expansive. There is the need to review the laws and to focus more on moderating the incidence of strike by "essential services" workers by procedural agreement.
2. Government's use of various laws however defined, in the intervention, of the trade union structures have generated the following issues:
   a. Widespread discrepancy among the unions over union jurisdiction arising from the effect of Decree No 4 that was used to reduce the 41 trade unions to 29.
   b. Limitation of the number of unions that can be formed by explicit mention of the Trade Unions that is recognised by law in the Trade

Trade Union (Amendment) Decree No. 4 of 1996 – Contrary to the fundamental right of Nigerian workers to assemble freely and associate with other persons and in particular, form or belong to any trade union for the protection of their interests, this Decree: disbanded the existing Trade Unions and substituted new ones created by the military regime. The Decree makes it impossible for any aggrieved person to obtain relief in any court of law. This ouster clause is contained in Section 8 of the Decree.

Unions Act. These include the NLC and the TUC. This is against the ILO conventions.

3. The trade union law's provision of compulsory registration has remained contentious because:
   a. an unregistered trade union is an illegal body, while
   b. it has the effect of workers having to obtain the consent of public authorities, through the office of the Registrar of Trade Unions, for a union to function.

   All these are against ILO Convention 87 which recognises the right of workers to form or belong to any union of their choice and Section 40 of the Constitution of Nigeria that guarantees the right to form or belong to any trade union.
4. Gaps in the labour laws resulting in the inability of the law to address unfair labour practices. In the Nigerian labour law, there appears to be no recognition of, nor explicit definition of actions and decisions to be regarded as "unfair labour practices" to address issues of staff unfair dismissal, "warning", "suspension" etc on account of union membership and general work relations.
5. Collective agreements are generally not enforceable in a court of law as there are no explicit provisions that recognise collective agreements.
6. Limitation of the principle of voluntarism through the automatic system of deriving check-off dues at source imposed by law (although a member can also contract out in writing) and excessive control functions of government on the senior staff associations who are deliberately denied automatic check-off system for deriving membership dues.
7. The law provides for an overwhelming power of the Registrar of Trade Unions which includes accepting/rejecting audited annual accounts of the trade unions[56] de-registration of a union, and approving ground rules for mergers and thus unilaterally determines the fate of trade unions.
8. Extensive procedures in the law for the registration of trade unions have the net effect of discouraging, if not rendering impossible, voluntary mergers and formation of federations.

Inappropriate, inadequate or dysfunctional collective bargaining units/structures

Issues general to the Public Sector

1. The Federal Government (instead of respective MDAs) is taken as (and plays the role of) the employer for public sector workers. This is because

[56] Aside from having powers to call for accounts of the union at any time, the Registrar may also institute civil or criminal proceedings against the union if not satisfied with the audited accounts!

either the "management" has abdicated their responsibilities or are improper mandated.

- With this arrangement, the Federal Governments occupies dual position of both the employer and the sovereign power.
  - In this regard, public sector workers and their representatives recurrently complain that the Federal Government almost always imposes its will as a sovereign power in bargaining with workers.
  - This arrangement (negotiating structure) which makes the Federal Government both the employer and the arbitrator is defective.
  - It creates the impression/belief that Government can "do and undo" and that "he who plays the piper dictates the tune".

2. Despite the sovereign issue raised by workers as above on the one hand, a number of workers and their representatives (e.g. ASUU, NASU) on the other hand consider the practice of bargaining directly with the Federal Government instead of their respective MDA more favourable because of the conviction that they can create more impact and achieve more in the bargaining process if they come together and bargain with the Federal Government.

   Also, workers and their representatives believe that not much can be achieved with their individual employers because their employers are funded primarily by the Federal Government; and there is also the belief that:

   - The Chief Officers of MDAs are political appointees who are significantly controlled by the Federal Government; and
   - The Federal Government is a major influence on the bargaining processes and strike actions at MDA levels. For example, the Federal Government instructed universities to stop paying the salaries of university workers during a strike action.

3. Closely linked to the issue of highly centralized bargaining process, is the one of having generalist (instead of specialists who better understand the peculiarities of the sector) bargain on behalf of Government. The Office of the Head of Civil Service of the Federation (OHCSF) bargains with workers in all MDAs, despite the fact that the MDAs reside in different sectors - Agriculture, Education, etc.
4. Non-recognition of individual or group bargaining units in the parastatals or the possibility of individual or group grievances. This issue has resulted in several attempts by employees of various parastatals to take themselves out of the unified salary structure (e.g. universities and polytechnics and other tertiary educational employees, NNPC, CBN, Police, Medical Doctors in Teaching Hospitals, etc).

The Main Civil Service

1. The current structure/grouping of collective bargaining units representing workers in the public service (Negotiating Council I, II & III) is defective. It does not allow for effective representation of the various workers groups. There is a need for more emphasis on a grouping of bargaining units along lines of profession / sector.
2. Emphasis is unnecessarily placed on splitting bargaining units along the lines of staff cadre (i.e. Junior and Senior Staff units) despite the fact that the common interest of all the staff cadres can be negotiated collectively.
3. Lack of clarity as to the recognition of who the "management" is for the civil service since employee management functions are performed by various public servants and bodies.
4. Problem with the representative structure of government:
   - The Federal government has made attempts to put in place a management structure for the public service. To this end, the NCE was constituted to perform the role of co-ordinating governments' position on this issue. However, it has been primarily focused on the review of collective agreements while other institutions have been largely responsible for Human Resource management.
   - There is no discernable structure for government management team. The ideal situation is for public sector employer negotiating team to be the Head of Service. Instead, a committee is usually hurriedly constituted in an emergency situation.

The Public Utilities

1. Poor bargaining practices due to:
   a. absence of productivity-based bargaining;
   b. existing conflict of interest of management staff during negotiations, who rather agree to union demands in order to retain their positions whether or not they are able to meet the demands or are poised to benefit from the outcome of the bargaining;
   c. decisions reached from collective bargaining are further subjected to other 3rd party approvals.
2. They are significantly affected by the twin issues of the "sovereignty" doctrine and classification as "essential services". This has limited their ability to develop a sustainable collective bargaining system, and for the further reason that the public utility companies exist as a monopoly.

Public Sector companies operating in near-private sector environment

1. Bargaining structures are largely centralised between the management at the Group Head Quarters and the representatives of the Branch

Executive Committees (BEC). Thus, demands specific to branch workers are not addressed.

2. From the above issue, the subsidiaries are also saddled with the task of interpreting the collective agreements centrally determined.
3. The bargaining situation is slightly weakened by the state ownership which limits the level of independence that can be exercised.

Higher Education and Research Institutions

Our finding shows that there is improper combination of bargaining unit for the tertiary institutions. This is so because bargaining is done between the unions and the Federal Government; instead of with their statutorily mandated employer which is the Governing Council of the respective institutions.

Faulty practices and application of collective bargaining principles and rules of procedures

1. ***Collective Agreements***

Collective agreements are either Procedural Agreements or Substantive Agreements.

- Procedural Agreements are documents containing the rules and procedures of collective bargaining as agreed by both parties. Typical contents of Procedural Agreements include:

- Definition of terms used in the agreements including reference to the negotiating parties
- The effective date of commencement of the collective agreements
- Objectives of the collective agreement
- The general principles that will govern the collective agreements
- Union representation (including employee and employer representatives)
- Union meetings and necessary facilities to support union meetings
- Provision for joint negotiating committee and the subject matter for negotiation by the committee
- Handling of grievances and discipline of members
- Collective bargaining levels and coverage
- Provision for any variation to the procedural agreements
- Provision for the termination of the procedural agreements
- Signatories/authorisation of the parties for the collective agreements
- Duration and review date of the agreement.

- Substantive Agreements contains the agreed terms and condition of employment. Typical contents of Substantive agreements include:

- Terms and Conditions of Employment

- Job Descriptions for each staff
- Hours of Work
- Holiday and Sickness Arrangements
- Pensions
- Overall Salary Structure and Pay Levels
- Health and Safety
- Equal Opportunities Policies
- Training and Recruitment
- Staff Amenities
- Redundancy and Redeployment
- Disciplinary and Grievance Procedures
- Relocation of Offices
- Provisions for Review of the Agreement
- Signatories/Authorisation of the Parties to the Substantive Agreement
- Any Other Item as Agreed.

The absence Procedural agreements (bargaining rules) in the public sector has been largely responsible for the issues faced by the collective bargaining system, while substantive agreements are also more of exceptions than norm. The general rule is to codify collective agreements and have copies of it deposited with the Ministry for Labour and Productivity.

Unfair collective bargaining practices by public sector employers

1. Intimidation of union executive committees and incarcerating their principal officers on undisclosed grounds (e.g. ASUU, PENGASSAN, NUPENG and the NLC).
2. Public sector employers have displayed scant regard for the contract of employment (and for individual and human rights) as reflected in arrears of wages and salaries, summary dismissals and mass sacking announced over radio and television.
3. Government's approach to productivity through mass sack tends to create the fear of job insecurity in the minds of the employees.
4. Public sector employers do not suffer any penalties for violating agreements due to the lack of a clearly defined legal status and implications of the agreements which makes the agreements binding on the parties.

2. ***Poor collective bargaining practices by trade union***

The level of technical skills displayed by some of the unions tends to be inadequate, thus their members approach to collective bargaining tends to be militant / confrontational in nature and their demands are perceived by government to be unrealistic.

Timing and content of collective bargaining

1. Typically, where collective bargaining occurs, the bargaining process is initiated after completion of the nations budgeting process and implementation is expected to commence anytime during the year but before the next budgeting cycle or backdated to a period prior to the negotiation. Thus, the Government always finds it impractical to accommodate any wage increases or pay any arrears not budgeted for.
2. Productivity does not feature much during collective bargaining processes and are not reflected in the communication to employees.

Values of collective bargaining are either not imbibed nor displayed by the bargaining parties

1. Bargaining is not usually done in good faith, e.g., refusal of public sector employers to honour collective agreements after completion of negotiation processes, even when the process goes as far as the IAP level. Government usually complains about inability to pay.
2. Poor representation of the parties on the side of government. The outcome of the bargaining processes are in a number of circumstances subject to secondary agreement because those who negotiate on behalf of Government do not have the final authority to commit Government, but go ahead to reach agreements with unions and the agreements end up to be overturned by superior authorities in Government.
3. Public sector workers and their representatives have certain impressions/ perception about the Government that the Government needs to be sensitive to and/ or address. These include the belief that:
    - Government lacks the willingness (not the ability) to implement satisfactory pay levels for public sector worker; that the Government always blames their inability on the economy;
    - Government lacks a democratic culture in bargaining; there is the belief that Government still adopts the military approach to bargaining, with the "obey the last order" concept;
    - Government sees unions as opponents not partners that can be negotiated with; there is the impression that Government does not genuinely subscribe to the concept of trade unionism, but is merely living with it because it is imposed by statutes and workers'/unions coercive potential;
    - Generally, there is a high degree of workers' distrust in the bargaining process with Government. Government needs to be sensitive to this and address it effectively.

Faulty dispute resolution procedure/process

Issues in the Conciliation and Arbitration stages in the dispute resolution process of the collective bargaining system are identified to include the following:

1. The procedures for dispute resolution are centred round the Minister. Typical practices include:
    i. Enormous power of the minister to unilaterally control the dispute resolution process ranging from mandatory deposit of copies of collective agreements to rejection of terms already agreed by the parties in industry.
    ii. Appointment of insufficient number of requisite judges for IAP and NIC in the past, thereby undermining confidence in the process/institution.
    iii. Awards are only communicated to the Minister (and not the parties) who can arbitrarily accept or reject the awards.
2. The stages of the dispute resolution procedure are compulsory, leaving no room for voluntary options without involvement of public authorities (except for the internal dispute settlement machinery).
3. The procedure is very cumbersome; taking some 50 days from apprehension to the NIC should the Minister decide to exhaust each stage – and this does not include the 30 days within which the NIC is required to make its award/decision.
4. Selection/ composition of the public employer negotiating team are typically done on an ad hoc basis.
5. Absence of an empowered Board and/or provision of relative autonomy to the public employer negotiating party to the negotiation process.
6. Delegates to ILO conventions and international meetings are mainly composed of officials from the Ministry of Labour and Productivity rather than complete representation of all the parties. This has the effect of inadequate representations at such gatherings.

PROPOSED COLLECTIVE BARGAINING AND WAGE ADJUSTMENT MECHANISMS

Recommendation Collective for Bargaining Mechanisms

The recommendations in this sub-section are based on the review of the main issues as identified in the preceding section, the guiding principles as prescribed in relevant ILO Conventions and recommendations, the leading practices from case study countries reviewed and the peculiar circumstances in Nigeria.

Thus, the Committee hereby propose the following recommendations:

The existing labour laws should be reviewed to ensure that the statutory provisions are in conformity with the principles prescribed in relevant ILO conventions and leading practices

As a first step, various problem areas in the labour laws that run contrary to the principle of collective bargaining need to be reviewed. Specific areas already identified for review include the following:

- make provision for the right for strike action by workers of general application;
- resolution of the problems with union jurisdiction arising from the compulsory determination of trade union bodies for civil service workers;
- introduction and clear definition of what constitutes unfair labour practice;
- recognise right to associate and engage in collective bargaining for all sectors, except the Police and Military;
- in sectors of the economy where strikes are not allowed, institutionalisation of joint consultative committee to have regular consultations should be encouraged e.g. in the Armed Forces and Police
- justiciability of collective agreements in the court of law to ensure awards are binding on the parties;
- compulsory codification and legalisation of penalties for any of the social partners that defaults, without permissible reason, on the collective agreement, etc.
- freedom of association and rights to collective bargaining that:
    - removes the requirement for the compulsory registration of trade unions and limitations on the number of federations of unions; unions, like companies, may be registered for record purposes and for ensuring no duplication of names etc; not as legal/administrative permission to exist and function;
    - guarantees the right of employees to vote, by election (open or secret depending on agreement) to establish unions, approve strikes etc;
    - basic workers' freedoms, rights and interests, such as freedom of association, the right to bargain collectively, non-discrimination, prohibition of forced labour, principle of voluntarism, equality of treatment etc. should be recognized and fully respected;
    - basic employers' freedoms, rights and interests, such as freedom of association, property rights and management requirements should also be recognized and fully respected; and

Review of the collective bargaining units/structure to ensure that they are effectively structured to achieving their objectives.

The importance of such a review cannot be overemphasised. There is an urgent need to restructure the bargaining units to become more effective in their functions.

4.1.2.1 The structure of the employee and employer bargaining units should be guided by the following key principles:

i. Where the legislation setting up the MDA allows the MDA to recruit and manage the employees, such an MDA can constitute a bargaining unit.
ii. A collection of such units in (i) above who operate in the same service area or industry, may choose to evolve into an industry-wide bargaining unit and decide on the structure and procedures to follow in their negotiations.
iii. Where the law forbids a trade union e.g. Armed Forces and Police, then there should exist Joint Consultative Committees.
iv. The political authorities should refrain from interventions, whether direct or indirect, with the activities of the unions that are bipartite in nature.

4.1.2.2 Structuring of bargaining units

Based on the principles espoused above, the following recommendations should apply to the public sector:

Main Civil Service

i. Structuring of collective bargaining at the Federal, State and Local Government levels.

Option 1

1. The representatives of both employers and employees from the federal, state and local government should collectively form a National Joint Negotiating Committee to decide and agree on the minimum level for the collective agreement that will be applicable to the entire public service.
2. The individual bargaining units at the federal, state and local government levels will thereafter derive their collective agreements from the minimum level established at the national level.

Option 2

Bargaining units should be localised to the federal, state and local government levels and they should bargain at their respective levels individually and decide on issues relating to their pay and conditions of services as well as generate their individual collective agreements.

ii. The civil service should:

1 retain the existing eight (8) employee union arrangement based on sector/categories while the national bodies should serve as advisory bodies to the civil service unions (where such exists).
2 discontinue the categorisation of employees into negotiating councils to allow for flexibility of the workers unions to constitute their own negotiating units collectively rather than by imposition.
3 allow bargaining units to have the freedom to decide on the level of bargaining which may be either at sub-sector level or enterprise-level or as considered suitable.

iii. Issues of wages and conditions of service should be negotiated by the bargaining units in line with national policies.

iv. Each bargaining unit should generate its own collective agreements (both Procedural and Substantive) and should be binding on all parties to the agreements, including non-unionised employees up to the extent applicable.

Essential Services
Since the national laws prohibit these categories from forming unions, we therefore recommend the formation of **Review Bodies** that would have the sole responsibility to review their pay and other conditions of services.

Tertiary Educational Institutions
We observed that the mandates of most tertiary educational institutions identify the Governing Councils as having the responsibility to employ and manage the various categories of employees of the institution.

We therefore recommend that:
i. the various employee unions in the institutions identify with this mandate and constitute themselves into bargaining units as applicable in order to negotiate with the University Council;
ii. the various employee and employer unions may on their own decide to constitute a joint committee either at the national or state level. Negotiations at the national level may be conducted to establish the industry-level the minimum standards applicable to the university system in line with the earlier defined principle;
iii. each individual institution may on their own modify the agreed industry-level collective agreements to address their peculiarities; and
iv. other issues of funding should be addressed through other relevant channels.

Other public sectors establishments
Most of the other public sector establishments comprise of public utilities establishments and other public sector companies operating in near-private

sector environment. The collective bargaining systems in these establishments have better evolved than in the main civil service.

Thus we recommend that the status quo be maintained while the various establishments develop innovative approaches to addressing collective bargaining issues peculiar to each establishment. Examples of such establishments include Water Board, Federal Inland Revenue Service, Pension Commission, Hospital Management Board, Teaching Services etc.

The above recommendations require that the following critical success factors should be considered in order to ensure effective implementation of these recommendations;

i. Autonomy of the establishments

The principle of a decentralised collective bargaining is better sustained in an environment of full autonomy, the right to conclude agreements, competence and appropriate mandate of the parties.

ii. Ability to Pay/Timing of Agreement

This is can be resolved in the following ways:

1. collective agreements are concluded prior to the budgeting process to ensure that the potential wage bill resulting from the bargaining process is factored into the proposed budget;
2. restructuring/reorganisation of the establishment to eliminate redundancies, wastages and more efficient allocation of resources for optimal benefits, etc.;
3. expansion of the revenue base, increase in allocation and optimal utilisation of the labour force.

iii. The MDA at all levels of government should be mission, goal and performance driven

This is to ensure that the benefits of decentralisation can be derived within the purview of limited resources and the increasing competitiveness among various institutions for performance.

Our review of case study countries shows that several countries especial in Europe have decentralised bargaining systems whereby there are federated, confederated and local employer. Consequently, employee unions are also formed at the national, regional and local government levels or their equivalents respectively. The federated unions negotiate at the national level to set the tone for collective agreements which are emulated by the states and local governments. The agreements are reviewed and use as reference in the state and local government levels. However, there are usually national policies that require to be adhered to. However, bargaining at each level of government is independent. Furthermore, most establishments have the mandate to conclude collective agreements with their workers to ensure full decentralisation, but within their budget limits.

The existing labour laws should be reviewed to ensure that the statutory provisions are in conformity with the principles prescribed in relevant ILO conventions and leading practices

As a member of the International Labour Organisation (ILO), Nigeria has ratified the ILO convention on freedom of association and collective bargaining embodied in conventions 87 and 98 since 17 October, 1960. By this, the nation has given the indication that it has adopted the principles of collective bargaining and this has been re-echoed severally by successive governments. However, the general consensus is that the principles are not being practiced as should have been and several cases of violation of the conventions have been cited.

We therefore recommend that the Government improve upon its practice of collective bargaining by fulfilling the following necessary conditions for effective institutionalisation of collective bargaining:

1. Give voluntary recognition to trade unions as one of the contracting parties.
2. Bargaining must be done in good faith. There must be willingness to give and take, reach agreements and limit demands to what is more realistic, etc. by all parties but especially by Government. Furthermore, the Government's actions prior and after negotiations should be such that they are capable of furthering an atmosphere of trust.
3. Hold regular meetings with representative unions to discuss and address issues of common interest, build better understand of each other's problems in order to find lasting solutions to questions on which their interests conflict.
4. Support of Labour Administration Authorities

   This implies that the Ministry of Labour and Productivity, Department of Establishment & Industrial Relations of the Establishments & Pensions Office and other relevant units in the public service will:

   i. provide the necessary climate for collective bargaining;
   ii. not support a party in breach of agreements concluded consequent to collective bargaining;
   iii. as far as is practicable, secure the observance of collective bargaining agreements.
5. Proper internal communication between the bargaining parties as a means of exhibiting openness rather than an atmosphere characterised by circumspect.

1.1.1 Legislation of collective agreements

1. Compulsory codification and assurance of the binding nature of collective agreement as a necessary step to developing concrete faith in the collective bargaining process.

2. Collective agreements must be complete in themselves and should include standard Procedure Agreements and detailed Substantive Agreements.
3. Recommended duration for collective agreement is 2 years or as may be determined by the parties.

1.1.2 *Review the category of "essential services" to ensure that it is in line with ILO principles and restricted to the Armed Forces, Police etc. Also, unionisation issues of essential services workers should be addressed through setting up of pay review bodies, which is in line with leading practices in UK and Canada.*

Review of the dispute resolutions mechanism

Our recommended options for the review of the dispute resolution process are as follows:

1. Discontinue the present dispute resolution process and in its place institute a labour relations commission that will be truly representative of the various parties and consultative in nature.
2. Modify the legislation to allow for an alternative dispute resolution mechanism which comprises of registered law firms, mediators and arbitrators that specialises in labour relations and whose function is to resolve dispute among aggrieved parties. Thus, both parties can collectively invite a mutually agreed upon mediator (i.e. law firm) to assist with resolving the dispute, and whose award will be binding on both parties.
3. Maintain the key structures of the dispute resolution system, but review the process for the following:
   a. Parties to a dispute should have the right to explore alternative dispute resolution procedure and not be compelled to follow the stipulated procedure.
   b. The chairman of the IAP should be rotated among the three parties to ensure fairness in representation.
   c. Awards should be communicated directly to the parties rather than to the Minister of Labour and Productivity. Also, the Minister should not have the right to withhold any awards for any reason.
   d. Other powers of the Minster of Labour and Productivity should be reviewed to ensure that it guarantees the needed freedom of collective bargaining and right to co-determination.

Building enduring capacity of people, organisations and communities, etc., for sustainable collective bargaining

If the recommendations of this committee are accepted and institutionalised, there will be a need to develop the capacity of the actors to ensure a sustained system.

Capacity building is defined as "the creation of an enabling environment with appropriate policy and legal frameworks, institutional development, human resources development and strengthening of managerial systems."[57] It is a long-term, continuing process, in which all stakeholders participate (ministries, local authorities, non-governmental organisations, user groups, professional associations, academics, etc.) to build a desired level of independence.

Therefore, our recommendations on capability building for collective bargaining in Nigeria's Pubic Sector include:

1. Develop a framework for capacity building to guide and support the collective bargaining process.

The capacity-building framework above is mainly focussed on the programs elements for building capacity but can be extended to cover support for change management. The framework emphasises five key action areas in broad context:

- Organisational development – refers to processes that ensure that the collective bargaining can be driven from the organisation itself through its structures, systems, policies, procedures and practices.
- Workforce development - refers to a process initiated within organisations to help ensure that the people working within its system have the abilities and commitment to contribute to organisational and community goals.
- Resource allocation - is an economic process and is concerned with the efficiency of resource allocation to ensure that it yields the greatest benefit.
- Partnership - refers to the development of effective partnerships to address collective bargaining problems.
- Leadership - is a function of training, experience and personality which seeks to foster the characteristics of leadership within people by developing and building leadership qualities in themselves and others.

1. Develop and administer trainings, educational programmes, seminars and workshops for relevant employee and employer groups (generic and specialised) on:
   i. negotiation skills;
   ii. principles of collective bargaining;
   iii. labour relations and regulations;
   iv. relevant institutions in the Ministry of Labour and Productivity;
   v. trade unions composition, structure and levels of organisation, etc.
2. Provide adequate resources, i.e. funding to facilitate effective capacity building programmes; and

[57] UNDP, 1991

3. Develop a broad and broadly shared knowledge base about capacity building for reference and the benefits of the community.
4. Efforts must be instituted to ensure that beyond the strengthening of labour administration services of the Ministry of Labour and Productivity, the Department of Establishment and Industrial Relations and other labour related units in the pubic service, more innovative means of enforcement must be developed such as effective empowerment of employers and employees and their representatives in monitoring and guaranteeing of rights, and providing for more effective checks and balances against abuses and violations.
5. Adequate representation at internationally organised conferences. Thus, the delegates from Nigeria should comprise of members drawn from the government, employers and employees and other key Human Resources Management and Industrial Relations experts, interests and stakeholders.

There is a need for regular and frequent meeting of employer and employees in the public sector (especially the public service) where issues are proactively discussed and resolved.

Chapter 17

EMPLOYMENT AND WORK RELATIONS IN THE NIGERIAN UNIVERSITY SYSTEM

INTRODUCTORY REMARKS

In 1962, there were four universities between the three political regions and Nigerian capital of Lagos, of which the Eastern Region, Northern Region and Western Region had one each and the fourth located in Lagos. The University of Ibadan, the oldest, was established in 1948 as University College, Ibadan, one of University of London colleges.

Some private universities emerged in the early 1980s, but all the 24 private universities established between 1980 and 1983 were abolished by the Federal Government in 1984 because "in the absence of proper guidelines for their establishment, they all turned out to be universities only in name."[1] In 1993, another law/decree which allowed the establishment of private universities and spelt out procedures for such was promulgated. A National Open University was established in 1983, closed shortly after and re-opened in 2001 to offer education through Open and Distance Learning mode. In 2024, there were 149 private universities, 63 state governments-owned universities and 62 federal universities, while some polytechnics are in the process of being converted to universities.

The universities are of different types and include such specialised institutions as universities of Technology; universities of Agriculture; Defence Academy; Open University; University of Petroleum Resources; and universities of Education.

A more comprehensive way of putting this is that colonial antecedents and legacy seemed to have pushed the involvement of the central or federal government in education largely in the direction of the tertiary level, some tokenism at the secondary level. What may therefore be regarded as the "federal education sector" in Nigeria comprises federal universities, federal polytechnics and colleges of technology, federal colleges of education, federal science and technical colleges and federal government colleges that are funded almost exclusively by the federal government from public resources.

---

[1] State Of The Nigerian University System And The Development of 10-Year Programme For System 2007 – 2016, submission of the NUC to the Honourable Minister of Education, April 2007, p. 2

But, education is on the Concurrent Legislative List in the 1999 Constitution. This means both the federal and state governments have legislative powers, as well as functional, in respect of education. Statutorily, the Federal Ministry of Education (FME) is at the apex of the regulation and management of education in the country and to discharge this mandate, the ministry is structured into eight departments and three statutory units. Although the FME has overall responsibility for formulating, harmonizing and co-ordinating policies and monitoring quality in service delivery in the education sector, the ministry is advised in the discharge of these responsibilities by the National Council on Education (NCE), which is composed of the Federal Minister of Education and the State Commissioners for Education (FME, 2005).

The other regulatory bodies set up by the federal government to ensure minimum standards at the tertiary level are the National Universities Commission (NUC), the National Board for Technical Education (NBTE), and the National Commission for Colleges of Education (NCCE). They are parastatals of the Federal Ministry of Education for ensuring effective administrative control of higher education in Nigeria. They plan, organize, manage, arrange funding, supervise and monitor provision and development of the tertiary institutions as may be appropriate to each commission or board. Each parastatal helps to ensure minimum standard and quality among the institutions. They also play the intermediary and advisory roles between the federal government and the institutional authorities (FME, 2005).

THE UNIVERSITY SYSTEM, UNIONISM AND LABOUR RELATIONS

The Nigerian Association of University Teachers was formed in 1965 in reaction to developments in the university system and Nigeria, comprising then of four universities located in Ibadan, Lagos, Zaria and Nsukka respectively.

The "decolonisation of the system" under the first four universities, followed closely by the University of Ife and what eventually became the University of Benin, saw a relatively smooth transfer of the academic management of the system into the hands of the first crop of indigenous professors, academics, and non-academics, a process which was not dominated by the blatant intervention of governments and traditional and political elites of the time.

The post-Civil War period ushered in a more complex university system with the creation and re-creation of states and most of which established their own universities and a flourish of private universities in more recent years. This has necessarily created challenges for regulatory authorities, themselves forced to elaborate their own structures and functions to ensure the development of objective measures of quality, a generalised university culture and governance system.

To represent and advance the interests of employees in the education sector are the Academic Staff Union of Nigeria Universities (ASUU), Non-Academic Staff Union of Universities and Allied Institutions (NASU), Senior Staff Association of Nigerian Universities (SSANU), Academic Staff Union of Polytechnics (ASUP) and Colleges of Education Academic Staff Union (COEASU) and the Senior Staff Association of Universities, Teaching Hospitals, Research and Allied Institutions (SSAUTHRAI). These unions articulate the collective grievances of their members as well as act as their bargaining agents during negotiations.

As for the potential members for unions in the university system, there were a total of 27,394 academic staff within the university system as at 2006 comprising Federal – 17,836 (65%), State - 7586 (28%) and Private 1972 (7%). Of these, Professor/Reader cadre constituted just 5,483 (20%), Senior Lecturer Cadre 6,475 (23.6%), while Lecturer I cadre constituted 15,436 (56.4%). There are a total of 72,070 Non-Academic staff comprising 30,275 (42%) senior Non-Academic staff, and a total of 41,795 (58%) junior staff. The system therefore had a grand total of 99,464 Academic and Non-Academic Staff, in the ratio of 1:2.6 in favour of Non-Academic Staff.[2]

Issues dominating employment and work relations at the macro-level reflected the times – period, socio-economic and political developments - as outlined below. While issues dominating work relations at the micro-level reflected the size and complexity of individual university. Over all, a comprehensive list of factors dominating, influencing and colouring work relations in the university system include:

- Duties and responsibilities in Unit/Faculty/Department/Section;
- Academic lectures (management, conduct, etc.);
- Academic Staff-Students relations;
- Admissions/credentials/verification processes/registration;
- Appointment of VC;
- Appointments/Elections of Deans and HODs;
- Budgetary allocations for academic programmes;
- Compulsory purchases of self-published works;
- Conduct of examinations;
- Cultism;
- Dereliction of duty;
- Disciplinary issues –admissions, sexual and other harassment of students, plagiarism, etc.

[2] Status Report On The National Universities Commission, 2008, p. 4

- Disciplinary procedure/process (Query system/feedback process/sanctions)
- Drug usage and peddling
- Employment/credentials/verification processes/ shortlisting of staff candidates/applicants
- Examination malpractices (no-show, impersonation, etc.)
- Examination questions – setting/leakages
- Exams/Supervision/Grading/Submission/compilation of results
- External examination system
- Extorting money from students
- Graduation requirements
- Groups, University Management and Community
- Hostel accommodation
- Internal generated revenue (IGR) and related matters
- Inter-colleagues relations
- Inter-groups dynamics
- Intimidation of both academic and non-academic staff
- Involvement with external groups (political groupings, societies, etc.)
- Placement issues
- Policy on fees
- Promotions and Placement
- Results and Certificate Award
- Salaries and fringe benefits
- Sale of handouts
- Senate (composition and conduct)
- Sexual harassment
- Staff Associations
- Students associations
- Students welfare
- University Council (composition and conduct)
- University Management and Groups
- University Management relations with other associations (cults, student union, external groups, etc.)
- University Management's policies and style
- Verification of credentials (staff and students)
- Welfare-related issues

EXTERNAL FACTORS IMPACTING ON EMPLOYMENT AND WORK RELATIONS IN THE UNIVERSITY SYSTEM

Regulatory and control framework

The external factors as identified here are only that much so because of their formal and legal statuses. Their being "external" is used advisedly because, in reality, it is often difficult to separate them, in many instances, from internal factors which we discuss below. For example, in the case of federally-funded universities, some decisions may be imposed on governing councils and vice chancellors by the Presidency, some others by the NUC, and against which staff and students may protest against a hapless university management. The NUC is supposed to serve as the initial contact point, and through which policy positions are routed by the Federal Ministry of Education, including as a conduit for channelling funds to the latter. Only a few years ago, the federal government began to bypass the NUC in the funding of university system. Any hiccups between the Ministry of Education and the NUC are not usually public knowledge, but the delayed appointment of the governing councils of universities, their composition, are pointed illustration of some negative impact of dilatory government's policies and subordinate-superior relationship between the Ministry and political leadership in and outside the Presidency, leaving many critical decisions pending to the annoyance of staff and students in the universities during that period of limbo. But historically, the external factor may conveniently be divided into four: i) military regimes; ii) Federal Ministry of Education; iii) the National Universities Commission; and iv) traditional and political elites.

Military regimes

Military regimes in Nigeria have been characterised by authoritarianism, arbitrariness, brazenness, disdain for procedures, checks and balances, and for civil institutions, all which are corrupting tendencies. Policy decisions and postings in ministries, government departments and agencies (MDAs) were affected by these. Both the 1979 and 1999 Constitutions enshrining the 'federal character principle' in recruitment and appointments merely served to elicit hostile reactions and aggravate feelings when adversely affected groups began to demand redressing imbalances in the post-1979 period but which post-1983 December 31 military regimes exacerbated with more arbitrariness in these matters.

In the case of tertiary institutions, and universities in particular, the military regimes harboured an unstable mixture of fear, hostility and contempt for intellect and intellectualism. In the immediate post-Udoji 1974 awards which made the permanent secretary earn more than the professor, which was hitherto not the case, in 17-scale salary structure, the public sector was plagued by strikes. To confront university teachers General Gowon arrogated more powers to the Visitor and which he used to appoint vice chancellors and punish. Building on this, Generals Babangida and Abacha summarily got rid of some Vice Chancellors and appointed sole administrators to them and to the NLC, NUPENG and PENGASSAN.

The military dictator could grant whatever monies he liked to any university, unilaterally slash the budget of ministries and parastatals, appoint a military Sole Administrator to a university and whose access to funds no Vice Chancellor could ever match. The Babangida regime had no problems with shutting down the universities for years, if that was the only means to deal with striking university teachers and students. We needed another general, but as a civilian President this time, to bring in the World Bank and the IMF to define "university autonomy".

Most of the vice chancellors and sole administrators appointed by successive military regimes, like their appointer, did not have much respect for university rules and regulations, other procedures, the University Senate, and senior colleagues and a new sub-culture of *impunity* became the norm. Employment, placements, promotions, admissions, disciplinary processes, award of contracts, research grants (where available), conference attendance, etc., were heavily and negatively impacted upon by the preferences of executive heads. Many statutory committees atrophied, while standing committees were either manipulated or stayed moribund, bypassed in largely personalized and caucus-driven decision-making process.

Delays in the passing of the federal and state budgets, in the implementation of the budget and the irregular timing of releasing funds have had unbelievably distorting effects throughout the university system. In fact, Abacha's regime practically did without a formal budget and meetings of his own cabinet. But, of more far-reaching ramifications has been "the envelope" concept of budget which grew out of Babangida regime's structural adjustment policy, characterised by massive budget slashing and cutbacks in public expenditure, removal of so-called subsidies, commercialisation and drive for internally generated revenue, and privatisation.[3] It meant all universities (and all MDAs) received substantially less of what they budgeted for, and the university councils and vice chancellors reacted with irregular payment of salaries even when they had to borrow from financial institutions as stop-gap measure, a cumulative reduction and stunting of programmes, abandoned and inadequate facilities and snail-speed infrastructural development, while consequent internally revenue-generating efforts had some positive outcomes, they were substantially negative in the forms of proliferation of legal and illegal

[3] See Otobo, D., *State and Industrial Relations in Nigeria*, Malthouse, 1988; Otobo, D. (ed.), *Further Readings in Industrial Relations in Nigeria*, Malthouse, 1992; and Otobo, D., *Labour Relations in Nigeria*, Vol. I, Malthouse, 1992 for useful coverage of industrial relations in this period.

academic and professional courses to augment statutory allocations, flagrant violation of NUC's carrying capacity guidelines in admissions, compulsory purchase by students of handouts and self-published books, dereliction of duty for private consultancies and business activities, corrupted admissions, examinations and disciplinary processes, intense and often bitter struggles over membership of certain committees thought more influential and "lucrative" because of a generalised focus on "making money", and frequent protests/strikes over compensation issues in the university system.

Federal Ministry of Education

Federal Commissioners/Ministers of Education under military regimes had very little autonomy and tended to rubber-stamp whatever were the decisions or policy options of the Supreme Military Council or Armed Forces Ruling Council, etc., on education over the years. Funding, admissions, appointment of top officials in federal secondary schools, teachers/technical colleges, polytechnics and universities were heavily influenced, if not dictated. The Minister of Education in several instances extended the tenure of some vice chancellors much beyond the periods provided for in the Acts establishing them. Of course, such decisions and actions undoubtedly impacted on the structures and processes within the universities concerned, including the conduct and comportment of academic and non-academic personnel therein.

Though since military regimes successive Ministers of Education have enjoyed substantial increase in autonomy and practical scope in decision making, most regulatory agencies in the education sector appear to have had greater autonomy too, but given the issue and circumstances some university managements have gone above the Ministry of Education, to the Presidency, National Assembly and other international development agencies. Granted the general concern for regime-sustenance and promotion of government policies, there would seem to be less focus on policy-making role of the Ministry for a drift towards policy implementation and thereby clashing or overlapping with those of specific regulatory agencies (e.g. Division of Tertiary Education with the NUC; Division of Primary Education with UBEC). The attendant mixed signals to tertiary institutions, especially the universities, reinforce *lobbying* at the highest levels as a major instrument for securing concessions and support for objectives and programmes. A university may then commence academic programmes with scant regard for guidelines as established by the NUC if it feels it has the ear of the Ministry or the Presidency.

Within the universities themselves, thus replicated, *lobbying* also became the main means of gaining the ears and support of university administration or management by academic and non-academic units, associations and individuals. This, in turn, served to undermine statutory and standing committees and other procedures for securing these outcomes.

And going with the times, an increasing number of ministry officials are appointed to membership of Governing Councils, choices often product of intense lobbying and outcome of a patronage system rather than on functional relevance and this in spite of the NUC's representation already in them as the regulatory body. Indeed, ministry policies are not routed through such officials, communication always sent directly to the vice chancellor, or through the NUC to the vice chancellor depending on the subject matter.

National Universities Commission

The National Universities Commission under military regimes functioned under difficult circumstances, the situation improving considerably from 1996. Where some of its Executive Secretaries were so inclined, especially during military dictatorships, functioned in largely autocratic manner, particularly where personal links or relationships with prominent members of a regime were all that mattered, this eventually led to the undermining of the status of the NUC as it was often bypassed by the Ministry of Education – e.g. in the funding of several activities of the universities - and had difficult relationship with JAMB. On some occasions, the highest regime authorities would bypass the Ministry of Education and the NUC and offer direct grants/donations/"gifts" to some institutions.

However in more recent times, the ability and capacity of the NUC to foster a better-functioning university system have improved tremendously, setting minimum standards, accrediting programmes at undergraduate and postgraduate levels (MBA), involved in facilitating provision of research funds and for conferences, and assisting those universities having problems managing themselves, etc. The critical point here is where the NUC through acts of omission and commission fails to get erring university administrations to mend their ways within its mandate, then the production of knowledge and skills in them would be suboptimal, while adversarial labour and work relations intensified.

Communities, local elites and politicians

The physical location of tertiary institutions, especially universities, has itself become subject to blatant political considerations, and when successfully influenced, it becomes one of the acclaimed achievements of some groups of traditional and political elites in their rivalry. Subsequent concessions demanded by them would cover the whole gamut of running the affected institution: recruitment, selection and placement of principal officers, contracts, admissions, examinations, promotions, to disciplinary issues of staff and students, the selection/appointment of the vice chancellor, registrar, deans and heads of departments, the push being for "daughters" and "sons" of the soil/locality or ethnic group. All of these obviously serve to condition the environment, comportment, conduct of, and tactics adopted by, personnel within these institutions in achieving their private and parochial objectives.

Another aspect of the politicization of physical location of universities (senatorial district, geo-political zone, state, local government, etc.) is the hurried establishment of so many of such institutions, with or without the approval of the NUC, accompanied by grossly inadequate funding, little physical and other infrastructure, poor staffing, poorly-built, poorly-equipped laboratories and lecture rooms, inevitably throw personnel therein into situations of so many aggravating factors, of fluid and barely functioning statutory and standing committees through paucity of numbers, lack of experienced hands and machinations of rival caucuses or groups, many practices hardly reflecting regular university culture and system, and local and political circumstances (e.g. budgets of state governments) and conduct of traditional and political elite have amplified divisive impacts.

Every now and then and aside from establishment and location of tertiary institutions in particular, traditional and political elites have sought to intervene in the education sector, from protesting against WAEC results, JAMB scores, cut-off points, admission quotas, number of professors from their areas of origin, to the fewness of vice chancellors from same. In accommodating some of these demands and in the case of vice chancellors, the phrase "senior academic" has been deliberately and liberally interpreted in a few instances to mean "senior lecturers and above" for senior lecturers to become vice chancellors in a few universities. In such universities, the demand for "democratisation" of the university system translated into senior lecturers, and in a few cases lecturer grade one, being "elected" heads of department and deans.

As for the private universities, flung and scattered all over the place due to the preferences of their proprietors, the more remote the geographical location and the distance from urban centres and bigger towns where some social amenities exist, the more glaring the paucity of facilities and amenities conducing to research, academic and teaching work, not to mention adequate decent accommodation for students. This partly accounts for the handsome fees currently prevailing in the private universities.

The budgetary process

Delays in the passing of the budget, in the implementation of the budget and the irregular timing of releasing funds have created a good deal of disharmony and disruption throughout the university system. It is tempting for many to maintain that not much can be done about this, from the National Assembly, Presidency, Federal Ministry of Education, the NUC and the vice chancellor. The budgetary process did not impact negatively on the university system till the late-1970s with the Obasanjo/Yar'Adua's regime, Gowon's regime having restructured the public sector with both the Adebo and Udoji Wages Commissions of 1970-1 and 1974 respectively. The burning issues thrown up by the two wages commissions were those of *relativities* and *comparability* of pay scales in the public sector, *not irregular funding* of the university system. Not many people are aware that before the 1974 Udoji Commission, for example, a university professor earned higher salary than a federal permanent secretary, and all permanent secretaries did not earn the same, a situation that was reversed under the unified salary structure which put emoluments of all public servants below that of a federal permanent secretary. Since 1999, most years are nearly half-spent before the budgets are passed by the National Assembly. All ministries, departments, and agencies (MDAs) barely operating efficiently during those times, and the university system starved of much-needed funds, and pushing staff in some universities to engage in forms of protests over irregular salaries and non-payment of certain allowances.

Collective bargaining and compensation policy

Wage bargain in the university system have also been partly driven by the desire of staff therein to opt out of the unified salary structure established by the Udoji Commission in 1974. The situation has been characterised by the following:

1. get employers to pay salaries regularly;
2. those universities owned by state governments negotiate with such state governments, while those funded by the federal government face a more complex set of bodies or institutions, from their governing councils, or NUC, the Federal Ministry of Education, to the Presidency and National Assembly. For example, the pretence of academic staff "negotiating" with individual university councils is gravely undermined by circular to the universities' authorities imposing an upper ceiling on increases and basic salaries; it is still a centralized system, and the respective councils do not have the authority to grant certain concessions. In the end, strikes then compel Presidency to listen, negotiate and implement.
3. relative lack of mandate on the part of government/university negotiators;
4. multiplicity of approving authorities, thereby reducing negotiations to mere identification of issues and options to be finally decided on elsewhere (Presidency);
5. poor composition of government's negotiating team. If the critical public sector players (Presidency, Finance, Establishment, Federal Ministry of Education, National Salaries, Incomes and Wages Commission, NUC, etc.) are represented, there should technically be no

grounds for anyone else overruling negotiated agreements. No president and his advisers can be better informed on relevant issues and budget implications of attendant agreements;
6. non-implementation of negotiated agreements;
7. inadequate and decaying infrastructure have accounted for several conflict situations in the university system, even if we disagree over the weight to be placed on this.

Goal-setting

Goal-setting includes curriculum development, general direction as reflected in admission policy, and manpower development. In practical terms, such is reflected in regulatory activities affecting minimum facilities for establishing a university, the determination of minimum academic standards, establishing ratio of undergraduate programmes to postgraduate programmes, qualifications of teachers, ratio of students to teachers, and ratio of teachers to support personnel, Visitation Panel Reports, Post-UME admissions screening, among others.[4] Accreditation of programmes in some instances has led to not only demonstrations by students, but also litigation, the two most widely publicised being that of Lead University taking the NUC to court over non-accreditation of its law and other degree programmes, and Lagos State University multi-campus policy and bewildering number of pre-degree programmes. Within these universities, as well as in several others, students and staff therein embarked upon extended strike actions, that of LASU lasting well over one academic session.

Autonomy issue

To fight university staff more effectively in mid-1970s, General Gowon increased the statutory powers of the Visitor and became such for all federally-funded universities. Among others, the power to appoint the vice

---

[4] Status Report On The National Universities Commission, 2008, p. 5, itemises them as:
- Expansion of Access to University education through the establishment of the National Open University of Nigeria and the licensing of 34 private universities;
- Significant increase in the level of funding to Federal Universities;
- Introduction of the Direct Teaching and Laboratory Cost Grant;
- Establishment of new academic programmes;
- Accreditation of academic programmes;
- Determination of carrying capacity/Admission quota for Nigerian universities
- Presidential intervention in Hostel Development and Management
- Deliberate war against cultism, sorting, sexual harassment and other institutional vices;
- Post-UME admissions screening
- Curriculum review
- Public hearing on Visitation Panel Reports
- Accountability in the Management of universities; and
- Efforts are also being made to stabilize the University Calendar.

chancellor he particularly cherished. The authoritarianism of military regimes since then served to distort and create disharmony within the university system, as they routinely bypassed the Federal Ministry of Education and the NUC. The military dictator could grant whatever monies he liked to any university, unilaterally slash the budget of ministries and parastatals, let alone of universities, appoint a military sole administrator to a university and whose access to funds no vice chancellor could ever match. The Babangida regime had no problems with shutting down the universities for years, if that was the only means to deal with striking university teachers and students. We needed another general as civilian president to bring in the World Bank and the IMF to define and foist on us a strange brand of "university autonomy". The federal government is said to have devolved autonomy legally since 2003 (though only gazetted in 2007), but it would seem continuing administrative practice of imposing certain decisions on vice chancellors, especially during conflict situations when even a director of state security services (SSS) in that state could order such immediate closure of relevant institution, makes a mockery of this brand of autonomy. I understand quite a few vice chancellors spend days on end in Abuja (and Governors' offices) "lobbying" for the release of supposedly routine statutory allocations. So much for autonomy!

Policy on fees

The pre-military regimes variety of pay-feeing arrangements in the country practically made it possible for any undergraduate and postgraduate student to afford the fees: federal scholarships, regional scholarships, federal bursary, regional/state bursary, indigent scholarship and loan schemes, and tuition-free education (Western Region), Commonwealth scholarship scheme, scholarship schemes of various international and American foundations (Ford, Rockefeller), etc. From the late 1970s till now, the shifting policies on fees have tended to generate disputes and disharmony within the university system, with that of LASU leading to a loss of academic session when the Governor of Lagos State increased tuition fees in 2010. The exceptions seem to be the recent crop of privately-owned universities where fees are on a "pay-or-leave-it" basis.

INTERNAL CONTENTS OF EMPLOYMENT AND WORK RELATIONS

The general thrust of this segment is not to provide ready excuse for those who violate procedures and misgovern any university, but to underscore four simple points which suffuse employment and work relations therein: i) that actual conduct is mostly based on *norms* and *values* people carry in their heads, and in this case learned and imbibed from the socio-culture of impunity and force fostered by nearly four decades of military dictatorships; ii) that these norms and values may change over time depending on circumstances (e.g. return to democratic politics); iii) these norms and values as reflected in practices may also be transmitted to younger generations; iv) that since socialisation is never perfect and individuals have a range of choices to make, there are sometimes competing values and practices - as reflected in the notion of "democratisation" of academic positions as used above.

The recency or newness of any university presents challenges of the sort that almost predetermine the comportment and conduct of personnel and thus work relations in largely predictable directions. Practically everything is rudimentary: the structure seems typified by fewness of academic and non-academic departments, of staff, of experienced and capable hands, of elaborate procedures and processes, of facilities and other infrastructure, etc., and centralization of authority and power. This tends to highlight and intensify interpersonal relationships between and among various categories of personnel, and bring students and lecturers into such close contacts which permit non-objective standards and measures in managing academic affairs and related matters. The emergent competing and rival groups in such small academic community become implacably opposed, utterances and activities consequentially more distorting and destabilizing of the institution and of the university system.

Of course, over time the law of increased numbers works in favour of more complex, stable, and better functioning structures, on the assumption of better funding and provision of facilities, etc., and more effective conflict-regulating mechanisms with wider acceptance and internalization of norms typical of a university culture and system. This suggests greater autocracy and centralisation of power and authority at inception, diluted over time with attendant adjustments in the conduct and comportment of academic staff, non-academic staff and students therein.

For the younger universities, the rate or speed at which relevant organs, units, etc., provided for by law are established would seem to have strong bearing on the conduct of some staff. The fewer the number, the more intense the competition for membership, while also assuming larger importance in the scheme of things; while the larger the number, either the more thinly staffed by members with varied skills and experience of the sort required, or may be dominated by a small group of either competent and/or politically well-connected people who are members of multiple committees and the like.

Management

The composition and conduct of governing councils, especially the role played by the pro-chancellor and vice chancellors. Where the chairman of the council believes and acts as the "chief executive officer" with a timid or sycophantic vice chancellor, the university authorities are likely to run foul of the university senate and staff to create disharmony in the system. Sometimes, such usurpation of roles by the chairman and some members of the governing council includes undue interference in the employment, admissions and promotion matters to the award of contracts.

1. And where the vice chancellor has the chairman and members of council in his pocket, so to speak, the chances of his/her being an arbitrary and authoritarian administrator are high, all conducing to corruption, disharmony and an institution plagued by petition-writing and caucuses of all descriptions (sub-ethnic, religious, political, etc.).
2. Where the governing council also acquiesces in a lazy vice chancellor abdicating his/her responsibilities onto the shoulders of a competent registrar, ensuing disharmony is intense because of fierce resistance from senior academic members of staff.
3. Where a power-hungry registrar engages a vice chancellor in a power tussle, the ensuing disharmony is also bad for the system and the institution.
4. The divide-an-rule tactics of some vice chancellors, creating antagonistic and rival factions or cabals, which then serve to complicate university senate proceedings, appointments and the management of faculties and of academic departments whose heads have to act out their loyalties in an equally divisive manner;
5. Succession management for positions of the vice chancellor and registrar and other principal officers of the university. This has often created factions, bitterness and hostility, including involving partisan traditional rulers and politicians.
6. Preponderant control of resources by senior non-academic staff (housing, etc.)
7. The ratio of resources devoted to non-academic staff in relation to others in the system, as a reflection of ratio of non-academic to academic is a perpetual source of disharmony and actually a threat to modernizing the university system by slowing down the process of having more intellectually productive and research-dominated universities. For example, a university having over twenty deputy registrars does not make much sense and may not be regarded as a cost-effective way of managing a university. Resources are thus strained, and spending over 70 per cent of income/subvention on salaries, wages and other entitlements in the face of barely staffed academic departments and laboratories can hardly keep a university in serious academic and teaching pursuits. One would have thought that increasing computerisation and adoption of other forms of information technology, aside from NUC's guideline regarding this, a more manageable ratio would have been achieved by now!

8. Manipulation of the promotion and grievance processing system. Allegations of discrimination, positive and negative, have at times plagued the promotion and grievance processing system, many academic and non-academic staff have stayed disillusioned as a result. Despite this, the system works on the whole and it is comforting to think that only an insignificant number of staff are so affected, but the demonstration effect is more extensive than at first realised. Several branches of ASUU have called out members on strike in some universities on account of such cases over the years.

Staff

a) An overwhelming number of universities in the country are newly established, the deleterious effect of this on the university system can hardly be overstated as alluded to above in discussing their recency. The fact is the military and academia (and managements of companies) are two institutions one only tampers with their hierarchies at the risk of devastating results; junior officers (coup plotters and caucus-members) bossing superior officers generate suspicion and hostility and breakdown of order, indiscipline, arbitrariness and personalisation of power and resources and counter-coups. In academia, respect and prestige grow out of research, publications and teaching, three activities that embody a *mentoring process.* Only professors are heads of departments, others less in rank are designated “acting heads of department”, and it is the norm for an elected Dean to nominate the head of department for the Vice Chancellor’s approval and appointment. Only professors are automatic members of the University Senate; a smaller number of lesser ranks are elected into it. Where a senior lecturer and those of lesser rank are “elected” “HODs” or “Acting HODs” by partisan groups created for that purpose, it serves to politicise the administration of an academic department, tainting all processes – employment, staff training, allocation of courses, mentoring, promotions, while encouraging disrespect for the hierarchy as the “democratisation” extends to the chairing of critical university committees and positions of Dean of Students Affairs and Deputy Vice Chancellors also.

It is no coincidence that it is only in the two or three universities in the country where a Vice Chancellor can be a senior lecturer over and above several professors who are willing to assume such responsibility that heads of departments are also “elected”. It is the rule of the inexperienced, who can only advance their ostensible academic careers through overtly political activities and actions that undermine relevant statutory and non-statutory bodies, while reducing the stature and position of the professor in the scheme of things with a flood of politically-produced ones – which then, in turn, affect the quality of decisions and management in the university system. The ensuing obviously distorting effects for such universities can no longer be denied even by the prime beneficiaries of such contrived and deviant arrangements.

Staff have a multiplicity of associations and unions representing the interests of academic and non-academic, with non-academic further split into junior and senior and technical cadres. Their activities have had mixed impact, some positive and others negative. The pursuit of less adversarial relations should be of greater benefit to the system.

The differentials between academic and non-academic (in some cases, even among the non-academic, there is a distinction between "admin" and "technical" staff) have remained conflict-inducing. I have never understood why a non-academic staff would demand equal or similar remuneration package with academic staff when basic criteria for engagement, job description, content, career path and for advancement are so dramatically different. In fact, I once overheard a deputy registrar claim the equivalent of an associate professor! But these are the kind of ideas and claims that generate conflict situations, and needless adding that many strikes have been called over differentials between academic and non-academic staff!

Then, of course, the politics of choice of vice chancellor, spawning ethnic, religious, political and cult allegiances and lasting animosities.

The mismanagement of students is one other factor, and such has created numerous conflict situations and disharmony. Students do have legitimate interests:

- affordable fees and accommodation;
- foul-smelling toilets and bathrooms;
- lack of water and electricity;
- checking of delinquent lecturers;
- ensuring integrity of examination process and of results;
- eliminating victimization and harassment in various forms;
- abuse of the examination process;

Students associations act as a counter-weight to internal and external cultism; i) indirectly check on mismanagement academic departments, faculties and thus of the university system itself; ii) while the banning of students associations/unions in some universities is largely counter-productive. The reason why academic and non-academic staffs have their associations is because they have interests to promote and protect. If they can do so, there is no sensible reason for preventing students.

Students

Students, who by definition are mostly young, creative, imaginative, idealistic, impatient, and risk-takers have contributed in no small measure to the existence of disharmony within the university system. Innumerable number of demonstrations, riots and mob action have characterised students' activism over the decades. The presence/absence and effectiveness of communication channels and institutional avenues for dialogue appear to hold key to minimising such disturbances, apart from addressing the issues promptly and adequately.

Cultism among students, in its current deadly and violent form, is a product of military regimes that entrenched the notion of "untouchables" in a socio-political environment characterised by arbitrariness, abuses and total lack of respect for basic human rights. Children of "untouchables" – that is, the "well-placed" Nigerian within and outside the university - are themselves also "untouchables". This has been a source of violence, fear, anxiety, physical harm and death in many campuses.

SOME STRIKES AND THEIR CAUSES

There is also a general agreement that conflict is inherent in employment relations. Over the years, the education sector in Nigeria has become a veritable theatre of conflicts rather than an incubator of human capital development. In actual fact the past three decades have witnessed quite a number of conflicts caused by factors that are both internal and internal to the sector. It should be noted that conflicts have been more prevalent at the tertiary level of the education sector.

The unending conflicts within the federal tertiary education sector have revolved around three major issues; funding, improved conditions of service and university autonomy/academic freedom. These issues have become particularly problematic since the 1980s when structural economic problems and the imposition of neo-liberal economic policies among other factors, have constrained the ability of the federal government to live up to its proprietorial responsibilities.[5]

The Academic Staff Union of Nigerian Universities (ASUU) has been frontally involved in addressing the conflict-inducing issues in its own fashion. The other unions have mostly taken a cue from ASUU struggles to make demands of their own, some of which bother on the ridiculous. A

[5] For an overview see: 'Strikes in Nigeria: Some Considerations,' *Nigerian Journal of Economic and Social Studies (NJESS)*, 1983, Ibadan, pp.301-318; The Nigerian General Strike of 1981', *Review of African Political Economy*, Sheffield, 1981, Vol.22, pp.65-81; 'The Political Clash in the Aftermath of the Nigerian General Strike of 1981,' *Review of African Political Economy*, Sheffield, 1982, Vol.25, pp. 104-112; 'Strikes and Lockouts in Nigeria: Some Theoretical Notes,' in Otobo, D. & Omole, M. (eds.), *Readings in Industrial Relations in Nigeria*, pp.221-232

good example is the demand for pay parity with academic staff of universities by their non-academic or support staff. Since the early 1970s, the union of university teachers has had cause to engage government in addressing some of the problems besetting the university system in particular and tertiary education in general. Not unexpectedly, many of these conflicts have resulted in strike actions which became preponderant since the early 1990s. The table below captures the strike profile within the federal education system.

S/No	Year	Issues at stake	Unions Involved
1	1974	Staff Welfare	NAUT
2	1980		ASUU
3	1981	Improved conditions Funding University autonomy	ASUU
4	1988	Improved conditions funding	ASUU & SSA
5	1991	Gross underfunding Conditions of service for academic staff Univ. autonomy and academic freedom	ASUU
6	1992	Funding Conditions of service Autonomy Parity in salary	ASUU(25-30 may, 20 July-Sept 4) SSA(14-16 Sept NASU (5 Nov. -4 Dec.)
7	1993	Implementation of 1992 agreement Parity in conditions of service	ASUU NASU & SSANU
8.	1994	Improved conditions of service Funding State of the nation	ASUU
9	1995	Review of the 1992 Agreement between ASUU and Federal government	ASUU
10	1996	Review of the 1992 agreement	ASUU
11.	1999	Improved conditions of service Funding University autonomy	ASUU
12	1999	Non-implementation of Oct. 1999 agreement	ASUU
13	2000	i. Review of basic salary ii. Funding iii. autonomy	ASUU
14	2001	Refusal of government to conclude negotiations	ASUU
15	2002	Non-implementation of 2001agreement	ASUU

16	2003	inadequate funding non-implementation of 2001 agreement disparity in salary implementation of allowances	ASUU, SSA & NASU
17	2004	Privatisation of federal government colleges and promotion of staff	Association of Senior Civil Servants of Nigeria
18	2005	Re-negotiation of 2001 agreement	
19	2007	Refusal of government to conclude negotiations	ASUU
20	2009	Conditions of service Autonomy Funding	ASUU
21	2012	Warning Strike	ASUU
22	2013	Warning strike Indefinite strike over "earned allowances"	ASUU ASUU
23	2017	Funding, Allowances and other issues	ASUU
24	2019	Funding for the revitalisation of public universities, etc.	ASUU
25	2020	Funding and Other issues.	ASUU

From the immediately above, there are hardly any of the strike actions that did not involve wage-related issues. But, on many occasions after securing concessions on wage issues, ASUU would still insist on government addressing the other issues before calling off their actions. This, however, cannot be said of the other unions who do not remember they have issues with government until ASUU secures agreements with government.

DISPUTE-SETTLEMENT MECHANISM

The collective bargaining machinery is one of the institutional mechanisms for the management of conflict in course of work. For meaningful collective bargaining, appropriate structures and machinery are created. There are two basic machineries for collective bargaining both in the public and private sectors in Nigeria. These are the National Joint Industry Councils for the private sector and the National Public Service Negotiating Councils I-III for the public service. The Councils which were recommended by the Udoji Public Service Review Commission (1972-74) cater for the following groups of workers:

- Council I- Association of senior Civil Servants of Nigeria.
- Council II
- Nigeria Civil Service Union (which caters for intermediate and junior non-technical grades, except in Customs and Excise and Immigration Department).

- Nigeria Union of Civil Service Typists, Stenographic and Allied Staff.
- Council III
- Civil Service Technical Workers Union of Nigeria
- Medical and Health Workers Union of Nigeria
- National Association of Nigerian Nurses and Midwives
- Printing and publishing Workers Union.
- Customs and Excise and Immigration Staff Union.*

It is important to point out that while negotiations take place in the private sector on a regular basis, the same thing cannot be said of the public sector. In spite of the existence of the appropriate machineries, there is not much bargaining in the public sector, including the educational sector. What obtains is the practice by governments to unilaterally fix wages and other conditions of work through wage commissions and tribunals as well as the use of tripartite committees whose decisions are still subject to official ratification.

In the educational sector, the various unions have often forced the government to negotiate with them. At times, it is not until the unions go on strike that government agrees to negotiate. In the absence of a standing negotiating body what obtains is the appointment of ad-hoc government negotiating teams, lacking the power to commit government during negotiations noted earlier. On occasions, after agreements are reached implementation committees are set up again and in the process fresh challenges are thrown up and without resolving outstanding matters. Then, traditional rulers, the National Assembly and prominent politician wade in with their various appeals to striking union members to utilise "dialogue" to resolve differences and other issues, almost as if years and months of exchange of information and meetings between unions' representatives and government officials were antithetical to dialogue!

What this suggests is a reluctance of state and federal governments to separate their role as an employer of labour from that of a "sovereign" political authority. This largely explains the failure of the collective bargaining machinery in the public sector with the attendant disruption of services across sectors by workers making legitimate demands and redressing legitimate grievances. The least government can do is to put in place a standing negotiating structure (instead of the prevailing ad-hoc arrangement) in the educational sector, comprising both the government and the union sides. More importantly, this structure should be used regularly while agreements reached should be respected by both sides.

* The military government proscribed this union in 1978.

FUTURE DIRECTIONS OF EMPLOYMENT AND WORK RELATIONS IN THE UNIVERSITY SYSTEM

It would be a pleasant surprise should employment and work relations in the university system depart in any substantial sense from current situation in the near future. First, the number of universities, especially private universities, shall increase tremendously in the medium run, and rightly so given a national population dominated by the young and teenagers, the burgeoning secondary level and thus pressing need for tertiary education. So would pressure on facilities prove them to be inadequate, as insufficient funding is likely to persist, and the older universities denuded of much-needed teachers, as well as increased number of retired teachers being reabsorbed on fixed-term contracts.

Second, it would take remarkable effort and drastic paradigm shift to move away from governments' ad-hocism and unilateralism in wage determination, not only in the university system, but also in the public services as a whole, a process largely left to naked self-interest and power-play between bureaucratic public sector and political elites and trade unions in the public sector.[6] For a federal permanent secretary who used to earn less than a professor up till 1974 but approved since 1999 thrice what is imposed on professors for himself/herself and justifies the differential on such patently flimsy and disingenuous grounds as permanent secretaries are fewer and are political appointees would suggest, among other things, agonising dwindling of professionalism and perverse but pervasive misconception of the notion of 'public service' and abuse of public office. It is almost as if one is being asked by this strange logic to think the responsibilities and functions of permanent secretaries and their efficiency and competence and of professors have somehow changed in different directions to warrant the contrived differentials. It has since 1974 looked as if the logic of "what's in it for me" espoused by top bureaucrats has drowned the idea of social policy for public good.

The point, of course, is that wage fixing in the public service can be based on scientific and verifiable criteria, as well as drawing a few lessons from comparative statistics and practices elsewhere. It makes little sense to impose salaries and allowances on university teachers and support staff without an eye on changes in the cost of living, wage differentials, nature/content of jobs and comparable pay within the public sector (such parastatals as military, NNPC group, DPR, judiciary, Central Bank, National Assembly), the economy and the university systems in rest of the world. And, there could also be wage indexation in order to address unanticipated changes in the prices of goods and services and to forestall easily avoidable agitations by

[6] Extensively discussed in Otobo, D., Bureaucratic Elites and Public Sector Wage-Bargain in Nigeria, *Journal of Modern African Studies*, Cambridge University Press, 24(1), 1986.

workers and their unions.[7] The wage bargain will thus continue to generate conflicts and protests within the university system and the public sector as current practices are not likely to be abandoned by present classes of political and bureaucratic elites.

Third, if the idea of a university is properly understood and taken a bit more seriously by proprietors and policy makers, then unreserved acceptance of a university as a place devoted to learning, research and teaching makes it a self-administered preserve and community of teachers and the taught, and not a place where thousands of non-technical support staff in each university, who far outnumber the former, have pensionable careers. It is not an issue of preference for one or other administrative or university model or structure, which apologists for the status quo often hide behind, but the reality of an ineffective, money-losing, rudderless but strategic company restructuring to survive, stay relevant and produce value for money in an increasingly competitive and nation-saving global knowledge production industry.[8] The NUC's guideline or recommended ratio in this respect has become counter-productive, encouraging gradualism as reflected in the policy of not replacing retiring non-technical support staff and adopting other measures thought to achieve "natural" attrition. Now, there are "directors" in various sub-units, including the Vice Chancellor's Office, who are higher than Deputy Registrars! The university system is in crisis and immediate, correcting measures are needed. A mandatory restructuring - starting with first and second generation universities - which reduces non-teaching staff by at least some ninety per cent would most likely achieve, among others, the following: i) ensure devoting available financial resources more to research and facilities; ii) reduce administrative overheads and provision for pensions dramatically; iii) freeing funds for other purposes such as staff development; iv) change the character of unionism and inter-group relations; and v) eliminate a group of conflict-inducing grievances and demands flowing from relativities in pay and non-money benefits. Things cannot be done in the same fashion and expect different results.

---

[7] I am mindful of the position of several economists on indexing of wages in "developing countries" being a hazardous undertaking, given greater swings/movements in prices of goods and services. I also know the existence of eye-popping wages and salaries in both public and private sectors in Nigeria which might, in fact, be reduced if they were indexed!

[8] Why should a university create an Exam & Records Unit/Dept which has two or more Deputy Registrars, several Senior Assistant Registrars, and complement of lesser positions numbering some twenty and more persons just to keep and retrieve data on students' results generated and stored by various academic departments themselves? In some universities, position of Director has been created, superior to Deputy Registrar, but subordinate to the Registrar, a result of push for career advancement by top non-technical support staff, this and other positions which technical staff who are more relevant to the production and imparting of knowledge are barred from!

Fourth, unionism, union tactics and strategies are unlikely to change in the short run. On ASUU in particular and some of its prominent members, the principles of separation of functions and collective responsibility seem to receive scant regard, especially since it insisted on and won the right to be represented on critical organs of the university and the union has some oversight functions in respect of motivational and disciplinary processes. If an ASUU member occupies a position and/carries out functions deemed in law and so described as "projection of management", like being a member of the University Council, then such a member and ASUU should have two choices open to him/her and it: i) be replaced; or ii) retain membership but be accountable to the University Council for his/her actions where such include divulging decisions and proposed policies to any person or body. But, if on the other hand and through agreements a union member occupies such a position as a representative of the union, then both that member and the union must accept the principle of collective responsibility for decisions reached in the Council or such statutory body.

Equally critical to achieving objectives for which universities have been established and for employment and work relations in the university system are the frequency and duration of university system-wide strikes and other forms of protest. For a country the size of Nigeria to have universities routinely shut down for months on end over wages/salaries and fringe benefits and whatever else cannot be taken seriously, and clearly signals, even in the face of self-denial, a failure of individual and collective leadership – more so of regulatory authorities, proprietors, and union leadership. Indefinite disruptions of the university calendar should not be happening, but there seem little prospects for that at the moment.

Fifth, the pressure for the upward review of fees is likely to grow in publicly funded universities - whatever the revenue-earning rate at the federal level and which most state governments also substantially rely on - with prevailing high rates in the private universities providing an uncomfortable benchmark. The outbreak of protests upon such review should be expected but should peter out once a sum considered reasonable by all parties is adopted. The same pattern is likely to be repeated at any point in the future when fees are reviewed upwards.

Sixth, it is early days yet to say with any great amount of confidence if and when even the largest private university may provide a liberal environment for both teachers and students, tightly controlled as at now, more so in those owned by religious or faith-based organisations. Chronic understaffing is likely to persist for a while, with previously retired university teachers, especially professors, and other part-time teachers comprising the bulk of the teaching faculty. Unionism would take sometime to take root, and whatever grievances exist among staff, managements are definitely more proactive albeit in an authoritarian or paternal fashion.

CONCLUDING REMARKS

Employment relationships within the university system, especially in federally-funded universities, are a fitful mix of adversarial relations and collaborationism largely because of the sometimes preference of federal and state governments, their proprietors, for a unipolar work order where the rights and feelings of the other parties involved are largely ignored, and the plurality of views/interests only notionally recognised. As long as university compensation packages are reduced and benchmarked against civil service director-level rates (instead of permanent secretary that has been the case all the while), and top bureaucrats and political public servants give themselves totally unjustified huge salaries and allowances, perpetuating incomprehensible wage differentials with those of the university system (professors' salaries were superior to and competitive with those of permanent secretaries, judges, generals, etc., before 1974), and physical facilities remain grossly inadequate, so would resultant effect be a troubled industrial relations climate.

Whatever else politicians and policy makers might be thinking, the tertiary education sector is far too important to this populous country, with a very young population, to be turned into a permanent theatre of conflict. And neither can the periodic and unconscionable extra-judicial killing of few vocal activists be part of an imagined solution. Between the totally unnecessary deaths of Mahmood Tukur Moddibo and Festus Iyayi, assassinated former ASUU presidents, we have more than thirty years of failure of all to do the needful to have a well functioning and stable university system. Issues and methods have remained the same. The latest example under the guise of "reform" is salaries of staff in federally-funded universities being paid directly by the Central Bank of Nigeria (CBN). If the main motive for this, which I suspect to be case, is the reluctance of some vice chancellors to obey political instructions during conflict situations to withhold salaries (and not just eliminating "ghost workers" as loudly proclaimed, a phenomenon restricted to main civil service and some parastatals in any case) obviously some powerful persons are having great difficulty seeing that the stability of any system and society hinges on the ability of all institutions to self-manage themselves – not centralized control, as operators of the Nigerian federation are slowly beginning to wake up to. The CBN can easily have and keep statistics of all employees in the public sector whose salaries and wages are funded by the public treasury without taking on the responsibility of paying lecturers' salaries itself. It would be interesting for the unions in the university system to test this in the law courts, given the Acts establishing each university! And for added measure, since the CBN usurped this responsibility, salaries have been running late, sometimes paid in the middle of the succeeding month! Another conflict-inducing seed has been planted and the planters still insist there is university autonomy and are likely to hound imagined "radicals" when the next set of strikes break out over late payment of salaries and other unresolved issues! *Deja vu!*

LABOUR RELATIONS AND DEVELOPMENT

Chapter 18

THE NOTION OF INTERNATIONAL LABOUR STANDARDS: CRITICAL OBSERVATIONS*

INTRODUCTION

In discussing *concepts* that have a long history, or *historical developments* generally, or the past, and *explaining* the nature of socio-economic development, and/or the *nature* of society, the *choice* of words or adjectives is very important. Such words or adjectives are carefully chosen, by persons and institutions that use them, to *convey particular messages* in respect of
a) causes of certain events or developments;
b) responsibility for those events or developments; and
c) choice of policy prescriptions/actions.

These are some of the reasons why controversies tend to surround the definitions and uses of many concepts in the social sciences in particular. With this at the back of our minds, we turn our attention to the notion of "international labour standards".

This chapter is a preliminary excursion on the notion of "international labour standards", a concept commonly associated with the International Labour Organization (ILO), with a view to encouraging critical engagement with, not of the ILO's use of it or the organisation's much-valued intentions but, the contexts under which it is being used.

The main burden here is to argue that, although the concept of international labour standards might have arguably gained general acceptance because their contents, according to the ILO, "are essentially expressions of international tripartite agreement on these matters," some of them have become political and strategic tools in the hands of some member-states, especially the G7.

We identify some of the factors responsible for this state of affairs to be
i) early industrialism;

---

* Paper presented at the National Conference on Workers' Rights and Labour Standards in Nigeria organised by the Department of Industrial Relations & Personnel Management, University of Lagos, Nigeria with the support of the Friedrich Ebert Foundation (FEF), Nigeria Office under the Auspices of the Memorandum of Understanding between the FEF and the University of Lagos, Held at the Gateway Hotel, Ijebu-Ode, 9-12 October 2007.

ii) modern colonialism;
iii) newly industrialising economies;
iv) International trade;
v) Globalization, strategic concerns and labour standards

The ILO was created in 1919 primarily for the purpose of adopting international standards to cope with the problem of labour conditions involving "injustice, hardship and privation." With the incorporation of the Declaration of Philadelphia into its Constitution in 1944, the Organization's standard-setting mandate was broadened to include more general, but related, social policy, human and civil rights matters, and the more popular of these have been the so-called "core labour standards" which the International Labour Organisation (ILO) identifies to be freedom of association, the elimination of all forms of forced or compulsory labour, the abolition of the most hazardous forms of child labour, and the elimination of discrimination in respect of employment and occupation.

The full list of these standards includes:

1. Freedom of association, collective bargaining, and industrial relations;
2. Forced labour;
3. Elimination of child labour and protection of children and young persons;
4. Equality of opportunity and treatment;
5. Tripartite consultation;
6. Labour administration and inspection;
7. Employment policy and promotion;
8. Vocational guidance and training;
9. Employment security;
10. Wages;
11. Working time;
12. Occupational safety and health;
13. Social security;
14. Maternity protection;
15. Social policy;
16. Migrant workers;
17. Seafarers;
18. Fishermen;
19. Dockworkers;
20. Indigenous and tribal peoples;
21. Specific categories of workers.

The ILO is thus responsible for establishing and monitoring international labour standards. It has no power to impose trade sanctions for violations of standards but relies, instead, on voluntary compliance and peer pressure.

The ILO brings together representatives of governments, labour organizations, and employers, and drafts conventions on labour standards subject to ratification by member countries. There are over 170 international labour conventions in force, although the number of countries that have ratified each convention varies considerably. Countries are bound to abide by any conventions they have ratified and are subject to regular supervision by the ILO. The ILO is empowered to investigate complaints about a country's violations of a convention made either by the country's own labour or employer organizations, or by another country. The ILO provides guidance and technical advice while seeking a cooperative solution. The ILO's tripartite structure, experience, and large membership make it well suited for consensus building.

We now flesh out the factors of early industrialism, modern colonialism; newly industrializing economies; international trade; globalization, strategic concerns and labour standards and briefly outline their impact on the notion of international labour standards and the uses to which some of them are being put.

EARLY INDUSTRIALISM

It is obvious that early capitalist industrialization in England and the rest of Europe pre-dates the formation of the ILO, so what is its relevance to international labour standards? Quite simply, the concern for labour standards of whatever description existed long before 1919: the exploitation of children, women and labour in general was of shockingly monumental dimensions during the Industrial Revolution, and it is often not pointedly remarked that social and political revolutions went on *pari passu* with economic changes of those times.

With some degree of simplification, we may claim that the rise and development of trades unions, struggles for removal of children from factories that they may go to school with the spread and institutionalisation of formal education, employment of women, hours of work, wages and payment systems, health and safety standards at work, etc., represented early attempts at establishing labour standards.

Some of such attempts were local, national and international on the parts of working peoples, revolutionary groups and their organisations, and whichever standards that were set over this period at all these levels were much against the opposition of private employers and state authorities. The limited and tentative successes that met such efforts, it is here argued, pushed the emerging class-ridden society into struggles for political franchise and other social and rights that characterised Europe from 1789 when the French Revolution occurred.

From this broader canvas, it is much easier to appreciate that the notion of labour standards – local, national or international – has been inextricably intertwined with prevailing ideas on decent society and power configurations at those same levels.

MODERN COLONIALISM

Whatever abuses, injustices, and privations that prevailed in general society and at work in industrialising Europe and North America were magnified beyond rational comprehension in the colonies. Secondly, most of the world was under colonial domination as at 1919 when the ILO was created by the League of Nations, a mothering organisation which was itself dominated by colonial powers.

In the 1920s and early 1930s, colonial powers were not particularly bothered by what were euphemistically called "labour conditions" in their respective colonies. Communal and labour rebellions in the colonies, the United States' anxiety over the possible spread of socialist and communist ideas and tenets with the Russian Bolshevik Revolution in 1917, and the ascendant activities of European and North American labour, socialist parties and humanitarian and other revolutionary groups, the post-World War II upswing in the activities of decolonising movements, induced a visible focus on legally addressing colonial "labour conditions" in the enactment of legislative pieces. Political imperatives in the colonies influenced the choice of "labour standards" to focus on: forced labour (as this was seen as cause of communal unrests, aside from imposed taxes), convict labour, child labour, legal regulation of trade unions, and disputes settlement mechanism. But, Emergency regulations during World War II superseded and undermined whatever legal protection any of these legislative pieces afforded the vulnerable groups at work and in the colonised territories. Colonial unionism was all about setting standards (physical, economic and legal) at work and within the emergent industrial relations systems.

NEWLY INDUSTRIALISING ECONOMIES

The emergence of newly industrializing economies from the 1970s, especially in Asia, served to create adjustmental problems for the pioneer industrialized countries, especially Britain, France and the United States of America. Explanations offered by most development economists in the Western industrialized economies - which were in ideological competition with industrializing communist and socialist bloc countries from 1949 – for the rapid economic development of these non-European societies ranged from the esoteric to the outrightly misleading, steeped in erstwhile racist superiority complex manifested in colonial misrepresentations of colonial subjects as culturally, technologically and economically inferior. In the absence of a "Protestant Ethic" which Max Weber[1] and others have identified to be the underlying philosophical engine of Western industrialization (although Italy and France, largely Roman Catholic, may require other explanations), we have been offered, among others, authoritarianism in social and political affairs, cheap labour and thus low wages, labour-intensive strategies, import-substitution industrialization strategy, scant regard for intellectual property, and communal life-style in accounting for economic development in the newly industrialising economies. Some of these, including land tenure systems, superstition, mass poverty, mass unemployment, mismanagement, corruption – especially in the post-colonial era – were earlier held by the same experts to account for lack of economic development.

INTERNATIONAL TRADE AND LABOUR STANDARDS

The regulatory framework for international trade in the immediate post-World War II period and which lasted till only a decade ago when it gave way to the World Trade Organisation (WTO), known as the General Agreement on Trade and Tariff (GATT), was established without the direct participation of most African, Asian and South American countries which were still colonies. Nor did a defeated Japan participate effectively. GATT basically laid the terms upon which goods may enter members' markets, regulations that clearly favoured the dominant economic and political powers, especially USA, Britain and France. So, also, were the structures and voting rights of the two financial regulatory institutions created along with GATT, the International Bank for Reconstruction and Development (World Bank) and the International Monetary Fund (IMF).

It was no surprise therefore that from late 1960s, most of the developing world, referred to as "South", were calling for a new international economic order to redress the unfairness of the international economic system, particularly as external debts mounted and poverty intensified and states remained unstable and politics volatile.

Then, once an increasing number of developing countries began to build up healthy surpluses from exports, not merely of primary products but also in an increasing range of manufactured goods, the dynamics of international trade also began to change as the governments in the more established industrialised countries took stock and fashioned counter-strategies.

From the late 1970s high unemployment rates and stagnant wages of unskilled workers in the United States and Western Europe raised anxieties, and many governments and policy makers advanced the argument that their own wages and benefits were being forced down by unfair competition from developing countries with much lower labour costs. The lower labour costs,

---

[1] Weber, M., *Economy and Society* vol. I ({1921} (New York, 1968),

they claimed, were possible because of failure to maintain international labour standards by governments in developing countries. Singled out in particular were child labour and freedom of association, especially in those Asian countries, including China, whose textile products outsold European and North American textiles and an industry that employed largely children and women. Such countries were accused of "social dumping". The impressive economic and technological achievements of the Asian Tigers, which further increased the range of manufactured products in competition with North American and European products, merely increased adversarial international trading relations as the western economies sought to further restrict access to their markets.

Aside from bilateral trade talks to impose quotas on entry of specific items, at various meetings of the World Trade Organisation and other multilateral trade talks, attempts have been made to impose what is referred to as "social clause". In this connection, Stephen S. Golub (1997) observed:[2]

> ...is the emergence of international labour and environmental standards as a major issue on the post-Uruguay Round trade agenda. Labour unions and human rights activists in developed countries argue that market access in the North should be conditioned on raising labour standards in the South, to prevent social dumping and a "race to the bottom" in wages and benefits.

Some trade items were banned by some Western governments on the grounds that violations of labour standards have taken place, or that enforcement was slack or weak. Collectively such trade sanctions are the controversial "social clause".

Naturally, developing countries have tended to view such social clauses as disguised protectionism and have fought vigorously against initiatives by the United States and other developed countries to give the WTO a role in the area of labour standards.

As summarised in the WTO's website:

> There is a powerful movement to include a 'Social Clause' - trade sanctions protecting workers' rights - into the rules of the World Trade Organisation (WTO), the global body that enforces trading rules. The WTO has the power to impose sanctions and many in the international trade union movement believe that this would help to enforce core labour standards. This is a controversial idea and many in developing countries fear that a Social Clause could be used for

---

[2]Stephen S. Golub, *International Labour Standards and International Trade,* IMF Working Paper 97/37 (Washington, April 1997).

protectionism, allowing rich countries to keep developing country goods out by claiming they are produced in sub-standard working conditions. Poor states will need time to re-adjust and put into place measures to ensure that children, for instance, are able to take up their education and are not forced into more dangerous work in the informal sector.

On the other hand, many developing countries believe the issue has no place in the WTO framework. They argue that the campaign to bring labour issues into the WTO is actually a bid by industrial nations to undermine the comparative advantage of lower wage trading partners, and could undermine their ability to raise standards through economic development, particularly if it hampers their ability to trade. They also argue that proposed standards can be too high for them to meet at their level of development. These nations argue that efforts to bring labour standards into the arena of multilateral trade negotiations are little more than a smokescreen for protectionism.

A DISCUSSION OF THE MAIN ISSUES

The discussion here draws mainly from the work of Stephen S. Golub (1997).[3] He notes that there are two main arguments - an "economic" one and a "moral" one - for the international harmonization of labour standards. The economic argument suggests that low wages and labour standards in developing countries threaten the living standards of workers in developed countries. The moral argument asserts that low wages and labour standards violate the human rights of workers in the developing countries.

In practice, it is not always easy to separate the economic and moral aspects. For example, the OECD's provision on child labour calls for "elimination of exploitative forms of child labour." Most parents care about their children, and what appears to be exploitative child employment may, in fact, be merely a family's desperate response to poverty. Limits on collective bargaining may also be defensible at times. In developing countries, unions often protect a tiny labour aristocracy to the detriment of the remainder of the work force. The principle of non-discrimination between men and women may not be accepted in some societies.

Labour costs

According to classical Ricardian trade theory, international differences in labour costs do not preclude mutually beneficial trade. On the contrary, international trade theory suggests that the gains from trade increase with the economic diversity of partners. Fears that high-wage countries are unable to compete with low-wage countries (the sweatshop labour

[3] *Op. cit.*

argument) often confuse the fundamental distinction between *comparative* and *absolute advantage. Classical trade theory teaches that overall differences in productivity (absolute advantage) determine wages, while sector-specific variations in productivity and costs (comparative advantages) determine trade patterns.*

For example, suppose wages and productivity in Malaysia's manufacturing sector are both 10 per cent of what they are in the United States but that the Malaysian/US productivity ratio is greater than 10 percent in simple products such as textiles and less than 10 per cent in sophisticated products like machinery. If skill-adjusted wages are about the same in all industries in Malaysia, as they should be in a competitive labour market, Malaysia's relative unit labour costs will be low in textiles and high in machinery. If so, Malaysia *will export textiles and import machinery. Of course, there are other determinants of comparative advantage besides sectoral labour productivity and labour costs. The important point is that both developed and developing countries benefit from specializing in what each produces efficiently, regardless of the overall level of labour costs.*

A key element in this argument is that if low wages reflect low labour productivity, any advantage accruing from employing low-wage labour is offset. Even if nominal wages are rigid (or, as is often alleged, artificially repressed) exchange rate adjustments could offset international differences in costs. Empirical evidence confirms that labour costs and labour productivity are related, although exchange rate movements and other macroeconomic shocks can sometimes induce substantial short-run deviations. Productivity and wage levels are closely related - *that is, international differences in unit labour costs are much smaller than differences in wage rates suggest - in most cases.* In fact, calculations indicate that unit labour costs in several emerging economies in 1990 were actually higher than those in the United States - the productivity gap is even bigger than the wage gap. There is also evidence that wages and productivity generally move together over time. For example, Korea had the most rapid productivity growth and the highest wage growth.

The unfair standards argument often focuses on *fringe benefits* and *safety conditions*, rather than *wages*, but it also confuses *comparative* and *absolute* advantage.

First, for a given level of labour costs, the division between wages and fringe benefits is largely irrelevant for international competitiveness, although it may not be a matter of indifference to workers.

Second, wages are the most important component of labour costs even in developed countries.

Third, mandating increases in fringe benefits, such as vacation and maternity leave, may simply alter the composition of labour compensation and not its total size.

Fourth, even when they do affect labour costs, weak labour standards, like low wages, are likely to be a consequence of low productivity and poverty, not an independent source of international comparative advantage. Economic development, cultural differences, or other national preferences may give rise to different choices about labour standards. These national characteristics, along with factor endowments and other more traditional forces, determine national comparative advantage. Low labour standards and low wages both reflect the abundance of unskilled labour and low productivity in developing countries.

The volume of trade is also inconsistent with fears about the competitiveness of low-wage countries. Exports of manufactures from developing countries to the North have increased rapidly, but the majority of these countries continue to run trade deficits in manufactures, since their imports have grown nearly as much as their exports. For many of these developing countries, manufacturing trade with the industrial countries is now quite large in relation to their national outputs (Brazil and India are exceptions). North-South trade in manufactures is, on the whole, much more important for the South than for the North, as measured by its share in their respective GDPs.

Human rights

Human rights activists believe that raising labour standards in developing countries will benefit workers in these countries and that some labour practices are morally intolerable. To analyse these concerns, it is important to separate labour standards relating to conditions of work--such as minimum wages, health and safety benefits, hours, and, possibly, the minimum age of employment--from labour rights--such as bans on forced labour, harassment, and discrimination.

Everyone agrees that improving living standards in the South is desirable. The question is how to achieve this. Attempting to mandate certain labour market processes, such as the setting of minimum wages, under conditions where they are inappropriate may not improve labour market outcomes. Most developed country labour standards are simply not feasible for many developing countries. Consider again the difficult problem of child labour. It is indeed deeply disturbing that young children in developing countries toil under harsh conditions for low pay. But the earnings of these children may be important to their families' and their own survival. Further, setting strict standards in a developing country's formal sector may consign children to even more degrading and less remunerative work in the informal sector.

Many developing countries do, in fact, have detailed labour standards, but these may cause more harm than good. In the North American Free Trade Agreement (NAFTA) debate in the United States, it was widely recognized that Mexico's legislated labour standards are, in fact, stronger than those of the United States and Canada, although enforcement of them is often weak. Labour market regulations such as minimum wages are often cited as a major contributor to the problem of economic dualism -- the twin evils of excessively high wages and high unemployment in urban areas -- in developing countries.

The pursuit of trade and labour market policies conducive to high growth is far more effective in raising incomes than mandated levels of wages and benefits. Such growth-oriented labour market policies need not follow *a laissez faire* approach. Government investments in education and training, in particular, are likely to be beneficial. The loss of access to markets in the developed world hamper the growth prospects of developing countries and thereby retard the upgrading of their labour standards. Trade sanctions are thus likely to be counterproductive as a means of encouraging improvements in such standards.

National labour market policies may at times enhance both efficiency and equity by remedying market failures. But why should this problem not be left to each country to decide for itself? One frequent argument is that the non-democratic political regimes in much of the South prevent the expression of the public's true preferences. Even if it is accepted that a developing country is not democratic, it does not follow that developed countries can legitimately impose higher standards or that doing so will raise welfare in developing countries. Instead, a more direct and effective method of expanding the public's voice in setting standards would be to encourage the spread of democracy in the developing world.

Finally, if the goal is to enhance the welfare of the South, trade sanctions hardly seem an appropriate and effective approach. T. N. Srinivasan[4] points out that the most effective way of raising standards for workers in developing countries would be to allow free international migration from low- to high-standard countries, an argument rarely made by proponents of harmonizing labour standards. Even if immigration is judged infeasible, direct income transfers, which could be used to upgrade living standards in the South, would be both more consistent with a humanitarian motivation and more economically efficient.

Some labour practices -- most obviously slavery and harassment of workers -- are almost universally regarded as unacceptable. However, as noted earlier, international consensus on the treatment of unions, child labour, and discrimination based on gender may be impossible. Without a clear basis for international agreement, enforcement of international labour standards could degenerate into protectionism.

---

[4] .N. Srinivasan, 1995, "International Trade and Labor Standards," in *Challenges to the New World Trade Organization*, ed. by Peter van Dyck and Gerrit Faher (Amsterdam: Martinus Nijhoff/Kluwer).

Another argument against harmonisation of basic labour rights is the arbitrariness of focusing on labour rights to the exclusion of other human rights problems, such as lack of freedom of expression. The focus on labour rights, rather than human rights in general, suggests that economic considerations, more than ethical concerns, underlie some of the calls for harmonization of labour standards.

Guillermo de la Dehesa (2007)[5] addressed the issue of social dumping in this manner, when he provided the answer to the question "Are developing countries engaging in 'social dumping'?"

> "Increasingly, the charge of "social dumping" is heard as a rational for protectionist measures against developing country exports. Many businessmen, labour unions and politicians in developed nations believe that lax working regulations and conditions, as well as weak political and social rights, provide developing country exports with an unfair advantage. *To counter this, they argue that either developing-country exports of cheap manufactured goods should be subject to anti-dumping duties to eliminate the "unfair" competitive factors, or these countries should impose higher labour standards.*"

These beliefs are wrong on several counts.

Is it dumping when low wages compensate low productivity?

First, according to basic international trade theory, each country should specialise in what it can produce competitively, exploiting its comparative advantages. Developing countries have lower wages due to their lower labour productivity and relative scarcity of physical and human capital. Their productivity disadvantage, however, is not spread evenly across all sectors. In labour-intensive sectors, their lower wages more than compensate for their lower productivity, so they tend to specialise in goods that are intensive in their use of low-skilled labour, cheap land, or abundant natural and energy resources. In other sectors, the higher wages of developed countries are more than compensated by their high productivity which stems from their abundant physical capital, technology and innovation; in these sectors it is the developing countries that cannot compete with the developed nation exporters. Moreover, both nations gain from focusing on what they do best and trading for the rest – a proposition that holds true regardless of the source of the comparative advantages.

Is it dumping when you pay higher wages in export sectors?

Second, "social dumping" is not dumping. Under WTO rules, dumping means the country in question is exporting at a price below

[5] 'Are Develioping Countries Engaging in "Social Dumping, ", CEPR, 23 May 2007

its domestic market price or below its production cost. This is exactly the contrary of what it is happening in developing country exports to developed countries. In these countries, wages in labour-intensive industries producing for exports tend to be higher than in those firms producing only for their domestic market and, as a consequence, their export products tend to have higher costs than similar products sold domestically. Many, if not most, exporting firms in developing countries are subsidiaries or affiliates of developed country multinationals or local firms that have outsourcing or off-shoring contracts with them. Robert Lipsey has marshalled conclusive empirical evidence that foreign-owned companies pay higher wages in both developing and developed countries.[6] Thus, only when exports from these foreign and domestic companies in developing countries were found to be subsidised by governments should a countervailing duty be justified.

Does imposing labour standards help poor nation workers?

Third, activists have for decades pressed for enforcement of "fair labour standards" to "level the playing field." While I believe it is an undeniable moral fact that everybody should embrace the goal of improving the wages and working conditions of workers in developing countries, it is also an undeniable economic fact that forcing these labour standards on developing countries may only make things worse for their workers while failing to have the desired effect of keeping more jobs in developed countries. Drusilla Brown, Alan Deardorff and Robert Stern have shown that, beside good intentions, there is no obvious case on welfare grounds for pursuing universal standards or even the harmonisation of standards on labour, the effect of which will most probably be negative for the very people that are in the greatest need for assistance.[7]

One common argument suggests that low-labour-standard countries reduce employment in rich nations via direct-export competition and the offshoring of jobs. This is refuted by empirical research. Mita Aggarwal has demonstrated that labour standards are lower in non-tradable sectors than in exporting ones and that developed countries imports of low labour standard products from poor countries are a *very small percentage* of total imports from developing countries.[8] On the FDI side, Dani Rodrik has

[6] "Home and host country effects of FDI," Robert Lipsey, NBER Working Paper 9293, 2002.

[7] "Child labor: theory, evidence and policy," Drusilla Brown, Alan Deardoff and Robert Stern, Discussion Paper 474, School of Public Affairs, University of Michigan, Ann Arbor, 2001).

[8] "International trade, labour standards and labour market conditions: an evaluation of the linkages", Mita Aggarwal, USITC Office of Economics Working Paper 95-06-C, 1995

shown that low labour standards are a hindrance rather than an attraction, for foreign investors.[9]

GLOBALISATION, STRATEGIC CONCERNS AND LABOUR STANDARDS

The globalisation of production facilities has led to and continues to lead to the loss of jobs in Europe and North America, further engendering antagonisms against a group of newly industrialising economies, India and China.

Equally important, the character of international trade has also changed considerably, comprising in the main exports and imports between subsidiaries of transnational or multi-national companies in different continents, and not necessarily between countries. So, in looking at labour standards in developing countries, it is advisable to make the following distinctions:

a) industrialising countries dominated by subsidiaries of trans-national companies;
b) industrialising countries dominated by national business companies;
c) imports-dependent countries but exporters of strategic minerals; and
d) imports-dependent countries and exporters of agricultural produce

While it can easily be demonstrated that subsidiaries of transnational companies pay wages higher than other local companies in developing economies, it is not necessarily true that they also encourage best physical work conditions, especially in agriculture and mining activities. There are certainly several foreign companies which have little regard for labour laws and thus labour standards.

But, this tends to beg the question of flagrant disregard for international labour standards in some sectors of local economies. The answer is probably best sought in the combined impact of military/politico-economic pressures of developed countries' governments and activities/policies and role of such international development agencies, financial and credit institutions as the IMF, World Bank, etc.

First, developing countries which gained political independence under non-revolutionary circumstances had governments and elites that were pretty much under the influence of erstwhile colonial powers.

Second, in the period 1948 to 1990, the Cold War era, Africa, Asia and South America were held hostage by civilian and military dictatorships that were sustained mostly by the West and a few by the East, in circumstances

[9] "Labour standards and international trade: do they matter and what do we do about them?" Dani Rodrik, in Robert Lawrence, Dani Rodrik and John Whalley (eds.) "Emerging agenda for global trade: high stakes for developing countries," Washington D.C., Overseas Development Council, 1996.

that saw the entrenchment of mass poverty, mass unemployment, massive external debts and utter disregard for human and other rights, including core labour standards.

Third, the development plans, economic policies and economic advisers were provided by erstwhile colonial powers through a series of technical assistance programmes and aid regimes. When the economies failed, causes of failure were claimed to be "indigenous" in origin, thereby disclaiming some responsibility.

Fourth, the last two decades of the IMF's structural adjustment programmes (SAP) have forced externally indebted countries into adopting policies inimical to the core labour standards, to the protection of employment, wages and incomes, to the right to strike and collective bargaining, etc. Indeed, these neo-liberal economic policies and external indebtedness have left little for financing primary and secondary education for children (in spite of the concern for child labour at the WTO and the ILO). In some cases, like in French-speaking West Africa, some governments have not been able to balance their budgets, pay public servants salaries without external aid nor devote enough funds to train required hands in the ministries of labour to enforce labour laws and thus labour standards.

Fifth, the G7 countries themselves have not ratified as many Conventions and Recommendations as most developing countries, nor have the monitoring and implementation of certain labour standards been better than in developing countries. For example, millions of migrant Mexican workers and several minority groups in the USA do not enjoy protection of any sort; rather, they are "sweated" by unscrupulous private employers.

Indeed, the sing-song of "international labour standards" on the part of the G7 has been calculating, strategic and recent. Stephen Golub (1997, *op. cit.*) notes that the mandate of the International Trade Organization (ITO), as enunciated in 1947 by the Havana Charter, called for countries to take measures against "unfair labour conditions." But the ITO was never implemented. It was replaced by the less ambitious GATT, which virtually ignored the issue of labour standards, except for a provision allowing countries to impose trade barriers on goods produced with prison labour.

This is in sharp contrast to the recent greater pressure for enforcement of international labour standards by the United States and some European countries and their repeated attempts to include violations of labour standards among the responsibilities of the new WTO and sidelining the ILO.

Sixth, there is a valid distinction between "child work", which is activity that children may traditionally carry out and as part of socialisation, even if they have money value and which they combine with going to school and "being children", and "child labour". Restrictions on child labour are contained in the International Labour Organization (ILO) Convention 138, which mandates countries to specify a minimum age of employment for children (not less than 15 years) so child labour below that age is considered illegal. To date, 141 countries have signed this ILO convention and some others, which have not signed the convention (including the USA), effectively outlaw child labour as well in their national labour laws.

Seventh, without condoning child labour, Eric Edmonds shows that only 1 in every 200,000 economically active children in the world, aged 10 to 14, are employed and only two countries in the world go above 1 in very 10,000.[10] Of that tiny fraction only 12 per cent of total working children in developing countries are employed in *exporting companies* and they have *higher wages* than those 88 per cent involved in *domestic production.* Their parents, in order to survive, need their children's' wages to complement their own meagre incomes.

CONCLUDING REMARKS

For strategic reasons, most diplomatic activities and military/politico-economic pressures most government bring to bear on one another appear to target the elimination of comparative advantages enjoyed by some countries. For example, the development of synthetic substitutes and alternative fuels come under this category.

It does appear that G7 countries take it for granted that the comparative advantage they enjoy in manufacturing and high tech industries should be accepted as normal, while "catching up" by countries in the developing world in same and other areas must have been achieved in less than competitive manner. Indeed, they hate to acknowledge, let alone admit, that their current positions have been achieved and maintained by protectionists laws and practices (aside from historical accumulation of capital during slavery and colonialism) against agricultural and labour-intensive manufactures produced by developing countries, which are exactly those goods the latter can export more competitively to the rest of the world.

Respect for core labour standards does not imply uniform labour conditions across developed and developing states, and not being uniform does not necessarily involve non-observance of labour standards. Nor is the claim true of rapid economic development occurring in the South depending on by-passing labour standards, because such other factors as skills, technology, effective management, effective communications, etc., all influence levels of productivity. Labour standards are but a minimal level

---

[10] http//www.voxeu.org/index.php?q=node/213#footnote11#footnote11; "Does globalization increase child labour?" Evidence from Vietnam," Eric Edmonds and Nona Pavcnik, NBER Working Paper 8760, 2002; ," Eric Edmonds "Child labour, NBER Working Paper 12926, 2007.

below which no member should sink.

We find from all of the above that labour administration, enforcement of labour standards, and the reform of labour law tend to be conditioned by globalisation, strategic concerns and tactics adopted by all parties in an increasingly competitive international economic environment.

Chapter 19

THE ECONOMIC CRISIS AND EMPLOYMENT*

INTRODUCTION

I should like to thank LAWAN for inviting me to give this short talk on the "Impact of Economic Crisis on Employment". Given the times and circumstances worldwide and in our country, the choice of topic is immensely sensible and commendable.

One challenge, however, presented by the topic is its breadth, dealing as it does with generic "economic crisis", a subject that has occupied the attention of social scientists, especially economists and political scientists, of violently opposed ideological persuasions, for the past two centuries at least!

If this is a challenge, the language of discussion is even more daunting, dominated by "isms" and technical jargons of the sort specialists and experts, like doctor's prescriptions, use to obscure very simple things or phenomena!

I am especially grateful that I have not been asked to proffer solutions to the Economic Crisis which I am sure would be left to some other speaker!

In the next hour or so, I shall attempt to do the following:

a) undertake a substantially non-technical discussion of our topic without, I pray, doing too much damage to the various views to be presented;
b) offer an overview of the global economic system and its workings;
c) offer a brief examination of the concept of "economic crisis";
d) pass comments on current global economic crisis;
e) explore the impact of economic crisis on unemployment internationally and locally; and
f) offer some concluding remarks.

GLOBAL ECONOMIC CRISIS

We talk of a global economic crisis today because we have a global economy, not because we have many countries. We have for several centuries had

* Text of lecture delivered at the workshop organised by the Labour Writers Association of Nigeria (LAWAN) at KS Motel, Ibadan, on 11 March 2010

many countries but not the kind of economic and financial crisis we are experiencing today.

We are all over the world experiencing economic crisis, not to the same extent or degree, because we share in or participate in certain global economic and financial institutions, which partly regulate and also comprise economic transactions between countries and between local and foreign or transnational companies.

In fact, the emergence of a national economy is also relatively recent. Economic activities and markets for products were local, each operating nearly exclusively of the other. A combination of factors which need not concern us here, including integrated air, land and sea transportation and advances in information technology, led to the expansion of local and regional economies into one complex whole where productive activities could be stimulated and monitored and computed to arrive at indices of national development. So, what is this global economy?

Global economy

- Comprises national economies
- Regional and Sub-regional economic groupings (e.g. ECOWAS)
- Regional and sub-regional financial and trade regulating institutions (e.g. African Development Banks- ADB)
- International trade, financial and development institutions/agencies
- Relevant UNO trade and financial agencies
- Transnational/multinational companies

Global economy- Structure

- Long-industrialised economies
- Newly industrialising economies
- Raw materials-producing economies
- Capital-intensive and rich economies
- Poor capital economies

International economic system

- Stock Exchanges
- Transnational/multinational companies
- The World Bank
- International Monetary Fund
- World Trade Organisation
- Regional and International Credit financial institutions

Workings of the International Economic System

- Market forces
- Deregulated markets:

i) Exchange rates;
ii) Finance and financial derivatives
iii) Shares and futures
iv) Services
v) labour
vi) Intra-continental and inter-continental business opportunities and interests gave birth to multinational or transnational companies, with subsidiaries located in all continents.
vii) Multinational companies compete for global markets and global sources of raw materials, with strategies fashioned to cope with or adapt to local circumstances of national economies.

LOGIC OF THE INTERNATIONAL ECONOMIC SYSTEM

Akin to this development is the issue of regional integration of otherwise independent states of European Community/European Union and ECOWAS, AU, etc., some having adopted common currencies.

Very striking has been the *internationalization of capital flows*. Instead of merely financing world trade, by the end of the 1980s banks and non-bank financial institutions have been dealing in currency exchanges, currency and commodity futures and so-called 'derivatives' of all sorts of a scale that not only dwarfed the conventional transactions needed for trade and investment, but made it impossible for the governments of even large economies to influence the value of their currency by intervening in the currency markets.

ECONOMIC CRISIS

The concept and notion of Economic Crisis derive from huge debates about the nature and workings of the capitalist system, especially since Karl Marx. An industrialising Europe was dominated by the doctrine of Classical Liberalism. Classical liberalism holds that individual rights are natural, inherent, or inalienable, and exist independently of government. It is a philosophy that upholds the *sovereignty of the individual*, with *private property* rights seen as essential to individual liberty.

Applied to economic matters and general social policy by a group of French, Continental and British economists during and since the times of Adam Smith and David Ricardo, it argues for minimum state involvement in the supply or production, pricing and distribution of goods and services. This has since been generally labelled *Laissez faire Economics*, especially after Adam Smith's books, *The Wealth of Nations* and *The Theory of Moral Sentiments* were published and in which, among other things, Adam Smith wrote of an "invisible hand" of the market mechanism, the infallible and most efficient value-allocating role of the forces of demand and supply.

So, what have these got to do with Economic Crisis? It did not take long to observe that the capacity of demand and supply to adjust themselves automatically was limited and not as smooth-sailing as supposed, that there were periods of scarcity and that aggregate welfare did not increase as rapidly as claimed. More crucially, like day always following the night, periods of boom or prosperity for businesses were always followed by period of recession or bust.

Karl Marx and his followers, socialists and communists developed thoroughgoing critique of the capitalist system, propositions which have all come to be known as the Crisis Theory. The Crisis Theory is concerned with explaining the *business cycle*, *recession* and *crises in capitalism*. Karl Marx noted that it is in the *nature* of the capitalism system to suffer from *periodic crises* because of its internal contradictions. According to him, "The *real barrier* of capitalist production is *capital itself* " and thus the crisis is *systemic*, not *random*. Prominent among the contradictions or factors identified by Marx are three, which have remained classic:

1. *The tendency of the rate of profit to fall* (As more goods and services are supplied because investors increase, prices reduce and profits fall as a result);
2. Under-consumption. If the capitalists win the *class struggle* to push wages down and labour effort up, raising the rate *of surplus value* (profits), then a capitalist economy faces regular problems of inadequate *consumer demand* and thus inadequate *aggregate demand.*
3. *Full employment profit squeeze.* Capital accumulation can pull up the demand for *labour power*, raising wages. If wages rise "too high," it hurts the *rate of profit*, causing a recession.

In Marxist or Marxian terms, all such crises are crises of overproduction and immiseration of the workers who, were it not for the control of society based on the accumulation of capital, i.e. by those successful in accumulation or their heirs, would be the determiners of both demand and production in the first place.

As such, Economic Crisis in its generic form thus refers to a period in which the normal reproduction of an economic process over time suffers from a temporary breakdown. This crisis period encourages intensified *class conflict* or *societal change* — or the revival of a more normal accumulation process.

It is a tenet of many Marxists groupings that such crises are inevitable and will be increasingly severe until the contradictions inherent in the mismatch between the mode of production and the *development of productive forces* reaches the final point of failure, determined by the quality of *their leadership*, the development of the *consciousness* of the various *social classes*, and other "subjective factors". Thus the degree of "tuning" necessary for intervention in otherwise "perfect" market mechanisms becomes more and more extreme as the time in which the capitalist order is a progressive factor in the development of productive forces recedes further and further into the past.

Marxists thus see Economic Crisis as part of the larger crisis of the social order under capitalism and liberal democracy.

KEYNESIAN ECONOMICS

At the end of World War II when all European economies lay in ruins, reconstruction and rehabilitation could not be based on market forces alone and the activities of entrepreneurs in a situation where capital was very limited and lives disrupted. Helped along by American Marshall Aid Plan, the State assumed a commanding role in rebuilding respective economies and which led to the rise and development of the Welfare State. Keynesian Economics are those prescriptions advocated by John Maynard Keynes and economists of his persuasion, measures designed to assist market forces rather than give them unfettered freedom as under *Laissez Faire* Economics.

Keynesian Economics thus attempts a "*middle way*" between *laissez faire*, unadulterated capitalism and state guidance and partial control of economic activity. Here attempts to address economic crises with the policy of have the State act as:

i) a temporary super-capitalist and pillar of the underlying private enterprise system with its increasing range of welfare policies; and
ii) actively supplying the deficiencies of unaltered markets through bailouts, subsidies, incentives, and other palliatives.

The post-World War II international economic system was designed at Bretton Woods, a small town in New Hampshire in the USA where the Allied Powers met in 1944. Aside from sorting out political issues, agreements on trade and other economic issues were contained in a document (and managed by an organisation) known as the General Agreement on Trade and Tariffs (GATT) – to which the WTO is a successor -, and the World Bank and the International Monetary Fund (IMF) were created to regulate the new system.

The new system was based on Economic Planning, representing an international consensus on the modification of *Laissez Faire* Economics, with member-states all adopting Development Plans for varying durations (5, 10,15, etc.). The lesson and wisdom now was the economic development could be planned for, and not merely the accidental or unintended, trickled-down effect of unrestrained market forces.

The role of the state/government in national economic planning and the international economy since the late 1950s was practically determined by the World Bank and the International Monetary Fund (IMF) – otherwise known as the Bretton Woods institutions – (and supported by the USA, Japan and other western countries) in the financial and trading regime they instituted for all member-countries. The financial and trading arrangements were designed to permit national governments to *manage* their economies so as to *maximise growth* and *employment.* Capital was not allowed to cross frontiers without government approval, which permitted governments to determine domestic interest rates, fix the exchange rate of the national currency, and tax and spend as they saw fit to secure national economic objectives. National economic planning was seen as a natural extension of this thinking, as were domestic and international arrangements to stabilize commodity prices. The *goal* of development was *growth*; the *agent* of development was the *state* and the *means* of development were these *macroeconomic policy instruments (Fiscal and Monetary).* These were taken-for-granted presuppositions of 'development theory' as it evolved from the 1950s onwards, until the mid-1970s, as we see below.

LIBERALISM AND NEO-LIBERALISM

Classical liberalism is a political ideology that developed in the nineteenth century in England, Western Europe, and the Americas. It is committed to the ideal of *limited government* and *liberty of individuals* including *freedom of religion, speech, press,* and *assembly,* and *free markets.* In the age of Laissez Faire Economics of that time till the 1940s when USSR, Eastern bloc countries emerged and Keynesian Economics or Welfare Economics became orthodoxy in the Western world, this remained the dominant ideology.

Neo-Liberalism

Broadly speaking, Neo-Liberalism seeks to transfer part of the control of the economy from public to the private sector, in the belief that it will produce a more efficient government and improve the economic health of a nation.

The concrete policies advocated by neo-liberalism are often taken to be John Williamson's *"Washington Consensus,"* a list of policy proposals that appeared to have been adopted by the Washington-based international economic organizations (e.g. International Monetary Fund (IMF) and World Bank). Williamson's list included ten points:

- **Fiscal policy discipline**; this is designed to help lower expectations for what the government can do to improve the lives of citizens. For example, the policy decision to maintain a reserve of unemployed as part of an inflation-fighting strategy combined with a public relations campaign that this *unemployment* is natural and cannot be defeated without huge deficits or *inflation.*
- **Redirection of public spending from subsidies** ("especially indiscriminate subsidies") toward broad-based provision of key pro-

growth, pro-poor services like primary education, primary health care and infrastructure investment;

- **Tax reform**– broadening the tax base by shifting the tax burden to the middle and lower economic groups and adopting moderate marginal tax rates;
- **Interest rates** that are market-determined and positive (but moderate) in real terms;
- **Competitive exchange rates**;
- **Trade liberalization** – liberalization of imports, with particular emphasis on elimination of quantitative restrictions (licensing, etc.); any trade protection to be provided by law and relatively uniform tariffs;
- **Liberalization of inward foreign direct investment** including commitment to unlimited transfer of earnings across foreign borders;
- **Privatization of state enterprises**; This occurs not only in the sense of the transfer of companies from the public to the private sector, but also in the conversion of social rights into marketable objects. Health and education, traditionally considered to be citizens' rights, become *economic interests* and, in many countries, are integrated into circuits of accumulation. In some cases, remaining public sector agencies and enterprises are encouraged to adopt *commercial* and *corporate management* and *organizational structures* (*corporatization*). With privatization of the public domain comes extractive fees for use of such resources and an increase in the overhead to the productive economy.
- **Deregulation** – abolition of regulations that impede market entry or restrict competition, except for those justified on safety, environmental and consumer protection grounds, and ***prudent oversight of financial institutions***;
- **Legal security for property rights**; and,
- **Financialization** of capital.

BACKGROUND TO CRISIS

What we call the "current crisis" is the effect of the rise and dominance of Neo-liberalism since the 1970s. The developments that facilitated the dominance of neo-liberalism included, among others, about a third of all trade between countries had come to consist of the movement of goods between different national branches of one or another multinational company. The mutual dependence of national economies implied by this fact was significant (obviously, it is not necessary for half of a country's capital assets to be foreign-owned for decisions taken in foreign countries to have a major impact on its fortunes);

But even more striking was the *internationalization of capital flows.* Instead of merely financing world trade, by the end of the 1980s banks and non-bank financial institutions were dealing in currency exchanges, currency and commodity futures and so-called 'derivatives' of all sorts of a scale that not only dwarfed the conventional transactions needed for trade and investment, but made it impossible for the governments of even large economies to influence the value of their currency by intervening in the currency markets.

But in the meantime control of capital movements had in any case also been abandoned as a deliberate policy decision, promoted, above all, by the USA. As competition with other industrial countries intensified, the USA borrowed abroad and became the world's largest debtor nation. As such it was obliged to give up its commitment to meet its dollar obligations in gold, which it did in 1971; and eventually, in 1973, the Bretton Woods system of fixed exchange rates was abandoned altogether.

This opened up new opportunities for international currency speculation and led to a new period of extreme instability in currency values and commodity prices, including the oil price increases of the 1970s and 1980s; these in turn led to vast new dollar balances being accumulated by the oil-exporting countries, and correspondingly vast expansions of borrowing, which drove up the total of international debt to previously unheard-of levels.

The abandonment of the post-war international trading regime was followed in 1979-80 by the abandonment of Keynesian economic policy in the Organization for Economic Co-operation and Development (OECD) countries, led by the UK and the USA. Deregulation in the USA and de-regulation and privatization in the UK were accompanied by high interest rates.

The governments of the other European industrial countries followed suit, either willingly or (in the case of France) because keeping interest rates significantly below those of other countries led to capital outflows that could no longer be prevented – 'Keynesianism in one country' – i.e. economic planning and management - was no longer practicable.

Capital exports were formally deregulated in the UK in 1979 and *de facto* everywhere else by the mid-1980s. Then, at the end of 1993, the conclusion of the 'Uruguay Round' of the General Agreement on Tariffs and Trade (GATT) negotiations inaugurated a further extension of global free trade, including the formerly sacrosanct agricultural sector, while further reductions in the regulatory powers of most industrial country governments were imposed by the European Union's Single Market and Maastricht Treaties and the North American Free Trade Agreement.

Most Third World countries, then, found themselves more vulnerable than at any time since they were first colonized. Their economies were least well-placed to prosper in the new 'global' market place. Primary commodity exports, other than oil, became steadily less significant as manufacturing became less commodity-intensive, and the overall share of the Third World in world trade fell dramatically. Faced with stagnating economies, and with per capita incomes declining from levels at which many people could barely survive already, they responded by increased borrowing abroad until servicing the debt led to balance of payments difficulties so acute that they were forced to turn to the IMF.

As a condition of further support the IMF and the World Bank then forced them to cut back government intervention in their economies, leaving these instead to be revived by the freer play of 'market forces'. This did not, of course, produce the anticipated results. Per capita incomes fell still further in all the affected countries (in sub-Saharan Africa, by over a quarter), while the debt-service burden (the proportion of export earnings spent on capital repayments and interest) of the 'low-income countries' (excluding China and India at the time) rose from 11.8% in 1980 to 24.5% in 1992. Under General Buhari in Nigeria, it rose to 40%.

The disciples of free movement of capital, now called 'neo-liberals', argued that:

- development was blocked by inflated public sectors, distorting economic controls and overemphasis on capital formation;
- *Governments* were *part of the problem, not part of the solution*; they were inefficient and often corrupt and hence parasitic, not stimulators of growth;
- The *solution* was to *privatise* the public sector;
- reduce the scale and scope of government spending; and
- give up all policies, from exchange rate controls to subsidies and redistributive taxation, that altered any prices that would otherwise be set by the impersonal forces of the market.

FINANCIAL CRISIS OF 2007–2010

As it is now an open secret, but also well documented by the *Wikipedia*, the free encyclopaedia for those of you seeking further details, the financial crisis of 2007–2010 was triggered by a liquidity shortfall in the United States banking system. It resulted in the collapse of large financial institutions, the "bail out" of banks by national governments and downturns in stock markets around the world.

How did this happen? Low interest rates and large inflows of foreign funds created easy credit conditions for a number of years prior to the crisis, fuelling a housing construction boom and encouraging debt-financed consumption. The combination of easy credit and money inflow contributed to the *United States housing bubble*. Loans of various types (e.g., mortgage, credit card, and auto) were easy to obtain and consumers assumed an unprecedented debt load. As part of the housing and credit booms, the amount of financial agreements called *mortgage-backed securities* (MBS) and *collateralized debt obligations* (CDO), which derived their value from mortgage payments and housing prices, greatly increased. Such *financial innovation* enabled institutions and investors around the world to invest in the U.S. housing market.

The policy of Deregulation entrenched by President Reagan in 1982 and pushed to its limits by George W. Bush turned "prudent regulation of financial institutions" to near-absence of regulation. The banks and other financial institutions took complete advantage of this and explored all possibilities:

- Banks borrowed even more money to lend out so they could create more securitization;
- Some banks did not need to rely on savings as much then, as long as they could borrow from other banks and sell those loans on as securities; bad loans would be the problem of whoever bought the securities;
- Some investment banks like Lehman Brothers got into mortgages, buying them in order to securitize them and then sell them on;
- Some banks loaned even more to have an excuse to securitize those loans;
- Running out of whom to loan to, banks turned to the poor; the subprime, the riskier loans.
- Rising house prices led lenders to think it was not too risky; bad loans meant repossessing high-valued property. Subprime and "self-certified" loans (sometimes dubbed "liar's loans") became popular;
- Some banks even started to *buy* securities from others.
- Collateralized Debt Obligations, or CDOs, (even more complex forms of securitization) spread the risk but were very complicated and often hid the bad loans.
- The sub-prime crisis came about in large part because of financial instruments such as securitization where banks would pool their various loans into sellable assets, thus off-loading risky loans onto others.
- For banks, millions can be made in money-earning loans, but they are tied up for decades. So they were turned into securities. The security buyer gets regular payments from all those mortgages; the banker off-loads the risk. Securitization was seen as perhaps the greatest financial innovation in the twentieth century!

While the housing and credit bubbles grew, a series of factors caused the financial system to both expand and become increasingly fragile, a process called *financialization.* Policymakers did not recognise the increasingly important role played by financial institutions such as *investment banks* and *hedge funds*, also known as the *shadow banking system*. Some experts believe these institutions had become as important as commercial (depository) banks in providing credit to the U.S. economy, but they were not subject to the same regulations.

These institutions as well as certain regulated banks had also assumed significant debt burdens while providing the loans described above and did not have a financial cushion sufficient to absorb large loan defaults or MBS losses. These losses impacted the ability of financial institutions to lend, slowing economic activity. Concerns regarding the stability of key financial institutions drove central banks to provide funds to encourage lending and restore faith in the commercial paper markets, which are integral to funding business operations. Governments also bailed out key financial institutions and implemented economic stimulus programmes, assuming significant additional financial commitments.

High default rates began to increase quickly thereafter in 2006. An increase in loan packaging, marketing and incentives such as easy initial terms and a long-term trend of rising housing prices had encouraged borrowers to assume difficult mortgages in the belief they would be able to quickly refinance at more favourable terms.

However, once interest rates began to rise and housing prices started to drop moderately in 2006–2007 in many parts of the U.S., refinancing became more difficult. Defaults and foreclosure activity increased dramatically as easy initial terms expired, home prices failed to go up as anticipated.

The bursting of a global housing bubble caused the values of *securities* tied to *real estate pricing* to plummet thereafter, damaging financial institutions globally. Questions regarding bank *solvency*, declines in credit availability, and damaged investor confidence had an impact on global *stock markets*, where securities suffered large losses during late 2008 and early 2009. Economies worldwide slowed during this period as credit tightened and international trade declined.

As housing prices declined, major global financial institutions that had borrowed and invested heavily in subprime MBS reported significant losses. (The term "subprime" refers to the credit quality of particular borrowers, who have weakened credit histories and a greater risk of loan default than prime borrowers – meaning expansion of higher-risk lending). Falling prices also resulted in homes worth less than the mortgage loan, providing a financial incentive to enter foreclosure. The ongoing foreclosure epidemic that began in late 2006 in the U.S. continues to drain wealth from consumers and erodes the financial strength of banking institutions. Defaults and losses on other loan types also increased significantly as the crisis expanded from the housing market to other parts of the economy. Total losses are estimated in the trillions of U.S. dollars globally.

When people did eventually start to see problems, confidence fell quickly. Lending slowed, in some cases ceased for a while and even now, there is a crisis of confidence. Some investment banks were sitting on the riskiest loans that other investors did not want. Assets were plummeting in value so lenders wanted to take their money back. But some investment banks had little in deposits; no secure retail funding, so some collapsed quickly and dramatically.

The problem was so large, banks even with large capital reserves ran out, so they had to turn to governments for bail out. New capital was injected into banks to, in effect, *allow* them to lose more money without going bust. That still was not enough and confidence was not restored. Some think it may take years for confidence to return.

Shrinking banks suck money out of the economy as they try to build their capital and are nervous about loaning. Meanwhile businesses and individuals that rely on credit find it harder to get, a spiral of problems result.

IMPACT ON THE NIGERIAN ECONOMY

In January 2009, the Governor the Central Bank of Nigeria listed the following impacts on the Nigerian economy:

- Commodity prices collapse (especially oil price);
- Revenue contraction (possible burst syndrome) ;
- Declining capital inflows in the economy;
- De-accumulation of foreign reserves and pressure on exchange rate;
- Limited foreign trade finances for banks—credit lines may dry-up for some banks;
- Capital market downturn, divestment by foreign investors with attendant tightness and possible second round effects on the balance sheet of banks by increasing provisioning for bad debt and decrease in profitability;
- Counter party risks vis-a-vis external reserves but CBN has taken measures to safeguard the reserves;
- Nigerian banks remain robust to withstand the shocks.

ECONOMIC CRISIS AND EMPLOYMENT

In a press release and found in its website, of the Geneva-based International Labour Organisation (*ILO News*), its Director-General, Mr Somavia noted that the global financial crisis could increase world unemployment by an estimated 20 million women and men.

Based on revised global growth estimates by the International Monetary Fund (IMF), the UN and early reports suggesting rising job losses for most countries where data was available, ILO Director-General Juan Somavia said the ILO's preliminary estimates indicated that the "number of unemployed could rise from 190 million in 2007 to 210 million in late 2009."

Mr. Somavia added that "the number of working poor living on less than a dollar a day could rise by some 40 million – and those at 2 dollars a day by more than 100 million."

Mr. Somavia also said that the current crisis would hit hardest such sectors as construction, automotive, tourism, finance, services and real estate. He also noted that the new projections

> "could prove to be underestimates if the effects of the current economic contraction and looming recession are not quickly confronted...This is not simply a crisis on Wall Street, this is a crisis on all streets. We need an economic rescue plan for working families and the real economy, with rules and policies that deliver decent jobs. We must link better productivity to salaries and growth to employment."

Mr. Somavia said his concerns included restoring credit flows; maintaining and enhancing social protection, including pensions, unemployment benefits, child support and health care schemes; ensuring enterprise access to credit to avoid layoffs, wage cuts, bankruptcy and permit recovery, respect for workers' rights and deepening social dialogue to deal with the impact on enterprises; ensuring ODA flows; rebuilding a regulatory regime for global finance; and moving quickly from recovery to sustainable development through investment and growth.

"We welcome the current calls for better financial regulation and a global surveillance system of checks and balances, but we must reach beyond the financial system," the ILO Director-General said. He noted:

> "Long before the current financial crisis, we were already in a crisis of massive global poverty and growing social inequality, rising informality and precarious work – a process of globalization that had brought many benefits but had become unbalanced, unfair, and unsustainable," he said. "We need to get the balance right and concentrate on rescuing people and production. It's about saving the real economy."
>
> "In order to keep open economies and open societies going, we must begin working together among relevant international organizations to develop a new multilateral framework for a fair and sustainable globalization. Trade talks are stalled; financial markets are on the

> brink, climate change continues; any reconstruction will have to find ways to integrate financial and economic, social and labour and environmental policies in a common sustainable development approach," (Ibid.).

As for sub-Saharan Africa, most politicians and policy-makers behave as if they are faced with very limited economic policy options for two reasons: a) their own uncritical orientations which impede the fashioning out of viable alternative policies; and b) the reality of globalisation of capital. There is enough evidence to confirm that policy-makers (already evidenced in the implementation of various structural adjustments programmes) intend to follow the path as laid down by the IMF and World Bank, hence all the privatisation programmes and deregulation policies.

It is instructive that such deregulation has been made a condition for undertaking a review of the abysmally low wages in the public sector in particular! Although, there appears to be some pockets of opposition to these measures, such has not been strong enough to lead to their abandonment: rather, the main civil service and many parastatals are still retrenching and other fiscal and monetary policies designed to ease the flow of capital and as added incentives to investors (elimination of excise duties in some cases and wholesale down-ward review of custom duties, among others) are being adopted in an *ad hoc* manner.

The impacts of globalisation and the current crisis on the economy and politics are thus multi-faceted, ranging from the impoverishment of a majority of wage-earners, continuing loss of members by way of down-sizing (restructuring, retirements, dismissals, etc.), abandonment of indigenisation schemes, and difficulties facing many companies (especially in the manufacturing sector faced by rising costs and competition from smuggled substitute products and administrative bottle-necks), declining capacity among union leadership due to wastages, attrition, and prevalence of younger and relatively inexperienced hands, the rapid growth in the number of rival non-governmental organisations (NGOs) many of which concentrate on some traditional concerns of the labour movement (civil liberties, human rights, child abuse, gender discrimination, occupational hazards, inequity and corruption, etc.) to deliberate anti-unionism tactics of both private and public employers, especially sub-contracting of operations and labour.

The increasing cases of 'rationalisations', 'down-sizing', mergers/take-overs, bankruptcies, technological changes, privatisation, commercialisation, removal of subsidies, and drastic cut-backs in 'public expenditure' have not only led to massive loss of jobs that can be 'organised', surviving on wages/salaries has become very difficult – in spite of those attractive remuneration packages for a class of employees in certain industries.

Many workers in Africa have become part-time workers in orientation, pre-occupied with how to supplement the pay packet (de-proletarianisation, de-industrialisation and pauperisation). Although there has been a corresponding growth in the development of certain skills and jobs accompanying rapid changes in technology, they are yet to be organised by unions.

Unemployment statistics for some countries (2010)

Country	*Unemployment %*
Australia	5.3
Austria	5.3
Belgium	8.0
Brazil	6.8
Cameroun	30
Canada	8.3
China	4.3
Denmark	7.0
Egypt	7.0
Finland	9.0
France	9.8
Gabon	21
Germany	7.9
Ghana	11.0
Greece	8.0
India	9.5
Ireland	13.8
Italy	8.6
Japan	5.0
Kenya	4.0
Malaysia	3.2
Netherlands	4.2
Nigeria	9.8
Portugal	10.5
Russia	9.2
Singapore	3.3
South Africa	23.5
South Korea	3.9
Spain	18.8
Sweden	9.0
United Kingdom	7.5
USA	9.7
Zambia	50
Zimbabwe	90

These statistics do not fully capture the employment effects of the Crisis. For countries like Japan that hovered around 2% unemployment rate, this more than doubled within a few months. And like Mr Somavia of the ILO had remarked, most countries were already facing increasing poverty and mass unemployment due to Globalisation before this Crisis kicked in.

Globalisation has accentuated the loss of autonomous regulatory power by States/governments. States and inter-governmental organizations have been since the 1980s playing a role in enforcing the rules of global economy and in enhancing national competitiveness, but their powers of shielding domestic economies from negative effects of globalisation have also diminished: especially affected is their capacity to deliver social goods that can help reduce poverty. 'Market forces' are now supposed to determine every transaction in the local economy, while the World Trade Organisation (WTO) and similar international rules (which favour the economically more advanced countries) and other tariff and non-tariff obstacles 'regulate' international trade. Thus, internally in most countries, xenophobia, ethnic, religious and other social divisions are on the increase, as aspirations remain unfulfilled.

CONCLUDING OBSERVATIONS

The impact of the Economic Crisis on Employment is very obvious: as businesses collapse, jobs are lost. As more persons lose their jobs and thus cannot meet their financial obligations (mortgage, credit card, rent, auto, medical, schools fees, etc.), those intermediary financial institutions to which regular payments of premiums are due also go out of business, and more people lose their jobs!

This is not to say that some jobs are not created; but not sufficient to make much difference especially if left to these same companies. This is why one measure is for the state or government to embark on job-creating ventures, especially construction of physical infrastructure that could inject immediate purchasing power into the system.

This then means one must begin to question some of the underlying assumptions of Globalisation as a theory of development and of Neo-liberalism as presented by their advocates. One of those assumptions is the claim that the best way forward is to have an unregulated economy where all transactions are left to market forces. From the current crisis, advocates of completely deregulated and liberalised economic environment have to accept that such an economy, local or international, does not exist. Even the USA government subsidises agriculture to the tune of $1 billion daily, and the European Union subsidises agriculture, health, education and a variety of social insurance schemes. In spite of WTO, regional, sub-regional, and continental groupings (EU, NAFTA, ASEAN, ECOWAS, SADCC, etc.) by definition erect barriers against liberalisation.

Another claim that should not go unchallenged is that globalisation is inevitable. Technical or technological advancement may have its logic, leading to further advances, but this should not be taken to mean that there are no alternatives to *laissez faire* economic doctrines embodied in neo-liberal positions. *Laissez faire* economic doctrines are some of the oldest ideas on development, underlying the early formulations advanced by Adam Smith and his contemporaries since late seventeenth century as we observed earlier. But *laissez faire* economic doctrines had to be abandoned in the 1930s for the same reasons as globalisation would likely to be abandoned sooner than later, namely that an unregulated market or private enterprise system is plagued by alternating incidents of booms and busts or depressions, and despite its acclaimed 'efficient allocation of resources', an increase in aggregate welfare is not achieved, let alone guaranteed.

Indeed, a critical point in relation to employment is that the period during which the world experienced the birth and growth of mass consumption society and greatest increase in the aggregate standard of living in human history was when extensive economic planning and state intervention occurred from mid-1940s till early 1970s. Another way of putting it is that since the mid-1970s when Globalisation/neo-liberalism gained ascendancy, mass poverty has been on the increase worldwide. So, it stands to reason that if people elect governments to improve their economic lot, laissez faire economic policies would certainly not do the trick in the short or middle run.

But, we are not here arguing that no good comes from deregulation! In the Nigeria case, for example, organised labour should encourage some degree of deregulation in sectors of the economy dominated by highly inefficient publicly-owned companies. It is not a question of whether government officials or staff of the NNPC or workers in the refineries should be blamed for the state of the refineries today. All of them are in the public sector, and if they owned any of the refineries as persons or investors, they would not have run them aground or put up with their epileptic performance. Deregulation and privatisation may be carried out in different degrees; no country has privatised all of its public utilities and service providers merely on account of market forces being the most efficient way of determining prices and of allocating resources. Even companies in the private sector collapse daily. A situation where only a few people control the importation of refined petroleum products is not good for consumers or the country – hence a degree of deregulation would prove beneficial.

Transparency in governance and business

Now that we know that wage employment takes place in both public and private sectors of the economy and within companies/organisations, and for meaningful employment (what the ILO refers to as "decent jobs") to exist, there should be increased concern for transparency in governance and business.

For political governance, activities directed at getting all to respect and protect human rights should be increased and encouraged. One way of doing this is for organised labour to network with other non-government organisations, including students' organisations, in civil society. No government should be allowed to insist on its own definition of 'human rights', of 'democracy' or reduce elections to declaring the well-connected victors rather than votes determining the results. With a consolidating civilian democracy, the trade unions have to respond proactively and reactively to a more benevolent socio-political situation characterised by positive expectation from the citizenry.

It should also be borne in mind that although a government may have the power (seized or constitutionally bestowed) to make laws, those laws that do not conform to laid down procedures in their enactment or violate those rights and privileges protected by the constitution can be declared *unlawful* by the courts. It is to avoid this that some military dictatorships introduce so-called 'ouster clauses' that prevent the law courts from even examining such laws. To this extent, a democratic environment is expected to assist the furthering and achievement of the rule of law and the development of a credible judiciary.

As for managing businesses in the public sector, the essential services will reinforce their continuing dominant position as the country's largest foreign exchange earner. One likely implication of this is either greater co-operation between the unions and state authorities, or more acrimonious relationship as governments might over-react to the sensitive position of these parastatals (e.g. NNPC group) in relation to its own interests and pre-occupations. My best guess is that collective bargaining would likely be a mixture of both attempts by governments to impose some terms, and other terms demanded by the unions and workers, depending on the compensation policies of private employers in the industry, social and political issues and nature of leadership on both sides.

The poor shape of the economy, if made much worse by official mismanagement or lack of effective management, shall continue to take its toll in terms of continuing loss of union membership through lay-offs, redundancies, 'rationalisations', declining turnovers and profits of firms, reluctance on the part of increasing number of employers to re-negotiate new agreements, declining membership dues, and inability of several unions to meet their financial and other obligations. It is left to labour to increase its ranks by organising casual and short-term contract workers, in addition to taking legal steps to compel employers to keep terms of agreement.

Second, a government alive to its responsibility and the future of the country should meet its obligations and also develop a more credible management of the oil and gas industry. Many jobs are likely to be lost, especially at the bottom of the ladder where a good deal of subcontracting of jobs is going on in the oil sector, and under a cross-posting policy for management staff an increasing number of positions are now being taken over by expatriate staff in virtually all sectors.

Transparency in Business

The relevant professional associations in Nigeria, especially legal and accounting, have not been of great help in promoting transparency and good corporate governance or practices. Concocted agreement and doctored "audited" accounts translate into loss of jobs in the end when the companies go under or restructure. Perhaps, self-regulation of these professional bodies in the area of corporate governance may not be adequate.

The quality of union leadership

The greatest challenge for organised labour in this dramatically changing socio-economic environment is the *quality* of union leadership. The trouble here would seem to be more in terms of *general orientation and vision,* than in formal education (not that this does not need to be beefed up) for, as I have always pointed out, the bulk of those in all Nigerian governments and the National Assembly were/are no better educated than union leaders. They have a role to play in encouraging both private and public sector employers to create more decent jobs and reduce unemployment, particularly impacting on official socio-economic policies that should take on board deregulation, privatisation, pricing of refined petroleum products, physical infrastructure, Niger Delta, etc.

Chapter 20

REFORM, NATIONAL DEVELOPMENT AND REFORMING THE REFORMER

INTRODUCTION

A modern meaning of the word "reform" would offer the following: a) to put or change into an improved form or condition; b) to amend or improve by change of form or removal of faults or abuses; c) to put an end to (an evil) by enforcing or introducing a better method or course of action; and d) to induce or cause to abandon evil ways (reform a drunkard). What all these meanings of "Reform" have in common is *improving upon a current situation* that is considered to be *unsatisfactory*.

Not that assured, as it were, historically, that the notion of reform was so straightforwardly optimistic and corrective, at least not in Medieval Europe and England to which its current usage may be traced. Indeed, it would be fair to assert that latter-day social scientists and historians appear to have *retroactively* applied the label to certain classes of decisions, actions, and measures of social and political actors. For example, a tyrant, warlord, king, or emperor or some such other absolutist political head in antiquity and right up to the fifteenth or sixteenth century devising ways and means of tightening or loosening physical and political control might not have thought in terms of "reform" as defined above. And, it is also unlikely that the amelioration of the conditions of victims of those sorts of actions and measures was the prime consideration given that the bulk of humanity passed as personal possession (slaves, serfs) of a few at the time.

But increasing social and political ferment in England and Europe from mid-seventeenth century brought into the fore dramatically rising and conflicting class interests, accentuated by burgeoning industrial capitalism and the violent overthrow of several absolutist monarchical regimes. The social and political metamorphosis of the "subject" into a "citizen" proceeded apace, and pressure for all manner of changes built up and exploded in mass riots in several instances. The emergent parliaments or legislative bodies, riddled with factions and corruption to varying degrees, responded to these pressures, but without necessarily solving all unfolding social and political difficulties. Inevitably from the logic of the situation, the direction of attention and scale of measures were always the outcomes of the balance of socio-political and economic forces and limited political franchise, including remnants of the old regime where not completely overthrown as was the case in England.

The mutations and emergence of "reform" in this period are partly captured by Helen Rogers (2014)[1] in her useful review of a book on the age of reform in Britain, where she explored "reform" as *aspiration* from the seventeen-eighties onwards as the book,

> …concentrated more on its origins than its legacy…reconsidered the age of reform in the light of the new historiography of the eighteenth century that shows the extent of governmental and institutional reforms, the vitality of 'pressure from without' and the emergence of social criticism…
>
> Nonetheless, the years 1780-82 saw the first use of 'reform' as a noun... This novel 'shift in vocabulary' can be seen as marking the inauguration of the 'age of reform', although '[a]ttitudes and practices changed less than the ways in which those attitudes and practices were expressed.'(p. 7) Henceforward, as Innes charts in her chapter tracing 'the fortunes of a word', reform became a slogan, though much contested...This book extends this historiography by examining 'pressure from within' and 'above', illuminating the deployment of reforming rhetoric in government institutions, professional bodies and elite culture…
>
> The verb 'reform' and the nouns 'reformer' and 'reformation', deployed in political and religious controversy for several centuries, increased in currency from the mid-eighteenth century. To 'reform' largely implied reformation – the *return to a former, less corrupted order*, or the revival and regeneration of manners and habits. While even Cromwell saw reformation in terms of *restoration*, the association of 'reform' with Puritanism and the Commonwealth and hence innovation and rebellion, tainted the word and…encouraged the development of 'improvement' as an alternative from the mid-seventeenth century…However, the evangelical awakening of the seventeen-thirties revived older Protestant associations of reformation, preparing the way for the 'reformation of manners' that would be seen as central to the purification of institutions as well as individuals. Under the influence of Enlightenment thinking and its

---

[1] Dr Helen Rogers, review of *Rethinking the Age of Reform: Britain 1780-1850*, (review no. 403) Rethinking the Age of Reform: Britain 1780-1850 edited by: Arthur Burns, Joanna Innes Cambridge, Cambridge University Press, 2003

> calls for legal and financial reform, the principle that institutional reform was a necessary precursor of moral reformation began to be established...
>
> Before 1830, to be a reformer meant principally to support parliamentary reform and other campaigns used different terms to define their objectives...The avoidance of 'reform' is explained by *its association with the French Revolution and hence violence, fervour and excess*: 'The very word fell into disrepute.'(p. 13) While Burke acknowledged the need for reform, its English application would be pragmatic: concerned with *adjustment* rather than *change*, *empiricism* rather than *speculation*. *Reform emerged as an alternative to revolution: as progress and improvement rather than dangerous innovation...*
>
> By the end of the eighteen-twenties, the term signalled *a gradualist alternative to revolution*, where on the Continent it retained its older connotation of innovation and consequently other words were deployed such as 'regeneration' and 'reorganisation'...
>
> British and continental experiences of the age of reform...the fundamental impression...remains of two quite different political universes.' (p. 313) Where in Britain and Ireland much agrarian reform was enacted by opponents of parliamentary reform, it was above all the emancipation of agriculture and the abolition of serfdom that animated European attacks on the *anciens regimes* and on much of the continent. It was not until 1848 that the liberation of rural society from pre-capitalist relationships was affected by revolution, rather than reform.

We may then see that the idea of political, social and other reforms had taken firmer root in England and Europe from late eighteenth century, given all the upheavals, but reforms were rather *piece-meal* in nature because of the logic of then unfolding capitalist industrialisation and other social practices wrought by a dying feudal order but under unceasing attack, a theoretical model that later underpinned Charles Lindblom's notion of incrementalism in public policy and public administration and of Robert Dahl's socio-political pluralism, and theories of choice and decision-making in the late 1950s.[2]

The Industrial Revolution and the creation of wage labour in their millions and the violence and resistance which accompanied and met the formation of workers organizations and their pressure to relieve deplorable

---

[2] Charles E. Lindblom, "The Science of Muddling Through," *Public Administration Review*, 19 Spring 1959, pp. 79-88

and inhuman work conditions brought the notion of reform into greater critical and sharper focus in Europe and Britain. A dominant l*aissez faire* capitalism or private enterprise economic system logically had room only for *market self-adjustments.* Thus the growth, fall and rise of businesses and prices, employment and unemployment and nature of work conditions respectively were essential ingredients and dynamics of *laissez faire* (free market) economy, taken as given and not to be tinkered with, but a claim which the very existence and reactions of organized labour and threatening socialist revolutions called into question.

For Karl Marx and many other Marxists, especially Lenin whose hands-on experience at state-restructuring taught him a few not all revolutionary things, reform in that century and subsequent periods stood for transformation, modification, or restructuring of an aspect of society, such as systems, institutions, or establishments, without destroying the foundation of the existing capitalist social structure. Socialist revolution is required for that. With subsequent socialist theorizing allowing for peaceful socialist revolution, reform in a capitalist system assumed a dual status; on the one hand, representing "concessions" by the ruling class to its class enemy and thus improved conditions of the working people in some respects (e.g., shorter hours, improved wages, and a host of what were subsequently known as welfare policies), then serve, in turn, as the precondition for their further struggle. That is to say, to maintain their power, the ruling classes agree to reforms, intending to weaken the pressure of the revolutionary forces and channel it into ordinary "reformism". While, on the other hand, reform may be "a preventive reaction, i.e. a measure to prevent the ruling classes from falling."[3] In principle, for Marxists therefore, the reformist approach obviously differs from the revolutionary approach because power is still retained by the ruling class after Reforms, whereas a proletarian-led revolution results in the transfer of power to a new class, the majority. It is thus the duty of working people and their organisations to push for the direct realisation of radical political and socio-economic transformation, the struggle for various reforms itself serving primarily as a means of strengthening class organisation and inculcating proletarian consciousness. If revolution triumphs, *true* reforms are carried out; if the revolution is defeated, the character and significance of the concession wrested from the ruling class will have proved insufficient. And, the struggle continues. This struggle for structural reforms is a special form of the revolutionary process as it focuses on basic structure of society. Reforms of this type, which go beyond ordinary reforms, therefore, are considered to be

---

[3] V. I. Lenin, *Poln. sobr. soch.*, 5th edn., vol. 15, p. 107; *Imperialism, The Highest Stage of Capitalism* (1916) in *Selected Works* (in one vol.) (Moscow, 1968) p.

a collection of gradual, fundamental transformations that do not "introduce" socialism in themselves but directly affect the foundations of the capitalist system, opening prospects for socialism. Collectivisation of agriculture and free education at all levels will be good examples.

The impulse towards the abolition of the Slave Trade (itself inimical to the emerging industrial capitalism which required physically liberated consumers who are free to make choices and with purchasing power to meet their wishes and tastes), the owning of colonies and the metropolitan formulation of colonial policies were themselves part-outcomes of ideological socio-political and economic turmoil and rivalries in Europe and Britain, later to be complicated by the implications of the 1917-1918 Bolshevik Revolution in Russia and subsequent emergence of the Soviet Union and Eastern Europe and Communist China in the late 1940s.

In modern parlance, from the late 1940s, reform had become mainstreamed, with various aspects of human development taken up by different agencies of the UNO and numerous international agreements and treaties signed and all governments routinely pursuing 'development' via Development Plans and Budgets. Flowing from these is what may be regarded as development, made up of various "reforms" targeting different sectors of society and the market, was increasingly determined *outside* national boundaries, certain institutional and legal frameworks for it being literally imposed by international financial and development institutions, agencies of the UNO, and continental and regional political unions or associations. The post-World War II fallout of ideological division of the world into the East and West thus produced two templates for reforms and development, one for capitalist economies, and the other for emerging socialist/communist economies.

It should be emphasized that the post-World War II political and ideological realignment, including the creation of the United Nations Organisation (UNO), marked the *dilution* of untrammelled reign of *laissez faire* economics and the rise of what became known as welfare economics, of which John Maynard Keynes and his associates were principal proponents. Systematic intervention in operations of the market, in order to increase welfare, was now entrenched, and reform was no longer totally or merely a response to demands of oppositional groups either but also inclusive of *deliberately* and *centrally conceived* and *implemented* social, political and economic projects contained in 'development plans' and doled out in yearly 'budgets'. From the late 1940s till early 1970s, in consequence, all prices and incomes were, *ab initio,* subjected to rigid regulation by central planning authorities, whatever the demand for a particular service or good might turn out to be. The contents of development plans and manner and timing of implementation were still subject to activities and preferences of competing social and economic forces domestically and internationally, of which the violent and non-violent or peaceful road to socialism or communism were the possibilities imperial powers were even keener to prevent in the colonies, especially having failed to do so in an ideologically and militarily divided Europe itself.

It would appear that the age of "development planning" fizzled out (after an incredible growth in mass consumerism, full employment and dramatic rise in standards of living over two and a half decades in the so-called economically advanced or industrialised countries) from early 1970s as economies stagnated worldwide in the face of inflation (stagflation), the dramatic and impressive advances in information and communication and computer technology from late 1970s and 1980s initially diverting attention from the fact of *globalisation* as a *forced return* to *laissez faire economics.* Globalisation ordinarily taken to mean the capacity of companies to invest and operate world-wide is nothing new. It is this tendency that led British and European companies and, eventually, countries to acquire colonies in Africa, Asia, South and North America in the first place after centuries of companies trading in slaves and other items; several companies were in Nigeria before Nigeria became Nigeria. What is new are the instruments for communication and speed of processing, storing, retrieving and transmitting information (ICT), all rendering global business operations and financial transactions much easier to co-ordinate and integrate.

Anyhow, back to our narration, over this period (that is, from 1948 till the 1980s) the State was involved in the provision of practically all forms of goods and services, and in many instances competing successfully against private sector rivals or producers. The provision of these goods and services, through the activities of parastatals (utilities) and state-owned companies, generated or created a massive public sector to supply and manage the welfare state. As it turned out, funding the welfare state was increasingly expensive as growth slowed and profits dipped, a situation crushing higher and higher personal income and corporate taxes failed to reverse. The set of influential measures proposed by Milton Friedman and like-minded economists in Europe and North America, borrowed and implemented to the letter by the American President, Ronald Reagan, and the British Prime Minister, Margaret Thatcher, referred to as "neo-Liberalism", basically was, as Mrs Thatcher reportedly famously put it, "rolling back frontiers of the State."

The large public sector in all countries was due for reduction and social and other services offered by parastatals deregulated and privatised to allow 'market forces' determine demand and supply. Among others, the structural adjustment programme (SAP) from late 1970s, a reform and development template, offered and driven by the IMF, the World Bank, other international financial and development institutions, with the full support of industrialised Western economies, *identified* and *imposed* a multi-fangled reform and development agenda: wage freeze, public sector mass retrenchment, currency devaluation, land reform, youth and women empowerment, skills acquisition programmes, fees charged in state-funded educational and medical facilities, commercialisation (and the eventual privatisation) of transport (road, rail and air) water, postal, telecommunications, electricity, and banking and financial services providers in the public sector, constitutionalism and democratisation of the political space or process (in autocracies and repressive regimes all over Asia, Africa and South America), etc., deregulation, liberalisation and privatisation!

Somewhat predictably, as it was in the *laissez faire*-dominated Europe and England from late eighteenth to mid-nineteenth century, as a result not only has the idea of reform become more contentious, so has the polity become more fractious as an increasing number of "reforms" seem disembodied, announced as required by "the system" or "the economy", leaving substantially untouched mass unemployment and mass poverty in many countries, while information technology and social media render it much easier for claims of policy-makers, governments and politicians to be debunked and "heating up the system". For example, any president or prime minister or minister announcing "I will create one million jobs this year" and who is never in a position to determine how many job openings the private sector's new and old companies might create over that same period, and with the reform template now *excluding* public sector job-creation of the development planning era, is either lying or is engaged in self-deception, a position or an illusion the teeming mass of unemployed youth, frequent mergers and acquisitions and restructuring or rationalisation and vocal oppositional groups easily contradict – not to mention the various "empowerment" and skills development schemes for the youth, women, etc., which themselves testify to the socio-economic paralysis of those groups in society where power, wealth and decent standard of life are yet to trickle down to via the "market mechanism".

Second, the institutionalisation of lobbying of civil servants and legislators by vested interest groups (informally and also via properly officially registered lobbying agents or companies in the USA) has tended to label certain official decisions, measures and projects as "concessions" to individuals or identifiable domestic and foreign interests. This flows easily from *laissez faire* economic doctrine, the accompanying dominant paradigm of society (which dismisses the existence and importance of social classes and impact on direction and nature of reform) as made up of various competing interest groups, the interest groups themselves free to pursue, protect and promote interest of their respective members within the legitimate framework or rules.[4] Implicit in this scenario is that the State's or government's attention *needs* to be *drawn* to an unsatisfactory condition by *those affected* for it to take remedial, if any, action. Also, *that* unsatisfactory condition competes (in market analogy) with *other* unsatisfactory conditions for that *same attention*. How does the government or policy-maker determine order of priority then? In the parlance of the theory of demand and supply, "effective demand" is achieved by those who have the means to and buy what they desire and want. Transposed, the interest groups who have the political connections and other means get what they want irrespective of what the Constitution says a government must do for the citizens and of what politicians promise during hustings. Indeed, the demands of some groups may be contrived to be mutually exclusive; the Beijing Convention may have recommended female representation at some 33.5%, while some groups seek to reduce, if not eliminate, such female presence at political and corporate structure or governance. It may then be said many types of reform are directed at meeting the needs of specific groups in the excluded presence of a development blueprint that accommodates *all kinds of needs* to varying degrees or extent. Some 170 million citizens demanding all-season motorable network of roads is not *effective* demand, if the government says it has other priorities, however determined, and international credit institutions and donor countries think such *social* investment is not a priority for *the economy*. Or, where only "bankable" projects may be embarked upon, with the criteria for being "bankable" determined by private, local and international financial institutions!

Third, and as alluded to earlier, a more fractious polity, aside from being part-outcome of improved avenues for voicing one's position on any matter (sometimes libellously, sometimes raucously, and other times subdued by teargas and other strong-arm tactics of law enforcement agencies maintaining "law and order" and "public peace"), is also traceable to the *reaction* of state authorities to the *drawing* of attention by those individuals, groups and communities so affected, to those *unsatisfactory conditions*. Quite often, due to a combination of factors, including ideological preferences and competition for and control of political power and sectional and narrower considerations, the needs advocated by some groups and persons seem to lose legitimacy before the eyes of state authorities - particularly legislators and presidency and coteries of "advisers" and "assistants", security and intelligence agencies - and such groups' activities

[4] Dahl, R. *Preface to Democratic Theory*, *Chicago* University Press, 1956; *Pluralist Democracy in America*, McNally, Chicago, 1967.

directed at protecting, promoting and pursuing their interests, ostensibly like other interest groups in society, attract negative labels - anti-government, subversive, ill-conceived, illegal, etc. - and dealt with accordingly. Countervailing reaction by such groups, persons and communities and state authorities' further actions all tend to create a seemingly vitriolic, unstable social, political and economic environment, held, locally and internationally, to be "unfavourable" to investment and development, including the relative absence of some of those physical and social infrastructures long-demanded by the groups and communities not so endeared to state authorities and other better connected interest groups at that juncture.

Fourth, not all types of reform outcomes are predictable and quantifiable from the outset, and as such many might have both *intended* and *unintended* consequences since many decisions/actions/measures are often based on *probable outcomes* envisaged in *scenario-building*. In fact, practically all major measures have positive and negative consequences with the best of intentions. As an example of what transpired under military regimes in Nigeria, a much-lauded loan scheme to farmers and small and medium scale enterprises (SMEs), implemented through deregulated financial services providers of all types - finance houses and scores of mushroom banks, and a handful of badly managed larger banks - anyone and everybody, including generals, top bureaucrats and businesses floated by the financial institutions themselves, became farmers and SMEs and were beneficiaries without envisaged improvement in production and supply of agricultural produce and vibrancy of and job-creation by SMEs. Or, the case of land reform through the infamous Land Use Act which handed over everybody's access to land to politicians, and which till date has not made supply of land for farming and other purposes any easier – and land acquisition regulatory officials imposing high charges especially in urban areas, that only a few can afford, for plots.

A few instructive points may be made in respect of both examples of reform measures in Nigeria. The first is that, in some instances, one comes away with the impression that a good many policy-makers and legislators have no rudimentary grasp of trumpeted economic models and attendant policy instruments. From Lindblom's unapologetic description of incrementalism, they just "muddle through", or "make do" with what is available by their own judgement or inclinations or what they have been asked to do. To these, the measure or reform is an act of faith, handed down by political authorities with a couple of persons implanted by the relevant international development and UNO agency on hand to guide the process. While for others, the ease with which models are sometimes confused with or regarded as reality is astonishing, if not shocking. Embedded in and core to *laissez faire* economics is *uncertainty*, hence *risk-taking* by producers and investors on the supply side. This is ignored and the major reform measures are instead trumpeted as panaceas to uncertain and fluid situations. It may, in defence of this, be argued that such posturings are marketing ploys to facilitate wider acceptance of announced policy or measure. Even at that, this is given the lie by state or political authorities digging in or proving recalcitrant to changing such a measure or policy in the face of contrary evidence (e.g. the Land Use Act which retired generals and their civilian cohorts always ensure is retained in the Constitution, and Babangida's infamous "There is no alternative to SAP") at greater economic cost to all and to "the economy".

The second, and which flows from the first, deregulation and uncertainty in market transactions mean risking-taking should be taken by those who wish to, individualised. In this case, by persons, families, communities and corporate bodies in private transactions. Production and buying decisions are private. For centuries, access to land in most parts of West Africa and areas which later became Nigeria was never centralised. With regards to agricultural productivity, from the 1890s to early 1960s when largely peasant farmers fed European and British industries with raw materials and respective local populations, access to land was private and communal, and it is doubtful agricultural production can compare favourably since the Land Use Decree (Act) was imposed.

Quite similar consideration may be extended to the oil and gas sector where Shell-BP and other crude oil-prospecting and producing companies for nearly half a century dealt directly with land-owning families and communities and sorted out compensations, and officially in recognition of "origin", the principle of derivation accounting for 50 per cent in the revenue sharing formula for *all* export proceeds or revenue between and among the politico-administrative units (regions) was agreed at collective negotiations. The post-Civil War military politicians and their civilian cohorts and spurious geniuses took crude oil out of the basket of exports, also as "reform", declaring it a "national asset", and via numerous legislations and operations of the National Oil Corporation (NAOC) and its predecessor, the Nigerian National Petroleum Corporation (NNPC), corralled the activities of the companies in that sector. With *state agencies* interposed between families and communities and the *private companies* over issues of access to land and degradation of the environment (ownership by the former of the crude oil in their land declared out of the question albeit in an ostensibly private enterprise economy) through spillages, emissions and noise not satisfactorily resolved, certain groups and communities in the Niger Delta region in particular have, from their reactions, become branded "anti-government", "militants", "unpatriotic", "disgruntled" and suchlike epithets. Reforms and conflict are still ongoing!

Fourth, the intricacies of implementation have often been the taken-for-granted but remain Achilles heels of many a measure. The attention-grabbing event has remained the initiating MDA or minister or Mr President making the well-orchestrated formal announcement and, where necessary, an enabling legislation decreed or enacted. In the era of neo-liberalism in particular, the frontal implementers may actually be in the private sector (say, banks, insurance companies and other financial institutions) where daily or weekly monitoring might actually prove infeasible because of their large numbers and physical distribution or locations, and elongated and bureaucratised feedback loop. In any case, where such profit-driven implementers consider their involvement less than profitable, nonchalance and obstructive tactics lead to delays and thus distortions in both the process and outcomes.

A related facet, paradoxically and ironically, is the not uncommon phenomenon of these private sector-embedded implementers metamorphosing into part-regulators too, cosier with representatives of international development and donor agencies interested in or sponsoring specific reforms or measures, or projects, wittingly or unwittingly explaining away deviations, different outcomes or lack of outcomes caused by themselves in course of "guiding" bureaucrats from their presumed advantageous position. The resultant "lack of implementation" phenomenon Nigerians so bemoan now, ironically, offer the basis for another round of foreign exchange-consuming 'capacity building' project for bureaucrats, as part of broader 'civil service reforms'. It may be objected that some bureaucrats, given type of qualifications and skills, the political decision of transferring them from their respective states, and general poor performance, training and re-training should be done. But such training does not have to be tied to a particular reform measure.

Fifth, there are instances where and when policy formulators and representatives of targeted segment of society so fully understand theoretical and other underpinnings of the measure or policy, but out of symbiosis or meeting of minds on both sides, or inertia, the implementation may run against its legal basis as evidenced, for example, in aspects of trade union law in Nigeria. Some ILO's Conventions (ratified by Nigerian governments) cover freedom of association and voluntarism, the right to organise, collective bargaining and all that, which are also recognised by the Nigerian Constitution of 1999. Yet, the trade union structure of industrial unions and senior staff associations, forcibly separating so-called junior workers from senior workers, has been legally imposed and Schedule III of the Trade Union Act, not to be seen anywhere else in the world, actually identifies the unions by name. Another provision imposes compulsory check-off system for collecting union members' dues (a purely internal matter of the trade unions), as well as imposing recognition of trade unions on employers! The Federal Ministry of Labour and trade union leaders appear quite comfortable with the situation, an apparent conceding of greater state intrusion by trade union leadership for the impossibility of dissenting members forming their own trade union by virtue of the Schedule III mentioned above, more regular income for union bureaucracies, among other pay-offs, the critic would argue. It might just as well be, on the other hand, as it played out that members, union leadership, and regulatory state agencies place greater premium on more institutionally and financially stable labour organisations than on dogged insistence on full compliance with relevant ILO Convention. Whichever the case, the lack of full compliance with these Conventions would always be the lurking shadow that will not go away, likely to be pursued by any of the parties under changing circumstances as "reform".

A second example is the "reform" of the National Industrial Court (NIC). In its original form, it was a voluntary and tripartite body on which sat representatives of the state, private employers and organised labour to foster voluntary settlement of trade disputes. Apart from long drawn-out procedure for sorting out matters brought before it and other financial constraints, the judicial officers therein were wont to protest also their "inferior" status to their counterparts in other arms of the judiciary. In 2006, President Obasanjo "reformed" the NIC, which basically was letting the judicial officers have same compensation or terms of employment as others in the judiciary, usurpation of the powers by the state to appoint all members and thus eliminating its voluntary tripartite structure, and strengthening the powers of an industrial court as final arbiter in employment relations matters. This is not to imply that the voluntary version of a labour court is necessarily more effective or that it is preferable; but that was what it was. Rather, attention is here drawn to the *direction* of the reform and to its *principal* beneficiaries, at least in the short run. Needless mentioning that the cost of litigation has escalated for employers, trade unions and workers who must now have lawyers to present and prosecute their cases as they do in the other courts! And it is a moot point if cases are settled more speedily now. Anyway, nearly a decade on, the Labour law reform bills, outcomes of tripartite committees funded by the ILO, are yet to be considered by the National Assembly! More reforms to come if and when it does so!

A third example is the status of a federal permanent secretary, the zenith for any civil servant at the federal level. General Babangida, as part of his own "reforms", not only changed the nomenclature of permanent secretary to "director-general", decreed them to be "political appointees" and to leave office with the appointing government or regime, thereby in one fell swoop truncating their careers and distorting career structure in the federal civil service. Although reversed by succeeding dictators, it took another general, President Olusegun Obasanjo, nearly two decades on, in another dose of reform, to surreptitiously amend relevant section of the Constitution to re-designate permanent secretaries as "political appointees", just for them to earn 300 per cent salary of what a permanent secretary used to earn, and nearly 350 per cent of the salary of the next-in-command, the director, and bring earnings of "political appointee permanent secretary" at par with those of legislators and other political appointees! Professors who, right up to the First Republic earned more than a permanent secretary were now reduced to the same level as directors in the ministries. Compensation differentials aside, to bypass usual processes and procedures that might have rendered this transformation difficult to achieve, the Revenue Mobilisation Allocation and Fiscal Commission (RMAFC) was underhandedly and unwarrantedly pushed into the business of evaluating and sorting out compensation issues of certain categories of public servants (political appointees in particular), the previously exclusive preserve of the National Salaries, Incomes and Wages Commission (NSIWC). We find here therefore one seemingly simple reform, as reactions and repercussions set in, that will likely trigger another comprehensive adjustment of wages and differentials in the civil service, and attempts to reverse the current structurally untenable position of political appointee permanent secretary.

Reform, we may now fruitfully admit, comes in various forms. One could reform a *process* or *procedure*, say, of designing and implementing leave roster, or payment of salaries of all federal public servants taken over by the Central Bank of Nigeria, or procedure for acquisitions and purchases, or method of payment and collection of personal or corporate tax, and method of preparing a budget, method or process of importing and distributing refined petroleum products. Or, reform might be of *institutional* type: a sub-unit of an organisation may be reformed, as well as the whole organisation may itself be restructured or reformed, rearranging span of control and positions and levels in the hierarchy, or how several organisations may, in fact, relate to one another (e.g. the NNPC Group). Or, it might relate to access to some *value*: social justice, freedom and mode of worship, procedure for accessing land, or funds for agricultural purposes, unemployment benefits, health and medical services, housing, education, right to vote, freedom of association, right to abortion, right to speak freely, right to free movement, etc.

Quite often, it should be sounded, a specific reform might not only involve the three forms, but also push for a rank-ordering of values, processes and institutions in one go. For example, the privatisation of telecommunications sector in the same breath imposed the provision of such services by private companies and individuals, leaving the security and protection of private data or information also in their hands, as well as the determination of mode and types of payment, and capping it all with the remarkable transformation of speed of communication and social relations. Communication at personal and organisational level now appear to be totally dependent on the operations of these private telecoms providers, the priority for most decision makers being acquisition of mobile phones, Internet access, use of short message system (sms), transmission of messages and documents via email and website development, thereby transforming the decision-making processes of, and how organisations and public administration work - not to mention success or failure of security and intelligence agencies! The individual is more likely to spend last penny on recharging the mobile phone than on a meal, while many organisations would keep their communications system running at the cost of delaying payment of salaries and wages, for example!

We noted in passing that the dynamism and directions of group practices, values, culture and constantly evolving socio-political and economic circumstances easily render certain anticipated outcomes false, some reforms redundant or counter-productive, and requiring further reforms to offset shortcomings. Whose reforms? Which outcomes? Whose shortcomings?

RATIONALITY IN CHOICES AND DECISION-MAKING

There is the unstated assumption of conscious and rational decision-making on the part of *initiators* and *demanders* of reforms, at least going by the definition of Reform in the opening paragraph, where a current situation may be seen and defined as being *unsatisfactory*. *Improving* upon existing situation thus implies a consideration of replacement (or modification) options and means for achieving the best or most appropriate option in the circumstances. By definition, then, individuals, families and organisations tend to make decisions rationally, where rationality represents a conscious attempt at making choices in the process of understanding and relating possible and actual means to possible goals.

But the resurgence of *laissez faire* economics, *neo-liberalism*, what constitutes most appropriate public policy and public administration is now more divisive and more contentious than ever, especially when the economy is in crisis and impoverishment along all dimensions is undeniably on the increase worldwide today. Welfare economics idea of “development planning”, the conception of policy making as a process of rational analysis culminating in a value-maximising decision – that is, arriving and implementing the best possible solution to a given problem - is challenged, and often derided, by those who espouse “incrementalism”, arguing that imperfect conditions, including state of communications and complexity of society facing the decision-maker (ambiguous and poorly defined problems; incomplete information about alternatives; incomplete information about the baseline, the background of the problem; incomplete information about the consequences of supposed alternatives; incomplete information about the range and content of values, preferences, and interests, and limited time, limited skills, and limited resources) favour several small incremental steps than a wholesale or comprehensive overhauling of existing policy or practice. It is thus more rewarding in such a state of affairs to trade off options (satisficing) and settling for what is practicable, and doable, since having to think through every possible alternative is not even feasible from this perspective.

It is has to be admitted that the scenarios outlined immediately above are commonsensical enough and might apply readily to a whole range of routine decision making, the decision maker relying on memory, precedence or experience, knowledge of similar occurrences and time constraint to opt for Choice A rather than Choice B. Indeed, certain choices are rendered predictable, if not inevitable, by custom, and others unreflectingly taken via habituation or rote, prejudged inconsequential. Even after making allowance for all these, it is doubtful that in considering the reform of certain *processes* or *procedures*, certain *institutions* and certain *values* there would be that large degree of ambiguity over the problem or unsatisfactory condition, plagued by incomplete information on alternatives and their likely consequences and about content of values, preferences and interests. Except it is an entirely strange or novel situation, an *adjudged* unsatisfactory condition has *an history*, one that over time, no matter how limited, must have thrown up effects or repercussions policy-maker and those affected negatively have lived with and attention of state authorities correspondingly drawn to. Let us take the reform of the supply of refined petroleum products to the Nigerian market as an illustration.

What is the problem to be addressed? In spite of producing and exporting crude oil, all refined petroleum products are imported. *So, it took some ten years, 1956 to 1965, for local refinery to commence.*[5] The time for

[5] The technical details are briefly this. In 1965 Shell/BP built Port Harcourt I as a topping and reforming refinery with a distillation capacity of 3 million mt/yr (60,000 bpd).

Port Harcourt II was built as a complex refinery with a distillation capacity of 7.5 million mt/yr (150,000 bpd). It came on stream in 1989.

The Warri refinery is a complex refinery with a distillation capacity of 6.3 million mt/yr (125,000 bpd). The refinery came on stream in 1978. It is managed jointly with a petrochemicals plant built in 1986 to produce 35,000 mt/yr of polypropylene and 18,000 mt/yr of carbon black.

The Kaduna refinery is a complex refinery with a distillation capacity of 5.5 million mt /yr (110,000 bpd). The first 50,000 bpd unit, built in 1980, was a fuels unit designed to run light Nigerian crude. It was later revamped to 60,000bpd by the addition of a pre-flash unit. In 1982, a 50,000 bpd sour crude unit was built, designed to provide feed to a lube base oil manufacturing plant, an asphalt plant, and an

considering possibilities and likely consequences could not have been a hindering factor here.

As for incomplete background information, until 1960, government participation in the oil industry was limited to the regulation and administration of fiscal policies. In 1971, Nigeria joined OPEC and in line with OPEC resolutions, the Nigerian National Oil Corporation (NNOC) was established, later becoming NNPC in 1977. With all its subsidiary companies, the NNPC controls and dominates all sectors of the oil industry, both upstream and downstream.

Nigeria's first oil refinery, at Alesa Eleme near Port Harcourt, began operations in late 1965 with a capacity of 38,000 barrels per day, enough to meet domestic requirements at the time. The refinery expanded production to 60,000 barrels per day after the Civil War but failed to satisfy the demands of a rapidly growing economy. An additional refinery, delayed by political manoeuvring over its location, was constructed at Warri, opening in 1978 with a capacity of 100,000 barrels per day. This plant was entirely owned by the NNPC, which starting in 1979 also held an 80 per cent interest in the earlier plant. Technical problems and shutdowns for routine maintenance reduced production, and the combined total of petroleum processed by the two plants in 1979 averaged 89,000 barrels per day - about 83 per cent of the domestic requirement.

In the late 1970s and early 1980s, the NNPC had substantial amounts of oil refined abroad (mostly by Shell) to make up the shortfall, and some oil was also processed in Cameroon, Ghana, and Ivory Coast. In October 1980, a third refinery, with a capacity of 100,000 barrels per day, began operations at Kaduna, but did not become fully productive until the mid-1980s. A fourth refinery was completed in March 1989 at Alesa Eleme, increasing Nigeria's refining capacity to 445,000 barrels per day. Domestic petroleum demand stood at 250,000 barrels per day, so a portion of the output of the four refineries could now be exported. However, by the early 1990s gasoline output was sufficiently short of the growing domestic demand to require that the NNPC still refine some gasoline abroad.

So, from the first refinery in the country which bought its own crude oil, refined, sold and kept proceeds of sales and duly declared dividends, to the subsidiaries of the NNPC which originally were self-governing limited liability companies and employed their own personnel to when, borrowing a

---

Linear Alkyl Benzate (LAB) plant. The plant was initially designed to run Venezuelan crude, but was later re-certified to produce lubes from Arab Light crude.

In 1987 the LAB plant was started up. The plant can manufacture 30,000 mt/year of LAB, 15,000 mt/year of benzene, and 30,000 mt/year of kero solvent, but has not operated since 1998. A drum plant was also installed, and a 6,000 bpd asphalt blowing unit.

leaf from the book of military politicians who moved everything to Abuja from Lagos, the subsidiaries were reduced to substantially internal units directly administered from NNPC Group Headquarters, and any refinery thereafter placing order for an urgently need part would pass through a bit over fifty-three steps, thereby making nonsense of supply chain management and institutionalizing frequent breakdowns, epileptic supplies of refined products especially as turn-around maintenance contracts were awarded above their heads to trading middlemen and those cornering the importation of refined petroleum products.

Then the spin-offs from the politics of federal character and internal dynamics of the NNPC group leading to over-manning and "oga-no-gree", an organogram where several categories of staff are "untouchables" irrespective of their positions in the hierarchy and reporting to no one in particular except to those who put them there. And amazingly, its pensioners' monthly pension exceed their previous monthly salaries as full-time employees, an incredible HR policy no doubt egged on by the two trade unions in the oil and gas industry and is certainly the most generous pension scheme anywhere in the world and whose formula HRM experts should pay a lot to obtain - but likely to prove unworkable in non-Nigerian circumstances.

So, some thirty years and more on, much-needed and predictable plain old *decentralization* of the NNPC group, under long-drawn out reform, becomes new buzz word "UNBUNDLING" and the politics of *re-naming* and *realigning* of respective jurisdictions of the subsidiaries and proposed methods of funding of joint ventures with multinationals and other foreign investors and employment possibilities assume the mask of *Petroleum Industry Bill* (PIB). My two favourite questions for nearly two decades to NNPC staff on the Chief Officers Course where I made presentation titled "Globalisation and Management of Public Enterprises" have been; one, the NNPC as an organization, what is its *core area* or *specialisation* if it is to be competitive and earn good returns on the public funds devoted to it? That is, what it is best at and can match or beat the competition, given that the era of jack of all trades by any business concern in a globalising world is gone. Exploration? Production? Refining? Second, if all the subsidiaries, as *limited liability companies*, specialised already, regain their full *autonomy*, what becomes of the very large NNPC Group Head Quarters? Both questions are usually met with uncomfortable silence and sighs and "This is Nigeria" remark.

What about ambiguity of content of values, preferences and interests regarding supply of refined petroleum products? As for the interests, the head of state or Mr President, First Ladies under military regimes especially, the Oil Majors, the handful of licensed and unlicensed importers, the so-called Independent Marketers, vested interests within the NNPC group, caucuses of ruling political parties and their local and foreign business fronts or partners and owners of storage facilities or tank farms strewn across the country are clearly unambiguous interests, dictating the importation, storage and distribution of the products.

Values and preferences would seem also not too difficult to make out: continued reliance on private sector-driven profitable importation of refined petroleum products, continuation of payment of "subsidies' to those importing, pump prices substantially fixed between state authorities and importers and independent marketers (despite a few very noisy public protests over the years spearheaded by organised labour and the existence of a tripartite Petroleum Products Pricing Regulatory Agency), institutionalisation of periodic acute nationwide shortages of refined petroleum products - with accompanying wrenching disorganisation of everyday life, sharp rise in cost of living (inter-and intra-city transport, food, etc.) and cost of running businesses (especially family, small and medium scale) and loss of millions of man-hours, a litre not really a litre at the pumps in many locations and cities despite valiant efforts of a short-staffed Department of Petroleum Resources (DPR), the unaccounted for over ninety by-products from local crude oil refined abroad, the right of pump attendants to sell to whomever they want, preventing, in the process and under the regulatory gaze of armed policemen and soldiers, the majority of end-users who have only jerry cans and smaller containers from buying, a thriving black market managed by rough-and-tumble young men on behalf of independent marketers who supply them above anyone else, endemic insufficiency of electricity, and so on *ad nauseam.*

Few will disagree with the conclusion that in this day and age, some sixty-one years, 1965 to 2025, could not have been too short a time for successive political leaders and policy-makers to "muddle through" and implement a policy for regular supply of refined petroleum products in Nigeria, public or private sector-driven. Many policies, like this one, carry grave economic, social and political consequences, in the final analysis, for all. Rising social and physical insecurity, for example, affect all even when one lives in a well secured or guarded property and drives a bullet-proof vehicle: you have to come out at some point, if only for some trial-and-error mechanic to replace the fake parts flooding the market via reforms, in the car! The dearth of well-staffed and well equipped medical facilities, public and private, portend reduced capacity to avoid preventable adverse medical conditions and deaths, and whether one affords to die in style in the UK or India or Malaysia or China or the United States of America, death is death and not only the poor are dying from all manner of ailments in a very stressful environment.

CONCLUDING COMMENTS

The burden of this brief comment on the idea of Reform is to reinforce the reality that what constitutes "life" sociologically is merely but a series of choices embodied in decisions made, most of them made in circumstances determined by others since we are quite unable to meet all our wants and desires alone. This is common sense enough. While at the collective level, public policy and public administration, among other factors, serve to constrain the range of choices so available by the type of reforms and their manner of implementation, feedback loop and chances of review and/or abandonment altogether. Sometimes, many choices are not freely made, if those are the only ones presented by the situation or context as created or designed by others. A persistently nasty life-style affects choices and decisions; it provokes. Those provoked and engaging in all manner of untraditional and unexpected behaviour may successfully be apprehended by the "law" and punished or jailed. However, when a large percentage of the population is so punished and jailed, that itself is a statement about the quality of life and type of society choices of reforms have wrought since no baby at birth is a criminal.

Second, whatever is labelled "reform" is far more complex than is initially supposed, whether by incrementalists or comprehensive rationalists. If we borrow from Herbert Spencer, a notable English eighteenth century philosopher and sociologist, that "every active force produces more than one change – every cause produces more than one effect," monitoring and efficacy of the feedback loop or arrangements would appear critical to the relative success of any policy and, more crucially, minimising adverse impacts. This, I believe, the rise and development of the NNPC Group, its relationship with the Ministry of Petroleum Resources, the National Assembly, the Presidency, other regulatory agencies (NAPIMS, DPR, PPPR, etc.) the Oil Majors, the Independent Petroleum Marketers Association of Nigeria (IPMAN), the trade unions and the consuming public in the supply of refined petroleum products have demonstrated convincingly.

Third, *emulation* is a strong impetus to advancement generally, but there are boundaries, peculiarities which are ignored at often very considerable cost. For example, British institutions (companies, managements, trades unions, public administration, educational institutions, law enforcement agencies, etc.) and way they function are far removed from their American counterparts although both run private enterprise economic system. There is no social institution that can be successfully borrowed inclusive of underlying cultural values and centuries of practices. Neither unsuccessful borrowing nor being guinea-pigs of lab-designed experiments and think-tanks scenario-building is desirable for the lives of over 200 million people, of whom an overwhelming proportion is desperately poor. By all accounts, there is nothing ambiguous about chronic poverty and lack of adequate social and physical infrastructures.

Fourth, whether from the perspective of society as made of various competing interest groups, and each sectional group actively organising to promote and protect such interest (pluralist doctrine) as discussed earlier, or Marxists who insist on a class divided society in which those who "own the means of production" share same orientation and destiny with policy-makers and public administrators and control the state apparatus, under neo-liberalism, it should be admitted, a policy of wholesale reduction or elimination of inequalities, especially poverty and unemployment, is never on offer because such is incompatible with the trickle-down logic and operations of market economy. The concern is not for society-wide social justice, it is argued, but the efficiency of the market mechanism in distributing scarce value – even where it is glaring that political parties, politicians and the business community do exercise preponderance influence over policies, policy-makers and public administration in Nigeria than other groups, for example. The irregular supply of refined petroleum products in Nigeria is still quite profitable after half a century – whatever the inconveniences or the negative social and economic impacts!

Some *individuals* and *companies now own* the crude oil deposits, like other minerals, through and after the military regimes, 'governing' political parties and state authorities impounded them as "national" assets by "law", the impounding "laws" being: 1) Petroleum Act 1969 (which gave the federal government ownership of all petroleum in Nigeria, including deposits in territorial waters, the continental shelf and the Exclusive Economic Zone); 2) Land Use Act 1978 (that vests all land in each state in the Governor, who holds it in trust for the peoples, and grants individuals and corporations rights of occupancy, rather than ownership); 3) Nigerian Minerals and Mining Act 2007 that gives the federal government control of all mineral resources in the country, and labels the owners "host communities" which "entitles" them to some pittance set aside in the Budget as part of the Revenue Allocation and Sharing Formula, depriving true owners, families and communities access and usage.

Most of the "reforms" suggested over the last two decades have related more to intensifying state control and centralisation of power, like under colonialism as already discussed, by deploying all law enforcement agencies (army, navy, air force, police, intelligence outfits, etc.) and the creation of new and armed to-the-teeth "special units" to roll back the life-saving activities of poverty-stricken communities that are now collectively criminalised as "illegal miners" – even in the embarrassing context of partly non-accountability and partly dubious accountability for outputs of legal mining activities (crude oil especially) and one of the ten largest producers of crude oil in the world unable for decades to refine enough domestically after millions and millions of dollars spent on so-called 'rehabilitation' of a few refineries, persistence of acute shortage of refined petroleum products, costly energy prices and deleterious effect on general prices of goods and services and quality of life!

A quick throwback to refresh even unwilling minds and memories about pivotal 'reforms' in the area called Nigeria: i) owned and occupied for centuries by different ethnic groups that fought and sorted out intra- and inter-ethnic conflicts, thereafter witnessed internal and externally institutionalised slave trade, the appearance of trading Europeans and companies that focused on where they could obtain agricultural produce and minerals, a process formalised and entrenched through decentralised colonial system of occupation and governance; ii) anti-colonialism of a coterie of local ethnic elites who eventually earned "Independence" of which their First Republic was based on colonially inherited decentralised political system and administration; iii) a system which "northern-dominated" military regimes that seized power via coups and three-year long Civil War terminated and centralised; iv) successive 'Republics', ostensibly civilian-led remained 'land of the Generals' and their cohorts in political parties and state agencies entrenching a centralised option. It is thus, for example, not totally unexpected, given antecedents, insistence on a continuing federal policy of free cattle grazing (that is private business), everywhere and through individual and communal farms (causing thousands of prematurely brutally ended lives via clashes) which, after all, by policy are on lands that are "national" property. The State then determines ownership of land and mineral resources, and thus individual and communal rights via legislation and enforcement practices. What exactly does one accurately call this type of country and society where the professional legal groups and their organs (lawyers, bar associations, judicial institutions, etc.), pro-democracy institutions and practices, intellectual community at all levels, so-called organised interest and human rights groups (especially trade unions), do not see those three pieces of legislation and attendant policies as threats to fundamental human and individual rights and freedom? What is this State? Reforming the Reformer…

BIBLIOGRAPHY

Abiodun, M. O., *Restructuring of Trade Unions in Nigeria*, 1976-1978, Salama Press, Jos, 1978

Adeogun, A.A. 'Strikes and the Institutionalization of Labour Protest: the Case of Nigeria.' Seminar on Third World Strikes, Hague, 1977.

Akinyemi, A.B., 'The Social Implications of Adebo,' *Quarterly Journal of Administration*, Ife, Oct. 1971-1972 July

Akpala, A. 'Industrial Relations Policies in Nigeria,' *Genieve Afrique*, vol. 10(1), 1971.

—. *Industrial Relations Model for Developing Countries: the Nigerian System*, Fourth Dimensions Press, Enugu, 1982.

— *Managing Industrial Relations in Nigeria: A Case Study of the Nigerian Coal Industry*, Dept. of Management of Univ. of Nigeria, Nsukka, 1984.

Alavi, H. 'The State in Postcolonial Societies,' *New Left Review*, vol. 74, 1972.

Allen, V.L. *The Sociology of Industrial Relations*, Longman, 1971.

Amin, S., *Neocolonialism in West Africa*, Penguin, 1973.

Ananaba, W. *The Trade. Union Movement in Nigeria*, Ethiope Publishing Company, Benin, 1969.

Anon, 'The Influence of International Labour Conventions on Nigerian Labour Legislation, *International Labour Review*, Vol. 82(1), 1960.

Baran, P., *The Political Economy of Growth*, Pelican, 1976

Berg, E.J. 'Urban Real Wage and the Nigerian Trade Union Movement 1939-1960: A Comment.' *Economic Development and Cultural Change, (EDCC)*, vol. 17(4), 1969.

Berg, E.J. & Butler, J. 'Trade Unions' in J.S. Coleman & C.G. Rosberg, (eds.), *Political Parties and National Integration in Tropical Africa*, Univ. of California Press, Berkeley & Los Angeles, 1964.

Bowers, P. 'The Mining Industry,' in PERHAM, M. (ed.), *Mining, Commerce and Finance in Nigeria*, Faber & Faber, 1948.

Cameron, D. *My Tanganyika Service and Some Nigeria*, London, 1939.

Clegg, H.A., *Industrial Democracy and Natonalisation*, Blackwell, Oxford, 1951.

Clegg, H.A., *A New Approach to Industrial Democracy*, Blackwell, Oxford, 1960

Cohen, R. 'Further Comment on the Kilby/Weeks Debate,' *Journal of Developing Areas*, vol. 5 (2), January 1971

-- *Labour and Politics in Nigeria*, Heinemann, 1974.

Cohen, R., Gutkind, P.C.W., and Brazier, P. (eds.), *Peasants and Proletarians*, Hutchinson, London, 1974.

Coleman, J.S. *Nigeria: Background to Nationalism*, Univ. of California Press, Berkeley & Los Angeles, 1958

Coleman, J.S. & Rosberg, C.G. *Political Parties and National Integration in Tropical Africa,* Univ. of California Press, Berkeley & Los Angeles, 1964.

Commons, J.R. *et al.*, *The History of Labor in the United States*, McNally, Chicago, 1967

Crowder, M. *The Story of Nigeria*, Faber, London, 1966.

— *West Africa Under Colonial Rule*, Hutchinson, 1968.

Dahl, R. *Preface to Democratic Theory*, Chicago University Press, 1956.

— *Pluralist Democracy in America,* McNally, Chicago, 1967.

Dahrendorf, R. *Class and Class Conflict in Industrial Society,* Routledge & Kegan Paul, London, 1959.

Damachi, U.G. and SeibeL, H.D. (eds.), *Social Change and Economic Development in Nigeria*, Praeger, 1973.

Dare, L.O. 'Nigerian Military Governments and the Quest for Legitimacy,' *Nigerian Journal of Economic and Social Studies,* vol. 17(2), 1975.

Davies, I. 'The Politics of the TUC's Colonial Policy,' *Political Quarterly,* vol. 35(1), 1958.

— *African Trade Unions,* Penguin, Harmondsworth, 1966.

Diejomaoh, V.P., 'Industrial Relations in a Development Contexts: the Case of Nigeria.' in DAMACHI, U.G. *et al.* (eds.), *Industrial Relations in Africa,* Macmillan, 1979

Dike, D.O., *Trade and Politics in the Niger Delta*, OUP, 1956

Dudley, B.J. 'Violence in Nigerian Politics,' *Transition,* vol. 5, 1965.

— 'Federalism and the Balance of Political Power in Nigeria,' *Journal of Commonwealth Political Studies,* vol. 4, 1966.

— *Parties and Politics in Northern Nigeria,* Frank Cass, London, 1968.

— *Instability and Political Order: Politics and Crisis in Nigeria,* University of Ibadan Press, Ibadan, 1973.

Dunlop, J.T. *Industrial Relations System,* Southern Illinois Univ. Press, Carbonsdale & Edwardsville, 1958.

Egboh, E.O., 'The Early Years of Trade Unionism in Nigeria,' *African Quarterly*, Vol. 8(1), 1968.

- 'Trade Union Education in Nigeria, 1940-1964.' African Studies Review, Vol. XIV, 1968.
- 'Pre-Trade Union Labor Relations in Nigeria,' *Insight*, V ol.7, 1972.
- 'Labour Relations in Nigeria: the Development of Joint Consultative and Negotiating Machinery, 1940-1964,' *Acta Africana*, Vol. II, 1972.

Ekundare, R.O. *An Economic History of Nigeria*, 1860-1960, Methuen, London, 1973.

— 'Salary and Wages Reviews Since 1946,' *Quarterly Journal of Administration*, Ife, Oct. 1971-1972 July.

Emiola, A. *Nigerian Labour Law*, Univ. of Ibadan Press, 1980.

Ezera, K. *Constitutional Developments in Nigeria*, Cambridge University Press, 1960.

Falola, T. & Ihonvbere, J. *The Rise and Fall of Nigeria's Second Republic*, Zed Press, London, 1985.

Fanon, F. *The Wretched of the Earth*, Penguin, 1973.

Fashoyin, T. *Industrial Relations in Nigeria*, Longman, 1980.

Federal Ministry of Information, Report of the Commission on the Review of Wages, Salaries and Conditions of Service of the Junior Employees of the Governments (Morgan Commission), Lagos, 1964.

- First, Second and Final Reports of the Wages and Salaries Review Commission (Adebo Commission), Lagos, 1970 and 1971 respectively.
- Report of the Structure and Salaries and Wages Review Commission on Public Services (Udoji Commission, Lagos, 1974.
- Report of the Tribunal of Inquiry into the Activities of the Trade Unions (Adebiyi Report), Lagos, 1977.

Federal Ministry (Dept.) of Labour, Annual Reports, Lagos, 1940-1969.

- *Quarterly Reviews*, Lagos, 1944-1968.

Flanders, A., *Management and Unions*, Faber & Faber, 1970

Fox, A. *Industrial Sociology and Industrial Relations*, HMSO, London, 1966.

— 'Industrial Relations: A Social Critique of Pluralist Ideology,' in J. Child (ed.), *Man and Organisation*, George Allen 8; Unwin, London, 1973.

Frank, A.G. *Capitalist Underdevelopment in Latin America*, Monthly Review Press, New York, 1969.

Freund, B. *Capital and Labour in Nigerian Tin Mines*, Univ. of Ibadan Press, Ibadan, 1981

Galbraith, K., *The New Industrial State*, Houghton Mifflin, 1967

Galenson. W., *Labour and Economic Development*, John Wiley, New York, 1959.

- *Labour in Developing Countries*, University of California Press, Berkeley & Los Angeles, 1963.
- *Comparative Labour Movements*, Prentice-Hall, Englewood Cliffs, New Jersey, 1953.

Geary, W.N.M. *Nigeria Under Colonial Rule*, Frank Cass, London, 1965.

Geiss, I., 'Some Remarks on the Development of African Trade Unions, 'journal of the Historical Society of Nigeria, V01.3(2), 1965

Goulbourne, H. (ed.), *Politics and State in the Third World, Macmillan,* London, 1979.

Gutkind, P.C.W. & Wallerstein, I. (eds.), *The Political Economy of Contemporary Africa,* Sage, Beverley Hills & London, 1976.

Gutkind, P.C.W. & Waterman, P. (eds.), *African Social Studies: A Radical Reader,* Heinemann, London, 1977.

Gutkind, P.C.W., Cohen, R., Copans, J. *(eds.), African Labour History,* Sage, Beverly Hills & London, 1978.

Hailey, Lord, *An African Survey*, OUP, London, 1938

Hinchcliffe, K., 'Labour Aristocracy - A Northern Nigeria Case Study,' *Journal of Modern African Studies* (JMAS), Vol. 12, 1974

H.M.S.O., Report by Sir F.D. Lugard on the Amalgamation of Northern and Southern Nigeria and Administration, 1912-1919, Cmd. 468, London, 1920.

Report of the Tudor Davies Commission into the Cost of Living in the Colony and Protectorate of Nigeria, No. 204, London. 1946.

Report of the Commission of Enquiry into the Disorders in the Eastern Provinces of Nigeria, No.256, London, 1950.

Hodgkin, T. *Nationalism in Colonial Africa,* Frederick Muller, 1956.

— *African Political Parties,* Penguin, 1961.

Hoogvelt, A. Indigenization and Foreign Capital: Industrialisation in Nigeria,' *Review of African Political Economy, 14,* January-April, 1979.

Hopkins, A.G. The Lagos Strike of 1897: an Exploration in Nigerian Labour History,' *Past & Present,* vol. 35, 1966.

— *An Economic History of West Africa,* Longman, 1973.

Hughes, A. & Cohen R., *Towards the Emergence of a Nigerian Working Class, 1897-1939*, Occasional Papers Series D, No.7, Faculty of Commerce & Social Science, University of Birmingham, 1971.

Hyman, R. *Industrial Relations: A Marxist Introduction, Macmillan,* London, 1975.

Ikime, O. (ed.), *Groundwork of Nigerian History,* Heinemann, Ibadan, 1980.

I.L.O., Mission to the USSR Reports, Geneva, 1927 and 1960

Imosili, C.I., 'Collective Bargaining in the Nigerian Private Sector,' *Labour and Society*, Vol. 9(4), 1984

Kassalow, E. & Damachi, U.G. (eds.), The Role of Trade Unions in Developing Societies, International Institute for Labour Studies, Geneva, 1978.

Kayode, M.O., 'Trade Union Finance in Nigeria,' in Damachi, U.G. & Seibel, D.H. (eds.), *Social Change and Economic Development in Nigeria*, Praeger, New York, 1973.

Kilby, P. 'Industrial Relations and Wage Determination: Failure of the Anglo-Saxon Model,' *Journal of Developing Areas (JDA)*, vol. 1(14), July 1967.

— 'A Reply to John F. Weeks' Comment,' *JDA*, vol. 3(1), October 1968.

— 'Further Comment on the Kilby/Weeks Debate: Final Observations,' *JDA*, vol. 5(2), January 1971.

— *Industrialization in an Open Economy: Nigeria 1944-1966,* Cambridge University Press, 1969

Kirk-Green, A. *Crisis and Conflict in Nigeria: Documentary Source-book,* vols. 1&2, OUP, London, 1971.

Lenin, V.I., *What Is to Be Done?* Foreign Language Press, Peking, 1975.

- *Collected Works*, Vol. V, Foreign Languages Publishing House, 1961

Lester, R.A., *As Unions Mature*, Princeton University Press, 1958

Lipset S.M, Trow M. & Coleman J.S., *Union Democracy*, Achor Books, Garden City, New York, 1956

Little, K. *West African Urbanization: A Study in Voluntary Associations in Social Change,* Cambridge University Press, 1965.

Lloyd, P.C. (ed.). *The New Elites .of Tropical Africa,* OUP for the International African Institute, London, 1966.

— *Africa in Social Change,* Penguin, 1971.

Lodge, G.C., 'Labor's Role in Newly Developing Countries,' *Foreign Affairs*, Vol.37, 1959.

Lozovsky, A., in Mccarthy, W.E.J. (ed.) *Trade Unions*, Penguin, 1972.

Lynd, G.E.,(pseudonym), The Politics of African Unionism, Praeger, New York, 1968.

Lugard, F.D. *Political Memoranda,* Lagos, 1918. *Report on the Amalgamation of Northern and Southern Nigeria and Administration, 1912-1919,* Cmd. 468, HMSO, London, 1920.

Lynd, G.E. (pseud.), *The Politics of African Unionism,* Praeger, New York, 1968.

Mackintosh, J.P. *et al. Nigerian Government and Politics,* Allen & Unwin, 1966.

Marsh, A., *Concise .Encyclopaedia of Industrial Relations*, Gower Press, 1979.

Martin, P.G., 'Strategic Opportunities and Limitations: the Norwegian Labour Party and the Trade Unions,' ILRR Vol. 28, 1974-5.

Marx, K., *Poverty of Philosophy*, 1847 (1955 edn.).

Marx, K. & Engels, F., *Manifesto of the Communist Party*, Progress Publishers, 1975 edn.,

Melson, R. 'Nigerian Politics and the General Strike of 1964,' in Rotberg, R.I. & Mazrui, A.A. (eds.), *Protest and Power in Black Africa,* OUP, New York, 1970.

- Ideology and Inconsistency: the Cross-pressured Nigerian Worker,' *American Political Science Review*, Vol. LXV, No.1, 1971.

-The Political Dilemmas of the Nigerian Labor Movement,' in U.G. Damachi, & D.H. Seibel, (eds.), *Social Change and Economic Development in Nigeria,* Praeger, New York, 1973.

Meynaud, J. & Salah-Bey, A., *Trade Unionism in Africa*, Methuen, London 1974.

Michels, R., *Political Parties*, English Language edition, 1911.

Miliband, R., *the State in Capitalist Society*, Quartet, 1969.

Millen, B.H., *The Political Role of Labour in Developing Countries*, The Brookings Institution, Washington, 1963.

Nicholson, I.F. *The Administration of Nigeria 1900-1960: Men, Methods, and Myths,* Clarendon Press, Oxford, 1969.

Nkrumah, K. *Neocolonialism: The Last State of Imperialism,* Nelson, 1956.

Okonjo, I.M. *British Administration in Nigeria: A Nigerian View,* Nok Publishers, New York, 1974.

Olukoshi, Adebayo, *Nigerian External Debt Crisis: Management and Problems,* Malthouse Press and NIIA, Lagos & Oxford, 1990

Orde-Browne, G. St.., *Labour Conditions in West Africa Report*, Cmd. 6277, HMSO, 1941.

Orr, C., 'Trade Unionism in Colonial Africa,' *JMAS*, Vol.4, 1966

Osoba, O. 'The Nigerian Power Elite, 1952-1965,' in P.C.W. Gutkind, & P. Waterman (eds.), *African Social Studies: A Radical Reader,* Heinemann, London, 1977.

Otobo, D. 'The Nigerian General Strike of 1981,' *Review of African Political Economy*, vol. 22, 1981.

— 'The Political Clash in the Aftermath of the 1981 Nigerian General Strike,' *Review of African Political Economy*, vol. 25, 1982.

— 'Strikes in Nigeria: Some Considerations,' *Nigerian Journal of Economic and*

Social Studies, Nov. 1983.

— 'Bureaucratic Elites and Public Sector Wage Bargaining in Nigeria,' *Journal of Modern African Studies*, vol. 24(1), 1986

— *Foreign Interests and Nigerian Trade Unions*, Heinemann, Ibadan, 1986.

— *& Omole, M., Readings in Industrial Relations in Nigeria*, Malthouse, 1987

— *State and Industrial Relations in Nigeria*, Malthouse, *1988*

— *Further Readings in Nigerian Industrial Relations*, Malthouse, 1992

— *The Role of Trade Unions in Nigerian Industrial Relations*, Malthouse Press, Oxford, 1992

— *Labour Relations in Nigeria*, Vol I, Malthouse, 1993

— *The Trade Union Movement in Nigeria*, Malthouse, 2000

— *Industrial Relations: Theory and Controversies*, Malthouse, 2000

— *Essentials of Labour Relations in Nigeria Vol 1*, Malthouse, 2016

— *Essentials of Labour Relations in Nigeria, Vol 2*, Malthouse, 2016

— *Essentials of Labour Relations in Nigeria, Vol 3*, Malthouse, 2016

— *Reforms and Nigerian Laobur and Employment Relations*, Malthouse, 2016

Oyemakinde, W., 'Pullen Market System: A Trial in Food Price Control in Nigeria 1941-47,' *Journal of the Historical Society of Nigeria* (JHSN), Vol. 4(4), 1969

Panter-Brick, K. (ed.) *Nigerian Politics and Military Rule: Prelude to Civil War*, Anthione Press, London, 1970.

Peace, A. 'Industrial Protest in Ikeja,' in de E. Kadt & G.P. Williams (eds.) *Sociology and Development*, Tavistock, London, 1974.

— *Choice, Class and Conflict: A Study of Southern Nigerian Factory Workers*, Harvester, Brighton, 1979.

Perham, (ed.) *Mining, Commerce and Finance in Nigeria*, Faber & Faber, London, 1948.

Perlman, S., *A Theory of the Labor Movement*, Kelly, New York, 1957

Post, K.W.J. *The Nigerian Federal Election of 1959: Politics and Administration in a Developing Political System*, OUP for NISER, 1963.

Post, K.W.J. & Vickers, M. *Conflict and Control in an Independent African State: Nigeria 1960-1965*, Heinemann, 1973

Post, K.W.J. & Jemkin, G.D. *The Price of Liberty: Personality and Politics in Colonial Nigeria*, Cambridge University Press, 1973.

Proehl, P. O. *Foreign Enterprise in Nigeria*, University of N. Caroline & OUP, Chapel Hill, London & Ibadan, 1965.

Roberts, B.C. *Labour in the Tropical Territories of the Commonwealth*, Bell,

London, 1964.

Roberts, B.C., & de Bellcombe, L.G., *Collective Bargaining in African Countries,* Macmillan for International Institute for Labour Studies, 1967

Roper, R.I. *Labour Problems in West Africa,* Penguin, 1958.

Roxborough, I., *Theories of Underdevelopment,* Heinemann, London

Sandbrook, R. & Cohen, R. (eds.) *The Development of An African Working Class,* Longman, London, 1975.

Sklar, R. *Nigerian Political Parties,* Princeton Univ. Press, 1963.

Smock, D.R., Conflict and Control in an African Trade Union: A Study of the Nigerian Coal Miners' Union, Hoover Institution, Stanford, 1969.

Sofola, K. *Report of the Commission of Inquiry into the Retail and Ancillary Trades in the Federal Territory of Lagos, Government Printer,* Lagos, 1957.

Sonubi, O., 'Machinery for Salaries and Wages Administration in Nigeria,' *Quarterly Journal of Administration,* Ife, Vol.6, 1971.

— 'Trade Disputes in Nigeria, 1966-1971,' *The Nigerian Journal of Social and Economic Studies* (NJESS), Vol.!5(2), 1973.

Streeten, P., *Frontiers of Development Studies,* Macmillan, 1972

Tamuno, T.N. *The Evolution of the Nigerian State,* Longman, 1976.

Toyo, E. *The Working Class and the Nigerian Crisis,* Sketch Publishing Corporation, Ibadan, 1967.

Turner, T. 'Multinational Companies and Instability of the Nigerian State,' *Review of African Political Economy,* vol. 5, 1976.

Ubeku, A.K. *Industrial Relations in Developing Countries: The Case of Nigeria,* Macmillan, London & Basingstoke, 1983.

Uvieghara, E.E., *Trade Union Law in Nigeria,* Ethiope, Benin City, 1976.

Warmington, N.A., A West African Trade Union, OUP, London, 1960

Warren, W.M. 'Urban Real Wages and the Nigerian Trade Union Movement, 1939-1960,' *Economic Development and Cultural Change,* vol. 15(1), October 1966.

— 'Urban Real Wages and the Nigerian Trade Union Movement, 1939-1960: A Rejoinder,' *Economic Development and Cultural Change,* vol. 17(4), 1969.

Waterman, P., *Division and Unity Amongst Nigerian Workers: Lagos Port Unionism 1940s-1960s,* Institute of Social Studies, The Hague, 1982.

— *The Communist Theory in Nigerian Trade Union Movement,* Occasional Paper, Institute of Social Studies, The Hague, 1974.

— 'Conservatism Amongst Nigerian Workers' in Williams, G. (ed.), Nigeria: *Economy and Society,* Rex Collins, London, 1976.

Webb, S. & Webb, B., *Industrial Democracy,* Longmans, Green and Co., 1897

Weeks, J. 'A Comment on P. Kilby: Industrial Relations and Wage Determination,' *Journal of Developing Areas,* vol. 3(1), 1968.

— 'Further Comment on the Kilby/Weeks Debate: An Empirical Rejoinder,' *Journal of Developing Areas,* vol. 5(2), Jan. 1971.

— 'Wage Policy and the Colonial Legacy,' *Journal of Modern African Studies* (JMAS), Vol.9(3), 1971.

— 'The Impact of Economic Conditions and Institutional Forces on Urban Wages in Nigeria,' *Nigerian Journal of Economic and Social Studies, vol.* 13(3), Nov. 1971.

Wiley, R.J., 'Trade Unions and Political Parties in the Federal Republic of Germany,' *ILRR,* 1974.

Williams, G. (ed.). *Nigeria: Economy and Society,* Rex Collins, London, 1976.

— *State and Society in Nigeria,* Afrografika, 1980.

Windmuller, J.P. 'External Influences on Labour Organizations in Underdeveloped Countries,' *Industrial and Labour Relations Review,* vol. 16, July 1963.

Yesufu, T.M. *An Introduction to Industrial Relations in Nigeria,* OUP for NISER, 1962.

— *The Dynamics of Industrial Relations: The Nigerian Experience,* University Press Limited, Ibadan, 1984.

Zack, A., *Labour Training in Developing Countries*, Praeger, 1964

INDEX

www.ingramcontent.com/pod-product-compliance
Lightning Source LLC
Chambersburg PA
CBHW050519240926
51846CB00003B/620
* 9 7 8 9 7 8 6 1 1 3 5 2 4 *